PRIDE AND FALL

OSPREY
PUBLISHING

For my Mother

Nos veremos en el cielo

PRIDE AND FALL

THE BRITISH ARMY IN AFGHANISTAN 2001–2014

Sergio Miller

OSPREY PUBLISHING
Bloomsbury Publishing Plc
Kemp House, Chawley Park, Cumnor Hill, Oxford OX2 9PH, UK
29 Earlsfort Terrace, Dublin 2, Ireland
1385 Broadway, 5th Floor, New York, NY 10018, USA
E-mail: info@ospreypublishing.com
www.ospreypublishing.com

OSPREY is a trademark of Osprey Publishing Ltd

First published in Great Britain in 2024

A catalogue record for this book is available from the British Library.

ISBN: HB 9781472868299; eBook 9781472868305; ePDF 9781472868282; XML 9781472868268; Audio 9781472868275

24 25 26 27 28 10 9 8 7 6 5 4 3 2 1

Maps by www.bounford.com
Index by Alan Rutter

Typeset by Deanta Global Publishing Services, Chennai, India
Printed and bound in Great Britain by CPI (Group) UK Ltd, Croydon CR0 4YY

Contents

List of Illustrations and Maps

Illustrations

Maps

Map 1: Afghanistan, 2011

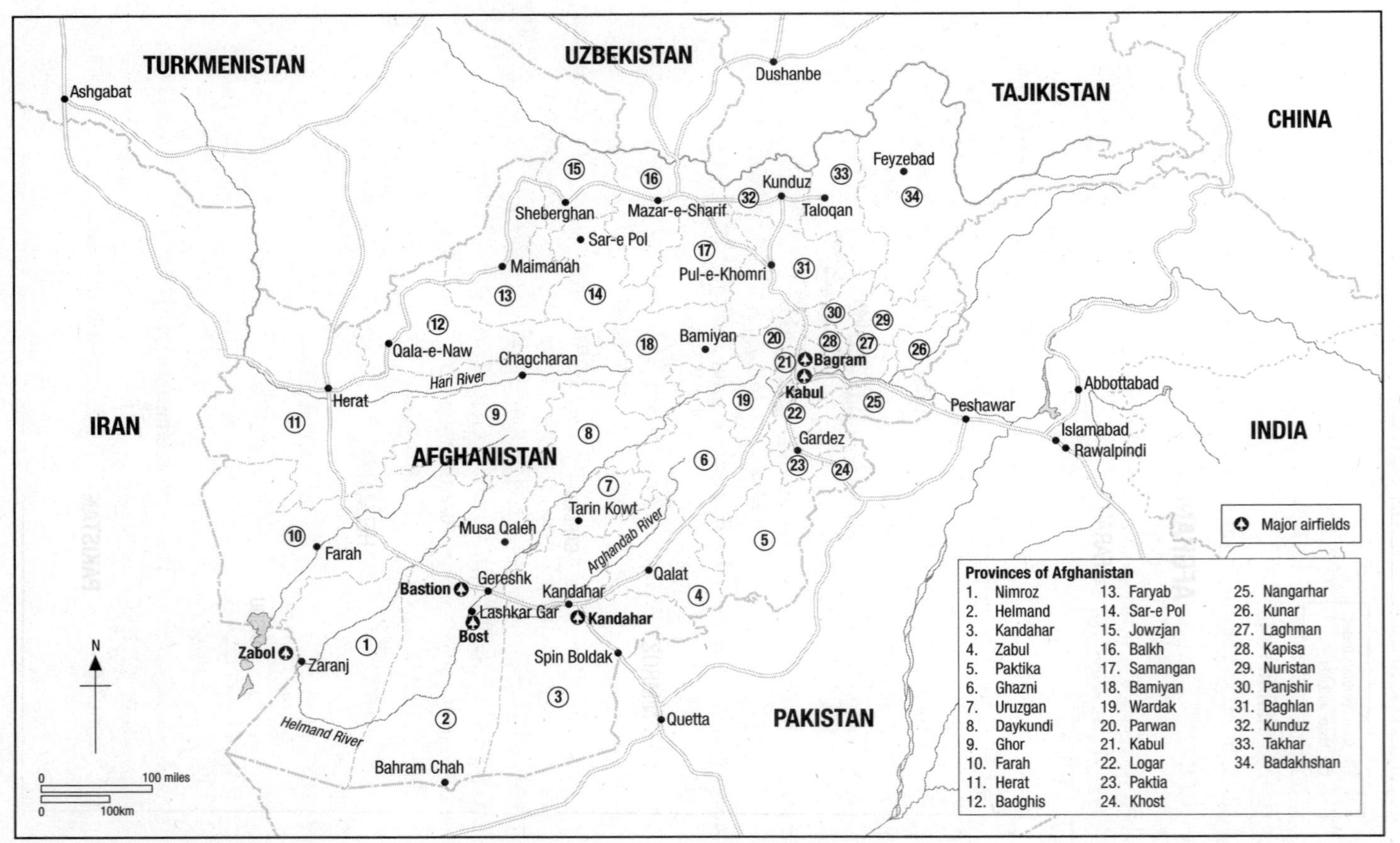

Map 2: Helmand Province, 2011

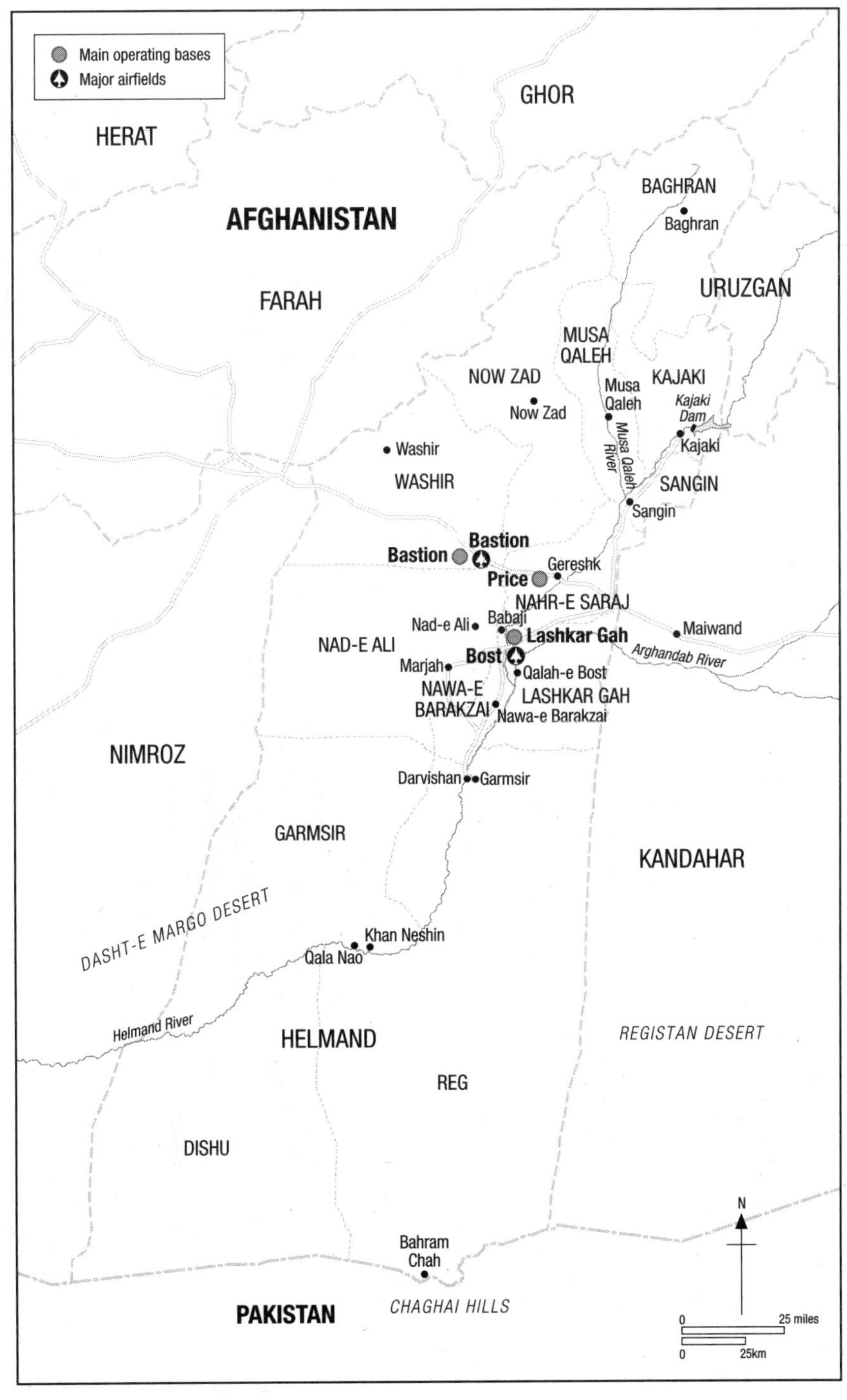

MAP 3: The high point of Task Force Helmand: Operation *Herrick 13*, October 2010 to April 2011

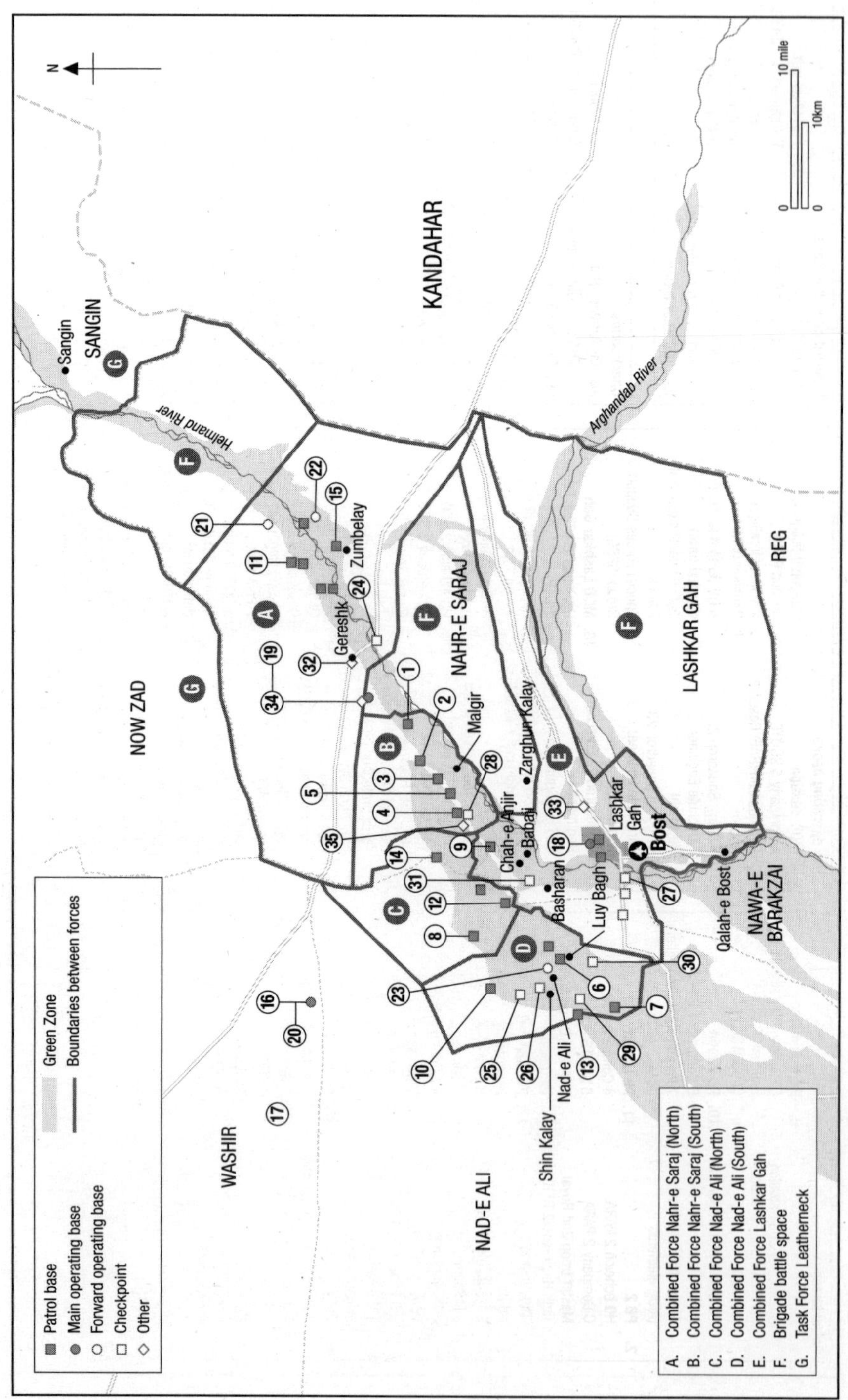

Patrol bases

1. **PB 1**
   D Company 2nd Battalion the Parachute Regiment (2 PARA)
   1st Battalion Irish Guards (1 IG) team
   Afghan National Army (ANA) elements
2. **PB 2**
   HQ echelon 2 PARA
   C Company 2 PARA
   Mastiff troop 2nd Royal Tank Regiment (2 RTR)
   ANA elements
3. **PB 3**
   E Company 2 PARA
   1 IG team
   ANA elements
4. **PB 4**
   B Company 2 PARA
   1 IG team
   ANA elements
5. **PB 5**
   B Company The Argyll and Sutherland Highlanders (5 SCOTS)
6. **PB Chilli**
   A Company 5 SCOTS
7. **PB Kalang**
   A Company 1 Royal Irish (1 R IRISH)
8. **PB Khaamar**
   A Company 3 PARA
   ANA combat elements
9. **PB Nahidullah**
   C Company The Royal Highland Fusiliers (2 SCOTS)
10. **PB Pimon**
    B Company 1 R IRISH
    7 Para Royal Horse Artillery (RHA)
11. **PB Rahim**
    4 Company 1 IG
    5 SCOTS team
    ANA 215 Corps *kandak* (battalion)
12. **PB Shahzad**
    HQ echelon 3 PARA
    B Company 3 PARA
    C Company 3 PARA
    Mastiff troop 2 RTR
13. **PB Silab**
    C Company 1 R IRISH
    Mamba counter-battery radar
14. **PB Wahid**
    Estonian elements
    1 IG elements
    ANA elements
15. **PB Zumbalay**
    A Company 1 IG

Main operating bases

16. **MOB Bastion**
    A Company 5 SCOTS
    12 Squadron (RAF) Reserve Node
    9 (Para) Squadron 23 Parachute Engineer Regiment
    51 (Para) Squadron 23 Parachute Engineer Regiment
    5 Squadron 22 Engineer Regiment
    52 Field Squadron TALISMAN (counter-IED)
    Counter-indirect fire (C-IDF) battery
    Hermes 450 unmanned air vehicle (UAV) battery
    Viking group 2 RTR
    10 Signal Regiment
    Electronic Counter Measures Force Protection (ECM-FP)
    216 (Para) Signals Squadron
    Desert Hawk medium unmanned air vehicle (MUAV)
    Brigade Reconnaissance Force (BRF)
    Joint Force Explosive Ordnance Disposal Group (JF EOD Gp)
    42 Engineer Regiment (Geographic)
    Task Force Helmand Provost Group
    Task Force Helmand Medical Group
    Weapon Intelligence Section (WIS)
    4 Military Intelligence Battalion (4 MI Bn)
17. **MOB Juno (location approximate)**
    Task Force 444 (Special Forces)
    Special Forces Support Group (SFSG)
18. **MOB Lashkar Gah**
    Headquarters Task Force (HQTF)
    Regimental HQ (RHQ) 7 Para RHA
    RHQ 4 Regiment Royal Artillery (4 RA)
    HQ echelon 2 SCOTS
    B Company 2 SCOTS
    Mastiff troop 2 RTR
    2 MI Bn
    D Company 5 SCOTS
19. **MOB Price**
    Danish Battlegroup
    D Squadron Household Cavalry Regiment (HCR)
    7 Para RHA
    5 SCOTS team
    Counter IED (C-IED) detachment
    ARTHUR counter-battery radar
    ANA 215 Corps elements
20. **MOB Shorabak**
    ANA 215 Corps combat support elements

Forward operating bases

21. **FOB Budwan**
    C Squadron Danish Battlegroup
    7 Para RHA elements
    1 IG teams
    ANA 215 Corps elements
22. **FOB Khar Nikah**
23. **FOB Shawqat**
    D Company 1 R IRISH
    1 IG team
    Mastiff troop 2 RTR
    ANA elements

Checkpoints

24. **CP Artillery Hill**
    ANA D-30 gun battery
25. **CP Blue 9**
    ANA elements
26. **CP Blue 17**
    ANA elements
27. **CP Bolan Shops**
    A Company 2 SCOTS
28. **CP Sabir**
    ANA elements
29. **CP Samsor**
    C Company 1 R IRISH
    ANA elements
30. **CP Shamal Storrai**
    5 SCOTS elements
    ANA elements
31. **CP Tapa Paraang**
    B Company 2 Royal Welsh (2 R WELSH)

Other

32. **Gereshk**
    Civil-military teams
    ANA elements
33. **Helmand Police Training Center (HPTC)**
    B Squadron Queen's Royal Lancers (QRL)
34. **Highway 1**
    E Squadron 1st Light Armoured Regiment
    ANA 205 Corps *kandaks*
35. **Vehicle Check Point (VCP) Dosti**
    ANA elements

Map 4: Distribution of tribal groups in Helmand Province

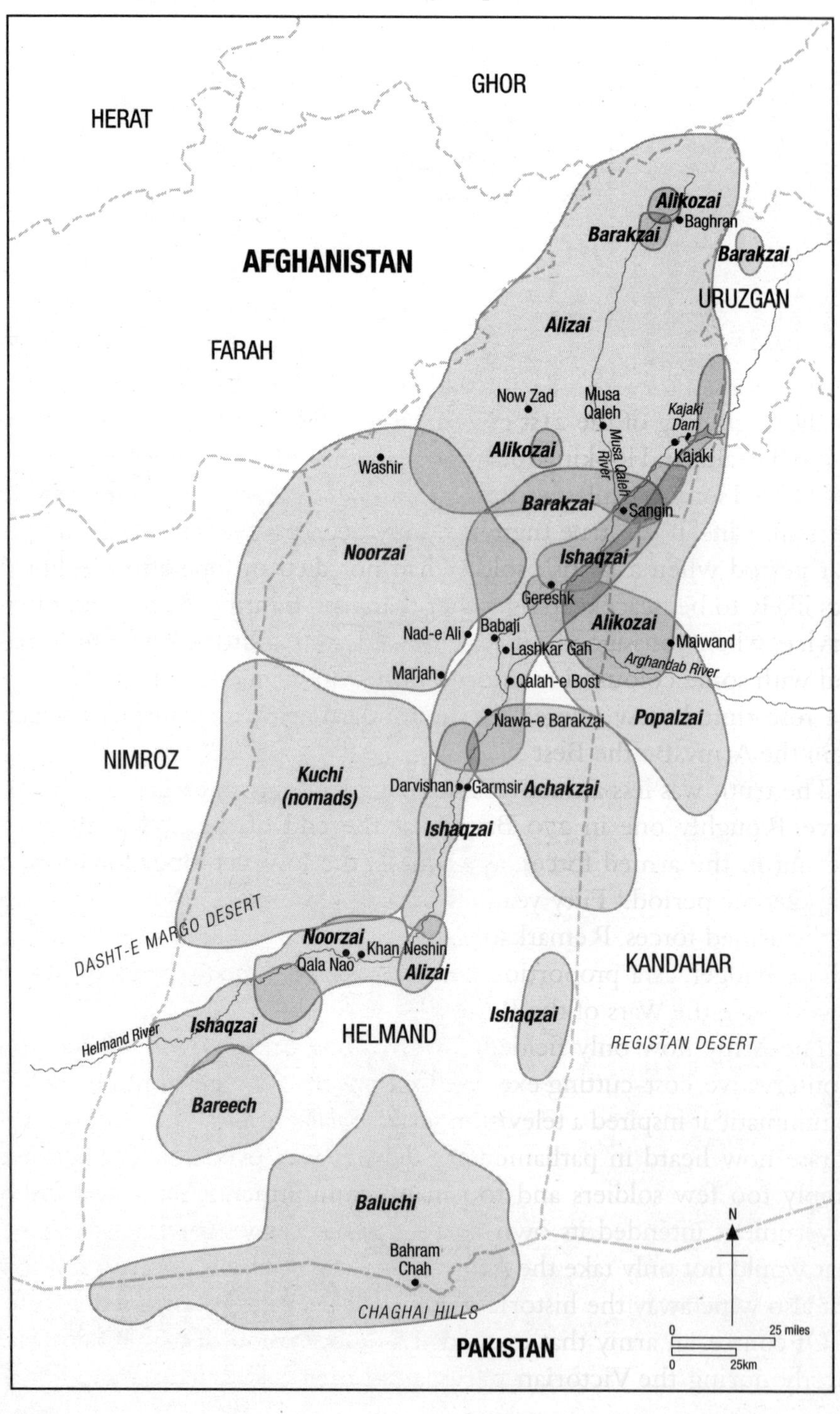
GHOR
HERAT
AFGHANISTAN
Alikozai
Baghran
Barakzai
Barakzai
URUZGAN
Alizai
FARAH
Now Zad
Musa Qaleh
Kajaki Dam
Musa Qaleh River
Kajaki
Alikozai
Washir
Barakzai
Sangin
Noorzai
Ishaqzai
Gereshk
Alikozai
Nad-e Ali
Babaji
Lashkar Gah
Maiwand
Arghandab River
Marjah
Qalah-e Bost
Nawa-e Barakzai
Popalzai
NIMROZ
Kuchi (nomads)
Darvishan
Garmsir
Achakzai
Ishaqzai
DASHT-E MARGO DESERT
Noorzai
Khan Neshin
Qala Nao
Alizai
KANDAHAR
Ishaqzai
Helmand River
Ishaqzai
HELMAND
REGISTAN DESERT
Bareech
Baluchi
N
Bahram Chah
CHAGHAI HILLS
0
25 miles
0
25km
PAKISTAN

Preface

At the beginning of the 21st century, if you were a young man or woman in good health and looking for some light adventure, then the British Army still offered some harmless escapism from the seriousness and responsibilities of civilian life. It was true there had only been one year in the entire post-war period when a British soldier had not died on operations – but this was likely to be peacekeeping rather than war-fighting. At the end of your service, when you signed off, you walked away a little fitter, a little wiser and with some colourful memories from your army days. This at least was the rose-tinted view offered by the modern army's recruitment slogan – 'Join the Army, Be the Best'.

The truth was less attractive. The Army had become a greatly shrunken force. Roughly one in 270 Britons at the end of the 20th century was serving in the armed forces, as a whole, the lowest proportion since the Napoleonic period.[1] Fifty years previously, one in ten Britons was serving in the armed forces. Remarkably, you would have joined an armed forces whose budget, as a proportion of general government spending, was the lowest since the Wars of the Roses.[2]

The Army now only fielded two divisions, the survivors of the savage, Conservative, cost-cutting exercise Options for Change 1991. The cull was so traumatic it inspired a television series, *Soldier Soldier*. The most common phrase now heard in parliamentary debates was 'overstretch'. There were simply too few soldiers and too many commitments. Yet a new Labour government intended its own cuts – Future Army Structures 2003–06 – that would not only take the Army below the symbolic 100,000 threshold, but also wipe away the historic Army built over three centuries.

Of course, an army that expanded as a federation of gentlemen's clubs, mostly during the Victorian period, and then ballooned during the two world wars, could not have survived. But it was the manner in which successive British governments pruned the defence hedge, while pursuing foreign policies requiring active military intervention, that attracted misgivings and criticism.

This was especially true of New Labour's idealistic leader: Tony Blair. 'A Force for Good' ran the rebuffed Ministry of Defence slogan. Britain 'must now be prepared to go to the crisis, rather than have the crisis come to us', argued the government's Strategic Defence Review 1998. This orthodoxy gestated an unchallenged jihadist domino theory: unless extremists were confronted, the dominoes would fall all the way back to a street in Britain. Of course, it was the British government's interventionism that was provoking home-grown terrorism, but this point could not be conceded.

It was against the background of this 'strange mixture of vainglory and miserliness'[3] as Professor Anthony King would describe Blair's partnership with his chancellor, Gordon Brown, that Britain's overstretched and ill-equipped army would find itself committed to a conflict in a harsh, alien land that would test it to the limits. This book tells that story.

1

The Planes Operation

On 14 September 2001, Secretary of State for Defence Geoffrey William Hoon rose to address a packed House of Commons.[1] The most shocking event in living memory had transpired just three days earlier in the United States. The moment deserved the gravitas of Churchill. In the event, a four-page address delivered to the expectant House fell flat. Hostile journalists perceived Hoon as a Blair acolyte and had already labelled the state secretary 'Geoff Who?' He would later reveal himself in rather unattractive ways. Entrapped in a media sting, Hoon boasted to an undercover reporter that what he was really looking forward to was 'translating my knowledge and contacts about the international scene into something that frankly makes money'.[2] From humble origins (the son of a railway worker), Hoon seemed to fit the mould of New Labour politician: the unembarrassed acquisitive socialist, keen on self-advancement. Rather than reassuring his fellow parliamentarians, the speech reinforced a growing reputation the government had acquired for spin over substance.

After expressing condolences to the American people, Hoon informed the House that in the wake of the recent terrorist attacks in the United States, his government was prepared and ready to protect the British people. A raft of melodramatic emergency measures was then announced, inflated by hollow boasts. No defence secretary had spoken like this since the outbreak of World War II and, in truth, it was eyewash. Historically, the home defence of Britain had always been neglected, except in moments of grave national emergency when invasion threatened. This position had not changed in September 2001.

The previous day, NATO had invoked Article 5 of the Washington Treaty, arguably the single most important measure taken in the wake of the September 11 terrorist attacks as it obliged European nations to provide military support to the United States. Once this genie was released from the bottle, it would prove very difficult for European governments to wriggle out of the commitment. Article 5 stated unequivocally: 'an armed attack against one or more … shall be considered an armed attack against them all'. This was the first time in the organization's history the key clause had been invoked. Britain had both obligation and interest in supporting the United States, even if – and Hoon prudently stopped short of saying so – this meant going to war.

On the other side of the Atlantic, an equally portentous resolution was agreed on the same day Hoon addressed the Commons. In a unanimous vote, Congress passed an Authorization for the Use of Military Force (AUMF), granting permission to the president to conduct whatever actions deemed necessary to hunt down the protagonists behind the September 11 attacks. The last time a US president had been offered such a free hand to wage war was in 1964 – the Tonkin Gulf Resolution. Lyndon B. Johnson pocketed this resolution then deployed it the following year, leading America into a ruinous war in Vietnam. George W. Bush would follow the same path, using the AUMF as the constitutional basis for a 'long war' on terrorism. With such an unfortunate precedent, congressmen may have been wise to reconsider granting their president such sweeping powers.

By chance, Britain was already in a position to pursue military operations in the Middle East because a task force was being deployed to Oman for pre-planned manoeuvres – Exercise *Saif Sareea II* ('Swift Sword'). This had been intended as a showcase of military capability as well as an exercise in defence diplomacy. Instead, the task force would now be readied for possible contingency operations in the region. Hoon asserted that Exercise *Saif Sareea II* demonstrated Britain's resolve to maintain its armed forces at a peak of professional effectiveness, as well as its solidarity with Arab allies. Commentators suggested the exercise was only taking place because of an Omani threat to defence sales. Over-stretched, over-budgeted and with simultaneous operations in Northern Ireland, the Balkans and Sierra Leone, the government had vainly sought to cancel the exercise.

Perhaps any defence secretary would have fallen short in the days following September 11, 2001. On that bright Tuesday morning, two civil airliners, American 11 and United 175, crashed into and collapsed the Twin Towers in New York, killing 2,603 people. American 77 crashed into a wing of the Pentagon, killing 125 civilian and military personnel. And United 93 crashed in Pennsylvania, following a struggle between hijackers and passengers, which resulted in the deaths of all on board the aircraft. A total of 246 crew and passengers were killed in the four aircraft, excluding the hijackers. In total, 2,974 people representing 90 nationalities were killed. At least 104 people jumped from the burning towers in New York, creating some of the most painful images of that day. It was the largest single loss of life on American soil from foreign attack, and it had been perpetrated by just 19, mostly Saudi Arabian, hijackers. Historically, it was the deadliest terrorist attack ever recorded. The defence secretary was absolutely right in one respect: 'To commit acts of this nature requires a fanaticism and a wickedness that is beyond our normal comprehension.' Perhaps the only consolation in the awful tally of dead was the number of children killed – remarkably just eight lost their lives in the September 11 attacks.

The attack on the Twin Towers created an appalling and iconic image, but of what? A Babel-like tower of words would be erected in their place analysing the significance of the September 11 attacks. The most prescient were written by Anthony Cordesman, the Arleigh A. Burke Chair in Strategic Studies at the Center for Strategic and International Studies,[3] just one week after the attacks:

> Invasions and efforts at regime change are a last resort. We must avoid military adventures and reacting to special interests. These include 'lobbies' calling for regime change in Afghanistan and Iraq … Nothing could be worse than sending major ground forces across hostile territory into the middle of nowhere in search of a dispersed and hidden enemy with no strategic objective other than to replace one bad regime with a fragmented one, and with the certainty of region-wide hostility and a long-term political backlash.[4]

This wisdom was ignored.

For those who saw it happen before their eyes, and for the billions who watched the replays on television screens, there was horror and disbelief. So improbable were the events that an F-16 pilot scrambled from Langley Air Base, on seeing a wing of the Pentagon burning, assumed a Russian attack. 'I thought the bastards snuck one past us,' he later told an inquiry.[5] President Bush was visiting a school in Florida when the attacks occurred. His reaction was visceral and defined the next eight years of his two-term presidency. Within minutes of the attacks, he called Vice President Dick

Cheney. 'We're at war,' he told him. 'Somebody's going to pay.'[6] Stubbornly, he held on to this *idée fixe* right up to the handover ceremony with his successor. Like the Texan sheriff he portrayed, and barely pausing to gather his thoughts, George W. Bush transformed into a war president. His resolve would remain undimmed, but if someone was going to pay, as he threatened, who would it be?

Within hours of the attacks, American intelligence agencies went into overdrive and spat out Osama bin Laden, al-Qaeda and Afghanistan. Yet bin Laden's pre-eminence, notwithstanding later transformations, was surprising. Despite the self-mythologizing, he had been a wealthy recruiting agent and facilitator who had played a peripheral role in the Soviet–Afghan War (1979–89). The CIA barely rated him, and his contribution to the resistance was judged marginal. Mostly, his skills appeared to be administrative and organizational. Like his construction magnate father, he was good at making contacts and winning contracts – and in the beginning he had his own money to back the projects. He would later become a relatively successful road construction manager in his own right in Sudan. When invited to Sudan, bin Laden not only offered construction services but also security services, or military training. He provided employment to ex-fighters, whether soldiers or mercenaries, contracted by client governments. In principle, this was no different from an American or British government contracting a security firm to provide quasi-military services in a war zone.

In August 1990, after the withdrawal of Soviet forces from Afghanistan, and on the eve of the first Gulf War, Osama bin Laden was not a terrorist. Rather, he was a young businessman with a certain reputation, in some circles, gained from his participation in the Soviet–Afghan War. Bin Laden's slide into a criminal existence was driven by three events: first, Iraq's invasion of Kuwait; second, the rebuff of his offer of assistance by the Saudi government; and third, the arrival of coalition – and in particular American – troops in his native Saudi Arabia. It was the latter in particular that darkened bin Laden's landscape. Even during this period, bin Laden was not emerging as a potential terrorist leader but more an aggrieved Saudi national with views shared by thousands of his compatriots.

Bin Laden was pushed into an outlaw life by the revocation of his citizenship and the seizure of his assets by the Saudi Arabian government in 1994. The quarrel was internecine, but bin Laden blamed America for his exile. The later *9/11 Commission Report*, published in the aftermath of the

September 11 attacks, would reveal in fascinating detail how bin Laden's gift for networking had turned him consciously, and perhaps sometimes unknowingly, into a financier and quartermaster for a wide range of desperadoes, malcontents and outright criminals. There was a sense that bin Laden was simply being milked – like his wealthy compatriots – by fellow Muslims who had become accustomed to viewing the Kingdom of Saudi Arabia as the fecund desert milk cow that it was. He seemed to enjoy playing the role of the wealthy Saudi rubbing shoulders with the wild-haired radicals living on the fringes of Islamic societies. It would be a stretch to say that bin Laden was completely gullible, but there was in his generosity a hint of carelessness, if not ignorance, of the groups he was helping and where his money was going. Did bin Laden really understand what was happening in Burma (subsequently Myanmar), Uganda, Bosnia or the Philippines – all countries with which he was associated? The period before the September 11 attacks was undoubtedly a sort of golden age for dreamers and jihadists free to move and communicate in ways that would become impossible after the attacks. This strange world of double values and flexible business arrangements is perhaps best illustrated by the fact that bin Laden opened offices of an organization called al Khifa, a subsidiary of the umbrella organization MAK (Maktab al-Khidamat), in six North American cities.[7] This behaviour suggested a business impresario seeking new opportunities, not an underground terrorist seeking to destroy America. At the time, *Jihad* magazine, published by MAK, was on sale in 49 countries (including the United States, for just $2.60).[8]

The analysis of terrorist networks also detailed how bin Laden was 'just one among many diverse terrorist barons'.[9] In fact, no terrorist attacks that took place between Osama bin Laden's first self-proclaimed fatwa against America in 1992 and the much quoted 1998 *Jihad Fatwa*, could be attributed *directly* to bin Laden himself. There was no direct evidence linking Osama bin Laden to the 1993 World Trade Center bombs; the 1995 Riyadh bomb; the 1995 Manila air plot; or the 1996 Khobar Towers bomb. It was not until 1998 that bin Laden would be linked directly with a terrorist attack against the United States (the Dar es Salaam and Nairobi embassy bombs). Even in these two attacks it could not be confirmed he was the main player, although the CIA and White House took a strong view that bin Laden was the mastermind. It was from this period that President Bill Clinton changed his mind on the Saudi and authorized what would be a series of aborted attempts to kill or capture the errant bin Laden.

The other important consideration related to the name al-Qaeda (or 'the base').[10] According to bin Laden, there was no such thing as an organization called 'al-Qaeda'. As author Jason Burke explained in *The 9/11 Wars*, 'al-Qaeda' in fact has multiple meanings, beyond the literal meaning of 'a base'. Post-September 11, bin Laden explicitly told Al Jazeera journalist Tayseer Allouni that the West had got it wrong – he had not founded a group with the specific name of 'al-Qaeda'. Rather, this was the name of a camp 'brother Abu Ubaida' had established in the Soviet–Afghan War, which Western reporting had subsequently inflated into an organization. He went on to claim that this 'base' had become 'a nation', illustrating the difficulties of interpreting this multi-layered Arab word. The sense bin Laden appears to have been conveying was that of 'al-Qaeda' as a foundation philosophy spreading across the *umma*, or Muslim world.

During the Soviet–Afghan War, the organization bin Laden ran jointly with the Palestinian radical Abdullah Azzam was the MAK, or 'Bureau of Services'. The two then seemed to fall out. In August 1988, 15 loose jihadists decided to establish a separate military group that would comprise a general camp, a special camp and a 'qaeda', or base camp (from the minutes of the meeting, an 'al-Qaeda al Askiriyah', or 'military base camp'). This group was a ragbag of characters including an Omani, a Nigerian, a Libyan, an Egyptian, an Iraqi and Saudi Arabians. A man named Abu Ayoub al-Iraqi was nominated emir, with bin Laden appointed as 'general emir'. The chief protagonists in the group appear to have been the Egyptians, notably Abu-Ubaidah al Banshiri, a former army officer, and the aggressive Mohammed Atef (Abu Hafs), a former police officer.[11]

Following the Soviet withdrawal, there appears to have been some sort of reconciliation between bin Laden and Azzam. By now, the former had decided that the Afghan war was over, and there was talk of migrating to Sudan to support the regime in its civil war against the Christian south. At the time, President Omar al-Bashir was offering an open invitation to numerous jihadist groups to support his regime. The Egyptians apparently convinced bin Laden to continue funding one of the training camps before he left – Azzam's original 'al-Qaeda al Sulbah', or 'solid foundation' for jihad elsewhere – but the words referred to a physical location, not an entity, and certainly not a terrorist organization. Bin Laden never referred to an 'al-Qaeda' in any of his fatwas or other pronouncements after his departure from Afghanistan. Whatever plans he had for promoting jihad, bin Laden chose first to return home in the winter of 1989, effectively ending his

Afghan adventure. He seems to have toyed with the idea of becoming a film producer, reflecting his lifelong fascination with visual media. Meanwhile, a core group of former Afghan jihadists known to bin Laden migrated to Sudan and bought properties and farms, collaborating with Islamic Jihad of Egypt. In Jeddah, bin Laden ran no militant organization and would not have been allowed to by the Saudi government anyway.

Following his expulsion from Saudi Arabia in 1992, bin Laden permanently decamped to Sudan. His business interests were numerous, as the list of trading companies associated with his name later revealed: Wadi al Aqiq Company, Taba Investments, Ladin International Company, Hijra Construction, Al Thema al Mubaraka, Al Khudrat Transportation, and the Khartoum Tannery. He even ran a peanut and sesame farm, and a fruit and vegetable business. Whatever else they may have been, bin Laden and his associates were keen entrepreneurs (though not that successful, as a weak Sudanese pound against the US dollar made for a difficult business climate). During this period of his exile, from 1992 to 1998, bin Laden was associated with two radical organizations, neither of which he tried to conceal. The first was called the Committee for Advice and Reform, set up in London offices in July 1994. He used this committee to bombard the Arab-speaking world (or anyone who cared to digest his invective) with salvos of propaganda directed against the Saudi regime. This was an especially low point in his life: cut off from his family, divorced by his wife, abandoned by his first and favourite son, and apparently losing $15 million in his Sudanese businesses.[12] The second was the International Islamic Front for Jihad Against the Crusaders and the Jews, announced alongside Ayman al-Zawahiri at a press conference in early 1998. It is notable that the other four signatories of this fatwa all titled themselves heads of jihadist organizations. Bin Laden alone signed in his name and belonged to no particular organization.

In CIA files, Osama bin Laden was simply known by his acronym 'UBL' ('Usama bin Ladin'). The CIA's own description of bin Laden in 1997 was 'extremist financier'.[13] Hundreds of wealthy Arabs might have fitted this description, funnelling money to Islamic charities whose funds ended up being used for extremist purposes. UBL was a cultural commonplace, not a maverick.

A longer and better description for UBL might have been the 'Osama bin Laden Finance Network'. Indeed, when President Clinton ordered the first cruise missile strikes against bin Laden, he only referred to him as a financier of terrorist groups.

American intelligence focus on bin Laden had a quality of accident about it from the beginning. Unable to find an internal candidate for a newly created post within the CIA's Operations Directorate, so the story goes, an outsider was recruited. When asked to pick a subject, the selected individual picked bin Laden because he happened to remember the name from a number of reports – thus did bin Laden find himself subject to scrutiny.[14] His value as a subject of study increased when a 'walk-in' ex-bin Laden employee, the Brooklyn-based Sudanese Jamal al-Fadl, offered to reveal the workings of the network to CIA officials. Al-Fadl, it transpired, had stolen money from bin Laden and was a temperamental witness. Nonetheless, an intelligence snowball effect followed. Was bin Laden important because he deserved to be, or because an intelligence reporting apparatus had accidentally elevated him to this position? The al-Qaeda title itself seems to have been created by American legal imperatives. To charge bin Laden under the Racketeer Influenced and Corrupt Organizations Act (RICO), he necessarily had to belong to an organization. Thus, it appears, was al-Qaeda born, in a literal sense, the bastard son of an American legal process and the testimony of al-Fadl. Who first coined the title al-Qaeda as the name of a terrorist organization remains unclear. The answer may well lie in FBI files. Al-Qaeda was only officially declared a foreign terrorist organization in 1999. Legally, 'al-Qaeda' came into existence on 5 February 2001 in hearings at the District Court of the Southern District of New York. At some point over this period, bin Laden started repeating the name in response to the American charges.

The final catalyst for bin Laden's descent into open terrorism appears not to have been his long-standing grudge against the United States (American forces were by now withdrawing from Saudi Arabia) but once again his own domestic circumstances – explicitly, his unresolved homelessness. In 1996 the Saudi government put pressure on the Sudanese government to expel bin Laden, forcing him to resettle in Afghanistan, the only country that would immediately take him, and the landscape of his youthful, romanticized past. The Saudi authorities then proceeded to seize his assets, dismantling bin Laden's business empire. These were difficult moments for bin Laden and another low point in his life. Exiled twice-over and now impoverished, bin Laden's relationship with the Taliban, facilitated by Pakistan's secret services, was not an instant success. Afghanistan remained a divided country with competing warlords, and bin Laden at first found it judicious to court both the Taliban and their opponents. But it was Mullah

Omar, the Taliban leader, who recognized the value of bin Laden's ad hoc security force and who provided the refugee with fresh employment. Within a year bin Laden had resurrected his business connections and was again operating profitably. A visitor to Afghanistan might regularly see bin Laden employees driving around in vehicles with Ministry of Defence number plates, and Arab fighters were being despatched to the front line (the 55th Brigade), to support the Taliban's inconclusive war against the Northern Alliance. As much as anything, it appears the greedy Mullah Omar was impressed and attracted by bin Laden's seemingly bottomless financial reservoirs. Soon the national air carrier Ariana was being used to fly over bin Laden's cash.

Mullah Omar was not the only individual to notice bin Laden's value as financial backer. The impoverished and unhinged Egyptian – Dr Ayman Mohammed Rabie al-Zawahiri, head of the Egyptian Islamic Jihad and co-author of the 1998 *Jihad Fatwa* – saw in bin Laden a mechanism for realizing his dreams of an Islamic revolution (or, more concretely, the overthrow of the Mubarak regime). Like bin Laden, al-Zawahiri's antipathy towards America was at root a protest against imprisonment, torture and finally exile from his own native country. Following that exile, it was al-Zawahiri's alliance with bin Laden that gestated the 1998 *Jihad Fatwa*, and it was the Egyptian Islamic Jihad – not al-Qaeda – that may have been decisive in the East African embassy bombings. One of the reasons why al-Fadl quit al-Qaeda and handed himself over to the FBI was precisely because the Egyptians had become so dominant: indeed, the eventual leader of the September 11 attacks was Mohammed Atta, an Egyptian.

Despite the uncertainty and a serious concern that he might be acquitted through lack of sufficient evidence, the CIA nevertheless planned and nearly executed a scheme to capture and arraign bin Laden in 1997. Sufficient intelligence noise had been generated to raise bin Laden's profile to the point where a kidnap operation was countenanced. Ironically, the operation was cancelled at the eleventh hour because it might have led to a loss of innocent lives. Had the CIA executed this operation, it still appears plausible Americans would have found themselves targets of Islamist extremists. Another trait of bin Laden was a tendency to inflate and believe in his own self-importance, a trait much in evidence in the interviews he gave to *TIME* magazine, the television broadcaster CNN and to the veteran journalist and Middle East expert Robert Fisk.

After the 1998 embassy bombings, American determination to bring bin Laden to justice hardened. Whatever ambiguities that may have existed before over his status and importance were set aside, and he became a priority target. A picture was painted of assumed prime culpability even when the evidence was sometimes acknowledged to be sketchy. The embassy attacks were claimed by the Islamic Army for the Liberation of the Holy Places, not al-Qaeda. When asked directly whether he was responsible for the attacks, bin Laden obfuscated, stating that the 'World Islamic Front' had issued a fatwa against Jews and Crusaders, but he stopped short of admitting responsibility. In 1999, a bin Laden aircraft hijack scare was raised, but the authors of the scare admitted, 'no group directly tied to Bin Ladin's Al Qaida's organisation has ever carried out a hijacking'.[15] In the meantime, several aborted attempts were made to kill bin Laden with cruise missile strikes over 1998 and 1999. As one CIA operator later put it, he 'should have been a dead man'.[16] The big missed opportunity was not, in hindsight, these CIA operations against Osama bin Laden but rather the Saudi government's consistent refusal to restore his passport and allow him to return to his homeland. An exiled bin Laden was a frustrated menace; a re-settled bin Laden would have been neutered. The unpalatable truth was that the Kingdom of Saudi Arabia was home to scores of bin Ladens expressing bigoted world views, and who channelled funds to dubious organizations. Mostly, the Saudi authorities kept such individuals under control by indirect pressure or, when they went too far and threatened the fragile order of the Kingdom, they were incarcerated. It was not too far-fetched to have imagined, at one stage, a reconciled bin Laden ageing in Jeddah, muttering occasional imprecations against 'the Jews and Crusaders' but causing no harm. This option never seems to have been seriously countenanced.

The next obvious country on America's hit list was Iraq. As with Iran, there was no evidence linking the Ba'athist regime to the attacks in New York. Saddam Hussein was a gangster and buffoon, but he had little truck with terrorist organizations, rightly fearing support to subversives might backfire and threaten his own regime. He little helped his case, as the Iraqi president was the single international leader who applauded the September 11 attacks, foredooming himself to an American response. In Cabinet meetings, Paul Wolfowitz emerged as the hawk pushing for punitive action against Saddam Hussein. A leaked email appeared to show that Defense Secretary Donald Rumsfeld also considered attacking

Iraq on the spurious grounds that Afghanistan offered few targets worth bombing. In the event, both were dissuaded from this course of action, but only for 18 months.

Afghanistan was then the clear target – 'not so much a state sponsor of terrorism as it is a state sponsored by terrorists', as one American official stated.[17] The CIA was well aware the Taliban-held southern half of the country had become home to several jihadist training camps, including bin Laden's camp at Tarnak, south of Kandahar. Mullah Omar had been repeatedly asked to hand over bin Laden and to close the camps. He had always refused. Pakistani involvement complicated the picture. Not only was Pakistan offering refuge and a transit point for jihadists, but its Inter-Services Intelligence Directorate, the ISI, was providing training and manpower in the Afghan terrorist camps. An attack on Afghanistan would, in one way or another, affect Pakistan.

Saudi Arabia could not be dismissed from the list. American authorities knew al-Qaeda was being sustained by the generous benefaction of wealthy Saudis and Gulf Arabs. The real paymasters of the September 11 attacks were this so-called 'golden chain', who had provided bin Laden with millions of dollars of funds, over many years, allowing him to play the Saudi rebel prince-in-exile. The key to this chain was held by the Saudi security services, and despite repeated appeals from American officials, the key was never delivered. The embarrassment of disclosure would have been too great. In a very real sense, bin Laden had mostly acted as a reckless conduit of other people's money – about $30 million annually, it was later estimated.[18] The post-September 11 world would demonize one man while ignoring the cabals of secretive, wealthy Saudis and others who provided the propellant for bin Laden's violent trajectory. None of these men would ever be brought to trial.

An indicted terrorist, the Pakistani Khaled Sheikh Mohammed was another potential suspect. His nephew Younis had been involved in the 1993 attack on the World Trade Center, and Mohammed had been involved in the 1995 Manila air plot, a foiled attack that bore similarities to the September 11 attacks. As a result of this plot, the US Attorney obtained an indictment against 'KSM' in 1996, but he escaped to Pakistan after being tipped off by a Qatari government official. During this period, the CIA was establishing its special Osama bin Laden unit. In this respect, KSM may have profited from the switch of attention. Had a special KSM Unit been set up instead, would the intelligence effort have led the US authorities to the September 11 plot? Did bin Laden play Guy Fawkes to the real agents of the plot, Khaled Sheikh Mohammed and the Egyptians?

Assessing KSM remains challenging. A large bibliography has grown around bin Laden, but remarkably, not a single book has been written about the actual mastermind and author of the September 11 attacks: Khaled Sheikh Mohammed. What is known about the individual is ambiguous. KSM was a melting pot of contradictory pasts and influences. Born in Kuwait, with Baluchi origins in Iran and Pakistan, he joined the Egyptian Muslim Brotherhood in his teens but also gained a mechanical engineering degree from North Carolina Agricultural and Technical State University.[19] He became involved in the Soviet–Afghan War but was sufficiently respectable to be personally recruited by a Qatari minister to act as a project engineer for the water and electricity ministry. Like bin Laden, he moved to the Muslim wild west of Afghanistan, where it appears the two men met, before finally settling in Karachi. He appears to have had links with some elements in the Pakistan Army. He was finally arrested in 2003 in Rawalpindi, home of the Pakistan Army. It transpired that he was lodging in the property of a Major Adil Abdul Qudoos. The major and two colonels were eventually convicted of subversion, but the trial revealed that associates of KSM, and by implication individuals with links to al-Qaeda, were being put up in Pakistan Army hostelries.[20]

It was in Khaled Sheikh Mohammed's head that the schemes that eventually crystallized into the September 11 attacks were distilled. And it was KSM who approached UBL, probably attracted by bin Laden's wealth. For his part, it appears bin Laden was initially lukewarm over the whole business of attacking North America. It was the Egyptian Mohammed Atef, one of bin Laden's subordinates, who convinced the latter to support Khaled Sheikh Mohammed, after the initial non-committal response. Gauging KSM is also complicated by the problem that his eventual capture and interrogations (which included 183 water boardings) revealed him to be a vainglorious man making probably false boasts. His broken English in public testimonies has added to the difficulties of understanding the mind of this mass murderer. Was there sufficient evidence, at the time, to lead American justice to Khaled Sheikh Mohammed, still living semi-clandestinely in Pakistan, rather than to bin Laden?[21] If there was, it was overtaken by an avalanche of anger directed at the popular hate figure Osama bin Laden.

The hijackers themselves offered no obvious target for a retaliatory attack. Who should the United States make pay, as President Bush vowed, when the hijackers included Saudi Arabians, an Egyptian, a Gulf State Arab and a Lebanese national? Fifteen of the 19 hijackers were Saudi Arabians. This group included two sets of brothers, the Hazmis and the Shehris. They were abetted wittingly and unwittingly by more Saudi Arabians, Moroccans, Yemenis, Jordanians and Gulf Arabs. By numbers alone, the provenance of the hijackers laid the guilt on Saudi Arabia's doorstep, but the Kingdom was an ally not an enemy.

The finger of blame, it seems, was always going to point at Osama bin Laden. Arab opinion assumed bin Laden's culpability. Palestinians cheered the attacks. In Pakistan there were marches in support of the attacks. Although bin Laden's complicity could not be confirmed, it was notable he was judged the prime suspect so quickly. It subsequently emerged the intelligence agencies were right to point the finger of blame at bin Laden, although understanding of al-Qaeda was distorted and imperfect.

Afghanistan as the omphalos of evil was over-stated. The idea of an attack involving hijacked aircraft had been circulating since the early 1990s. The selected 'pilots' received their tradecraft training and elementary training on flight simulators in Karachi before proceeding to America to undertake flight training. The radicalization of the suicide attackers crucially took place in Saudi Arabia. For many years the Kingdom had been fermenting and exporting an extremist, intolerant and potentially explosive Islamic world view, necessarily tolerated by the West. In the first decade of the 21st century this ideology finally detonated, with terrible consequences for the Arab world. For the suicide attackers, the *casus belli* was not America or even Israel; it was Chechnya. The lead September 11 attackers had been attempting to reach the Caucasus to take part in the jihadist war against Russia. It was the successful blocking of the smuggling routes into Chechnya that led to the diversion into Afghanistan. This was accident not deliberate planning. The later justification that British troops were fighting in Afghanistan to keep Britain safe from terrorism never acknowledged that the terrorism had been geographically dispersed from the beginning. Afghanistan was everybody else's accidental transit point, not the root of the terrorism. The root was in Pakistan, where Khaled Sheikh Mohammed was based, and it was the meddling and encouragement of Pakistan's intelligence services that was decisive in establishing clandestine camps in Afghanistan. At one stage there were scores of such Pakistani-sponsored terrorist camps, known to Western as well as the Indian intelligence services, but nobody confronted Pakistan over this matter. If any country had the claim to be the geographical locus of the September 11 attacks it was Pakistan, not Afghanistan. The ideological locus, indisputably, was the Kingdom of Saudi Arabia.

Whether or not Osama bin Laden may be considered the terrorist mastermind of the September 11 attacks, there are no serious doubts he was heavily implicated and they would not have taken place without his support. Bin Laden provided funds to jihadist and terrorist organizations, including Khaled Sheikh Mohammed. He set up training camps in Afghanistan that acted as incubators for jihadists. He actively groomed the young men who became the September 11 hijackers. He provided ideological inspiration and a conduit for anti-American vitriol. He was cognizant and approved of the attacks, whether or not they were his idea. He encouraged Khaled Sheikh Mohammed to complete the operation. The Saudi hijackers themselves felt they were undertaking a martyrdom operation for 'Sheikh Osama'. For these reasons and despite all the uncertainties, it was with justification that within days of the attacks, Osama bin Laden, al-Qaeda and Afghanistan became the main targets.

What surprised was that a man so loudly bent on attacking America should have so equally loudly denied any involvement in the attacks. Five days after the attacks, a bin Laden statement was broadcast on Al Jazeera television denying culpability. Amazingly, for someone so vainglorious, Osama bin Laden showed no desire to claim authorship for the most spectacular terrorist attack in history. If one of the aims of the attacks was to enhance his reputation, this seemed remarkable coyness (a significant segment of the Arab world was celebrating him as a hero anyway, and jihadist recruiting boomed).

Two interviews followed: the first with the Al Jazeera journalist Tayseer Allouni, and the second with the Saudi cleric Ali al-Ghamdi. In the former, he justified the attacks on the United States in a long-winded ramble. In the latter, he indicated that he knew when and where the attacks were going to take place (remarking that he had expected three or four floors to collapse, not the entire buildings). It was not until 2004, against the background of a US presidential election, that bin Laden broadcast a statement fully admitting knowledge but again not responsibility for the September 11 attacks.[22] Osama bin Laden, in fact, would never claim credit or direct responsibility for the 'Holy Tuesday operation'. Despite the leaking of hundreds of Guantanamo prisoner reports and scores of subsequent interviews with people who may be considered primary sources to the events, no coherent account has ever emerged describing how bin Laden planned, masterminded and directed the September 11 attacks.

A plausible explanation is that he just didn't. It *was* ultimately the work of Khaled Sheikh Mohammed, abetted principally by his associate Ramzi bin al-Shibh. The CIA's original assessment of bin Laden may have been accurate all along – ultimately, he had been an 'extremist financier'.

In the aftermath of September 11, such equivocating would have fallen on deaf ears. Osama bin Laden became the most wanted criminal on earth because America needed a bogeyman. Hot on the heels of American revenge was a media machine stoking a good cop versus bad guy story. The problem with the rush to kill or capture Osama bin Laden was that America was proposing to do this by invading a country and toppling its regime – and Article 5 of the NATO charter had just been invoked. The soon-to-be announced Operation *Enduring Freedom* would drag NATO to war, or not quite. As the US Department of Defense (DOD) fully understood, only a handful of NATO partners could actually be counted on to fight a war. From this short list, perhaps only one or two had useful military capabilities. One of these countries with a potentially useable military capability was Britain. The day after the attacks a single DC-10 flew heads of the Secret Intelligence Service (SIS), Security Service (MI5) and Government Communications Headquarters (GCHQ) to Washington, DC, one of the few aircraft allowed to fly over American airspace in the immediate aftermath of September 11. Nine days later, the president of the United States held a telephone conference with the British prime minister. The subject of the conference was the forthcoming war and Britain's participation in that war. Blair responded to the tocsin calls by making 37 trips and flying 40,000 miles over the next eight weeks, drumming up support for the war. If a single period were needed in the aftermath of September 11 to highlight Britain's status as America's dependable military ally, this was it.

The conference also marked the beginning of one of the most unlikely political alliances between two contrasting world leaders. Bush was an ineloquent Texan Republican, prone to gaffes and with little experience of foreign affairs. He read little and preferred to receive information through verbal briefs. He lacked the charisma and oratory of his predecessor, Bill Clinton, hiding instead behind a bluff, joking persona that sometimes verged on smirking sophomore. His values were Christian and conservative. His appeal to voters was uncomplicated – if you voted for Bush, you voted for God and America. There was also a hint – at least before the September 11 attacks – that Bush Junior was developing into one of the laziest presidents in history. The number of days he was spending in his ranch in Crawford, Texas, rather than at his office in Washington, did not go unnoticed. His British counterpart could hardly have been more different. Tony Blair was the young, energetic leader of a reformed socialist party: New Labour. He played rock guitar, swept away the fusty Conservatives, and ushered in a period of 'Cool Britannia'. This domestic frivolity belied an enthusiastic and serious appetite for foreign affairs. Tony Blair's wide smile became one of his signature features, but he was not a prime minister afraid to bare fangs and go to war.

The two leaders became united by a shared messianic belief that military force can be a force for good – the phrase that became the Ministry of Defence's official motto during the Blair premiership. Daily reminders of the purpose of military power spread across the government department in hundreds of posters, corporate mugs and mouse mats. To hold the belief that military force can do 'good' required a suspension of the messy realities of warfare, as well as a naïve and simplified world view. Both leaders trumpeted such simplicities, leaving the details and the unpleasantness of actually running wars successfully to subordinates. Churchill's warning that the national leader who gives the signal for war 'no longer becomes the master of policy but the slave of unforeseeable and uncontrollable events' was never truer than in the Bush–Blair partnership.

The September 11 attacks gave wind to the so-called Blair Doctrine, a phrase coined by the media rather than by the prime minister. This doctrine, such as it existed, offered a world view so simple and persuasive that it would be uncritically adopted by the Conservative–Liberal Democrat government in 2010. The ideas that informed the doctrine had already fermented in the prime minister's mind when he spoke on 22 April 1999, at the Economic Club in Chicago, at the height of the Kosovo conflict. Five criteria for 'a more active and interventionist role in solving the world's problems', crucially outside UN auspices, were posited: be sure of your case, exhaust all other options, ask if military operations can be reasonably prosecuted, prepare for the long term and confirm that national interest is at stake. Reportedly, these criteria were originally coined by Professor Lawrence Freedman at King's College, but whatever their provenance, they would anyway be ironically ignored in the subsequent invasion of Iraq. The key point about this doctrine was that it had a humanitarian impulse. This chimed with Foreign Secretary Robin Cook, who had entered office with a determination to pursue an ethical foreign policy. It also linked with the 1998 Strategic Defence Review, which cast the armed forces as 'a force for good'. Blair did genuinely and honourably seek a more effective international mechanism for resolving humanitarian crises, and the personal investment he made in these ideas would eventually bear fruit in the UN-endorsed concept of the Responsibility to Protect (R2P).

The doctrine received its fullest expression in a speech delivered in Banqueting Hall shortly after the attacks, but by now its foundation had subtly changed:

> What is clear is that 11 September has not just given impetus and urgency to such solutions, it has opened the world up … one illusion has been shattered on 11 September: that we can have the good life of the West irrespective of the state of the rest of the world … Once chaos and strife have got a grip on a region or a country trouble will soon be exported.[23]

Dealing with this anticipated export of 'trouble', in practice, meant the despatch of military forces to faraway lands before 'they' do 'harm to us'. This policy may have had merit if it in any way reflected Britain's military capabilities, which it unfortunately did not, and if it was not fatally weakened by a supreme disregard over whether such interventions would actually work. The formula was so self-servingly justified, so apparently above the necessity for debate, that, in effect, there was none. The last half-century had witnessed an exceedingly long roll-call of chaos, strife and 'failed states', none of which had led to any harm being done to 'us'. Nor was it evident in 2001 that any state, or more pertinently 'non-state actor', to use the modern euphemism, was threatening Britain. To live in Britain at the beginning of the 21st century was to live in a totally unthreatened country and one of the safest in the world. No intelligence agency uncovered any Islamist terrorist plots against Britain in the aftermath of the September 11 attacks, for the simple reason that there were none. These considerations were swept aside by the armada of billowing words. The world had to be fixed and no corner was beyond the reach of the Blair broom: the Middle East, Africa, Russia and the United Nations. If this was 'Utopian', the prime minister was unapologetic. 'So let us seize the chance of this time,' he told the audience of City worthies. 'Future generations will not forgive us if we fail' – sentiments so grotesquely ironic it seems harsh to point out that he would both fail and leave behind a wake of angry Britons wholly unprepared to forgive him the chaos he helped trigger.

America's plan for toppling the Taliban regime, which Britain would be invited to join, was a dusted-off variant of a scheme devised by the CIA under the Clinton presidency. Broadly, it involved two planks: first, the Taliban would be classed as a terrorist regime and ostracized in international forums; and second, funds would be channelled to the Taliban's arch enemy, the Northern Alliance, who would topple the regime with American military assistance.[24] Ironically, American officials had previously kept the Northern Alliance at arm's length, partly to appease Pakistan, and partly because this confederation of Tajiks, Uzbeks and others was viewed as a minority grouping unlikely to ever wield power in a predominantly Pashtun Afghanistan. Now the hillbillies of the north were a key ally. This plan reflected a complementary shift in doctrine across the Atlantic – the very real Bush Doctrine – or America's right to act pre-emptively against potential enemies, which in fact had roots in a cauldron of ideas generated in the fall days of the Clinton presidency. The Clinton-era Operations *Infinite Reach* and *Infinite Resolve* thus readily mutated into Operation *Enduring Freedom* and ultimately a 'Global War on Terrorism'.[25]

It was this intersection of ideas – both interventionist – that transformed Blair's original impulses and fixed London's support for Washington. The Blair Doctrine had been about doing something to resolve an existing humanitarian crisis; the Bush Doctrine was about acting pre-emptively and aggressively against an imagined, possible future threat. These were two quite different ideas, but as no British government dare challenge an American orthodoxy, it was a matter of inevitability that a British prime minister would end up adopting, or at least partnering with, the Bush Doctrine. That Blair believed in these imagined threats made the switch easy.

What emerged from this coincidence of Anglo-Saxon interventionist impulses was a jihadist domino theory, articulated with religious certainty in Washington and chanted by London. Fifty years had passed since Eisenhower made an allusion to falling dominos, long enough for two generations to forget how the thrall of this monolithic idea had led America to a tragic communion with Indochina. Now the dominos were repositioned. If terrorists and their supporters were not dealt with, wherever they harboured, then it was just a question of time before the dominos would fall, and Western cities would be under attack. In the wake of the September 11 attacks, who would have questioned this canon, any more than question the Red Menace in the 1950s?

What exactly would Britain's role be within the inevitable American military response? On 4 October, Geoff Hoon returned to the House of Commons to present the answer to this question. He opened with a forgivable error of fact. It was clear, he asserted, that some 6,000 people had been killed in the September 11 attacks, doubling the body count. Somewhere between 14,000 and 17,000 people had in fact entered the Twin Towers that morning – it was, in the end, miraculous that more people had not been killed. Although it was not known at the time, after American nationals Britain had suffered the most fatalities. Sixty-seven Britons lost their lives, including two brothers from Ipswich, Anthony and Timothy Gilbert, who worked for the same financial firm.

Hoon's warning was clear: 'The time for forceful military action against Usama bin Laden, his associates, and, if they do not act, those who support them, is coming.'[26] In turn, Britain would do whatever was required to support an American military campaign: 'We have made it clear to our US allies that we will offer them every assistance in the action they take.'[27] This was not, as it happened, empty rhetoric. There was a real eagerness, even over-eagerness, to demonstrate the useful military contribution that Britain could make. This sincere willingness to support the American cause was matched by an equally real fear that British military assistance would be spurned, or that a token contribution would be accepted, but no more. It was a remarkable measure of the unequal nature of the Anglo-American partnership at the beginning of the 21st century that the government should be agitated on this point. American indifference to a possible British military contribution was not entirely misplaced. The political value of an Anglo-American coalition escaped no one, but within the Pentagon there were individuals who did not rate the contribution of a middle-sized power with down-sized, under-resourced armed forces. Over time, American diffidence towards its allies would change, but in the winter of 2001 Britain represented a political fig leaf, not serious military muscle.

If Hoon made it clear that Britain was prepared to go to war over this matter, he left the details of Britain's military contribution and the likely missions that British forces might undertake deliberately vague. The important point was to express solidarity with Washington. Attention then turned to the 20,000-strong force in the Middle East, including almost all of 3 Commando Brigade, participating in Exercise *Saif Sareea II*. This naval task force, commanded by Rear Admiral James Burnell-Nugent, included the aircraft carrier HMS *Illustrious* and the amphibious transport HMS *Fearless*, with escorts provided by HMS *Cornwall* and HMS *Southampton*. The task force also included two submarines, HMS *Trafalgar* and HMS *Triumph*, as well as seven support ships. Crucially, the two submarines were armed with American Tomahawk missiles. Around 50 RAF aircraft in various roles were also taking part in the exercise.

How would the task force be used? On this point, the defence secretary could not help indulging in some party-politicking:

> The Strategic Defence Review leaves us well placed to take on and defeat international terrorism. We have significantly improved capabilities – reconnaissance, intelligence, surveillance, target acquisition, precision strike, rapid deployment, and sophisticated command and control – all of which will play their part in the campaign against international terrorism.[28]

This cheerleading was for a domestic audience. Nobody in the Pentagon, after the embarrassing British performance in Kosovo (Operation *Allied Force*, 1999), believed him. Within 18 months the boast would sound hollow after a British Army division was stalled for three weeks outside Basra by a small number of lightly armed Ba'athists, even as two American divisions advanced 500 kilometres north to Baghdad, swatting all opposition.

American scepticism over the value of the British maritime task force off the coast of Oman was well founded. The aircraft carrier and amphibious transport were old and in constant need of maintenance. A joke circulated that HMS *Illustrious* should be renamed HMS *Impediment* because it offered little real military capability and got in the way of larger American carriers. The 16 Sea Harriers it was carrying were just for show. None of the deficiencies highlighted in Kosovo, such as the lack of an adequate targeting pod, had been addressed, and the aircraft did not have the range to reach Afghanistan anyway without multiple refuels. Plans would be hurriedly made to replace them with helicopters that might at least offer some utility. The RAF was little better placed to support an American-led war in Afghanistan. In the end, the only support American planners requested was tankers (because of an incompatibility between US

Air Force and US Navy refuel nozzles which British tanker aircraft could overcome). The RAF would be reduced to acting as service stations in the sky for American aircraft. The vaunted reconnaissance capability which the defence secretary alluded to rested on the Canberra, an aircraft about to be retired after half a century in service. There were no credible plans to replace this museum piece. The intelligence, surveillance and target acquisition capability relied on two variants of the Nimrod, an aircraft that was patched up dangerously during the Falklands Conflict, and eventually exploded over the skies of Afghanistan, with the loss of 14 lives. The replacement aircraft, another Nimrod variant, was sitting on drawing boards and developing into another procurement scandal. The claimed precision strike capability was also not credible. When British forces rolled into Iraq in 2003, the RAF would still be waiting for an adequate precision strike capability to support ground troops. Unwilling to cause civilian casualties, pilots resorted to lobbing inert concrete bombs, a plainly useless gesture. The 'sophisticated command and control' supposedly enjoyed by Britain's armed forces was a Byzantine mess of ageing systems that could not keep up with the pace of modern warfare. One of the reasons why Britain's armed forces *had* to operate under an American umbrella was precisely because they lacked the information technology systems to operate coherently. About the only element of the British task force the Pentagon could rely on was the ever-dependable Royal Marines. The remainder of the capabilities that the defence secretary claimed simply did not stand up to military scrutiny. The truth was that Britain was ill-prepared for war and the Americans knew it.

There was another reason why Hoon could offer little detail on the forthcoming military operations in Afghanistan: D-Day was only three days away. American military planners had worked overtime following the September 11 attacks, and at the heart of their efforts was Donald Rumsfeld's vision of 'war lite'. This would not be a war fought by a large army manoeuvring tanks, artillery and great logistic trains across the plains of Afghanistan. Building up such a force and projecting it to land-locked Afghanistan would have presented insuperable problems even with American transport resources. Neighbours – Russia, Pakistan and Iran – would have fretted. The entire operation would have taken much longer, eroding the momentum generated following the September 11 attacks. As importantly, American public opinion wanted swift revenge. President Bush, initially criticized for his reaction in the immediate wake of the attacks, was eager to atone for early hesitancy and deliver that revenge. Operation *Enduring Freedom* would be a war fought by around 350 special forces soldiers and by American air power.[29] Among this special forces contingent would be troopers from 22 SAS and marines from the SBS. These soldiers would be the only British servicemen invited to join the American show.

On 7 October, at one o'clock in the afternoon, Eastern Daylight Time, President Bush announced the initiation of military operations:

> Every nation has a choice to make. In this conflict, there is no neutral ground. If any government sponsors the outlaws and killers of innocents, they have become outlaws and murderers, themselves. And they will take that lonely path at their own peril. The battle is now joined on many fronts. We will not waver; we will not tire; we will not falter; and we will not fail. Peace and freedom will prevail.[30]

Reaching for the political fig leaf that this was a coalition operation, and not just an example of the American superpower wielding its club, Bush took special care to mention 'the staunch friend, Great Britain'. The British government duly obliged by launching a salvo of American-built Tomahawk missiles from HMS *Trafalgar* and HMS *Triumph*, at H-Hour, at targets supplied by American intelligence. Five days later a second salvo was fired, after which British stocks were exhausted.

2

International Rescue

Afghanistan, 2001–05

Operation *Enduring Freedom* was a strange war. The collapse of the Taliban regime was precipitous, an indication of the fragility of the movement and the wider bankruptcy of the Afghan state. Air strikes started on 7 October, and just over one month later the victorious Northern Alliance was walking into an undefended Kabul. One American soldier was killed by enemy action. The Taliban mostly fled to their southern hinterlands. Pakistani fighters re-crossed the border to the safety of the ungoverned tribal areas. The Arab foreign legion skulked away to the mountainous Tora Bora region of eastern Afghanistan. With them retreated Osama bin Laden. He fled in such haste a television crew guided by locals was able to film his abandoned town house, noting among other domestic details the large supply of medicines Osama bin Laden appeared to be taking. Soon after the investment of Kabul, Hamid Karzai, a Pashtun chosen by Washington to lead a re-founded Afghanistan, was appointed the unelected chairman of an 'Afghanistan Interim Administration'. Within six months, the Pentagon would kill or capture 16 of 25 al-Qaeda leaders, and 21 of 27 Taliban leaders on its most wanted list.[1]

How did America succeed so stunningly? At the time, success seemed far from assured, with many commentators predicting America would be sucked into an Afghan quagmire, like the Soviets before them. These warnings were not without foundation. American soldiers were effectively joining a civil war that had been in progress for over five years without resolution (or since 1978, taking the longer view). The two opposing sides were a hotchpotch of alliances and misalliances, each with competing aims and a tendency to switch sides when conditions changed. The only certainties in this civil war were the implacable hatred between the Taliban and the Northern Alliance and the fact that neither side had the strength to win the war. The Pentagon itself, it appears, had doubts, with some planners anticipating the proposed special forces war would fail, and the 101st and 82nd Airborne Divisions would need to be deployed to sort out the mess.[2]

The Taliban offensive that swept the movement to power in 1996 had failed to entirely defeat the confederation of tribes collected under the banner of the Northern Alliance and led by the charismatic Ahmad Shah Massoud. Three static fronts had emerged with fixed defensive lines. About 50 kilometres north of Kabul on the Shomali Plain, Massoud permanently deployed a few thousand fighters to protect the gateway to the Panshir Valley, the heartland of the Northern Alliance and the scene of bitter fighting during the Soviet–Afghan War. A second front was held at Takhar. A third front existed in an enclave at Darrah-e Suf, south of the Uzbek city Mazar-e-Sharif. After the capture and ransacking of Mazar-e-Sharif by the Taliban, Abdul Rashid Dostum, the notorious Uzbek warlord, had fled to exile in Turkey. In the spring of 2001, Massoud had enticed the moustachioed general back to Afghanistan with the promise of a triple alliance between Dostum's own men; the Shia Islamic Unity Party (Shia Hizb-i-Wahdat Islami), led by an individual named Mohammad Mohaqiq; and Massoud's lieutenant in the area, Ustaz Atta Mohammed.[3] It was a typical Afghan arrangement. The persecuted Shias needed security, Dostum wanted to regain his old fiefdom, and Massoud sought reinforcements in his war against the Taliban.

It was to these three fronts that American and British special forces detachments deployed over the next two weeks following the initiation of the ground war, based on a long-standing CIA plan known as the 'Blue Sky Memo'.[4] What they found was a ragbag of militias, each owing allegiance to their immediate commander, full of fight but without the means to break the deadlock on the front lines. The stalemate could only be broken by American air power, but this was being used to pursue a classic air campaign against strategic rather than tactical targets. That the planners of the air campaign chose to fall back on a template first used in the first Gulf War and later refined in the Kosovo War betrayed a lack of understanding of the true situation on the ground. There were very few strategic targets of any worth in Afghanistan, and these posed no threat whatsoever to American forces anyway. On the first day of the air campaign, 16 air strikes were conducted against surface-to-air (SAM) sites, 12 were conducted against airfields and four were conducted against command and control centres.[5] By day five, the number of missions flown against SAM sites, airfields and command centres had dwindled to zero – there was nothing left to attack.[6]

The frustration at American targeting was such that, in an improbable twist, Iranian intelligence began to feed the CIA with grid references of worthwhile Taliban targets, pleased to see these former enemies get their comeuppance at the hands of the Americans. The frustration was also being felt by America's new-found ally, the Northern Alliance. The few air strikes called to support the militias on the front lines generally involved a pair of aircraft dropping a handful of bombs. The war was never going to be won at this pace, and criticism of the war plan became vocal. Defense Secretary Donald Rumsfeld began to manifest frustration with his service chiefs. America needed to demonstrate progress on the ground.

On 30 October the US theatre commander-in-chief General Tommy Franks travelled to Dushanbe and held meetings with representatives of the Northern Alliance.[7] The outcomes from this meeting were immediate. More special forces detachments were deployed to the front lines, and the air campaign switched decisively in support of the ground war. The three Taliban fronts at Taloqan, Mazar-e-Sharif and Shomali were all targeted. Mazar-e-Sharif, in particular, received the brunt of the American bombing effort. In the first week of November, two-thirds of all bombs landed on the Taliban front lines encircling this city.[8] Converting this expenditure of high explosives into tangible results on the ground, however, was not without military and political ramifications.

American focus on Mazar-e-Sharif was driven by both political and military considerations. After two decades of bending to Pakistani sensibilities in the region, American policymakers were still finding it hard to get tough with Pakistan's rulers. The Taliban were Pakistan's client. The capture of Kabul and the dethroning of Mullah Omar were still viewed with horror by many Pakistani officials, unable to accept these would be the inevitable consequences of the Taliban refusal to hand over Osama bin Laden. The latter's eventual escape would, in part, be the result of Pakistani fretting over American intentions in Afghanistan and America's sensitivity to these concerns. In this sense, the military campaign was hobbled from the outset, and its primary objective – the capture or killing of Osama bin Laden – was always likely to have been difficult.[9] The capture of the

Uzbek Mazar-e-Sharif, never a Taliban city anyway, was much less likely to stir Islamabad.

The Northern Alliance had already attempted to take the city in the third week of October but failed. On 4 November, the offensive resumed. The following day, after a brief but violent battle, the nearby Keshendeh fell to Dostum's fighters on horseback. In a bold gesture, Uzbek cavalry at one point charged Taliban T-55 tanks, an assault witnessed by amazed and impressed American Green Berets. Five days after the offensive started, the loose coalition of tribesmen entered the city of Mazar-e-Sharif. It was late evening, and the Taliban used the darkness to scatter, leaving behind all their heavy equipment. At last the joint American–Northern Alliance war had its first real success on the ground. In a symbolic gesture, several pieces of the World Trade Center were buried in the city.[10] Only small pockets of Taliban, in the end, fought to the death in Mazar-e-Sharif.[11] Many more, mostly Pakistani prisoners, were slaughtered outright in revenge killings. This was not just an army in retreat; this was an army without a stomach for the fight.

The lack of fight seemed to deepen with Taliban equivocation over the entire rationale for the war. Mullah Omar had never sought confrontation with the United States, a country he knew nothing about and whose emissaries he never met because they were not Muslims. The war came to Mullah Omar because of his misjudged stance over Osama bin Laden. More worldly Afghans in the Taliban government could see the brewing storm and were unhappy over its predictable consequences. Nobody, it seems, was able or willing to persuade Mullah Omar to change his mind. When the storm broke, self-survival took over and most chose to seek shelter rather than brave the elements.

The collapse of Mazar-e-Sharif produced a snowball effect which caught everyone by surprise. The day after the fall of Mazar-e-Sharif, Dostum captured his old fiefdoms of Sheberghan, Sar-e Pol and Maimanah, where the British would later set up a temporary base. Qala-e-Naw fell soon afterwards. Within a week, Dostum was celebrating his return to scenic Bamiyan, where two famous Buddhist statues carved into a cliff face had been destroyed by the Taliban. Again the Taliban fled offering no resistance. When Kabul collapsed a week later to Tajik forces led by Fahim Khan, it was journalists scrambling to keep up with the Northern Alliance columns who beat American forces to the city. In western Afghanistan, Ismail Khan, another Tajik, seized Herat.

In the wake of these operations an episode occurred that revealed the depth of support offered by Pakistan to the Taliban. It was not just Mullah Omar or bin Laden who failed to foresee America would launch a ground invasion and prevail swiftly. The Pakistani Inter-Services Intelligence Directorate, the ISI, also seemed to get caught out. Scores of Pakistani intelligence officials and army officers now found themselves trapped in the Kunduz pocket and facing almost certain death. General Musharraf had no choice but to appeal to the Bush government to allow a rescue mission to recover the stranded spies. Over several nights starting on 5 November a series of secret flights were given permission to land in Kunduz, to rescue the Pakistani intelligence officers (dubbed 'Operation *Evil Airlift*').[12] The very people who had once supported bin Laden were being allowed to escape, protected by American air power.

With the collapse of the northern fronts, only Kabul held out but it was becoming increasingly obvious the Taliban regime was in its death throes. A motley caravan of Northern Alliance T-55 tanks and assorted armoured vehicles pointed itself south and began to roll up the fleeing Taliban on the Old Road to Kabul. A single American B-52 bomber was all that was needed to hurry the Taliban along their way.[13] The offensive started on 12 November. By the following grey morning, following a two-hour bombardment, the Northern Alliance was parading through the streets of the city from which it had been ejected five years earlier. Excited mobs led Western journalists to photograph the few dead Taliban that could be found, like roadkill. The unthinkable had happened, but for American forces the celebrations were muted. Osama bin Laden, who rented a house in Kabul, and who appears to have fled to the city from Kandahar expecting a strike against his Tarnak Farm compound, had vanished. There were rumours, counter-rumours and false sightings, but nobody really knew where the fugitive had fled.

The consequences of the fall of Kabul were strangely anti-climactic. The Taliban regime had been defeated but the war was far from over. The main prize was at large. Mullah Omar, the Taliban leader, had also vanished, reportedly smuggled over the border on the back of a motorbike. According to the Pakistani journalist and author Ahmed Rashid, Mullah Omar in fact hid in Helmand and only made the passage of forced exile in the winter of 2002, when it was apparent that American forces were staying in Afghanistan and effectively protracting (in his eyes) a vindictive war against Pashtuns.[14] Following him into exile in Quetta were the former head of the Taliban army, Mullah Akhtar Osmani; the hard-line, one-legged Mullah Dadullah; and his former interior and defence ministers, Mullah Abdul Razzaq and Mullah Obaidullah Akhund.

There was no surrender, and a peace treaty was an unthinkable as well as an impractical proposition. Pockets of Taliban (in fact mostly foreign fighters) still existed throughout the territory of Afghanistan. Militias continued to roam the countryside – nobody knew how many or where. With the traditional fighting season now drawing to a close, some chose to lay down their arms and return to their farms. The Taliban pocket in Kunduz, mainly refugee fighters from Mazar-e-Sharif, quit the fight on 24 November, encouraged by a demonstration of American air power.

Two weeks later, in the south, Afghanistan's soon-to-be interim president Hamid Karzai accepted the bloodless surrender of Kandahar on 6 December. The fall of this city was also anti-climactic. US Marine Task Force 58 had already seized a desert airstrip around 80 kilometres south of Kandahar (the same airstrip used by Osama bin Laden and wealthy Gulf Arabs on hunting trips). Now renamed 'Objective Rhino', it served as a base for a move north to the city. With American and Pakistani support, a former, brutal warlord, Gul Agha Sherzai, advanced from the Pakistani border leading a reconstituted Barakzai tribal militia. Karzai's Popalzai kinsmen marched from Uruzgan in the north, and the western approaches to the city were sealed by Alikozai tribesmen who had broken their alliance with the Taliban. Reportedly, it was Mullah Naqib, the Alikozai leader, rather than Karzai, who was instrumental in persuading the Taliban to hand over power peacefully. Another account suggests the Helmandi Rais Baghrani played a key role.[15] The latter would then be accused of sheltering Mullah Omar, creating an American obsession with Baghran in northern Helmand, Rais Baghrani's heartland. The British would eventually pay dearly for this fixation, finding themselves drawn into a pointless sweep of northern Helmand – Operation *Mountain Thrust* – when they eventually deployed a task force to the province in spring 2006.

The fall of Helmand was similarly quick and virtually bloodless.[16] American aircraft bombed a camp in Bolan (an area just west of the provincial capital Lashkar Gah); a hill south of the commercial capital Gereshk, used as an artillery base; a purported Taliban headquarters in the same town; and, oddly, a cotton gin which the British had originally built. The Alizai Sher Mohammed Akhundzada then crossed the border from Pakistan with the soon-to-be president Hamid Karzai and mobilized fighters in northern

Helmand. In the south, a Noorzai named Abdul Rahman Jan who had been evicted by the Taliban returned from Iranian exile and retook Marjah District, after some stiff fighting. By the end of November, the Taliban had fled, leaving Helmand to a four-way power tussle between another Noorzai named Isreal Khan (who somewhat opportunistically declared himself governor), an ex-mujahid Hazifullah Khan, Abdul Rahman Jan and Sher Akhundzada. The latter won the contest endorsed by the Americans notwithstanding the majority of his fighters were Taliban who had simply switched sides. The commercial capital Gereshk at first went to an ex-Harakat* mujahid named Khan Mohammed, but he was eventually displaced by the American-backed ex-Hizb-e Islami† mujahid Mir Wali, who was given command of the 93rd Division, such as it existed.[17] The first Western soldiers reportedly entered Lashkar Gah on 31 December, marking the beginning of what would be a 14-year involvement in the province.

With the Taliban's traditional stronghold surrendered to a fellow Pashtun, at least the internecine Afghan war was over for that winter. American forces hunting Osama bin Laden were drawn to the Tora Bora mountain range south-east of Kabul, where all leads seemed to point. This was wild and difficult country, covered in the lower reaches with conifer forests that afforded plenty of protection to anyone evading a hunter force. The mountainsides were riddled with caves that offered concealment from the air as well as protection from aerial bombs. This is where the last lines of the first act of the war were written. Bombers dropped 15,000-pound 'Daisy Cutter' bombs and 5,000-pound GBU-28 'bunker busters' to winkle out the mostly Arab fighters that had fled to Tora Bora. All of this was to no avail. In some cases evidence of occupancy was found, and corpses. Mostly the air strikes appeared to destroy vacated positions. As Anthony Cordesman observed, little about Operation *Enduring Freedom* gave confidence that Western forces had learned how to fight an irregular enemy.[18]

Crucially, however many Arab fighters were or were not caught in the Tora Bora mountains, Osama bin Laden was not among them. The very

* A traditionalist, Islamist political movement and one of the largest of the mujahidin groups.

† Hizb-e Islami was one of the larger mujahidin factions and a rival to the Taliban which it periodically clashed with in pitched battles.

Afghan militias co-opted by American special forces to winkle him out, actually helped to smuggle him out. This was suspected at the time by the American commanders on the spot and should have rung a bank of alarm bells in Washington, but did not. Bin Laden's evasion had one inescapable implication. The war, now dubbed the 'Global War on Terror', would go on. This was a problem. Nobody in the Pentagon, still less in Whitehall, had given serious consideration to act two of the war. There was no back-up plan. Lord Frederick Roberts's famous conundrum, first posed in 1879, had no answer in the winter of 2001: 'The two questions therefore which chiefly exercised the minds of people in authority with regard to Afghan affairs, were, what was to be done with Afghanistan now we had got it, and, who would be set up as Ruler with any chance of being able to hold his own?'[19]

Operation *Enduring Freedom* had been an updated version of the Clinton-era Operations *Infinite Reach* and *Resolve*. These envisaged stamping on an enemy and paid little attention to what followed afterwards. What emerged was a military plan outside a political, cultural or social context. In other words, what emerged was no plan at all.

Britain's part in Operation *Enduring Freedom* (named Operation *Veritas*) was almost invisible and would have remained so but for the actions of an Afghan cameraman who filmed British special forces soldiers firing wildly over the ramparts of Qala-e Jangi fort at Mazar-e-Sharif, following an attempted jail-break by Taliban prisoners.[20] Qala-e Jangi became the most extensively reported single event of the war because of the coincidence of at least three television crews at the fort when the fighting erupted. Over 200 Taliban prisoners were killed in this controversial incident.[21] Television footage later showed dozens of bodies strewn across an open courtyard of the fort. None was armed and many had their hands bound behind their backs. At least two British servicemen were also wounded in one of several American air strikes on the fort. If a similar incident involving a massacre of prisoners and British troops had occurred in Bosnia or Kosovo there would have been demands for a public inquiry, but this was Afghanistan, and Taliban lives (or Pakistani and Arab lives, as it seems most of the 'Taliban' prisoners were in fact foreigners) were a debased currency. Calls by Amnesty International to investigate the deaths were rejected by Washington and London. Nobody questioned too hard what actually happened at Qala-e Jangi, and the incident was swiftly buried, along with the bodies, following the collapse of the Taliban regime.

The public face of Britain's involvement in the short war to oust the Taliban regime was presented by the faces of Royal Marines from B Company, 40 Commando, who arrived on the night of 15 November to secure Bagram Airport north of Kabul, blinking in the lights of media cameras. Dressed in a mix of green and desert camouflage, as if confused by their ultimate destination, they stepped off the ramp of the RAF C-130 with the swagger of new boys joining an old war. It seemed an apt metaphor for Britain's entire subsequent involvement in Afghanistan.

What they found was chaos, and not a little suspicion. The airport was derelict and littered with the debris of previous fighting. Unexploded ordnance lay everywhere. When the airport was finally declared safe, over 200 unexploded pieces of ordnance had been recovered (which was a modest number compared with Kabul Airport, where French soldiers ended up disposing of 70,000 anti-personnel mines).[22] There was no running water or electricity. Everything that was needed to survive had to be flown in. The MOD's new-found enthusiasm for expeditionary warfare was about to be put to the test. Locals who remembered the arrival of Soviet troops at this airport had to be calmed down by the marines. Gun-toting Afghans soon joined the British contingent, but nobody was really sure whether they were there to assist in guarding the airport or to keep the British constrained within the airport compound. Within a few weeks this first 'footprint' swelled, with the arrival of American soldiers bringing additional resources, vital communications and the confidence of a force that meant to stay.

If it was evident that this Anglo-American force intended to remain in Afghanistan at least for the foreseeable future, it was not clear it had a meaningful post-war plan. British campaign objectives ranged from the fanciful to the nebulous. The problem with the goals was not just their naïve worthiness, but the fact that no British government would seriously countenance the true cost of putting back together the Afghan Humpty Dumpty. More relevantly, nor would an American government. The coalition had not resourced or prepared a long-term post-war strategy. Partial victory and its consequences had not been considered. From the very beginning, the finishing line had been blown over by the desert sands. As Cordesman warned:

> In war, more than any other human activity no one should begin what they are not prepared to finish, and few modern wars will have outcomes

> where desirable governments, economies, societies, and patterns of alliance magically occur simply because the fighting ends. The officer who cannot adjust to this reality is unfit to wear his or her uniform. The political leader unwilling to face this reality is, at best, a recipe for military futility and, at worst, a recipe for disaster.[23]

As if keen to sow these seeds of disaster, an ebullient British prime minister confidently told the country: 'We are not here just for today, tomorrow, [or] next week.'[24] Britain's commitment to Afghanistan would indeed become long term and burdensome, but the prime minister who made the commitment would be long retired and forging a lucrative career in international consultancy.

For the coalition, which by early December meant a loose and uneasy alliance of NATO countries, some political arrangement was urgently needed to fill the vacuum created by the deposition of the Taliban regime. The Bonn Agreement, hastily drafted under the auspices of the German government on 5 December, aimed to address this question. Four stages were envisaged to create a stable political future for Afghanistan. First, an Afghan Interim Authority (AIA) would be set up under the Western-appointed Hamid Karzai, a moderate Pushtun. In the second phase, an Emergency Loya Jirga – or meeting of Afghanistan's power-brokers – would convene in June the following year, to select a Transitional Authority. This would be followed by a Constitutional Loya Jirga in December 2002 to determine Afghanistan's future constitution. If the plan held, the last stage would involve presidential elections in December 2004, followed by parliamentary elections in 2005. Holding the plan together would prove a difficult task hampered by internal rivalries, a barely functioning government and Western reluctance to over-committing in Afghanistan. Two implications were clear: for better or for worse, the little-known Hamid Karzai would be Afghanistan's de facto president for at least the next three years, and possibly longer. And second, the AIA would be run by the victors of the war, creating the impression that the whole scheme had been a reward for the Northern Alliance and punishment for the majority Pashtun population.

In all these deliberations the Taliban were conspicuous by their absence, which would later be viewed by many as a strategic mistake. This would lead to the fallacy of the 'missed opportunity' (much like the 1945 'missed opportunity' relating to Ho Chi Minh). It is the case that several key

Taliban leaders made peace overtures to Karzai in December. This group included Mullah Omar's chief of staff Tayyeb Agha; his deputy, Mullah Baradar; defence minister Mullah Obaidullah; and Mullah Abdul Razzaq, the interior minister. But the argument that the Taliban may have been engaged in peace talks in Bonn was totally spurious. The Bush government made over 30 attempts to negotiate with the Taliban before launching Operation *Enduring Freedom*, all fruitless. The Northern Alliance had no intention of welcoming its recent enemy to the negotiating table and would not have done so even if pressed. And lastly, a dogmatic and simplistic Western categorization of Taliban as terrorists foredoomed any chance of reconciliation. Even if some Taliban representatives had been admitted to Bonn, what could they have possibly negotiated? A Western crisis industry – the so-called 'Kosovo crowd' – had already swung into action with its army of experts and consultants, all mapping out what was good for Afghanistan, and eyeing lucrative contracts. There was nothing *to* negotiate: the Western experts already had the answers.

Perhaps the most surprising appointment in the new political arrangement was that of Hamid Karzai himself as chairman of the Ruling Council. A Popalzai from Kandahar, Karzai belonged to an established political dynasty. His grandfather and father served as deputy speakers in the Senate and Parliament respectively, and an uncle had served as Afghanistan's representative in the United Nations. Karzai himself served as the deputy foreign minister in the Rabbani government. During the Soviet–Afghan War Karzai mostly acted as fundraiser, based in India where he had studied for his master's degree. Like many Afghans, he welcomed the emergence of the Taliban but then broke with the movement when it became evident they were being used as a proxy by the ISI. During this period he came into frequent contact with the CIA, never failing to warn them, so he would later allege, of the dangers posed by this fanatical movement. The Taliban repaid him by assassinating his father in Quetta where the family lived in exile.

Karzai had not been a mujahid. Nor did he have the charisma or the romance of the Northern Alliance leaders. In a nation of hirsutes, he sported a bald head and trimmed his beard. His eyes seemed to rest in the far distance with an expression of melancholy. He did not look like the obvious leader to lift Afghanistan out of its dark past. But Karzai had other attributes which made him attractive to the Americans – notwithstanding that he was almost mistakenly killed in an air strike. In an improbable twist,

15 minutes after cheating death from the air strike, he received a telephone call informing him the Bonn Conference had appointed him head of the newly established Afghan Interim Authority.[25]

Karzai was educated, a fluent English speaker and a conservative, Pashtun moderate. He was also ambitious, an ambition which he literally wore on his body, dressing himself in a signature green gown and Karakul hat previously worn by Afghan kings. The war had been won with the Tajik Northern Alliance, but the peace would have to be won by a Pashtun, Afghanistan's majority ethnic group. For all these reasons, and for lack of any other credible candidate following the death of Ahmad Shah Massoud, the crown fell in Karzai's lap. In a nation where symbolism mattered, Karzai received a Durrani tribal coronation at the Sher-e-Surkh shrine near Kandahar, in much the same way as his Taliban rival, Mullah Omar, confirmed his own kingship of the same confederation of tribes by donning the cloak of the Prophet Muhammad, a relic also kept in a Kandahar shrine. To most Western politicians, charmed by his courteousness and respectability, Karzai seemed the best of the bunch.

The Bonn Agreement not only mapped out Afghanistan's immediate political future; it also 'called for the deployment of an international force to Afghanistan to assist the new Afghan Interim Authority … with the provision of security and stability for Kabul'.[26] Shortly after the conclusion of combat operations on Operation *Enduring Freedom*, the globe-trotting CENTCOM (Central Command) commander General Tommy Franks met with British military counterparts. It is not known whether Defence Secretary Hoon was involved or indeed what civilian oversight there was in the meetings. Franks did later describe Hoon as a good friend and was fulsome in his praise of British commitment. All that is known with some certainty is that as a result of some backroom dealing between the military men, the concept of this international security force in Afghanistan took shape. No European partners were present or, it seems, were even aware the Americans and British were holding such discussions.

For European nations likely to provide the foot soldiers, the eventual agreement was importantly undertaken under UN auspices (UN Security Council Resolution 1386, agreed on 20 December). Nobody, however, wanted to step forward to take the lead. The European NATO countries (with the exception of Britain) were very reluctant to be drawn into an American war. For the Americans, with the unfinished business of finding Osama bin Laden and destroying any remaining terrorist camps, constraining the Europeans to Kabul was a key concern. Importantly, Washington also demanded that any NATO forces deployed in Afghanistan should fall under a single American-led command. The Pentagon, however, did not want to become involved in a UN or peacekeeping operation, so the ball inevitably was passed to the British. The British in turn were supportive of the American single command proposal (not least because they realized they could not run an operation in Afghanistan without American airlift and other key military resources), but were reluctant to commit to more than a three-month deployment – a reluctance which European chancelleries conspiratorially suspected was part of a cunning British ruse to satisfy American demands, before slipping out of the country just as the real trouble started.

Eventually a compromise was reached (American negotiators foot-dragged the longest until it became apparent they could not hope to shift the reluctant Europeans). An International Security Assistance Force (ISAF) would be stood up for six months, after which time it was anticipated the AIA would be able to take over security responsibilities in the capital – a measure of just how unreal Western expectations were at this time. There would be two separate commands, as the Europeans demanded, and the latter would remain within Kabul, as the Americans demanded. Who would lead this force was left open to further negotiations, but it looked likely this would be a British-led operation, not a NATO operation, supported principally by Germany and France. Nobody was offering to step forward beyond the three-month period tentatively offered by the British. It was messy, unrealistic and an augury of the Byzantine nature of ISAF. American dismissiveness of the Europeans over this period should not be underestimated. Walt Slocombe, the under secretary of defense for policy during the second Clinton presidency, would later describe the allies, in an unguarded moment, as stupid, wobbly and wimpish.[27] The biggest fear for American policymakers was that European military forces and their political masters were simply not up to the task.

What followed was a British charge from which no European government could later retreat. The figure leading this charge was Major General John McColl, the general officer commanding 3 (UK) Division. Just behind the charging general, it may be assumed, was the figure of the prime minister, Tony Blair. Part of McColl's confidence seems to have stemmed from the deployment of a task force headquarters just three months previously, which suggested that a British-led mission was feasible

(Operation *Bessemer* – Macedonia). Over four days (14–17 December) he made a lightning reconnaissance to Kabul. On his return he informed the defence secretary the British Army could – and it may be intuited, should – deploy a task force to Kabul. The following day Hoon informed Parliament that Britain had stepped forward and offered to establish the first international security force in Kabul. By this stage, there had already been a joint US–UK presence at Bagram Airport for a month. Two days later, the announcement of the establishment of a peacekeeping force was made at Bonn.

The decision in the end surprised no one. As America's closest military ally and the only NATO country that had joined Operation *Enduring Freedom* at its inception, it followed naturally that Britain, now enjoying a toehold in the country, should take the lead in consolidating the international presence in Afghanistan. For the prime minister, this was an opportunity to demonstrate the relevance of British forces to sceptical Americans. To critics, Britain had slipped into the role of America's charlady, without much discussion or prompting. The short timeframes meant the MOD had to work feverishly over the holiday period to warn off units and make preparations for their deployment. Units that had been expecting a routine return to barracks after Christmas leave found themselves urgently packing equipment, ordering maps and hunting for any information they could find on Kabul and the situation in Afghanistan. The unit chosen to lead the British task force, 2nd Battalion the Parachute Regiment, was at high readiness anyway, but the unfortunate timing of the operation in the middle of leave compressed timings further.

The pace then quickened even more. McColl returned to Britain for just three days before returning to Kabul. The day after his return to the Afghan capital, on 22 December, the Afghan Interim Authority was stood up. The British Embassy formally opened its doors on 23 December. The first British soldiers to deploy to Kabul, signallers from 3 (UK) Signal Regiment, were allowed to spend Christmas with their families but were Afghanistan-bound on Boxing Day, their morale sagging like their over-fed stomachs. On the penultimate day of the year, marines from B Company, still camped in the dilapidated Bagram Airport, set off on the very first British joint patrol with local Afghan security forces. Neither side understood each other, but the event was staged for the media and not to improve security in the Kabul environs. It would be the first of thousands of such patrols. At 0730hrs on 1 January, McColl formally activated the ISAF HQ at the Old Sports Club in Kabul. The gesture was symbolic, as the headquarters would not be fully manned and running until mid-February, but the symbolism counted. The man who best understood this was the prime minister. On 4 January, Tony Blair landed at Bagram Airport, repeating the gesture he had made in Kosovo. The Muslim Kosovars would be eternally grateful to Blair for his solidarity; the Afghans, less fulsome in their appreciation.

In truth, the initial ISAF deployment was shambolic and bedevilled with tensions. The speed with which McColl had acted alarmed European allies, who refused to link up with the rudimentary communications infrastructure established in Kabul for fear it would imply subordination to Operation *Enduring Freedom*. The seeds for the later fractured command arrangements were sown in that first month. As a result of exaggerated attitudes over the threat (which was non-existent), the RAF would only fly under the cover of night, and insisted on the wearing of body armour. The more sensible European contingents flew by day and deployed more quickly and efficiently than the British. This left the lead nation in the uncomfortable position of leading somewhat from the rear. Despite McColl's confidence, the British lacked adequate expeditionary equipment and soon became known as 'The Flintstones', a nickname echoed by 'The Borrowers' moniker earned in the second Gulf War the following year (in the Korean War, of course, the British were known as 'The Woolworth's Boys' – there is an unfortunate history of deploying British soldiers on the cheap). Some judged the presumptuous British had become the laughingstock. 2 PARA arrived without their ammunition, to the consternation of the paratroopers. McColl's personal dynamism and competence were never in question, but behind him was a creaking and in some parts a broken machine. And behind McColl was a prime minister who aspired to play a pivotal role in international affairs but whose government was not fully supporting the armed forces.

By the time the prime minister's flight had returned to Britain, his defence secretary was explaining to the House the composition and purpose of the British task force. A Military Technical Agreement (MTA) had already been signed four days previously in Kabul by the self-appointed Afghan interior minister, Yunus Qanuni, and by the British representative, McColl. 'The force,' Hoon explained, 'will be charged with assisting the Afghan Interim Authority in the maintenance of security in Kabul and its surrounding areas.' Hoon was at pains to emphasize that this was a separate mission to Operation *Enduring Freedom*: 'The force will have a particular mission (known as Operation *Fingal*), distinct from Operation *Enduring Freedom*. But The United States will provide essential enabling support to deploy and sustain the force.'[28]

This was a candid admission that Britain, and the remainder of the NATO countries offering troops to support the first ISAF mission, would be dependent on American resources. Rumsfeld's jaundiced view of 'old Europe' seemed to be confirmed – the allies across the Atlantic could not, when challenged, project even a modest security force, without American assistance. 'Let me be clear,' the defence secretary concluded, 'the International Community is sending the force to assist the Afghans, not to interfere in their affairs.'[29] It was a sincere sentiment, if staggeringly off the mark.

There was less sincerity, or perhaps just ignorance, over the circumstances surrounding the signing of the MTA. The majority of the Afghan powerbrokers in Kabul, led by Defence Minister Fahim Khan, were against the ISAF deployment, and indeed were opposed to any foreign troops at all in Afghanistan. A moderate camp proposed a maximum of 1,000 troops but stipulated these be based outside Kabul and confined to barracks. Karzai was encouraged to agree to the deployment of a modest Western force. The interlocutor on the Western side was McColl.[30] At this stage there were no European officials, military or civilian, involved in the discussions in Kabul. This was unfortunate as it was almost certain a NATO commitment, however modest, would follow, notwithstanding the foot-dragging in European capitals. The actual number '5,000' appears to have been a back-of-fag packet UN number. Remarkably, it seems the British were privately touting as many as 25,000 soldiers. As in so many other instances of the Afghan story, the solution was not what the Afghans wanted, but rather what was imposed by a Westerner, and with some rather casual arithmetic. Sensitivity over the issue was such that the MTA had just two signatories and one witness: McColl, Qanuni and a Brigadier Kratzer acting as witness for Lieutenant General Mikolashek, the nominated NATO Coalition Forces Land Component Commander in Europe.

Had the fate of Afghanistan ever been signed off so speedily by just two individuals, one a foreigner, and neither enjoying any political legitimacy whatsoever over the Afghan people? Did the new foreign secretary, Jack Straw, who did not visit Afghanistan and who was anyway pointedly side-lined by Blair, know what had actually transpired in Kabul? Were Afghan reservations over this Western-imposed solution honestly communicated? What discussions had taken place, and between whom? Were the Europeans kept fully informed? It seems not. When the news got out there was considerable surprise and some anger in Afghanistan. Who had agreed to this? Who had been consulted? For ordinary Kabulis, there was just confusion: the British paratroopers were assumed to be Russians, and a Gurkha reinforcement company, bizarrely, was thought to be the vanguard of an invading communist Chinese force.

The hurriedly formed British task force turned out to be a ragbag of units. The headquarters was drawn from 3 (UK) Division, but a second tactical headquarters drawn from 16 Air Assault Brigade also deployed, setting a pattern of multiple layers of command that became a feature of the war. The British were only deploying about 1,800 soldiers, but they were deploying a divisional HQ, elements of a brigade HQ and a battalion HQ to command the force – a highly unbalanced ratio of staff to front-line soldiers by any measure. 2 PARA deployed as announced but required support from a Gurkha company to make up the numbers. From the beginning it was evident the British Army would struggle to find sufficient infantry to meet its commitments. Elements of 33 and 36 Regiments Royal Engineers deployed to build the necessary camp infrastructure. 30 Signal Regiment provided strategic communications. Support troops were drawn from a number of units, including 13 Air Assault Regiment of the Royal Logistic Corps and 16 Medical Regiment of the Royal Army Medical Corps. The British contingent would not be shouldering the burden alone. In total, 18 other NATO countries* eventually offered troops, commonly specialists like doctors and engineers, which ensured that there was a multinational stamp on the operation.

This force was commanded by McColl, the personality on the British side who more than any other actor created the momentum for the British mission in Kabul, and effectively acted as ISAF's midwife. A former Royal Anglian – like the Chief of the Defence Staff, General Mike Walker – he proved the perfect choice for the delicate mission. McColl combined a taxonomic eye for detail with a firm grasp for broader, strategic considerations. He had a reputation for setting rigorous standards. His headquarters ran like clockwork, and it was thanks to his personal drive that the ISAF HQ was established in record time, despite all the difficulties.

*Austria, Denmark, Finland, France, Germany, Greece, Italy, New Zealand, Netherlands, Norway, Portugal, Romania, Spain, Sweden, Turkey, Belgium, Bulgaria and the Czech Republic.

Over the next six months he would need patience and tact, qualities he enjoyed in abundance. The model general later rose to become Deputy Supreme Allied Commander Europe, the second-highest military post in NATO and the highest a European general could aspire to. In McColl, a hesitant and later grateful Labour government seemed to have found their man.

However, McColl was the first in a succession of senior British officers who became drawn to the problem of Afghanistan and who felt strongly that Britain had an obligation to help the Afghan people. During the Algerian War (1954–62), a French negotiator observed, '*Algérie montait à la tête*' – 'Algeria got to your head' – and the same thing happened to a generation of British Army officers in a way that was not true of their American counterparts.[31] For the Americans, Afghanistan would always be about September 11. When revenge was finally exacted ten years later, against a backdrop of mounting casualties and costs, the desire to continue fighting a futile war waned. For the British Army, Afghanistan became a matter of pride as well as obligation, although London's enthusiasm for supporting American wars would wane.

In faraway Kabul the customary winter rains which turned the capital into a place of misery and mud were finally easing. The scent of spring, combined with the surge of international goodwill, was heady stuff and it provoked the 'Kabul effect'. This was a delusion that what was happening in the capital city could be replicated throughout Afghanistan – the malignant gene of the Taliban displaced and replaced by the virtuous genetic material of international benevolence. The delusion set in because no Western troops (other than American special forces units chasing shadows in the hills) had set foot outside Kabul and its environs. Afghan politicians working with the international community were all Kabul-based, and they told ISAF and donors exactly what they wanted to hear, parroting the mantras of reconstruction as if they were Western politicians on a campaign trail.

Over the first few months the Kabul effect would engender many strange and wonderful sights. Bianca Jagger, a critic of the American invasion, and a women's rights activist, was spotted in downtown Kabul, flanked by burly British paratroopers. Her visit would make not a jot of difference to the beggary and destitution that was the daily lot for many women in Kabul, but it fed a media-machine promoting a story that 'good' was being done for Afghanistan's oppressed womenfolk. She was even coaxed into providing the perfect quote: ISAF, she told an approving McColl, was acting as 'a force for good'. Lawrie McMenemy, the football coach, turned up in Kabul, armed with club strips and a clutch of footballs. He organized a symbolic football match on a snow-bound pitch in the city's only sports stadium, where the Taliban had once held executions. A platoon of Gurkhas was press-ganged into acting as cheerleaders for the event. The goodwill match almost backfired when the crowd became rowdy and local police weighed in with the usual brutality, but the ISAF public relations officer was careful to omit any mention of crowd trouble in his post-match report. Geoff Hoon made an appearance on 6 February and was feted by his Afghan hosts. McColl – acting in his capacity as diplomat as well as soldier – was cajoled into cutting ribbons and planting trees as his hosts staged events to demonstrate Afghanistan's rebirth.

It was really nothing of the sort. This cosmopolitan city – Afghanistan's only cosmopolitan city – was simply rebounding after the lid of Taliban oppression had been lifted. And there was also another quite different Kabul effect in evidence. Government officials were beginning to consume Western aid money with the voracity of white sharks, which was provoking a property boom as well as the sudden apparition of luxury cars on Kabul's grimy streets.

For the troops deployed on Operation *Fingal*, soldiering in Kabul mirrored the routines of peacekeeping operations in Kosovo or Bosnia, only in a far poorer environment. There were sangars to construct, sentry posts to man and ablutions to build. The devastated infrastructure meant that almost everyone was surviving in very basic conditions and living off ration packs. Huge stocks of ammunition were secured and destroyed: by the time 2 PARA handed over to 1 Royal Anglian on 15 March, about 3 million items of ordnance had been destroyed, the overwhelming majority land mines.[32] Kabul's reputation as the most mined city in the world was not undeserved. In keeping with the 'hearts and minds' approach, the paratroopers mounted patrols in the city, engaged with the locals and reported on possible Quick Impact Projects, or QIPs. Over 200 such projects of varying sizes were proposed (but not all were funded or completed).[33] Joint patrols were mounted with the Afghan National Police, and the first battalion of a new National Guard was raised (but not paid, which caused its almost immediate disbandment). It all seemed humdrum and benign. There was one incident in which paratroopers opened fire and killed the occupants of a car that appeared to be acting suspiciously, but the incident was quickly smoothed over. A reporter who had the temerity to remind a 2 PARA officer of the fate of the last British garrison to decamp in Kabul was brusquely reminded, 'The last lot weren't 2 Para.' Unbeknown to both, on 11 February an ominous milestone had been passed. On that day, the ISAF nominal role stood at 2,497 troops, or exactly the same number of soldiers in the ill-fated Kabul Field Force of 1879.

Optimism was reflected by the defence secretary when he addressed the House of Commons in mid-March:

> It is clear that this action has been remarkably successful. Afghanistan is now a very different country. The Taliban government, which harboured the Al Qaida terrorists, is no more. Terrorist training camps have been put out of action. The first steps towards recreating a functioning state have been taken. Aid agencies operate with increasing freedom. Refugees are beginning to return to their homes.[34]

At this stage – just five months into the operation – the total contingent of forces had risen to 4,600 troops drawn from 18 countries.[35] The hero of the hour, McColl, was lavished with praise for his role in bringing together this disparate alliance under a British-run headquarters. From Whitehall's perspective it was almost too good to be true. No British general since World War II had been responsible for leading a multinational brigade on such a tricky operation. This was de facto NATO's first ground war, in the same way that Kosovo had been NATO's first air war, and a Briton was in charge. As importantly for the Treasury – eyeing suspiciously the possibility of an extended commitment – Turkey had agreed to assume command of the ISAF operation in the summer, and the Turks would be followed by a joint German–Dutch brigade. But the Germans and Dutch only agreed to assume leadership of the mission on the basis there would be no expansion of the mandate. At the same time, more interventionist voices were arguing for the deployment of Joint Regional Teams, or JRTs, across Afghanistan, as a compromise that might square the circle of competing American, European and Afghan interests. Although no plans had yet been made, this would all be a prelude to a NATO headquarters assuming command of the operation in August 2003, a renewed UN-mandate issued in December 2003 and a progressive expansion of ISAF beyond Kabul in 2004. However, such were the misgivings over deeper involvement in Afghanistan that exactly the opposite message was being signalled.

By this stage it was evident British government policy was increasingly at odds with itself. On the one hand, the defence secretary was strongly hinting at a British withdrawal. On the other, Downing Street was making promises to Washington of a continuing British commitment in the newly declared 'war on terror'. On 20 March, Parliament was informed commitments in Kabul did not alter the government's 'determination to draw down the number of British troops deployed as part of the ISAF'.[36] Rumours that the mission would expand were also scotched. 'Let me make clear,' Hoon warned, 'that speculation that the ISAF will become a NATO force or a European Union force or anything other than a "coalition of the willing" is just that – speculation', a naïve assertion, as by the following year this is what it would become.[37] Service chiefs had no inkling that by the following spring Britain would be mounting a full-scale invasion of Iraq. Hoon himself was being kept in the dark. About the only person who appears to have enjoyed tacit understanding of Washington's intentions was the prime minister himself, Tony Blair.

In Hoon's calculations, the principal reason for reticence over engagement in Afghanistan lay not so much in concerns over future commitments but in the baggage that Britain's armed forces were already carrying: the perennial fear of 'overstretch' that dominated military debate during this period. Treasury pressure to limit costs was undiminished. Indeed, Hoon alluded to 'overstretch' in his 20 March statement and sought to reassure the House that the new and possibly open-ended commitment to Afghanistan would not place an impossible strain on the armed forces.

If the chancellor, Gordon Brown, was also hoping to limit the financial liabilities imposed by this new military commitment his hopes were about to be dashed, because mission creep was already setting in. In one of those unfortunate moments when a politician holds himself a hostage to fortune, Hoon had told the Commons, just two days earlier, that notwithstanding Britain's handover of responsibilities to Turkey, additional troops were, in fact, going to be deployed to Afghanistan – but, he added categorically, 'In no sense is it "mission creep".'[38] Of course, it was. Hoon had gravely underestimated his prime minister's willingness to support American military interventionism.

These first seeds of mission creep were announced, like all bad news, at the end of the speech. At the beginning of 2002, the British government found itself in an increasingly difficult but not unfamiliar position. Washington was entirely unimpressed with the British contribution in

Afghanistan, dismissing ISAF as a sideshow to the war on terror. From the Bush administration's ungrateful perspective, there was a mismatch between Blair's rhetoric and his willingness to actually contribute soldiers to fighting the remnants of al-Qaeda in Afghanistan – the only war that Washington cared about. Tony Blair, now being drawn into a secret trajectory to war in Iraq, had little option but to find troops – but from where? One option would have been to re-task the Kabul-based troops, but the handover between 2 PARA and 1 Royal Anglian was already underway, and besides, such a re-tasking would have fatally undermined the ISAF mission. Another option was to deploy the army's standby battalion. At the time, this was 1 Royal Irish, but it was judged the unit was insufficiently prepared for undertaking such a demanding task. The baton instead was passed to the Royal Marines.

As if pulling a rabbit out of the hat, Hoon told the Commons, 'We have held 45 Commando ready for offensive operations in Afghanistan for precisely this purpose.'[39] This was not strictly accurate, but two companies of 45 Commando were in the Indian Ocean on board HMS *Ocean*, an amphibious assault ship that had taken station following the withdrawal of HMS *Fearless*. To create a properly balanced land force, the two companies of embarked marines would be joined by the remainder of the commando who were sitting in Arbroath in Scotland, as well as by elements from 29 Commando Regiment Royal Artillery and 59 Independent Commando Squadron Royal Engineers. The RAF would contribute three Chinooks to ferry the force.

The justification for this deployment would be repeated by British politicians over the forthcoming years, with increasingly less credibility – Britain had to be in Afghanistan, because 'Al Qaida and Taliban elements have the ability and the desire to launch attacks right into the heart of nations like ours' – despite the lack of any intelligence that this was the case.[40] This questionable justification – the jihadist domino theory – was capped by a glib and dishonest assertion that would also become wearisomely familiar to the British public: 'Our exit strategy is that we will leave when the task is completed.'[41] The truth was that, 13 years later, Britain's 'exit strategy' – all exit and no strategy, as Henry Kissinger quipped of ISAF's withdrawal – would be entirely based on electoral calculations, financial constraints and the imperative of acting in lock-step with Washington, not a judgement on whether the task had been completed. This was, of course, true of every other ISAF-contributing nation.

For the marines ostensibly despatched to chase al-Qaeda out of Afghanistan – Task Force Jacana – the experience proved an unsatisfactory business. The 1,700-strong battlegroup began deploying in early April, and the final elements of the force withdrew at the end of July. Before deploying, HQ 3 Commando Brigade drafted an astute intelligence estimate.[42] 'The principal motivation for all Afghans,' the report judged, 'remains financial, tribal loyalties and a common distrust/hatred for foreigners.' Presciently, an unknown author pencilled in the margin, 'Xenophobia likely to re-emerge as expectations of a better life fail to emerge.'

Although the MOD was keen to portray Task Force Jacana as a success, the marines were far more realistic in their perception of the mission in Afghanistan. The vastness of the country had impressed. 45 Commando was well aware that it was only leaving boot prints in a handful of hills and valleys. The rest of the country, which the commandos only saw from the air – the thousands of square kilometres of dramatic mountain ranges, deserts and fertile valleys – remained *terra incognita*. This highlighted a point persuasively argued by characters such as Barbara Stapleton, a political advisor to the European Union Special Representative to Afghanistan, who enjoyed a privileged perspective and observed the ISAF mission unfold in the early years. Afghanistan needed a heavy footprint of international troops at the beginning, but the very opposite happened because of the American obsession with the war on terror. Confining the Europeans to Kabul fatally undermined Afghan confidence at a juncture when that confidence needed most reassurance.[43]

Task Force Jacana had escaped the constraint of remaining in Kabul, because it had in effect been invited to take part in Rumsfeld's 'war lite' – a war fought by special forces units and aerial precision strikes. The manner in which the Taliban regime had tumbled like a house of cards had only served to reinforce a dogmatic belief that this was *the* way to wage war. The so-called Powell Doctrine of the first Gulf War, which involved the massing of vast conventional armies, had been turned on its head within a decade – so the proponents of 'war lite' argued – by the 'Revolution in Military Affairs' which made this new, smart war the only game in town. The problem with 'war lite', as it turned out, was that it was not decisive after all.

As far as the marines were concerned, the Taliban and al-Qaeda had not so much been beaten as simply vanished into the hills. The Americans themselves were discovering this, notably in Operation *Anaconda*, a bungled mission that resulted in a large number of casualties and some surprising resistance by a group of fighters. In their post-operational report, the marines argued there was no reason why the Taliban and al-Qaeda could not simply lick their wounds, re-arm and return. This view was shared by independent observers such as Anthony Cordesman.[44] In the post-Bonn euphoria, few were listening to these siren voices. In the context of the Afghanistan War, 45 Commando's deployment was ultimately trivial, but in the light of the Iraq War it was hugely important, because it set a precedent of British acquiescence to Washington's demands for British 'boots on the ground' from which the Blair government could not back down.

If the Europeans, corralled in Kabul or taking part in fruitless counter-terrorist operations like 45 Commando, were beginning to develop one perspective on the operation in Afghanistan, the Americans were developing quite another. By the summer, the few hundred American special forces soldiers had grown into a divisional-sized joint force. About 7,500 soldiers from 10th Mountain Division (whose commander notoriously commented that the division didn't really do mountains) were deployed to Afghanistan. There were a further 1,000 American servicemen in Pakistan, 1,000 in Kyrgyzstan, 1,700 in Uzbekistan and 13,000 afloat.[45] These two forces – ISAF and American forces committed to the continuing Operation *Enduring Freedom* – were pursuing quite different missions and the tensions were beginning to show. In testimony to the Defence Select Committee, ten years later, General Robert Fry, then Deputy Chief of Defence Staff (Commitments), neatly summed up the contradiction:

> Those two things were profoundly inimical to each other, and in fact to conduct a counter-terrorist campaign in that way was almost mutually exclusive to a peace support operation, because if you happen to be dropping bombs on people and killing them in significant numbers, they are unlikely to be susceptible to the blandishments of political accommodation.[46]

On Capitol Hill, disunity over war aims became public. Influential senators such as Joe Biden, Tom Daschle and John McCain questioned both the mission in Afghanistan and a growing suspicion that the Bush government was about to embark on further military operations in the Middle East. This was, of course, a reference to the Pentagon's preparations for war in Iraq, Washington's worst-kept secret, and it provoked stinging criticism from

Senator John Byrd: 'Instead of concentrating on completing our operations in Afghanistan, the Pentagon seems to be looking for opportunities to stay longer and expand our presence in the region. We seem to be good at developing entrance strategies but not in developing exit strategies.'[47] He could hardly have been more prescient.

By coincidence, NATO was due to hold a summit in November, in Prague, to formalize the accession of seven new members, and it was clear to all participants the alliance were heading for a diplomatic showdown. Two key questions had to be addressed that would dog NATO in Afghanistan for many years, and neither had an easy resolution. What exactly was the mission, and who was in charge? The Americans, appealing to good military principles, continued to argue for a unified command led by the United States. For the majority of Europeans, nervously hearing war drums beating over Iraq, this option was totally unacceptable. A multinational leadership, the preferred European option, was equally unacceptable to the Americans after the fraught experience of Operation *Allied Force* in Kosovo. If the allies were at odds over command arrangements, they were also at odds over the mission. For the Pentagon, war came first. For the Europeans, reconstruction came first (albeit a small number of nations were now contributing special forces units to assist in the Global War on Terror). Predictions that the Prague Summit would lead to serious fractures in NATO – just over a year after the September 11 attacks – proved overly pessimistic. The organization's eternal capacity to compromise saved the day, even if the outcomes were unsatisfactory from the point of view of the operation in Afghanistan.

The United States would continue to mount Operation *Enduring Freedom*, while NATO would assume leadership of a separate ISAF mission, with a reconstruction mandate. George Robertson, the NATO Secretary General, appears to have played the deal-maker role. Crudely, NATO needed a mission, relations with Washington needed to be repaired, and Afghanistan seemed a good fit. The European allies pledged to undertake a comprehensive review of their 'activities and working procedures', code for the lack of expeditionary force capabilities in their armed forces. For Donald Rumsfeld, who was frequently close to despair over European lack of military punch, this was a small victory. They also pledged to continue to support the operation in Afghanistan, but as the separate ISAF mission. Keen to avoid any fighting, the Europeans unrealistically insisted, 'the responsibility for providing security and law and order throughout

Afghanistan resides with the Afghans themselves'.[48] For the Americans, notwithstanding the new and renewed commitments from European allies, the Prague Summit ultimately was a letdown. Once again, the Europeans had failed to show mettle, reinforcing the sense that America could only rely on its own resources, and perhaps a handful of willing allies. If the Prague Summit did not lead to the collapse of NATO it was because another war was about to detonate in the Middle East that would completely overshadow Operation *Enduring Freedom* and change the dynamics of this central Asian war. By the time the last lights were switched off in the conference halls in Prague, America, and its military ally Britain, were just four months away from invading a former foe: Saddam Hussein's Iraq.

The controversial and hugely divisive decision to topple the Ba'athist regime in Iraq would have profound consequences for the ISAF mission in Afghanistan. The flawed and exaggerated intelligence on Weapons of Mass Destruction (WMD) – an American paranoia that had circulated in intelligence circles since before the first Gulf War – fatally compromised Operation *Iraqi Freedom* and its British counterpart, Operation *Telic*, even before the mismanaged intervention began to unravel. Public opinion in Europe turned against the very idea of invading Iraq before a single shot was fired, and European capitals, including London, witnessed some of the biggest protest marches ever recorded in the post-war era. Middle Eastern opinion was indignant. As the hour of invasion approached, the cloth spun by the weavers in Washington and London became increasingly fabulous. It was a classic example of the Emperor's New Clothes: everybody was pretending to see the Weapons of Mass Destruction, because they believed everybody else was seeing them, and the moment was just waiting for a child to step out of the crowd and cry out: 'But there aren't any!' Unfortunately, nobody found the moral courage to do so. If it became increasingly clear, as Iraq belatedly opened its doors to UN inspectors, that the country was in an awful, dilapidated state and posed a threat to no one, it also became transparent that the Bush administration was determined to depose Saddam Hussein regardless. It was a moment of foolishness, compounded by clumsiness, and hundreds of thousands of Iraqis would lose their lives or livelihoods as a result of the American–British invasion. While America floundered with its worst foreign policy decision since the Vietnam War, Iran grew in influence, and the seeds were sown for the fracture of Iraq and reincarnation as a nursery for Islamist terrorism. A worse strategic outcome could not have been manufactured.

The consequences of Operation *Iraqi Freedom* were felt across Afghanistan and Pakistan. President Musharraf seems to have calculated the American switch of focus would imply a withdrawal from Afghanistan.[49] A probable American withdrawal was anticipated by the ISI even before the invasion of Iraq. This organization continued to provide covert support to the Taliban even as it pledged support for America's war on terror.[50] Mullah Omar and the deposed Taliban hierarchy also expected American troops to withdraw within a short period. When it became obvious that America was not quitting but instead preparing to invade a second Muslim country, it seeded the conviction that this was nothing less than an assault on the *umma*, the Muslim nation, by the world's superpower. Mullah Omar's first public pronouncements and the Taliban's first attacks post the regime's fall from power, date to this period. It was the invasion of Iraq that acted as the catalyst for the resurgence of the Afghan Taliban, a not unimportant point.

Even as Operation *Iraqi Freedom* was launched, American and European negotiators agreed in April 2003 to roll out the ISAF operation across Afghanistan in a series of four stages, over three years. The impetus behind what would become the expanded and mired ISAF mission did not therefore come from Afghans. It was basically the by-product of internecine Western tensions and NATO politics.

The importance of being seen to contribute, rather than making the hard contribution of 'boots on the ground', created an embarrassing diplomatic spectacle. On 11 August 2003, NATO officially assumed command of ISAF, with the operation run from the Allied Joint Force Command (JFC) Headquarters in Brunssum under command of a German general, Egon Ramms. A total of 1,700 soldiers from 40 nations crammed into the new headquarters in Kabul – more soldiers than the European NATO countries had actually deployed in the rest of the country at this stage. It was painfully obvious this was an invitation to a party no country wanted to be seen to be declining, but nobody wanted to step onto the dance floor either.

NATO needed a plan for expanding its mission, and the mechanism for the subsequent roll-out of ground forces would be based around the concept of the newly coined Provincial Reconstruction Teams, or PRTs (the first was established by US forces in Gardez). According to Jack Fairweather, the original concept appears to have been coined by future Chief of the Defence Staff Nick Carter, then serving as a colonel in the ISAF headquarters.[51] In principle, the idea was simple. Each of the larger NATO countries would individually, or jointly, assume responsibility for a geographical area of Afghanistan, establishing a regional command headquarters and logistics base to support the PRT. These would be the so-called 'lead nations'. Smaller NATO countries would be expected to contribute forces in support of the lead nations. Any country (such as Britain) deploying a sizeable task force would also establish its own national headquarters, which implied a third layer of command. In total, from Brunssum in the Netherlands to a brigade in Afghanistan, there would be four layers of headquarters. In the case of a national headquarters, this would be answering not only to the ISAF chain of command but also to its own strategic headquarters and ministry of defence. For British forces, this was the Permanent Joint Headquarters (PJHQ) at Northwood. Irregular units such as 22 SAS answered to their own chain of command, and ultimately to the prime minister. As if these elaborate command arrangements were not complex enough, there was also the direct and indirect influence of operations being conducted under the name of Operation *Enduring Freedom* within these newly allocated ISAF regional commands. Nations that flatly refused to be associated with Operation *Enduring Freedom* could not prevent operations conducted under American auspices from taking place within their regional commands. As these were invariably special forces operations, they were seldom informed that an operation was taking place at all. In the case of Britain, the military contribution was already compromised, as British forces had established a foot in both camps. The answer to the question – was Britain a contributor to ISAF or an auxiliary to the American Operation *Enduring Freedom*? – could not be comfortably answered. To add to the friction, national caveats – the rules that stipulated what any particular contingent may or may not do – ran to dozens of pages. No military operation in modern history had been attempted under such convoluted command arrangements.

In Kabul, in spring 2002, 2 PARA had been replaced by 1 Royal Anglian. For the Royal Anglians, the second infantry unit to serve on Operation *Fingal*, life in Kabul was humdrum, if not boring. Conditions for the soldiers slowly improved as military engineers and civilian contractors began the significant task of building permanent structures for the burgeoning multinational force. There was routine patrolling to fill the time, in a peaceful if shattered city, and the weather improved. A Private Darren George was killed in April, following an accidental discharge of a weapon, but this was about the only incident of note to report. On 3 June

– the occasion of the Queen's Golden Jubilee – a beacon was lit on a hill overlooking the city by the youngest soldier in the regiment, a Private Watts. The Royal Anglians duly handed over to Turkish counterparts, and it seemed the British commitment to ISAF had been successfully concluded, at least for another year. A small support element remained in Kabul, but this was not an onerous commitment. Returning units fed back positive if dull reports. 'The British are good at this game' was the main message received in Whitehall. There was hubris over the British 'can-do' attitude compared with the reticence of European partners. Overall, the picture painted of Afghanistan was that of a mostly benign if impoverished country. Compared to the drama that was about to unfold in Iraq, Afghanistan seemed a cakewalk.

In March 2003, a sister battalion, 2 Royal Anglian, took up the reins of Operation *Fingal*. This unit would remain in Afghanistan until October, when it would be replaced by 2 Royal Gurkha Rifles. In May, the defence secretary announced in a written statement that from July the United Kingdom would lead a PRT in Mazar-e-Sharif and the five surrounding provinces. To signal this new phase in the British mission, the operational codename *Fingal* was complemented by a second codename, Operation *Tarrock*. The former referred to the Kabul-based British contingent and the latter to PRT operations in northern Afghanistan.

One year later the codename would change again. Unlike the American practice of literal, two-word codenames (such as Operation *Enduring Freedom*), the British used a random word generator to create single code words. In 2004, the computer threw up the surname of a 16th-century metaphysical poet – Herrick. Nobody could have guessed at the time how weighted a word this would become in the British Army's consciousness. Unlike the parallel operation in Iraq (Operation *Telic*), it had the virtue that it was not a name that could be readily subverted ('Telic' became jokingly known as 'Tell Everyone Leave Is Cancelled', a reflection of how the army was struggling to meet its manpower commitments).

The foundations for the Mazar-e-Sharif PRT were duly laid in July 2003 (a smaller outpost in Maimanah would be added later in the year). A New Zealand contingent followed suit and established a PRT in nearby Bamiyan. The Gurkhas manned this first British PRT from October 2003 until April 2004. The Urdu-speaking Gurkhas had a natural affinity with the Uzbeks, Tajiks and Hazaras of northern Afghanistan. With some pride, the battalion reported it had made good progress. The Gurkhas patrolled and showed 'presence' while projects were focused on building up the local government (rather than building clinics or schools, the later staples of reconstruction efforts). A potential flare-up between rival warlords was successfully defused that summer. Military observation teams were despatched around the countryside. A quick reaction force undertook a handful of arrest operations with the local police. Kabul's streets were patrolled and trainers were attached to an American-led Task Force Phoenix which provided Embedded Training Teams (ETTs) at the Afghan Army NCO School. A modest number of QIPs were started. Over the deployment, there was just one fatality. On 28 January 2004, a 23-year-old Territorial Army soldier, Private Jonathan Kitulagoda, serving with the Rifle Volunteers, was killed in a suicide attack. Four of his comrades were injured in the attack. At the time, such incidents remained rare, but his death was a reminder that Afghanistan could be a dangerous place.

The Gurkhas in turn were relieved by the Green Howards, whose tour lasted until autumn 2004. This battalion formed the first Afghanistan Roulement Infantry Battalion, or ARIB. The experience, unfortunately, proved a disappointment. The Green Howards found an ISAF mission that was complex, confused and under-resourced. The plan was that the UK PRT, based on the ARIB, would be military-led and deploy for up to two years. It would initially comprise some 50 troops who would liaise with Afghan military forces in the region. These latter would provide the PRT's support and protection. Civilian staff from the Foreign and Commonwealth Office (FCO) and the Department for International Development (DfID) would be responsible for providing political and development advice respectively. The government made just £1 million available to its development adviser in the Mazar-e-Sharif PRT in 2004. This was the equivalent of sending two coach-loads of soldiers with a kitbag of money, to an area the size of Scotland, and instructing them to fix the place. This was much less money than a single opium-poppy-growing valley made.

If the British were indulging in military 'tokenism' (like the remainder of NATO contributors), there were some glimmers of hope. Regular consultation exercises were established with UN agencies and NGOs, to avoid duplication of effort, but there was a certain amount of friction between these various agencies. Despite these good if very modest intentions, the British PRT 'ultimately amounted to crisis management'.[52] One problem was tensions between the military and the civilians from the FCO and DfID, a foretaste of what would follow in Helmand. The second problem was the scale of the effort. When the British handed over the PRTs to Swedish and Norwegian contingents just over a year after establishing the bases, the overwhelming majority of Afghans in the five provinces would not have even been aware that a British military force had co-existed among them. It had been a near-invisible, token military deployment designed to appease NATO politics rather than address the needs of the Afghan people. This behaviour was was being repeated throughout Afghanistan by the other ISAF partners.

The sluggish expansion of the ISAF mission was further exacerbated by a collapse in interest in the whole problem of Afghanistan on the part of the Bush administration. In spring 2003 Operation *Iraqi Freedom* had been hailed as a great military victory. Just one year later American troops found themselves mired in a vicious sectarian war that was in danger of spiralling out of control. The size of the challenge facing America in Iraq, coupled with the strategic importance of the country, completely trumped the perceived backwater of Afghanistan. As with so many wars in the past, Afghanistan was in danger of becoming a forgotten war. Without American pull, the ISAF donkey was ambling.

Notwithstanding the halting progress being made by ISAF, it was clear that a second international conference would have to be held to coordinate the mission and set goals for the next five years. The Berlin Conference in early April 2004 brought together donor countries, as well as ISAF-contributing nations, under one tent and in a growing mood of uneasiness. As with all the conferences held on Afghanistan during the first Karzai government, it began with an inventory of false and self-deluding successes. Two Loya Jirgas had been held: the first had established the country's new constitution, and the second had confirmed Karzai as the unelected president. In fact, the first Emergency Loya Jirga had been a shoddy affair manipulated by the US Special Representative Zalmay Khalilzad and the UN chief Lakhdar Brahimi. In the estimation of Afghan expert Thomas Ruttig, it was at this Loya Jirga that the West began to lose the 'hearts and minds' of Afghans who had trusted in the international mission.[53]

The second Constitutional Loya Jirga was similarly manipulated by Khalilzad, who imposed a presidential system of government on Afghanistan, despite almost half the delegates strongly objecting to the proposed constitutional arrangement. As damagingly, a Single Non-Transferable Voting (SNTV) system was imposed (only shared by the Pitcairn Islands, Vanuatu and Jordan).[54] Karzai went along with this because it fractured political opposition and enhanced his power. In this respect, Khalilzad played the same damaging role as the luckless Paul Bremner in Iraq, unrolling conceptions of Western governance that went against the local grain.

The bunkum of the Berlin Conference could not mask European fears over becoming sucked into an American war. Once again, the Europeans emphasized that law and order was a matter for the Afghans, even though Afghanistan lacked any credible security forces at this stage. Neither was ISAF prepared to get involved in tackling the opium trade, although it was obvious to everyone that the most visible by-product of the American-led invasion was a boom in the cultivation of the opium poppy. Despite the rhetoric at the Berlin Conference, the expansion of ISAF forces proved a far more difficult and slow process due to the growing realization that any forces deployed to the south might be drawn into open fighting against an expanding insurgency.

The British, at this stage, had no immediate plans for redeploying south. On 29 June 2004, in Istanbul, Blair announced that Britain would resume leadership of the ISAF operation, but by deploying HQ Allied Rapid Reaction Corps (ARRC) to Kabul, not by making any specific commitment in south-west Afghanistan. This was a politically motivated decision to avoid further commitments in Iraq – rather than a strategic decision taken by the MOD – but it would have profound implications for the army that would be required to re-balance from Basra to Afghanistan.[55] Within one year of the invasion of Iraq, Operation *Telic* had become a toxic liability for the Labour Party, acutely so after confirmation there were no Weapons of Mass Destruction. For the beleaguered prime minister, the imperative was to get out, but without snubbing the Americans. Afghanistan provided a legitimate escape route: a 'bad war' would be swapped for a 'good war', so some reasoned.

The presidential election was nonetheless held in October 2004 against the backdrop of uncertain security. The occasion was embraced with genuine enthusiasm on the part of the Afghan people, and in the event there was little violence, despite Taliban threats that the elections would be disrupted. Electoral fraud was brushed under the carpet. President Karzai, the only real contender to the presidential post, initially failed to secure the necessary 50 per cent majority. The newly agreed constitution pointed to a second-round vote, but Western backers had no appetite for seeing their man challenged in this way, so the inconvenient constitution was bypassed by the very people who had imposed it on Afghanistan. This lesson in *realpolitik* was not lost on Afghans.[56] Possibly 70 per cent of registered voters participated in the 2004 presidential elections (8.1 million votes, of which 40 per cent were women), which was as close as Afghanistan was going to get to universal suffrage and a higher voting participation than several European countries. These voters, ultimately, were cheated.

On 5 December 2004, with great fanfare, President Hamid Karzai was duly sworn in as Afghanistan's first democratic president. The international community congratulated the new president but the fact remained that he was taking over a narco-state. Exactly a week after the inauguration ceremony, a UN-sponsored conference was held in Kabul to address the Afghan narcotics trade. It was attended by flocks of Afghan and international delegates. The US grandly pledged $780 million to assist Afghan counter-narcotics operations. The newly installed president boldly promised the delegates, 'we will fight the poppy', but the facts of the opium trade were sobering. Over 60 per cent of Afghanistan's GDP was accounted for by this drug. A record-breaking 130,000 hectares of the opium poppy had been grown in the previous planting season – Afghanistan now accounted for 87 per cent of the world's opium supply.[57] The message from the Berlin Conference had reached Afghanistan, but other than throwing money at the problem, no credible strategy was offered, not least by Britain, which Blair had volunteered as the lead counter-narcotics nation.

At this stage ISAF had about 8,000 troops in Afghanistan (from 37 contributing nations), and very few of these had ever strayed outside the immediate environs of the capital, or indeed the ISAF HQ. The parliamentary and district elections due to be held in September 2005 would provide an opportunity for widespread back-scratching and corruption, as the Kabul government sought to strengthen its position by cutting deals with former warlords and other unsavoury characters. ISAF, blinded by the apparent success of Afghanistan's first presidential election, seemed oblivious to this next certain evolution of Afghan 'democracy'.

ISAF shifted over 1,000 tonnes of ballot papers, 403 tonnes of polling station furniture, 150,000 ballot boxes, 120,000 bottles of indelible ink, 150,000 voting screens and 34,000 polling stations throughout the national territory. Once in Afghanistan, a network of 18 cargo aircraft was used to ferry the ballot materials across country, supported by a fleet of 1,200 trucks. Afghanistan's long-suffering domestic animals found themselves surprising participants in the democratic process: 1,247 donkeys, 306 horses and 24 camels completed the deliveries to the more remote areas.[58] Despite the backroom dealing, corruption and currying of favours, it was a success of sorts. Half the Afghan population voted in the parliamentary and provincial council elections.[59] Women, who had been excluded from society by the Taliban, were now in government and formed a quarter of the total number of legislators sitting in the 351-member National Assembly. The enterprise had taken four years to complete, but it seemed, at last, to be on its way.

This, at least, was the official view. The reality was quite different. Around 80 per cent of the members of the Lower House (Wolesi Jirga) were the old power brokers: warlords, mujahidin and local strong men.[60] The quarter of seats reserved for women and other minorities were in fact a reserve quota imposed by Westerners. But for this quota, the entire legislature may well have been hijacked by the usual crooks. The single non-transferable voting system, deliberately designed to break up powerful blocks, had the unintended effect of creating a fissiparous and hopelessly unruly parliament.

Any visitor to Kabul over those four years would have witnessed visible changes to the capital. Even accepting the self-serving Western propaganda with due caution, it seemed the patient was gradually recovering. Afghanistan (which still mostly meant Kabul) was booming. Officially, the country experienced a 30 per cent hike in economic growth in the first two years following the collapse of the Taliban regime. It was no wonder the 2004 USAID brochure on Afghanistan was entitled *Afghanistan Reborn* and came with a splash of photographs and statistics portraying a central Asian country rising phoenix-like from the curse of war.

The British lead in reconstruction and development was assumed by the recently created Department for International Development. DfID's charter rested on an act of Parliament, the 2002 International Development Act. This act was drafted in support of the UN Millennium Goals and included a rosary of developmental goals, such as achieving a 'reduction in poverty', 'sustainable development' and 'improving the welfare of the population'. These were not aims that anyone could particularly disagree with, but they produced violent disagreement on how they should be achieved.

From 2001 to 2006, DfID would claim to spend over £500 million on reconstruction and development in Afghanistan, making it the second-largest donor after the US. In one of the last acts by the outgoing Tony

Blair, Britain agreed to commit a further £330 million from 2006 to 2009. Regardless of the true aid sums it was clear from the outset that DfID stood out from the other donor agencies. Unlike the Americans who believed reconstruction should follow the military operations, DfID took the view that the priority task was to stand up a working, centralized, Afghan government. This went by the euphemism 'capacity-building'. While it was accepted that Afghanistan needed a credible government in Kabul, the majority of donors were sceptical that pumping money into Kabul was the best way to get Afghanistan back on its feet. The problem with DfID's stance was that it wholly ignored Afghan culture and was wildly unrealistic. As Center for Strategic and International Studies (CSIS) author George Hyman put it in a grisly post-mortem a decade later, most Afghans had little or no experience of central government in their daily lives. They did not expect or want it. The West, led by organizations like DfID, was attempting to set up far more 'government' than rural Afghans cared for, wanted or needed.[61] DfID would court controversy in other ways which would become critical after the British deployed to Helmand.

At the outset of the ISAF mission, DfID contributed just £2 million towards reconstruction, but this trivial sum came with caveats. Rather than viewing itself as a joint partner with the army in Britain's foreign policy, DfID took the dogmatic view that no funds could be used 'to contribute to the military effectiveness of the British Army'. As the only effective task that 2 PARA and later 1 Royal Anglian could possibly undertake was some light, developing world do-goodery (the QIPs proposed by soldiers that DfID objected to) this somewhat undermined the very purpose of the soldiers. Furthermore, DfID took the view that the British Army should be treated like any other NGO bidding for funds. The professional NGOs knew the abracadabra spells needed to unlock DfID's treasure chest and get hold of British taxpayers' money (a 'Holistic Female Empowerment Action Programme' was hardly likely to trip off a paratrooper's tongue), so this put the soldiers at a disadvantage. In an unnecessarily insulting gesture, DfID also refused to delegate any financial authority to General McColl, which placed him in an embarrassing position as his German subordinate – a colonel – turned up with €600,000 in his pockets. Lastly, to the enormous frustration of the soldiers who were keen to achieve results quickly, DfID was terribly slow in releasing funds.

A related and major problem was the phenomenon of hollow pledges, an especially virulent disease at international donor conferences. It was more than probable that the individuals involved in these failed programmes knew perfectly well they would not take off. A culture of deceit was so institutionalized in the Western aid industry they were allowed to run anyway, before dying natural deaths.

For the British in the north, the Stage 1 expansion of ISAF had been a relatively smooth affair. In September 2004, six Harrier GR7s were deployed to Kandahar to support Operation *Enduring Freedom*. These would represent the first steps of what would become a significant RAF presence in Afghanistan. In the late autumn of 2004, the Green Howards ARIB at the Mazar-e-Sharif PRT was relieved by the Worcestershire and Sherwood Foresters. This was the first unit to serve in Afghanistan under the new operational codename, Operation *Herrick 1*. The official date of the start of the operation was 1 October. The 'Woofers', as they were known, returned to Britain in March 2005, unimpressed by the evolving operation. Worthwhile intelligence was almost non-existent. The fleet of vehicles deployed in Afghanistan was inappropriate, unreliable and too small. Communications were terrible – civilian mobile telephone became the default means used to ensure that messages were passed. It was rumoured pilots resorted to painting mobile telephone numbers on the undersides of their aircraft. Most damningly, the soldiers complained of the lack of helicopters. To constrain costs, the government had curtailed sending helicopters to support the British PRT in northern Afghanistan. This meant the British were dependent on two German helicopters that would only fly under restrictive national caveats. It was a completely unsatisfactory situation, and it meant that British soldiers were extremely wary of placing themselves in circumstances where they might require a casualty evacuation.

The Gurkhas relieved the Worcestershire and Sherwood Foresters for their second tour of Afghanistan in as many years and found none of the problems raised by the returning units were being addressed. Operation *Herrick 2* evolved into a story of good intentions undermined by a lack of resources. Vehicles were literally falling apart. Authorization was granted to procure local 4x4 SUVs. The lack of a robust communications infrastructure was seriously affecting operations. Patrolling an area of roughly 500,000 square kilometres without a single helicopter was completely unrealistic. This was military 'tokenism' at its worst.

The last British infantry battalion to serve in central Afghanistan, before the redeployment to Helmand, was the Royal Gloucestershire, Berkshire and Wiltshire Light Infantry.[62] This battalion's deployment coincided with a spike of unrest near Mazar-e-Sharif. On 19 October, a British vehicle patrol was attacked. A Lance Corporal Steven Sherwood was shot in the chest and killed, the first British soldier to die in combat on Operation *Herrick*. As well as the usual litany of complaints, chief of which was that no lessons from the previous deployments were being addressed in any meaningful way, the commanding officer, a Lieutenant Colonel Brown, made the prescient observation in his post-operational report that it was only with the development of a competent and credible Afghan army and police force that the international forces would be able to withdraw from Afghanistan. This obvious insight seemed to get entirely lost within the grandiose plans being hatched in Kabul for ISAF's expansion. A last chance to re-evaluate the mission in Afghanistan passed unnoticed.

In February 2005, NATO announced ISAF would be further expanded into the west of Afghanistan. This process, Stage 2 of the ISAF expansion, began on 31 May 2005, when ISAF took command of two Italian-led PRTs in the provinces of Herat and Farah as well as a FOB in Herat, also provided by Italy. Later that year, two further ISAF-led PRTs in the west became operational – in Chagcharan, led by Lithuania, and Qala-e-Naw, led by Spain.

After the original establishment of the ISAF mission in Kabul in 2001, led by a British HQ and supported by an infantry battalion, the British government had been assiduous in reducing its commitment to Afghanistan. The next three years had witnessed 'military tokenism', a pattern repeated by all the contributing ISAF nations. In the summer of 2004, at the Istanbul NATO conference, the government had announced it would deploy the headquarters of the Allied Rapid Reaction Corps (ARRC) to Kabul to command the NATO Stage 3 expansion into a new Regional Command South. The culmination of this process would be the Stage 4 expansion into Regional Command East, at which point ISAF would assume responsibility for all Afghanistan. Shortly before the Istanbul announcement, Lieutenant General David Richards was informed that he would command the ISAF mission.[63] His posting would start in January 2006. At the time, there was a hopelessly unrealistic expectation that Stage 3 would start in September 2005. In fact, the handover of southern and eastern Afghanistan from US forces did not begin before the spring of 2006 and would be completed in the late autumn. So, by the end of 2004, as the British handed over their PRTs to Nordic contingents and were redeploying to Kabul, it was known that an increased British commitment would be required to support the planned ISAF expansion. This commitment would almost certainly involve sending at least a reinforced battalion to south-west Afghanistan.

Shortly after the announcement of Stage 2 expansion, the Blair government took the firm decision to redeploy the British mission in ISAF to southern Afghanistan, as part of ISAF's Stage 3 expansion. Specifically, the decision to deploy to Helmand appears to have been taken in March or April 2005, or some nine months after the Istanbul announcement.[64] According to John Reid's subsequent testimony, his predecessor Geoff Hoon signalled British intent to redeploy south at a NATO conference in Nice on 10 February 2005. In April, with Reid about to assume the post of defence secretary, the service chiefs agreed to the deployment south starting in September (a quite impossible deadline given ISAF's foot-dragging). Two months then passed between the first statement of British intent under one defence secretary and Helmand becoming fixed in British sights under his successor.[65] By the time the first British reconnaissance teams were despatched in May 2005 to visit PRTs established in Uruzgan, Kandahar and Helmand provinces, the British commitment to Afghanistan had been reduced to the single Gurkha company conducting patrols in Feyzebad District in north-eastern Afghanistan, as well as the security battalion in Kabul manned by the Royal Gloucestershire, Berkshire and Wiltshire Light Infantry. This unit would briefly send a company to Helmand, the first to serve in the province (and the first to serve under the Operation *Herrick 4* banner).

It was to prove a momentous decision, but the path that led to this decision was unclear. Lieutenant General David Richards, who would command ISAF the following year, confessed to not knowing how the British task force ended up being committed to the little-known province of Helmand. Neither could Reid shed light on the decision, as it was taken before he assumed his appointment as defence secretary. Everyone agreed, in General Richards's words, that the ISAF mission needed 'gingering up'.[66] But this commitment had less to do with military hubris and more to do with the political toxicity of the Iraq War. By now, the Blair government was looking for a way out, while not wishing to be viewed as a weak ally by Washington. The ISAF Stage 3/4 expansions offered such an opportunity. The British would take over the ISAF show and shift their commitment to this less toxic war. It was a 'good war', from a political perspective. From a military perspective, assuming the lead nation role naturally implied that Britain would have to do more than indulge in the 'military tokenism' of the last three years. Merely redeploying a single infantry battalion to the south would have been inappropriate. Task Force Helmand would have to be a more substantial force, in line with Britain's status as ISAF lead nation. The unanswered question at the time was: how much more substantial?

On 7 July 2005, John Reid, newly appointed to take over from the embattled Geoff Hoon, made the simple announcement that Britain would also be establishing a PRT in Helmand Province (in fact, taking over the American-built PRT). This announcement followed the May reconnaissance. Reid only officially confirmed the mission in a statement on 26 January 2006, six months later.

In fact, three Goldilocks options were worked up, but it was always the case that the third option (the largest force package) would eventually be chosen. Despite later criticisms from the task force commander, Brigadier Ed Butler, that the mission was wilfully and culpably under-resourced, he received the maximum package, within Treasury-imposed constraints. There was no casualness or optimism on the part of the planning staffs at PJHQ, and nor were the concerns of the deploying formation 16 Air Assault Brigade ignored. The planners involved were working within tight financial caps. Despatching soldiers on the cheap, to faraway lands, was practically a British Treasury tradition. Butler was unfortunately joining a long list of unlucky commanders from the past.

Three factors ultimately determined this maximum force package. First, there was political necessity – Britain had to be seen to be offering more as lead nation. The second factor was Defence Secretary John Reid's cautious nature. Following events in Iraq, there was an understandable desire not to get caught out. The larger force was an insurance policy. A third factor was Richards, but his reasoning was different. Like Butler, Richards was unimpressed by the levels of commitment and preparations for the deployment of his force – the ARRC – and he had arguments both with superiors in MOD and NATO. Eventually, he impressed on Reid in a secret meeting that a strong British force should be deployed to south-west Afghanistan.[67] This took place in Berlin in mid-September 2005, coincident with Reid attending a NATO conference. Richards went behind the backs of the Chief of the Defence Staff (CDS) and Director of Operations, Major General Robert Fry, to hold this meeting, despite the fact that the former, General Mike Walker, had reassured him that he would be appropriately supported. According to Richards's account, it was at this meeting that Reid promised Richards the additional resources he was demanding.

By this stage, Richards was diverging from fellow senior officers in the MOD. The principal reason for this difference in perceptions was that the latter could see no compelling reasons for a strong force. It was important to recognize that Helmand was peaceful at the time. Major General Peter Wall, the Deputy Chief of Joint Operations, thought there was a 'relatively quiescent population', which was true. Just three American soldiers had been killed in Helmand in five years. Four police chiefs had been assassinated, but this was hardly unusual.[68] British advance parties despatched in May 2005 to visit PRTs established in Uruzgan, Kandahar and Helmand provinces had driven about openly in Land Rover Snatches, vehicles that would later become notorious because of their vulnerability to roadside bombs, without meeting any hostility. There were discussions over how many civilian minivans the British task force would require to ferry staff, a remarkable measure of the MOD perception that the mission would be essentially peaceful. Nobody had challenged, still less attacked, the small reconnaissance force. One of the officers who took part in this reconnaissance later returned as a brigade commander and was quoted as having reported there was a fight waiting to happen in Helmand.[69] This seems an observation taken out of context and re-warmed for posterity by critics of the mission. There were no Cassandras at the time because there were no reasons for doom-laden prophetic utterances. General Mike Jackson would later make the point succinctly: 'No intelligence was put in front of the Ministry of Defence which said, "What you're about to do will result in mayhem." Had that been so, I think there would have then been a very serious discussion as to whether that plan was viable or not.'[70]

There may not have been Cassandras warning of mayhem, but there were voices warning of a potentially difficult mission. Ed Butler recalled:

> ... both the preliminary operations teams, the special forces teams, who had been out in theatre, the individuals who pulled together the joint UK campaign plan for Helmand, all came up with the same sort of recommendations. They said that we were underestimating how long it was going to take; we did not have sufficient resources or know what was the actual mission going to be [sic]. All these points were very clearly

made by December 2005 ... I asked and I certainly never got those questions answered.[71]

It was later suggested the MOD had recommended Helmand Province as the first British choice on the grounds that it fitted with Britain's role as lead nation in counter-narcotics. The prime minister merely gave his assent. It appears that as early as the summer of 2004, at least the possibility of a British deployment to Helmand had been raised.[72] Another version suggested that the decision came from Downing Street, possibly encouraged by the FCO. Later evidence given to the Defence Select Committee indicated the MOD produced a paper entitled 'Why Helmand?' in the first half of 2005.[73] This was submitted to the Chiefs of Staff Committee and was subsequently endorsed by the prime minister's office. Apparently, this paper was later 'lost' (to the possible relief of its authors, who thus escaped the judgement of history). Whatever justifications were made in the 'Why Helmand?' paper, the more prosaic explanation was that the Canadians pushed to assume control of Kandahar, which left the British with little option but to pick up the leftover Helmand Province.

Certainly, there were ambiguities over accountability in decision-making, exacerbated by the change over of key personnel. At PJHQ, Air Marshal Glenn Torpy was replaced by Major General Nick Houghton. Crucially, Houghton, who was serving as a senior British representative in Iraq, left his job in mid-March 2006, 'span round', and found himself in command of operations in Afghanistan, as the Chief of Joint Operations, at the beginning of April.[74] He had some background knowledge of Operation *Herrick*, but appointing a new general in this key post, at such a crucial stage of an operation, was injudicious at best. With PJHQ transfixed by an imminent major British operation in Basra (Operation *Sinbad*), Houghton stood little chance of getting to grips with his brief just when it mattered most. This command change was compounded by a change at the very top of the military hierarchy, with Air Marshal Jock Stirrup assuming the post of CDS on 28 April (the day before 3 PARA conducted its first patrol in Helmand).

It was also the case that the arithmetic of the deployment was suspect. It appears Major General Fry, a highly intelligent officer, may have been the owner of the broken abacus. Tasked with scoping the Afghanistan commitment over 2004, under the auspices of a strategic planning group, it seems Fry and his team became the unwitting originators of the good war-bad war dichotomy.[75] Specifically, Fry made the graphic linkage between troops drawing down from Iraq, and troops ramping up in Afghanistan. This later infamous PowerPoint slide illustrated not so much hubris as an unfortunate arithmetic based on the most optimistic assumptions. *Even with* the drawdown from Iraq, the downsizing British Army would struggle to meet its Afghanistan commitments. Hoon had been warning about 'overstretch' since the beginning of operations in Afghanistan, *before* the Labour government's defence cuts (under Future Army Structures 2003–06). It was as if the inconvenience of arithmetic that simply did not stack up could not be allowed to act as an impediment to military commitments, spawned by Blair's interventionist and ambitious foreign policy. When General Richard Dannatt subsequently took over as Chief of the General Staff (CGS), he straight away questioned the arithmetic and got into trouble over making remarks that the army was 'running hot'.

The MOD planning team was following political direction, but it was perhaps not entirely blameless. The projection offered in the PowerPoint was only realistic if the Basra task force did indeed withdraw, and if a future commitment in Afghanistan remained stable. But what if neither of these assumptions held? In the event, total withdrawal from Basra was five years away, and the Afghanistan mission would be anything but stable. Were these possibilities discussed? Did anyone raise the uncomfortable 'what ifs'?

A subsequent allegation made by the British ambassador, Sherard Cowper-Coles, that the British Army sought to reinforce the operation in Helmand to save itself from further cuts, was also unfounded.[76] General Richard Dannatt may or may not have made the passing remark to Cowper-Coles in the summer of 2007 that the army had to 'use them or lose them' (referring to the battlegroups being withdrawn from Iraq), but this was not the reason why more troops were requested for Helmand (Cowper-Coles reportedly later apologized for making the allegation). The planned downsizing of the army was already underway. There were no plans to downsize further, and nor was a commitment to Afghanistan in any way an influence on the future restructuring of the army. All these matters had already been deliberated during the first Blair government. The reason why the operation in Helmand was reinforced was because the argument was quickly made that the first task force had been hopelessly under-resourced, most notably by Butler, who before the task force even deployed repeatedly warned of the under-resourcing and lack of commitment. At the end of the war, the under-resourcing of Operation *Herrick 4* became an often-repeated *mea culpa* from now-retired senior officers, but this was a complete red herring. The reason why the task force got into difficulties was because it became embroiled in unnecessary spats with the tribes of northern Helmand. It would have made not an iota of difference if twice as many soldiers had been sent. More soldiers would have just spread and exacerbated the fighting, as happened over the succeeding years.

Butler was right to highlight that his brigade was being despatched to Helmand 'on the cheap'. But this only mattered if you set yourself the impossible task of securing Helmand. Nobody gave Butler this mission. He was, in fairness, specified a totally inadequate list of wishful good intentions which amounted to a parody of a mission (delivering good governance, security and development), but it was his responsibility to cut his cloth accordingly. The later argument made – that 'no plan survives contact with the enemy' – was weak. They do. Otherwise there would be little point making plans. Bad plans don't, and nor do plans that are basically discarded. The latter happened, and *not* because of contact with the enemy. Task Force Helmand abandoned 'the plan' within a few weeks of arriving in theatre *before* it became entangled in the fighting that came to be known as the 'platoon house' sieges. Indeed, it abandoned the plan before it had even fired any shots, or encountered 'the enemy'.

What was clear was that as a result of this somewhat confused and opaque decision-making the MOD would send a task force to Helmand either in late 2005 or early 2006. In Brigadier Andrew Mackay's later condemnation, this was done with 'eyes shut and their fingers crossed'. In the words of another serving officer, 'There was institutional denial and ignorance.'[77] Voices that suggested caution were drowned out by a lobby that argued for 'cracking on', despite the lack of intelligence and resources. This view of a precipitate British entry into Helmand became part of the myth of Operation *Herrick 4*, but it is not supported by the facts. What was striking about the decision was the extreme caution demonstrated by John Reid, who eventually delayed the mission by four months, weathering significant criticism for doing so. The better description of the British entry into Helmand was given by Matthew Parris in *The Times*, many years later as the task force withdrew:

> Thus, not quite by accident yet never really by design, people who should have known better, people who could have known better,

> and people who simply wouldn't focus inched each other towards a steepening downward slope. Of course nobody could have known that the Helmand operation must fail; but many should have known that it was a huge and imponderable risk.[78]

John Reid's announcement that a British task force would be deployed to Helmand Province in the spring of 2006 was the key decision of his short tenure as defence secretary. Geoff Hoon had inherited armed forces committed to peacekeeping in the Balkans and looking forward to ending their long overdue stay in Northern Ireland. A gentle decline was on the horizon. By the time he handed over to John Reid, Britain had gone to war in Iraq and was now trapped by its consequences. The world had been turned on its head and the old certainties had been wiped away. Seeing this was proving hard work. There was still a sense in the MOD that the events of the last two years had been a blip and that 'business as usual' would be restored. For the government this became a matter of absolute urgency as the political liability of Iraq tore the Labour Party apart and ended the career of its most successful premier in the modern era.

John Reid first visited Afghanistan at the beginning of October 2005, four months after assuming the post of defence secretary. His visit was confined to Kabul and he did not venture to Helmand to see for himself where the government was proposing to deploy the British task force. In Kabul he attended the re-opening of the city's second-oldest school – the Abdul Ghafor High School – where he cut ribbons and accepted flowers from girls dressed in colourful tribal costumes. The real purpose of his visit was to finalize the arrangements for the Stage 3 and Stage 4 expansions of the NATO mission, which would see ISAF take over responsibility for all Afghanistan from US Joint Task Forces. After the foot-dragging manner in which some nations had approached Stages 1 and 2, the American delegation was keen to inject firmer commitment and a sense of urgency into the European partners. In the end, despite the messy arrangements, the timetable would be largely met, albeit with the four-month delay. For the US Army unit languishing in forgotten Helmand the moment could not come too soon.

The last piece of the diplomatic framework, before the deployment of the British task force to Helmand, was laid by the Afghanistan Compact, a conference held in London in January 2006 attended by 60 countries. The conference was subtitled with the optimistic slogan 'Building on Success'.

The sense that the fragile, impoverished and corrupted state of Afghanistan might actually be slipping into war was passed over. In line with DfID's mandate, the Afghanistan Compact was about Afghanistan fulfilling its millennium goals. This conference would be Tony Blair's swansong on Afghanistan before retiring bruised from the fiasco of Iraq. The unrealism of the Afghanistan Compact could be gauged by the genre of articles the *ISAF Mirror* in Kabul was printing at the turn of the year: warm stories about French nurses visiting a village outside Kabul, or of ISAF helicopters delivering blankets to a village in northern Afghanistan following a landslide, or Spanish soldiers ferrying a burns victim to a hospital. No mention of the war – the great taboo subject in NATO.

For the Afghans, led by President Karzai, the important point was the money. A total of $10.5 billion was pledged. But as critics pointed out, these headline figures were deeply misleading. Money pledged did not mean money obligated, still less money spent. A proportion of the pledged money came from funds that had already been pledged at the Bonn, Tokyo and Berlin conferences – a fraudulent accounting trick routinely played by donor countries. These were not additional funds at all. Trying to unravel the opaque spending mechanisms and accounting procedures of 60-odd countries was an impossible task. And much of the money was simply being embezzled by Afghan officials. No matter how much blood was pumped into the patient it was only succeeding in keeping the patient alive, because blood was still leaking from untreated wounds. What the Afghanistan reconstruction plan was achieving, mainly, was holding up a mirror to the intractably complex world of foreign aid – a world of worthy intentions and deep, pocket-lining cynicism in equal measure, of life-saving aid, but also of colossal mismanagement, waste and corruption. This was the Kabul colourfully described in Jason Burke's seminal *9/11 Wars*: on any street you could equally meet a saint or a crook.

For Western donors like Britain, the Afghanistan Compact was about setting targets, another staple of the Blair governments. These rolled out like manifesto pledges: minefields to be reduced by 70 per cent; primary school enrolment to be increased by 75 per cent; hunger to be reduced by 5 per cent annually (how anyone was proposing to measure the hungriness of the Afghan population was not clear); electricity in rural areas to be increased by 25 per cent, and so it went on, a litany of promises that could be massaged by statistical manipulation by the time the next international conference came around to demonstrate that progress had in fact been achieved. Security was not ignored, and within this raft of proposals it was agreed the Afghan security forces would be increased to about 70,000 by 2010. It was a measure of how far 'The Afghanistan Compact' was from the reality of Afghanistan that, by 2010, four times this number of Afghan security forces were being demanded to fight the expanding Taliban insurgency.

At the heart of ISAF's expansion strategy were the PRTs or Provincial Reconstruction Teams. To Barbara Stapleton, the political advisor to the European Union Special Representative, this strategy proved unbalanced and flawed.[79] The PRTs followed national agendas and failed to cooperate and coordinate between themselves. There were tensions between the military and the civil agencies. The civil agencies themselves bickered. PRTs began to mirror the fractured state of Afghanistan by ignoring instructions from the centre if they judged them irrelevant. Some PRTs – like the British PRT in Mazar-e-Sharif – were given such meaninglessly small amounts of reconstruction money that it is doubtful whether they achieved any tangible impact in their provinces. Attempts to align PRT operations – through conferences, steering groups, executive committees – all failed. Instead, the aid effort became 'Balkanized', with governments that had contributed to ISAF more concerned with demonstrating spurious success to their electorates than with achieving real success. The voice piece of this shambles was the *ISAF Mirror*, which, it was joked, was used by local Afghans as wrapping paper. Page after page offered examples of ISAF 'progress' as the country slid deeper into insurgency. The PRTs experienced, as Stapleton put it, 'the paradox of development', namely that what you expect to happen is confounded by what actually happens as a result of your good intentions. There was no rigorous auditing mechanism for the activities of the PRTs. There was too much focus on inputs (the headline targets beloved of politicians), and unflattering outputs were skipped over. Instead of the imagined virtuous circle, a vicious spiral set in.

For the NGOs, ISAF were a bunch of arrivistes who did not understand the nuances of aid and reconstruction. For the military, the NGOs were dogmatic do-gooders who were failing to take a more pragmatic approach to the situation in Afghanistan. The number of NGOs operating in Afghanistan, drawn like bees to the honeypot of reconstruction money, was staggering – over 2,500 were registered with the Afghan Interim Authority.[80] The overwhelming majority of these were the appropriately named one-man 'suitcase NGOs' – or Afghans more than happy to fill their suitcases with free Western money. This shadowy world of aid was a sensitive if not taboo subject. Only a few intrepid reporters, such as Linda Polman in her investigative book *War Games: The Study of Aid and War in Modern Times*, dared tackle the subject.[81] Polman found what many suspected: Western do-goodery commonly worsened already dire situations by provoking rampant corruption. Polman coined her own phrase for 'suitcase NGOs'. She dubbed them MONGOS, 'My Own NGO', or people getting rich by dispensing 'consultancy' in developing countries. Foreign correspondent Jonathan Foreman also tackled the subject in *Aiding and Abetting*, a book that exposed how a great deal of British government aid channelled through organizations like DfID was simply being stolen or squandered.[82] Foreman had some credibility, as he had worked in Iraq and Afghanistan and had witnessed at first hand the waste. These intelligent books made no difference because DfID was a protected department, immune from forensic inquiry that would no doubt have left ordinary Britons aghast at what was actually happening to their taxes siphoned off to developing countries.

Out of this increasingly chaotic situation emerged the Provincial Stabilization Strategy, which ran for a year without visible results, before giving way to another initiative, the Regional Development Zones or RDZs. These also proved fruitless and were replaced by the Afghan Development Zones or ADZs, as if Afghanistan could be won over by rolling out acronyms. It was an ADZ centred on Lashkar Gah and Gereshk that would be the centrepiece of Britain's Helmand Plan, the scheme that would inform the deployment of Task Force Helmand. The ADZs would be part of an 'ink spot strategy', the idea being that the military would clear an area of insurgents to allow reconstruction to take place. As Stapleton shrewdly noted, in Afghanistan, the plan commonly substituted for the action. As reform processes came up against the political constraints that often rendered them ineffectual, the tendency was to start another process and abandon the former one.[83]

By now, another problem had beset the PRTs. In Afghan eyes, they were deeply compromised. American special forces units started operating from them (or Afghans believed they did), causing mayhem in their search for 'terrorists'. Afghans were detained in PRTs. The PRTs dealt with corrupt officials and unintentionally strengthened their positions. On occasions, tribal leaders simply refused to have anything to do with PRT initiatives.

As importantly, many simply did not understand the purpose of the PRTs – the communication of ISAF's intentions was abysmal. Stapleton concluded her analysis with a metaphor. The international community was dealing haphazardly with symptoms, while dodging causes. Far from sailing towards a better future, Afghanistan was heading for an iceberg, and Western squabbling was akin to rearranging deckchairs on the *Titanic*.[84] It was on this sinking ship that the Blair government embarked Task Force Helmand.

3

A Particularly Difficult Operation

Operation *Herrick 4*, March 2006–October 2006

General Sir Mike Jackson, the Chief of the General Staff, could have been forgiven for describing Britain's latest theatre of operations as 'miles of fuck all and a river'.[1] Helmand, the province where the British Army was about to deploy a reinforced parachute battlegroup, was mostly uncharted territory. In the 19th century it was known as Hilmand, a spelling which persisted in some gazetteers. The boast of a local hothead that the British had been beaten in the past and would be beaten again was not quite accurate. The British had never really paid great attention to Helmand, except for a brief period during the first Anglo-Afghan War. The only town of note, Girishk – the modern-day Gereshk – had been briefly invested and a fort built. It was still serving as a prison when the British returned at the beginning of the 21st century. A second fort was built in central Helmand in the 1880s, in Nad-e Ali, that the British would take over and turn into a forward operating base.

The reality was the imperial British were wasting their time in Afghanistan, but each time it took a setback, escalating costs and an increasingly sceptical home government to end the misadventure and order the withdrawal back to India. Throughout, more sensible minds found themselves having to rein in those fascinated by the Great Game in Central Asia. In 1885, Lord Salisbury complained to Roberts:

> We are still the victims of an incurable attack of 'brag'. We cannot reconcile ourselves to the truth that if we will not provide cloth enough for the coat we want, we must cut down our coat to the cloth we have

> got. So many of our amateur, semi-military programmes go on the assumption that we had [a] large army.

Surely, Lord Salisbury's ghost hung over every Blair war cabinet.

One hundred and twenty years after the first British incursion into this corner of Afghanistan, little had changed. A major who deployed to the town of Sangin in 2006 remarked on arrival: 'Imagine England, then remove all the roads, the power supply, the communications, all the structure of government, and there's no money but there's corruption and drugs.'[2] This was perhaps the first thing that impressed military planners – the sheer scale of the place and the near-total lack of anything resembling a modern infrastructure. How would the modern soldiers cope against 'the united horrors of climate, treachery and barbarous warfare', in the words of the memorial plaque to the 44th Regiment wiped out at Gandamak in the First Anglo-Afghan War?[3]

Helmand Province stretches for 300 kilometres, from the Pakistan border in the south, to the district of Baghran in the north, which pokes into the side of neighbouring Uruzgan Province. The southern border, ill-defined by the Durand Line, runs for 160 kilometres following the low-lying Chaghai Hills. It is open, barely policed and criss-crossed by dozens of ancient smuggling routes. In the far north, Helmand becomes mountainous, narrowing into a 50-kilometre-wide salient. Neither the southern border nor the northern valleys had ever been successfully controlled by the provincial governments. The internal borders are equally lawless. Helmand shares them with six other provinces: Nimroz, Farah, Ghor, Daykundi, Uruzgan and Kandahar. Within those borders, the province is divided into 13 administrative districts, the most prosperous being Lashkar Gah (meaning 'Place of the Soldiers'), the seat of the provincial capital, and Nahr-e Saraj, where Gereshk, the commercial capital, is located. The only other settlements of any significance are Sangin, a town with a population of about 20,000 at the heart of the opium trade; Musa Qaleh, a smaller settlement in northern Helmand; Now Zad, in the far north-west; and Garmsir in the south. The province itself was only created in 1941.

The defining feature of Helmand is the river that goes by the same name, the longest in Afghanistan.[4] The classical world knew it as the Erymandrus, and without it Helmand would be like neighbouring Nimroz, a mostly uninhabited desert. Archaeological evidence shows that human civilizations had been exploiting the life-giving river since at least 3,000 BC. It is the only perennial watercourse between the Indus to the east and the Tigris–Euphrates to the west. The river runs roughly from north to south, bisecting Helmand into two equal halves. Unusually, it is a river destined never to complete a natural journey to the sea. In the far south the river curls west, dispersing in a boggy area of underground aquifers known as the Sistan Marshes, before finally running its course in the Hamun-e-Helmand lake region, on the Afghan–Iranian border. The name Helmand was well chosen. It means 'many dams', an echo of the other name by which it is known: the *hazar shakha* or 'thousand-branch river'. In the spring the river coils from Kajaki District in the north to Dishu District in the south, forming hundreds of rivulets and sandbars along a wadi bed, swollen with winter rains. When it flows as a torrent the river can easily tip over a truck unwarily attempting to ford. In the height of summer, a man might cross the river at its widest point, skipping from sandbar to sandbar.

If the Helmand River is the province's blessing, it is also its curse. An aerial image of Helmand reveals why. The majority of the province is a tawny colour, indicating rocky desert, or a darker brown, indicating mountain. Running through the middle of the province is a thin ribbon of green showing cultivated lands on both banks of the Helmand River. A Lance Corporal Boyd who served with 2 Mercians (Worcesters and Foresters) described this ground perfectly:

> I realised that it was not desert at all but more like secondary jungle; jungle in places which gave the enemy excellent cover and most tree lines offered the opportunity for the enemy to spring ambushes. Along each tree line, more often than not, there's a culvert that runs from tree line to tree line. Each field is roughly 150m to 200m square with tree lines and varying sizes of streams dividing each field.[5]

Like the more famous Nile, the Helmand River delineates the boundaries of life and death. The gravel desert to the west of the river is known as the Dasht-e Margo, or 'desert of death'. To the east is the sandy Registan Desert. For centuries the thin strip of fertile land between these two deserts had been dominated by a handful of tribes. In the modern era an influx of outsiders had arrived, encouraged by irrigation projects. The Soviet–Afghan War tangled the tapestry of tribes still further.

To better harness the potential of the Helmand River, American engineers embarked on a series of ambitious projects that would transform

Helmand into 'little America' and give the province its modern-day topography. This was Helmand's golden age, and older residents still recalled this period with fondness. Forty years later, an Afghan chef in a Lashkar Gah guesthouse was still turning out stick-in-the-rib dishes and could reportedly sing the words to 'Deep in the Heart of Texas'.[6]

The centrepiece of the projects was a dam, built in 1953 near a village called Kajaki Sofla in the north. The Morrison-Knudsen project was overseen by a young American engineer named James Dunn who took to dressing in traditional Afghan garb. Over 100 metres tall and 250 metres wide, the dam created a reservoir of shimmering turquoise beauty, the Band-e Kajaki. The purpose of the dam was to generate electricity for the growing Helmandi economy, spurred by canal building and reclamation projects further south. The turbine hall itself would only finally be completed in the 1970s, before work had to be abandoned following the communist takeover. The power infrastructure needed to distribute the electricity, however, was never completed, turning Kajaki into a white elephant. Thirty years later, a dedicated band of local workers and a single American engineer known as 'Kajaki Bob' were keeping the last turbine running. When the Soviets arrived, they took over the dam and built a small airstrip on the other side of the river, alongside an existing small settlement named Tangye. Over the course of the war, fierce fighting depopulated the area, creating a legacy of antipathy towards foreigners that would rebound against the British. After the Soviet withdrawal, the locals returned to the area and built a bazaar on the abandoned airstrip. The 100-metre-long wooden bridge joining the bazaar to the dam in the meantime began to rot and was no longer safe except for light vehicles.

After Kajaki Dam, the most important project undertaken by American engineers was the reclamation of land in central Helmand. This was undertaken under the auspices of an organization eventually titled the Helmand Arghandab Valley Authority (HAVA), and built on work by Japanese engineers undertaken in the 1930s. It created the prosperous new farming district Nad-e Ali that would become important to the British (Nad-e Ali is 'the Call of Ali', the poem attributed to one of the wives of the Prophet Muhammad). Between 1953 and 1973, 5,000 farming families were resettled in the area, representing a wide range of ethnic and tribal groups.

To coordinate the project American engineers proposed building an entirely new town at a point on the Helmand River that was equidistant between the reclaimed lands and anticipated markets. This point was Lashkar Gah just north of the ancient and now abandoned site of a former Ghaznavid fort. Then known as Lashkari Bazaar, the site also fulfilled another important criterion, namely that it possessed 'natural beauty and potential for healthful living'.[7] The site was chosen by an American engineer named Frank Patterson, and he estimated that over 1,000 American workers and their dependants would need offices and homes. Over a ten-year period he hoped the economic stimulus would grow the town to a population of about 10,000, which proved a wild underestimate.

There is no memorial to Frank Patterson but there should be, because he became the founding father of Helmand's largest town and eventual provincial capital. In many respects, the idealistic and hard-working Patterson created Helmand Province. The site of the ancient capital – first trashed by Genghis Khan and finally razed by Timurlane – had been overshadowed for the last 500 years by the more prosperous Gereshk. All that remained of its former glory were some old medieval ruins, a dilapidated roadside bazaar and a handful of farms. Now the American turned around the relative importance of the two locations. Modern houses with large gardens were built alongside an administrative city centre. Tree-lined boulevards were laid out. The new housing estates also followed the traditional American grid pattern and contrasted with the warren of compound houses in the sprawl of suburbs built later by Afghans, attracted to Lashkar Gah by the economic boom. Locals would say when the Americans built the houses, there were no walls. The walls came later, with the Soviet occupation and collapse of civil order. In the rejuvenated Lashkar Gah, a smart new hospital, schools and government offices were built. Public gardens, a sports stadium, a bank, a cinema and club house were added. The Helmand River was spanned with a modern bridge. An ornate mosque, Helmand's architectural jewel, was built. An airstrip, Bost Airport, was added south of the town. A light industrial park sprung up. This was Yankee frontier spirit at its energetic best. When the British arrived in 2006, Lashkar Gah had a population of 150,000 and was a mixed, relatively cosmopolitan town. Frank Patterson's vision had flourished in ways he probably never imagined.

The Helmand Valley Reclamation Project had important demographic consequences. Above all Helmand was tribal, or as a 19th-century Briton would have put it, 'barbarous'. This tribal mix was greatly complicated by the influx of migrants and the deliberate creation of areas of heterogeneous tribal identities. A hierarchy of *kor* (family), *khel* (clan group) and *zai* (tribe) defined your identity. *Zai* literally means 'son of', hence the Barakzai, a large tribe in Helmand, are 'the sons of Barak'. A primitive but rigorous democracy governed the everyday life of communities, dominated exclusively by men. Each family group had its mosque, which acted as the communal hall, and in some settlements as cemetery. There was little need to stray beyond the boundary of fields which defined your clan or tribal area. A girl could grow up, marry, bear children and die without ever having left the immediate environs of the dozen compound farm buildings that made up her village. Beyond this world there were the modern political creations of a head of district, and a provincial governor, but these were distant figures. Kabul – seat of the national government – was utterly remote. Following the New York terrorist attacks, most Afghans only had the vaguest sense of the import of the events that were about to change their lives. America may well have been on the moon. So for that matter could London, Glasgow or Belfast. Several years after the entry of the British in Helmand, this was still the case, with many farmers still ignorant as to why British soldiers were decamping in their fields.

Southern Afghanistan is dominated by Pashtun tribes. There are two major confederations – the Durrani and Ghilzai – comprising 60 major tribes and over 400 clans. The largest tribal group in Helmand are the Durrani Pashtuns, who have also been the dominant confederation in Afghanistan since the end of the 18th century. Well known to the British, they were described in a 1936 Indian Army guide to the Pathans (the common name for the modern-day Pashtun) as comprising eight sub-tribes, all of which were still recognizable when the British task force marched into Helmand 70 years later. The Indian Army knew them as a tribal group straddling both sides of the Durand Line, a point of some strategic significance when the British found themselves fighting the modern-day descendants in the form of the Taliban movement. As part of a policy of pacification, the British recruited from the Durrani confederation – as they did from many compliant Pathan tribes – but did not find them to be especially good soldiers.[8] They made far better guerrillas.

By the time the British returned in 2006, the tribal map had grown more complex and mixed. The Barakzai, divided into seven branches, still dominated the capital Lashkar Gah and were also strongly represented south of the capital, in Nawa-e Barakzai District and in Nahr-e Saraj District. They also maintained a lodgement in Maruf District in Kandahar Province. As this tribe controlled some of the prime opium-poppy-growing land in central

Helmand, it was heavily implicated in the narcotics trade. The Barakzai were part of the 'aristocratic' Zirak branch of the Durrani confederation, along with the less numerous Alikozai, Achakzai and Popalzai.

The other tribe that had come to dominate this illicit trade was the Ishaqzai, who would become implacable foes of the British. The Ishaqzai were a virtual narco-tribe because they were strongly established in two key areas: Sangin in the north and Dishu in the south. Sangin was the centre of Helmand's opium trade and held its largest market. As opium poppy cultivation expanded in Helmand, it would become the centre of the narcotics trade in Afghanistan. Dozens of opium processing labs were established in outlying settlements especially to the north of the town. Dishu was important because it sat on the Pakistan border and hosted the infamous Bahram Chah market, a beehive for cross-border smugglers. In Dishu and neighbouring Reg, the Ishaqzai shared the spoils with Baluchis, the inveterate travellers and smugglers of the lawless border lands. Ishaqzais were also strategically placed in Lashkar Gah, Gereshk, Garmsir and Now Zad. Periodically, drug wars would break out between the tribes, and such a clash happened between the Ishaqzai and the Alikozai in 2006, which the British misinterpreted as a Taliban eruption. The other important point about the Ishaqzai was that they belonged to the lesser Panjpai ('five fingers') branch of the Durrani confederation, together with the Alizai and Noorzai. This made them the natural enemies of the aristocratic Barakzai.

The Alizai, who divided into three branches – Hassanzai, Pirlai and Khalozai – were the other great players in Helmand. The Alizai had always been present in northern Helmand, as the 1936 Indian Army guide recorded, but in later years the tribe had grown to become one of the most numerically strong throughout Helmand. Squeezed by population growth, the Alizai had begun to encroach southwards into Ishaqzai and Alikozai lands north of Sangin (eventually provoking a clash in 2007 which the British optimistically hoped signalled a tribal revolt against the Taliban). The Alizai were also in conflict with the Popalzai over control of Highway 1 east of Gereshk. The tribal heartlands were in Musa Qaleh District, where the opium poppy was cultivated on an industrial scale, but the Alizai were also well represented in Baghran and Kajaki. Although the Alizai belonged to the lesser Panjpai branch of the Durrani confederation, the tribe dominated Helmand politics thanks to the leadership shown by the Akhundzada family during the Soviet–Afghan War. When the British first drove into Lashkar Gah, Sher Mohammed Akhundzada, a relative of the mujahidin leader, was governor of Helmand Province.

Lastly there were the Noorzai, a tribe strongly represented on both sides of the Durand Line. The days when the Noorzai were mainly a poor tribe with a foothold in Gereshk had long passed. During the 1950s, Noorzai had flooded into Nad-e Ali, grabbing prime land. They were followed by Baluchis, Kakars, Kharoteis and other Pashtun tribes. Uzbeks and Tajiks from the north also settled in Nad-e Ali, as well as the exotic Hazaras, regarded as satanic by the Taliban. Noorzai also migrated south to Garmsir, an important junction for smugglers travelling between Lashkar Gah and the Pakistan border. Their presence in Spin Boldak, the main border crossing point south of Kandahar, and the existence of Noorzai communities in Baluchistan, endowed them with a formidable smuggling network. Noorzai dominance of Nad-e Ali naturally set them against the Barakzai in Lashkar Gah. This rivalry would come to a head in the summer of 2008 when the Barakzai would try to push poppy eradication initiatives away from their lands in Nawa-e Barakzai and onto Noorzai lands in Nad-e Ali.

Any survey of Pashtun tribes in Helmand – including the one just offered – was necessarily a simplification. The two urban centres, Lashkar Gah and Gereshk, like all large towns, had mixed the tribal tapestry. The combination of the economic boom in the 1950–70s, followed by the trauma of war and civil war, had complicated Helmandi society further. The strength of tribal loyalty varied, and cross-tribal cooperation was as evident as inter-tribal rivalry. The Taliban had scratched the picture further by encouraging pan-tribal power structures (although only among their own favoured Pashtun tribes). Anyone seeking to understand Helmand through its tribal delineations was as likely to be confused as illuminated. Four years after deploying to Helmand, the British would still not have accurately mapped or fully understood the tribal dynamics of the province.

At the heart of Pashtun culture was the *puktunwali* code, known in the 20th century as *pashtunwali*. This code of conduct was not written anywhere, and it has been argued it was a construct of early British anthropology seeking to gain an understanding of the Pathans. A 1938 British Army guide advised that *puktunwali* was 'framed on principles of equity and retaliation'.[9] The three maxims of the code were protection (*nanawatai*), retaliation (*badal*) and an obligation to demonstrate hospitality, or *mailmastia*. *Badal*, or retaliation, was the duty of any man subjected to injury or insult. Failure to exact *badal* resulted in loss of face within the clan or tribe. Every male tribesman killed by a British soldier was incitement to *badal*, and the more tribesmen the British killed, the wider the blood feud extended, like an uncontrollable Ponzi scheme. If any single factor was going to unhinge the British campaign in Helmand it was this ancient impulse to blood feuds, as indeed it did. This was understood but never resolved by the British, who continued to kill tribesmen to the very end, guaranteeing that the final British soldier to leave would do so with the sound of a vengeful bullet whistling past his ear.

When British cartographers finally compiled a general tribal map of Helmand Province in 2007, they needed a 23-bar colour code.[10] It was this map, as much as any other single document, that eloquently illustrated the complex web of power relations in which the British had become embroiled. In the 19th century there may have been a political officer who could speak the language, who had 'gone native', and who could guide a military commander through this maze of tribes (although political officers were frequently ignored), but no such animal existed in the 21st-century British Foreign and Commonwealth Office, still less in the Department for International Development (DfID).

All these tribes lived in characteristic adobe, walled compounds, the 'million Alamos', as the American ex-special forces officer turned journalist, Michael Yon, would describe them.[11] Building technology had not advanced since biblical times. Almost all were one-storey buildings and seldom higher than 10 feet. Furniture was extremely sparse: inside one might find a corn bin (*kandu*) for immediate use; some beds (*kat*), stools (*katkai*) and cots (*zango*). Children were everywhere. Cooking was done over open fires or clay ovens. In the courtyard there were often sheds for the domestic animals as well as a much larger corn bin, the *khamba*, in which a year's supply of grain was held. Small fruit gardens and even flower gardens were cultivated in the larger compounds. Soldiers could generally distinguish the headman's house by the size of his garden. Modern-day soldiers would joke that this house was readily identified because it was the only house in the village with glass in the windows.

The tribesmen that would turn against the British were accurately described in a 1945 platoon commander's guide to frontier warfare:[12]

> They are a poor but hardy race. Brought up in an atmosphere of hereditary blood feuds, they are experts in self-preservation, and every boy learns

> to handle a rifle at an early age. They have many good qualities, among which manliness, hospitality, a sturdy spirit of independence, and a good sense of humour predominate; but on the other hand the trans-frontier Pathan is often fanatical, cruel and treacherous.

In the 60-odd years that elapsed between the drafting of Indian Army Pamphlet No. 16, 'Platoon Leading in Frontier Warfare', and the arrival of the British task force in Helmand, nothing had changed, or it seemed, had been learned.

The most salient fact about Helmand Province, other than its complex tapestry of tribes, was that it was at the centre of Afghanistan's opium trade. When *Janes*, the defence journal publication, published a lengthy article examining the imminent deployment of the British task force, it was entitled 'British forces enter "Opiumland"'.[13] This point seemed self-evident, but the British task force was determined to avoid becoming embroiled in a drug war. British policy towards the poppy cultivation was summed up by Royal Marine Colonel Gordon Messenger in *The Independent* on 23 February 2006: 'There will be absolutely no maroon berets [of the marines] with scythes in a poppy field.'

Three protagonists would become indelibly written into the story of the initial British deployment into Helmand, Operation *Herrick 4*. The first was the Secretary of State for Defence, John Reid. His father had been a postman in South Lanarkshire and his mother had worked in a factory. He left school at the age of 16 and was largely self-taught, gaining a PhD in economic history as an adult. He struggled with alcohol and nicotine and eventually controlled both addictions. Anyone who dealt with John Reid could not help but be impressed by his combative and direct manner, earning him a reputation as the Labour Party's 'attack dog'. This old-fashioned socialist, steeped in a Scottish tradition of self-help and common sense, would be richly rewarded in the New Labour project, eventually holding seven different Cabinet posts.

Like the remainder of the Blair Cabinet, Reid had no war experience, but he compensated for this lack of experience with good sense. His importance to the story was paradoxically his absence from the narrative at a crucial juncture. Reid was the single personality who may have saved Operation *Herrick 4*. In one of his last acts as defence secretary he questioned an expansion to the British mission – then being requested in Helmand – that would involve the deployment of British troops outside the agreed areas of Lashkar Gah and Gereshk. Following his departure on 5 May, this was overturned. In the end he quit his post, having served one day less than a full year.

The second protagonist in the drama was Brigadier Ed Butler, a contrasting personality to the defence secretary. Butler was the scion of a distinguished Conservative family. His grandfather 'Rab' Butler had been Winston Churchill's chancellor. His father, Adam Butler, had served as a junior minister under Margaret Thatcher. He joined the prestigious Royal Green Jackets, unofficially known as the 'Black Mafia' because of the number of generals this regiment churned out. His operational experience was exceptional: he had completed three tours of Northern Ireland (where he gained a Mention in Dispatches), as well as serving in the first Gulf War, Bosnia, Kosovo and Sierra Leone. He undertook SAS selection and proved one of the outstanding candidates of his intake, later returning as a squadron leader and earning a Distinguished Service Order in Afghanistan. He was one the army's youngest brigadiers, his soldiers respected him and fellow officers reckoned he was destined to reach the top. Inoculated by his Eton education, Butler spoke and wrote in good English, in an age when army officers had taken to writing in an impenetrable house style laden with jargon and euphemisms (his post-operational report read like a clear, intelligent essay, contrasting with some reports authored later in the war). Despite increasingly exasperated efforts to make sense of the mission, Ed Butler would become the quarry in the traditional Afghan game of *bushakzi** – except that his pursuers would be British government officials urging him to accede to the requests of the governor of Helmand; President Karzai who quickly became critical of the British mission; and the American military leadership in south-west Afghanistan. There were also hints that senior British Army officers whispered against him. General David Richards ticking off Butler for threatening to act in unilateral ways was unfair, and may have contributed to the later view that it was all Butler's fault.[14] In subsequent testimonies, senior figures bent over backwards to defend Butler, perhaps reflecting a sense of guilt over the way he was treated. Shortly after his return from Afghanistan he would resign from the army, citing family reasons. The army would lose one of its best talents, the first high-profile casualty of the war.

*Literally 'goat-dragging'. An equestrian game in which riders compete to gain control of a goat or calf carcass that has been decapitated and dehoofed.

The last protagonist – Lieutenant Colonel Stuart Tootal – was the most junior but in some respects proved the most important British actor in Operation *Herrick 4*. This inversion of rank and responsibility was not accidental. For periods over the summer of 2006, British foreign policy in Afghanistan was effectively being delegated to this mid-ranking officer, with backing from Butler, but without the necessary support from the Kabul Embassy, or from a British government distracted by domestic concerns, and without the full support of PJHQ, which viewed Afghanistan as a sideshow. Tootal had originally joined the Queen's Own Highlanders, a strong family regiment created from an amalgamation of the Cameron and Seaforth Highlanders. Later in his career he volunteered to serve with the Parachute Regiment. It was in the Parachute Regiment that Tootal found his home. When he was appointed commanding officer of the 3rd Battalion, a unit with a reputation as one of the hardest to manage, he was delighted. Tootal was a passionate man: he would without embarrassment describe his paratroopers as 'beloved'. He was also a thoroughly professional and committed officer. He would be pitched into Afghanistan with scant intelligence and minimal resources and be asked, ultimately, to undertake an impossible mission. Like his immediate superior, Ed Butler, with whom he enjoyed a close relationship, he too would resign from the army, angered by the aftercare given to wounded soldiers.

By the middle of 2005, the first two stages of the ISAF mission to Afghanistan had been completed with the deployment of PRTs and modest national contingents, to all but the south-west and eastern provinces of the country. With the deployment of British, Canadian and Dutch contingents to Helmand, Kandahar and Uruzgan respectively, the third stage would be completed. In October 2006, the final and fourth stage would be finalized, and this would allow the separate American Operation *Enduring Freedom* to surrender its regional commands to the wider ISAF operation in Afghanistan, and to focus on counter-terrorism. As terrorism and insurgency had become indistinguishable, by implication, this meant counter-insurgency operations.

John Reid chaired the so-called 'Reid Group'. This ad hoc committee included Nigel Sheinwald, Tony Blair's foreign policy advisor; a junior Foreign Office minister usually delegating for Foreign Secretary Jack Straw; a junior minister delegating for the development secretary, Hilary Benn; the Chief Secretary of the Treasury; senior military and civil service officials; and other advisors. It was later stated that discussion within this group was at an abstract level and did not consider detail – which is to say it was probably no discussion at all.[15] Some individuals later capitalized on having 'the inside track' on the Reid Group by writing articles for the Royal United Services Institute (RUSI).[16] These pieces were notable for what they did not say, rather for than what they did say. The fact was the average Briton reading the essays would not have come away knowing when the decision to enter Helmand was taken or why, who was in the room, who dissented, what follow-up actions were proposed, what questions were raised or what concerns were expressed.[17]

Britons, in fact, would never learn who was behind 'the Helmand decision' and a war that cost the lives of over 450 British servicemen and women, and more than £37 billion in national treasure. Some laudable *mea culpas* aside, the essays mostly served as a dispiriting reminder of cosy relations between individuals and organizations in Whitehall; the manner in which nobody must be seen to be responsible when a colossal blunder is made; and the impressive reach of brooms sweeping under deep carpets. The answers lay somewhere in the triangle of Prime Minister Blair, Defence Secretary Hoon, Foreign Secretary Straw, and their associated advisors and senior officials (including some senior military officers). The military axis fell between the Operations Directorate in MOD Main Building and PJHQ. Some protagonists published memoirs, but they were all apparently absent at the relevant meetings.

The single person who did emerge with (almost unqualified) credit from this period was John Reid. From the outset, the defence secretary was at pains to emphasize the British mission was about reconstruction and the spread of formal governance to areas ISAF had not yet reached: 'Let me stress once more,' he told Parliament, 'We are deploying this potent force to protect and deter. The ISAF mission is unchanged. It is focussed on reconstruction.' With a nod to the Treasury, he indicated that the commitment would be limited both in time and money: 'This will be a three year deployment. It will cost around one billion pounds over a five year period.'[18] Then, in April 2006, he uttered the infamous sentence in Kabul: 'We would be perfectly happy to leave in three years and without firing one shot because our job is to protect the reconstruction.'

These words were later widely quoted to ridicule the defence secretary as the purported reconstruction mission turned into a brawl. The ridicule was misplaced, but there were questions hanging over this toxic choice of words. It appears, from Butler's testimony, the phrase was actually coined by Butler in a meeting that morning, but to make exactly the opposite point – that the task force was almost certainly going to fire shots.[19] Reid borrowed the phrase later that afternoon and turned it on its head.

As far as Reid was concerned, the Helmand mission *was* an extension of stabilization operations the army had been conducting in Mazar-e-Sharif and before that in Kabul. Butler later offered the astonishing revelation that on Reid's visit to Kabul on 23 April, he told Butler that nobody in the MOD had briefed him that Operation *Herrick* was a counter-insurgency mission, and he questioned why the reconstruction mission was being effectively supplanted by a more aggressive mission.[20] This division of opinions – which nobody appeared to address in the build-up to the operation – finally came to a head in this last week of April; a little late, as the paratroopers were already arriving in the province.

The possibility of confrontation was not dismissed. Reid acknowledged that some factions in Helmand might wish to derail the British PRT. But he was alluding to militias, of which there were at least a dozen in Helmand. The 'Taliban' were a secondary consideration, and if found, of course would be confronted. Al-Qaeda was dirty linen that belonged in the basket of the separate Operation *Enduring Freedom*. Nobody demonstrated hindsight when Reid uttered the sentiment. Major General Wall, who was closely engaged in intelligence assessments of the period, later testified that, 'We were ready for an adverse reaction, but to be fair we did not expect it to be as vehement as it turned out to be.'[21] Some claimed wisdom afterwards. Notwithstanding these exculpations, the puzzling aspect of Reid's wish is that it could not possibly have come true. Butler, in this respect, was right.

British soldiers were already firing shots in Helmand. A British special forces contingent was taking part in unhelpful US-led operations that were riling the locals and generally causing trouble. The first British casualty of the year was a Royal Marine, presumably serving in the SBS, wounded in action in mid-March, before the arrival of the task force. This special forces campaign had an indirect and subtle influence on the British task force. Butler had already served two tours in Afghanistan with 22 SAS. These experiences seemed to strongly bias his perception of the mission. In his view, 'we knew that we were going to generate a pretty angry reaction'. Furthermore, 'We knew full well and made very clear to PGHQ [sic] and others in 2005 … that we had underestimated both the enemy, their response and their capabilities and the nature of the terrain.'[22] As soon as he arrived in Afghanistan, in the first week of April, 'I had [discussions] with the embassy, the security services and the ambassador, we were very clear … the Taliban … were going to take the fight to us.'[23] Self-persuaded by this negative scenario – which it appears was shared, if not reinforced by the SIS (MI6) station – Butler then set about trying to persuade Reid that a fight was not only inevitable but necessary.

His belief that there was a 'fight waiting to happen' was strengthened by two suicide car bomb attacks outside the Lashkar Gah PRT on the first two Fridays of April. However, these attacks may have been subjected to a certain amount of over-interpretation. The first was actually against American contractors, almost certainly provoked by unrest over opium eradication programmes. The second, although it did involve a British military vehicle, may not necessarily have been directed against the British. The insurgents, much like ISAF, were not especially good at distinguishing their enemy. It could have been another mistaken attack against 'the Americans'. But in Butler's predisposed mind this was proof of 'cause and effect', which demanded the response of 'going north' after the Taliban, 'to keep us free from attacks'. 'If we just sat in our bases in Lashkar Gah, Gereshk and Bastion,' he later reasoned, 'the Talib would come and attack us there, which they had already done on two occasions [the two suicide attacks].'[24]

When Reid arrived in the third week of April, Butler set about persuading him of this point of view:

> For five days I stayed with him shoulder to shoulder, briefing him on what the issues were, what the challenges were, the lack of intelligence, the lack of a very clear mission, these competing missions. We also started discussing at that stage the whole issue of northern Helmand, delivering what became known as the Sangin effect. We always knew that Sangin was going to be an issue we were going to have to grapple with, even though it was outside the Afghan development zone—the triangle, as people referred to it. He was in no doubt when he left of the seriousness of the situation we had got into and *what we were going to have to do about it* [author's emphasis]. I would challenge those who would say that the Secretary of State at the time was not aware of what *we were likely to have to do in order to fulfil our mission* [author's emphasis].[25]

Butler's own testimony therefore suggests that he had already made up his mind. The reconstruction mission intrinsic in the Helmand Plan, which remarkably 16 Air Assault Brigade had no part in formulating anyway, was going to be ditched, or at least suspended. Butler has not described Reid's reactions to his arguments, and the latter has been silent on the matter. It is unlikely Reid turned a complete deaf ear to Butler's arguments, but by the former's testimony neither does it appear he was fully persuaded. Did he mollify Butler, but privately disagree? When he left office, just two weeks later, he had not authorized, and indeed was questioning, any move north. Five weeks later he reported being surprised by the move north, which seems somewhat disingenuous, as he was aware of Butler's intentions. This period – and what the two protagonists said and did not say – remains one of the key puzzles of Operation *Herrick 4*.

Old Afghan-watchers did point out that Helmand would be a different proposition to the largely peaceful north of Afghanistan, but it was one thing to warn against the general lawlessness of the south-west – a factor that everybody acknowledged – and another to predict that Britain would be embroiled in a war that would cost much blood and treasure. Nobody really knew how many 'Taliban' there were in Helmand. Some thought there might be a few hundred fighters, mostly in the north, skulking in their old heartlands and making money from the opium trade. This was an assessment derived from the American obsession with labelling the tribal leader Rais Baghrani a 'Taliban commander'. The probable truth was that there were very few actual 'Taliban' in Helmand at all – that is, fighters owing direct allegiance to Mullah Omar and seeking a return to the old order. Instead, there were armed groups who over the last 20 years had made a living as Hizb-e Islami and Harakat mujahidin, militiamen owing allegiance to powerful landowners, bent policemen, crooked security men, bandits, narcotics traffickers and highway toll collectors. There is evidence that by 2005, Mullah Omar's Quetta Shura had appointed Taliban shadow governors in Helmand, but it is unclear what power or status they held, or how many fighters they actually commanded.[26]

Aside from these tensions in the British camp, there was the American commander in southern Afghanistan, Major General Benjamin Freakley. In early 2006, he indicated publicly that he would mount one last major offensive against the Taliban in Helmand, Kandahar and Uruzgan before handing over to ISAF and Richards. This referred to what became known as Operation *Mountain Thrust* (May–July 2006). There was the taint of unfortunate American arrogance in this decision. ISAF, under Richards, was meant to have taken over from US forces (Combined Joint Task Force 76) in the spring of 2006, coincident with the arrival of 3 PARA, the lead unit in Task Force Helmand. However, the Americans were somewhat sceptical of ISAF's competence and capabilities. A decision was therefore taken to delay the handover for three months (Richards finally assumed full command on 1 August). During this period CJTF-76 would sort out the Taliban and thus set the conditions for ISAF's successful transition. This implied that all ISAF forces, for that period of three months, would fall under the American general. The likelihood was that British forces would fire shots – plenty of them – because the American general would co-opt the ISAF allies, British, Canadians and Dutch, into his offensive. This is exactly what happened.

Then there was Richards. The British general was involved in the decision-making that led to his assumption of full command being delayed. He interacted with the American general and with Canadians who were similarly affected through this period. Naturally, he was determined to demonstrate that American doubters were wrong. In the national chest thumping world of NATO, the way you did this was by mounting operations. Butler has written how there were rumblings, presumably from the American camp, of a NATO strategic failure. The pressure was on. Reid may have been coming in peace, but the top British general was not. Following Operation *Mountain Thrust*, ISAF under Richards intended to mount its own offensive, Operation *Medusa*. Notwithstanding all the other good ideas that Richards brought with him and his wariness of the American muscular approach, as he put it, he also intended to show his biceps. In his memoir *Taking Command*, Richards displayed self-confidence and devoted several pages to Operation *Medusa* (which, in fact, was something of a fiasco; the Canadian contingent experienced a number of setbacks including a blue-on-blue incident, and the British suffered an air accident involving a Nimrod that left 14 dead). Richards suggested Butler may have been acting in rogue ways, but there is a case that he was being somewhat the rogue, if by rogue one means doing exactly the opposite of what the defence secretary had just stated in public he hoped not to do, namely, fire shots.[27] Indeed, Richards was proud he was something of a maverick.

A division then appears to have grown between the MOD and PJHQ, who had one conception of the mission, and Butler, Richards, the Americans and the Canadians, who had another. The former were seeing a basically benign stabilization operation, and the latter were talking and training for war. Reid seems to have been caught uncomfortably between the two blocs. He was certainly aware of Richards's views, as he was of his military advisors' opinions in the MOD. But Richards did not 'belong' to Reid, or the MOD; he was answering to the NATO chain of command. He was also aware of Butler's assessment of the situation, acutely and tardily in his last two weeks in office.

By late 2005, a British plan was devised over several weeks at Kandahar Air Base, by military and civilian experts, for the deployment to Helmand Province. The so-called Helmand Plan was long on management-speak and meaningless, development buzz-phrases, but this did not necessarily condemn it to failure. At the heart of the plan was 'the comprehensive approach' – a marriage of military security and civilian reconstruction. In John Reid's words: 'We in the British Government have undertaken an unprecedented degree of cross-governmental co-ordination to ensure that this is a fully integrated package addressing governance, security and political and social change.'[28]

Afterwards it would be claimed that no plan survives contact with the enemy, but this was weak justification for the collapse of the Helmand Plan. The central problem with the Helmand Plan was that the military deviated from it almost immediately, and the civilians – despite Reid's best efforts to encourage serious DfID participation – did not show up. There were also many flaws in the detail that deserve to be bared, if only to demonstrate how far 'the plan' was from the reality. As plans do not fall from heaven like manna but are conceived in men's minds, this is another way of saying that many officials' minds languished a fair and reckonable distance from reality.

First and most obviously, the Helmand Plan was devised without consultation and advice from the people it was supposed to be assisting – the Helmandis themselves. It was a scheme largely devised by Westerners who believed they knew what was good for Helmand. To these experts, Pashtun villagers were essentially children awaiting a guiding hand to lead them to a better place. The second and related flaw was that the Westerners based these well-meaning intentions on frankly very limited knowledge. It was remarkable just how little the British actually knew about the province where they were deploying a 3,000-strong task force. In 16 Air Assault Brigade, a single lieutenant colonel had been tasked to 'mug up' on Helmand. At PJHQ, a more comprehensive effort was made under a Brigadier Paul

Newton to understand Helmand. Everybody was aware of the intelligence failures in Iraq, and avoiding a repeat of these shortcomings was 'absolutely on the tip of our tongues throughout this whole period'.[29] These efforts, however, proved inadequate. It would take several years before the claim could be made that the British understood Helmand. General Richards would later argue, when quizzed over intelligence failures, 'there was just no way we could do it' because no ISAF troops had actually visited large areas of Helmand.[30]

This was not fully accurate, as the Americans had been in the province for five years. British knowledge of Helmand was poor, because for unexplained reasons – and this is the other great puzzle of Operation *Herrick 4* – the British did not engage with the Americans. A possible explanation for this failure was simply a lack of intelligence personnel in Whitehall. Over this period the government was determined to sell off Churchill's wartime office and the historic Old War Office Building (eventually to a Spanish hotel consortium) and to squeeze the downsized Defence Intelligence Staff (DIS) into just half a floor of the adjoining Ministry of Defence building. DIS had never been so small in its history. In a way this suited the Blair administrations, because 'the intelligence' had become what a small circle of individuals around the prime minister decided it should be. DIS was providing electronic wallpaper to a Cabinet Office across the road which had already taken its decisions heedless of intelligence. The capstone foolish decision had been the invasion of Iraq. The fiasco in Iraq was now sucking any available manpower. The Afghanistan desk was minimally manned (this was also true, incidentally, of PJHQ). And what intelligence was passed by the Americans – the tapestry of militias the Americans had been working with, for example – was ignored anyway.

Secondly, the plan was predicated on imaginary resources and capabilities. In the last years of the Blair premiership, foreign policy increasingly seemed to be based on phantom divisions and paper organizations. Britain had volunteered to lead on counter-narcotics – the principal reason, it seems, why the British deployed to Helmand in the first place – but Britain had no experience in leading counter-narcotics campaigns. There was not even an equivalent of the American Drug Enforcement Agency (DEA), the one organization that could claim real and global experience in counter-narcotics. Remarkably, the Afghanistan counter-narcotics programme was placed in the hands of the FCO and SIS – two organizations with no expertise whatsoever in this field.[31] The notion that Britain could effectively lead a counter-narcotics campaign in Afghanistan was pie-in-the-sky. Over eight years, it appears no individuals in the government departments involved in this charade had the moral courage to tell their political masters so.

Most critically, Britain had no organization capable of supporting reconstruction in a hostile environment, or in plain English, a war. Much would be written about the rights and wrongs of reconstruction, and there was certainly mutual ignorance on the part of the military and civil agencies, but these differences and arguments obscured the central fact that DfID gained its charter in end-of-century Blairite froth to promote lofty and idealistic millennium goals. The organization was not set up to deal with the practicalities of achieving real goals at the sharp end of war zones. DfID basically disbursed billions of pounds of British taxpayers' money, largely by transferring it to opaque funds run by multilaterals such as the World Bank. In a triumph of hope over experience, it then made claims over how this transfer of British taxes was making the world 'better' through the meeting of often dubious and in some respects deceitful targets related to millennium goals. DfID did not 'do reconstruction'. To operate effectively, or indeed at all, it needed Non-Governmental Organizations (NGOs) and other development experts. In normal circumstances, these were more than happy to siphon fat consultancy fees from DfID. But in 2006 the 'experts' were in very short supply in Helmand. As soon as the fighting flared up, they quit the province altogether, along with the nervous DfID staff.

Despite protests to the contrary when later criticized, DfID had always been reluctant to deploy to Helmand. Tootal recalled that the number of civilians deployed to Lashkar Gah could be counted on one hand – they then quit altogether when the shooting started.[32] The organization had to be pushed and prodded into supporting the military mission, eventually through the creation of an entirely new organization called the Civil Stabilization Unit, when failure could no longer be concealed. From the beginning there was a total mismatch between the vision of a prime minister who staked Britain's reputation in Helmand and one of the key government departments (which he created) that was meant to translate that vision into effective policy. At the outset of the Afghan mission, Major General McColl had been given the meaninglessly small sum of £2 million to support reconstruction.[33] When the British task force deployed to Helmand, only about 5 per cent of British aid to Afghanistan was directed to the province by DfID. By ISAF's own graphs, Helmand Province, the most troubled in Afghanistan, was receiving the second smallest amount of aid money in the entire country.

The claim that 'DFID works closely with other UK Government departments including the MOD' was an empty one.[34] DfID staff wanted to remain in the relatively congenial world of the Kabul diplomatic circuit, providing funds to support 'development goals'. The very first page of the organization's slick, glossy brochure made this plain. DfID also sought to build up Afghan central government 'capacity' – a laudable and important goal if the Karzai government was ever to stand on its own feet – notwithstanding that rampant corruption was almost certainly draining millions of pounds of British aid money. Living in portakabins in Lashkar Gah, supporting the British Army, was not at the top of DfID's agenda in the summer of 2006.

There was an argument then that the central plank of Britain's involvement in Helmand was rotten before the mission even started. What cannot be hidden is that the British knew this, or should have known this. DfID's record in Iraq was already causing serious disquiet. DfID staff did not co-locate with the army HQ, increasing friction and complicating cooperation. When the situation in Basra deteriorated in 2005–06, the army launched Operation *Sinbad* to re-establish security in the city. DfID refused to support this operation (American Commander's Emergency Response Program, or CERP, funds were used to support reconstruction). Instead, citing a dangerous working environment, DfID moved base to more agreeable hotels in Kuwait. It seemed to accord with the national zeitgeist that a government department was prepared to undermine British foreign policy on health and safety grounds. The British so-called 'comprehensive approach' was an unfolding disaster in Iraq, but either Whitehall was simply brushing this under a very thick carpet, or the true state of affairs in southern Iraq was not being honestly communicated to ministers. The same pattern would be repeated in Helmand. Nothing, it seems, was being learned.

Fourth, the plan was apparently based on an inappropriate and hubristic appeal to the Malayan Emergency, the so-called 'ink spot strategy'. Linked to this was the other article of faith of counter-insurgent theorists, 'winning hearts and minds'. Foreign Minister Kim Howells's observation on the matter was difficult to improve: 'I remember a very distinguished and clever general explaining to me on a big sheet of paper how they would have an ink blot approach to Helmand province. They would have an ink blot here and an ink blot there and they would gradually join them up and then control the whole area. It was completely bonkers.'[35]

It *was* bonkers, for two reasons. First, because the British did not do 'ink spots' in Malaya; they did old-fashioned population control. And second, 'ink spots' were not a British idea anyway. The term *tache de l'huile* was coined by the French high Catholic Marshal Hubert Lyautey. Lyautey viewed himself as the Louis XIV of the colonies and was determined to spread conservative, Catholic French values in expanding 'oil spots' – or counter-insurgency as evangelism. In Helmand, as MP Adam Holloway later quipped, there was more a 'violently flicked ink splatter'.[36]

The British were proud of their counter-insurgency campaign in Malaya and it was frequently contrasted with America's poor experience in Vietnam, but this false nostalgia for British know-how in counter-insurgency wars contained a trap. The differences between Malaya and Helmand were so manifest, anyway, that it is difficult to understand what the promoters of the 'ink spot strategy' were seeing.

'Hearts and minds' in Malaya was a political slogan, not a military strategy – it was an appeal to Malays to reconcile. Indeed, General Sir Gerald Templer viewed the phrase, which he used in a newspaper interview, as 'nauseating'. The ill-tempered general was quite clear the military strategy was to kill CTs (Communist Terrorists), not win friends. This instruction was expressed with characteristic bluntness on the first page of the army's counter-terrorist manual.[37] 'The job of the British Army out here,' he wrote, 'is to kill or capture Communist terrorists.' Over the years the mythologized phrase became the foundation stone of counter-insurgency theories despite overwhelming evidence that the chances of soldiers winning 'hearts and minds' were pretty slim even in the best of circumstances. One only had to point to Northern Ireland, where the British Army spent 30 years hated by Catholic enclaves in Londonderry and Belfast, no matter what it did or how it behaved. In Malaya, the British themselves conceded that trying to win Chinese 'hearts and minds' was a pointless endeavour and gave up.

There was another profound flaw with 'the plan'. Whose plan, exactly, was the brigade supposed to be following? At any one stage there were as many as six plans, according to Butler.[38] ISAF promulgated an Afghan-wide strategic plan. At PJHQ, a second strategic plan was drafted – the plan, in fact, which 16 Air Assault Brigade was supposed to be adhering to – the British plan for the Stage 3 expansion of the ISAF mission (known as the 'Prelim Ops Plan'). This was the plan that Reid understood and endorsed. But the brigade was subordinated to a southern Afghan regional command with its own general and staff, and this headquarters also promulgated an operational plan, which it expected the British task force to follow. And lastly, there was the campaign plan drafted by the headquarters staff of the brigade itself. This plan, ultimately, was the plan which the brigade seemed to cling to, mainly, it seems, because it was understood by its authors. One civilian observer could not fail to notice that some of the brigade staff had clearly not even bothered to read the wider Helmand Plan.[39]

This competition of plans – mixing strategic, operational and tactical concepts in dubious ways – was ultimately disastrous for the British. They all ended up in a trash can anyway. What was intended as an ISAF mission was almost immediately entangled with the quite separate American-led Operation *Enduring Freedom*. The separate, overlapping plans were trumped by Major General Benjamin Freakley, the US commander in south-west Afghanistan, with his own plan for the British task force.

Lieutenant Colonel Tootal's chain of command within this set-up was extremely confused. Because a Canadian brigadier, David Fraser, already commanded ISAF troops in south-west Afghanistan, it was deemed inappropriate that Ed Butler should exercise direct command, which is why the unlucky Butler initially ended up in Kabul. But because it was also judged inappropriate that Brigadier Fraser should be giving commands directly to the British commanding officer in Helmand, a deputy, Colonel Charlie Knaggs, was posted to the Lashkar Gah PRT. In practice this meant that Fraser had to pass his orders through Knaggs, who would then transmit them to Tootal, who would then have the right to confer with Butler, if there were doubts over the task given to the British. Butler in turn had to juggle the conflicting demands of his own superiors; Freakley, the American general; an anxious British ambassador and FCO; and a PJHQ with limited understanding of the situation in Helmand.

This shambolic command structure was not the only problem Lieutenant Colonel Tootal would face. He also had to contend with special forces units operating in an uncoordinated fashion in his backyard. This failure to coordinate special forces operations with the operations of the wider army was not accidental but rather an accident waiting to happen. In the modern period, 22 SAS had developed the attitude that it was really quite separate from the rest of the 'green army' and only answered to its own chain of command. In the case of US special forces units, the problem was even worse. Lieutenant Colonel Tootal had no idea what units were working in Helmand and nor was he informed of impending operations. Even before the British arrived, a poll revealed that 70 per cent of Helmandis judged that ISAF troops were conducting 'improper actions' and 38 per cent did not want Western troops in the province.[40] This was the legacy of American special forces operations that Lieutenant Colonel Tootal was about to inherit. In Helmand, a British special forces mission known as Operation *Malaya* was already underway, but, as adumbrated, was completely uncoordinated with the main mission.[41]

At the beginning of May, Lieutenant General Richards would be taking over the command of ISAF IX.* This intelligent and urbane officer, who would rise to become the Chief of the Defence Staff, had clear ideas on the purpose of the mission, but he too would find himself thwarted by events and timings. Crucially, ISAF would not take over southern Afghanistan from American forces until 31 July. Over the first three months of the deployment, the British mission, effectively under operational command of the American Ben Freakley, would unravel.

It was unquestionable Richards displayed a certain self-regard. Nonetheless, here was a general with some sound ideas and convictions, which to date had been short in ISAF. Richards's vision was enlightened but it was never championed or resourced. Five priorities were proposed to restore stability to Afghanistan: reconstruction, development, governance, relations with Pakistan and lastly security, or fighting. In Richards's view, ISAF's mission was to deepen Afghan governance, allowing reconstruction to take place and, importantly, allowing the Afghan security forces to take the lead. To achieve this aim he promoted the concept of an integrated Policy Action Group, or PAG, and championed the creation of ADZs, or Afghan Development Zones, ill-advisedly using Helmand as an example. Securing the population, the central plank of the later McChrystal doctrine, was also General Richards's key idea: 'My Guiding Intent is for all those in Afghanistan who are opposed to the use of violence for political ends

*The ninth rotation of the ISAF mission.

to actively unite their efforts in order to secure the Afghan population as a whole from hardcore Taliban and other insurgents. We must give the former the incentive, the means, the resolve and the courage to stand up to the latter.'[42]

In offering this vision, Richards was acutely aware that time was not on ISAF's side. Too many expectations had been raised that had not been fulfilled. The insurgency had grown stronger because of Western neglect, not because the Afghan people welcomed a resurgent Taliban. Richards was also keen to work with and not against the grain of Afghan culture. 'We should seek to re-invigorate valued and trusted traditional forms of influence and authority,' he argued. 'Let local people decide on specific priorities and feel a sense of project ownership … we must listen much more closely to … the people and be less inclined to apply western precepts to a socio-economy that has its own dynamic and requirements.'[43] Unsurprisingly for a man conscious of the importance of this subtle approach, he found that pan-government strategic integration was 'woeful' (echoing John Reid's private fears over DfID) and resolved that the shortcomings should be addressed as a matter of urgency.[44]

Richards also recognized the importance of Pakistan long before the term 'Af-Pak' was coined. He met with President Musharraf (the two generals seemed to have liked each other), and he championed regular meetings with Pakistani counterparts through a series of working groups and committees. He promoted the creation of the Joint Intelligence Operations Centre in Kabul, which included six Pakistani intelligence officers working alongside ISAF and Afghan counterparts. All this was highly free-thinking at a time when ISAF and in particular Operation *Enduring Freedom* was effectively ignoring the importance of the southern neighbour.

Significantly, Richards foresaw a *mobile* role for ISAF, not a ground-holding role. In a valedictory presentation as ISAF IX Commander entitled *Theatre Command*, Richards included a slide subtitled 'Restoring People's Confidence', which showed governance, development and security bubbles all within a larger Afghan National Security Forces (ANSF) bubble. *Outside* this bubble were smaller 'ISAF/ANA (Afghan National Army) Manoeuvre' bubbles protecting the inner Afghan-led core. Whether or not this was a realistic vision, it was a world away from the course of action Task Force Helmand would follow. General Richards was the closest the British came to producing a modern Gerald Templer. In the modern army, with its six-monthly rotating posts, he never got his chance.

Ironically, some in the Pentagon envisaged exactly this role for Richards. Following a visit by Defense Secretary Donald Rumsfeld, the idea was mooted that the newly appointed Commander ISAF might serve an 18-month tour. The British general interpreted this as an endorsement of his sound leadership. It was, and Rumsfeld had been impressed, but for different reasons. For American policymakers the Taliban had been 'defeated'. The trick now was to persuade a British government to act as America's cleaning lady in Afghanistan. In Richards, Rumsfeld saw a suitable candidate to don the apron and rubber gloves. This position would be abruptly reversed within a few months, with the controversial 'Musa Qaleh deal' that would raise perennial fears over a perceived British lack of fight.

Lieutenant Colonel Tootal also had a clear idea of the mission. In a staged media interview, he explained the forthcoming British deployment in terms of force protection for reconstruction teams that would rebuild roads, schools and hospitals, as well as providing security to the Afghan National Army that would tackle the narco-trade.[45] 3 PARA, of course, would achieve none of these aims.

This was the public face of the mission. In private, Tootal held a quite different view. In December 2005, he had undertaken a reconnaissance to Zabul, rather than Helmand, where he was hosted by an American unit. The reason for this odd choice of location remains obscure. The visit seemed to make a strong impression on him. Tootal came away with a sense that Western forces were engaged in an outright war with the Taliban, not a Peace Support Operation (PSO), the official description of the forthcoming British mission. In his memoirs, Tootal would not mention this trip. This recce influenced the training undertaken by 3 PARA in Oman, which focused on fighting as much as winning 'hearts and minds', and led to a list of demands for additional equipment. A photograph published to accompany the news article showed a Private Bennis squatting on a bergen reading a book entitled *Hunting Al Qaeda*. At least this paratrooper seemed to share his commanding officer's private view of the purpose of Operation *Herrick 4*.

The 3 PARA battlegroup that deployed to Helmand was much larger than a normal peacetime battalion, but it would nonetheless be swallowed like a desert caravan in Helmand's never-ending space. It was perhaps symptomatic of a peacetime army that just three members of the battalion, all Falklands veterans, had experience of real war.[46] The total British deployment numbered about 3,150 troops.[47] One third (1,180) fell under the 3 PARA battlegroup. This compensated, at least at the beginning, for the fact that 3 PARA's establishment strength of 645 men had been financially capped at 552, a commitment it was unable to meet anyway. The battalion actually deployed 50 paratroopers short of this capped figure. When another 100-odd paratroopers were deleted from the order of battle, because of Rest and Recuperation (R&R) or other reasons, Tootal really only had around 400 infantry to meet all the commitments thrown at him in Helmand (in an area of roughly 60,000 square kilometres, or the equivalent of three Wales). It was a hopelessly inadequate number, even if the operation had unfolded relatively peacefully.

There was a certain irony to this, as critics later made two simultaneous and contradictory charges: first, that the army had deliberately argued for a strong force, to get into a fight; and second, that the MOD had hopelessly underestimated the task and sent a weak force. Neither allegation was true.

The parachute battalion proper consisted of three 'line companies'; an ISTAR company (a pompous military acronym for a reconnaissance company); and a support company, which included heavy weapons such as mortars. As the battalion was undermanned, it was at first reinforced by a platoon of Royal Irish and a second platoon of Territorial Army paratroopers. By the end of the tour the battlegroup would almost double in number with attached infantry companies from other regiments, a policy of 'augmentation' that disguised the overstretch the army was suffering. These included further companies from the 1 Royal Irish Regiment, 2 Royal Regiment of Fusiliers, 2 Royal Gurkha Rifles and an Estonian mechanized infantry platoon.

The battlegroup's armoured reconnaissance was provided by D Squadron of the Household Cavalry Regiment (HCR), veterans of the invasion of Iraq in 2003. Unfortunately, the troopers and their precious Scimitar reconnaissance vehicles would not arrive in Helmand until July. Even following their deployment, in Brigadier Butler's judgement, the task force was suffering a 45 per cent shortfall in vehicles, of all types.[48] Artillery support was provided by 105mm light guns manned by I Battery of 7 Royal Horse Artillery. 18 Troop, an unmanned aerial vehicle (UAV) troop, completed the complement of gunners. Unable to fly the nearly useless existing British UAV in the army's inventory (Phoenix), the gunners resorted to flying the American Desert Hawk mini-UAV, a hand-thrown drone with limited range and endurance. Signals support was provided by 216 Parachute Signal Squadron, specially reinforced by invaluable LEWTs, or Light Electronic Warfare Teams. Engineers were sourced from 23 Regiment Royal Engineers, which deployed one of its combat field squadrons (51 Squadron).

On paper this appeared to be a well-balanced formation, but there were serious deficiencies that would become glaring gaps as the operation unfolded. Most notably, there were insufficient helicopters to support the force. 18 and 27 Squadrons RAF were deploying six CH-47 Chinooks. In practice, this meant that on a routine basis perhaps half this number was actually available because of financial caps on flying hours, maintenance schedules and the need to provide a Chinook to support casualty evacuation. At most, the RAF could surge four aircraft, or enough to lift one company and its equipment. 656 Squadron from 9 Regiment Army Air Corps completed the Joint Helicopter Force, with the first operational deployment of eight WAH-64D Apaches. These magnificent machines would play a key role in the Helmand campaign, but they also represented an asset that had to be husbanded carefully because of financial caps on flying hours. Butler's warnings over the unrealistic and miserly restrictions on flying hours came to pass within one month of arriving in Helmand: 'By May … We were some 20% over our hours for support helicopter [sic] – Chinooks – we had six of them. We were already 11% over on our attack helicopter hours.'[49]

In fact, this was inevitable. The operational budget for the Apache had been capped at a totally inadequate £2 million. By the following summer it leapt to £34 million (the Chinook operational budget similarly jumped from £18 million to £77 million).[50] These numbers inescapably showed that the handful of helicopters sent to Helmand in 2006 had been sent 'on the cheap' and did not enjoy the necessary budgeted flying hours to properly support the mission. The responsibility for this lay squarely on the Treasury.

The first company – A Company – arrived at the newly built Camp Bastion, 20 kilometres west of the provincial capital Lashkar Gah, on 15 April. The brigade officially assumed command of its new AO (area of operations) on 1 May 2006. With only one undermanned battalion of paratroopers, Lieutenant Colonel Tootal's options were, to say the least, limited. Camp Bastion was the only sizeable camp with a logistic infrastructure in place that could support the extended, anticipated operations. The camp also benefited from albeit rudimentary communications that would prove vital.

With members of the task force HQ decamped in the provincial capital of Lashkar Gah, Tootal really had no option but to establish his battalion HQ in the logistics base, but this was not ideal. It would mean that he would be isolated from his line companies, 50 kilometres to the east and north, located in forward operating bases or FOBs. Such was the difficulty of the terrain and the lack of a road infrastructure these distances typically took two or more days to cover. Breakdowns were frequent and convoys got lost. The British only had a sketchy knowledge of the ground: the state of fords, or the trafficability of wadis, which would have to be discovered by trial and error. The companies would be very isolated indeed.

American and Canadian engineers expanding the ISAF mission from Kandahar had already built two forward operating bases in Helmand, FOB Price immediately west of Gereshk (built in the summer of 2002), and FOB Robinson. A third FOB – Juno – was being used by special forces units, although the British special forces contingent initially parked itself in FOB Price. Keen to make an impression, A Company was deployed to FOB Price within two weeks of arriving in Helmand and conducted its first familiarization patrol in the town on 29 April, coincidentally the anniversary of the fall of the Taliban. The main recollection of this first British patrol in Helmand Province was the debilitating heat.[51] The town itself appeared peaceful if wary of the newcomers.

The other ISAF base, FOB Robinson, built 5 kilometres to the south of Sangin, was a more austere location. FOB Robinson had been originally intended as a base for the ANA, but after a violent confrontation between local tribesmen and the corrupt police, a Canadian infantry company had been despatched to stiffen the base. The Canadians were still holding the line when the British arrived. On 26 April, just one day after the task force activation party arrived at Lashkar Gah, Butler held an impromptu *shura* (meeting) in Sangin such was the level of hostility this base attracted from the townspeople.

Having started to lay out his forces, like counters in a game of Risk, what exactly was Lieutenant Colonel Tootal supposed to do next? The vagueness of his all-embracing mission – the 'what' of the mission – hid profound flaws in the 'why' and 'how' of the mission. His task was to support central government authority (which only existed in the imagination of Kabul-based civilians); and to collaborate in PRT-led reconstruction with local Afghan governmental departments (the PRT was non-functioning, and effective local governance in Helmand was also non-existent). 3 PARA was also supposed to take over the training of 1/205 Brigade from the Americans, in reality a paper battalion of demoralized ANA soldiers. In keeping with his judgement that 3 PARA had to be ready for anything, Tootal deployed the single A Company at Gereshk, and held back the remainder of his battalion as an Operations Company Group, supported by a number of platoon-sized Quick Reaction Forces (QRFs). These eventually formed the Immediate Reaction Teams (IRTs), a Helmand Reaction Force, and a Regional QRF. At the time, this seemed the wisest option.

The Americans had already built a camp for the ANA – Camp Tombstone, at a cost of $68 million. The funereal association in the name was hard to miss, and it was no surprise the Americans were desperate to get away. By the time the British arrived late to take over the task, parts of the camp had already been stripped and sold off by the ANA.[52] The unit was meant to be 1,000 strong, but a third had deserted. The overwhelming majority were illiterate. Many were ill. Many were short-sighted but could not afford to buy spectacles. Few could tell the time. Few cared to train still less fight. They had no kit to speak of and were quick to sell off attractive items in Lashkar Gah.[53] Like their brethren in the police (the ANP), they set up checkpoints to extort money from the locals. 3 PARA would never engage in the ANA training mission – a failure that was never explained by any of the *Herrick 4* protagonists – and the British only seriously threw themselves into training the Afghan security forces when it became obvious that this was the only viable exit strategy out of the mess of Helmand. Faced with this unsatisfactory panorama, the paratroopers fell back on the old staples of establishing 'presence' in the heart of some distrustful communities that had never seen a British soldier, still less understood why they were there, patrolling and attempting to win 'hearts and minds'.

This vacuum in direction and purpose could not last long. Two personalities then entered the story that would derail the British mission and uncork the bottle of insurrection. The first was Major General Benjamin Freakley, the commander of Combined Joint Task Force 76 (the umbrella designation for all units engaged in operations in southern Afghanistan), who simultaneously commanded 10th Mountain Division. General Richards would be taking over CJTF-76 with the establishment of the ISAF Regional Command South HQ (considered an honour, as this would place a British general in command of American servicemen, the first time this had happened since World War II). But crucially, 3 PARA would remain within the command chain of CJTF-76 until 1 August.

This was Freakley's swansong before handing over to the British, a matter which seemed to ill-suit his temperament. The American general was a red-blooded Virginian, a scion from heartlands that have produced so many of America's top brass. Freakley was an alumnus of the strict Virginia Military Institute (VMI), a military college that has produced more generals than any other in the United States. VMI would have been proud of their graduate: Freakley proved a motivated individual and this drive had served him well. He had led combat units at every level of command and he had taken part in both Iraq wars. This was his third war. Commissioned as an infantry officer, he sported parachute wings, air assault wings and a Ranger Tab. He had dozens of meritorious and distinguished service medals. Freakley could not be criticized for failing to do his duty.

But what Freakley offered in raw military efficiency he seemed to lack in cultural openness. Freakley was a patriot with an apparent blind spot for anything beyond the shores of continental North America. When interviewed by a reporter shortly after the arrival of the British task force, he declared: 'I love our country. I think anybody that's ever been a day or two out of America in any other country [has more] respect for what America stands for.'[54] One of the most emotional moments in his life, he confessed, was seeing a sea of American flags in Iraq.

Freakley's myopic optimism made him an unreliable interpreter of the true evolving situation in Afghanistan. At a Department of Defense teleconference on 16 March – on the eve of the British arrival – the general assured his interlocutors in Washington that there had been 'significant accomplishments' and that 'this nation of Afghanistan clearly is moving forward every day'.[55] In this particular respect, Freakley was playing a similar role to that of the hapless General Paul Harkins in the Vietnam War. Harkins had self-confessedly been the guy with the goodies: just tell Washington what it wants to hear. Freakley, unfortunately, due to his optimism too easily slipped into this frame of positive reporting.

With five years' experience in Afghanistan, his understanding of the enemy was certainly accurate – ISAF was facing a mix of criminals, Taliban, some foreign fighters, remnants of al-Qaeda and ex-warlords running lawless militias. But his assessment of the future was fatally complacent: 'I will tell you my sensing right now is the Afghan National Army and the coalition forces have the initiative. We're taking the fight to the enemy.'[56] When asked directly whether he thought the Taliban was getting stronger, he replied without equivocation 'no'. Nor did he ask for reinforcements.

Pressed whether more troops were required, the general boasted to his audience of the capabilities of the newly deployed 'modular force' – a fancy concept the US Army was selling to the Pentagon at the time – adding, 'I think we have the force that we need to defeat this threat' – a sharp contrast to Butler, who straight away realized that ISAF was chronically undermanned for the task.

The general appeared to have difficult relations with the British contingent, despite public protestations that he looked forward to working with the British and that the coalition would work well. The reality was that Freakley, as overall commander of ground forces in south-west Afghanistan, would nominally command Brigadier Ed Butler. As a young officer, Freakley had attended a British Army infantry course. Whether or not the experience had left him with a jaundiced view of British Army officers, he appeared to quickly develop an antipathy for the Etonian Ed Butler. Later he would confess that he had felt like punching Butler on one occasion. Freakley gave the impression that this was his turf and that he alone understood the game. Furthermore, in his view, the late-arriving and casual British were simply not trying hard enough.

The second character who would walk onto the stage and trip the British was the very person anointed by the British themselves to govern Helmand Province – 'Engineer Daoud'. The first British incursion into Afghanistan in the mid-19th century had been driven by a desire to replace Afghanistan's ruler with a more compliant, British-approved ruler, a tale told brilliantly in William Dalrymple's *The Return of a King*. In 2005, the British repeated the same folly. The previous governor, Sher Mohammed Akhundzada, an amiable, bushy-bearded Helmandi, had been deemed unacceptable by the FCO on the grounds that he was corrupt, enjoyed connections with the Taliban and was heavily involved in the opium poppy trade. That this might be the normal state of affairs in Helmand seemed to have escaped the judgement of British officials pressing for his dismissal. That it was precisely these factors that made him useful was also passed by. In a widely reported story, 9 tonnes of opium were found in the governor's offices. Akhundzada claimed this opium had been impounded from dealers. It appears he was telling the truth; the opium had in fact been seized from his close rival Mir Wali.[57] Similar stashes had been confiscated in the past.

However, what followed beggared belief. Seizing their chance, some individuals in the British Embassy colluded in a plot to discredit the governor by ordering a raid – effectively setting him up – after being informed of the existence of the stash via the American PRT in Lashkar Gah and US Embassy in Kabul.[58] This was playing the 'Great Game' in the most idiotic fashion. It is still unclear who played the parts of Lord Auckland, Macnaghten or Burnes in the modern version of the play. According to Jack Fairweather, the British ambassador Rosalind Marsden was the motor behind his deposition.[59] Ed Butler has written that SIS was responsible.[60] Probably both were, because both departments had their hands in the counter-narcotics pot of money and needed to demonstrate success. Whoever was behind the asinine plot, it was the *fons et origo* of all subsequent ills in Helmand and the price was paid with the lives of British soldiers and marines. Before a single shot was fired, the task force stood little or no chance of succeeding in Helmand, thanks to two government departments that were never summoned to answer for their foolishness.

'SMA', as Sher Mohammed Akhundzada was known, could have been the perfect interlocutor, offering the British a back door entrance into the corridors of power in Helmand. He held no grudge against the British and welcomed the new arrivals. He had co-existed peacefully with the presence of American and Canadian soldiers in his province (the Americans were well aware of his drug dealing, but pragmatically chose to ignore his criminal activities because of his close relation with President Karzai). The Americans also worked with and not against the many militias, although not always sensibly. Helmand elders respected him as nephew of the legendary Mullah Mohammed Nasim Akhundzada, the commander of Harakat-e-Inqilab-e-Islami, who led the mujahidin resistance in northern Helmand. He could have been the friendly rascal who introduced the British to all the other villains. Instead, he was turned into an enemy, and with his dismissal an opportunity was lost. General Richards would later politely hint that he viewed the sacking of SMA as a mistake.[61] President Karzai would also rue in public Akhundzada's dismissal at the promptings of ignorant British officials.

His dismissal had a certain comedic quality. The Akhundzadas could no more be marginalized in Helmand than MacDonalds in Scotland. He re-appeared in the Upper Chamber of the Afghan Parliament, and his brother, Amir Mohammed, took over as deputy in Helmand. The British were made to look ridiculous. To add insult to injury, Sher Mohammed Akhundzada had maintained a private militia, a normal practice for a powerful local leader. One British newspaper later suggested that as many as 3,000 fighters answered to the governor.[62] With the loss of the governorship, it appears that a proportion of Akhundzada's militia decided to switch allegiances and fight for the 'Taliban'. Sher Mohammed Akhundzada naturally maintained relations with his former commanders, now freelance 'Taliban', thus ensuring that he kept a foot in both camps.[63] The British could have had several hundred gun-toting Afghans on their side, eager to have a crack at anti-government gangs, for a fee. Instead, they were turned into enemies. The British-appointed Engineer Daoud had no fighters. It was hardly surprising that Helmand's elders turned their backs at this toothless, British-appointed governor.

Mohammed Daoud fitted a naïve FCO view of a suitable governor for Helmand Province. Akhundzada was a turban-wearing, illiterate provincial who had never travelled. Daoud by contrast was a suit-and-tie-wearing Westernized Afghan with impressive qualifications and a career in international organizations. In exile in Quetta, he had been President Karzai's neighbour (which gave the appointment a whiff of nepotism). The flaw was not in the choice of these two contrasting candidates but in the character of the British diplomatic service. The political officer of the British Empire, an individual who spent years immersed in the culture of his adopted country, who learnt the language (probably picking up a local mistress along the way), and who felt entirely comfortable supping with the devil, had vanished. As Rory Stewart, a former diplomat himself, pointed out in *Can Interventions Work?* – a highly intelligent critique of Western interventions co-authored with the American Gerald Knaus – as late as 2009 the FCO was arguing there was no need for its staff to even learn Pashto. The army in the meantime was valiantly teaching basic Pashto to its 20-year-old soldiers.

The imperial political officer would not have set at the top of his to-do list 'do good', or 'spread Western values'. His modern successor was a six weeks on, two weeks off, tick-box bureaucrat with poor understanding of the local culture (the notion that an official deserved two weeks' leave after just a few weeks in-country would have quite astounded the 'politicals' who were used to spending years in isolated posts).[64] Service to your country had long been replaced by self-service and an obsession with allowances, expenses and entitlements. The gap between the modern FCO official and the culture he or she was meant to be interacting with was huge: the award-winning *Times* reporter Christina Lamb recalled watching an FCO and DfID team showing bemused elders in Gereshk a BBC David

Attenborough nature programme, for what purpose can only be guessed.[65] Daoud would have been viewed with suspicion as a 'white Afghan' by a 19th-century-India hand (characters like Sir Robert Warburton, who served for many years as assistant commissioner in Peshawar, and who was the son of an Anglo-Irish father and Afghan mother). The old India hand would have sniffed about for the real powerbroker, drunk tea with him and not hesitated to hug his interlocutor, however unpleasant kissing the cheeks of a foul-breathed, bearded bigot. The modern British diplomat, by contrast, could only be comfortable with his Afghan mirror image, educated, Westernized and English speaking. Out went the country bumpkin and in came the technocrat.

Daoud was appointed as the new governor, at the request of the British government, on the grounds that he was honest. This may have been true, but honesty was an exceedingly volatile currency in Afghan politics. President Karzai's own family was rumoured to be implicated in the narcotics industry. Afghan members of Parliament included an unsavoury mix of warlords, criminals, drug barons and a known paedophile. Kim Howells memorably quipped in an answer to a parliamentary question on corruption in Afghanistan: 'This is not Surrey; it is Afghanistan, and it is a pretty rough neighbourhood. To say that we can do nothing there until we have proved that every single provincial governor is as pure as the driven snow is to be on the road to nowhere.'[66]

Daoud was not a bad man – indeed he was a competent administrator – he was just the wrong person. In May 2006 he was also an uncertain and nervous individual. His appointment was the first big blunder committed by the British in Helmand Province.

The dismissal of Akhundzada was badly received. In Daoud's first *shura* held in the provincial capital of Lashkar Gah he got a rough reception. What better way, then, to make an impression than to flash heavily armed foreign soldiers in the faces of the local elders who had snubbed him? The opportunity to use the British in this way would come soon and it showed up Daoud at his flighty worst. Daoud would always contest that he pushed the British into acting in precipitate ways, but in Butler's recollection it was precisely the newly appointed governor who most strongly peddled the spectre of a Taliban army over-running Helmand:

> If the black flag of Mullah Omar flies over any of the district centres, you may as well go home because we'll have lost our authority to govern

> in Helmand, and if we lose our authority to govern and our ability to govern, then that will threaten the south. Kandahar will be next. We'll lose the south before you've even started. What are you going to do about it?[67]

Daoud's nervousness was transmitted to the FCO, who had 'equities' in the new man, and this in turn was pushed back onto the newly arrived task force who were urged to act.[68] It was during this build-up phase, as 3 PARA were arriving in Helmand, that reports of increased violence began to raise tensions. With the arrival of spring, the hibernating Taliban appeared to be returning to the fray – or were they?

The town of Baghran in the far north was reportedly in Taliban hands. This proved to be an exaggeration; there was no meaningful governance in the north at all, and there never would be. ISAF would just give up on northern Helmand. The tribes were managing their own affairs – and feuds – as they had always done. What they did not want was corrupt rule, and labelling opposition to corrupt rule as 'Taliban' was crass. In Baghran the squabble was, as ever, between Rais Baghrani, the leader of the Khalozai clan, and the Akhundzadas who dominated the Hassanzai branch.

At the beginning of 2006, the American special forces contingent in Helmand, Task Force Bayonet, had handed over to Task Force Aegis, and levels of violence noticeably rose. Gereshk, where FOB Price had been built, experienced its first suicide attack in January. In February, Sangin witnessed a gun battle between locals and the police which left seven policemen dead. There were five further shoot-outs in and around the town that month. The newly built FOB Robinson, just south of the town, in particular became a source of local resentment. On 16 March, even as the first elements of the British task force were arriving at Camp Bastion, the first British soldier wounded in action was recorded – an assumed SBS marine evacuated from FOB Price. Two weeks later a great mêlée broke out in Kajaki Olya between the police and a reported 100–200 villagers. Whatever the rights or wrongs of the grievance, the villagers seemed to have got their revenge. In May, an improvised explosive device (IED) was placed outside a compound targeting the police chief's family.

For the next two months the level of tit-for-tat shootings rose significantly. The American Task Force Aegis and FOB Robinson appeared to be at the centre of much of the trouble. Whatever the soldiers were up to, it was clearly riling the locals. Suicide bombers were apparently being primed in Lashkar Gah, and increasingly alarmist reports suggested that Taliban in the north were on the march and the towns of Now Zad and Musa Qaleh were imperilled. On 17 May these reports seemed to be confirmed when a gun battle erupted in Musa Qaleh which reportedly left two dozen policemen dead. Again, it was almost certainly a dispute between Baghrani and Akhundzada, and the disorder was put down by one of Akhundzada's militias. This was an Afghan solution to an Afghan problem, but the 3 PARA Pathfinder Platoon was despatched, at the behest of Daoud, to deal with the incident. Just over a week after John Reid left office, stating that British forces should *not* deploy to northern Helmand, the instruction had been ignored.

Three days later, on 20 May, paratroopers were again despatched north to deal with a reported 'Taliban' threat to Kajaki Dam. Once again, Reid's stricture was being ignored and nobody it appears was questioning this change of mission. They found no Taliban, although it was clear there was a general hostility towards the provincial government at Kajaki. Concurrently, an incident occurred near the town of Sangin in which two French special forces soldiers were reported missing by Afghan soldiers, after what appeared to have been a deliberate ambush. They may have been mistaken for opium poppy eradication teams which were provoking significant friction in the area. Their mutilated bodies were later recovered by A Company on 21 May. On 22 May, it was reported the town of Now Zad was about to fall following a gun battle between a police chief, an unsavoury paedophile named 'Haji' and local tribesmen.[69] Again, a paratrooper company was sent to quell the violence – this time the newly arrived B Company – and once again they found a peaceful town. On 23 May, after significant pressure from Daoud, the Pathfinders found themselves once again making the journey to Musa Qaleh to deal with reported 'Taliban'. On 24 May, Daoud summoned the British commander at the Lashkar Gah PRT and demanded that a British force be despatched to Baghran to rescue a government official who was being threatened by 'Taliban'. After some rushed arrangements, two Chinooks loaded with A Company headed off to mount the rescue (named Operation *Bag Wrap*). The operation proved to be an anti-climax. The threat had been exaggerated and the stricken official, far from cooperating with the paratroopers and obeying their instructions at the rendezvous, almost scuppered the mission.

All these incidents had been relatively trivial by Afghan standards, even if they were increasing. Bouts of violence had flared up in Helmand in the years before the British arrived, and these had been resolved by the local powerbrokers. The notion that northern Helmand was about to fall to a Taliban army – an argument that would be later used to justify the actions that 16 Air Assault Brigade took – was greatly overplayed. Classified documentation later released by Wikileaks (the record of 'SIGACTS' or 'Significant Actions') reveals this was simply not the case. What the secret reporting clearly showed was this: first, that local corruption was causing periodic flare-ups; second, that there were unresolved clan disputes in the province, largely driven by drug feuds and land disputes; third, that American special forces units were stirring this mix unnecessarily; and last, that wherever the Americans had built a base, there had been resentment and eventually a spiral of attacks.

Task Force Helmand was ultimately responsible for the actions it took in the summer of 2006, but there is strong evidence that a misguided American special forces campaign in Helmand contributed to undermining the British operation before it even started. To Helmandis, the aggressive Americans were known as the 'specialporce'.[70] This label meant many things to many actors: patronage, weapons, money and the chance to see off rivals by hinting to the 'specialporce' that an individual was a 'Taliban'. This Afghan game was played with some gusto. The other magic word was 'terrorist', which clearly excited the Americans and sent them chasing after marginal and, it appears, completely innocent Helmandis who were unscrupulously sold for bounties.[71] As one prominent Helmandi commander later remembered, he was never able to work out why the Americans were 'so stupid'.[72] To be fair, 'stupid' was also the word used to describe the British. Scots Guards officer Leo Docherty, who resigned over Operation *Herrick 4* and then authored an intelligent book decrying the folly of the mission, shared the sentiment.[73]

The spark that eventually detonated the powder keg of Helmand was lit in the near-biblical and impoverished settlement of Now Zad. It is difficult to conceive, scanning photographs taken by soldiers who served in this isolated outpost, how Now Zad, a 'shite-hole' in soldiers' language, could have possibly mattered to anyone. The round fact of the matter was that it did not.

Now Zad – which means 'New Born' in Farsi – was a forgotten town at the end of the line. It had one barely functioning medical clinic and one dilapidated school. Like most 'towns' in Helmand, it was comprised of a single bazaar road, the length of a running track, around which a maze of compound houses had been built. Perhaps 7,000 people called Now Zad home. Around half were Ishaqzai, originally from the Sangin area, with Noorzai, Barakzai and Alikozai making up most of the remaining tribal groups. During the Taliban era, the Ishaqzai and Noorzai had joined forces and apparently supplied many fighters and commanders to the cause.[74] Due to falling water levels, the population in Now Zad had been dwindling for several years and average farm sizes had fallen to less than 2 hectares. The western escarpments bordering the town were marked by the evidence of some old quarries. Pylons had once been erected, but they were still waiting for an electricity grid that never reached the town.

Now Zad had been completely neglected by the Afghan government for decades and effectively ran its own affairs. The small force of ANP stationed in the town was untrained, corrupt and in league with the local narcos. When the Taliban took over Helmand, the locals had happily sided with the new order, rather than tolerate a rapacious local government. For an outsider it had the squalid banality and anonymity of all those places where soldiers have died, which instantly provoked the question: why did this place matter? The Soviet Army had built a firebase on a small conical hill overlooking the settlement, and later abandoned it along with a spiked gun. Half-filled trenches still existed on the hillside, like gaps caused by pulled teeth. When the British arrived, they would build their base over the palimpsest of the old Soviet gun positions. The town was declining, and just about the only rentable economic activity was the opium trade.

On 22 May, B Company of 3 PARA deployed to Now Zad. They arrived at the behest of Daoud, convinced that the town was about to fall to the Taliban. There was no warning and there was no explanation to the locals. The unexpected arrival of B Company, however, produced no reaction. Far from being a town about to fall to the Taliban, Now Zad gave the impression of being a place lost in rural somnolence. The residents of the town and the surrounding villages may have been taken unawares by the arrival of these aliens, but there was no hostility.

The paratroopers busied themselves restoring the old police station – a large, dilapidated compound house on the bazaar street without running water, electricity or toilets – to a liveable state. For 11 days nothing happened. Then on 2 June, 10 Platoon of the Royal Gurkha Rifles, commanded by a 24-year-old Lieutenant Paul Hollingshead, arrived in Now Zad. The Gurkhas had been sent to relieve the paratroopers, but there was a second motive behind the arrival of these reinforcements. Along with the Gurkhas, two more companies of paratroopers (A and D Companies) would be arriving in Now Zad, joined by the battlegroup's tactical HQ and the Patrols Platoon. It was now Freakley's turn to push the British into undertaking a petty and ultimately disastrous mission.

American forces were mounting a much larger operation – Operation *Mountain Thrust* – in northern Helmand. It would be the last of the futile sweeps carried out by American forces in this area. 3 PARA would become part of this wider effort and launch the battlegroup's first major operation. It was called Operation *Mutay*, and it was scheduled to take place on 4 June.

The aim of Operation *Mutay* – a cordon and search operation – was to apprehend a local 'Taliban' commander. The intelligence for this operation came from the Americans in Kandahar keen to get the British into the fight. In private, this amounted to frustration on the part of General Freakley at what was perceived to be the lack of a British desire to fight.[75] Why this particular commander mattered – if that is what he was – was difficult to understand. He lived a 20-minute walk from the police station, where the paratroopers had been camped for almost two weeks. Not a single hostile shot or gesture had been directed at the British. Did the British, who had only just arrived in Now Zad, have any real sense of who he was or what his standing was in the local community, or why, even, he represented a threat to the provincial government in Lashkar Gah? It seems unlikely.

'Taliban' were not outlaws in Helmandi eyes. Probably every one of the province's village, town and district leaders could have been described as 'Taliban' inasmuch as they had once accommodated and lived peaceably with the previous regime. Some may have embraced the Taliban with enthusiasm, and some may have merely tolerated Taliban rules, but you had to be very careful before casting the Taliban stone at anyone, lest it bounce back and hit you. As one local journalist laughingly later told an American researcher, you could not live in Helmand without having friends in the Taliban.[76]

On the morning of 4 June Operation *Mutay* rolled out. The appearance of so many soldiers could not have gone unnoticed. As a Gurkha platoon drove towards the compound where the reported Taliban commander lived, they stumbled across some young men. One of the men ran inside a compound and re-appeared with a rocket-propelled grenade (RPG) launcher on his shoulders, which he fired off in the direction of the surprised Gurkhas. It missed. The Gurkhas responded with small arms fire, and a general mêlée broke out. The impetuous youth who fired the RPG was killed – the first tribesman to be killed by British forces on Operation *Herrick*. Soon the entire area echoed with the sound of gunfire. In a town where every man owned a rifle, this was a clarion call to arms. 3 PARA's blooding in Helmand Province was about to turn into a very long day. The local response to this unexpected and unprovoked aggression was disorganized and random. Groups of armed men began to appear in the hedge lines and ditches ready to take on the intruders. They were elusive and seemed to be everywhere. The Gurkhas had managed to successfully extract themselves, carrying a policeman who had been shot in the stomach, but two Chinooks' worth of paratroopers who landed north of the target area, including Lieutenant Colonel Tootal, would spend the next four hours locked in running battles.

For the over-excited, and over-brave tribesmen, it proved a lethal experience. With Apaches and an American A-10 loitering overhead, the armed villagers were easy prey. By the end of the day the battlegroup reported killing over 30 'enemy', although this number would later be revised downwards to 23 local people in the post-operational report. Nothing of significance was found: a few bullets, a grenade and some opium bags. Such a find would not have been untypical of the average compound in Helmand. No soldier had been killed or injured. The better trained paratroopers had smashed the locals in a bloody day's fighting, although there had been some close moments. The young soldiers who took part in Operation *Mutay* were no longer green – they were now combat veterans, and there was a real sense of elation in the British camp. As one paratrooper put it, it had been good fun.[77] For the tribesmen a quite different emotion was being experienced. As dusk fell, a profound sense of shock seized Now Zad. The aliens who had arrived two weeks ago with their smiles and promises had proved to be murderers.

The echoes of the shots fired in Now Zad rebounded all the way back to Sangin (where it appears the tribesmen may have originated). They then travelled north to the town of Musa Qaleh and forked right, reaching Kajaki. All of northern Helmand was set alight by the news. Before Operation *Mutay* the British had not fired a single round in Helmand Province.[78] After the events in Now Zad, the ammunition expenditure graph spiked like a runaway hyperinflation chart. The brigade would add an ammunition expenditure annex to its post-operational report; for future historians, the graphs in this annex, itemized by day, week and month, clearly reveal the story of Operation *Herrick 4*. Following a lull, Now Zad broke out into a general rebellion. It would last for over 100 days. By the end of the month

Sangin had detonated in the face of the British. The 'siege of Sangin' would wax and wane for the rest of the brigade's deployment in Helmand. Musa Qaleh was next, and Kajaki soon followed. Everywhere the British would find themselves under siege from an irate local population.

It would later be insinuated the 'Maroon Machine' needed little invitation to swing a punch. A serious author like Professor Anthony King would assert that Operation *Herrick 4*, in this respect, had been a reflection of the aggressive airborne ethos.[79] This was unfair. It was coincidental that a parachute battalion had been involved – it could have been any line infantry battalion. Freakley would have attempted to get any British unit into the fight, as he did the Canadians. 3 PARA had not deployed to Helmand looking for a fight, although Tootal expected one. Both Butler and Tootal were under immense pressure to 'do something' from a number of actors – they did not seek gratuitous action. Tootal could not have refused to undertake Operation *Mutay*. He was a subordinate commander within a wider American-led operation. It would have taken government-level intervention to stop Tootal's participation in the American operation. No British cabinet would have dared act in this way and anger Washington.

Operation *Mutay* took place because of the coincidence of overheated minds in the personalities of Governor Daoud and General Freakley. In this mix, Britain's foreign policy in Afghanistan effectively fell on the shoulders of a paratrooper lieutenant colonel, newly arrived in a country he barely understood, who was then despatched on a misguided mission to a remote town, to thwart an imagined Taliban threat. Tootal, ultimately, was the fall guy (although he did not view the events in this way).

The consequences of *Mutay* were immediate and irreversible. The task force quickly became fixed defending platoon houses, and commanders did what commanders are always tempted to do when a plan unravels – they began to ask for more troops. When Lieutenant General Dannatt, C-in-C Land and about to be appointed CGS, visited Helmand just one week later, Butler made exactly this request: 'he asked for additional troops and more helicopter support to make up for that lost manoeuvre capability'.[80] The alarm bells, at this stage, should have been ringing.

Following Operation *Mutay* an uneasy calm descended on Now Zad. The same was not true elsewhere in northern Helmand, where word of the British massacre had spread.

One week later, on 11 June, the battlegroup suffered its first combat fatality – Captain Jim Philippson, a gunner – killed by gunfire when a patrol based at FOB Robinson tried to retrieve a Desert Hawk mini-UAV it had lost on the far bank of the Helmand River. The situation then deteriorated further. On 13 June, A Company was again called out to rescue an American convoy ambushed near Sangin. On 17 June, following intensive American pressure, a small detachment was sent to Kajaki Dam. French Force (named after the officer in charge) drew blood in a mortar exchange, and the British were then requested to deploy a permanent guard at the dam. On 18 June, inter-tribal fighting flared up in Sangin and a local politician's son was wounded in a gun fight. Pressed by Governor Daoud, A Company was despatched to Sangin to rescue the wounded man on 21 June (Operation *Clab*). He turned out not to be badly wounded, but as at Kajaki, once a British force had deployed to one of these northern locations, there were calls for a permanent presence and A Company would soon find itself stuck in Sangin. On 27 June, two British special forces soldiers were killed outside Sangin and B Company was sent to recover the bodies. On the same day, a patrol from C Company patrolled to a village called Zumbelay, east of Gereshk, accompanied by the *Sunday Times* reporter Christina Lamb and her photographer Justin Sutcliffe. This was a mixed Barakzai and Khugyani settlement. The aim of the patrol was to spread 'hearts and minds', but the paratroopers were ambushed and were lucky to escape with their lives. Unbeknown to the soldiers, Zumbelay was where a number of ex-Hizb fighters who had been serving in '93rd Division' found themselves unemployed when the Americans decided to disband the old Afghan Army. They were hardly likely to welcome Westerners. Some had since offered their services as 'Taliban'.

Published on 2 July 2006, the story of the gunfight at Zumbelay caused a sensation. Up to this point the government had been assiduous in promoting Operation *Herrick* as an essentially benign stabilization operation. Now Britons were reading dramatic accounts of paratroopers fighting for their lives. As a result of the *Sunday Times* story there would be a clamp down on embedded reporting, although this was denied by the MOD (Ed Butler's subsequent testimony contradicts the MOD's position, and asserts that there was indeed an attempt to stifle negative reporting).[81] It was too late anyway. The genie had been let out of the bottle, and a narrative of reconstruction had been replaced by a story about destruction. As Christina Lamb wrote: 'The ambush of our lightly armed patrol not only was unexpected but also brought into question the entire strategy being pursued by the British in Helmand, the huge province they have taken on.'

For the newly appointed defence secretary, Des Browne, the turn of events in Helmand was a cause of concern. Iraq, as he later admitted in evidence to the Defence Select Committee on 29 March 2011, consumed his time: 'I was totally focussed on Iraq in the initial days, so from my point of view, having forces deployed in two environments, and conducting two wars was challenging.' He first visited Helmand in mid-June (immediately after General Dannatt) and then in early July, when he directly posed the question why the British were becoming involved in fighting and not reconstruction. The answer he received – that the British had been sent to support the Afghan governor in Helmand, and that this implied confronting the Taliban – was unsatisfactory. It was a measure of just how quickly this orthodoxy was established that Des Browne felt obliged to issue a statement that gave an official stamp to the mythology of Operation *Herrick 4*. His justification for the change of mission is worth quoting in full for two reasons. First, because it cemented a fallacy that would dominate British operations for much of the war, and second, because it was discussed at Cabinet level and received the endorsement of the prime minister, Tony Blair:[82]

> The original intent was to tackle the challenges incrementally, spreading security and reconstruction from the centre of Helmand out. But commanders on the ground grasped an early opportunity. They saw the chance to reinforce the position of the local Governor and the Afghan army and police by going into Northern Helmand, and challenging the impunity of the Taleban there. In doing this, we moved faster towards achieving our ultimate objectives, but extended ourselves. This is a development we must respond to. But it is our actions that have brought about this development, our decisions and our determination to grasp the challenge. It is not, as some suggest, a failure to anticipate a violent response to our arrival. Yes the violence has increased, but that was inevitable. We are challenging the power of the Taleban and other enemies of the Afghan government, and they are reacting. But despite their efforts, we are spreading security.[83]

The notion that 3 PARA had spread across Helmand chasing fugitive threats because it represented an 'opportunity' was claptrap (although the paratroopers certainly now faced a 'challenge'). They had done so because Daoud and Freakley had pressed them to do so. They also did so because Ed Butler believed the war would have to 'go north'. The weasel phrase actually came from a PowerPoint presentation given by Butler to Browne in the June visit, in which the former argued that the platoon houses deployment was acting as a block to a potential Taliban advance against central Helmand – again, an indication of just how quickly the Operation *Herrick 4* myth was established.[84] The argument that an increase in violence was inevitable was also weak. It was the British task force that provoked the violence, as General Jackson later conceded, by poking a stick in the 'Taliban anthill' and causing the ants to run around.[85] The American Operation *Mountain Thrust* undoubtedly contributed to this needless stick-poking. Before the arrival of the British, Helmand had been lawless, but not especially violent by Afghan standards; just three American soldiers had been killed in the province in five years. Far from moving the British more quickly towards their 'ultimate objectives', Operation *Herrick 4* was a setback from which the British struggled to recover for the next four years, until the arrival of 22,000 US Marine reinforcements. Every subsequent defence secretary would feel obliged to repeat this mythology. Two years later, the balanced John Hutton made the assertion that if the British had not gone into northern Helmand in 2006 the Taliban would probably control Helmand and Kandahar, a quite exaggerated retelling of history.[86]

For 10 Platoon left manning the police station at Now Zad, this spin was of little relevance. The lull that followed Operation *Mutay* did not last, and soon they found themselves under attack day and night. All pretence of patrolling was abandoned, and the small force fell back on defending the outpost. The Gurkhas would later compile a map of Now Zad showing all the insurgent firing points. In total, there were 37 – the whole town had ganged up on them. To counter the increasing threat, a second Gurkha platoon was despatched to Now Zad on 2 July (11 Platoon commanded by Lieutenant Angus Mathers), and command was assumed by Major Dan Rex.[87] At this stage the British had not abandoned the hope that the situation might be resolved through dialogue. On 11 July, Major Rex organized a *shura* with the town elders to explain the purpose of the British mission and to emphasize that he did not seek confrontation. The *shura* was poorly attended and his words fell on deaf ears. The elders simply wanted the British to leave, the same message they would receive elsewhere in Helmand. After the failure of this *shura*, an outright attempt by the local tribesmen to oust the British from the police station began in earnest. A wave of attacks followed, reaching a crescendo two days later when the station came close to being overrun.

Faced with this outburst of violence, the British compensated for their numerical inferiority by resorting to air power. This did not stop the attacks – they would continue unabated for another two weeks – but the aerial bombardments did destroy the bazaar. This destruction was mirrored inside the police station, which began to resemble a rubbish dump. On 16 July a further batch of reinforcements was sent, which included a mortar detachment and machine-gun team manned by Royal Fusiliers. This allowed the Gurkhas to hit back at the Taliban mortar teams as well as engage the attackers at longer ranges. The intensity of the fighting in Now Zad over the month of July was reflected in the ammunition expenditure: 30,000 rounds of 5.56mm ball, 17,000 rounds of 7.62mm link, and 2,000 rounds of .50 cal were expended.[88] Over a two-week period, 28 assaults were repelled, and the soldiers reckoned they accounted for 100 insurgents. The British themselves were very fortunate not to have suffered fatalities.* Shamefully, no Gurkhas received gallantry awards for this desperate defence of the Now Zad police station.

On 30 July the relief of the beleaguered force finally got underway. Over 500 troops were committed in Operation *Oqab Qurbani*, which included a company of paratroopers and a company from 2 Royal Regiment of Fusiliers (that would directly relieve the Gurkhas).[89] HCR provided armoured support, and 7 Royal Horse Artillery was stood by to provide artillery support with light guns. The intention was to hold Now Zad for a matter of days before withdrawing, following a negotiated settlement. The settlement never happened, and A Company, led by the Fusilier Major Jon Swift, ended up spending over 100 days under siege – the longest in recent history and an epic worthy of imperial forebears. For the duration of the siege the Fusiliers lived on rations. This was the longest sustained period on rations recorded in the modern British Army, and it provoked scientific interest when the soldiers returned home.[90]

The luck enjoyed by the Fusiliers cannot be overstated. By now the British were occupying a split position between the police station and the small, conical hill immediately west of the station which the Russians had once occupied. The tenacity of this enemy deeply impressed the British. Some local tribesmen demonstrated bravery so suicidal it was suspected they were taking drugs. The isolation that the Fusiliers felt was increased

* Three casualties were suffered, one relatively serious.

by the indifferent manner in which they were treated by the airborne staff at Bastion Camp. They received no regular updates on events happening elsewhere in Helmand, and they received no items from the scarce trickle of equipment that was reaching the province. Frequently, they ran very low on ammunition. In the entire siege the Fusiliers received just two telephone calls from the brigade HQ – a scandalous abandonment. As one officer put it, they often 'did not have a clue what the rest of the battlegroup was doing'.[91]

By the end of the siege, when marines arrived in October, the Fusiliers had endured 149 gun battles as well as mortar and rocket attacks. To repel the attackers they called air strikes roughly once every three days. Twenty-eight bombs were dropped on Now Zad, a place no bigger than an English village. This amounted to 18 tons of high explosives which, unsurprisingly, completely trashed the once thriving bazaar.[92] The mortar detachment fired off more than 1,000 bombs – or more than a peacetime battalion would fire off in training in several years. The machine gunners rattled off 58,000 rounds, with one soldier, Fusilier Dean Fisher, becoming a media celebrity because he personally fired off almost half this amount.[93] Churchill's self-satisfied description of 'blind credulity and fanaticism, now happily passing away from the earth, under the combined influences of Rationalism and machine guns' aptly described the Fusiliers' defence of Now Zad.[94] Like the Gurkhas before them, the Fusiliers were overlooked in the operational awards list and received no gallantry medals for their feat of endurance. According to the locals, as many as 170 tribesmen may have been killed and probably three times this number were wounded.[95] In a valley with a population of about 7,000, this meant everyone knew someone who had been killed or injured by the British. An unstoppable blood feud had begun.

The experience at Now Zad began to be repeated throughout other supposedly threatened towns in Helmand Province. Brigadier Ed Butler would later defend the decision to man the district centres on the grounds that it kept the fight north of Highway 1 and away from the provincial capital. The succession of the platoon house sieges would be described, after the event, as a necessary and inevitable 'break-in battle'. 16 Air Assault Brigade expected a fight and got it. This post-hoc justification is not credible. Lashkar Gah and Gereshk were not under threat and never would be. To suggest there was a Taliban army waiting to sweep south and overrun Helmand was fantasy. The break-in battle which the British referred to was not started by the 'Taliban', who ignored the newly arrived forces for two months (or six months, if the date of arrival of the British is taken from the beginning of the construction of Camp Bastion). The fight was started by the British, who provoked a chain reaction of violence. American operations in Helmand did not help matters. Manning the district centres had exactly the opposite effect claimed by Butler. It provoked a southward migration of insurgent gangs as well as fomenting tribal insurrection elsewhere across Helmand.

It is to jump ahead in the story, but the point is so central it must be made now. The day after the last British soldiers quit Helmand, on 27 October 2014, former commanding officer of 22 SAS Richard Williams wrote an opinion piece in *The Times*. It was telling that he waited until this moment before speaking out, and it begged the question how many other now retired British Army officers were sitting on the truth but keeping silent. He wrote:

> What, I was asked, was the SAS view on the effects of replacing the cash-rich but soldier-light American development team in Helmand with a cash-poor but paratrooper-secured British operation, which aimed to spend less money on development while simultaneously disrupting the narcotics industry and forcing a change of the provincial governor? Leaving aside the military weaknesses of not enough helicopters, air support or medical facilities, and woefully inadequate communications … we highlighted the most significant weakness in the plan to the visiting military planning team from London. This was led, surprisingly, by a submarine officer from the Royal Navy.
>
> We forced upon the visiting sailor our view that no amount of fighting spirit and enthusiasm would secure a peace if the fragile balance of power in the province was disrupted, if aid spending was reduced or if the governor was replaced … Our message was simple: don't challenge the status quo for now, build relationships locally over the long-term based on an increased amount of development aid, and keep the operation as low profile as you can and you might be able to achieve sustainable progress.

Williams was absolutely right. In two paragraphs he sentenced the failure and folly of Operation *Herrick 4*. In the same article, he further adumbrated the failings of the military leadership and called for an inquiry into the conduct of the war. He was probably right in this demand too, but two other government departments carried equal responsibility for the mess. The FCO and SIS destroyed the fragile balance of power in Helmand by sacking Governor Akhundzada. And DfID totally failed to provide meaningful reconstruction. Tootal and his paratroopers were the fall guys for the failings of many officials who escaped inquest and censure.

The next town to flare up was Sangin, which had been at the heart of Helmand's opium trade since the 1970s. It is an unfortunate pathology of some military operations that an objective can take on the character of an irrational obsession, an observation once made by Henry Kissinger. In the summer of 2006, the town of Sangin gained this dubious distinction. Unfortunately for the British and US marines that followed, the pathological obsession lasted almost seven years. During this period the two allies would each suffer over 100 fatalities 'securing' Sangin, and scores of young men would be left maimed – single, double and triple amputees. The purpose of this sacrifice – to deny the insurgents a town so thoroughly corrupt, so anti-government and anti-Western, so beyond any reasonable hopes of meaningful reform – would have been quixotic, if it had not been tragic. The death toll among the local tribes, of course, was far higher, and parts of the town ended up as rubble. Nobody, in the end, won in Sangin.

The name meant 'heavy' or 'solid place', and it was once a caravan stopover on the confluence of the Musa Qaleh and Helmand rivers. The main north–south route in Helmand, Route 611, passed through Sangin, and the modern town had grown along the length of this gravel track. The town itself had a population of perhaps 20,000, but with the adjoining villages that merged into the outskirts of the town, this population doubled. The town centre had grown on either side of a shallow wadi – the Sangin Mandah – that ran east to west into the Helmand River. On Thursdays this wadi filled with market stalls and animals. North of the wadi, across a concrete bridge which the soldiers nicknamed 'The Sangin Flyover', was a bazaar area that had been laid out in a grid pattern. The shops followed the traditional Afghan style of a single, box-shaped unit with a grill front. When the fighting broke out, this area would become deserted, spelling economic disaster for the traders.

South of the wadi, Route 611 divided at a Y-junction. East of the junction were Sangin's only prominent tall buildings: a dilapidated hospital, some Soviet-style flats and shops and the improbably named 'Florida Hotel'. The soldiers renamed it 'The Red Hotel' from its colour and it became a well-used firing point. West of the Y-junction was Sangin's main mosque – a large, flat building with 12 domes – more compounds and administrative buildings, and the district centre. The track leading to the district centre became known as the 'Pipe Range' from the number of gun battles that erupted there. Later it would be renamed the 'Avenue of Hope', which provoked predictable cynical observations. The district centre itself, later named FOB Jackson after the first paratrooper to die there, included the police station and the governor's offices. The British would lease a half-built two-storey brick building within the compound, which ironically belonged to one of Sangin's better-known narco-traffickers, a man named Haji Lal Jan. When the Taliban moved back into Sangin in December 2013, the redoubtable Jan was still standing, another example of Afghanistan's great survivors. South Sangin trailed away along Route 611, an area which included more bazaars and 'millionaire's row', a collection of large, garish houses built by some of Sangin's opium barons. The whole town sat inside a bowl surrounded by rocky, undulating ground and compound buildings that spread out in an ill-defined sprawl into the surrounding desert and 'Green Zone', the term coined for the fertile Helmand River Valley.

Sangin was a town that always threatened to spill over into violence from inter-tribal competition over the narcotics trade, a volatility that the British paratroopers poorly understood. The recent troubles in Sangin dated to the distribution of patronage following the fall of the Taliban. Supported by American special forces, the Alikozai Dad Mohammed was appointed head of the provincial National Directorate of Security (NDS). He in turn appointed two brothers, Gul and Daud, as Sangin district governor and police chief, decisively ousting his rival, the Ishaqzai Atta Mohammed. This provoked a low-level war for control of Sangin's lucrative drug bazaars that was simmering when the British arrived. The Alikozai–Ishaqzai rivalry was further fanned by American special forces who fell for Dad Mohammed's 'intelligence leads' and began pursuing Ishaqzai 'commanders', adding to the sense of alienation of this tribe.[96] When the British arrived, the Barakzai Khan Mohammed, an Akhundzada ally, was chief of police. The ex-governor, Gul Mohammed, had just been murdered by Ishaqzai, along with 32 family members, and this provoked his brother Dad Mohammed, now a member of Parliament, into drawing the British into Sangin by portraying these events as a 'Taliban' assault.[97]

Three days after the arrival of B Company in Now Zad, on 25 May, the 3 PARA Patrols Platoon, reinforced by 1 Platoon, arrived in the district centre of Sangin after receiving reports that the town was about to fall to the 'Taliban'. As with the deployment to Now Zad, they found a peaceful if somewhat tense town. Anxious to unwind the commitment to effectively garrison Sangin, Lieutenant Colonel Tootal ordered the withdrawal of the Patrols Platoon but was forced – for political rather than military reasons – to leave 30-odd paratroopers to man the district centre and to act as an OMLT (Operational Mentoring and Liaison Team, pronounced 'omelette'). The British four-year occupation of Sangin District Centre effectively began on 30 May with the unlucky 1 Platoon, 3 PARA, commanded by a Lieutenant Hugo Farmer. A short mission turned into a sojourn of several weeks (albeit 1 Platoon was extricated from its OMLT commitment, so the deployment was not continuous). As at Now Zad, the British paratroopers did not find themselves under attack. In fact, according to Hugo Farmer, the locals were basically curious and mostly friendly.[98] Farmer recalled, 'The first week or so went well until a separate military operation [a special forces operation] to the South caused public opinion to move sharply against us. The locals complained of broken promises of peace. That night the base was attacked for the first time by heavy small arms fire from multiple firing points.' Soon, the platoon was being attacked roughly every four hours 'night and day'. The same pattern would be repeated across northern Helmand.

In mid-June, 3 PARA received three high-profile visitors, Generals Dannatt, Richards and lastly Des Browne. At least Browne questioned why the task force was becoming embroiled in local fights. None, however, appears to have been sufficiently alarmed as to fundamentally re-evaluate the unexpected developments in Helmand. This was a lost opportunity and probably the last chance to save and re-set the mission.

A series of violent spats then sparked another call for British reinforcement, and three weeks later, on 21 June, A Company, commanded by Major Will Pike, was loaded on four Chinooks and dropped off immediately west of the Sangin District Centre in a wadi. The paratroopers had returned in strength. The reason for this second deployment was the 'rescue' of Khan Mohammed's son. According to Governor Daoud, Mohammed's son had been seriously injured in a fight with the 'Taliban'. There had been a local punch-up, but the governor almost certainly knew that the population in Sangin was in almost open rebellion against Khan Mohammed, the corrupt police chief. Mohammed was a notorious bully who had reportedly raped a girl. Opinion in the town almost certainly applauded the retribution, which had been delivered by the Ishaqzai, not the 'Taliban'. As with previous clashes with the ANP across Helmand, the locals resolved the problem themselves without the need for British intervention and chased the police chief out of town. Butler was aware of these shenanigans and remained wary. Lieutenant Colonel Tootal also opposed the mission, and he was backed by Butler. The appearance of British troops might add fuel to the fire, and the 3 PARA battlegroup was already overstretched. Nobody wanted to be seen to be backing a corrupt and unpopular official.

The day after the arrival of A Company, a *shura* was held attended by Daoud. It ended in failure, with the elders informing the governor they would have to consult with the Taliban before agreeing to a permanent British presence.[99] The de facto truce only lasted a week. On 27 June, just south of Sangin, an SBS team mounted an operation to arrest a 'Taliban leader'. The paratroopers in Sangin knew nothing about the operation. Captain David Patton, serving with the Special Reconnaissance Regiment, and Sergeant Paul Bartlett, a marine, were killed in the operation. A Gurkha contingent – 12 Platoon commanded by a Sergeant Major Trilochan Gurung – crashed out from FOB Robinson to rescue the men but fell into an ambush and ended up calling artillery and aerial support to extract itself, leaving behind a destroyed Land Rover WMIK. The vehicle was hit by six RPGs, but the crew baled sharply and were unscathed. The following day, B Company was flown to the area and the two bodies were retrieved. For the locals this botched operation was a signal that the truce was definitely over. The elders made one last attempt to persuade the British to leave, and that night the 'siege of Sangin' began in earnest.

On 30 June local tribesmen appeared to make a concerted effort to overrun the base but failed, with heavy losses on their side. The British responded with artillery fire and aerial bombardments, destroying parts of the now vacated town centre. The sheer weight of fire directed at the besieged paratroopers was inevitably going to take a toll, and the British luck ran out on 1 July when a 107mm rocket scored a direct hit on the tower in the district centre. Corporal Peter Thorpe, a signaller, and Lance Corporal Jabron Hashmi, a rare Muslim soldier serving with the Intelligence Corps, were killed instantly by the strike. Five other soldiers were wounded. The shock of taking casualties was profound. This event changed the game and the mood of the soldiers.

Two days later, B Company relieved the exhausted A Company. It did not take long for the newly arrived company to be blooded. On 5 July,

Private Damien Jackson was shot and killed just south of the base. The 20-year-old from South Shields was the first British paratrooper to die in action in Helmand. For Major Giles Timms, the loss of one of his men proved a serious test of his leadership (Jackson was actually serving in 1 Platoon, A Company – the platoon had volunteered to stay behind in Sangin, as B Company was short of one of its platoons). Psychologically, no paratrooper wanted to concede defeat, but equally everyone knew that the fight in Sangin was pointless. Trying to motivate his men to step out of the district centre when virtually every patrol was coming under fire required special strength. Ingenuity was also demanded as the paratroopers sought ways to out-fox their opponents. After another week of heavy gun battles another *shura* was called on 15 July, attended by Daoud, Butler and Tootal. Again it failed – by now, the elders just wanted the British to leave. Regardless of this failure, the British still needed to address the pressing matter of resupplying the besieged base. On 18 July, a resupply run was organized, led by a Canadian company from FOB Robinson mounted in light armoured vehicles, or LAVs. The Canadians joked about having to rescue the paratroopers, but they were also appalled by the conditions the British were enduring in Sangin. It was the first glimpse that outsiders had of the seriousness of the British position. Tootal and Butler were also becoming increasingly vocal over their concerns while acknowledging the political reality that they would not be allowed to withdraw from Sangin.

If the British were thinking privately of withdrawal, General Freakley was urging more aggression. On 14 July, 3 PARA had mounted an operation to capture a reported Taliban commander who lived just north of Sangin. Operation *Augustus* was an American-inspired operation with the ambitious goal of driving away the insurgents from the town centre and creating a security cocoon around the beleaguered district centre. It was part of the wider, ongoing Operation *Mountain Thrust* that was committing Canadian and American troops to similar operations in the Kandahar area. The follow-up reconstruction mission, in which it was hoped to engage with local elders, would be known as Operation *Rana*. Tootal had doubts that attacking a Taliban commander would make any significant difference to the situation in Sangin, perhaps with some wisdom gained from the experience of Operation *Mutay* in Now Zad, but it went ahead anyway.

In a post-operation meeting in Kandahar, General Freakley criticized the British for failing to do enough in front of an audience that included Daoud and the Canadian brigadier, David Fraser.[100] The criticism, unsurprisingly, fell badly on the British who felt that their desperate attempts to hold the line across northern Helmand were simply not being appreciated. As anticipated, Operation *Augustus* had no effect at all on the siege in Sangin. Indeed, it inflamed the situation further. With no more troops to juggle, on 27 July, Tootal duly redeployed A Company to Sangin to take over from B Company.

A Company, now commanded by Major Jamie Loden, found themselves in a farcical situation. The few ANP in the base would have nothing to do with the paratroopers and would not even wear uniforms. The ANA platoon appeared to be taking drugs and running some sort of paedophile ring.[101] Determined not to allow the gunmen to feel they were winning this contest of wills, Loden drove his men on through that blistering August. The firepower used by the British just to move a few hundred yards was extraordinary. After 20 August, Loden recalled, every patrol leaving the base was supported by two GR7 Harriers, a troop of 105mm guns, a mortar line, Scimitars and heavy machine guns manned by sappers in the sangars. In short, it was madness.

Over the first two weeks of August several paratroopers were wounded by small arms fire or shrapnel. On 20 August, three more paratroopers were wounded when a section was ambushed in thick vegetation. The section commander, a tough Yorkshireman called Corporal Bryan Budd, charged the enemy. His body was later found within yards of three tribesmen, conjoined in death. For this action he was awarded a posthumous Victoria Cross, the first of the war. It later emerged that Budd may have been shot by his fellow paratroopers. Whether or not this was the case, his courage and self-sacrifice were not in question. On 29 August, A Company was again relieved by C Company, supported by a platoon of Royal Irish. By this stage, Loden's men had fired off more than 20,000 rounds of small arms ammunition, over 500 mortar bombs and more than 650 artillery shells – all to justify walking the distance of the 'Pipe Range' before withdrawing back to the security of the base. Sangin was not being 'dominated' by this firepower. It was simply being trashed. The attacks on the Sangin District Centre diminished in September but they never petered out completely On 6 September the battlegroup suffered its last casualties at the district centre when a lucky mortar strike wounded four Irish Rangers, one of whom subsequently died of his wounds. At the height of the siege of Sangin, in July, the British had held off 44 attacks against the district centre.

The third location where the British found themselves under siege was Kajaki Dam. Following Operation *Enduring Freedom*, the Americans had proposed restoring the turbine hall, but the project had never quite got off the ground. When the British arrived in 2006 the dam was being guarded by a local militia led by an ex-American special forces soldier called John Kravinach. The other American at the dam was a grizzled engineer called George Wilder, who had been working on the single surviving turbine since 2004. His Afghan colleague, an engineer called Sayed Rassoul, had been working at the turbine hall for almost three decades. The militia was routinely shot at and mortared, and the Americans were keen the British help by deploying a permanent force to the dam. The problem for Tootal was that he had no troops to spare.

On 17 June, after more pressure from General Freakley, the platoon-sized French Force deployed to the dam under the auspices of Operation *Barcha*. French Force included a mortar detachment and heavy machine guns, two weapons the civilian guard force lacked. Captain French decided the best way to end the routine of sniping was to play the villagers' own game. By now the locals had become so confident they set up their mortars at the same place and time, in full view of one of the security outposts. Unsuspectingly, the fighters arrived in their pick-ups to begin another attack and were ambushed by the paratroopers. One mortar bomb appeared to achieve a near direct hit, killing or injuring most of the gunmen. The paratroopers celebrated, and the attacks against the dam stopped for the next week. Using this success as an excuse, Tootal withdrew French Force, but after renewed pressure from the Americans, he was forced to establish a permanent presence at the dam shortly afterwards. The British occupation of Kajaki Dam had begun.

Kajaki was different from the rest of Helmand and would always remain so. The main reason for the difference was the ground. It was very hard for either side to actually hit each other because the hills offered perfect visibility to any defender. Once local fighters realized they could no longer approach the dam with impunity because they were being watched, they resorted to ineffectual long-range attacks. No British soldier would ever be killed or even wounded by these attacks. This logic would also apply against the British – every British casualty at Kajaki was suffered when the British chose to sally out of the dam to attack the locals. It was a stalemate from the beginning, but it would take three years and over 20 fatalities before the British finally accepted the pointlessness of what they were doing and decided that holding the dam was sufficient (incidentally, the US Marines who took over pursued the same futile game, and also incurred casualties, until it was their turn to leave). The Soviet Army fought a bitter stalemate in this area and the British were about to repeat the experience.

The paratroopers sent to Kajaki were ignorant of this history. To them, the ritual attacks were more than just an annoyance; they were a provocation that had to be confronted. In an effort to take the fight to the villagers, the paratroopers would become involved in the most controversial incident of the battlegroup's deployment, when a team of snipers accidentally strayed into a minefield and suffered mass casualties.

The first week of September had already started badly for British forces in Helmand. On 2 September, XV302, a Nimrod MR2 surveillance aircraft, detonated in mid-air over Afghanistan, killing all 14 crew including a paratrooper and marine. The aircraft had only just taken off from Kandahar Air Base and crashed in front of Canadian troops preparing for Operation *Medusa*. At first, it was mistakenly reported as a crashed Ariana 727, but an American Chinook despatched to the scene soon confirmed the grim truth. 34 Squadron RAF Regiment deployed a flight to the crash site and spent the next 36 hours recovering body parts and equipment, a task compounded by looting locals. The gunners were lucky not to fall victims themselves to an opportunistic insurgent attack, repeating the experience of six Royal Military Policemen controversially killed in Anbar, Iraq, in 2003. Failed by their radios, the RAF men were saved by their flight commander who used his Nokia mobile phone to call for help.

For the 3 PARA battlegroup, 6 September proved the blackest day. Three soldiers were killed and a further 18 were injured in three separate incidents. The first setback took place precisely on the hillside observation posts (OPs) at Kajaki when a section strayed into an old Russian minefield below the OPs. The eventual tally of dead and injured was shocking. A severely wounded Corporal Mark Wright, who would be awarded a posthumous George Cross for his leadership and bravery, died of his wounds en route to Bastion. Corporal Pearson lost his left leg and was awarded the Queen's Gallantry Medal. Drummer Barlow also lost his left leg and was awarded the George Medal. Lance Corporal Hale suffered an amputation of his right leg. Lance Corporals Craig and Hartley were both badly injured, and Private Prosser had suffered shrapnel wounds to his chest. A single paratrooper had been left standing.

The minefield incident at Kajaki Dam then developed twists that tarnished the ordeal the men had endured. The first came from Andrew Walker, an Oxford-based coroner who became a thorn in the MOD's side. The fact that there were several contradictory versions of the events of 6 September at Kajaki, and these amounted to conflicting and at least confused witness statements, did not seem to blow his sails off course. This is not to incriminate Tootal, but this officer alone wrote three versions (a report following the events which drew heavily from communications logs and included useful, detailed timings; a second in his post-operational report on returning to Britain; and a third in his book). These versions did not fully match in details.

In the case of the Kajaki Dam incident, some individuals may have been tempted to nuance their statements to support a particular viewpoint. The key charge made by the coroner was that the MOD had failed the troops by not deploying a helicopter equipped with a winch to Afghanistan – a requirement that was judged 'obvious'. What the inquest did not emphasize was that none of the helicopters in southern Afghanistan belonged to the British task force anyway, whether or not they were equipped with a winch. They were all pooled within a combined force that served all ISAF units regardless of nationality. Helicopters with winches were available – US Black Hawks. The tragedy was that one of the American helicopters developed a technical fault. The whole affair had hinged on a moment of bad luck, which was then compounded by the paratroopers who unluckily set off more mines. None of this could be attributed to a MOD official in Whitehall. Neither was it 'obvious' that helicopters with winches were required. The incident at Kajaki Dam would prove to be a unique event. There was never a subsequent call to rescue soldiers from a minefield, by helicopter, for the remainder of the war.[102] No matter – the Ministry of Defence should 'hang its head in shame' was his harsh judgement on the Kajaki Dam incident.[103]

For the surviving paratroopers these headline-grabbing verdicts were gratefully received. They were opportunistically suing the MOD for £5 million, for 'breach of duty of care', supported by MPH Solicitors, a firm based in Manchester that specialized in compensation cases for soldiers. The basis of the action was the ministry's failure to provide 'adequate information and intelligence' – or, as it was reported, mapping showing the assessed minefields.[104] This remains a puzzle, as the first-edition GSGS map of the Kajaki area clearly showed a mined area immediately south-west of the OPs as a red hatched circle. In a bizarre last twist to this dubious episode, in 2013 it was announced a film would be made of the Kajaki Dam incident, demonstrating perhaps an enduring British love affair for military disasters, but also the compulsive power of myth-making.

Of all the platoon houses the British took over in the summer of 2006, the police station at Musa Qaleh was probably the most claustrophobic and dangerous. Situated in the middle of the town and surrounded on all sides by buildings, it had poor fields of fire and, critically, no obvious landing site. Over two months, Chinooks were only able to land six times to resupply this beleaguered outpost.[105] The station included a prison and was situated next to the town's main mosque, which would be destroyed by an aerial bomb. The defenders of Musa Qaleh came to be known as the 'Musa Muckers', bonding in the adversity of their long siege. For the hierarchy, Musa Qaleh was always a mistake. General Richards thought it so, as did Brigadier Butler, but both men were trapped by political decision-making that was overriding military common sense.

When the British arrived, the police station was being run by Police Chief Abdul Wali Koka, known to the British as 'Coco', after the clown. There was in fact nothing clownish about 'Coco'. Police Chief Koka was a great survivor from past wars and he enjoyed local respect – a rarity in Helmand (he was finally caught by a suicide bomber in 2012, but survived with serious head injuries). Importantly, he seemed to know everyone, including the Taliban. 'Coco' was as much a part of the circle of powerbrokers in Musa Qaleh as the Akhundzadas. He never undercut the British, although he could be a very frustrating person to work with when pursuing his own vendettas.

The town he reigned over was smaller than Sangin and home to perhaps 10,000 inhabitants. Musa Qaleh meant 'Moses' place' or 'settlement', and the original village had grown on the east bank of a river by the same name, just north of a wadi formed by a tributary named Baghni River. For most of the year, the Musa Qaleh River was fordable to vehicles, and the British would use its pebble bed as a bridge to their base. There was a single north–south running bazaar road that ended on a roundabout with a minaret. This minaret was the only distinctive structure in the town and a source of some local pride. The bazaar road forked west at the minaret, leading to the river, 400 metres further down the track. This was where the district centre would eventually be located, near an unfinished two-storey brick building, which the soldiers would nickname 'The Hotel'. Like the

Fire Support Group Tower at Sangin, the British would occupy and fortify this building, abandoning the police station in the middle of the town. To the north of the district centre, near the banks of the river, was Musa Qaleh's 'hospital', a whitewashed building offering basic medical care. The river beach that ran north from the district centre to the hospital filled with market stalls on Thursdays. South of the district centre the ground was covered in orchards, commonly frequented by children minding livestock. The town also boasted a dentist and a school, which the Taliban would close when they took over the town.

The first British force sent to Musa Qaleh was the Pathfinder Platoon, whose role within the 3 PARA battlegroup was to act as long-range reconnaissance force. This role was completely compromised by the Musa Qaleh deployment. They arrived on 14 June to take over from a small American force with instructions that they would only spend a matter of days in the town. Their stay eventually lasted 52 days, during which time they were under attack on 26 of those days. At one point they ran out of food and they frequently ran very low on ammunition. As in Now Zad and Sangin, it was the foreign soldiers, not locals, who caused the problem.

The fighting erupted after an American convoy transiting through Musa Qaleh at the end of June was shot at. The Americans responded to this attack with overwhelming force, which one paratrooper described as resembling a scene from *Apocalypse Now*.[106] As in other locations in Helmand, the British were paying the price for an aggressive American ethos that created an unbridgeable gap between the locals and Western soldiers. For the Pathfinders, later reinforced by 6 Platoon from B Company, holding the police station became a grim and dangerous business. Enemy mortar and rocket fire proved very accurate, far more accurate than that experienced at any of the other district centres and raising suspicions that Pakistani instructors were coaching the locals. The enemy mortar men had found their range, successfully landing over 90 mortar bombs within the compound and eventually wounding 14 of the defenders with shrapnel and splinters.[107] Every casualty was an evacuation headache, as it meant risking a helicopter to extract the casualty. As in Sangin, the British responded with mortar and artillery fire (from an American battery) as well as aerial bombs, with similar destructive effects on the town centre. It was an indication of the heaviness of the fighting that a Royal Irish mortar platoon deployed to reinforce Musa Qaleh would fire off a quarter of all mortars bombs expended on Operation *Herrick 4* (851).[108]

Anxious to support the beleaguered Pathfinders, a relief was attempted on 6 July (Operation *Ketab*), which failed in the face of withering fire and multiple ambushes. A second attempt mounted on the following day also failed. Faced with such stiff opposition, the battlegroup drew back and prepared a major operation to reach the paratroopers. On 21 July, with the relief force in place west of the town, a third attempt was made to relieve the police station, supported by a Danish reconnaissance squadron mounted on Eagle APCs. This too was beaten back. The failure of these relief operations sank morale within the base, but the defenders had little option but to hold on until help arrived. On 24 July, perhaps emboldened by the parlous state of the besieged force, local fighters mounted their strongest attack to date and managed to destroy one of the sentry positions. This proved to be a turning point. Exhausted by their attacks, it was now the turn of the locals to draw breath. On 26 July, the Danes finally got through, to the immense relief of the dirty, bearded paratroopers who had not seen a friendly face for almost two months. This was still not the end for the Pathfinders, who would have to wait another 11 days before their British replacements arrived. At least they were now in little danger of being overrun – the Danish contingent brought with them six precious heavy machine guns, as well as a rare female machine gunner called Anna, who became known to the British troops as 'Combat Barbie'.

Judging that the outpost still faced a severe threat, the recently arrived D Squadron HCR was subsequently ordered to deploy to the town on 1 August. This was a challenge, as the Combat Vehicle Reconnaissance (Tracked), or CVR(T), on which the squadron was mounted, were very old and prone to breakdowns (the troopers self-deprecatingly referred to themselves as the 'Antiques Roadshow', such was the lack of faith in their machines). The deployment, which was undertaken in haste and with no infantry support, turned into a fiasco. Approaching the outskirts of the town, the squadron was caught in a well-executed ambush. One of the vehicles – a Spartan command vehicle – ran over a large IED, killing three of the occupants and severely burning the driver (who would subsequently be invited to the wedding of Prince William and Catherine Middleton in the spring of 2011). A second vehicle, a Scimitar, was also lost in the gun battle. It was only the actions of Corporal of Horse Mick Flynn, a 46-year-old Falklands veteran, that saved the day.[109] Under accurate fire and forced to abandon his own Scimitar after receiving several RPG strikes, Flynn rallied the survivors and organized the rescue of the burned and unconscious

Spartan driver. For this bravery he was awarded a Military Cross. On this occasion, the villagers had clearly won the contest and D Squadron was forced to abandon the mission and return to Camp Bastion.

The Danish reinforcement was greatly welcomed but proved to be short-lived. When the conditions at Musa Qaleh became apparent to Danish policymakers, a decision was taken to withdraw the force. For the British, this was a body blow they could do little about. Every nation committed to the ISAF mission had the right to fall back on national caveats. For the Danes, the isolation of the base at Musa Qaleh, and in particular the difficulties of carrying out casualty evacuation, were simply unacceptable. The British had raised exactly the same concerns, but British policymakers could not, or would not, stand up to American pressure to remain in Musa Qaleh.

Tootal in the meantime had to mount a fifth relief operation in as many weeks to finally withdraw the Pathfinders. On 6 August, Operation *Mar Chichel* ('Snakebite') kicked off, involving more than 500 British troops with the aim of flushing away the gunmen from Musa Qaleh.[110] By now, knowledge of the ground had greatly improved, and the British had a much better idea of the likely enemy firing points. With the Royal Irish Somme Platoon and mortars securing the dry river bed west of the town, B and C Companies conducted an air assault into Musa Qaleh. To intimidate the locals, Canadian LAVs provided fire support and created an armoured corridor to the police station. In a pattern that would become familiar to British troops, the enemy, faced with these overwhelming odds, melted away after a brief gun battle, but not before catching out a resupply column and killing a soldier from 13 Air Assault Support Regiment with a roadside bomb. The entire operation was undertaken in searing temperatures, with the thermometer hitting 47 degrees centigrade. Sapped by this inhuman heat, body armour was shed at local commanders' discretions. To avoid ambushes, the paratroopers found themselves having to blast their way through the thick compound walls using demolition charges. In less than a day, the town was cleared, leaving the paratroopers in command of a battered and largely deserted landscape. As a relief operation, *Mar Chichel* was a success. There were now close to 170 men in the base – but this would make them even more vulnerable to casualties.[111]

The idea of pulling out of Musa Qaleh was not the first time the British had considered withdrawing from a district centre. By mid-July it was increasingly obvious to everyone, from Brigadier Ed Butler downwards, that the task force had taken on too many tasks and was dangerously and unsustainably stretched, even with the reinforcements from 2 Royal Regiment of Fusiliers. On 22 July, 3 PARA had offered to withdraw from Now Zad (an offer that the pressed Gurkhas would gladly have supported), but this was rejected on the grounds that it would mean a loss of face. The same argument was consistently used to justify the continued presence in Musa Qaleh, even though with each passing week the British toehold in this northern town was becoming increasingly untenable. The Danes, unimpressed by such arguments, did withdraw, leaving behind an ad hoc collection of Royal Irish and paratroopers known as Easy Company.

The biggest fear that preyed on Butler was the consequences to the campaign if the Taliban succeeded in shooting down one of the Chinooks. At Musa Qaleh, due to the location of the only available landing site, this was no longer a possibility – it was becoming a probability. The risks taken by the Chinook crews of Flight 1310 on the first Operation *Herrick* deployment were extremely high. By the end of the deployment 18 Squadron would receive more gallantry awards than any RAF squadron since the end of World War II. Flying conditions were appalling due to dust 'brown outs', even without the risk of enemy fire. Navy pilot Nichol Benzie offered just one example of the risks daily undertaken by the Chinook crews. As he recalled, he was attacked regularly and heavily on most missions. On one occasion, his helicopter was attacked by seven separate machine-gun posts.[112] Later it was discovered his machine had been hit extensively, fortunately missing vital components. The experiences of Major Mark Hammond, a marine on secondment who was awarded the Distinguished Flying Cross and later wrote a book, were typical of the hazardous flying conditions endured by the Chinook crews. On 6 September Major Hammond undertook three casevac missions, all under fire, in Sangin and Musa Qaleh. In one of these missions his helicopter was hit by machine-gun fire and he narrowly escaped being downed by an RPG. Undeterred, he returned with a fresh helicopter and successfully evacuated the casualties.

If conditions in Musa Qaleh police station were becoming intolerable for the defenders, they were equally bad for the civilian population witnessing the destruction of what was previously a thriving market town. Over the course of September, I Battery, 7 Royal Horse Artillery reckoned they had expended over 2,300 artillery shells and over

270 bombs had been dropped (including 70 2,000-pound bombs!) over northern Helmand.

Finally, on 13 September, after two months of fighting and secret three-way negotiations between London, Kabul and Lashkar Gah, a ceasefire was finally declared at Musa Qaleh, brokered by Haji Shah Agha, a tribal elder. This was an enormous relief to the British, who had been struggling to find a way out of the military and political impasse. The siege was finally over, but the deal provoked great controversy. Butler, who had been pressing for a withdrawal, came close to taking the unilateral decision himself. This seemed to jolt PJHQ, as well as raise eyebrows. The newly arrived General Richards also wanted an exit but argued that it had to be managed within an acceptable political framework. Under the terms of the ceasefire, it was agreed the gunmen would stop interfering in Musa Qaleh in return for a British withdrawal. Both sides would save face, and both sides would be able to claim a victory of sorts. The Americans, naturally, were unhappy about the deal and saw British 'softness' in these machinations. In the US Congress, the Musa Qaleh deal was openly described as a British 'disaster'. London flapped but could do nothing to alter the perception of a British retreat. About the only people who were unequivocally happy with the deal were the soldiers of Easy Company, who were at the end of their tether. Three Royal Irishmen had been killed and 17 wounded in northern Helmand – one-third of the force that deployed. The Taliban also celebrated and filmed the final British withdrawal for propaganda purposes.

There was still one more obstacle to overcome, and this was actually vacating the police station. After much bartering, the British eventually left in a convoy of colourful Afghan trucks on 17 October, escorted by the town elders. Both Richards and Butler would commend Musa Qaleh as an example of the way forward, and it well might have been. Whatever the misgivings of the critics, this was undeniably 'an Afghan solution to an Afghan problem'. Kabul also applauded the deal for this reason. Perhaps the most candid assessment of the whole business came from one of the members of Easy Company, Ranger Devine, quoted in James Fergusson's incisive account of Operation *Herrick 4*, *A Million Bullets*. The whole business had been pointless, he opined. All that happened was that the town was destroyed and the Taliban eventually moved in.[113]

As 3 PARA prepared to hand over to 3 Commando Brigade at the beginning of September, they had much to reflect on since suffering their first fatality in mid-June. There had been nearly 500 contacts with the enemy. The battlegroup had expended 480,000 small arms rounds – a phenomenal ammunition expenditure rate when it is understood the fighting was largely confined to a handful of besieged outposts. 'Bull's Troop', the gunners supporting 3 PARA, fired over 200 missions amounting to a daily expenditure rate of about 40 shells.[114] The artillery fire had been boosted by the expenditure of over 3,000 mortar bombs. It was hardly surprising that quarters of Now Zad, Sangin and Musa Qaleh were reduced to rubble. The Apaches experienced teething problems in their first blooding and only loosed off around 4,500 cannon rounds and half a dozen Hellfire missiles. The first British soldier to receive support fire from an Apache turned out to be a Gurkha – Rifleman Rupendra Rai. The helicopters did nonetheless prove their usefulness on the battlefield and quickly earned the nickname 'The Mosquitoes' from the Taliban.

The battlegroup had suffered 15 dead and 46 wounded – casualty figures that had not been experienced by the Parachute Regiment since the Falklands Conflict. An enemy body count of 700 was claimed, but this was an inflated figure. Nobody was recovering bodies; the paratroopers mostly hunkered behind sandbags, firing off thousands of rounds at invisible enemy behind walls. The claims were simply not believable.

These statistics were really only the footnotes to an unpalatable truth: Operation *Herrick 4* had been a fiasco. First, it was clear to all those who had taken part in the fighting over the summer that the strategic plan did not match reality. 16 Air Assault Brigade's own assessment of the status of the operation was nothing if not honest. The intelligence had been woeful; the communications simply inadequate for the distances involved; the reconstruction plan a fantasy manned by phantom staff; and the Afghan National Army a force that would not be ready for independent operations for a number of years. There had been serious operational and tactical errors.

The campaign was lost over five crucial weeks, between the last week of April and the end of May. Over this period, John Reid handed over to his successor Des Browne, and the former's crucial instruction that the mission not be expanded beyond its original remit was lost. A new CDS, Air Chief Marshal Jock Stirrup, took up office in the last week of April. At PJHQ the key post of Chief of Joint Operations was handed over to General Nick Houghton, who had just returned from Iraq and whose focus inevitably returned to that country. Indeed, over the period of Operation *Herrick 4*, the posts of defence secretary, Chief of the Defence

Staff, Deputy Chief of the Defence Staff, Chief of Joint Operations and Chief of the General Staff all changed. The only continuity was represented by Wall in his post as Deputy Chief of Joint Operations. The two senior officers in-country were not properly in the ring – General Richards was still waiting to assume command at the end of July, and Brigadier Butler was marginalized in Kabul and Kandahar, as well as by awful command and control arrangements. Four high-level visitors arrived in Helmand – Richards, Dannatt, Wall and Browne – but none was sufficiently alarmed to intervene. The key British government departments, the FCO and DfID, played weak and sometimes unhelpful roles. Margaret Beckett was appointed foreign secretary on 5 May, lasted one year, and was conspicuous by her absence and lack of engagement in Afghanistan. The British Embassy did not appear to engage at all in the unfolding disaster in Helmand. Hilary Benn, the international development secretary, visited Kabul once. When later pressed by the opposition to explain exactly what Britain had achieved with a reported expenditure of £400 million of aid in Afghanistan, he gave the astonishing reply that the 'information is not available and to obtain it would incur a disproportionate cost', a most arrogant *de haut en bas* put-down by a left-wing politician to British tax payers.[115] In Helmand, Governor Daoud was panicking, and in Kandahar General Freakley was fretting over British lack of fight. Karzai did not help matters. The British prime minister was battling to save his reputation from the fallout of the invasion of Iraq. A more toxic combination of characters and circumstances would be hard to imagine.

It would have taken great moral courage and imagination to stop the clock and rethink the strategy. These were not qualities absent in senior British officers, although Butler would, after the final withdrawal in 2014, allege a lack of moral and professional courage, as well as 'self-denial and self-deception'.[116] Certainly Ed Butler did not lack moral courage. But the campaign – or war more properly – had gained that quality that all wars gain very quickly: momentum. The unstoppable train of the next rotation could not be halted by the inconvenient fact of failure. The failure would have to be deepened before the strategy was re-thought. Remarkably, for the next three years, every succeeding brigadier inherited the original campaign plan, largely unchanged. The only thing to do was to go on. Waiting for Godot was hardly a worthwhile strategy, but in the absence of a campaign director as in past British counter-insurgency wars, this was what the British did.

The task force took decisions – against the uncertain panorama in which it found itself – which would have enduring consequences on every succeeding brigade. The district centres at Musa Qaleh, Now Zad and Sangin had been bitterly contested for no measurable reward. The conclusion drawn from this stalemate was not that British troops should withdraw from the district centres – as they ultimately would from Basra in Iraq – but rather that these buildings held iconic status and should be defended at all costs. To pull out would be to concede defeat. No matter that these might become urban Alamos – as in fact they became – the point was to demonstrate that the symbol of lawful authority in each of these towns was occupied by ISAF and its Afghan allies, and not by gun-toting bandits from the surrounding countryside. Having established security, reconstruction, it was argued, would surely follow. Three years later, a patrol leaving the district centre in Sangin to walk 800 metres to a satellite patrol base could take as long as 24 hours – such was the level of threat and hostility to British troops in some district centres. Whatever else was being achieved, neither security nor reconstruction was on the list.

In the end, all the task force managed to do was buy time for an unpopular governor, while constantly running the risk of running out of resources, faced by a resourceful enemy and suspicious civilian population. Brigadier Butler was clear that 'an Afghan solution to Afghan problems' was required – a mantra that would be repeated tirelessly by future commanders – but there was a near complete absence of Afghan solutions, just the problems. And buying time raised difficult questions. At what human cost? For just how long was a British government prepared to buy time for a bunch of venal local politicians, narcos, petty tribal leaders and outright criminals?

Despite this disastrous start, Brigadier Butler did not view Operation *Herrick 4* as a complete failure. In his view there was always going to be a fight and it would have been naïve to think otherwise. The fight – when it erupted – had been contained away from the two main population centres of Lashkar Gah and Gereshk. Highway 1 had become a de facto front line. The Taliban had been given a bloody nose, and 'footprints' had been established. The Musa Qaleh deal had been a good deal and possibly offered a blueprint for the future. These arguments supported what became the mythology of Operation *Herrick 4* – namely that the British had engaged in the necessary 'break-in' battle, laying foundations for future brigades to secure and develop Helmand. This reasoning was summarized by a returning officer who argued that it had been a particularly difficult operation, but the battlegroup had always expected a fight, and reconstruction would follow the spread of security.[117]

Butler bequeathed two important lessons to his successor. The first was that this was an Afghan war that Afghans should fight, not the British. The second was that the British task force had become static and fixed. Unfixing the force had to be managed as a matter of urgency. In Tootal's phrase, the British had to become 'dynamically unpredictable'. This task would fall to the marines.

4

Unfix the Force

Operation *Herrick* 5, October 2006–March 2007

Brigadier Jeremy ('Jerry') Thomas, the commander of 3 Commando Brigade, inherited a situation in Helmand that would not be repeated. There was no fighting in the province's two principal towns, Lashkar Gah and Gereshk. A truce had been negotiated in Now Zad. Another truce was called in Sangin, which would hold intermittently almost until the end of the brigade's tour. The British had withdrawn from Musa Qaleh and the town had been handed over to the elders. Only in the lawless north at Kajaki, and in the equally lawless south, in Garmsir, were the British facing an openly confrontational situation.

The chance to seek some sort of province-wide deal to capitalize on these truces and to restore calm was never pursued. London was still shell-shocked by the events of the summer. Foreign Secretary Margaret Beckett was mired in negotiating a withdrawal from Iraq and was paying insufficient attention to the supposed reconstruction operation in Afghanistan. Defence Secretary Des Browne was still struggling to get to grips with his portfolio. In Kabul, the British ambassador was about to be replaced. At Northwood, PJHQ was creaking under the pressure of running two wars.

In the army's own historical study of its long campaign in Northern Ireland a conclusion was drawn:

> The initial period after the arrival of a military force in a peace support or peace enforcement operation has been described as the 'honeymoon period'. That suggests that there is a period (variously given as 100 days or three months) in which to put things right. The term 'honeymoon

> period' is a misnomer. *It is not a honeymoon. It is the most important phase of the campaign.*[1]

That honeymoon period had been botched, but there was still a chance, in the autumn of 2006, to recover the situation.

In Afghanistan, nobody took responsibility for the campaign.[2] One of the lamentable features of the war was the manner in which labyrinthine and diffuse political and military command relationships abrogated commanders of ultimate responsibility, inhibiting anyone from showing leadership and seizing the war by the scruff of the neck, which it needed. It would take an American general, Stanley McChrystal, to demonstrate that leadership, but by the time he arrived in 2009, the ISAF mission had already spiralled out of control. In Helmand, the governor should have led the political process, but he proved weak and panicky. The sacked Akhundzada, who had been keeping the peace for five years, must have gloated at the chaos caused by his dismissal. Karzai, whose national leadership was provoking questions, never visited the province. The ISAF regional and national commanders were busy 'running the war'. British diplomacy was ineffectual. The notion of striking peace deals was not even on the cards.

Thomas was almost a perfect fit for the war in Helmand. Youthful and with a wide boyish grin, he epitomized the stereotype of the marine as 'thinking man's soldier'. One of a dwindling number of Falklands veterans, Thomas had subsequently alternated between command and intelligence posts. It was the experience he gained in the latter appointments that provided him with firm foundations for tackling the insurgency in Helmand. Intelligence is central to counter-insurgency wars and Thomas understood this intuitively. Indeed, the marines began to talk of Operation *Herrick* as an 'information operation' first, so struck were they by a near absence of reliable, ground truth intelligence. Of all the brigadiers that served in Helmand – along with Brigadier Andrew McKay, but for different reasons – Thomas held the most distinctive views on how to run a counter-insurgency war. This vision was not taken up. The winter of 2006 marked the single window when the British might have adopted a mobile warfare approach to the insurgency. After this period, it became a static slugfest and campaign of attrition.

In the mid-1990s, the British Army adopted a 'manoeuvrist' approach to warfare. The word did not even exist in the dictionary, which perhaps should have raised questions. The self-confessed author of the manoeuvrist approach was the Royal Engineer Mungo Melvin. After leaving the army with general rank (and, incidentally, becoming a fine military historian), he dismissed his own coinage as 'a load of old rubbish', adding, 'I should know, I made it up.'[3] But what did Melvin make up and why?

To understand the roots of 'manoeuvrism' (which also did not exist in common English), one had to go back to the first Gulf War (1990–91). This conflict proved a huge shock, and not just for potential foes. Just 16 years separated this war from the humiliating scenes of America's precipitous withdrawal from Saigon in 1975. Those who predicted American decline were totally confounded. The majesty, reach and technological superiority of America's armed forces were – to use an American term – awesome. In Britain, the war provoked torrents of military froth which would have pernicious effects, and not just in doctrine (the unreal and later abandoned Future Rapid Effects System (FRES), for example, had roots in this period).

During the war, Major Mungo Melvin served as 1st (UK) Armoured Division's G5 Plans lead. It was Melvin who undertook the operational analysis and ultimately devised the scheme for the British ground campaign. He later rose to become Director Land Warfare. The inspiration for 'manoeuvrism' came from the flimsiest linkage of the Coalition Force's wide flanking manoeuvre west of Kuwait City and Basil Liddell Hart's 'indirect approach'. The post-war British Army account of the war made this link explicit, with a lengthy quote from Hart's 1932 *The British Way in Warfare* prefacing the introduction.[4] Later in the document it stated, 'The plan relied heavily upon the indirect approach … Basil Liddell Hart described the concept, with some prescience, in 1932.' The facts, however, were different. A VII (US) Corps planning team convened in Germany in late November 1990, and the thoughts of Basil Liddell Hart were not on their minds. Unsurprisingly, the American plan was based on American doctrine: Fix-Isolate-Destroy (the Republican Guard). In effect, the British Army's account of the war painted a British veneer over what was actually an American plan.

The linkage was flimsy, anyway, because the Coalition Force was always going to mount a flanking manoeuvre (the plan was so obvious it was appearing in media articles, to the consternation of Central Command). And second, basing doctrine on the ideas of the eccentric, self-promoting Basil Liddel Hart was probably not wise. The 'indirect approach', a somewhat dubious concept, critics have argued, first appeared in *The British Way in Warfare*. Hart originally considered the 'circumnebular approach', but this would not sell. The 'indirect approach' proved a hit and publisher's dream, or as a biographer has put it, the phrase became his 'signature tune'.[5] What he actually meant is too involved to discuss here. Wavell, who was sympathetic to Hart, jokingly remarked, 'with your knowledge and brains and command of the pen, you could have written just as convincing a book called the Strategy of the Direct Approach'.[6]

Hart was an outstanding military historian (his accounts of the two world wars remain classics). The clarity and concision of his Edwardian English were envious, contrasting with the windy pomposity of the modern British Army's 'military speak'. He did offer valuable insights into strategy and tactics. Like all his generation, he was scarred by trench warfare and made an appeal for 'tank-pace warfare', as he described it. It was unfair that he was ultimately ignored and even snubbed by contemporaries. His ideas deserved better appreciation but not in the pretentious 'manoeuvrist approach to warfare'. Over and above these considerations there was the irony that when faced with a real war, the British Army abandoned the 'manoeuvrist approach' anyway – whatever it really meant, or what serving officers imagined it meant. Task Force Helmand became a fixed, static and dispersed force mired in attrition warfare – the very opposite of 'manoeuvrism'.

Whether or not Thomas consciously followed 'manoeuvrism' or was simply acting from pragmatic common sense, his brigade followed three simple principles: do not hold ground, do not get fixed and remain mobile. For Thomas, 'manoeuvrism' meant mobile warfare, in the classic sense, stripped of the many additional meanings added by later military doctrine authors, elaborating on Melvin's original coinage. Follow, in other words, the hard-won lesson of his predecessors and become 'dynamically unpredictable'. 3 Commando Brigade in 2006–07 would be the *only* British brigade to divide the campaign map into a series of manoeuvre boxes – every other brigade would carve up Helmand into static, battlegroup areas. Planting troops, like Roman legionnaires in isolated posts to ward off the barbarians, was not serving great purpose. Rather, it was leading to petty squabbles in the Green Zone (the fertile Helmand River Valley).

It was Thomas who coined the phrase 'courageous inactivity', three years before McChrystal coined the more famous phrase 'courageous restraint'. He understood that every needless bullet only served to stir the pond more. All tactical engagements favoured the enemy, whether or not the marines were able to give the gunmen a bloody nose, for the simple reason that every punch-up created further unrest and the impression of an ungovernable province. Killing the enemy could be entirely counter-productive, as every dead tribesman created another ten seeking revenge. The wisdom of this Royal Marine was not heeded by army successors. One of his subordinates, Lieutenant Colonel Matt Holmes, the commanding officer of 42 Commando, put it quite plainly. Body counts were pointless, he argued. The pool of available fighters was endless. If Task Force Helmand pursued an aggressive approach, it would only lead to strategic failure.[7]

Thomas's brigade was the first and last to view the war through this lens, with the exception of 52 Brigade under Brigadier Mackay. From the spring of 2007, collating enemy kill statistics – so reminiscent of the Vietnam body counts – became a feature of the campaign. However, this did not imply a defensive outlook on the part of the marines. 3 Commando Brigade would act in aggressive ways, although Thomas did not, at first, seek confrontation. There was no patrolling, as Holmes later observed, just for the sake of showing 'presence'.[8] Like Butler, he strongly argued this was an Afghan war that should be fought by Afghans. He also understood that the imposition of Western paradigms would never succeed in Afghanistan, but convincing others of this key point proved his biggest challenge. His brigade operations officer, a Major Lee, observed that Afghans simply did not conform to Western ideas, and any attempts to impose such ideas on them should be resisted.[9] Afghan solutions had to be found to Afghan problems. This advice was also disregarded, particularly by the PRT and the civilians who set about imposing Western constructs on Helmandis.

Thomas wrote his operational report in three parts – the only brigade commander to do so. The first part he authored before deploying to Helmand, setting down his ideas on what he thought the campaign was about. The second part he wrote mid-way through the tour. The last part he completed after the brigade had returned to Britain. In this regard he left behind a valuable record of a commander thinking through a problem without hindsight, as the events unfolded, and later with the benefit of reflection. It was unclear whether this marine's post-operational report was greatly read (or at all) by the army. Certainly, there was nothing in how the successor brigade acted that suggested his advice was taken.

Thomas arrived with a plan that was eminently sensible. 3 Commando Brigade would focus on development in the original ADZ (Afghan Development Zone) between Lashkar Gah and Gereshk. After all, this was the plan the British were supposed to be following. Concurrently, he would use mobile forces to interdict and keep off balance insurgents in the north and south of the province. Lastly, he would train up the ANA and ANP, a task that the predecessor brigade neglected and then was unable to address because it got caught up in the platoon house sieges. From the outset Thomas was clear that it was only by bringing the Afghans along that the British would be able to disengage. It was, in the end, an Afghan not British insurgency.

The plan unravelled for several reasons. First, Thomas was let down by the civilian agencies. In the polite euphemism used at the time, there was a 'developmental pause' in the British reconstruction effort in Helmand. Second, he was let down by the governors. Daoud was sacked and his replacement Assadullah Wafa proved corrupt and anti-British. Third, he was let down by the Afghan National Army. The single *kandak* (battalion) in 3/205 Brigade went AWOL en masse, leaving the marines as the only official military force in Helmand. A second untrained *kandak* was despatched from Kandahar, and it was to the commando's credit that by the end of the tour this new lot were taking part in combined operations. Fourth, he was let down by the intelligence, or its near absence. 3 Commando Brigade had set about with the intention of conducting precise, targeted, intelligence-led operations. It came as a shock to discover that intelligence was so thin the commandos had to collect information in the crudest of ways – by 'advancing into ambush', as the marines joked. Thus they began to refer to Operation *Herrick 5* as an 'information operation'. This lack of intelligence was exacerbated by the final departure of the Americans, on whose resources every ISAF contingent relied. Fifthly, he was let down by the Bowman radios. In the verdict of the brigade signals squadron: 'Terrain and frequency allocation/management has significantly degraded BOWMAN comms in Helmand for both H4 and H5. Due to the dryness of the desert terrain, HF and VHF comms have been unstable ... Man pack radios, restricted by terrain and real estate for antenna placements, have hindered any efforts to run and maintain an all informed 24hr BOWMAN Fires' net.'[10] Lastly, he was let down by the highly unrealistic and under-resourced British campaign plan. Thomas simply did not have sufficient troops to fulfil the ambitions of the Helmand Plan, even if the panorama had remained relatively benign. After deploying his marines to the British 'footprints', inherited from the paratroopers, he was left with just one company (an ad hoc India Company) to pursue the main mission in the ADZ.

Thomas welcomed the Musa Qaleh deal and hoped the same would happen in Now Zad. He reluctantly accepted the political impossibility of withdrawing from Sangin and understood the importance of securing Kajaki Dam. These tasks, along with holding the southern outpost at Garmsir, swallowed virtually his entire force.

The absence of worthwhile intelligence was inexcusable. In Iraq, the army commissioned retired Brigadier Ben Barry to undertake a candid assessment of the campaign's failures. His chapter on intelligence was damning. It opened with the sentence that there had been 'complete failure' in the four elements of the intelligence cycle: direction, collection, collation and dissemination. The subsequent official army report somewhat softened the language but even so concluded, 'Overall, it appears that the significant weaknesses in tactical intelligence and ISTAR [Intelligence, Surveillance, Target Acquisition and Reconnaissance] were an example of multiple failures to adapt resulting in a tactical intelligence capability that even after six years of the campaign had failed to establish many of the pillars of successful intelligence in previous COIN campaigns, including Malaya and Northern Ireland.'[11]

The root problem – across the army – was that nobody was in charge, still less responsible. Historically, the British had understood the importance of intelligence in counter-guerrilla warfare, as it was known. An intelligence director was appointed. A comprehensive, 'joined-up' intelligence structure was set up. The modern army seemed to throw this all away. Instead, in Helmand, intelligence was drained of leadership and continuity by the six-month deployment cycles. Each departing brigade haemorrhaged intelligence and left behind incomprehensible files abandoned by the new team who would duly re-invent collation and reporting systems.

There was no incentive to address this failure because it was being rewarded. In the past you faced dismissal; in the modern army, paradoxically, an unfortunate situation was manufactured where failure was being rewarded with promotions and gongs. Everybody 'jingled with trinkets' (medals), to invoke the wartime joke, from the repeated failures in Iraq and subsequently Afghanistan. The root reason did not lie with the army but rather in government spin. If the armed forces were 'delivering' – in the awful phrase of the period repeated by government ministers in Parliament – and if 'progress' was being made, as successive foreign secretaries insisted, then rewards were due. For a soldier of a previous generation it would have seemed astounding that not a single senior officer was sacked (and no minister resigned) in 'two wars' worth of mistakes', borrowing Anthony Cordesman's phrase.[12]

Three years later, when the task force mounted the major operation of the year (Operation *Panchai Palang*, summer 2009), the brigade intelligence officer wrote: 'I was horrified to discover that there were no historical files or documents for us to draw on other than a dated Danish CIMIC report.'* He added, 'This despite the fact that Babaji had been in our AO [area of operations] for over three years and at least two British operations had been conducted there before.' As a consequence, 'the commander and the BGs [battlegroups] had to operate with very significant gaps in their knowledge'. Such intelligence incompetence would have been unimaginable in the post-war counter-guerrilla campaigns of the British Army when, ironically, an Intelligence Corps did not exist, or only in rudimentary form,† as the organization had been dismantled at the end of World War II.

Perhaps the most egregious failure was witnessed at the end of the campaign. As the British withdrew it became apparent that thousands of secret documents and other materials could not be accounted for (a particular offender was PJHQ, which seemed a black hole for secrets). Potential embarrassment for the Intelligence Corps was acute. The defence secretary at the time (Michael Fallon) was not informed. Instead, the whole affair was hushed up.

As well as abandoning the 'manoeuvrist approach', the British also abandoned their counter-insurgency doctrine although Thomas (and later Mackay) would attempt to follow its dictates. British experience of 'small wars' over two centuries was second to none, so it was unsurprising this experience produced a significant body of official and unofficial literature on fighting insurgencies and rebellions. What emerged from this long history of small wars were three important principles: political primacy, minimum force and unity of effort. On all three counts, in Helmand, the British failed to follow their own doctrine. This collective amnesia recalled

*The observation was made by the SO2 J2 of Task Force Helmand Op *Herrick 10*. 'CIMIC' stands for 'Civil Military Cooperation'.

†The Intelligence Corps was properly re-constituted in 1956 after being run down following the end of the war. In typical British fashion, it was restricted to just 100 full regular commission career officers to cut costs. This cohort became known as the 'Hundred Club'. 'The Corps Renewed 1957–90' in Andrew Clayton, *Forearmed: A History of the Intelligence Corps*, Brassey's (UK) Ltd, 1993.

Wellington's observation that nobody in the British Army read doctrine, except as an amusing novel.

3 PARA's direct replacement in September 2006 was 42 Commando, commanded by Lieutenant Colonel Matt Holmes. The commando comprised four sub-units: Juliet, Kilo, Lima and Mike Companies. Over the course of the tour, 42 Commando would swell to 1,500 personnel and comprise 11 companies, including Danish and Estonian contingents. Lima Company, which arrived first, was deployed to Sangin (Operation *Platinum*). It was subsequently rotated through Camp Bastion and Now Zad, and finished the tour where it began, taking part in an operation to 'retake' Sangin. One company from the Rifles took over the responsibility for holding Sangin in their absence (in fact, C Company 2 Light Infantry, about to be amalgamated into the Rifles 'super-regiment'). Kilo Company was temporarily sent to the American–Danish base FOB Price, on the outskirts of Gereshk, before being relieved by Juliet Company. Kilo Company then redeployed to Now Zad, relieving the pressed Royal Fusiliers (Operation *Silica*). One troop was later sent to Kajaki. Juliet Company would remain at FOB Price for the remainder of the tour, a considerable luxury compared to the sub-units that were rotated between bases. Mike Company – the last to deploy – was kept at Camp Bastion as an immediate reserve known as the 'Ops One Company'. For the first two months, this company barely deployed: a reflection of the general truce that appeared to take hold over most areas of Helmand. One troop from this reserve company was deployed to take over Athens and Normandy OPs at Kajaki. It would only remain on the mountain for a month before being relieved by a troop from Kilo Company, which was itself relieved by Mike Company for the second half of the tour. Mike Company would subsequently relieve the Rifles company in Sangin, in late February (Operation *Platinum 2*).[13]

This detail matters because it is important to understand that although 3 Commando Brigade was numerically larger than the preceding deployment, which was essentially based around a single, reinforced battlegroup, the newcomers were not so numerically superior they could significantly change the pattern of dispositions laid down by their predecessors. Troop numbers were still far too low to cope with the geographical size of Helmand and the growing scale of the insurgency. ISAF was either demonstrating blind optimism or terrible complacency in its troop levels.

During the handover, Butler and Thomas had both agreed the most important military task was to 'unfix the force' and to restore mobility to the battlefield. The reality was that without a significantly larger force the British footprint would become fixed in a handful of locations, whatever Brigadier Thomas's intentions. An additional Rifles company was committed to holding Now Zad; Whiskey Company from 45 Commando became the force protection company for 28 Engineer Regiment; and India Company made up from 'odds and sods' in 45 Commando became the protection company for Lashkar Gah. Only Zulu Company was truly available to undertake mobile operations, and it was quickly sucked into holding the town of Darvishan in the south.

In the end, the sum total gain from deploying all of 3 Commando Brigade, less 40 Commando, was to take over responsibility for one more besieged outpost: Darvishan in Garmsir. Politicians struggled to understand this hard arithmetic of military force. They saw and announced the headline figures of another thousand troops and appeared to believe (or wanted to believe) this implied more results, and success. For the first half of the war in Helmand, this was the self-deluding trap of British governments.

Thomas hoped for the possibility of a withdrawal from at least some of the northern platoon houses but this was dependent on Daoud striking some sort of political deal with the tribes. Daoud's capital had become exhausted and in December he was replaced by a 70-year-old, non-English-speaking governor called Assadullah Wafa, who proved a disastrous replacement. The corrupt Wafa seemed to arrive with an antipathy for Westerners as a result of his experience as governor of Kunar Province, where an American air strike had resulted in the deaths of a large number of civilians. He made little effort to cooperate with the British and on occasions he demonstrated outright hostility towards what he viewed as outside interference in Afghan affairs. Thomas's other vain hope was that reconstruction would take off. DfID disappointed again, leaving the commandos with little to offer but empty promises.

The first decision Brigadier Thomas took was to end the ineffective command arrangements that had hobbled the paratroopers. The entire brigade headquarters was ordered to pack up and move to Lashkar Gah (Operation *Fossil*). It took about three weeks to shift everyone from Kandahar, with the paucity of available transport, but the disruption was worth the trouble. Until almost the end of the campaign, Lashkar Gah would remain the location of the British task force HQ, with Camp Bastion about 20 kilometres to the west acting as the logistic hub. Kandahar Air Base would remain the centre of air operations for Regional

Command South, with a smaller army presence. The move to Lashkar Gah meant that the military staff would now be co-located with the civilians working in the PRT, headed by David Slinn, an ex-ambassador with Kosovo experience. Slinn was part of the wider 'Kosovo crowd' that had gravitated to the rich pickings of Afghanistan. Unfortunately, their intellectual baggage of templates and stabilization concepts were not transferable from a European to central Asian country. This did not deter them from attempting to do exactly that anyway.

Who exactly was in charge – at least in Thomas's mind – remained an open question. Within the so-called Afghan Development Zone – essentially the areas surrounding Lashkar Gah and Gereshk – he felt the PRT should take the lead. Outside this zone, the military should take the lead.[14] In practice, the civilians were providing no leadership at all, and the military were predictably filling the vacuum. This ambiguity would bedevil the British war in Helmand for years: there was no political primacy, still less unity of effort, two of the cardinal principles of counter-insurgency. Strictly, the senior civil servant in Afghanistan, the British ambassador, was the government's senior representative, and he or she therefore out-ranked all military officers. But the ambassador was based in Kabul, so powers were delegated on a day-to-day basis to the PRT leader, Britain's senior civil servant in Helmand. However, practically no meaningful reconstruction was taking place; the Afghan Development Zone was a hollow phrase. This inaction could not last forever. In fact, it only lasted about two months by which time the military resumed aggressive operations. The lack of urgency of the civilians was almost inevitably overtaken by the dynamism of the marines. This would be the story of 3 Commando Brigade. It would be a tour of two halves, with the first half dominated by tenuous truces, and the second by a series of aggressive operations that started with a bang in January and would see the marines mounting operations right across north and south Helmand.

There was another reason why the marines' tour presented this somewhat schizophrenic aspect. Thomas's espousal of 'courageous inactivity' was a complete anathema to the Americans. Much like Butler, he found himself under pressure to 'do something', with bullets preferably. This urge to action was compounded by ISAF, now led by the Dutch, who for reasons of national prestige also felt compelled to demonstrate resolve.[15] Squeezed between these two actors demanding action, and without support from a disengaged Whitehall, the marines duly obliged by doing what they do best – fighting.

Before these pressures mounted, Thomas turned his attention to the original mission, as laid out in the Helmand Plan. This was to support reconstruction and development in the Helmand ADZ. There was little happening in the way of reconstruction. However, in one town, Gereshk, existing infrastructure appeared to be under threat. Gereshk was Helmand's commercial hub, and although it would never be seriously threatened by insurgents, the reported presence of lawless groups on the outskirts of the town could not be ignored. Of special concern was a hydroelectric dam on the Nahr-e Bughra Canal just 2 kilometres north-east of the town which provided electricity for Gereshk. The corrupt ANP who guarded this dam were constantly being sniped at by Barakzai villagers, and it was decided to establish a better protected, permanent presence by building two PVCPs (Permanent Vehicle Checkpoints) about 350 metres north of the canal on the main track leading into Gereshk. Ironically, this was exactly where the Russians had also built a security post, which the locals naturally remembered.

Operation *Slate 1*, as it was called, was mounted on 5 November and involved Whiskey Company as well as engineers from 42 Squadron.[16] The group left FOB Price early in the morning in a package of 16 Vikings and Pinzgauers and arrived at the dam as dawn was breaking. It was not long before the first mortar bombs began landing. What followed was a pattern that would be repeated many times over the years wherever engineers set about building security force bases. The locals would attempt to disrupt the work by sniping and firing mortars or rockets, and the British would retaliate with even more firepower.

This particular gun battle lasted 12 hours – as long as it took the sappers to complete the structures, despite the fire directed at them. By the end of the day one policeman had been killed and the marines reckoned they killed over 20 gunmen.[17] Apache and fighter aircraft had been used to suppress the enemy. The fighting, however, did not stop there, with Mike and Juliet Companies both involved in helping Whiskey Company extract back to FOB Price. The entire operation took over 24 hours to complete; one Viking was destroyed and two marines were wounded. It may have amazed the marines who took part in this first operation to know that six years later the front line would be exactly where they had left it.

Following the success of this mission, it was decided to mount Operation *Slate 2*. This involved Mike Company, used to protect the engineers as they built a PVCP immediately south of the town overlooking a bridge on Highway 1 known as Tom (the other two bridges in the area were predictably known as Dick and Harry). As in the first operation, the marines came under mortar fire, which on this occasion was so accurate that it was attributed to a Pakistani trainer. For the next two months Gereshk remained relatively quiet. Juliet Company mounted a cordon and search mission east of Gereshk (Operation *Castella*), but this yielded little. As long as the marines did not provoke the locals, then it seemed the latter mostly ignored the marines. The dead chill of the Afghan winter may also have contributed to this lull in fighting.

For the marines in Lima Company based at Sangin, the daily routine involved making improvements to the base, rather than gun battles with the locals. The truce negotiated at the end of 3 PARA's tour held for two months, by which time the marines handed over to C Company, 2 Light Infantry.* This company would be confined to FOB Jackson and forbidden to patrol in an effort to defuse tensions. This time was used to try to build relations with the town elders, but with little to offer, British promises sounded hollow (there was no FCO or DfID representation in Sangin, and the marines were not allocated funds to pursue reconstruction projects themselves). It was another wasted opportunity and a failure of the civil half of the British mission in Helmand. Over the next three months, the light infantrymen continued to improve the defences of the Sangin district centre and suffered just two ineffectual attacks (the elders assured the soldiers the attacks had not been perpetrated by the 'Taliban' but by some disgruntled locals). The same locals also attempted to encourage the British to leave by cutting off their water supply, without result. In the same way that the marines were unable to make any progress, so the soldiers found themselves essentially holding a fort in the middle of a hostile population and with nothing to offer to that population. All of this could have been avoided or at least defused. Trouble had brewed in Sangin for many months even without the British presence. Addressing the basic grievances of the townspeople (and the grievances in Now Zad and Musa Qaleh) was never attempted.

*Which was about to be amalgamated in the Rifles 'super regiment' of five battalions.

The departure of Lima Company from Sangin did not mean the marines had entirely vacated this volatile part of northern Helmand. In December, Whiskey Company from 45 Commando was deployed to FOB Robinson, 5 kilometres south of the town, alongside a troop of light guns from 29 Commando Regiment Royal Artillery. It was actually Thomas's hope that all British troops might then be pulled out of Sangin and be based at Robinson, where their presence would not provoke so much hostility. Had this plan been followed through, it may be observed, Task Force Helmand would have saved itself over 100 fatalities and countless amputees. Another sensible proposal was thwarted by unhelpful political interference, and American hostility to perceived British withdrawals. Ironically, this attitude would rebound spectacularly when US Marines eventually assumed responsibility for Sangin, suffering terrible losses themselves.

The marines would remain at FOB Robinson with the task of carrying out intelligence-gathering patrols in the Green Zone, establishing a pattern that would mark future British operations. The justification for these patrols – that they provided an opportunity to gather low-level intelligence and gauge the 'atmospherics' – in practice meant finding out how hostile the mainly Ishaqzai villagers were feeling on any particular morning. Whiskey Company encountered this hostility on its very first patrol mounted in the New Year (Operation *Magma*). The 'atmospherics' were as ghastly as the phrase itself. The company was surrounded by gunmen, the Bowman radios failed, making control exceedingly difficult, and 160 artillery shells (as well as support fire from Apaches and F-18s) were required to extract the marines safely. By the end of the afternoon the atmosphere smelt of gunpowder, rather than the illusory perfume of 'hearts and minds'.

While Whiskey Company was discovering the reality of the 'atmospherics' in the Upper Gereshk Valley, Mike Company finally withdrew from Kajaki, having been relieved by Kilo Company, and in turn prepared to relieve the light infantrymen holed up in Sangin District Centre since November. The relief was only intended to be short term to make up a gap before the imminent deployment of a company from the Royal Regiment of Fusiliers to Sangin (Operation *Platinum 3*). The marines of Mike Company could not have guessed how unlucky this decision would be. The handover took place in late February, and almost as soon as the last grateful soldier left the base on the last Chinook, another round of fighting erupted in Sangin. The sudden flare-up was almost certainly connected to the US-led Operation *Achilles*. Like *Mountain*

Thrust and *Medusa* (the two major operations in the preceding tour), *Achilles* was another example of quite futile and ultimately self-defeating attempts to clear entire districts of 'Taliban'. The only and predictable outcome of these operations was to stir anger among the tribes and boost insurgent recruiting. The British part of *Achilles* would be the 'recapture' of Sangin, a town that did not need recapturing, just good governance. It seems Thomas was entirely against the notion of attacking Sangin but was overruled by ISAF politics. Knowledge that the operation was about to take place was widespread. It appears probable the townspeople associated the arrival of the marines with the start of the operation, and it was this that provoked the fighting. Recapturing Sangin, in this sense, became a necessary self-fulfilling prophecy.

The intensity of the attacks, which lasted about two weeks, a usual period before ammunition stocks depleted, surprised the marines of Mike Company. There were literally hundreds of gun battles in early March as well as unpredictable mortar and rocket attacks. The fact that the locals' marksmanship was abysmal offered little relief – the tribesmen had completely failed to kill a single British soldier in Sangin since the preceding September – but the arithmetic of chance was such that eventually they would get lucky.

The luck turned against the marines on the fourth day of the attacks, when a mortar bomb landed on the three-storey Fire Support Group Tower, lacerating one of the marines with shrapnel. This was the tallest building in the base, and it was inevitably used as an aiming mark. The marines could not abandon the sangars built on the roof of the building because this would allow the insurgents to draw even closer to the base. Their only option was to hunker down and hope. Manning the tower required great reserves of nerve and never more so than in the first week of March, when the townspeople made a concerted effort to oust the company from the base. A few days after the successful mortar hit on the tower roof, an RPG struck one of the sangars, instantly killing a lance bombardier and mortally wounding a second. The casualties continued to mount after a grenade attack claimed two more marines, both seriously wounded. Then a double strike with grenades and RPGs claimed the life of a sergeant major, Mick Smith, who had been sent as a relief for the two killed lance bombardiers, and seriously wounded another marine. The popular sergeant major who made a strong impression on the marines with his courage under fire was hit in the face by a grenade and stood no chance. Mike Company had now suffered seven casualties in as many days, and the intensity of the attacks did not seem to diminish.

The gunmen, however, were not having it all their own way. As well as facing aerial attacks, the troop of 105mm light guns based at FOB Robinson, just 6 kilometres away, had also wreaked considerable destruction on the areas of the town adjoining the base which the gunmen were using for cover. The main bazaar was entirely abandoned and derelict. The 'Pipe Range' – the main track leading to the base – had suffered extensive damage. And the locals – inevitably under such a weight of counter-fire – had begun to suffer significant casualties. Throughout the offensive the marines were able to monitor enemy chat using their ICOM scanners. It was evident from the intercepts that the townspeople had had enough. Like the paratroopers before them, the marines had held the district against sustained attack and demonstrated the British could not be dislodged. This would be the last such deliberate and sustained attack against a major British base. For the rest of the war the insurgents would switch tactics, avoid head-on confrontations and opt instead to fix the British with sniping and IEDs. At the end of the first week of March, as if it had only been a passing storm, the attacks ended and Mike Company handed over to C Company of the Royal Regiment of Fusiliers. The Fusiliers would suffer no fatalities or significant attacks during their tenure at the base, confirming that the gunmen had been exhausted attempting to dislodge Mike Company from Sangin District Centre.

The two-week assault on the district centre had, nonetheless, rattled the brigade staff. With Operation *Silver* imminent (the British part of *Achilles*), Brigadier Thomas could have been forgiven for the naïve hope that this deeply hostile town could realistically be cleared of troublemakers; the idea was as far-fetched as clearing Londonderry or West Belfast of Irish nationalists. Sangin was a town in revolt. Everybody knew somebody involved in the insurgency. If the locals were not actively attacking the British, they at least sympathized with the gunmen. All that would be achieved in an outright assault on the town would be more destruction. The gunmen would be driven underground for a brief period, but the resistance would re-seed and grow back like a weed.

The size of the town alone was a problem. Sangin sprawled over 16 square kilometres – an area that required at least a brigade-sized force, which Brigadier Thomas did not have. Operation *Silver* would have to concentrate on the town centre and ignore the outlying areas.

It was only possible to mount the operation thanks to the arrival of Task Force 1 Fury, a reinforced battalion of American paratroopers from 82nd Airborne Division.

Operation *Silver* was the largest operation undertaken by 3 Commando Brigade. It involved all of 42 Commando, C Squadron of the Light Dragoons, an Estonian mechanized company and a Dutch armoured reconnaissance squadron. The main assaulting force was provided by the American Task Force 1 Fury, pushing into Sangin from the south, using Route 611 as the axis of advance. C Company of the Royal Fusiliers acted as the anchor and held the district centre throughout these manoeuvres. The fire support was intensive. Artillery sub-units included: 28/143 Battery (Tombs's Troop), 127 (Dragon) Battery, an American light gun battery, a battery of Canadian 155mm guns and the commando's mortars.

While the marines undertook clearances of the north-east area of the town, the paratroopers of Task Force 1 Fury pushed north along Route 611, effectively squeezing the insurgents out of the town centre. The entire operation took four days, and by the time it was called off Sangin was a deserted and badly damaged town, especially around the central bazaar where the strongest resistance had been encountered. Operation *Silver* was judged to have succeeded, but its success recalled the Vietnam saying, 'We had to destroy the village in order to save it.' Sangin had joined Now Zad, Musa Qaleh and Darvishan as a trashed and half-deserted town. In the eyes of the marines, success was simply measured by the number of times they were attacked on a daily basis. Before Operation *Silver* the district centre had been attacked four to five times daily. Following the conclusion of the operation, a more tolerable average of two daily attacks was recorded.

In the far north, a quite different tale unfolded. The story of the marines' occupation of Kajaki became a paradigm of the stalemate that followed. All the British casualties at Kajaki were self-inflicted either from straying into minefields, as the paratroopers had done, or from accidents (including a fratricide incident that resulted in three deaths), or from aggressive and ultimately fruitless actions undertaken by the British to clear the Alizai villages north of the dam. Once these actions were over, the de facto front line simply re-established itself, more or less where it previously ran. The raw fact was that the British never had the numbers to do more than hold the dam itself, and the villagers in the surrounding area were so hostile – probably from their experiences with the Soviet Army – that reconciliation was impossible. Militarily, the best the British could hope to achieve was to arrange the front line so that it suited them and not the hostile tribes. This was achieved by 3 Commando Brigade and was an important legacy the marines bequeathed to successor brigades.

In October, when the marines first took over responsibility for the dam, they were only able to deploy one troop for its defence. This troop occupied the two OPs on the eastern side of the mountain overlooking the dam – Athens and Normandy – as well as the FOB next to the dam. The obvious first task was to occupy the western half of the mountain, not an easy task on a bald rocky feature with the ever-present threat of Russian mines (indeed, this was the only vital task, as once the entire mountain was in British hands, the tribesmen could not hope to seriously threaten the dam as all approaches were visible from the mountain). However, the marines were so stretched they would be unable to undertake this task until the beginning of January, when an entire company – Mike Company – was deployed to Kajaki to permanently occupy the western positions.

Several operations followed: *Clay*, at the beginning of the year, to clear the area surrounding Tangye village immediately west of the dam; *Volcano*, at the end of January, to clear Barikju village; and *Kryptonite*, in mid-February, to clear Chinah and Shemali Ghulbah. The aerial support mustered to support these operations was lavish. Major Lucas, the battery commander for 42 Commando Group, recalled, 'One company group operation in KAJAKI had a Nimrod MR2, a B1B bomber, 2 F16s, 2 AH [Apache attack helicopters], mini-UAV and mortars in support, all of which made for a very busy and dynamic battlespace.'[18]

Kilo Company then took over and mounted the last operation in the area, *Knight*, which kicked off on 6 March. The aim was to clear the last two villages in the local area – Machi Kheyl and Bagar Kheyl – suspected of harbouring insurgents. The problem for the marines was that it was evident civilians were also still present in the villages. The marines of Kilo Company would either fight to clear the villages, or if it became apparent the insurgents had fled, they would attempt to engage with the locals. This double and contradictory mission would, in the event, prove too ambitious.

The plan was simple but risky. The company tactical HQ would be set up on 'caves and shrine hill', an area from which both villages could be observed. A fire support group would then establish a gun line south of the easternmost village, Machi Kheyl, while two troops would approach Bagar

Kheyl from the south following a track that ran past a cemetery. The track would act as a boundary for the two troops. Overhead, Kilo Company would be protected by a pair of Apaches and two USN F-15s. The Kilo Company commander – Major Sutherland – also had a Desert Hawk UAV feeding imagery to his tactical HQ. The risk lay in a 200-metre stretch of open and slightly rising ground which the marines would have to cross before reaching the village. H-Hour was set at daybreak, and with none of the aircraft or UAV sensors detecting the presence of enemy, the marines were ordered forward to the first set of compounds at the southern edge of Bagar Kheyl.

They reached within sprinting distance of the village when the entire front seemed to erupt with gunfire. In fact, the company had long been spotted by sentries who demonstrated good fire discipline and waited until the last moment before opening fire on the advancing marines. Marine Benjamin Reddy was killed, and a second wounded (hit by three rounds in the chest which were stopped by the body armour). The surviving marines went to ground and spent the next hour trying to extricate themselves from the fire-swept fields south of the village. They finally managed to find dead ground, and a pair of Apaches were used to attack the suspected insurgent firing points. This allowed the marines to resume the assault, but they found the intricate maze of walls and compounds difficult to negotiate and potentially hazardous. Two more marines were shot attempting to enter a compound, and it became clear that clearing Bagar Kheyl was going to prove a tough fight.

Over the course of the day Kilo Company found numerous tunnels and rat runs that the gunmen were using to evade their pursuers, and there were several lucky escapes, with armed individuals suddenly appearing out of nowhere in the midst of the assaulting marines. As the day progressed, the extent of the defences became 'horrifyingly clear' with a tunnel system running the entire length of the village.[19] Many of these over-excited defenders paid with their lives. By midday both sides were calling for reinforcements – a platoon from the Rifles joined the fight from 'caves and shrine hill', and more villagers were detected moving south. By early afternoon it was decided to end the operation, which was concluded with a significant aerial bombardment of suspected insurgent positions. Kilo Company claimed that it killed about 40 gunmen – almost certainly a gross exaggeration – but it also suffered four casualties, including the single fatality.

The marines judged Operation *Knight* a success. Their superior training and tactics had demonstrably been the difference between the two sides. Insurgent activity in the area declined in the immediate aftermath of the operation. But this was the very point which the British never reconciled satisfactorily. The short interludes in the fighting that followed a British clearance operation had no long-term significance. Like the reservoir of water the marines were protecting, the levels of fighting merely rose again with the next rainfall of weapons and recruits. Bagar Kheyl was never cleared of insurgents. It was destroyed, deserted by civilians and eventually re-occupied by insurgents. The same was true of every other village in the area. Six years later, when US Marines were based at Kajaki, the two sides were still fighting over exactly the same ring of villages 42 Commando had 'cleared'. The front line had moved not a jot.

Fifty kilometres to the west, the other half of Kilo Company took over responsibility for the town of Now Zad. The situation here was frankly awful. The town was partially destroyed and abandoned. A Company of 1 Royal Fusiliers had just endured the longest siege in living memory in appalling conditions. Determined to renew negotiations, a truce was arranged with the town elders. This only lasted about three weeks but it did allow some clearance of the war damage in the bazaar. After that the marines found themselves in exactly the same position as the Royal Fusiliers. A front line ran along a wadi about a kilometre east of the town. All the ground east of this wadi belonged to a hostile local population, and all the ground west – effectively Now Zad town – was no man's land. The British dominated the ground as far as their weapon ranges. There were frequent sniping and mortar attacks on the base, and despite Kilo Company's best intentions no substantial progress was made other than some token Cash for Works projects clearing debris from the town centre.

For two months the marines resisted provocation, but in the end the temptation to take the fight to the locals proved too strong. On 8 December, Kilo Company mounted a large fighting patrol on the edge of the front line, to the north-east of the town. A day-long gun battle ensued, in which Corporal Hewett was awarded a Military Cross for leading his section out of a precarious situation. The patrol achieved nothing except to whet the appetite of the marines for another confrontation. On 12 December they set out again, and this time the patrol went badly awry, with a Marine Richard Watson, a 23-year-old from Caterham, receiving a serious gunshot wound from which he later died. The patrol was aborted and, once again, nothing was achieved. For the locals, these patrols were intolerable infringements of the front line. For the marines, the patrols were justified as a demonstration of British resolve to patrol. The truth was that without greater numbers – and reportedly the Russians had deployed a battalion to this area – the marines could not hope to substantially change the status quo in Now Zad. Like the stalemate at Kajaki, aggressive British patrolling was simply a way of causing self-inflicted casualties. In January, Kilo Company was relieved by Lima Company and the game went on, without resolution.

To fulfil Brigadier Thomas's vision of mobile warfare – or 'unfixing the force' – a new, composite unit had to be created. This task fell to Juliet Company based at FOB Price. The idea of creating desert 'flying columns' appears to have been mooted by Brigadier Butler – perhaps unsurprisingly given his SAS background – but without the troops to create such a force, the idea largely remained on the drawing board. Tootal actually did create a prototype MOG (which initially stood for Manoeuvre Outreach Group) using the Patrols Platoon, half a squadron from the HCR and an Estonian platoon. This grouping was used with some success on several operations. The credit for getting the idea off the drawing board, however, must go to Brigadier Thomas and his marines. The re-founded MOG was re-labelled a Mobile Operations Group. The supposition that ordinary Helmandis were sitting in villages waiting for the friendly arm of an outreach group was wishful thinking. The latter title was the accurate description of what the MOGs were and did.

A MOG comprised a group of about 40 vehicles, which included artillery, mortars, an electronic warfare team, a mortar locating radar and a UAV detachment. Repair and recovery vehicles and a medical team were also included in the package. Heavy weapons were provided by the Fire Support Groups mounted in Vikings and Land Rover WMIKs. In the words of Major Murchison:

> A MOG is simply 'Manoeuvre' and 'Patrolling' in the enemy's backyard. Initially, the primary task was to gain intelligence on the environment and Taliban activity, however, MOG ops increasingly were to relieve pressure, albeit temporarily on the fixed locations, demonstrate resolve, dominate key terrain, interdict lines of communication, so disrupting Taliban activity, whilst remaining configured to destroy opportune targets that interfered with the Mission.[20]

After leaving Price, a MOG could stay out in the desert for two to three weeks before returning to base to resupply. It was classic, World War II raiding.

In practice, 'mogging', as it became known, became an 'advance to contact'. The MOG would establish a desert leaguer, then the manoeuvre group (WMIKs and Vikings) would probe the edge of the Green Zone to test the reaction of the locals. Invariably, the reaction was hostile. Major Murchison recalled that on *every occasion* (author's emphasis) they attempted to enter the Green Zone, they were shot at.[21] Over the course of the winter, Juliet Company would become involved in dozens of gun battles conducting MOG operations. The obvious conclusion to draw from this reception was that the British had provoked a rural insurrection in Helmand Province. This conclusion, however, never seems to have been drawn. Instead, a 'Taliban' narrative continued to inform official reporting, even though the everyday experience of the marines was one of universal tribal hostility to the British presence. This should not have surprised. After the violence of the summer, the appearance of British troops only meant one thing to Helmandis, and it was not 'hearts and minds' or the promise of aid and reconstruction.

The MOG would, on occasions, be augmented by the Brigade Reconnaissance Force (BRF), as well as by C Squadron of the Light Dragoons. These Geordie cavalrymen were initially met with some scepticism by the marines until they realized their worth. Led by a Major Ben Warrack, the Light Dragoons proved imaginative and enterprising. Like the marines, Warrack found that any intrusion into the Green Zone inevitably led to gun battles. A typical sequence of events would see women and children leaving the area and young men arriving on the scene, drawn like 'moths to a light'. Within an hour the hedgerows would be echoing with the sound of gunfire. Appreciating that he was involved in a cat-and-mouse game against an elusive foe, Major Warrack used ruses and feints to draw out the gunmen, on one occasion staging a fake IED strike to provoke them into revealing their positions. The cavalrymen also rode their luck. On one occasion, an insurgent fired an RPG at point-blank range at a Scimitar. Somehow, the warhead passed between the commander's and gunner's heads. The shocked crew returned fire with the turret machine gun and also missed. On another occasion, a Scimitar suffered an RPG strike that fortunately only caused relatively minor injuries to the crew, who continued to fight on from their vehicle until rescued. The Light

Dragoons would end their tour without suffering any fatalities, a testament to their luck, but also to their canniness. Despite the rundown state of their vehicles, they managed to spend over 100 days on the move and reckoned that they covered 3,000 miles. Tens of thousands of rounds were expended in scores of gun battles.

3 Commando Brigade had inherited six 'footprints' from the paratroopers, all in the centre or north of Helmand: the Lashkar Gah PRT; FOBs Price and Robinson near Gereshk and Sangin respectively; Sangin District Centre; the police station at Now Zad; and Kajaki Dam. It was clear, however, that a sixth location would have to be invested. Fifty kilometres south of Lashkar Gah sat the town of Darvishan in Garmsir District. The town itself was little more than a one-street bazaar located between the Helmand River and a prominent canal, but its location made it all-important to controlling the southern half of Helmand Province. A small OMLT led by the Royal Irish had been deployed to Darvishan during 3 PARA's deployment, and they had found a suspicious town in an area threatened by insurgents. Before the arrival of the Royal Irish, a Taliban gang had taken over the town and reportedly raised the Pakistani Jamiat-e Ulema flag, suggesting ISI involvement, before being kicked out.[22]

Darvishan sat at the head of a lozenge-shaped area of fertile land about 15 kilometres long and 10 kilometres wide. To the west of the town was a rocky desert plateau which ran into the Dasht-e Margo, the 'Desert of Death'. To the east of the town was the sandy Registan Desert. A gravel track following the west bank of the Helmand River, Route 605, connected Darvishan to the capital Lashkar Gah. North of Darvishan a thin Green Zone belt followed the course of the river and its matrix of American-built canals, gradually widening near the provincial capital. South of Darvishan the cultivated belt narrowed again, closely hugging the dwindling river across a wild and desperately poor area. About 70 kilometres south of Darvishan the river kinked sharply to the west in an area the marines would nickname the 'Fish Hook' because of its shape. If you carried on driving south for another 120 kilometres across the barren desert you would reach the Chaghai Hills and the Durand Line, the border with Pakistan, not recognized by Afghanistan. South of this border was Baluchistan, a troubled region.

A traveller transiting either south or north through this part of Helmand would naturally be drawn to Darvishan. It was the only substantial settlement in a hundred-kilometre radius of otherwise uninhabited desert. This barrenness was recent, perhaps only a few centuries old. A string of old forts and scores of ruins testified to a fertile belt of land that had since turned dry. Hundreds of desert tracks now converged on the town from all points of the compass, most lasting no more than a season before being wiped away by sandstorms and the annual winter rainfall. When the British turned up at Darvishan it was mostly a smuggler's transit point, and a natural stopover point for fighters travelling north from Pakistan. During the Soviet–Afghan War this route had gained in importance, eventually dragging Helmand into a war that had mostly been confined to Kandahar. The population was very mixed: around a third was Noorzai, and a quarter was Alikozai. Andars represented a substantial minority. In addition to these three principal tribes there were at least another 15 tribal groups, including Ishaqzai, Alizai, Achekzai, Uzbeks, Tajiks and Hazaras. The small team of Royal Irish deployed to the town became holed up in a dilapidated agricultural college that was subsequently renamed FOB Delhi. About 10 kilometres to the south-west of the town was a second base, FOB Dwyer, where a gun line was established.

Darvishan desperately needed reinforcements, and these were initially based around the BRF and a MOG made up from Zulu Company. The BRF's first task was to find out more about the area. British intelligence on southern Helmand could be written on one side of paper. The marines even lacked mapping, which prevented them from extending their patrols much beyond Darvishan. Operations were also limited by the availability and range of helicopters. Given that the BRF was getting into gunfights whenever it approached the Green Zone (in the end it would be involved in 72 fights), nobody wanted to take the risk of suffering a serious casualty in this remote and inaccessible area.[23] These fighting patrols continued for about two months, supported by the Light Dragoons, before a decision was taken to push the insurgents away from the town and reinforce the small British force with a permanent company deployment. This would involve holding an artificial hillock known as JTAC Hill overlooking the 250-metre-long bridge that spanned the river on the west side of the town (JTAC was named after the Joint Terminal Attack Controllers, who used this high ground as a vantage point), as well as a checkpoint in the centre of the town, and an eastern checkpoint overlooking the canal at a bridge (later christened 'Balaklava Bridge'). At the bottom of the canal, under the bridge, was a rusting Russian armoured car, evidence of previous fighting in this area.

The plan to clear Darvishan was unimaginative, under-resourced and bound to end in failure.[24] On 5 December, Zulu Company broke camp in the desert and entered Darvishan in darkness. C Company of the Light Dragoons, comprising 16 Scimitars, remained on the flank on the western side of the river, and a section of Vikings was despatched to the eastern flank alongside the canal. Overall command of the operation was vested in Colonel Magowan, the commanding officer of the IX Group (Information Exploitation Group). As dawn broke, Zulu Company was ordered to advance in line, across a 1,000-metre frontage, much like soldiers on a World War I battlefield.

For the next 12 hours Zulu Company became locked in an unwinnable tussle over a few hundred square metres of muddy fields. Despite artillery fire, as well as support from a pair of Apaches and a Harrier GR9, the villagers held their line and even began to threaten to outflank the marines. At a critical moment a USN F-18 strafed the enemy positions and accidentally killed Marine Jonathan Wigley. Wigley had joined the Royal Marines at the age of 17. He died a 21-year-old, his entire short adult life dedicated to the service. A second marine almost had his arm ripped off by a cannon shell. This signalled the end of the assault. What began as an attempt to clear the enemy from the area south of Darvishan became a casualty evacuation exercise. Zulu Company eventually made it back to FOB Delhi, then spent the night under constant mortar fire from the irate insurgents. The remaining locals in Darvishan fled the town, turning it into a ghost town. The whole operation had been a disaster, and a second Now Zad had been created. It would be over a year before the locals had the confidence to return.

While Zulu Company mulled over its next move in Darvishan, the BRF had been sent 20 kilometres to the south to raid a collection of compounds in a village called Koshtay. There were actually two Koshtays within 1,500 metres of each other. The area identified from signals and aerial intelligence as the insurgent base was roughly between the two Koshtays near a canal. The problem for the marines was that the only approach to Koshtay was across the Helmand River.

Operation *Talisker* – as the mission was called – was the most audacious raid carried out by the marines during their tour and was reminiscent of classic commando raids.[25] As the marines had no boats, it was decided to swim the 100-metre-wide river, despite the fact that at this time of year the waters were icy. This would involve stripping off at the home bank, wading across the river with equipment floated as improvised rafts, and then dressing again on the far bank. On the return journey the procedure would have to be repeated. The raid was conducted in the early hours of the morning on 10 January, and to avoid detection just one troop crossed the river. This group then had to cross over 2 kilometres of broken and boggy ground, in complete darkness, before reaching an observation position near a sluice gate by a canal, about 250 metres short of the suspected insurgent compound.

The marines reached this point at about 0400hrs. Two snipers were then tasked to shoot sentries seen on the MX-15 surveillance camera of a Nimrod MR2 supporting the raid. Although the raid commander Captain Milne had no visual downlink, he did have radio communications with the aircraft. The gunfire awakened the area, and Milne decided to play his trump card straight away: 12,000 pounds of high explosives dropped in one pass from a USAF B-1B. The British were culturally coy about firepower, and sometimes criticized their American ally on this score, except when it suited them. The fact was that no British aircraft could simultaneously drop this amount of GPS-guided bombs in a single pass, and, as importantly, loiter in the area to allow the ground troops to line up the attack. The thump and flash of the bombs was breathtaking. A pair of Apaches then fired off Hellfire missiles and rocket pods at the smoking buildings. The original plan involved searching the area, but Captain Milne changed his mind and decided to withdraw. Individuals did in fact survive the bombing: the surveillance camera on the Nimrod MR2 recorded 'hot spots' fleeing the area.

Four days after the Koshtay raid the marines in Garmsir once again decided to take the fight to the Taliban by assaulting one of their strongholds called Jugroom Fort, just 6 kilometres south of FOB Delhi. The aim of Operation *Glacier Two* was to raid the fort and destroy whatever insurgent infrastructure might be found at the site before retiring to the relative safety of the forward operating base. The operation was again led by Colonel Magowan, and included the BRF and C Squadron from the Light Dragoons. The assaulting force would be drawn from Zulu Company, supported by the Armoured Support Squadron in Vikings. The latter's mission was to drive the marines onto the objective.

Raiding Jugroom Fort presented the marines with serious problems, not least the size of the objective and the ground. The name itself was somewhat misleading. There was an old mud brick fort at this spot, but it sat within a cluster of villages and compounds. Just 800 metres north of the fort were two hamlets, and beyond these another three villages. In an immediate 500-metre radius of the fort there were perhaps 50 structures or buildings of one type or another, many protected by the traditional perimeter wall. This was at least a reinforced battlegroup objective (two years later, an American regimental-sized force finally captured Jugroom Fort). Magowan was proposing to undertake the raid with one company.

If this was not challenging enough, the fort had been purposely sited to create difficulties for any assaulting force. The only realistic approach was from the south-western flank, effectively attacking the rear of the fort, but this entailed crossing very difficult ground. The marines would have to ford the Helmand River, negotiate another 300 metres of boggy ground criss-crossed by numerous ditches, ford a second water feature and finally cross 200 metres of open ground south of the fort. The distance from the western bank of the River Helmand – the marines' line of departure – and the southern edge of the fort was over 600 metres. This ground was in a slight bowl at the end of which was the fort itself. In effect, the marines were going to advance down a gallery range, or what was for the defenders a near perfect killing area. This could only be attempted in darkness, which would make the task even more treacherous.

In the event, the assault was a fiasco. Zulu Company, mounted in the Armoured Support Group Vikings, crossed the river, and like some latter-day charge of the Light Brigade rode straight into a hail of machine-gun and RPG fire. In fact, the charge was only conducted by two troops, as it was deemed that one troop should be kept in reserve on the sand spit on the River Helmand. It was madness, and a minor miracle that more marines were not instantly killed or injured. Within about a quarter of an hour five marines were wounded, and the company was now faced with the prospect of having to mount a mass casualty evacuation across open ground and under fire. To make matters worse, the Bowman radios were packing up, which meant orders could only be transmitted by shouting. Appreciating the seriousness of the situation, the Armoured Support Group and Zulu Company commanders mutually agreed that to continue with the raid would be folly, and they requested permission to withdraw. Magowan granted permission, but it then took a further 20–30 minutes to pass the order to marines now scattered outside and inside the fort fighting for their lives. In all, the two troops spent about 45 minutes in this killing area, achieving little more than setting themselves up as targets. A hasty and somewhat chaotic evacuation was organized by Warrant Officer Shepherd, the Zulu Company sergeant major, and the battered marines withdrew back over the river.

Only a short time passed before it was realized that one of the marines, Lance Corporal Mathew Ford, a 'gentle giant', was missing. Then an RAF sergeant monitoring the UAV feed from the Desert Hawk spotted the lifeless body of Lance Corporal Ford slumped against the exterior wall of the fort. At the time nobody wanted to believe that he might be dead and, regardless, a rescue mission would still have to be organized to retrieve the body.

Warrant Officer Mark Rutherford, an Apache pilot, was credited for proposing the rescue plan that was eventually adopted, for which he would be awarded a Military Cross. The scheme was daring: two Apaches would swoop down on the body, carrying four marines strapped to the wings of the aircraft. Lance Corporal Ford's body would be tied to one of the airframes and the Apaches would return to the safety of the tactical HQ. Using the Apache helicopters in such an unorthodox way had never been attempted before, and by now it was half past nine in the morning. The four men who undertook this hazardous mission, selected for no better reason than they happened to be in the vicinity when the plan was proposed, were: Captain David Rigg, a Royal Engineer officer; Regimental Sergeant Major Hearn; Marine Robertson, the commanding officer's signaller; and Marine Fraser-Perry, who was making a cup of tea at the time. Captain Rigg would receive the Military Cross for the recovery of the body. For the others there was at least the satisfaction that they had done their duty to a fellow marine.

The operation almost turned into a second disaster. The Apache carrying RSM Hearn and Marine Robertson missed the body altogether and landed inside the fort. The two men jumped off, started running in the wrong direction and had to be retrieved by one of the crew who jumped out of his aircraft and chased after them. The second Apache landed at the right spot, but Marine Fraser-Perry became disorientated and also ran off in the wrong direction. Only Captain Rigg found the body, and the task of lifting or even dragging the lifeless Lance Corporal Ford proved a physical impossibility. After a terrible struggle and under intermittent fire, Captain

Rigg, Marine Fraser-Perry and eventually Warrant Officer Rutherford, who also dismounted his Apache, succeeded in carrying Lance Corporal Ford to the awaiting helicopter. With everyone safely re-attached, the two Apaches withdrew with the ghoulish sight of Lance Corporal Ford's body hanging limply underneath one of the helicopters.

The media went wild over the story. This was just the sort of tale of Royal Marine derring-do the country needed in the depths of the post-Christmas hangover. What the media did not report was that the Zulu Company commander was relieved of his command and replaced by a newly arrived major. This was an injustice. The raid on Jugroom Fort was always recklessly over-ambitious. The plan – and crucially the fire plan – had been devised by Colonel Magowan and his staff, not the Zulu Company commander. The company had been tardy at arriving at the fort, but this could not be attributed to its commander. And once in the fort there was little Zulu Company could do, hampered by a breakdown in their radios and under heavy fire. The marines would never again attempt a similar raid and lessons were learned, but the raid cost one company commander his job and one marine his life. The British task force spokesman, Lieutenant Colonel Rory Bruce, tried to justify the mission with bullish words, but the results were never credible:

> Our intention was to show the insurgents that they are not safe anywhere, that we are able to reach out to them and attack whenever and wherever we choose, even where they think they are at their safest. To that end, the mission was a success and the insurgents now know we can and will strike at any time.[26]

If the marines were holding the line in the south and centre, and even managing to take the fight to the enemy, in the far north another twist to the story unfolded. The Kajaki 'security bubble' was about to be expanded and Now Zad was stalemated, but the town located halfway between these two locations – Musa Qaleh – fell to the Taliban in January. Led by Mullah Abdul Ghaffour, who had reportedly become angered by American air strikes, the insurgents overran the police station, expelled the elders, and staged a few hangings *pour encourager les autres*. Some reporting suggested that Taliban from Sangin had been involved, taking orders from Pakistan. Mullah Abdul Ghaffour would himself be killed by an air strike, but the town would not be reclaimed by ISAF until the end of the year. For the British, the collapse of the Musa Qaleh deal was a serious blow. The Americans had never believed in the British 'hands-off' policy, and this latest twist seemed to confirm their reservations. Brigadier Thomas could only watch the situation unfold, knowing that without further reinforcements – it would take a full brigade operation to recapture Musa Qaleh – there was little he could do. By the beginning of the year, 3 Commando Brigade was already stretched to breaking point just holding on to the few gains it had made. The series of operations that were undertaken over January and February to push the insurgents away from Kajaki and Darvishan, as well as the final operation to retake Sangin, could never have taken place if the marines had been ordered to expel the Taliban from Musa Qaleh. There were simply not enough troops.

Even in the depths of a miserable Afghan winter, 3 Commando Brigade felt there was some cause for optimism. The marines had managed to train up two ANA battalions of 3/205 Brigade. Security might be handed back to the Afghans if this effort were reinforced. From the perspective of the task force HQ the enemy in turn appeared to have been weakened. This was wishful thinking; the fighting season was over, and this seasonal aspect to the fighting in Afghanistan, more than any other factor, accounted for the drop in insurgent activity. British intelligence reading the runes saw enemy morale falling when all that was plummeting was the temperature. Even in the fighting off-season, Helmand could be a dangerous place. The brigade eventually suffered 12 fatalities and 84 wounded over the course of the winter fighting. Only two of the fatalities had been caused by roadside bombs, and one fatality – Marine Gary Wright – had been killed by a suicide bomber in Lashkar Gah at the start of the tour. Despite Thomas's intention to avoid unnecessary fighting, it had been a violent six months. There had been 821 gun battles (300 more than the paratroopers experienced in the summer), and over 1 million pounds of high explosives had been expended, including over 30,000 shells and mortar bombs. Supporting aircraft had dropped 750 tons of bombs in over 200 air strikes. 42 Commando alone had expended 21,000 81mm mortar bombs and 11,000 105mm shells.

Setting aside these statistics of military effort, independent polling suggested that any optimism in Helmand was premature. Indeed, what most polls seemed to indicate was that the British entry into Helmand had been a disaster which had provoked a province-wide insurrection. Four out of ten Afghans believed that the Taliban had become stronger, and a majority of Afghans believed that the government should negotiate a peace settlement with the insurgent movement.[27] Just over half supported the idea of a coalition government, undermining notions that the Taliban were viewed by ordinary Afghans as irredeemably beyond the pale of political accommodation.[28] One quarter of Afghans reported Taliban in their district, and one in ten judged that they had a strong influence in their area.[29] Depressingly for ISAF, polling indicators suggested a decline in support for ISAF and an increase in support for the Taliban, especially in the south-west. In 2006, three-quarters of Afghans living in the south-west opposed the Taliban. Within a year, only half opposed the Taliban, and almost 15 per cent supported the movement.[30]

Reconstruction and development had been a grave disappointment. Some minor refurbishment had been undertaken in Lashkar Gah hospital and in 11 schools. Wells had been dug, a few bridges repaired and generators distributed. In total, around 50 modest projects had been started. No reconstruction, however, was taking place in the volatile areas of Helmand where it was most needed. Even the peaceable residents of Lashkar Gah stirred when a pot of reconstruction money was controversially spent building a recreation park on the west bank of the Helmand River (in fact, the refurbishment of an existing, disused park with a Ferris wheel). If any single project illustrated the gulf between British reconstruction and the reality of Helmand Province in the early days of the war, it was the notorious $800,000 Bolan Park project. The project came about because it 'ticked boxes' in DfID forms rather than because it served any pressing need in a war zone. The park was supposed to provide an outlet for women ('empowerment' of women was a DfID millennium goal). Leaving aside the laughableness of Western interference in Helmand's deeply conservative, male-dominated culture, Lashkar Gah's womenfolk, it was pointed out, could not reach the park anyway without a male chaperone. It was an ignominious end to a year of meaningless British non-reconstruction in the Afghan Development Zone.

Brigadier Thomas had sought to fight a mobile counter-insurgency campaign but in the end found himself fixed like his predecessor Ed Butler. Without more troops, better intelligence and crucially more helicopters, the options were always going to be limited. The reality that the British had provoked a general insurrection was not acknowledged, which was the bigger failing. A hopeless and hostile governor, an equally feeble British reconstruction effort, continuing American sweep operations and the marines' own aggressive operations had all ultimately undermined the mission and deflected Thomas from his original intention, which was to support the ADZ between Lashkar Gah and Gereshk. But what Thomas did not do was add to the British 'footprints'. Not a single additional base was invested, and indeed Thomas sought albeit unsuccessfully to withdraw from some of the platoon houses. His was the only brigade that would be able to make this claim. Despite all the impediments, Thomas had stuck to a philosophy of mobile warfare. When 3 Commando Brigade handed over to its successors in the spring of 2007, there was still the chance of 'unfixing the force'. A political settlement was still on the cards, if only political actors on the British and Afghan side would step forward to end the unhappy situation in Helmand. None did, and the chance to 'unfix the force' once and for all would not be taken because the successors – 12th Mechanized Brigade – arrived with a quite different view of how to win the war in Helmand.

5

Take the Fight to the Enemy

Operation *Herrick 6*, April 2007–October 2007

The spring of 2007 marked an important milestone for Britain's armed forces. The attention, however, was not on Helmand, but rather hundreds of kilometres away in Basra. Desperate to reduce the political liability of a deeply unpopular war, the outgoing Blair government began the process of British withdrawal from southern Iraq – a retreat in some eyes – that would prove almost as controversial as the original invasion. The speed with which this happened was precipitous. On 8 April British forces handed over their base at the old Shatt Al-Arab Hotel to the 10th Division of the Iraqi Army. Ten days later an announcement was made that the troubled Maysan Province, which the British had never successfully controlled anyway, had been handed back to the Iraqi authorities. A week later, the giant Shaibah Logistics Base just outside Basra City was also handed over to the Iraqi Army. British forces were now based in just two locations: at the airport and in the symbolically important Basra Palace. American insistence kept the British locked up in this foothold, which no longer held any military value except for an American special operations contingent monitoring growing Iranian influence in Basra Province. For the insurgents, Basra Palace had become a mortar range. For the soldiers of the Rifles, the last British regiment to serve inside the city before the final British withdrawal, conditions were miserable. The palace received daily attacks, and there was little the British could do except take cover and accept the steady trickle of casualties. Every resupply was a major operation. One jaundiced observer noted people were dying just to deliver toilet paper to the soldiers.

This intolerable situation could not be sustained, but the British still needed some face-saving solution to quit the city once and for all. The deal struck proved controversial. In return for a prisoner release, including a prominent insurgent leader, a pledge was made that the British could leave Basra Palace unmolested by the insurgents. Anxious not to hand over the buildings to extremists, it was also agreed the Iraqi Army would assume control of the palace. In September the Rifles finally withdrew to Basra Airport, flags flying defiantly from their vehicles. True to their word, the insurgents allowed the British free passage. The British government portrayed the withdrawal as part of a staged plan to hand over security to the Iraqi Army but few believed the spin. For the Americans, the British had been 'defeated'. For the government of Prime Minister Nouri al-Maliki, the British had proved a let-down. In Baghdad, British officers suffered the daily embarrassment of having to explain the British position to sceptical Americans. The central justification – that the Iraqis were capable of maintaining their own security – later appeared hollow when an Iraqi-led operation to clear insurgent groups from Basra City collapsed. The British-mentored Iraqi troops had to be stiffened by American soldiers sent south to the restore the situation. The British commander was not even in the country when these events unfolded, having taken leave. Such was the inglorious end to Operation *Telic*.

If the story in Iraq was one of retreat, in Afghanistan the army was about to engage in its biggest killing spree since the first Gulf War. By the end of the six-month tour, 12th Mechanized Brigade would claim to have killed over 2,000 Taliban and foreign fighters. The body count was exaggerated, but it was true that a level of violence had been visited in some districts of Helmand, not experienced since the Soviet occupation. Before Operation *Herrick 6*, the two sides had been trading punches. In the summer of 2007, the British dynamited the ring. The outcomes of this period of incessant fighting would be profound. The British would be led into thinking their war was winnable. The tribesmen would retrench, rethink tactics and emerge stronger.

12th Mechanized Brigade was commanded by the 43-year-old Brigadier John Lorimer, a Cambridge graduate and Arabist who had already commanded a brigade over a difficult tour in Basra the previous summer. The Lorimers, it seemed, were drawn to the Middle East – the newly arrived brigadier was the great-grandson of an Edwardian Arabist.

John Lorimer was a paratrooper who combined innate intelligence with the aggressive ethos of the Parachute Regiment. Operation *Herrick 6* would mark a sort of early apogee in the British campaign in Helmand. No other army brigade would mount as many offensive operations, with as much ambition and sweep, as 12th Mechanized Brigade in the summer of 2007. Much of this was due to the brigade commander, who proved a vigorous leader. Confident in his abilities, and served by a team of equally capable commanding officers, he set a relentless tempo of operations despite numerous difficulties with equipment and, in particular, awful problems with the Bowman communications system. He was the only Helmand brigadier who took his brigade to war in Iraq and Afghanistan, and this may have reinforced his confidence.

The aggressive approach seemed to pay off, or so the British first thought. 12th Mechanized Brigade did not 'butcher and bolt' in the manner of early 20th-century, punitive, expeditionary campaigns, but the brigade clearly thumped the tribes in northern Helmand. Six brigade operations and a score of battlegroup operations were mounted. No other brigade inflicted as much damage or killed as many fighters, whether genuine Taliban or local 'ten dollar Talibs'.* The brigade forced insurgent gangs to lie low, and it was in no small measure thanks to the offensive operations conducted over the summer of 2007 that the successor brigade 52 (Lowland) Brigade was able to enjoy such a quiet tour that winter. That this did not prove to be a winning tactic in Helmand was down to three principal factors.

First, there was no credible and resourced plan to exploit military operations with reconstruction and development programmes. The civilians were still at the tail of the column and in no hurry to catch up with the vanguard. For this reason the 12th Mechanized Brigade tour would be remembered as an exercise in 'mowing the lawn', an ultimately futile activity as the valley tribesmen experienced fighting but no reconstruction. This would decisively turn local opinion against the British, especially in the Upper Gereshk and Sangin valleys. Here, the tribes never forgave the actions of 12th Mechanized Brigade, and every subsequent brigade paid for this in revenge-taking. Second, the Afghan security forces were in no shape to support let alone consolidate British clearance operations.

*The term referred to non-ideological local gunmen who simply viewed fighting for the insurgency as another seasonal revenue stream.

Western military clout without an 'Afghan face' was always going to appear as naked aggression that had to be resisted. And last, the point of this campaigning was now no longer to interdict the 'Taliban' and push the trouble away from the ADZ, as 3 Commando Brigade had attempted, but to establish more British bases in the contested areas. No other army brigade would ever be able to match the operational tempo of 12th Mechanized Brigade because no other brigade possibly could: the manning bill for the expanding number of patrol bases would effectively fix the force in dispersed locations across Helmand. Over time, Task Force Helmand would become static, hugely expensive to sustain and without a sufficient mobile arm. The seeds for this were sown by 12th Mechanized Brigade. The argument that Afghans saw security in terms of numbers of bases was persuasive but it did not disaffirm the need for mobile operations. Nor did it mean that British soldiers had to man the bases. In this respect, Lorimer repeated Johnson's mistake in Vietnam – their war became our war. The mantra of Ed Butler and Jerry Thomas – that this was an Afghan war that had to be fought by Afghans – was buried. The dictum that Task Force Helmand had to be 'unfixed' was discarded. As a consequence, every succeeding brigade was forced to follow in Lorimer's path, including 52 Brigade, which tried to reverse course.

Much criticism of the brigade, however, was harsh. Insufficient troops – and crucially, poor FCO and DfID support – could not be laid on the shoulders of Brigadier Lorimer. Other actors now entered the picture over this crucial summer. On 17 May, Sherard Cowper-Coles took over as the new British ambassador in Kabul. Cowper-Coles proved a jovial but controversial character. He seemed ill at ease with the military. On a flight to Helmand, he ungenerously recorded in his FCO blog that some army officers were reading books, pretentiously was the suggestion, as if surprised army officers might just be intelligent and reflective. His main role in the play would be to act as a brake on military operations, taking his cue from a nervous government that sought to limit British commitments and casualties. Later in the war he would be mischievously – and, in his testimony, wrongly – quoted by a French satirical newspaper, suggesting the war was lost. After retiring from the FCO he would write a book critical of the entire strategy in Afghanistan and of what he perceived to be the military dominance of Whitehall.

In other respects, Cowper-Coles's case was strong. He held a deep and justified suspicion of optimistic military reporting. Unlike his military counterparts, he could not see the reasons for optimism and was dismayed by the steady stream of reports suggesting progress. He strenuously argued for a political not military solution – a point that few could argue against, but which was proving as difficult to achieve as a military win.

Cowper-Coles was also an astute observer of the many petty follies of the war: the mendacious Afghanistan conference industry; the circus of Western developing world 'experts' lining their pockets; the endless coordination meetings by Westerners for Westerners; the pernicious effects of the six weeks on and two weeks off work routine and the obsession with allowances; the hollowness of the Helmand Plan; the pointless production line of PowerPoints, as if the war could be won by accumulating bullet points, to invoke Maxwell Taylor's quip from the Vietnam War; and not least, the turgid language of British Army staff work, so far removed from the plain English of previous generations; all this he recorded drolly in his memoirs (he went so far as to wonder whether the pompous mumbo-jumbo and impenetrable jargon which had become fashionable with British Army officers was being deliberately used to disguise the fact that the army was losing its war).

The new defence secretary, Des Browne, re-entered the story, now more forcefully. Like his predecessor, a Catholic Scotsman and Celtic supporter, Browne was known as a 'safe pair of hands'. He proved to be a hugely influential defence secretary, not only for his longevity (he served from 5 May 2006 to 3 October 2008) but because he persuaded the Treasury to open the purse strings and then presided over the biggest (and necessary) re-armament programme of a British Army at war in a generation.

The last character who would have a significant influence on attitudes towards the war was General Richard Dannatt, the recently appointed CGS. Dannatt, a former Green Howard, took over in the autumn of 2006, just as Operation *Herrick 4* was winding down. He quickly courted controversy by making strong remarks about the rationale of British operations in Basra. A strongly committed Christian, Dannatt would do more to raise the profile of his army than any other senior officer. In doing so he became a thorn in the Labour government's side and ultimately, it appeared, sacrificed his own career.

12th Mechanized Brigade arrived in Helmand in unseasonably cold weather and heavy downpours. The threat of a Taliban spring offensive hung in the air. According to Governor Wafa, over 700 insurgents had crossed over from Pakistan and were heading for Sangin. These included Chechens and Arabs as well as Pakistanis.[1] Mullah Dadullah, the most able Taliban tactical commander in south-west Afghanistan, was promising a summer of violence on Al-Jazeera television and offering gold to anyone who killed ISAF soldiers. There were rumours of a mass suicide bomber offensive.

With the deployment of the brigade, the British task force levels rose again to around 5,800 strong. Helmand was now divided into three battlegroup areas of responsibility: north, centre and south. The two commando battalions were replaced by three infantry battalions: 1 Royal Anglian, commanded by Lieutenant Colonel Stuart Carver; the Worcestershire and Sherwood Foresters (about to be renamed 2 Mercians under an army downsizing programme), commanded by Lieutenant Colonel Richard Westley; and the Grenadier Guards, commanded by Lieutenant Colonel Carew Hatherley. The latter deployed with a Second Lieutenant Folarin Kuku, the regiment's first black officer in its 350-year history.[2] Armoured reconnaissance continued to be provided by a squadron from the Light Dragoons. The brigade was also supported by a 140-strong Somme Company from the London Regiment, an impressive commitment from reservist soldiers.

The infantry battalions themselves were also substantially augmented. 1 Royal Anglian's three line companies were doubled with a Grenadier Guards company (Number 3 Company), a Danish company and an Estonian company. 1 Royal Anglian was also supported by a company from the Theatre Reserve Battalion (C Company, 2 Royal Regiment of Fusiliers). To make up numbers, additional infantrymen were also recruited from the Gibraltar Regiment, a sister regiment (in fact, infantrymen from eight different regiments served in 1 Royal Anglian, an indication of just how overstretched the downsized infantry had become). In total the battlegroup jumped from a normal peacetime strength of about 600 to over 1,500 all ranks. The Viking 'battlefield taxis' used by the marines were left behind in Helmand, with their marine drivers. 1 Royal Anglian was allocated one troop of these vehicles. The battlegroup was also the first to receive a company's worth of Mastiffs, a 28-ton American vehicle with significant levels of protection.

1 Royal Anglian companies were initially deployed to the British 'footprints' across Helmand. A (Norfolk) Company was deployed to Now Zad; B (Suffolk) Company occupied FOB Robinson; C (Essex) Company

invested Kajaki Dam; and D (Cambridgeshire) Company assumed the reconnaissance and support weapon roles. A Royal Anglian contingent was also deployed to the multinational FOB Price near Gereshk, where they were joined by Inkerman Company of the Grenadier Guards. Guardsmen from Queen's Company and Number 2 Company were sent to Camp Shorabak, the ANA camp built adjacent to Camp Bastion, where they would act as mentors for the 1st Battalion of the ANA 3/205 Heroes Brigade. The Guardsmen were quick to notice their Afghan charges had 'a fairly lax approach to uniform ... punctuality, or indeed any of the normal traits one associates with good military men' but that they made good 'scrappers'.[3] The BRF was relocated to Camp Bastion, where it was judged it might be better employed from this more central location. Over the course of the next six months, soldiers would find these were only temporary homes as the brigade mounted a series of offensive operations that demanded the rapid relocation of platoons and companies from one base to another.

For Brigadier Lorimer, the important task was to seize the initiative. The British deployment to Helmand had been surprised by the level of resistance it met. It had clung by its fingernails to a number of outposts in the face of daily attacks. It had battened down during the bitter Afghan winter. Now it was time to play the game in the enemy's half again, and not be too concerned by 'worriers' fretting in the stands (a word he used in his post-operational report). The mission had not changed. The British task was to create security in the increasingly questionable Afghan Development Zone, to promote reconstruction and development, and to encourage better governance. Even as the fresh brigade arrived, Sangin had 'fallen' to 3 Commando Brigade, which seemed to augur well for the new fighting season. In fact, what had happened was that the local resistance in the town had simply melted back into the Green Zone. This was where Brigadier Lorimer was determined to make a difference. 12th Mechanized Brigade would not nibble at the edges of the Green Zone, in the manner of 3 Commando Brigade. The new brigade would break through the crust of the enemy defences, join the towns of Lashkar Gah, Gereshk and Sangin, and create an enduring presence in the Green Zone. Afghans respected 'boots on the ground', or so it was judged, and this meant marching into the enemy's territory and building bases right on his doorstep. So the brigade marched off to war, floating on ideas that sounded good on paper, and to the trumpet blasts of military terms that, like arrows drawn on maps, made perfect sense in a parallel world of wishful thinking, but made less sense in the real world of Helmand's fields and villages.

Lorimer intended to 'hit the ground running', and 12th Mechanized Brigade certainly did that. Sergeant Parr, serving with Chin Troop of 127 Gun Battery, was asked to fire his gun within 27 minutes of arriving at FOB Robinson, which probably set a record from bringing a gun into action on arrival at a forward operating base.[4] This troop was commanded by a female officer, Lieutenant Jenny White. Within the first few weeks, her troop would fire off a further 927 shells in support of the infantry operating within the range of the guns at FOB Robinson.[5]

Between April and June, the 1 Royal Anglian battlegroup undertook a series of ambitious operations in the Green Zone. To all intents and purposes these were 'search and destroy' missions but on a trivial scale compared to Vietnam-era operations. In Operation *Junction City* (1967), to give one example, a fleet of 200 helicopters was employed. For the majority of their operations, the Royal Anglians were allocated just one – the casualty evacuation helicopter. The aim was to flush out the enemy and to force him to fight or flee. For the British the justification for these operations seemed strong: the wastefulness of 'mowing the lawn' would only become apparent later. The widespread use of roadside bombs that would immobilize British soldiers by the following summer had not yet become a feature of Taliban tactics. The display of overwhelming force seemed to intimidate the fighters who put up limited resistance before dispersing. The Royal Anglians actually suffered no fatalities from these mobile operations, which may have reinforced the justification that the tactic was right. By comparison, Suffolk Company would suffer 13 casualties in just two days in May when it was sucked into fruitless, attritional shooting matches in the Sangin area.[6]

The first of these operations was codenamed Operation *Silicon* and involved almost 2,000 troops. The operation was one of a series of missions undertaken still under the umbrella of Operation *Achilles*, the broader American campaign to wrest northern Helmand Province from imagined Taliban control. The aim was to clear insurgents from a village called Deh-e Adam Khan in the Upper Gereshk Valley, deep in Barakzai tribal lands. The Royal Anglians may have reflected this same area had ostensibly been 'cleared' by the marines in their very first operation, six months ago, and the old front line had simply reasserted itself. The newcomers would have to do it all over again. Six years later, when the last British and Danish soldiers finally quit Gereshk, villages in this area had still not been 'cleared'.

H-Hour was set for 0500hrs on 29 April. As well as the 1 Royal Anglian battlegroup, a troop of Light Dragoons mounted in Scimitars, the BRF, a Danish reconnaissance squadron, an Estonian mechanized company and two US special forces detachments took part in the operation. A total of six ANA companies were also mustered to help search compounds and to act as interpreters. Artillery and mortar support was provided by six light guns from 28/143 (Tombs's Troop) and six mortars from the Royal Anglian mortar platoon. Surveillance was provided by a USAF U-2, a Nimrod MR2, two teams of Desert Hawk UAVs and two Light Electronic Warfare Teams, or LEWTs.

It was estimated that 1 Royal Anglian might face 'up to 1,000 fighters', an exaggeration, but Operation *Silicon* still turned out to be a hard slog due to the resistance of the Barakzai villagers.[7] One of the memorable features of this operation was actually the weather, rather than tribesmen shooting back at the soldiers: the battlegroup had to endure a sandstorm, followed by a rain storm, followed by sapping heat. Most of the fighting experienced by the soldiers involved random shooting matches against an invisible enemy. At first the countryside would seem peaceful. Then a tree line would erupt with gunfire, and a battle would follow that could last for several hours.

For the majority of soldiers who took part in the operation, the villagers proved an elusive foe. Private Muhammad Khan, serving with the Royal Anglians and acting as the 'eyes and ears' at the front of his patrol, remembered spotting the enemy on only one occasion. Mostly, he recollected the heat, the weight of the equipment and the exhaustion.

The only casualties suffered by the Royal Anglians were two soldiers who collapsed with heat exhaustion and a third who was hit by shrapnel. This was a very cheap victory. Most of the fighters who were killed appeared to have been caught by Apaches at the end of the day as they attempted to leave the area. Despite the expenditure of tens of thousands of bullets and thousands of pounds of high explosives over the course of the day, just eight dead fighters were found.[8] A further three wounded Afghans were evacuated to Camp Bastion field hospital. This did not stop the battalion from reporting they had killed at least 95 insurgents but that the true figure was probably much higher.[9] The tendency to exaggerate kill counts remained an irresistible temptation for British commanders.

A Grenadier Guards officer mentoring an ANA company seemed more impressed by the 'gutsy' Taliban than by his ANA colleagues.[10] A year into the war, the reliability of the ANA was already becoming a serious cause of concern for the British mentors. The figures being quoted by ISAF for numbers of trained ANA simply did not reflect the reality on the ground. An example of this mismatch was the experience of Lieutenant Colonel Bramble, serving with 19 Regiment Royal Artillery, 100 kilometres away to the south, in FOB Dwyer. Bramble's job was to train Afghan gunners, but just holding on to his students was proving the bigger challenge. Paying the ANA their overdue wages only served to encourage the Afghan soldiers to desert. The best incentive to retain the soldiers was a certificate. Afghan soldiers placed great value on receiving a certificate from the British Army, however meaningless. Still, the numbers of soldiers he was training remained pitifully small. Just six ANA gunners were presented certificates for attending command and observation post courses.[11] It is worth recalling that at this time ISAF was claiming over 40,000 ANA had been trained, although it also conceded that only about 22,000 were 'consistently present for combat duties'.[12]

Following Operation *Silicon*, on 10 May, Lorimer was invited by Governor Wafa to address a *shura* of over 400 of Gereshk's tribal elders. This was the first opportunity for the governor and the British task force commander to speak directly to the tribes. Lorimer's message was one that would be repeated endlessly by British commanders:

> We have provided support through a number of projects in Gereshk in recent months, including investment in health, education and municipal services. In addition the Kajaki dam project will bring new roads, better irrigation and employment to the Upper Gereshk Valley. It is a great opportunity which will brighten your future, but it needs your help and can only work if the Taliban are kept out.[13]

The problem with this message in the spring of 2007 was that it was entirely hollow (by DfID's own reporting, just £6 million had been spent on 130 QIPs over 2006–07, a meaninglessly small sum).[14] Lorimer was in the uncomfortable position of having to make promises to tribesmen who knew very well that the British were all talk and no action. Indeed, Helmandis had jokingly begun to refer to the British as the 'note-takers', observing their propensity for paperwork but little action. Keeping the Taliban out was not an easy message to sell to the elders when the majority were related to or knew tribesmen who had taken up arms against the British. To consolidate the gains from Operation *Silicon*, a base was built on the edge of the Green Zone: FOB Inkerman. Over time, this base would become one of the most notorious and beleaguered of all the British outposts.

Undeterred, the brigade mounted a second operation – Operation *Lastay Kulang* ('Axe Head') – which took place in the last week of May and ran into the first week of June. Again it involved the 1 Royal Anglian battlegroup supported by Danish, Estonian and American troops. The main objective of the operation was to clear a large village called Putay in Alikozai tribal lands, about 12 kilometres north of Sangin.

Private Ed Garner described the action as they drew close to the first compounds:

> I hopped over a small ditch at the corner and just as I looked up an automatic weapon opened up about 20 meters to my half-right as the rounds thudded into the wall between the 3 of us that had exposed ourselves to the gunman. My world was well and truly in slow-mo as Martin, LCpl Andy Howe, the section commander and I fired on automatic into the tree where the fire had come from. I smiled as some geezer half jumped, half fell out of the tree and scrambled around the corner of the compound at the base. 'How did that twat manage to get away?' I joked to Martin.[15]

What followed was a typical village fight, as described by Lance Corporal Bill Drinkwater:

> For the next couple of hours we played cat and mouse with several Taliban through alleyways, trenches and little rat-runs like some speeded up Laurel & Hardy film. I'll never forget when I moved around a corner and an enemy RPG gunner saw me and flapped and fired his RPG from the hip landing about 5m in front of him. I don't know who was more scared, me or him, but he somehow got away with it.

Drinkwater's description of the ensuring gun fights unintentionally highlights the inherent contradiction in what the British were attempting to do. The company entered Putay to win 'hearts and minds', but instead, 'all hell broke loose'. The soldiers found themselves dodging salvos of

RPGs and unable to cross the open ground because it was being raked by fire from insurgents hiding in a maize field. Eventually, Drinkwater and his mates took cover in a ditch to avoid the 'mayhem', and a US A-10 providing close air support settled the matter. After this display of American air power there was little resistance.

The coordination of both the air and artillery support for Operation *Lastay Kulang* was undertaken from a makeshift fires cell that had been set up at the Sangin District Centre. Such were the difficulties of travel in Helmand that the gunners who made up this team had taken 16 hours to drive from FOB Price to Sangin, a distance of barely 30 kilometres. When they arrived, Sergeant Steel recalled they were met by a painted sign that read 'Welcome to Sangingrad'.[16] The bleak joke raised a smile, despite the ordeal of the journey.

To suggest that 12th Mechanized Brigade was simply acting like the biggest bully in the neighbourhood, picking fights, would be an over-simplification. Reflecting on these first two operations, Lorimer was clear that the key to success was not the fighting but precisely the reconstruction:

> When we close with the enemy, with the Taliban, we beat them. But the critical part, as I said before, is what happens after that. It's the reconstruction and development, which we are taking forward with colleagues from the Foreign and Commonwealth Office and the Department for International Development on behalf of the government of Afghanistan. Also we're making sure that the government of Afghanistan get their representatives out on the ground to engage with the locals.[17]

In truth, this was putting a brave face on an inadequate situation. At Lashkar Gah, a bureaucracy had grown that swelled the brigade HQ to three times its normal peacetime establishment. At the head of the PRT was the Helmand Executive Group (HEG) led by the FCO's David Slinn. The HEG included the deputy commander of Task Force Helmand as well as representatives from the FCO, DfID, the US State Department, USAID (which was actually funding the majority of reconstruction projects in the British area of operations), a counter-narcotics officer and representatives from Denmark and Estonia. This group was further augmented by a first political secretary, media officers, legal advisors and finance officers. Despite an outward show of unity, it was a disparate body with widely differing agendas. The US State Department was keeping an eye on the British as well as the Taliban. The FCO and DfID appeared to be playing the part of two nervous spinsters trying to avoid anything that might ruffle their comfortable worlds. The counter-narcotics officer was caught between a British lack of ideas and an American desire to pursue eradication.

Only the Danes seemed to be making any meaningful progress with reconstruction in Gereshk. Between September 2006 and May 2008, a nine-strong Danish CIMIC team in Gereshk would implement 255 small- to large-scale projects; more than the British were managing with their much larger bureaucracy.[18] Six years later, as the ISAF national contingents began their withdrawal, an unholy row broke out over infrastructure left behind by PRT-sponsored projects, specifically the British-sponsored projects. It transpired that just 70 per cent of claimed clinics were actually functioning, and of 336 registered 'schools', only 164 were actually open and less than a third had 'proper buildings'. It was telling that the Helmand Education Director Mohammed Nasim Safi, who reported this information, also pointed out: 'The schools funded by Denmark … were of a high quality and had been built in the right locations, providing education for a large number of students.'[19] DfID 'success statistics', quoted by politicians in Parliament to demonstrate 'progress', had been so much spin.

The real problem with the PRT was that it thoughtlessly imposed Western notions on Helmand, totally ignoring the advice of Brigadiers Butler and Thomas (and General Richards) that ISAF should work with and not against the grain of Afghan culture. Reporting to the HEG was a raft of 'working groups', which seemed to grow in inverse proportion to the reconstruction actually taking place on the ground. In the round there was a Governance Working Group, an Influence Working Group, a Sustainable Development Working Group, a Security Sector Reform Working Group, a Stabilisation Working Group and a Counter-Narcotics Working Group. These naturally generated lucrative work for expert 'consultants' who produced dozens of spreadsheets, held long meetings and rarely if ever left the safety of the PRT. There was no representation in the forward operating bases or at district level, where it really mattered. The civil servants worked six weeks in theatre and were then entitled to two weeks' leave. Given this generous work practice, projects inevitably lacked coherence and personal accountability. The civilians also cost a king's ransom in allowances and security, and they were completely dependent on the military for their accommodation, feeding and transport. Unsurprisingly, relations between the soldiers and civilians were strained and sometimes downright hostile.

The Western-staffed HEG and its associated working groups did not work in isolation. These related through weekly meetings and further working groups with Governor Wafa's Helmand Provincial Council, the Provincial Security Committee, the Helmand Security Shura, the Combined Provincial Command Team, Joint Provincial Coordination Centres, various Provincial Development Committees and the district governors (where they existed). These Afghan bodies were entirely artificial organizations promoted by the British. Unlike their counterpart Western organizations, they tended to produce little or no paperwork, as the members were almost all illiterate. At one stage the entire cast of elders serving in the Helmand Provincial Council was illiterate, including the governor himself. None spoke English. There would be few more eloquent illustrations of the gap between the reality of Helmand, based on tribal loyalties and networks, and the Western-imposed architecture of executive teams, working groups, committees and sub-committees that blossomed within the unreal confines of the Lashkar Gah PRT.

The military contribution to reconstruction and development also remained inadequate. A Development and Influence Team or DIT was formed. The DIT was commanded by a lieutenant colonel and its function, as a staff sergeant who worked in the DIT explained, was to 'Come in, speak to the local population, see what they immediately need and what we can do for them. We can provide the locals with basic fresh water, electricity and help them with basic road improvements.'[20] This was 'military tokenism' of the sort that had characterized the British deployment in Mazar-e-Sharif in 2003–04. The DIT comprised just ten sappers from 26 Regiment Royal Engineers. This was little different to awarding a contract to a firm of ten handymen to cover an area the size of southern England.

During this period, the Lashkar Gah PRT was managing a budget of about £8 million, which was all that Britain had actually committed to reconstruction in Helmand (and not the misleading £500 million headline figure routinely announced by politicians to Parliament or at donor conferences), and it had overseen a small number of building refurbishment programmes, which was all that had been achieved one year after British troops deployed to Helmand.

Counter-narcotics – a purported reason why Britain had volunteered to take responsibility for Helmand by the outgoing Blair government – remained a dismal failure. According to the United Nations Office for Drugs and Organised Crime (UNODC), poppy cultivation had increased by 17 per cent in 2007, from 165,000 hectares in 2006 to 193,000 hectares. Opium yields had improved from 37 kilograms per hectare to 42.5 kilograms per hectare. Total potential opium production had swelled from 6,100 tonnes in 2006 to 8,200 tonnes, a 34 per cent increase. Helmand accounted for 53 per cent of the Afghan poppy industry, and it was estimated that Helmand farmers made $528 million from opium in 2007; or about 50 times the sum of money offered as aid by the British government. Four-fifths of farming families in Helmand cultivated the opium poppy, which was providing about one-third of their annual income. Crucially for Taliban revenues, about two-thirds of all opium was being processed in Afghanistan. This was where the big profits lay. As many as 60 laboratories were operating in the six districts controlled by Taliban gangs in Helmand.[21] The nexus between farmers, drug traffickers and the Taliban was tight and highly lucrative, and it was all happening under the nose of the British.

The challenge facing the British was that the opium and heroin trades were transnational and involved a huge number of players. The 18-year-old soldier deployed to Helmand was not just taking on some petty dealer with a bag of opium paste. He was indirectly challenging a wide range of characters across the region: corrupt Afghan government officials (including, allegedly, the president's brother); corrupt Afghan and Pakistani police; Iranian, Afghan and Pakistani traffickers (known as the 'Quetta Circle'); trucking mafias; Pakistani and Arab shipping mafias; corrupt Pakistani secret services; the Iranian Al Quds force; Uzbek narco-gangs (perhaps controlling 70 per cent of the heroin trade in central Asia); Arab drug cartels mostly based in Dubai; and Turkish criminal gangs – to name the main players. Helmand was at the centre of this spider's web of multi-billion-dollar criminality. In this respect and without hindsight, the naivety which the British government demonstrated when it sent a single reinforced battalion to Helmand in the spring of 2006 was breathtaking.

Regardless of the failures in reconstruction and in tackling the illicit drug trade, the war had to go on. In the second half of June, the Royal Anglians mounted Operation *Ghartse Ghar* ('Mountain Stag'), a second sweep of the Green Zone north of Sangin. A Taliban commander called Tor Jan had made a mockery of the earlier Operation *Lastay Kulang* by reimposing Taliban control in the area north of Sangin, a situation the British felt obliged to reverse. Two days before the operation started, an emotional but terse Tony Blair handed over the premiership of the country to his chancellor and rival Gordon Brown, in a packed House of Commons. The leader of the opposition, David Cameron, sportingly led the applause for the departing Labour leader. The prime minister who led Britain into Helmand Province, and who even by the most optimistic projection of three years would never have overseen the conclusion of the mission, left after just one year.

Tony Blair had been a war prime minister. He had believed in using the armed forces as a force for moral good. This dispensation of good from the barrel of a gun had backfired in Iraq, tarnishing the last years of his ten-year premiership. Afghanistan had also backfired, but now the problem was being handed over to a prime minister who was much less interested in foreign adventures and who would only 'get the war' when it threatened his office. Gordon Brown's disinterest in military affairs did not disqualify him from being a keen judge of military campaigns. One of the paradoxes of his premiership was that he instinctively saw through the confident assessments of his military commanders. He never believed the war could be won with one more push. Instead, he harboured the visceral distrust of politicians tired of being told by the generals that the war will be over by Christmas. Trapped by an electorate that laid all the blame for the mismanaged war at the government's door – now his front door – he was forced to act against his instincts and bow to the demands of the war machine. Only in the last six months of his government, facing electoral meltdown, did he bang his 'clunking fist', but by then it was too late.

For the Royal Anglians in Sangin, the national change in leadership was as remote as it was irrelevant. The battlegroup would be revisiting an area it had ostensibly cleared of insurgents just three weeks previously. The objective would be the village of Jusyalay, a small Barakzai settlement just 5 kilometres north of the town of Sangin. As with the previous two sweeps, Danish and Estonian troops, as well as US special forces teams, took part in the operation. The village was in machine-gun range of FOB Inkerman – the newly built forward operating base on the edge of the Green Zone – and it was suspected that many of the local men were implicated in attacks that had been launched against this base ever since it had been built. The operation involved some risk, as the RAF was refusing to fly casevac helicopters into the Green Zone after the downing of an American Chinook.

The fighting was at close quarters. In one incident, a well-led group of insurgents counter-attacked Suffolk Company and with a single, close-range RPG shot managed to wound five soldiers. Private Thompson described what happened:

> We were blown up in a ditch ... and an RPG shot out of a bush, hitting me in the chest. My Osprey body armour saved my life so I was lucky. There was a big dent but I wasn't allowed to keep it as a souvenir. My leg snapped in half. I was in agony but the blokes helped me out of the trench and then I was shot in the face. Back at Bastion, doctors removed the bullet ... I won't be able to go back on the frontline but I don't really mind. I reckon you've got three lives and I used up two of mine.[22]

Private Perry, who was standing next to him, received 157 separate shrapnel wounds over his body and survived the experience.[23] Having suffered eight casualties in three days (the company had actually started the operation with two understrength platoons), it was clear the Suffolks had run out of soldiers. A platoon of Grenadier Guards was flown in to reinforce the exhausted company. The operation would continue for a further five days but the main fighting was now over.

Following Operation *Ghartse Gar* there was a decline in attacks in the local area, but this was only a temporary respite. The British could not hold Jusyalay, and beyond some token ditch-digging they had nothing to offer in terms of reconstruction. Within a month the status quo ante had been restored, and FOB Inkerman was once again a base surrounded by a hostile population. Faced with this resurgent opposition, the brigade would run Operation *Leg Tufaan* ('Small Storm') from 16 June to 10 July, in what was now a fourth attempt since May to clear the troublesome Sangin and Upper Gereshk valleys. Over the course of the operation, a base was built on the edge of the Green Zone north-east of Gereshk (FOB Sandford, named after Lance Corporal Paul 'Sandy' Sandford, who was killed fighting in the Upper Gereshk Valley). In a break from the usual state of affairs, 2 Mercians, who led the mission, were highly impressed with their Afghan counterparts, reporting that the operations could not have been conducted without the ANA. FOB Inkerman continued to act like a magnet, attracting local attacks which reached a climax at the beginning of August.

Whenever the soldiers patrolled out of their bases, they would be met by volleys of rifle fire and hostile villagers. These greatly misnamed 'ground domination patrols' only served to create front lines that would eventually encroach on the bases themselves. Casualties were also inevitably incurred. When Essex Company patrolled to the village of Regay in mid-August, Private Tony Rawson was killed, shot through the head.[24] The villagers had no hope of overrunning a base like Inkerman, but a lucky rocket strike against one of the sangars wounded four soldiers and killed the base commander, Captain David Hicks, a popular officer who had stood in for the company commander while the latter was on leave.

The penultimate sweep operation was called *Chakush* ('Hammer'), and it ran from 16 July to 9 August in stiflingly hot weather. The aim of the operation was to clear insurgents from the villages of Heyderabad and Mirmandab and to establish a second patrol base in the area (subsequently called FOB Arnhem, an appropriate name as it proved a FOB too far and would eventually be abandoned). Naturally, this was not the end of the matter. From 30 August to 2 September the brigade was again forced to mount another operation (Operation *Palk Ghar*) to relieve pressure on the district centre in Sangin and FOB Inkerman. At the conclusion of this final sally into the Green Zone, the battlegroup reckoned that it had killed 40 insurgents. Over the course of seven battlegroup operations the Royal Anglians had succeeded in wearing down the tribal resistance, but the effects were always temporary and quickly reversed. PowerPoint slides showing how the number of incidents had declined following an operation were measured in one or two weeks. Within a month attacks had returned to former levels of intensity or got worse. This second set of statistics was not being so widely advertised.

In London a perception of mounting success was created by this wave of operations. In mid-July, the House of Commons Defence Select Committee published a report that broadly presented an optimistic view of the British campaign. Defence Secretary Des Browne welcomed the report, gratified by its recognition that 'we are performing well against a challenging background'. The arena of parliamentary committees was unlikely to provide a damning criticism of the war effort to date, but the committee members could not fail but notice that British reconstruction in Helmand was decidedly thin, and the problem of helicopter availability had still not been resolved.

Although 12th Mechanized Brigade's main effort through the spring and summer was to establish government control in the Gereshk–Musa Qaleh–Kajaki triangle in northern Helmand, the task force retained responsibility for one outpost in southern Helmand, the company base FOB Delhi, established by the marines in Darvishan. Ever since the marines had occupied the derelict compound at the abandoned agricultural college, Darvishan had become a thorn in the side of the British. Unable to commit more than a hundred men to the defence of this town, the task force found itself trapped in an irresolvable siege situation. It was a repetition of the platoon house sieges of the previous summer, and with no end in sight. The fighting had caused a collapse of economic activity in the town, which had emptied of all civilians, and the Taliban front line was just a few hundred metres away. During the marines' stay at Darvishan they had discovered that the only way to outflank the insurgents was to attack from the west, across the Helmand River. Although this was a major water feature, it was also fordable in places. To the east of the town, an American-built canal blocked all movement. The bridge that had existed over the canal had been destroyed, and a Russian armoured car rested at the bottom of the canal. In late spring, the decision was taken to open up this eastern flank by building a 30-metre medium girder bridge, or MGB, over the canal. Although the erection of an MGB was a routine engineering task, the Royal Engineers had not built a bridge in combat conditions for many years.

Operation *Bataka* was commanded by Lieutenant Colonel Angus Watson, the commanding officer of the Light Dragoons battlegroup, and involved a company from the Worcestershire and Sherwood Foresters, and Number 3 Company from the Grenadier Guards. An ANA company also supported the operation. The bridge, later christened Balaklava Bridge after a Grenadier battle honour, was erected in a matter of hours by 40 sappers from 26 Engineer Regiment on 21 June, in the early hours of the morning. Working in full body armour and in darkness significantly increased the workload, but the bridge was completed by dawn. To deter insurgent attacks, Number 3 Company raided east beyond the bridge and a permanent checkpoint was built at the site. Operation *Bataka* was a success, but one that could not be exploited. The British company in Darvishan would not be strengthened, and it was not until the following summer, when US Marines deployed to Garmsir, that the Taliban were finally pushed away from the area and the town re-opened. Lieutenant Colonel Watson's assertion that the bridge 'will provide a bigger space into which civilians can move back and continue the expansion of government and security in this area' proved a premature hope by about 12 months.[25]

In August, Suffolk Company left behind the Green Zone and relieved Essex Company at Kajaki. The level of hostility towards the British presence at the dam remained unabated. In the first month, just one Royal Anglian patrol did not come under enemy fire on leaving the safety of FOB Zeebrugge.[26] This hostility was matched by the continued inaccuracy of the enemy fire. The chances of being hit were very remote, despite the expenditure of thousands of rounds of ammunition. Essex Company had taken casualties, but these had all been self-inflicted. A patrol early in the tour had stumbled on an IED that resulted in a soldier losing his foot. Later during the deployment it was decided to raid the nearby village of Mazdurak. These raids achieved little more than stirring up an already confrontational situation. During this first raid, Essex Company came close to having a soldier captured by villagers after a Private Craig Gordon was hit three times by close-range fire. He was rescued even as he was bleeding to death in a desperate action by one of the section commanders. A second soldier – a guardsman – was subsequently shot and blinded in one eye, and this incident required mounting a second rescue. Three more soldiers would be seriously wounded before the company ran out of bullets and momentum and the operation was abandoned.

The lesson from these experiences, perversely, was to keep having a go at the villagers despite the risk of incurring casualties. Suffolk Company did eventually suffer three fatalities when three privates – Aaron McClure, Robert Foster and John Thrumble – were killed accidentally on 23 August in an air strike. McClure and Foster were teenagers. They had already taken part in over 40 gun battles. Thrumble, barely out of his teens, had served a tour in Iraq. The bomb that killed them landed in the middle of a compound, decimating the section occupying the building. A Corporal Parker, who had been on the roof of the building, was reduced to his boxer shorts and boots, all his equipment and clothing ripped off his body. A second severely wounded soldier, Private Lee, helped him off the roof. In the confusion and still under fire, Private Foster's body was left behind, unnoticed under the rubble, and a patrol would have to be despatched later that evening to recover the corpse. Foster's lifeless body was finally found at 0200hrs. The forward air controller who called in the two USN F-15s had accidentally given the wrong grid to the American pilots. This incident seemed to sum up the futility of the confrontation at Kajaki Dam that had long descended into a ritual play between two performers trading lead insults on a daily basis. In the gaps between these exchanges of gunfire, the Afghan employees at the dam and at the security posts scurried to their workplaces like commuters intent on avoiding an imminent rain storm. The timings of these attacks became routine to the extent that Major Borgnis, the Suffolk Company commander, recalled predicting to a visitor when the next attack would begin. On this particular occasion it was at 0520hrs (although it actually started eight minutes early, as if to thwart the accuracy of his prediction). What followed was a typical dawn gun fight at Kajaki. The soldiers fired off 6,000 rounds, probably failing to hit anyone or anything. The mortar detachment at the base lobbed 237 mortar bombs. And a circling pair of American fighters dropped three 500-pound bombs on likely enemy fire positions.[27] The whole show lasted about an hour and a half, and it was not inconceivable that no one was actually killed or even wounded by the exchange of fire.

If this was already a stalemated war, it was also a technological war of measure and counter-measure. Over the course of the summer, 12th Mechanized Brigade began to benefit from the arrival of new equipment denied to the paratroopers and marines.

In Helmand, the British Army desperately needed a well-protected wheeled vehicle – or a tough truck sufficient to carry a section of infantry. Only American industry could be counted on to produce such a platform. It was called the Cougar and it rolled off the production lines of Force Protection Incorporated in Ladson, South Carolina. The British renamed it Mastiff. The story of this vehicle was one of quintessential Yankee can-do, and it highlighted the comparative weakness of British industry.

Mastiff proved one of the outstanding success stories of the war. The key to its virtual impregnability to roadside bombs lay in its design. The vehicle stood high above the ground with wheel arches that deflected rather than contained blast. The engine block was mounted well forward of the crew compartment. In the event of a high-explosive detonation, it sheared from the main hull of the vehicle. The steel hull was strengthened with additional armours and spall liners. All this protection meant that it was not until almost the end of the war that the British finally suffered fatalities in a Mastiff (in June 2013 a massive 200-kilogram bomb on Route 601 ripped open the back of the vehicle, killing three soldiers – no vehicle would have survived such a blast). This record was a unique achievement in military engineering design. The British Army had never fielded a combat vehicle in its entire history in which it was suffering precisely no combat deaths. A single Mastiff would eventually set what appeared to be a record, surviving five separate IED attacks. The troops, understandably, respected it. The debt to American defence industry was huge.

Protection against roadside bombs was becoming paramount, but the capability to strike the elusive enemy was equally important. To front-line commanders it was evident the British Army also needed a precise mallet. Again, British defence industry could not supply such a weapon, but American industry could. The Lockheed Martin Guided Multiple Launch Rocket System or GMLRS was first fielded by 35 Battery (the Welsh Gunners) in the summer of 2007. It arrived with a great deal of expectation and excitement. GMLRS was an upgrade of an existing system sold to the British Army in the 1980s. GMLRS fired a single XM31 unitary rocket carrying a 200-pound warhead out to 70 kilometres. It never failed and its accuracy was stunning.[28] This weapon was dubbed the 'silent killer'. Unlike aircraft that signalled their presence with engine noise, it fell virtually noiselessly, giving no warning to its intended victims. B Troop, 39 Regiment recalled the first rocket launch from FOB Robinson:

> We arrived into FOB Rob and started settling into our new campsite location. Once the ammunition arrived two days later we could report ready and wait for the missions to come in. Three weeks later we were still waiting. Then one fine morning Sgt Berry broke his duck, and he did so in some style. He fired two, 3 rocket closed sheaf missions in support of operations.[29]

Striking precisely was only one half of the so-called targeting cycle. Finding the enemy was the other. 12th Mechanized Brigade had already deployed with a hand-thrown American mini-drone, the Desert Hawk. This had a range of about 10 kilometres and a limited endurance of about one hour. In the late summer, 57 (Bhurtpore) Battery received the first of the newly leased Israeli Hermes 450 UAVs (the British drone operators were trained in Tel Aviv). These medium-altitude UAVs had a range of 150 kilometres and an endurance of 14 hours. Initially only two aircraft were leased, and there were delays in setting up the operation, but once established the Hermes 450 battery provided a reliable set of airborne eyes for the British task force. Capable of night and day tasking and with the ability to pinpoint targets with accurate geo-coordinates, Hermes 450 was the natural bedfellow of GMLRS.

The last significant piece of new equipment fielded by the brigade was the Javelin anti-tank missile (the previous brigade had been similarly equipped). Also produced by Lockheed Martin, Javelin was the first ever 'fire-and-forget' missile bought by the British Army. This cutting-edge technology was originally developed to counter the massed tanks of the Warsaw Pact. Unlike conventional anti-tank missiles that used wire-guidance from launcher to target, the Javelin only required the operator to 'gate' the target within the sight picture and to press the fire button when the missile launcher achieved lock-on. Once launched, the missile flew in an upwards trajectory before crashing down onto the target. There were no tanks in Helmand, but the missile served equally well as a man-killer, albeit an extremely expensive one. Each missile cost over £70,000. To the soldiers, firing a Javelin was 'throwing a Porsche' at the Taliban. Competitions to become the first 'Javelin millionaire' became the game, although it is doubtful that any one individual managed to fire off a million pounds' worth of missiles. The Javelin had a range of over 2 kilometres, which gave the British an important advantage in standoff engagements. The penetration enjoyed by the missile against the thick adobe walls of Helmand's compounds was another matter. Over the course of war, scores of Javelin were fired at rock-hard compound walls to no great effect.

Perhaps one of the biggest challenge facing the brigade, as it mounted operations across the Green Zone, was its communication systems. By the end of the 1990s the army's ageing Clansman radio system needed urgent replacement. For a combination of reasons, the provision of a modern, secure, digital radio network for the British Army turned into a procurement horror story. Ten years elapsed and hundreds of millions of pounds were spent on a possible candidate system (Archer) that was subsequently cancelled. After a decade of failing to meet the programme goals, the MOD then jumped precipitously and signed an ambitious £2.4 billion deal to procure the Bowman radio system. A 'big bang' approach would see the army converted to the new radio system in a rolling programme whose scale drew sceptical comments from industry commentators. The sceptics, it turned out, were right. Bowman, soldiers joked, stood for 'Better off with map and Nokia'.

Complaints were received that the radios were heavy and the batteries had insufficient life. Patrols discovered that they had to take risks and keep radios switched off unless they ran into trouble, to save battery life. The radios also initially interfered with the ECM, or Electronic Counter-Measures, a phenomenon known as 'communications fratricide'. The range of the radios in the Green Zone proved disappointing – on occasions VHF sets could only communicate over hundreds of metres. The HF sets, which should theoretically have afforded long-range communications, were similarly disappointing. Crucially, Bowman failed to provide 'Situational Awareness', or the plotting of the locations of vehicles or personnel on digital map views. As one officer put it, the communications of the brigade were 'simply unbelievable' and bore 'more resemblance with military preparations in 1914 than 2007'. Urgent upgrades would be implemented to rectify the problems with the Bowman radio system, but not before confidence had been lost.

The difficulty of using the Bowman radio system in Helmand provoked a rash of emergency procurements. Commercial TACSAT became the default. To provide 'situational awareness' a second commercial tracking system (with servers based in Texas) was rushed into service. The Iridium telephone became popular as a back-up. Secret information could not be exchanged. Nor could headquarters exchange images or video. Any large operation required a laborious transfer of personnel by helicopter for face-to-face discussions because of the failures of a radio system whose chief selling point had been that it would provide secure, digital communications.

Political sensitivity over the problems of the Bowman radio system was acute (especially after an incident in Iraq in which six military police were killed, unable to raise help). Commanding officers returning from theatre who tried to voice their concerns were asked to restrain their language. In the end, Task Force Helmand muddled on with an erratic and hybrid radio network. In a further twist to the army's problems, two years later, a future strategic communications system known as Cormorant was also ditched (after a further expenditure of over £100 million). In its place, a reliable Israeli commercial system was bought instead.

Resupplying this enlarged force had become a significant logistic operation. The brigade had deployed with 10,000 tonnes of equipment, all of which had had to be flown to Helmand then distributed to the various forward operating bases and patrol bases. In a typical week the brigade was consuming about 250 tonnes of ammunition (or 25 Hercules aircraft loads) – this figure alone should have alerted the distracted Labour government that it had become embroiled in a serious war. The number of ration packs delivered exceeded 88,000 man days. A further 56 tonnes of fresh food were being delivered each month and about 18 tonnes of mail.[30] This operation struggled to meet the demands of the task force, lacking both modern asset tracking systems and manpower. A study by the National Audit Office in 2007 discovered that the average length of time a unit had to wait for priority one, two and three items was two weeks, three weeks and 13 weeks respectively. This implied that a priority three item ordered in the second half of the tour was likely to arrive in Helmand after the unit had returned to Britain.

Even as the brigade unrolled its operations it was learning surprising lessons, or perhaps revisiting old lessons. Despite the advantage of possessing a range of modern surveillance technologies, the insurgents remained a difficult enemy to spot and target. Their cunning was the same guile recorded by General Skeen, writing on frontier wars in 1932: 'Their power of moving concealed is outstanding, not only in moving from cover to cover, but in slipping from light to shadow, and background to background. It has to be seen to be believed.'[31] 'Human-wolves', with red eyes from watching their victims, were required to spot the elusive Pathan, the general advised, adding, 'one can't help admiring these folk, and if we don't take lessons from their doings, we deserve all we get'. This was the open question – were the British learning or were they getting all they deserved?

Afghans were encountered who believed the British were Russian troops. This was a truly biblical land, utterly cut off from the realities of the outside world. The British were only just beginning to understand how little they understood. The lack of willingness on the part of Afghans to take a leading role in the problems of their country also came as a profound and disappointing shock. The expansion of the British mission in Afghanistan had been predicated on a fantastic assumption that an Afghan Army could be trained in two or three years. Now planners were beginning to talk in terms of tens of years. The difficulty and complexity of working in a multi-lingual coalition was also beginning to sink in. There was no thin red British line in Helmand. It was a rainbow coalition, with no pot of gold at the end. As well as the presence of American troops, Helmand was shared with Danes, Czechs and Estonians. The largest contingent, a reinforced Danish battalion, occupied the midriff around the commercial town of Gereshk on the banks of the River Helmand. A Jordanian special forces company would later join the expanding force, one of the rare deployments of a Muslim contingent to assist Afghan co-religionists.

The biggest visible change was the expansion of the British 'footprints'. 3 Commando Brigade had avoided fixing itself in bases and had sought to fight a mobile counter-insurgency war. 12th Mechanized Brigade reversed this approach. By the time the brigade handed over in the autumn, British forces had built 31 new FOBs and patrol bases (although not all were manned by British soldiers). This was a clear signal of future intent and began the process that would see literally hundreds of security locations, from checkpoints to major bases, constructed in Helmand. After 2007 the British task force would always be a dispersed, fixed and an increasingly defensive force.

On 19 September, the brigade mounted its last major operation – Operation *Palk Wahel* ('Sledgehammer'). It seemed an apt name, as this is what the soldiers had been swinging all summer. The aim was to clear the village of Zumbelay (scene of the gunfight that provoked the *Sunday Times* newspaper story the previous summer). Following the clearance, a FOB would be built about 4 kilometres north of the village near a smaller settlement called Khan Nikah Radirah, in the middle of the Green Zone. The advantage of this location was that it stood on a slight hillock. FOB Keenan, as the base became known, would consequently enjoy commanding views of the surrounding area. For the local tribesmen at Zumbelay, who had once fought a pitched battle against a company of paratroopers, the arrival of about 2,500 soldiers on the edge of their village must have been a considerable surprise. In addition to the Grenadier Guards battlegroup that had taken part in the previous operation in the Gereshk Valley (Operation *Chakush*), the British task force was augmented by the newly arrived 1 Royal Gurkha Rifles and the Right Flank Company of the Scots Guards mounted in Warrior armoured personnel carriers. Brigadier Lorimer had originally requested the deployment of a company of Warriors to Helmand but had been turned down. Now the Warriors were finally being deployed, but with the successor formation, 52 (Lowland) Infantry Brigade. As if in vindication, Brigadier Lorimer bagged one of the Warriors to act as his Tactical HQ for part of the operation. The penny-pinchers at Whitehall had been beaten, if late in the day. Operation *Palk Wahel* was concluded on 1 October without British fatalities. On returning from the operation, however, a convoy carrying Gurkha soldiers ran over a roadside bomb. Captain Alexis Roberts, a popular officer who had been Prince

William's platoon officer at the Royal Military Academy Sandhurst, was killed instantly. He left behind a widow and two young daughters and his death predictably made headline news in Britain.

Captain Roberts was the first soldier to die from the successor brigade. For the departing brigade, September had also been an unlucky month, in particular for the Worcestershire and Sherwood Foresters. In June three soldiers from the regiment had been killed in separate incidents. With the handover imminent, it appeared the regiment would get off lightly. Then, on 5 September, two privates were killed in Garmsir. The youngest, Ben Ford, was a teenager. Three days later, Sergeant Craig Brelsford and a South African, Private Johan Botha, were killed in an ambush. During this confused incident that happened at night, six other soldiers were wounded. A Lieutenant Simon Cupples who was leading the platoon rallied his men and made four attempts to recover the wounded and killed from the beaten zone of the ambush. Three stricken soldiers were evacuated in this way. On a fifth attempt to recover the last body, Cupples was beaten back by the sheer weight of fire. Leaving behind a fallen comrade was quite unconscionable, so Cupples reorganized his remaining men and led a final rescue attempt that succeeded in recovering the body. For this desperate and inspirational leadership Cupples was awarded the Conspicuous Gallantry Cross. Sergeant Brelsford, who had placed his body between the line of fire and the casualties, was awarded a posthumous Military Cross.[32] On 20 September, another two soldiers were killed in an accident. In their last month in Helmand the regiment's fatality rate had doubled. The Grenadier Guards, by comparison, suffered five fatalities between the beginning of May and the end of their tour.

For the 1 Royal Anglian battlegroup it had been an especially arduous six months. Over 100 company and platoon operations had been conducted by the men of East Anglia – a quite unprecedented operational tempo in the British Army's recent history. Nine Royal Anglians had been killed (three by friendly fire), and the battlegroup as a whole had suffered 12 fatalities. Sixty-eight soldiers had been wounded in action, and a further 85 had been lost through non-combat-related injuries. Overall the battlegroup lost one-fifth of its strength – 165 men.[33] This sort of attrition had not been experienced since the Falklands Conflict. The difference between this latter conflict and the expanding war in Helmand was, of course, their duration. For how long could Britain's downsized infantry battalions sustain this level of attrition? The Royal Anglians had been involved in 354 gun fights, or roughly two for every day of their six-month tour.[34] The soldiers expended over a million bullets, twice the number that 3 PARA expended the previous summer. More than 500 grenades were posted. A large number of the newly procured Javelin missile were fired off – 87 in total, representing over £6 million's worth of missiles to kill gunmen armed with AK-47s. The regiment lobbed over 18,000 mortar bombs, called over 160 artillery fire missions and requested more than 150 close air support missions.

The increase in aerial bombing was arresting. The soldiers had, in effect, bombed and blasted their way across the Green Zone. In August 2005, NATO aircraft had dropped just 20 bombs in Afghanistan. By the following summer (when the 3 PARA battlegroup was fighting for survival in the platoon houses) this figure jumped to 242 bombs. A year later the figure had almost tripled, to 670 bombs.[35] By historical standards these were not large numbers, but the damage was localized and concentrated. The British contribution to this aerial bombardment remained modest. Harrier GR9s over the course of 2007 dropped 110 Paveways (guided bombs), and, astonishingly, 76 dumb or unguided bombs – a measure of the inadequate state of the RAF four years after the Blair government had taken the country to war in Iraq. Over 700 close air support missions had been requested, or more than one a day.

A frustrating twist to this tale of destruction was the manner in which compensation payments were granted to Helmandis. The civil servants at the Lashkar Gah PRT ruled that no compensation be paid to farmers whose compounds had been taken over by gunmen. As the farmers had little choice in the matter, this unrealistic ruling implied that little or no compensation would be paid, a proposition that Lieutenant Colonel Stuart Carver, the commanding officer of 1 Royal Anglian, found completely unacceptable. Unlike the civil servants who never ventured outside the walls of the PRT, he was acutely aware of the frictions and uncertainties of war. Eventually, after extensive lobbying, $100,000 was released for compensation payments. This was drawn from an ISAF rather than DfID fund, just as the battlegroup was leaving Helmand.

1 Royal Anglian claimed that it killed over 1,000 Taliban, and the brigade as a whole later claimed over twice this number.* The numbers

* Brigadier Lorimer reported 2,350 insurgents killed (*The Infantryman*, 2007).

were exaggerated. The Royal Anglians did kill and injure a significant number of fighters, but nowhere near the number claimed. Leaving aside the accuracy of the enemy body count, there was a more serious question – what was the point of this attritional approach to warfare? Five years into the Soviet invasion of Afghanistan the CIA estimated 40,000 insurgents had been killed, but the insurgency had grown stronger not weaker.[36] The British had an awfully long way to go before reaching these astronomic kill-count figures, and their chances of success appeared as unpromising as those of the Soviet Army.

1 Royal Anglian was the last British infantry battalion to play by the 'Brecon rules'. The platoon and section tactics adopted by the soldiers were recognizably those taught at the army's unforgiving infantry school in the hills of the Brecon Beacons. Fire and manoeuvre, the maintenance of momentum and offensive spirit were all evident. Within a year these tactics would become quite impossible, partly because of the loads infantrymen were being asked to shoulder and partly because of the threat of IEDs. Royal Marines – famed for 'yomping' across the Falkland Islands – would report that a realistic daily marching distance for the average foot soldier had been reduced to just 800 metres.

12th Mechanized Brigade as a whole had been involved in more than 800 gun fights, or a weekly average of 30.[37] Impressively, just under half of these actions had been initiated by the brigade. Brigadier Lorimer could justly claim that he had taken the fight to the enemy. By the following summer, 2 PARA would be reporting that the vast majority of gun battles were being initiated by the insurgents (yet another echo of the Vietnam War). The brigade's six-month deployment had coincided with a period of relative lack of restrictions over the use of close air support (not to be confused with rules of engagement, which were always rigorous from the beginning).[38] 12th Mechanized Brigade consequently enjoyed a golden age of close air support. Close to 3 million pounds of high explosives had been expended in Helmand's Green Zone, including over 40 of the new GMLRS rockets. Soon, nervous ISAF commanders would limit the use of aircraft in support of ground operations. When 19 Light Brigade mounted a major five-week operation two years later, just ten bombs were dropped. The aircraft were far busier than the attack helicopters because there were more of them, but the six British Apache still managed to mount over 70 missions in support of the ground troops (183 hellfire missiles were launched). The brigade as a whole fired off

10,000 shells and another 10,000 mortar bombs. It had unquestionably gone to war.

Over the course of the summer fighting 12th Mechanized Brigade had been helped by a series of American-led decapitation operations that weakened the Taliban leadership, forcing it to rethink its tactics. In total, three members of the ten-man ruling *shura* were killed. They included Mullah Obaidullah, the former Taliban defence minister who had maintained links with insurgent groups in eastern Afghanistan, and Mullah Akhtar Osmani, the former 2 Corps commander in Kandahar who had contacts with both bin Laden and Iranian sympathizers. Most significantly, Mullah Dadullah Lang, the Taliban's most ruthless and charismatic battlefield leader, was caught off guard and killed in the border areas. Dadullah 'the lame', so-called because he lost a leg in the Soviet–Afghan War, had been a thorn in Mullah Omar's side because of his independent nature. He had also displayed strong psychopathic tendencies in the past, reportedly once beheading eight prisoners and filming the event. Still, he could not afford to lose one of his best lieutenants. Faced with these heavy losses, Mullah Omar issued a decree ordering his district commanders to adopt hit-and-run tactics. Many would take heed of the last piece of advice and take up temporary, self-imposed exile in the sanctuary of Pakistan.

The fighting experienced over the summer proved fertile soil for acts of bravery. There were 184 gallantry awards that year, including five Conspicuous Gallantry Crosses, 28 Military Crosses and three Distinguished Flying Crosses. The Royal Anglians alone won six Military Crosses, a highly unusual tally for a single regiment. One of the most popular winners of a posthumous Military Cross was Captain David Hicks. Due to retire from the army, Hicks had volunteered to extend his service to see out the Afghanistan tour before being killed in the attack on FOB Inkerman at the beginning of August. Two Royal Anglian company commanders were awarded Military Crosses for inspirational leadership in battle, along with a Corporal Robert Moore, who despite being shot in the arm and losing a fillet of muscle, continued to command his section until relieved. A young lad from South Uist in the Hebrides was awarded a Conspicuous Gallantry Cross for driving a civilian plant vehicle in full view of gunmen bent on killing him. Lance Corporal Donald Campbell, serving with the Royal Engineers, continued to operate the plant, disregarding bullets pinging off the unprotected vehicle, until he managed to successfully lay a bridge.[39] A 22-year-old Private Luke Cole serving with the Worcestershire and Sherwood Foresters was also awarded the Military Cross. A Territorial Army soldier who in peacetime worked as a forklift driver, Cole was caught in an ambush and lost part of his leg. He continued to fight, even after a second bullet hit him in the stomach, stuffing his shirt into the open wound to staunch the bleeding. The citation read like an incident from the Second World War.[40]

By the time 12th Mechanized Brigade's campaign in the Green Zone began to wind down in preparation for the handover to the replacement brigade, a tone of hubris had begun to replace the optimism of the spring. The question raised by the end of the summer – what had been the overall effect of the military campaign? – had no clear answer. There was no national or provincial political solution in sight. The ANA was clearly not ready to undertake major military operations and would require close mentoring for several years. The poppy crop had enjoyed another bumper year, which would fill the Taliban's coffers over the winter months. Nobody had fully anticipated the debilitating effects of the heat. Hundreds of tonnes of bottled water had been shifted to keep the troops moving. Understanding of Helmand's 'micro-environments' – the tribal affiliations and rivalries – had been poor and, as a consequence, some operations had been clumsy. Despite the mantra that the population was at the centre of British counter-insurgency doctrine, that population had proved determinedly hostile and resistant to 'hearts and minds'.

Given these reservations, had the brigade achieved its mission? It was always unlikely 12th Mechanized Brigade would downplay its own achievements. Thirty-two soldiers had been killed, including three Danes and one Estonian. At the sharp end, officers like Major Dominic Biddick, who commanded Norfolk Company, felt his soldiers had shown 'what the British Army is capable of'.[41] From the viewpoint of the task force HQ, Lorimer had set out to plant British flags in the Taliban's backyard, and this is what his brigade had done. On returning to Britain he wrote:

> For most of the summer, 12 (Mech) Bde was in the thick of the fighting, averaging 85 hours per week in contact. It was pleasing to see that a 'normal' ground manoeuvre brigade could more than 'hack' it, despite the challenging terrain, horrendous climatic conditions and ferocious enemy activity. We undoubtedly broke the back of the Taliban in Helmand, at

> least for this year. When we departed theatre, they had suffered significant losses, their command and control was fractured and the morale of their fighters was very low. They had nothing to look back on in 2007 with any degree of satisfaction.[42]

A conclusion was drawn that security had improved and that conditions were now set for reconstruction. In an interview with *The Observer* newspaper at the Lashkar Gah PRT, Lorimer offered the following long-term view: 'If you look at the insurgency then it could take maybe 10 years. Counter-narcotics, it's 30 years. If you're looking at governance and so on, it looks a little longer.'[43]

At least the outgoing commander could not be accused of being over-optimistic. His boss, Defence Secretary Des Browne, told American counterpart Robert Gates at a meeting in London on 11 October: 'Our key to understanding success is about recognising that Afghanistan is a long term effort. Progress there is measured in terms of whether we are heading in the right direction. On these metrics, the mission is being successful and is seeing success.'[44]

A marine warrant officer writing in *British Army Review*, however, questioned the whole basis of the British campaign. At the heart of this campaign was an obsession with holding ground, the very opposite of a mobile approach to warfare. Watching the news, he could not help but notice that 12th Mechanized Brigade had been fighting over exactly the same ground where he had fought, and indeed where 3 PARA had squabbled with the locals. We seem, as he put it, to be fixated with holding ground.[45]

He was right. The British were fighting over the same ground and would continue to do so virtually for the remainder of the war (or until relieved by US Marines). Security, far from improving, was worsening. The virtues of agility and manoeuvre taught in staff courses had evaporated in the heat and mud of Helmand's Green Zone. The vision of an agile and mobile counter-insurgency campaign was entirely sunk in the fields and ditches between Sangin and Gereshk in the summer of 2007.

While the army struggled with its war in Helmand, Kabul seemed remote and even detached. With 128 diplomatic staff, the British Embassy in Kabul was one of the largest in the world. Ambassador Sherard Cowper-Coles took to blogging, and some of his offerings were eye-popping. In one blog, he described jumping around playing a wicked game of

Nintendo Wii boxing with Richard Rose, the spokesman for DfID in Afghanistan.[46]

The impression given by this and similar blogs was awful. This was Britain's most senior representative in Afghanistan, playing Nintendo boxing with the spokesman of an organization that was failing to achieve any meaningful reconstruction, hundreds of kilometres away from a front line where British soldiers were dying on a weekly basis. Rome burned while Nero fiddled?

6

The Prize is the Population

Operation *Herrick* 7, October 2007–April 2008

At one minute past midnight on Wednesday 10 October 2007, Brigadier Andrew Mackay, commander of 52 (Lowland) Infantry Brigade, assumed command of Task Force Helmand in southern Afghanistan. One of the features of the British war – at least for the first three years – was the manner in which incoming brigade commanders sought to tackle the counter-insurgency in the light of their own preconceptions and beliefs. British responsibility for the war ran from the office of the prime minister, to the defence secretary, via the Chief of the Defence Staff (CDS) in Whitehall, to the Chief of Joint Operations (CJO) in PJHQ. None took responsibility. Nobody was in charge.

In the absence of firm political direction, as well as a lack of campaign leadership from PJHQ, Helmand had become a laboratory for counter-insurgency theories. The failure of 'the comprehensive approach' also created a vacuum which the task force commanders more than readily filled. As CDS Air Chief Marshal Jock Stirrup would later remark with some frustration over his army colleagues, 'It was my experience – I think I am right in saying that I had nine brigade commanders in my time as CDS – that everyone discovered counter-insurgency afresh all by himself, or at least that is the impression one got, going up there. It became a bit frustrating.'[1] This led to the allegation that too many brigadiers were 'seeking the bubble reputation even in the cannon's mouth',[2] in the Shakespearean phrase – or more prosaically, they were writing their own promotion reports by mounting 'signature operations'.

Never was the contrast between two brigade commanders more acute than between Lorimer, the outgoing brigade commander, and Mackay. Both sincerely believed they had the right approach to counter-insurgency. Both were intelligent and reasonable men. Both brought experience and impressive commitment to the job. It was noteworthy then that both chose exactly opposing approaches to the task of suppressing the insurgency.

Brigadier Andrew Mackay was not one of the glamorous younger brigadiers in the army. He sported no parachute badges or commando daggers. His extensive experience in post-conflict environments included staff and command appointments in IFOR, SFOR and KFOR;* overseeing justice and security reforms in Kosovo; and training police in Baghdad. He belonged to an older generation of soldiers and he was immensely loyal to his brigade. 52 Infantry Brigade was a 'territorial brigade' rather than a front-line brigade. Based at Edinburgh's Redford Cavalry Barracks, the brigade's main business before the war had been humdrum regional training and civic events, not fighting a real enemy. 52 Infantry Brigade had great experience in organizing military tattoos and none in fighting the Taliban. If the army had not been downsized, the brigade would never have been raised to fighting strength and sent on operations – it was a measure of continuing manpower problems that this regional brigade was being mustered at all. Everybody was conscious of the brigade's lower league origins, and Brigadier Mackay was determined to put doubters in their place.

One of the main problems facing Mackay, as intelligent commentators like Anthony Cordesman persuasively argued, was that the war in Afghanistan was not the war that ISAF had wanted or planned for; it had metamorphosed from a legitimate act of self-defence in response to the September 11 attacks into a drifting counter-insurgency without clear purpose, rationale or adequate resources. Historian Donald Mrozek's description of the Vietnam War would have served equally well for Afghanistan: the conflict had become 'a creature with no creator'. The creature had outgrown the master, leaving behind pathetic self-deception and 'the ache of irresolution'.[3] 'Mission creep' had spread with viral speed. NATO was now embroiled in several wars, against several actors across Afghanistan, ranging from former warlords in the east to criminal gangs in

*Implementation Force (Bosnia and Herzegovina), Stabilisation Force and Kosovo Force

the south-west, and none of these wars had an obvious or speedy resolution. In this war, Cordesman argued, Taliban-bashing was proving fruitless.[4]

An all-embracing and comprehensive civilian as well as military strategy for resolving this mess was entirely absent. Instead, ISAF had a plethora of 'plans', no sooner promulgated than changed by the next general on a six-month tour, and a civil mission that was badly failing to offer any credible programmes. In the unimpeachable judgement of another Vietnam War author – an anonymous contributor to the Pentagon Papers – 'premises were transformed into conclusions, desiderata institutionalized as objectives, and wish took on the character of the force of imperative'.[5] Such was ISAF in 2007.

The insurgency was only one among many intractable problems. The opium poppy crop had reached record levels. Since 2002, the United States alone had provided over $1.5 billion to stem the production and trafficking of illicit drugs in Afghanistan. Despite American and more modest British efforts in counter-narcotics, the UN estimated that by the time 52 Infantry Brigade arrived in 2007, opium poppy cultivation had increased again by 17 per cent from 165,000 to 193,000 hectares. About four-fifths of farming families in Helmand grew the opium poppy, which provided them with 35 per cent of their annual income. In 2007 this was estimated at $528 million.[6] This implied that four-fifths of Helmand's farmers enjoyed some sort of relationship with the Taliban, as it was the insurgents who provided the protection to the farmers and traffickers. The overwhelming vested interest was not weighted in favour of a defeat of the Taliban. The income derived by the Taliban was not less than $50 million – applying the crude 10 per cent *ushr* tax – but from numerous spin-off businesses, including heroin production, it was almost certainly higher. Across the country the UN estimated that the total value of opium and its derivatives was equal to at least a third of Afghanistan's licit economy.[7] This was a country addicted to criminality.

The Afghan National Security Forces were too small and incapable of dealing with the myriad problems facing Afghanistan. There were perhaps just 20,000 ANA, of which probably one quarter were absent from duty anyway, and just over 60,000 ANP. Absenteeism and corruption in the latter was endemic. A US Government Accountability Office report soberly noted that just one of the 72 police units established post the 2001 invasion was actually capable of operating alongside Western forces.[8] Six years after the US-led invasion, Afghanistan still had no nationwide judiciary system, which made the police at best ineffectual and at worst rapacious dispensers of corrupt justice. Traditional mechanisms for solving disputes as well as the prompt Taliban justice system prevailed across wide swathes of rural Afghanistan.

Reconstruction also remained at too small a scale, and the different national PRTs were not coordinated. In terms of international trade, Afghanistan's exports were naturally dominated by illicit narcotics, which had an estimated total value of $2.7–2.8 billion per year, according to the World Bank. By contrast, officially recorded exports were estimated at several hundred million dollars. In 2005, the most recent year for which data was available, development assistance from international donors was estimated at $2.8 billion, or over a third the size of the national economy. How much of this pledged money was actually spent (and how) could not be explained with any confidence. ISAF remained a divided alliance – divisions that would be exposed as Brigadier Mackay found himself relying on American boots and firepower to recapture Musa Qaleh. At the beginning of 2007, when 52 Infantry Brigade deployed, there were 107 national caveats in place within ISAF. The military ideal of 'unity of action' had to grind through the sand-clogged cogs of these caveats every time ISAF attempted to launch a multinational operation.

Nationwide, violence had grown by over 30 per cent. In 2006, there had been a monthly average of over 400 attacks. By 2007, this had climbed to a monthly average of 566 attacks.[9] In 2002, there had been just 22 IED attacks in Afghanistan. By 2007, there were this many IED attacks every week.*[10] A suicide attack was now happening every three days, and Afghanistan was becoming a prohibitively dangerous country for aid workers – 40 had been killed, and double this number had been abducted in the previous year.[11] A US CENTCOM brief reported that only 183 of some 1,767 armed illegal groups had pledged to disband and hand in their weapons (somewhat putting the problem of the 'Taliban' in perspective). This meagre result had yielded (along with cache finds), an astonishing total of almost 30,000 light weapons and over 4,000 heavy weapons. The total amount of ammunition collected was just over 9,000 tonnes.[12] Privately, Western diplomats assessed that there were at least 3,000 illegal militias still at large in Afghanistan.[13] 'The Taliban' was truly

*The numbers were 2002 (22 IEDs), to 2003 (83), 2004 (325), 2005 (782), 2006 (1,931) and 2007 (2,615).

a label of convenience that barely reflected the fractured, armed state of Afghanistan. The number of weapons and tonnage of ammunition still at large could only be speculated. It was probably not an exaggeration to assume that every man of fighting age in Afghanistan owned at least a rifle.

In short, ISAF was badly failing the Abrams Test, named after General Creighton Abrams, who closed America's war in Vietnam. The general, weary of being assured that a district in Vietnam had been secured, posed the challenge: if he could not walk somewhere during the day, or drive somewhere at night, without protection, then security had not been achieved. Nowhere in Helmand passed the Abrams Test, or ever would.

52 Infantry Brigade deployed with four infantry battalions, an increase of one battalion on the previous brigade. The Coldstream Guards, commanded by Lieutenant Colonel George Waters, deployed in late September, although the battalion complete would not arrive in Helmand until the end of October. The lack of RAF transport aircraft to fly the infantry battalions in one lift to theatre (or an unwillingness to bear the cost of contracting civilian aircraft) meant that units were still arriving in Helmand in dribs and drabs, 18 months after Lieutenant Colonel Stuart Tootal, the 3 PARA commanding officer, had complained about the disruptive effect this caused. The principal role of the Coldstream Guards would be to act as mentors for the ANA as well providing manning for the newly formed Joint District Coordination Centres in Kajaki, Sangin, Gereshk and Garmsir. These JDCCs were viewed as key to coordinating one of the pillars in the British strategy – 'Security Sector Reform' – or the training of the ANA and ANP. This, as every previous unit reported, continued to be a source of great frustration. Captain Russell, who commanded the Reconnaissance Platoon and was responsible for training an ANP company, commonly recalled turning up for work and finding 'thoroughly high coppers who only have an interest in the monetary side of their work'.[14]

Of the remainder of the battalion, Number 1 Company was deployed to Kabul, where it would remain for the duration of the tour, providing security for the British civilian mission in the capital. This was compensated by taking under command the Right Flank Company of the Scots Guards mounted in Warriors. This company would fight a gruelling war, deployed in the field for all but 12 days of the tour. One would probably have to go back to World War II to find a British Army company spending such an extended period living out of the back of armoured vehicles. By the end of the tour, the Warriors had become the guardsmen's homes. The insurgents came to know them as the 'Desert Devils'.

This left only a single Coldstream company – Number 3 Company – to undertake operations in the Green Zone. This company was deployed to the Battlegroup North area, in FOB Keenan, where it would later be joined by a Danish contingent.[15] The guardsmen took over the base from A Company of the Worcestershire and Sherwood Foresters. On completing his reconnaissance of the various outposts, Lieutenant Colonel Waters noticed just how basic living conditions were at FOB Keenan, possibly, he mused, to encourage his guardsmen to 'get out and find the Taliban'.[16] Later in the tour, Waters would revisit this company and find himself stuck for five days because of the 'disgraceful' lack of helicopters. His complaint was wholly justified – the entire brigade was being supported by just seven helicopters of which, on any given day, probably four were available. When the operation to recapture Musa Qaleh was mounted, this was, in fact, the maximum number of support helicopters the British could muster.

The second infantry battalion was provided by the Green Howards (2 Yorks) whose regimental head was the new CGS, General Richard Dannatt. A Company was deployed alongside 40 Commando in Sangin and took over the manning of Waterloo, Tangiers, Nijmegen and Blenheim patrol bases. The majority of this battalion was split into four OMLTs to act as mentors to the ANA. This important training role would be overtaken by events later in the tour. In November, a company of the Green Howards was deployed to FOB Arnhem to release the Right Flank Company of the Scots Guards, that would take part in the major operation of the brigade's tour – the expulsion of the Taliban from Musa Qaleh. The remainder of the battalion would also be committed to this operation. A Company, together with the Reconnaissance Platoon, would be left behind in Musa Qaleh, following the conclusion of the operation, to take over a newly established district centre in a half-built 'hotel' on the edge of the town. Before the arrival of the British, this building, which was adjacent to the governor's offices and a barracks, was being used to store opium – a perfect illustration of the nexus between the local Taliban, drug traffickers and the civil authorities. The Green Howards also importantly provided the core of the BRF which initially assisted the Coldstream Guards with 'hearts and minds' tasks in the Lower Gereshk Valley, and later became involved in the retaking of Musa Qaleh.

The third infantry unit was drawn from 1 Royal Gurkha Rifles, which deployed with three rifle companies. A and C Companies were deployed to Kandahar where they acted as the regional reserve and were later joined by B Company of the Royal Welsh. B Company was deployed to southern Helmand and took over FOBs Dwyer and Delhi. The latter base would host Prince Henry of Wales, covertly deployed to Helmand following a gentleman's agreement with the media that would later be broken. The Gurkha native language, Nepali, was sufficiently related to the Pashto and Dari tongues to allow basic communication with the locals – an important advantage which the British soldiers in the task force did not enjoy. The Gurkhas were also superb soldiers. In their six-month tour they suffered just one fatality (from an IED strike), a testament to their professionalism.

The fourth infantry unit for the brigade was provided by 40 Commando. Although the marines had only just left the province six months previously, the combination of a lack of army infantry units and the 'arms plot' (essentially the system of rotation of units) meant that a marine commando had to be 'borrowed' to take the brigade to full strength. This unit was deployed to the Battlegroup North area and operated from Sangin, Now Zad and Kajaki. The Marine Armoured Support Group equipped with Vikings also remained with the brigade.

C Squadron of the HCR in the meantime had taken over from the Light Dragoons and deployed to the Battlegroup South area (FOBs Dwyer and Delhi), where it was judged the tracked Scimitar vehicles would be best employed in the open desert. Later in the tour the HCR would form a composite battlegroup that would take part in the operation to reclaim Musa Qaleh. To the disappointment of the cavalrymen, very little had changed since their tour in the summer of 2006. Most of the vehicles they were driving were older than the troopers – just keeping the Scimitars on the road without constantly having to stop to deal with breakdowns was a major challenge.

The failure to provide the Royal Armoured Corps with a new reconnaissance vehicle – to replace a vehicle whose design dated to the 1960s – was a procurement headache that had simmered without resolution for decades. The army had originally procured 486 Scimitars. Scimitar, part of the larger CVR(T) family of vehicles, was actually a success story and an innovative vehicle in its time. Like so many other British defence industry success stories of the post-war period, it then withered in the infertile soil of chronic defence procurement mismanagement. All the hard-won expertise from the war was lost, piece by piece, and succeeded by a plague of programmes notable for silly abbreviations and little else. Over the next 40 years, the replacement so-called Family of Light Armoured Vehicles (FLAV) programme became the Future Family of Light Armoured Vehicles (FFLAV) programme; which became the Tactical Reconnaissance Armoured Combat Equipment Requirement (TRACER) programme; which became the Multi-Role Armoured Vehicle (MRAV) programme; which became the impossibly futuristic Future Rapid Effects System Specialist Vehicle (FRES-SV) programme; which eventually became the troubled AJAX programme – and not a single vehicle was added to the fleet of the Royal Armoured Corps. Not one.

By the time the British Army deployed to Helmand, the original Scimitar fleet had shrunk by a third, of which only about 160 vehicles were still working.[17] Within three years, the government would be forced to tender a contract to restart the production of the CVR(T) (with BAE Systems) because the surviving vehicles were literally falling apart. They were also too vulnerable to IEDs, and eventually an upgraded vehicle based on the Spartan chassis with a raised floor – CVR(T)2 – was brought into service.

52 Infantry Brigade was also supported in Helmand by enlarged Danish and Estonian contingents. The British were extremely fortunate with these two allies and relations were excellent throughout – not a small achievement given the tensions generated in a war. Transfer of authority of the Gereshk area to the Danish battlegroup was finally formalized during the 52 Infantry Brigade's tour, releasing British troops for operations elsewhere. The Danes remained at FOB Price located to the west of Gereshk and also took responsibility for the ring of patrol bases east of the town. The Danish battlegroup was roughly comparable to a British battlegroup but included unique resources, not least the only tanks in Helmand, a troop of Leopard 2A6s. The now 30-strong Danish CIMIC team was also proving highly effective and embarrassingly showing up the lack of British reconstruction programmes elsewhere (the Danish reconstruction plan was in fact adopted by the British PRT in Lashkar Gah, although complaints over resources persisted).[18] The Estonians provided a mechanized company whose soldiers proved doughty fighters, some having previously fought for the Soviet Army in Afghanistan. This company would take over responsibility for Now Zad, a town completely gutted by fighting, which it handed over to US Marines in the following year.

52 Infantry Brigade benefited from new equipment that had begun to arrive in theatre with the previous brigade. The two Israeli Hermes 450 UAVs, leased by the British government, were beginning to provide useful intelligence. The feed from these aerial platforms was played on large screens at the task force HQ, but more importantly, Fire Support Teams (FSTs) on the ground, equipped with American Rover III terminals, could also view the footage. This capability was greatly welcomed, but British dependency on foreign expertise and technology was again exposed. Civilian contractors were also needed to keep the UAVs flying (and crucially to land the UAVs safely). The Hermes 450 detachment was joined in November by the RAF's first Reaper UAV and in early December by an upgraded variant of the mini-UAV Desert Hawk. Both were American manufactured. The British would be conducting armed Reaper missions by the summer of 2008.[19] For the RAF that had just retired its last Canberra – a museum-piece aircraft – Reaper represented salvation. 39 Squadron was reformed as a UAV squadron, and 1115 Flight decamped to Nellis Air Force Base in Nevada (from where the British had to fly their Reaper because the American-owned infrastructure required to support Predator operations was not budgeted). Nobody in 1115 Flight likely protested at the inconvenience of being posted to Nevada.

The problem of IEDs was also being addressed more convincingly; the original Ebex mine detector was phased out and replaced by the more sensitive two-tone German Vallon mine detector. Over time this latter mine detector would be supplemented by more sensitive and specialized detectors, again all foreign manufactured, as British defence industry had lost this basic capability.

Brigadier Mackay was probably the most thoughtful task force commander who served in Helmand and he would later resign his commission, it was speculated, from a sense of disappointment over the manner in which the war was being prosecuted. From the outset Mackay was clear that, in the words of the much-quoted adage: 'the insurgent wins if he does not lose and we lose if we do not win'.[20] Nobody could disagree with this, but what did winning mean? Did it necessarily mean winning battles? Or winning ground? Or was the task force just winning time for a lagging political process? For Mackay, what really mattered was winning the population, and at the heart of his counter-insurgency philosophy was the phrase 'the prize is the population'. In this respect, Mackay played John the Baptist to the Messiah McChrystal.

Countering the tide of positive reporting from Helmand, Mackay was ruthlessly honest about the limitations and challenges facing the British task force, as well as his own frailties. 'How could anyone,' he conceded with some humility, 'capture the totality of what we are engaged in?'[21] Nobody, he argued with some truth, not even the Afghans, truly understood the complex interplay of tribal relationships and power struggles bubbling in Helmand.

The enemy that seemed to have been well beaten by 12th Mechanized Brigade's summer offensive could not be underestimated. 'Insurgents are the living proof why man is at the top of the food chain,' he wrote.

> If we are the most creative, treacherous, loyal, aggressive and determined life form yet to evolve then the insurgent as a species is in robust good health. Insurgents are not impressed with conventional power either. They respect it but constantly seek ways round it and are forever displaying remarkable levels of ingenuity. We also underestimate, at our peril the resilience of the Taliban and its capacity to regenerate.[22]

What Mackay wanted from his officers and men was questioning and open minds, not orthodoxies: 'The successful counter-insurgents are those that are able to join the dots that create a vision that others have not seen, think laterally, integrate capabilities that no one else had thought of and who constantly question perceived wisdom.'[23]

Winning for Mackay could not be achieved by defeating the Taliban in any military sense. Winning was about perception. It would only be achieved by wresting the consent of the population away from the insurgent. Mackay would later write a thesis expounding his philosophy of 'influence operations' and leave it as a parting shot to the army he loyally served for 29 years.[24] 'If you wish to capture the operational design of the counterinsurgency campaign in Helmand in two sentences it is this,' he wrote, 'we will CLEAR, HOLD, BUILD where we can and DISRUPT, INTERDICT, DEFEAT where we cannot.'[25]

This should not have been a forlorn hope given the general unpopularity of the Taliban, but the British, so far, had made very heavy weather of it. In the same way that Thomas had warned that every bullet discharged was a potential tactical victory for the Taliban, so Mackay argued that every action undertaken by British soldiers created a perception in the eyes of the local tribesmen, positive or negative. It behoved the counter-insurgent therefore to scrupulously ensure that every action represented a positive influence, as only by influencing the perceptions of the population would that population be won over. Bluntly, 'the more force is used, the less effective it is'.[26] Mackay was so firm on this point he prohibited body counts, which he viewed as 'a corrupt measure of success', and he insisted no such statistics be presented on PowerPoint slides (a side rebuke to the previous brigade that had been quite keen to boast over how many insurgents it claimed to kill).[27] Nobody should be fooled, he argued, by the difficulty of the task the British had set themselves: 'In this business anything that resembles 70% is good enough.'[28] By some measures the task force was falling short of even this B minus.

There was a counter-argument to this philosophy of 'influence operations', and it was that the people did not want to be won over – most Helmandis just wanted ISAF to leave. Lord Frederick Roberts's famous quote (which would be used to headline an exhibition on Britain's Afghan wars at the National Army Museum in London) carried an important germ of truth: 'We have nothing to fear from Afghanistan, and the best thing to do is to leave it as much as possible to itself. It may not be very flattering to our amour propre but I feel sure I am right when I say that the less the Afghans see of us the less they will dislike us.'

In the winter of 2007 ISAF could not take this option. Whether they liked it or not, Helmand's farmers were going to see a lot more of the Westerners for the foreseeable future. The second strong counter-argument was that a now aroused enemy would not be 'influenced' and could only be killed. This task, as we shall see, fell to the American Task Force 1 Fury, which was much less impressed with notions of mysteriously 'influencing' the Taliban into defeat.

This then was Mackay's counter-insurgency philosophy: persuasion, not force, lateral thinking and not literal thinking, the population and not the insurgent as the prize – but how was it being interpreted by his brigade 'outside the wire'?

Once the companies had settled in at their several bases, familiarization patrols and the odd gun battle with locals soon became the daily routine. Traditionally, the winter had always been the fighting off-season in Afghanistan, partly because of the weather, and partly because of the lack of cover. When Number 3 Company of the Coldstream Guards took over FOB Keenan, roughly 15 kilometres north of Gereshk, they found themselves under immediate attack from local gunmen. The base was no more than a large compound by a village called Khan Nikeh Hadirah, but the thick mud-brick walls offered good protection against the inaccurate enemy fire. Major Charles commanding the company described the first attack:

> As luck would have it on our first night in role after the previous company had left the Taleban decided to greet us with a combined attack of mortars, small arms fire and rocket propelled grenades! Thankfully such are their poor operating skills they failed to hit the target. We however were more precise. But this did not put off the Taleban as they came again the very next night only this time an hour later. This time with more weapons at our disposal we managed to give them even more of a bloody nose, so much so that since this failed attack they have not bothered us again.[29]

After these futile attacks on the newcomers, the gunmen changed tactics and started ambushing patrols mounted from the base. These attacks similarly failed to cause any casualties and the attacks began to peter out. The guardsmen themselves also had to curtail patrolling due to the unreliability of the generator in the base which meant they could not recharge the batteries for their radios or ECM equipment. In the end there was a temporary stalemate brought about by poor logistics on the British side and a cultural indisposition to fight in cold weather on the Afghan side.

The deterioration in the weather saw the level of attacks drop dramatically, although the threat of a chance encounter with armed villagers never went away. In fact, FOB Keenan was not attacked again until 6 December, which the guardsmen attributed to their lack of patrolling, having been forced to maintain a platoon at constant readiness as a Quick Reaction Force (QRF) for the brigade.[30] This suggested that a peaceful *modus vivendi* was being maintained, *not* by patrolling, but by staying out of sight and thus not giving the locals an excuse to start a gun battle. This insight seemed to bypass everyone. In their entire six months at FOB Keenan the guardsmen only bothered to mount two deliberate operations (Operations *Spotty Dog Bark* and *Growl* in January), which barely met any resistance. If one example could be plucked from Operation *Herrick* 7 of sensible, low-key counter-insurgency tactics and 'hearts and minds', the experience of Number 3 Company of the Coldstream Guards would be it.

For local, mainly Ishaqzai tribesmen in nearby villages the pressing business became compensation claims. When it became apparent that the guardsmen were prepared to pay compensation for war damage, a trickle of claims turned into a torrent. A free weekly medical clinic also became popular, and the guardsmen donated loudspeaker systems and blankets to local mosques to generate goodwill. A *shura* was held, which had its comical moment when an American helicopter flew overhead:

> This [*shura*] went down extremely well and was only briefly interrupted when the tent that the thirty odd attendees were sat in took off and then promptly collapsed – an American Chinook decided to hover over the Shura ... The scene was reminiscent of something from the Monty Python Show as a group of thirty hysterical Afghans struggled to pull themselves out of the tarpaulin crying with laughter.[31]

The tent may have collapsed, but the persistence paid off and meetings like this led to more *shuras* and confidence-building with the local population.

Organizing these confidence-winning measures – ultimately setting foundations for the success or failure of the British mission in Helmand – was a responsibility laid on very young shoulders. In Number 3 Company, the entire effort was being run by a Lieutenant Law and a small team of dedicated NCOs. Major Charles, again, described this side of his soldiers:

> The men have been showing their softer side in dealing with the locals. A 2 year old girl was brought to our camp the other day with injuries to her head and shoulder. The level of medical assistance and knowlegde [sic] out here is extremely basic so her parents could do little for her. However, LCpl Constantine did some stirling [sic] work whilst getting through most of his sweet selection, before she was extracted back to Camp Bastion for some proper medical attention ... Aside from the medical condition the little girl required it was evident that her physical size was far smaller than that expected of an average child of the same age back in the UK. Clearly undernourished, the provision of food for families is a real concern.[32]

Ultimately, Number 3 Company's experience at FOB Keenan revealed the overstretched nature of the British task force. It was noteworthy this was the single British company conducting 'hearts and minds' operations in the entire task force, as Mackay would have wished it. Every other available company was holding besieged outposts or eventually was drawn into the operation to recapture Musa Qaleh. This was far too little effort devoted to winning over the population, and it represented a terrible imbalance despite Brigadier Mackay's determination to focus on the population rather than on fighting.

Elsewhere, the poorly resourced nature of British operations in southern Afghanistan, 18 months after the initial deployment, could not be hidden. Some units were simply forced to improvise as they went along. The experience of B Company of the Royal Welsh was typical. The entire battalion had initially been ear-marked for operations with 52 Infantry Brigade in Afghanistan. At short notice this posting was changed, and the battalion was ordered to prepare for operations in Iraq. At even shorter notice (with the commanding officer already in Iraq conducting his reconnaissance), this decision was reversed again and it was decided to send just one company to Iraq and a second to Afghanistan. The root of the problem, as ever, was the debilitating under-manning of the chopped infantry regiments. Over this period, every single infantry regiment that survived the culling of Future Army Structures (FAS 2003–06) was routinely undermanned by as much as a company. This created an impossible headache for planners trying to meet commitments in both Iraq and Afghanistan.

Given the uncertainty of their final destination, B Company had little time to prepare adequately before being deployed to Afghanistan. The plan was that the company would form a new theatre reserve for the entire ISAF command in south-west Afghanistan and be based at Kandahar. Once in theatre, however, the company discovered that no resources had been allocated for it to fulfil this new role, and everything the company needed to go to war was sitting in Camp Bastion. Eventually the company was allocated a batch of spare Land Rover Snatch vehicles. Due to the lack of helicopters, numerous operations were abruptly cancelled. Poor communications exacerbated their difficulties. In some instances, the company headed off on an operation only to discover that a different set of orders had arrived, too late. Remarkably, the Welshmen saw out the entire tour without any ECM equipment – an unthinkable situation within one year. Despite these unsatisfactory conditions, the soldiers managed to mount a number of effective operations and returned home without suffering any fatalities.

But this was a portrait of a task force held together with black masking tape and bungee cords; an army fire-fighting with scant resources, not an army equipped to do its job.

By the time 52 Infantry Brigade approached the mid-way point of its tour, it was evident the Taliban had effectively stalemated British forces in the south in Garmsir and in the north at Kajaki. Sangin and Now Zad remained relatively quiescent compared to earlier levels of fighting. Musa Qaleh had become a safe haven for assorted drug barons and Taliban, and it was clear that the town would have to be recaptured. Despite this, the brigade felt that by pursuing a measured counter-insurgency strategy (COIN rather than Hi-COIN, which amounted to open fighting), some rewards were being reaped. The mentoring of the ANA was progressing, a process that would culminate during the operation to retake Musa Qaleh. The 'footprints' inherited from 12th Mechanized Brigade had been retained, and 36 Engineer Regiment had added a further four patrol bases as well as numerous checkpoints. The headquarters set-up had been retained and expanded. The Lashkar Gah PRT was now crammed with military and civilian personnel in dwindling and limited real estate.

The problem of IEDs was worrisome but not overwhelming. In the summer of 2006, the 3 PARA battlegroup had encountered 80 IEDs. The commandos that followed them dealt with 137 such devices. 12th Mechanized Brigade encountered 344, and 52 Infantry Brigade would encounter even more. All this significantly increased the workload on the 60-odd strong Joint Force Explosive Ordnance Disposal (JFEOD) group, which included only one Improvised Explosive Device Disposal (IEDD) Team, as well as a High Risk Search Team and Conventional Munitions Disposal Team. Every combat fatality incurred by 52 Infantry Brigade would be caused by an IED – the only brigade to suffer this experience. For some, this single statistic was proof the Taliban had switched tactics from conventional stand-off to 'asymmetric warfare'. This was a simplification of a more complicated picture. The widespread use of IEDs was always going to increase as bomb-making skills spread. And the Taliban never stopped ambushing or engaging in gun battles with British forces, even after the IED became the principal weapon in their armoury.

Intelligence – always the capstone in counter-insurgency – was slowly beginning to improve, although serious deficiencies remained. Mackay had urged every soldier to see himself as an intelligence gatherer, but the British were still a long way off gaining a comprehensive understanding of their patch of Afghanistan. One of the most effective means of achieving this was by using commercially available short- and long-wave radio receivers, or ICOM scanners. These were proving a ready way of intercepting insurgent communications. The insurgents knew full well their conversations were being listened into and often traded insults with the Afghan interpreters working for the British. Cannier and more disciplined commanders enforced radio silence, but the average insurgent foot soldier was a compulsive talker. These intercepts provided information at the tactical level.

At the operational level, better information was beginning to flow through various means, including the cultivation of informers. SIS opened a sub-station in south-west Afghanistan, and the British special forces contingent, originally known as Task Force 42 (the designator number would change over the course of the war), acted as a conduit for 'actionable intelligence'. Often the best sources were the Afghan soldiers themselves. The British were constantly surprised by how quickly the indigenous soldiers spotted 'an absence of the normal and the presence of the abnormal', which usually signalled impending trouble. To most British soldiers, Afghans were largely indistinguishable. The ANA, naturally, could straight away detect an out-of-place regional accent, or the typical features that distinguished a Pashtun from a Tajik or Uzbek.

Keeping this expanding force supplied, watered and fed was beginning to prove a gruelling challenge. The 6,000-kilometre air bridge was the quickest route to Helmand, but arriving in theatre could still take 48 hours, and the limited number of available aircraft meant that the bulk of heavy supplies had to be transported by sea. The lead time for an item arriving via Pakistan, on the ship-borne route, was between two and three months, and the land passage remained vulnerable to brigandage and insurgent ambushes.

For the army mechanics of 1 Equipment Support Battalion REME, Helmand was proving a logistic nightmare. Conventional army doctrine espoused a 'forward repair' policy, with the deployment of Light Aid Detachments or LADs with sub-units. In Helmand this proved wholly unfeasible and the doctrine had to be turned on its head. Instead, a 'hub and spoke' scheme had to be adopted, with casualty vehicles recovered back to Camp Bastion rather than repaired at the forward bases.

However, this is where the problems started. No bespoke vehicle repair facilities had been planned or built for Operation *Herrick*. The IT infrastructure was inadequate, complicating every task, from ordering spares to maintaining repair rosters. Publications pertaining to new equipment or vehicles were not available. Vehicle breakdowns were so frequent that an impossible demand was placed on the limited numbers of recovery crews driving antiquated Foden vehicles (which themselves broke down and had to be recovered). The situation became so acute (over 600 recoveries had been undertaken by the previous brigade) that additional recovery crews had to be collected in Britain and sent at short notice to Helmand (incidentally, without the usual pre-deployment training, such was the crisis that had developed and the lack of recovery crews in the downsized Royal Mechanical and Electrical Engineers).

Due to the lack of spares and the difficulties with ordering spares, a World War II-style cannibalization policy had to be adopted. Repair jobs could take two or three times as long to complete because the appropriate spare part had to be first removed from another vehicle. Added to the time needed to recover a vehicle to Bastion and then return it to its crew, this meant that a significant proportion of the army's vehicle fleet in Helmand was permanently off the road. The vehicles that were on the road were always on the cusp of breaking down again. When the task force undertook the operation to recapture Musa Qaleh in December that year, a quarter of its trucks broke down. In the Crimean War, Sir John Burgoyne had lamented, 'nine-tenths of the evils of the army were attributable to the want of transport'. A century and a half later, a British expeditionary force was once again labouring with inadequate vehicles, vehicles so old they were falling apart, and a maintenance system unfit for purpose. These frustrations were publicly voiced by the brigade's deputy chief of staff, Major Nick Haston, who resigned his commission in protest at the shambolic support given to front-line troops. He was the fifth officer to resign in protest in a war that was barely a year old.* That something was clearly wrong with the way in which the government was supporting the army could hardly be hidden.

The poor state of the road fleet placed great demands on air resupply. In 2007, there were over 12,000 tactical airlift sorties and more than 500 air drops.[33] The workhorses of this effort were the RAF's C-130Js that conducted low-altitude night missions to resupply FOBs using an air-dropped container delivery system (aircraft that would be retired

*After Brigadier Butler, Lieutenant Colonel Tootal, Major Pike and Captain Docherty.

in the near future to cut costs). Between May and December 2007, crews delivered nearly 1,000 containers with 800 tonnes of food, water, ammunition, fuel, generators and even power plants for broken-down vehicles. Without these air drops the tempo of operations could not have been sustained because there were insufficient helicopters to service the requirement for cargo lift.

The lack of helicopters was causing not only military friction but also a political storm. By December 2007, the pressure on the Labour government to address this very public issue reached a crisis point. One week before Christmas, Defence Secretary Des Browne announced that a £62 million contract had been awarded to convert eight mothballed Chinook Mk3 into the support helicopter role. These notorious airframes had once been intended as special forces helicopters, but a procurement wrangle over software with the manufacturer had left them permanently grounded. Now they would be returned to the air (or at least six of them were, because two had already been cannibalized), but this would take several years. In the meantime, the task force would have to struggle on with its limited helicopter fleet. The burden on the Joint Helicopter Force (JHF) continued to rise over this period. Between May 2007 and the following summer, the number of passengers lifted jumped from 4,377 to 31,824.[34] Total freight increased from 779,500 tonnes to 1,130,000 tonnes. Casualty evacuations also inevitably increased from 375 to 607.

The climax of 52 Infantry Brigade's tour was Operation *Mar Karardad* ('Snakebite'), the expulsion of the Taliban from the town of Musa Qaleh. Everybody knew it was coming but nobody could agree on how it should be undertaken. The town elders had run the town for 143 days after the British withdrawal in September 2006, but for the last ten months the Taliban had held the town. Musa Qaleh was not just a military problem (which, taken in isolation, was straightforward), but rather a political problem with many ramifications. For the Americans, the failed Musa Qaleh deal was still the stone in the shoe in their relationship with the British. Ever suspicious that their ally lacked the will to fight, these fears were being reinforced by events in Iraq where a controversial British withdrawal was unfolding. For the Afghan government that initially welcomed the Musa Qaleh deal and British withdrawal in 2006, Taliban domination of the town was an affront and an embarrassment that had to be reversed. A violent Fallujah-style operation, however, was not favoured. For the British, who always regretted being drawn into Musa Qaleh in the first place, there was a certain frustration that what should have been an example of British subtlety and good sense turned sour after heavy-handed American air strikes in the area provoked a Taliban reaction. Regardless of their previous differences, all three partners knew they had to succeed in Musa Qaleh to restore the credibility of the Afghan government.

52 Infantry Brigade did not arrive in Helmand with a plan to retake Musa Qaleh. If circumstances had been different, the Taliban may have enjoyed another winter in charge of the town and the task would have been handed to 16 Air Assault Brigade, the successor brigade. A plan arose by chance, as a result of an unexpected defection, and it occurred early in the tour. On 30 October, Right Flank Company of the Scots Guards, based at FOB Arnhem, was ordered to redeploy with its Warriors to Shah Kariz, a small village east of Musa Qaleh, to protect an ex-Taliban commander. The name of this commander was Mullah Abdul Salaam, and in the fullness of time he would become a byword for corruption and dashed hopes.

How Mullah Salaam entered the picture encapsulated all the contradictions bedevilling the war in Afghanistan. Northern Helmand was dominated by the Alizai tribe, which as we have seen was divided into three principal sub-tribes: the Pirzai, Hassanzai and Khalozai. Abdul Salaam was a Pirzai. Rural settlements tended to be dominated by a single sub-tribe, but in Musa Qaleh all branches were mixed, creating a fractious environment. Sher Akhundzada, the former governor of Helmand deposed by the British, had never stopped scheming in his Alizai heartlands. The loss of Musa Qaleh – his town – had been a grave loss. Seeing an opportunity to retake the town by backing a marginalized Taliban commander, Akhundzada, now with a seat in the Afghan legislature, persuaded President Karzai that Mullah Salaam should be championed and encouraged to evict his former Taliban colleagues from Musa Qaleh. Karzai had a sympathetic bent towards Akhundzada whom he felt had been unfairly treated by the British.

In a brilliant piece of detective work by Michael Martin, it appears an ingenious game of Afghan duplicity was played on Karzai (as well as on SIS, which got involved in the Salaam saga).[35] There were in fact three Mullah Salaams, like a riddle in a story from the *Arabian Nights*. SIS was backing *the* Mullah Salaam, the Pirzai former ex-Taliban. Karzai, it appears, thought that Mullah Salaam was an Alizai/Khalozai ex-Baghrani commander, whose brother Zakir was in Guantanamo. Zakir coincidentally was released on the day Musa Qaleh was finally secured, and Martin suggests Karzai may have conflated Zakir's imminent release with his brother switching sides. Sher Akhundzada, it appears, craftily did not advise Karzai that he was confusing two Mullah Salaams. Lastly, there was a third Noorzai Mullah Salaam who had been a Taliban corps commander (he played no role in the plot).

The plan hatched by the wily Akhundzada was seductive. If it worked, it could be claimed that an Afghan solution had been found for an Afghan problem and there would be little bloodshed. The story may have unfolded thus anyway, but others disagreed. For the ISAF Commander, General Dan McNeill, the whole scheme sounded hare-brained. McNeill may have trusted in God, but after that he trusted in firepower. The Taliban were only going to leave if ISAF kicked them out. For the British ambassador, Sherard Cowper-Coles, any military operation that threatened to result in heavy casualties was an anathema, so he too backed the Karzai plan. Mackay was not privy to these discussions but he inherited their outcomes. Mullah Salaam would be protected – by British soldiers – until such time as a joint military and political plan could be concocted to recapture Musa Qaleh, hopefully before the end of the year. For all the niceties and finessing, it was in the end Dan McNeill who was proved right. Musa Qaleh would only be retaken with military muscle and the application of violence, and because the British could not or would not do it, this meant American military muscle.

In preparing orders for the operation, Mackay's staff would, following standard staff work, draw an 'effects schematic' on a wipe board, summarizing the plan to retake Musa Qaleh (an effects schematic was essentially a wish-fulfilment sketch which listed various 'effects' a commander intended to visit on his enemy, in a triumph of hope over experience). It was telling that the 'effects' Mackay intended to apply to Musa Qaleh were: 'Divide, Disrupt, Dislocate [in order to] drive a wedge between Tier 1 + Tier 2 EF [Enemy Forces] and allow the tribal elders to restore GoIRA [Government of the Islamic Republic of Afghanistan] authority'.[36] This was pure fantasy. The single 'effect' that counted was 'kill the enemy', which Mackay could not countenance. The American paratroopers were entirely comfortable with this idea and delivered the necessary kicking.

The preliminary phase of the operation – the protection of Mullah Salaam – was British-led. It was called Operation *Mar Changak* and it kicked off on 2 November with the march north of the Right Flank Company of the Scots Guards, accompanied by a squadron of the King's Royal Hussars

(KRH) mounted on Mastiffs, one commando company and an artillery troop. To distract the Taliban, the BRF deployed on 11 November and 'demonstrated' to the west of the Musa Qaleh wadi. The Scots Guards, who were needed elsewhere, were replaced three weeks later by C Squadron of the HCR, mounted on Scimitars. The British were not alone in the area as an American Green Beret unit – Task Force 32 – had been operating south of Musa Qaleh since October. The conflict between regular units and special forces units had still not been resolved, and 52 Infantry Brigade would experience the frustration of special forces raids about which they had not been informed.

At Musa Qaleh the British continued to cling to the hope that less destructive 'influence operations' might do the trick, while the Americans, sceptical over the efficacy of this approach, pressed for a direct assault. Operation *Mar Changak* had only been in progress for a week when 52 Infantry Brigade was warned that a full assault on Musa Qaleh was looking an increasingly likely possibility. The news apparently caused some dismay to the British who wanted more time to allow their 'softly, softly' approach to work.[37] A unit of American paratroopers, Task Force 1 Fury (the very title may have made Mackay wince), commanded by Lieutenant Colonel Brian Mennes, was ear-marked for the operation. Mennes had a classic, rugged military face with a paratrooper's haircut to match that straight away told you he meant business. With a special forces background, his instincts were aggressive rather than pacific. His paratroopers had been in Afghanistan almost a year compared to their British counterparts, who had only been in theatre two months. Because the operation would take place in a British area of responsibility, Brigadier Mackay would be in command, but he now found himself in the uncomfortable position that the bulk of his combat power would be American, and these soldiers would be unwilling to answer to British sensitivities.

British frustrations were matched by American impatience over the whole business of Musa Qaleh. Dan NcNeill had, in fact, made five offers to recapture Musa Qaleh, all of which had been rejected by President Karzai.[38] Now a half-baked Afghan plan was being proposed and Afghan commanders were boasting they could retake Musa Qaleh without ISAF assistance. On the ground, Sher Akhundzada was suggesting the matter could be resolved by the Alizai themselves without outside interference. None of this washed with the American general who had become far too canny about his allies.

One factor did play in McNeill's favour. Cowper-Coles, another voice against military action, was on leave. Without the British ambassador scotching any attempt to mount an aggressive operation, McNeill had free rein to propose a realistic alternative. The Americans – Task Force 1 Fury – would do the heavy lifting, but the Afghans would be allowed to take the credit for the recapture of the town. The British would play a secondary role guarding the flanks of the town, even though a British commander would nominally command the operation. The compromise seemed to satisfy everyone, and without a British veto, McNeill acted quickly, presenting the decision as a fait accompli on 18 November to Brigadier Mackay.[39]

When the two coalition partners sat down to agree the details of the plan, disagreements arose straight away. From Lieutenant Colonel Mennes's point of view, the British simply did not understand the mechanics of executing a large air assault operation.[40] British planners wanted to split his paratroopers, whereas Mennes wanted to abide by one of the cardinal principles of war: concentration of force. The British wanted to approach from the south, the usual route. Mennes wanted to achieve surprise by arriving from an unexpected direction. There was talk of an Afghan lead under Brigadier Mohayadin, which Mennes, like his boss, Dan McNeill, did not find credible. And there was British touchiness over American 'heavy metal' blazing Musa Qaleh and reducing it to a pile of ruins. This fear was amplified by a horrified Cowper-Cowles, who returned from leave to discover that the operation to retake Musa Qaleh had been sanctioned in his absence. In a deliberately planted email, Cowper-Coles indicated that the assault force would refrain from overtly aggressive actions during a forthcoming visit of the new prime minister, Gordon Brown, to save any potential embarrassment.[41] This would not be the last time the British ambassador attempted to interfere in military operations in Helmand, and it incensed the military staffs.

These disagreements came to a head in the first formal planning group that descended into an open debate between the three 'M's: Mohayadin, Mackay and Mennes. The British had been meticulous in planning the preparatory phases of the operation, as well as in proposing a plan for the follow-on stabilization phase, but had left wide open the thorny question of how the Taliban were actually going to be defeated. The hope – a naïve hope in Mennes's view – was that the Taliban would somehow be persuaded to leave by the show of force. A veteran of the retaking of

Sangin, Mennes simply did not believe in this vague, British notion of psychological persuasion. Sangin had been retaken by firepower, not leaflet drops. What really stuck in the maw of the Americans was a British insistence that no large munitions be used in Musa Qaleh town centre, without prior authorization from the British General 'Jacko' Page, commander of Regional Command South.[42] This was unacceptable to Mennes. His men would be taking the risk – because the British were incapable or unwilling to mount the operation – and now the British expected him to follow rules of engagement that would increase the risk further. From Brigadier Mackay's viewpoint, what was at stake was his entire philosophy of 'influence operations' and winning over the population. Musa Qaleh could be the experiment that proved his thesis right, if only he could persuade the Americans to embrace his way of thinking.

Not all the British, it may be noted, believed in this policy of restraint. At least one officer judged the staff officer insisting on a prohibition of large munitions was an 'idiot'.[43] After lengthy and heated debates, a template for a plan was agreed. Task Force 1 Fury would recapture Musa Qaleh according to Mennes's plan, but the paratroopers would desist from entering the town centre in broad daylight, allowing the Afghans to take the honour.

The operation to retake Musa Qaleh – Operation *Mar Karardad* – began on 2 December with a move by Bravo Company, 40 Commando into blocking positions on the Musa Qaleh wadi, north of Sangin. Prior to this move, 4/73 (Sphinx) Special Observation Post Battery had already set up observation posts overlooking Musa Qaleh. This sub-unit, it was later claimed, would endure the longest desert patrol mounted by the British Army since the end of World War II. The BRF had also deployed to the vicinity of Musa Qaleh. With the bridgehead secure, the Scots Guards motored to Shah Kariz for the next phase of the operation.

The 25-kilometre drive north took 48 hours across difficult desert terrain. The purpose of this move was to meet up with militiamen who would protect Mullah Salaam for the duration of the operation. This Afghan-side of the operation, in which SIS had a hand, turned into farce. On 5 November two clapped-out buses escorted by a Czech special forces team arrived at the rendezvous point. They were full of disorientated militiamen, many of whom were ex-Taliban, and all of whom seemed to be in a sour mood.[44] The militiamen loaded their weapons and became hostile. An attempt was then made to disarm the men, which caused tensions to rise still further. Eventually, a peace was brokered and the militiamen were driven to the nearby village of Shah Kariz in British vehicles. Mullah Salaam was either not expecting this protection or was distrustful of the strangers and refused to accept the militiamen. When the convoy arrived he was not even at home, and it took a good while to track him down on a mobile phone number, by which time darkness was falling. Back at the 52 Infantry Brigade HQ at Lashkar Gah, Mackay lost his temper with the SIS liaison officer, and the whole business was being described as a 'cluster fuck'. A wildly unrealistic order was then transmitted to the British ground commander to disarm the fighters and to recover $64,000 which they were carrying. He wisely declined to follow this order, and eventually the militiamen found their way back down south. Mennes had been right – if the matter had been left to the Afghans, Musa Qaleh would have remained in Taliban hands.

Even as this drama was unfolding, the second element of the British force, led by the commanding officer of HCR, Ed Smyth-Osbourne, began its move from Assembly Area Apollo to blocking positions at Objective Vulcan near a village called Yatimchay, about 7 kilometres south of Musa Qaleh. This force comprised C Squadron HCR, B Squadron KRH, the reconnaissance platoon of the Coldstream Guards and an Afghan company. They would later be joined by the Right Flank Company of the Scots Guards who surrendered the pointless task of protecting Mullah Salaam. It was a measure of British reticence to get involved in fighting that this potent force of tracked and wheeled vehicles – Scimitars, Warriors, Mastiffs – was kept out of danger and relegated to acting as a block. If Smyth-Osborne's task force had simply been ordered to continue motoring north to Musa Qaleh, only a 20-minute drive away, supported by the marines, it is difficult to see how the Taliban could have stopped him.

Far to the west of the HCR battlegroup, the third British force – a composite task force of Afghan soldiers mentored by B and C Companies of the Green Howards (2 Yorks), led by the BRF, began the long desert journey from Camp Bastion to the western edge of Musa Qaleh. In total, the convoy stretched for over 16 kilometres and was impossible to hide. The purpose of this force was to act as a second diversion and then to enter the town, once it had been cleared by the American paratroopers. Ironically, the Green Howards battlegroup – which was also deliberately kept away from the fighting – would suffer the most British casualties through mine strikes.

D-Day was set for 7 December. Alongside the roughly 4,000 strong ground force, an armada of aircraft had been assembled to support the assault, including every strike platform available to American forces in Afghanistan: B-1B bombers, F-16s, F-18s, A-10s, AC-130 gunships and AH-64 Apaches – all to see off a small number of gunmen armed with Kalashnikovs and RPGs. The latter two aircraft would prove the most effective killers. This aerial force was supported by American surveillance assets that included Predator and Reaper UAVs, an RC-135 Rivet Joint collecting signals intelligence and an E-8C JSTARS collecting imagery intelligence. An American E-3 Sentry AWACS aircraft coordinated all the aircraft movements over the tight airspace. The British contribution was meagre: a single Nimrod MR2 and Harrier GR9. The latter followed strict British rules of engagement and apparently never engaged the enemy.

Every available helicopter in south-west Afghanistan was bagged to support the air assault of Task Force 1 Fury. Even this armada of 21 helicopters only included 12 Chinooks – the largest and most useful of the transport helicopters – crewed by a mix of British, Dutch and American pilots.[45] The insufficiency of helicopters was again plaguing coalition operations.

The original plan had envisaged landing the entire force in Wuch Mandah, a wadi 4 kilometres north-west of Musa Qaleh. This was protected from view of the town by a spur of ground. To the dismay of the British, immediately before landing the paratroopers, an inferno of air and artillery firepower would be unleashed on 34 targets – the standard Vietnam-era tactic of 'prepping' the battlefield.[46] This depended, of course, on someone with hostile intent actually being at the nominated targets. Typically, the intelligence had been greatly exaggerated (one of the RAF helicopter pilots remembered being assured they were all probably going to die). As the airborne armada circled, it became clear there was no enemy. This created a dilemma that the American fire planners could not bypass. The carefully worked-out fire plan needed an enemy. The American pilots could not destroy compounds gratuitously even by their own rules of engagement. As the minutes passed and fuel began to run low it became apparent the fire plan would have to be abandoned (it was not entirely, as some guns opened fire anyway). Without a fire plan, Lieutenant Colonel Mennes switched to landing the entire force in the Arhad Mandah, another wadi a further 4 kilometres away from Musa Qaleh. It would mean a longer and harder approach march for his paratroopers and all surprise would be lost.

As if to add insult to injury, the paratroopers landed in full view of the British BRF, which had simply driven to the same spot.

The paratroopers that landed in Arhad Mandah now faced a stiff trek to their start lines. Laden with ammunition and stumbling over rocky undulating ground, they only finally arrived on the outskirts of Musa Qaleh at daybreak on 8 December. The key feature that dominated the town was the Roshan Tower, the telecommunications mast set on a 1,089-metre bluff 3 kilometres north-west of the town that offered panoramic views of the entire area. Surprisingly, there was no Taliban presence on this hill, which A Company swiftly occupied, followed by the battalion tactical headquarters. For the rest of the battle, Lieutenant Colonel Mennes, and later Brigadier Mackay, would follow events on the ground from this eyrie, much like 19th-century commanders surveying a battlefield through a spyglass.

The seizure of the Roshan Tower in effect determined the outcome of the battle before a single shot had been fired. There was only one footpath to the top of the Roshan Tower (from the south-west), and anyone attempting to climb the hill faced cliff faces on three sides. While A Company settled on their commanding height, B and C Companies began a pincer movement on the town, advancing from the north and south respectively. C Company was the first to make contact just after dawn and B Company soon followed. For the remainder of the day, all three companies found themselves tied down in a slugging match against a nearly invisible enemy and struggled to make any progress. To A Company's surprise, a suicidal attempt was made by a group of locals to attack the telecommunications mast. This was easily repelled, but then the paratroopers took casualties when they decided to abandon the safety of the hill and chase down gunmen who had got away. Some of the fighting that day was at very close quarters, and Task Force 1 Fury was lucky to escape with so few casualties. By the evening everyone was exhausted, having barely slept in the previous 24 hours, and Mennes called a halt to any further offensive actions.

At daybreak on 9 December the round of fighting resumed. Despite lavish artillery and air support offered to the paratroopers, insurgent resolve seemed undiminished. The stack of aerial surveillance platforms flying over the battlefield was also struggling to clearly identify enemy positions. By the end of the day, during which there was a lull in the fighting to undertake an ammunition resupply, the paratroopers had only been able to make yards against their determined opponents. As night fell Mennes was joined by Brigadier Mackay, whose presence so far forward at the tactical headquarters caused some irritation. To the Americans it felt like snooping and interference in what was an all-American battle. Mennes may have validly posed the question why 40-odd British armoured vehicles were parked just south of the town, and not lending him support.

The luck of the Taliban was always going to run out eventually given the huge odds stacked against them, and the turning point seemed to come in the evening of 9 December.[47] A Predator spotted a Taliban heavy machine gun being wheeled away in the dark, and the crew was successfully attacked by a strike aircraft. One of the survivors then led the watching UAV to a building which was confirmed to be the source of a large number of insurgent radio transmissions. A second, 2,000-pound bomb completely flattened this building. This strike seemed to flush out more fighters. Unbeknown to the Taliban, two AC-130 Spectre gunships were circling overhead viewing the entire spectacle. It became a turkey shoot. By the end of the engagement the crews reckoned they had either killed or wounded 50 insurgents. For the Taliban on the ground the entire experience must have been very demoralizing. The sense that there was nowhere to hide in the darkness from these monstrous aircraft only added to their demoralization. Mennes now ordered his companies to press forward in the dark, exploiting the battering that had been wreaked by the gunships. Facing much lighter resistance, the paratroopers closed on the edge of the town centre by dawn on 10 December.

What should have followed on the morning of 10 December was a rapid investment of the town centre. But for the sluggishness of the British and their ANA charges, this is what would have happened. Instead a whole 24 hours passed while the British reorganized their forces which – with the exception of the BRF – had not taken part in the fight for Musa Qaleh. The HCR battlegroup had originally been deployed to a southern blocking position to intercept any 'squirters' heading south. Radio intercepts indicated that some Taliban, possibly field commanders, had indeed evaded south. None of these were captured. The battlegroup was now ordered to redeploy to the east of the town, where it was suspected more Taliban were fleeing. By the time the battlegroup arrived in its new blocking position, the Taliban that had chosen to flee along the eastern route had long disappeared in the direction of Kajaki. In the end the British failed to take a single prisoner. To the west, the Green Howards battlegroup spent the entire day preparing to move with the ANA companies, but did not actually move a foot forward.

Faraway to the south, Prime Minister Gordon Brown arrived at Camp Bastion for the long-planned pre-Christmas visit. The relief in the British Embassy that the operation had unfolded without heavy British casualties was now overtaken by a desire to rush out a 'good news story'. Could the prime minister announce the recapture of Musa Qaleh, the embassy enquired? No – the brigade answered flatly.

On the morning of 11 December the Green Howards battlegroup and ANA finally marched to Musa Qaleh. They arrived at the southern outskirts of the town at about lunchtime and began to probe forward, with C Company clearing the western half of the town and B Company clearing the eastern side. Some of the ANA soldiers profited from this leisurely march by helping themselves to marijuana plants.[48] The distance they had to cover to the town centre – a roundabout marked by a minaret – was a 15-minute walk, but a chronic British risk aversion coupled with an exaggerated sense of the Taliban threat meant that by sunset they had only advanced about half this distance, or about 500 metres, in four hours. In the entire afternoon nobody saw any insurgents, or indeed any civilians. The place was deserted. The soldiers could have strolled to the centre with hands in their pockets. Instead, they stopped short and bedded down for the night in deserted buildings. Musa Qaleh would have to wait yet another day before it was officially liberated (which did not stop Kabul announcing the recapture anyway).

Finally, on the morning of 12 December, 48 hours after the American paratroopers had sent the Taliban running, Musa Qaleh was 'liberated'. To commemorate the event a photograph was taken of Brigadier Mohayadin, the ANA commander, raising a triumphant fist in front of Musa Qaleh's only noteworthy building – an ornate minaret on the roundabout in the town centre.

In the succeeding days, house searches began to reveal old weapon caches, bomb factories and stashes of opium. Three drug laboratories were found and about 2,000 kilograms of opium, a fraction of Musa Qaleh's output in the last ten months when it had been free of government control. Somehow these figures then became wildly inflated so that within days reports of 60 opium laboratories and $500 million's worth of opium were being bandied about, or more than the total profit of all Helmand's farmers in a good year. The spin and counter-spin then went into overdrive as a

Chinook's worth of reporters flown in three days after Brigadier Mohayadin raised the Afghan flag managed to find some unhelpfully honest locals who were more than forthcoming in relating to the media circus just how many of their innocent relatives had been killed in the fighting.

Ultimately, views on the recapture of Musa Qaleh depended on which perspective you chose to view the operation from. For Brigadier Mackay, Musa Qaleh had the character of a philosophical and emotional cause. He was desperate to show there was another way of conducting counter-insurgency operations that did not involve destroying the village in order to save it. The decisive actions would not be the military operation but what followed: the rebuilding of the town and its institutions, such as they existed. Following the operation he wrote:

> With some hard won experience behind us, the work of our predecessors, a better sense of how the enemy operate and the beginnings of all activity being influence driven we are, I believe, making headway. We do have to bear in mind however that in an insurgency of this nature the insurgent wins if he does not lose and we lose if we do not win ... That said I have also come to realise that there is not a single individual, group or organisation (including, if not more so, Afghans) who truly understand how tribal alliances shift, the true impact of the tribal make up and how individuals gain or lose authority within the ebb and flow of the insurgency. We have therefore to rely partly on our instincts, partly on continually improving our situational awareness (objectivity rather than subjectivity should be the aim) and mostly on getting our approach right.[49]

He was right, of course, but the Americans also understood this – it was a pot of $13 million (all American funds) that was allocated for the reconstruction of Musa Qaleh. For Karzai, living in the bubble of Kabul, Musa Qaleh was a vindication of his policy of supporting loyal tribesmen who had turned against the Taliban. It mattered not that the loyal tribesman in question, Mullah Salaam, was a hopeless inept individual whom the British would have to mollycoddle and eventually bypass in order to get anything done in Musa Qaleh. The errant Mullah did not actually show up in the town until almost two weeks after its capture. Whitehall, also out of touch with the realities on the ground, lauded this success story, which had fortuitously coincided with the prime minister's visit to Afghanistan. The British ambassador's fears of a public relations disaster never materialized. For Lieutenant Colonel Mennes and his paratroopers, now nearing the end of their arduous tour, the retaking of Musa Qaleh was just another operation which they executed with customary efficiency. The real victor was Sher Akhundzada, who now found the path clear to reassert his authority over the district.

In the short term, it was easy to be cynical about Operation *Mar Karardad*. The town's reconstruction, led by the grandly named but unfortunately incompetent British Musa Qaleh Planning Group, was faltering at best. The town mosque destroyed in the fighting was still not rebuilt three years later when the British left (US Marines would eventually rebuild the mosque and the town minaret). The main bazaar road was laid with tarmac but six months later was full of potholes again. (DfID supported this task, ironically, on health and safety grounds, in a war zone where neither health nor safety were measured by pot holes in roads but rather by bullets and bombs.) A school was opened and some medical assistance was offered but these were token gestures. Mostly the town picked itself up by its own efforts, and crucially because the fighting ended. This was Mackay's legacy and it was not an unimportant one. In time, the Taliban returned but now they were kept away from the town. A ring of small patrol bases would sprout around the perimeter of Musa Qaleh, creating an effective security bubble. These acted as magnets for the insurgents and kept the fighting away from the town centre. The approach needed patience, and whatever other faults the British had, a lack of patience was not one of them. Unlike Sangin, the British would be able to look back on Musa Qaleh, the town that had caused them so many problems in the summer of 2006, and claim that some progress towards pacification had been made. This achievement was set by Brigadier Mackay and 52 Infantry Brigade, and it was one of the substantial successes of the British war in Helmand Province.

Much like 3 Commando Brigade in the preceding winter, 52 Infantry Brigade significantly stepped up its operations in the second half of the tour. In the former case this had been catalysed by a sense that something had to be done to push back insurgents encroaching on the handful of British bases. In the latter case, the retaking of Musa Qaleh seemed to awaken the insurgency from its traditional winter hibernation. It was ironic that both brigadiers, Thomas and Mackay, who strongly espoused calming the situation and avoiding confrontation, ended up swinging the British club at the Taliban anyway.

This upswing in operations coincided with a period of foul weather which severely tested both men and equipment. Christmas had barely been celebrated (21,000 sacks of mail, weighing over 170 tonnes, were sent to Afghanistan that year) before the task force found itself in action again.[50] Lieutenant Colonel Waters recorded the effect this had on the troops who faced prolonged periods exposed to the elements:

> A number of people have noted that the wind, rain and most particularly, the mud have made Southern Helmand rather more like the infamous training grounds of Brecon than anyone thought. Bouts of torrential rain and the resultant mud made patrolling decidedly tricky. The rain was quickly followed by a prolonged cold snap which has seen night time temperatures down to minus 12. Operating in cold weather is one thing but when there is nowhere at all with significant heating to warm up at the end of the day is [sic] does make for quite robust soldiering.[51]

From 1 January to 4 February, 40 Commando based at Sangin mounted Operation *Ghartse Spike*, a series of company-level operations designed to disrupt insurgent groups that had filtered south from Musa Qaleh towards Sangin. This was followed by Operation *Mar Kheshta* ('Snake Brick') on 8 February, which involved soldiers from the Scots Guards, the KRH and a troop of 105mm light guns from 4 Regiment Royal Artillery. To ensure an 'Afghan face' to the operation, the strike itself, in a village called Mosulmani, 15 kilometres north of Sangin, would be conducted by an Afghan *kandak* mentored by British soldiers. As well as disrupting an insurgent group, it was hoped to seize an opium laboratory. In this respect, Operation *Mar Kheshta* marked a small milestone because it was the first, deliberate counter-narcotics operation mounted by the British since their arrival in Helmand.

From 16 to 26 February the task force mounted Operation *Mar Taqeeb*, aimed at disrupting Taliban that had migrated into the Upper Sangin Valley. This was followed by a combined Anglo-Danish operation just north of Gereshk that resulted in the building of a new base – FOB Armadillo – that would become a permanent Danish company outpost. The HCR battlegroup in the meantime mounted Operation *Mar Jaang* (10–14 March), which sought to push back Taliban that had re-infiltrated into the Musa Qaleh wadi, south of the town. The last such mission was Operation *Gharste Dagger*, mounted from 18 to 31 March, which also involved B Company of 40 Commando. The target in this case was the village of Sapwan Qala, just north of Sangin, where a group of Taliban had regrouped and were protecting a suspected drugs laboratory. Marching in darkness, the marines arrived at the village at dawn and discovered over a tonne of morphine base – the precursor of heroin – as well as weapons, identity cards and evidence of financial transactions, some of which were in English.

With all eyes focused on Musa Qaleh and northern Helmand, it was easy to forget that to the north and south the British task force was engaged in almost daily gun battles with insurgents. For the marines at Kajaki, like their predecessors in operation *Herrick* 5, the daily routine involved patrolling, sniping and the occasional raid. On occasions – as happened during a raid on the village of Khevelabad in early November – matters could go horribly wrong. Caught in an ambush, four marines were wounded. Under fire, it took the efforts of the entire company and a supporting F-15 that dropped a 2,000-pound bomb, to evacuate the casualties.[52] By the end of the day, the marines had fired off almost 20,000 rounds and launched three Javelin missiles.[53] For all this expenditure of ammunition, nothing changed on the front line.

On other occasions, a certain improvisation and almost reckless bravery coloured the raids. Determined to clear old Russian trenches on Shrine Hill, Charlie Company set off with a newly arrived and inexperienced bomb disposal officer, a splendidly named Major Ian Scattergood. The first bomb was found at the base of the ridge. Scattergood cleared this by hand. Arriving at the top of the ridge, he came under fire but continued to clear the trenches, finding and dismantling a second bomb attached to a rocket. Scattergood was duly awarded a Military Cross for this action.

In the south of the province, Garmsir was proving one of the most violent districts in Helmand, as well as the most beleaguered. Captain Yambahadur Rana, the officer commanding B Company, 1 Royal Gurkha Rifles at FOB Delhi in Darvishan, recalled a typical day, starting and ending with mortar fire: 'It is normal to wake up in the morning firing [a] few mortar rounds on to the heads of infiltrated Taliban. This goes on; on and off almost all day before it gets dark and nights are generally quiet. Within a month they had a troops in contact (TIC) almost every day.'[54]

As the Gurkhas were naturally gifted marksmen, real pride was experienced when one of the soldiers managed to hit the elusive enemy with a single well-aimed shot: 'Sgt Bhaktabahadur Sherchan killed one

Taleban at approx 250 metres in one shot who was recovered by Afghani [sic] National Police. He was shot right on the chest. After all Sgt Bhakta is an Army 100 shot. Well done!'[55]

Mostly, the enemy remained shadowy and elusive, although B Company reckoned they probably killed about 40 Taliban who had taken their chances attacking the base. The toughness of these Nepalese mountain men was also evident. In one day-long gun battle at Balaklava Checkpoint at the eastern end of the town, Private Laldhoj Gurung was struck by a bullet that somehow missed his Osprey body armour and entered his right chest. Oblivious to the pain, he continued to fight on. His section commander only appreciated the seriousness of his wound when he saw the blood-stained body armour. The hardy Private Gurung was eventually evacuated and would fully recover from his wound.

While B Company was slugging it out in Garmsir, the two sister companies were experiencing a very different tour as the regional reserve based in Kandahar. This placed them under the multinational chain of command of the Regional Command South commander – a Canadian general – rather than under Brigadier Mackay in Helmand. The operations they undertook were essentially intelligence-led raids that sometimes ended in success but mostly ended in frustration. All were coalition operations, a novel experience for a Gurkha battalion drawn from its insular base in Brunei. As the majority of these missions were undertaken in the mountainous belt to the north of the city, the Gurkhas experienced extreme climatic conditions throughout this period. One of the biggest challenges they faced was the unreliability of the Bowman radios, which provoked angry comments from the commanding officer. The VHF radios experienced frequent fill dropouts and manifested poor range. Eventually the Gurkhas adopted World War II-style drills and hand signals to overcome these difficulties. As much as anything the tour became a human and equipment endurance test.

Newly arrived in theatre, A Company was first deployed on Operation *Palk Wahel* in support of the operation to clear insurgents from the village of Zumbelay, north-east of Gereshk. This took place in the last week of September, and the heavy summer of fighting had clearly taken its toll as the Gurkhas only experienced one gun battle in the entire two weeks they spent in the Green Zone.

After an interlude, A and C Companies then took part in a three-week-long, Dutch-led mission called Operation *Spin Ghar*, which was mounted at the end of October. The objective of the operation was to assault and destroy a reported Taliban redoubt 200 kilometres north of Kandahar in an area known as Baluchi Valley. The lack of enemy gave the whole show a holiday atmosphere. One Gurkha chiefly remembered the experience because of the habits of the Dutch chefs rather than the threat of the Taliban insurgents: 'A special mention must go to a few people ... the Dutch chefs who constantly sent out frozen food for the boys to eat. I now feel there will be a new Gurkha tradition of putting cold meat down your underpants for defrosting before making it into a sandwich.'[56]

Before Christmas the two companies would take part in four further missions – one in Helmand and the remainder in Kandahar Province. Operation *Breshna*, the first mission, was conducted in support of an American special forces detachment – Task Force 32 – which was given the task of clearing an area called Chenartu Valley. Like Operation *Spin Ghar*, it turned into a physically gruelling and mostly pointless flog. Chenartu Valley had been cleared every year since 2005, when Task Force Bayonet first ventured into Taliban strongholds at Ordobagh, Zamto Kalay and El Bak. As soon as American forces left, the insurgents simply returned to the villages.[57] C Company infiltrated by night on foot and secured a helicopter landing site for A Company, which followed the next day. Four days were spent searching the valley before the operation was abandoned. Nothing was found.

Immediately following this operation, A Company were redeployed to Helmand to support 40 Commando as the southern block in the operation to retake Musa Qaleh. C Company in the meantime took part in two Canadian-led operations to clear insurgents from Panjwai District west of Kandahar. At the turn of the year the pace of operations picked up once again. The two companies deployed on Operation *Sohil Laram 1*, a Canadian-led mission that would last four weeks and that took the Gurkhas to the mountain massif that forms the northern border of Kandahar Province. Major Paul Pitchfork, the officer commanding A Company, had nothing but admiration for his men who endured this four-week ordeal in the mountains: 'As usual, the boys were superb. Every day they set off on patrol after a night sleeping on the frozen ground wearing everything they had brought with them, and some (including myself!) using two sleeping bags. Never once did I hear anyone complain.'[58] Pitchfork's inspirational leadership over the course of the six-month tour would earn him a Military Cross.

The second mission – Operation *Sohil Laram 2* – also involved A Company working alongside a Canadian battlegroup. In this case the target was the compound of a suspected Taliban chief in the area of Maiwand. Operation *Sohil Laram 2* was the last operation undertaken by the Gurkhas before handing over to the incoming 3 PARA. Although the Gurkhas performed stoically in extreme weather conditions and difficult mountainous terrain, their tour as the regional reserve force was largely a disappointing experience following poor or exaggerated intelligence leads. This was wasteful employment of enthusiastic soldiers who might have been better employed supporting Brigadier Mackay's vision of winning 'hearts and minds' rather than chasing shadows in the hills. The Gurkhas' ethnic and linguistic empathy with Afghan tribesmen – perhaps their most important quality in the context of what the British were trying to achieve – was not exploited.

The other serious flaw was the transient nature of the operations – a flaw recognized by their commanding officer, Lieutenant Colonel Bourne. The principal lesson he drew from his battalion's experience was that there was little point pursuing Taliban gangs if no meaningful ISAF presence or reconstruction followed. With this single insight, Bourne effectively sentenced the last six, futile years of Operation *Enduring Freedom*. His men had covered a vast geographical area. But their presence in the villages north of Kandahar had amounted to fleeting visits by foreign soldiers who subsequently departed leaving nothing behind. The locals knew these foreigners would probably not visit again, if at all, for many months. Their goodwill lasted only as long as the last dust trail vanished on the horizon. If the prize was the population, this was not a strategy for winning that prize.

The Gurkhas' bravery and endurance – especially tested in Garmsir – was never in question. Corporal Agnish Thapa was awarded a Military Cross for dragging a mortally wounded soldier across 100 metres of open ground and under fire. Rifleman Bhimbahadur Gurung repeated the feat, charging across open ground to thwart a Taliban flanking attack and then doubling back across the same bullet-swept ground with a wounded colleague over his shoulders. He was also awarded the Military Cross. A third Military Cross was awarded to Corporal Mohansingh Tangnami, who led his section in a ten-hour gun battle and constantly exposed himself to enemy fire. To the Gurkhas – a deeply traditional people – emulating the wartime feats of 'our forefathers' was an almost sacred duty. As one of the medal winners later remarked: 'Now I can tell them stories.'[59]

In March 2008, the regional brigade that had been viewed with some suspicion by the rest of the army prepared to hand over to the paratroopers of 16 Air Assault Brigade. The soldiers had become veterans, and 52 Infantry Brigade had confounded the sceptics. Over six months, Task Force Helmand suffered just nine combat fatalities, the lowest casualty rate achieved by any British brigade before withdrawal in 2013–14, when the task force effectively stopped fighting. Total fatalities including accidents represented just 0.16 per cent of the total deployed force, a fact Mackay would use to defend his counter-insurgency philosophy.[60] This included three marines killed almost at the end of the tour in separate IED attacks in Kajaki and Sangin. The youngest British fatality, Trooper Jack Sadler, was just 21. The oldest was a 51-year-old reservist, Senior Aircraftsman Gary Thompson, who left behind a widow and five daughters. Part of the explanation for this collapse in British casualties may have been a result of the thumping 12th Mechanized Brigade delivered to the tribes in the previous summer. The foul weather experienced that winter was another factor that probably discouraged fighting. But recognition was also due to Brigadier Mackay, who sought to impose a more enlightened and less belligerent approach to counter-insurgency. Ungenerously, Mackay's passionate attempts to encourage a different approach to the war were viewed by some as self-promotion. The lessons learned by 52 Infantry Brigade were duly collated and presented to the rest of the army – this was also typical of Mackay.[61] But there was an old joke circulating in the army: a lesson was only learned if something was actually done about it. Otherwise it remained a 'lesson identified'. As 16 Air Assault Brigade unpacked its weapons and broke open ammunition boxes, the truism behind this joke was about to be confirmed.

7

Fixed Again

Operation *Herrick 8*, April 2008–October 2008

One of the odd aspects of the British war in Helmand, at least in the early years, was an unjustified mood of optimism that seemed to infect the replacement brigade. The commanding officer of 23 Engineer Regiment (Air Assault) wrote on his arrival in the province in the spring of 2008: 'I have been struck by how much has changed since I was out here 6 months ago. The country really is developing – and mostly for the better.'[1] His brigade commander later voiced the opinion that the war might be reaching a tipping point. Given the torrid six months the brigade was about to experience, what were they seeing?

For many months, independent observers had been warning the situation in Afghanistan was deteriorating rapidly. Britain was now facing an escalating war, and this had never been part of the calculation. Nobody had posed the difficult question: what happens if the war intensifies and spreads across Afghanistan? The assumption was always that 'the war' had been won in 2001 and operations in Afghanistan were about stabilization and reconstruction. Two years into Operation *Herrick*, the sense that this was an entirely new war – a Pashtun nationalist war underpinned by the opium trade – was still not properly recognized. The possibility of defeat was hardly countenanced, although 16 Air Assault Brigade would raise the prospect by the end of the tour. The true costs of continuing on the same path were inadequately assessed, or not scoped at all. Bringing the war to an end was vaguely couched in terms of an 'exit strategy' that existed only as a set of principles, not concrete plans. It was personalities like Rory

Stewart, ex-soldier and diplomat, who offered the counter-arguments to this optimism:

> We need a policy which reflects our actual capacity rather than our hubristic fantasies. We cannot win a counterinsurgency campaign against the Taliban. We do not control the borders with Pakistan, where insurgents find safe havens and support. Our troop numbers are limited and so is our understanding of local structures. Nato is divided and uncoordinated. The Afghan government lacks the capacity to provide the level of support which we require. The local population is at best suspicious of our actions. In Helmand, where we have increased the troop presence from 200 to over 7,000, our gains can only be temporary. It is more dangerous there for foreign civilians than it was two years ago, before we deployed our troops.[2]

Operation *Herrick*, far from a success, was heading for failure.

In an interview for the *Los Angeles Times* in mid-January, a deadpan Robert Gates bluntly warned that within NATO there are 'some military forces that do not know how to do counter-insurgency operations'. His comments echoed the sentiments of the pessimistic and influential *Afghanistan Study Group Report*, co-chaired by retired General James Jones and Ambassador Thomas Pickering.[3] Their verdict was bleak. Afghanistan now stood 'at a crossroads', and the 'light footprint' needed to be replaced urgently with the 'right footprint', or more troops. The redoubtable Anthony Cordesman was similarly critical. 'What happens if the war escalates in cost, time, and impact?' he asked. Answering his own question, he advised, 'Keep the war limited; if the war goes sour, get out.'[4]

While it was the case that Afghanistan was backsliding towards steeper levels of violence, this pessimism needed to be qualified. The overwhelming majority of insurgent attacks were occurring in just 33 districts (8.2 per cent of the national total), and were affecting about 4.9 per cent of the population.[5] The portrayal of Afghanistan as a country wracked by widespread insurgency was inaccurate. The problem for the British was that these facts were largely irrelevant – British troops were parked in the epicentre of the insurgency. It mattered little that the insurgency was barely visible in Herat or Badghis. In Helmand the levels of violence had rocketed and the situation was clearly worsening, not improving.

At the helm of the newly arrived 16 Air Assault Brigade was Brigadier Mark Carleton-Smith. Originally commissioned into the Irish Guards, he had served as a squadron leader and commanding officer of 22 SAS on operational tours in both Iraq and Afghanistan. He would be the second ex-special forces officer to attempt to solve the puzzle of Helmand, and like his predecessor Ed Butler, he would leave the province a disappointed man.

There were other similarities between the two men. Both were old Etonians. At 42, Carleton-Smith was the youngest brigadier in the British Army. He seemed destined for the top, even if his directness reportedly rubbed against conventions. Brigadier Carleton-Smith had warned that the deployment of British troops in Helmand might provoke an insurgency, after completing a reconnaissance of the province in 2005.[6] Whether or not this was a remark taken out of context and later resurrected for posterity, Carleton-Smith's brigade indisputably now faced a growing insurgency. The word insurrection would not be coined for another year by *The Economist* (Anthony Cordesman described the resurrected Taliban as a 'Pashtun-driven insurrection' as far back as May 2004, but was ignored as usual).[7] It was now a matter of academic debate whether the British were facing an insurgency or outright rural insurrection. For Carleton-Smith, the deteriorating security situation posed a challenge, as he had strongly argued that a less violent campaign stood a greater chance of success. One officer who attended his pre-deployment pep talks remembered him echoing John Reid's sentiment that it would be better to return home claiming no bullets had been fired, rather than boasting about the number of battles that had been fought.[8] 'We are not fighting a war,' he was quoted as saying, 'we're supporting a democratically elected government to prosecute a counter-insurgency campaign, the nature [of which] is much more political than it is military.'[9] The army even published an updated 200-page doctrine pamphlet entitled *Countering Insurgency – A Guide for Commanders*, in which the first principle for counter-insurgency was defined as 'political primacy and clear political aim'.[10] The problem was neither existed.

For the paratroopers who deployed to Helmand in the spring of 2008, this was an opportunity to redress the wrongs of their first deployment two years earlier. Like their brigadier, they too would leave disillusioned. The possibility of success for 16 Air Assault Brigade was undermined before the paratroopers even set foot in the province. Their deployment was always likely to be flawed because the brigade was sent to Helmand without a credible plan for taking the campaign forward. Both Whitehall and PJHQ offered little beyond 'do more of the same'. Neither the overall strategy nor the broken Helmand Plan was seriously reviewed or questioned. Additional resources – critically in reconstruction – were never provided. The sense that Britain was at war was discounted. For policymakers in London, Operation *Herrick* was still a stabilization operation that had wobbled at the beginning but which now appeared to be back on track with casualties at a manageably low level. The campaign was about restraining budgets, constraining troop numbers and limiting casualties – not winning. This complacency was dangerous folly. To stand still in Helmand was to fall back. The landscape, like the often-quoted scene of the Red Queen in *Through the Looking Glass*, was continually moving forward. The Taliban, unlike Whitehall policymakers, were playing to win.

The Task Force Helmand handover was followed by a change of command in ISAF. On 3 June, General David McKiernan took over from General Dan McNeill. He would be President Bush's last general in Afghanistan. McKiernan arrived with high expectations. He had commanded the ground campaign in Operation *Iraqi Freedom* and proved to be a decisive and quick-thinking commander. He also came with experience of peacekeeping operations in Bosnia-Herzegovina and Kosovo. President Karzai welcomed the new general with one of the great understatements of the war: 'Your tasks will not be easy,' he told him.[11] McKiernan barely needed reminding. 'Bottom line,' he commented in his inaugural interview, 'there is no military solution to the problems here.'[12] In this respect, McKiernan would be the last American general to play the fall guy in Afghanistan. He would entrench the strategy of clear-hold-build and give fresh impetus to training the Afghan security forces, but he would never be given sufficient resources to accomplish the task. His successors – notably General McChrystal – would steal the limelight, but it was McKiernan who laid the foundations.

The recapture of Musa Qaleh by the previous brigade meant the British task force was once again as stretched as ever across a geographical space it could not hope to adequately control. The four British battlegroups were spread out across 19 bases and four geographical areas: Battlegroup North (2 PARA); Battlegroup North-West (The Argyll and Sutherland Highlanders – 5 SCOTS); Battlegroup South (The Royal Highland Fusiliers – 2 SCOTS); and Battlegroup Centre, held by the Danish.

Carleton-Smith was acutely aware of this overstretch and was determined not to allow the British task force to be committed to additional districts in Helmand. The manpower and logistic bill for fighting an essentially static, defensive war from forts, rather than an agile, mobile war, necessarily implied that the British were going to dig in and mostly attempt to hold on to their few gains.

Although 16 Air Assault Brigade was known, at least in the popular imagination, as the Paras, only one parachute battalion was actually available to Carleton-Smith. The 1st Battalion was permanently committed to supporting British special forces operations in Afghanistan, and the 3rd Battalion had been detached from the British task force to act as a regional reserve based in Kandahar. A more accurate description of Carleton-Smith's command would have been the 'Celtic Brigade'. In addition to The Argylls, supported by companies from The Highlanders and Royal Highland Fusiliers, the brigade also included 1 Royal Irish Regiment, commanded by Lieutenant Colonel Ed Freely. All these units taken together would represent the biggest concentration of Celtic regiments of any of the Operation *Herrick* deployments to date. Compared to their Scots brethren, the Ulstermen seemed to draw the short straw. Of all the towns in Helmand, Sangin had already developed the worst reputation. This was where C (Ranger) Company deployed, as part of the 2 PARA battlegroup, with smaller detachments located in Tangiers, Waterloo, Blenheim and Tufaan 3 patrol bases. The Royal Irish also took over the responsibility for guarding Kajaki Dam and for mentoring the ANA at Camp Shorabak. Additional teams deployed to Gereshk and the Upper Gereshk Valley in support of the Danish battlegroup. To make up the numbers needed to meet all these commitments, 116 members of the Royal Irish Territorial Army battalion were mobilized from their civilian jobs. No other British Army infantry battalion would manage to mobilize as many of its reservists in one tour. As so often in the past, Irish loyalty to the Crown was second to none.

The combination of Sangin and a large number of volunteer civilian soldiers might have suggested the Royal Irish would pay the heaviest price on Operation *Herrick 8*. The reverse proved true. The regiment almost managed to reach the end of the six-month deployment without suffering a single fatality. The achievement of the Royal Irish to stay ahead of the gunmen in the most hostile town in the province could not be denied – the battalion would in fact suffer fewer casualties than any other British unit deployed in these badlands over the course of the war, and many fewer than were suffered subsequently by the US Marines who took over the town. The Royal Irish's unique accomplishment in Sangin deserves recognition.

This could not be accounted for by a lack of hostility on the part of the mainly Ishaqzai and Alikozai tribesmen. As one Ulsterman recalled:

> Sometimes you just know that you're wasting your time by the way an individual looks at you. It can speak volumes out here. All too often we are greeted by 'Stinkeye' a term referring to the, '*I really don't want you here infidel*,' look. Other times you patrol an area and it's as if Amy Winehouse has reproduced with an angry version of Borat to produce hundreds of grumpy individuals baying for your blood. Oddly enough you could patrol the exact same area an hour later and you're as popular as Cindy Crawford at a stag do.[13]

Luck may have played its part, and it was true the density of IEDs had not yet reached the saturation of later years. But sound tactics also surely contributed to the low casualty rate. Irish warmth may also have worked on the normally icy locals. An exchange of words typically proved a fruitful experience:

> Foreigners will never be welcomed openly in public due to the threat of the Taleban, however once in compounds and out of sight of strangers they are most sociable. Most groups of males will invite you to sit, enjoy tea and air their problems with you. Traditionally and in no particular order these problems are Pakistan, the establishment of Pashtunistan, the Afghan National Army and the kafir (infidel i.e. you!).[14]

It was interesting that at least in this officer's perception, ordinary residents of Sangin blamed 'Punjabis', or Pakistanis, for their ills.

The Sangin-based company did finally suffer a fatality at the end of the tour. The soldier killed was Ranger Cupples, whose life story was archetypal of the great Irish diaspora. Justin Cupples was born in the United States, the son of Irish migrants. After the September 11 attacks he joined the US Navy and served on Operation *Iraqi Freedom*. Imbued with a sense of double patriotism, he returned to County Cavan, the family's ancestral home, and joined the British Army. As he described it, he still had unfinished business with the people who had perpetrated the September 11 attacks. Along the way he picked up a young Lithuanian bride who had also migrated west searching for a better life. Ranger Cupples never did get to grips with al-Qaeda. He was killed by a roadside bomb, conducting one of many routine patrols around the district centre.

With Ranger Company of the Royal Irish holding the central ground in Sangin and its satellite stations, the remainder of the 2 PARA battlegroup, commanded by Lieutenant Colonel Joe O'Sullivan, deployed its companies north and south of the town. B Company went to FOB Inkerman and C Company to FOB Gibraltar. D Company was deployed to the multinational FOB Robinson, where it was supported by the Royal Scots Dragoon Guards (Scots DG) mounted in Scimitars. One platoon from D Company was detached from the company and sent north to guard Kajaki Dam.

What the paratroopers found, at whichever base they deployed, was a landscape scarred by almost two years of fighting:

> Most of the locals who lived in the Green Zone close to the FOB have moved out of their compounds … In the Green Zone there are a lot of these compounds, and many are empty. Some of these are used as firing points by the Taliban, so whilst on patrol we have to look for these firing points. Some compounds have been destroyed by air assets long before we came here. Some areas are smashed to pieces.[15]

Despite the war damage, it would have been wrong to portray rural Helmand in the spring of 2008 as uniformly hostile to the British soldiers. One of the surprising aspects of patrolling in the Sangin Valley was the encounter with the genuinely friendly local farmer, whatever his motives for displaying hospitality towards the foreign soldiers. There were also the ubiquitous children who could descend on a patrol like pecking starlings, before vanishing back to the compounds: 'Local children often approach the section on [sic] masse, demanding sweets, pens, and pretty much anything you haven't tied down to yourself. As you can expect this can get quite frustrating, not to mention a somewhat dangerous distraction, but on the other hand, it does mean one thing ... you're safe.'[16]

Equally, it would be too easy to accuse the paratroopers of spoiling for a fight. The airborne mentality was certainly evident. The officer commanding D Company expressed this ethos without embarrassment when he enthused, 'The greatest pleasure in commanding … paratroopers, is that you don't have to give them any motivational pep talks to close with and kill the Taliban. The greater challenge is in holding them back, like a pack of baying Alsatians!'[17]

It would be simplistic to take such statements as evidence that 2 PARA deployed to the Green Zone with blind, aggressive intent. On deploying to FOB Gibraltar, C Company organized weekly *shuras* and planned a series of modest reconstruction projects. For the first two months, there was barely any fighting. The sister companies similarly deployed to their respective bases with the intention of winning 'hearts and minds'. The fight came to the paratroopers rather than the other way round, and the turning point arrived at the end of the poppy harvest.

In the first week of June, FOB Gibraltar was attacked with rockets, which provoked an angry reaction from the locals who feared British retaliation. Then, on a hot Sunday morning in the same week, a B Company multiple (large patrol) stepped out of FOB Inkerman to undertake a routine patrol. The intent of the patrol was to collect low-level intelligence and to gauge the 'atmospherics' of the area. The patrol was uneventful until it reached a small cluster of compound farms at about 1100hrs, a few hundred metres from the base. When the paratroopers passed one of the farms a young man stepped out to observe them. He seemed harmless, perhaps even high on drugs. As Private Daniel Gamble, the patrol's linguist, moved forward to practise some Pashto phrases that he had spent 40 weeks learning on a long language course, the young man detonated a suicide vest. Gamble died instantly. Two other paratroopers died alongside him, Privates Nathan Cuthbertson and Charles Murray. They were both just 19 years old. With the deaths of these three paratroopers, British fatalities in Helmand passed the symbolic 100 mark.

The suicide attack that killed the three B Company paratroopers had a profound influence on the manner in which the soldiers would operate for the remainder of the tour. The change in mood was exacerbated by what appeared to be a coordinated attack on FOB Gibraltar. A second bomber was forestalled by a quick-thinking patrol, but three days later a C Company multiple was ambushed, which resulted in the death of two more paratroopers. A line was crossed and the paratroopers became more overtly aggressive and bent on killing insurgents. This, in turn, provoked cycles of violence within the settlements of the Gereshk and Sangin

Valleys, where every Afghan family group was related and where horizons stretched not much further than the next village. 'Hearts and minds' in the Green Zone was largely abandoned. All locals were ordered to remain at least 50 metres from the troops. In a procedure that unfortunately recalled controversial images of Israeli checkpoints in Palestine, anyone who wanted to draw closer had to lift their shirts to show they were not concealing a bomb.

Stopping and searching Afghans sometimes had its comical moments, as a soldier serving with The Argylls recalled: 'This is where the very diligent Pte Howie was searching the locals and found what would appear to be a foreign object under his clothing which aroused his suspicions. He then asked the local to remove the object and with a beaming smile the local produced 1 x Erect part of his person much to Pte Howie's disgust.'[18]

Such moments aside, stop and search was a disaster, particularly for the paratroopers in the Green Zone. Without the possibility of interaction, however difficult, the soldiers were just another occupying force routinely humiliating the locals. Mutual incomprehension turned to alienation and then to sullen hostility.

By the height of the summer every patrol leaving FOB Gibraltar or FOB Inkerman had a high chance of becoming engaged in a gun fight. Bereft of ideas, the British continued their patrols throughout this period, and the locals duly replied with volleys of gunfire and RPGs. Each of these futile spats was another opportunity to create a blood feud. The paratroopers, with their superior training and weaponry, were much better at drawing blood, especially when they were able to call for support from Apaches or from the gun battery at FOB Robinson. But laden as they were like pack mules, they were unable to exploit their successes.

British infantry were literally becoming fixed by the weights they were being ordered to carry. Measurements taken in Helmand in the summer of 2008 showed that the weights carried by infantry sections typically amounted to 74.14 kilograms for section commanders, 65.35 kilograms for grenadiers, 72.41 kilograms for light machine gunners and 69.14 kilograms for light-support-weapon gunners.[19] The unpopular Osprey body armour alone weighed 9.98 kilograms. While undoubtedly saving lives – a Gunner Carl Jordan serving with 7 Royal Horse Artillery had the distinction of having been saved twice on separate occasions by his body armour, earning him the nickname of 'bullet magnet'[20] – it remained unpopular with the infantry.

A subsequent article in the *British Army Review* pointed out that the loads soldiers were being asked to carry were well in excess of the weight that could legally be loaded on animals like pack horses and mules – in some cases, soldiers were carrying twice the legal limits.[21] Seaside donkeys, the article pointed out, were not allowed to carry as much weight. With this load – in some cases equalling the body weight of the soldiers – just crossing a few hundred metres of broken ground represented a major physical effort. Tactical options, such as outflanking the insurgents, no longer became realistic. Fire and manoeuvre was out of the question. Some soldiers did not adopt prone firing positions because they knew they would struggle to get up again. Dealing with a casualty effectively ended a patrol because it was taking at least six men to carry one casualty.

In the daily tit-for-tat gunfights across hedgerows, the villagers rarely scored a hit. 2 PARA would experience over 400 gun fights, on one day becoming involved in 14 shootouts with locals.[22] Tens of thousands of rounds were fired at the paratroopers over a roughly five-month period, which resulted in the deaths of just four soldiers. This amounted to bullying by the British, who were so superior that the willingness of the villagers to risk their lives by taking pot shots at the patrols was arresting. The Tom on the front line did not, naturally, see it this way. Any bullet winging in your general direction was a potential danger. Every punch up with the villagers was an adrenalin rush, followed by a state of nervous exhaustion and a flood of relief. Private Smith, serving at FOB Inkerman, was 'quite surprised at how well organised the Taliban are and the way they surround us, plus the rates of fire they put down', even if the fire was wildly inaccurate.[23]

The daily routine of gunfights across hedgerows and ditches affected soldiers in different ways. Some paratroopers enjoyed this circus. There was a buzz about being caught up in a battle that sharpened senses and heightened emotions in an intoxicating way. For Private Goodall, who had only recently walked into the army from 'civvy street', war was incomparably more exciting than his former humdrum life: 'On the plus side the feeling of a contact or walking into an ambush, there's no feeling like it, that's when 2 PARA work best, I can't see myself in a civilian job after the contacts I've been in knowing we made it out alive, just!'[24]

Others, like the paratroopers in D Company, were motivated by feelings of revenge:

> Every man in the company is extraordinarily determined to get their own back against the Taliban on behalf of their mates ... They say that there is nothing better than being in the midst of your fellow soldiers in situations like this; I can vouch for that without hesitation. I'm afraid that this won't give all of you back home many restful nights but it is better to be straight with you.[25]

Some became worn by the repeated grind but repressed their fears. The fact that very few paratroopers were being killed did not mean that few were being injured. In fact, the injury rate was so high it continually threatened to debilitate the companies to a point where they were no longer effective. Private Smith, who had been surprised by the well-drilled Taliban tactics, also recalled: 'My platoon alone has lost 8 toms [privates] due to various circumstances, everyone wants to get on the ground and get the job done, but most of the toms in the FOB are constantly back filling other platoons to make numbers up, so blokes are often very tired plus less enthusiastic about being out on the ground again.'[26]

Combat injuries only accounted for a proportion of the wounded. There was also a weekly bill of DNBIs, or disease and non-battle injuries. C Company reckoned that one in three of the paratroopers deployed to FOB Gibraltar in the end succumbed to some sort of injury or illness during their tour, although the company 'only' suffered five combat fatalities.[27] Tellingly, three of the five were point men, the most exposed position in the patrol.

Fighting in the Green Zone had three distinct seasons. During the opium poppy harvest in April and early May there was little fighting, as a large influx of workers migrated to Helmand, some of whom would remain behind to earn more money fighting as seasonal 'ten dollar Talibs'. During the wheat planting in May and June, the fighting would once again resume, with both sides testing each other's strengths and weaknesses. Late summer was perhaps the most dangerous time, with the maize crop exceeding head height, providing excellent cover for the insurgents. 2 PARA patrols operating from FOBs Gibraltar and Inkerman found that there was an 80 per cent chance of a gun fight every time they left their bases. And as the paratroopers observed, it was the insurgents who held the initiative, with the vast majority of the gun battles being started by them. The same observation was made of the Viet Cong in Vietnam.

The biggest fear, unquestionably, was provoked by IEDs rather than by enemy gunfire. It was this weapon that afforded the Taliban the only hope of redressing the imbalance between the two adversaries, and it was used extensively. When the Royal Irish found six IEDs in a single day in Sangin, it was considered a great novelty and was widely reported. Within a year, five times this many IEDs were being uncovered in Sangin on one road. The widespread use of the roadside bomb, which almost seemed to catch the British unprepared despite their recent difficult experience in Basra, was nothing new. In the 1930s Pathan tribesmen employed 'tin-can bombs', as they were then known, to ambush Indian Army troops, recycling ordnance in the same manner as the Taliban: 'Our "dud" shells and aeroplane bombs have provided the tribesmen with a supply of high explosives, which he has latterly been turning to good account in the making of tin-can bombs, which are generally buried and lightly covered with sand on "kachcha" road or track. When found they must be treated with the greatest respect.'[28]

By the summer of 2008, the rise in the number of roadside bombs significantly increased the workload of the Bastion-based JFEOD – basically, there were never enough of these soldiers to deal with the rising number of IEDs. A typical call would come as a '10 liner' giving the grid reference of the suspected device. A team would then deploy by helicopter to destroy or render the bomb safe. Even with the assistance of a mechanical wheelbarrow this entailed great risks to the bomb disposal officer. In the summer of 2008 the JFEOD would lose one of its most charismatic and experienced operators – Warrant Officer 'Gaz' O'Donnell – a popular soldier who had already received a gallantry award in Iraq. Even the most experienced bomb disposal officers, it seemed, could get caught out. O'Donnell had been tasked to clear five IEDs discovered near a three-storey building south of Musa Qaleh, known as US Patrol Base (USPB). B Company, 1 Princess of Wales's Royal Regiment (1 PWRR) provided protection in Warriors, but the operation proved hectic. One Warrior, crewed by a Lance Corporal Kelly, took three hits from RPGs, blinding the driver.

To outwit the bomb disposal officers, some Taliban bomb makers constructed their IEDs to initiate either by downward or upward pressure.

Anyone lifting such a device would be killed instantly. In O'Donnell's case, it appeared he unwittingly set off such an anti-lift device. He died clearing the last of the five of the IEDs, at the end of a blisteringly hot day under fire. His sacrifice would be recognized with a posthumous bar to his George Medal. A fellow warrant officer – Benjamin Kelly – would be awarded a Military Cross for recovering O'Donnell's body. That summer was also noteworthy because a Captain Louise Greenhalgh made history as the first female and Territorial Army bomb disposal officer deployed on operations. Appropriately, in her civilian life, Louise Greenhalgh was a risk assessor. By the end of 16 Air Assault Brigade's tour, the JFEOD had dealt with over 800 roadside bombs – a massive jump on the previous year.

For the sections that daily ventured from the patrol bases, the only sure protection was mine-sweeping every step of the way. This was undertaken with the new German Vallon mine detector in a drill known as Operation *Barma*. It added a verb to the English language – to barma – and 'barmaing' became a way of life for the soldiers of the task force. It called for sharp senses, nerve and mental stamina. Good Vallon men became prized but they also became exhausted and vulnerable to enemy snipers. A Corporal Jamie Kirkpatrick, of 101 Engineer Regiment (Explosive Ordnance Disposal), named his Vallon after his 15-month-old daughter, Holly. His expertise at finding IEDs meant that he inevitably led from the front. At the height of the summer fighting his luck ran out and he was shot and killed in a clearance operation near the notorious CP Kings Hill.[29] Vallon men were a breed apart, an exclusive club and one whose members knew they were playing Russian roulette every day they stepped out to patrol. The range of standard section formations – double file, column, extended line, arrowhead – were replaced by a single formation – the 'Afghan snake'. Every soldier tried to place his feet in the boot prints of the soldier preceding him to stay inside the safe lane cleared by the Vallon man – although this measure did not offer an absolute guarantee of safety.

The month of June proved to be the most difficult month. The passing of the threshold of 100 fatalities was met with a predictable rash of media articles questioning the point of the war. These served to increase the nervousness of the Labour government over the drift and conduct of the campaign. Gordon Brown's government was already facing what appeared to be a spiralling global financial crisis that threatened to provoke a severe recession, if not depression, if the more gloomy prognostications were to be believed. A year into his premiership and with his leadership under question from backbench rebels, the last thing Gordon Brown needed was a 'bad war'. The mission in Afghanistan was beginning to look just like that sort of war, even as Britain had managed to extricate herself from Basra.

In the Westminster Hall debates held on 17 June, Adam Holloway, a former Grenadier Guards officer and now Conservative MP, was scathing of the government.[30] (Holloway, unusually, spent his gap year after school with the mujahidin during the Soviet–Afghan War.) The war in Iraq had been 'crazy and unnecessary'. The operation in Afghanistan was 'incompetent and half-cocked'. The excuse that 'we are where we are' was barely acceptable as a foreign policy strategy. Holloway's attack carried some credibility, as uniquely he had visited Helmand twice at his own expense, and he was the only British politician who had investigated local opinion before the arrival of the British task force in 2006. What he found was 'a pretty quiet place' – a far cry from the war zone that Helmand had become by 2008. Holloway's litany of British failures made painful hearing, but what really struck at the core of the government was his questioning of the rationale of the entire mission. The sacred cow that Britain was engaged in a war in Afghanistan to keep British streets safe from terrorism was 'nonsense'. In Holloway's words: 'The effects of our over-ambitious and ill-resourced plan has been further to radicalise large numbers of people across the Muslim world … to assert boldly that al-Qaeda will return to Afghanistan in a meaningful way is almost ridiculous.' This was an argument the British government could not concede. The jihadist domino theory had to be sustained. If the whole business of 'keeping Britain safe' – repeated *ad nauseum* by politicians – was flawed and overblown, if the dominos were not going to fall, then why were British soldiers dying in Helmand in the first place?

More and more, Afghanistan was beginning to look, feel and smell like Vietnam. The latter was a war, as historian Donald Mrozek astutely observed, where 'any solution attempted could in turn generate new problems; thus, the risk was that these problems would fan out in geometric fashion from a common but quickly forgettable point of origin. Each new problem could then call attention in its own right, potentially distracting interest from the broader goal to which the original solution had been devoted.'[31] Borrowing Mrozek's analogy, Helmand had become a Zeno paradox: infinite steps in a geometric convergence, and no apparent forward movement. Were British soldiers really keeping other Britons safe by picking fights with Pashtun tribes in villages in south-west Afghanistan? What was the point of it all?

Among the fatalities that helped tip the total over the 100 mark was Corporal Sarah Bryant, serving with the Intelligence Corps, the first woman to die in combat in Afghanistan. That a woman had been killed was emotive enough, but Corporal Bryant was also an attractive young woman with a sunny smile and this seemed to make the death more poignant. The media seized on her death as a newsworthy story and followed the progress of her body back to Britain, covering her funeral. There was a twist to the story that gave it more wind. Corporal Bryant had died in a Land Rover Snatch along with three other colleagues from the Territorial Army SAS.

The Land Rover Snatch had already become a *cause célèbre* in Iraq as the exemplar of poor equipment foisted on betrayed troops by an incompetent government. In the heat of the debate some facts were lost and judgements were distorted. Corporal Sarah Bryant, along with her three colleagues, did not, in the end, die because she was travelling in a Land Rover Snatch, for which culpability could be laid on the ministry. She died because of an improbable coincidence of circumstances and because the unlucky crew struck a massive IED. The Snatch was barely recognizable after the blast. The only vehicle that would have withstood the blast that killed Corporal Sarah Bryant was the American Cougar, specifically designed for bomb disposal operations, and then adapted by the British as the Mastiff infantry troop carrier. Even the Warriors were vulnerable to IEDs of this size as the Gurkhas would discover later in the year in Musa Qaleh.

Just over a month after this tragedy, a second tragedy unfolded at Kajaki Dam, which had been the bitter scene of the costly mine strike during 3 PARA's tour in the summer of 2006. Despite the fact that the situation at the dam was entirely stalemated, the British could not resist mounting aggressive patrols against the villages north of their base. These achieved nothing and they put the lives of the soldiers at risk. On 22 July, such a patrol unravelled with terrible consequences. That evening, an X Company patrol decided to occupy a vacated compound with the intention of using it as a sniper's lair. One of the X Company snipers, Lance Corporal Tom Neathway, moved a sandbag that had been placed near a window to create a better firing position and set off a booby trap. He later described the sensation of being blown up as similar to a rugby tackle. The explosion caused the traumatic amputation of both his legs and left his right arm dangling by its tendons. His life was saved by a cool-headed South African, Lance Corporal Jan Fourie, who dealt with the injuries promptly. The first phase of the casualty evacuation was undertaken on the back of a quad bike, which was the only transport immediately available to the paratroopers.

In the meantime, a Vector ambulance was despatched to meet the quad bike from FOB Zeebrugge. The soldier at the wheel of the vehicle was Corporal Jason Barnes, an armourer serving with the Royal Electrical and Mechanical Engineers, who volunteered to act as the ambulance driver. Crashing back down the track that led to FOB Zeebrugge, the Vector struck a second IED. With the driver's seat directly over the wheel arch of the vehicle, Corporal Barnes stood no chance and was killed instantly. X Company now had a fatality as well as the injured Neathway from the first booby trap to deal with. Lance Corporal Neathway would survive his terrible injuries as a triple amputee, the second of the war.* A year later he would feature in a documentary that revealed both his remarkable courage as well as the personal calvary faced by servicemen in his predicament. In an unfortunate twist to the story, it would subsequently emerge that he was bullied within his regiment – shameful behaviour that was only finally acknowledged after he repeatedly sought justice from the MOD.

For the task force, the weekly routine revolved around mounting platoon or, more ambitiously, company-sized patrols. 16 Air Assault Brigade also mounted six task force-level operations over the course of the summer. Two were disruption operations in areas that had been visited on several occasions by preceding brigades (the Upper Gereshk Valley, the Upper Sangin Valley and Musa Qaleh). One was an extended relief in place of 24th Marine Expeditionary Unit (24th MEU), the first of the US Marine units to arrive in southern Helmand (Operation *Oqab Jarowel*). Following withdrawal from Iraq in 2006, the US Marine Corps had lobbied to take a lead role in Afghanistan. Helping the struggling British was an obvious mission and assistance was gratefully received by the Brown government. A strike operation was also conducted north of Musa Qaleh in mid-June (Operation *Oqab Luma*). The last involved the deployment of the Afghan special forces unit, Task Force 444, to the Lashkar Gah area following disturbances in Marjah, west of the provincial capital, at the end of the tour (Operation *Oqab Soba*). The single largest operation, which was reported extensively in the media and which required the redeployment

*After Marine Mark Ormrod MBE.

of around 2,000 ISAF and Afghan troops, involved the delivery of a third turbine to Kajaki Dam.

The failure of the government to address the management of the war decisively was painfully revealed by the controversy over the deployment of 24th MEU to assist the beleaguered British company holding the abandoned agricultural college FOB Delhi, at Darvishan. The situation at Darvishan in many ways summed up all that was wrong with the British mission in Helmand. As well as FOB Delhi, the British had set up a checkpoint (known as Ypres) on an American-built bridge spanning the Helmand River, and built a reinforced observation post on a tumulus overlooking the bridge (JTAC Hill). A second British outpost called Vittoria was set up in a two-storey building 500 metres east of JTAC Hill, next to an old clinic known somewhat optimistically as Haza Joft Hospital. At Balaklava Bridge, a further kilometre to the east, another checkpoint was established. North of the road was the crumbling ANP station, prison and the abandoned L-shaped bazaar. Darvishan was a dying town when the Royal Marines deployed there in the winter of 2006, and the British presence seemed to deal it a mortal blow. The town was vacated, the bazaar closed and a front line formed about 500 metres south of Route 605. The marines raided Taliban positions but lacked sufficient numbers to dislodge their enemy. The Taliban in turn sniped, mortared and fired rockets at the British. The Gurkhas took over from the marines, and 18 months later, when A Company of The Argylls, reinforced by reservist soldiers from 3 PWRR and a Yeomanry contingent, took over FOB Delhi, nothing had changed.

For the newly appointed Governor Gulab Mangal the 'loss' of Darvishan was an unacceptable affront. Regaining the town and revitalizing the local economy had become one of his highest priorities. With limited troop numbers there was little the British could do to change the balance of power in the south. The Americans, with their superior troop numbers, could make the difference. The proposal to use 24th MEU to force the insurgents away from Darvishan – effectively to push the front line a further 10 kilometres south to create a 'security bubble' around the town – was resisted by both by the FCO representative in Lashkar Gah, Michael Ryder, and by his political masters in London.[32] Fraught diplomatic traffic bounced between London and Lashkar Gah as British officials attempted to thwart the American proposal. In effect, Whitehall policymakers preferred the stalemate to a successful offensive that might force London to increase the British commitment (because more troops would be required to hold the expanded security cordon). If The Argylls based at FOB Delhi had known that officials in Whitehall were prepared to leave them in their desperate situation indefinitely, rather than accept an American offer of assistance, they may have been less inclined to risk their lives on a daily basis.

A tension between civil servants (and their political masters) fretting over the British commitment to Helmand, while soldiers died, was crudely exposed. To his great credit, Brigadier Carleton-Smith refused to endorse the FCO position and Whitehall caved in. For the American negotiators, military and civil, this pantomime performance only served to fuel suspicions that the British camp was divided and weak. This chimed with a broader fear in the summer of 2008 that all the European NATO allies were on the brink of folding, highlighted in a critical report to Congress.[33] For the British Army, these civilian machinations caused deep anger. The suspicion of a government 'stab in the back' – which some saw as the reason why the campaign in Iraq had ended in embarrassment and ignominy – was revived. Government officials were sending a strong signal that they really did not care whether the army 'won' in Helmand. The balm of a government spin machine would smooth over the eventual political and military outcome, as it had done in Basra. What mattered was avoiding commitment and restraining costs. For the army, winning in Helmand had become a vital cause, especially after Iraq. There was also a moral debt to the dead. Government spin doctors viewed casualties as 'bad news days'; the army as fallen comrades. The division between these two pillars of state was not in the imagination of Americans observing their British counterparts. In the summer of 2008, the Labour government sailed dangerously close to losing the loyalty of the army.

Operation *Azada Woza* ('Stay Free'), the 24th MEU mission led by Colonel Peter Petronzio to expand the security bubble in Darvishan, began in early May. His command was slightly larger than a typical USMC expeditionary unit. In addition to 1/6 Marines (the veterans of Guadalcanal), the unit brought its own battery of M777A2 155mm lightweight howitzers, the first time that this British-designed gun had been deployed with a USMC unit. Ironically, the M777 – a British-manufactured gun that was unarguably effective in Helmand – was not procured by the MOD, even as it was winning favour with foreign armies. 24th MEU also deployed with a reinforced air wing comprising a Marine Medium Helicopter Squadron (HMM 365), and strike aircraft. An additional USMC contingent – 2/7 Marines – was tasked under separate command with training Afghan security forces. The motto of this unit was 'Ready for Anything – Counting on Nothing', which seemed appropriate for its new task. All these deployments were meant to be short term, but the marines ended up staying in Helmand until November.

The Argylls assisted the US Marines at the start of the operation by securing their left flank and forward passage of lines. After that it was an American show. The US Marines were surprised by what they discovered. A dense network of trenches, rat runs, tunnels and underground bunkers had been built in a belt south of Darvishan. The threat of IEDs was ever present. The Taliban however were no match for the 2,500-strong force. Colonel Petronzio leant on the door and it swung open. Over the next three months a ring of checkpoints and observation posts were built at key canal crossing points and track intersections: Nijmegen, Hamburger Hill, Hassan Abad, OP Rock, Myhand, Tuffan, Pamir, Sharnahad and the most southerly, Masood. Jugroom Fort, which had cost the life of Lance Corporal Ford and led to the daring retrieval of his body, was finally wrested from the Taliban. Although government officials had capitulated to Carleton-Smith, no additional British troops were made available to man these new bases once 24th MEU left, so they were handed over to the ANA and ANP. Before it redeployed, 24th MEU distributed $832,000 in CERPs (Commander's Emergency Relief Program funds) to locals to kick start the reconstruction process. The US Marines also handed out a total of $784,700 in battle damage aid. The British had no comparable financial mechanisms. However, to ensure momentum was not lost, a British MSST (Military Stabilization and Support Team) was deployed to Darvishan, and this would be followed by a small team from DfID.

24th MEU's operation in Darvishan gave blood to a dying patient. The bazaar re-opened. Locals returned to farms they had abandoned because of the fighting. There appeared to be genuine gratitude that the Taliban had been ejected (although this was a common enough response elsewhere in Helmand from a population hedging its bets between the two warring sides). The backwater of Garmsir District suddenly became fashionable. The military bridge at Balaklava was replaced by the Royal Engineers with a bigger and better bridge. Major General Peter Wall, in his capacity as the senior Royal Engineer in the British Army, attended the opening of the new bridge with the governor of Helmand. What may have galled the Americans was the manner in which the British quickly took the praise for the rejuvenation of Darvishan. The FCO had wanted nothing to do with the place. Now the town was recast as a British 'success story'. DfID blogs and defence media articles gushed with stories of Darvishan's renaissance. The fact that Whitehall had initially opposed the operation was entirely buried.

Britain was now fighting a real war in a far-off land. Much closer to home, Britain found itself fighting a financial war that nobody had anticipated. In the summer and autumn of 2008, a series of chain events in the global financial markets provoked a massive credit crunch. Unthinkable emergency measures were taken to restore liquidity to the financial markets, most of which involved some form of 'quantitative easing', or the pumping of billions of funds of public money into banks close to bankruptcy. This was not the turn of events that a wartime government needed, and the question was inevitably raised – would the banking bailouts sink the war effort? Britain was still committed to maintaining a presence in Iraq, and this was not cheap. The original invasion had cost an estimated £1.3 billion. Five years later, the greatly downsized Operation *Telic* was still costing the tax payer an annual £1.4 billion.[34] Whatever successes the British had achieved in Basra, cost-cutting was not one of them. In comparison, operations in Afghanistan, at the time, had seemed a bargain.

The dream of a cheap war, of course, had to come to an end. By the following year, the cost of war in Afghanistan had doubled, and by the end of the first winter of Operation *Herrick* it was just short of £200 million. The following year the reported cost jumped to £738 million. As the financial crisis loomed, inter-departmental fighting broke out as Treasury officials tried to pass on the costs of military operations – up to this point funded from contingency funds – back to the MOD. This was the reckoning which the ministry had feared might come one day, but which it had tried to stave off, mainly through the process of procurement through the Urgent Operational Requirements (UOR) mechanism. This allowed the ministry to pass a fat lump of its costs to the Treasury, thereby protecting an already strained defence budget. By 2008, £3.5 billion had been spent on UORs. In the previous year, 240 UORs had been delivered, and another 300 were in the pipeline. The credit crisis inevitably exposed this accounting trick. The true cost of the war suddenly became evident. In 2007–08, operations in Afghanistan cost a reported £1.5 billion. By the following year they had jumped again, to £2.3 billion.[35] The overall cost of both campaigns, eight years after British troops first entered Afghanistan, and six years after the invasion of Iraq, was £13 billion.[36] This was money that a Labour government, weakened in the polls, would rather not have spent on foreign interventions, but in the uncomfortable context of a £50 billion bailout of the banking system, neither was it ruinous.

A financial crisis was not the only problem facing the British war effort. Over the previous three decades, Britain's defence industry had been run down. The demise of Royal Ordnance was the archetypal example. This company had manufactured ammunition for the country's armed forces since the Tudor period. No other enterprise was so interwoven with the history of the British Isles. Soldiers need bullets and plenty of them. Royal Ordnance was allowed to wither because it was argued as a matter of political ideology that Britain would be able to source its ammunition requirements more cheaply through open competition (not uncommonly, foreign firms championed and subsidized by their respective governments; indeed Royal Ordnance collapsed because it was being undercut by foreign competitors, a scenario that did not appear to trouble the civil servants awarding the contracts to the foreign firms). There was no need to sustain this state-owned manufacturer, so went the argument. Let markets decide. The problem with this free-market ideology was that war decided instead.

When the Labour government committed Britain to operations in Iraq, and then subsequently to Afghanistan, it quickly became apparent that the ammunition bill was going to be much higher than a cost-cutting Treasury had anticipated. Not only could Britain now not supply its own ammunition requirements, but neither could foreign suppliers; furthermore, sourcing ammunition from abroad was proving prohibitively expensive. In 2004 there had been a demand for 90 million bullets. Five years later, the ammunition bill had climbed to 236 million bullets (a 5.56mm bullet cost 20 pence and a 7.62mm bullet 40 pence).[37] There was only one solution: to re-invent the industrial wheel and revive an ammunition manufacturing capability in Britain. It may have come as some shock to the government to discover that the country, which as late as 1985 had 16 ammunition factories employing 19,000 people (when Royal Ordnance was privatized under the Thatcher government), now had precisely one wartime-era ammunition factory. Britain had never been so unprepared to go to war in its entire history as a modern state.

The vital factory was located at Radway Green in Cheshire. Its infrastructure was so obsolete it needed an £83 million cash injection to modernize the facilities (leased by BAE Systems). For the successors of British Aerospace (who, after acquiring Royal Ordnance cheaply, proceeded to close factories and enforce redundancies), this represented a bonanza.

Under a fashionable Private Finance Initiative (PFI), BAE Systems signed a 15-year deal with the Labour government to exclusively supply the British Army's ammunition requirements – effectively supplanting Thatcherite ideology with another equally contentious New Labour ideology, as PFIs were eventually discredited and abandoned.* The cost of this deal was an estimated £2 billion, but the growing demand for ammunition would probably raise this figure to £3 billion. This was not a bad return on an historic entity which the Thatcher government sold off for just £188.5 million. The whole saga challenged the assumptions of the original privatization: if Royal Ordnance had not been eroded to extinction, would the British taxpayer have had to fork out quite so much to provide the army with its most basic requirement – bullets?

At the end of August, 16 Air Assault Brigade mounted the biggest operation of its six-month tour, indeed the biggest operation attempted by British forces to date in Helmand Province. The troops had known for months the operation was likely to be mounted, but the timing could not have been worse. After five months of attrition warfare, accidents and routine illnesses, the brigade had lost over a battalion's worth of soldiers. To mount Operation *Oqab Tsuka* ('Eagle's Summit') soldiers would have to be scraped from every infantry unit in Helmand. The lack of helicopters and the sheer logistic difficulties of repositioning all the men and materials needed for the task meant that the operation started a full month before the proposed D-Day, to stand any chance of meeting its deadline. Many of the troops were exhausted from a summer of hot fighting and had their sights fixed on homebound flights, not the enemy. It would be the last major effort undertaken by the brigade before handing over to its successor.

Operation *Oqab Tsuka* showed the British at their determined best and self-mythologizing worst. At stake was a $200 million USAID-funded project to deliver a third turbine to the Kajaki Dam. This project had been proposed in the early stages of Operation *Enduring Freedom*, when American soldiers first explored the upper reaches of the Helmand Valley, building a new police station at Kajaki village and funding a clinic and school. The countryside had been benign then and it seemed an obvious and useful reconstruction project, potentially restoring electricity to tens of thousands of homes that had been cut-off from Helmand's rickety power

*In another twist, the owners then sold the site to a consortium of Korean institutional investors in 2017.

grid since the days of the Soviet occupation. For USAID, Kajaki Dam was unfinished business from the 1970s – what better way to restore American prestige? In fact, the proposal to add a third turbine to Kajaki Dam was flawed from the start. The turbine alone would serve no purpose. What was required was a major refurbishment of the entire power grid, such as it existed, as well as the construction of hundreds of kilometres of new supply lines. This second phase of the project was never seriously assessed or resourced. If ISAF was engaged in 'gesture strategy', to borrow Max Hastings's memorable phrase, then this was 'gesture reconstruction'. When fighting flared up at Kajaki, effectively creating a front line within shooting distance of the dam, the project stalled anyway. Now 16 Air Assault Brigade would be entrusted with reviving this moribund project.

The British ambassador, Sherard Cowper-Coles, and the civilian head of the PRT in Lashkar Gah, Hugh Powell – in the usual way – were both completely set against the operation. If an operation was likely to result in many casualties – or unpleasantness for political masters in London – then civilian officials tried to veto the operation. This had almost happened with the deployment of 24th MEU earlier in the summer, but FCO fears had been overridden by the robust attitude of Brigadier Carleton-Smith. Now it was about to play out again.

In Operation *Oqab Tsuka* the army spectacularly shot itself in the foot by producing a wildly pessimistic assessment of the likely risks of the operation. In the overheated atmosphere of the task force HQ at Lashkar Gah, staff officers estimated that an operation to deliver the third turbine to Kajaki, by driving up Route 611, would result in about 50 British fatalities and they began to dub the mission 'Operation Certain Death'.[38] This was a ridiculous assessment of the risk. The threat of an imaginary Taliban division grew in the minds of apoplectic government officials in the Helmand Executive Group, who began to describe the operation as 'totally mad' and potentially disastrous for the entire British presence in Helmand Province.[39] Cool heads were needed and an alternative plan to driving the length of Route 611 to the dam (which would have provoked a fight with the Taliban but not on the scale envisaged). The real problem was that engineer reconnaissance had revealed that nearly 70 culverts would have to be reinforced to take the weight of the load carriers.[40]

The proposed alternative route – baptized Route Harriet – essentially followed a little used dirt road that diverted north from Highway 1 across a deserted rocky plain in northern Kandahar Province (passing not that far from Maiwand village, the scene of the British rout in 1880). About 30 kilometres short of Kajaki the track swung sharply west and sneaked along the bed of a wadi known as Ghowrak Pass. The total distance of this circuitous cross-country route was 180 kilometres, and the convoy would end up completing the epic journey at an average speed of about 1 mile per hour. Ironically, the British already knew about Ghowrak Pass (or should have known), because A Company of 1 Royal Gurkha Rifles had patrolled this pass at the beginning of the year. The haemorrhaging of intelligence continued to be a feature of the war in Helmand. During the Vietnam War, American army officer John Paul Vann observed: 'We don't have twelve years' experience in Vietnam. We have one year's experience twelve times over.'[41] The same phenomenon was being repeated in Helmand with each brigade re-inventing the intelligence wheel every six months.

That the mission took place at all was due to pressure placed on the British by the American ambassador, Bill Wood, and by informal understandings between the two soldiers General McKiernan, the American commander of ISAF forces, and Brigadier Carleton-Smith. It was a damning comment on British political oversight and military command of the war in Helmand that the most significant mission undertaken in that year should have come about as result of back room deals between two operational commanders and American diplomatic pressure.

Just getting the massive turbine to the dam would prove a significant challenge. The turbine components weighed about 200 tonnes so they necessarily had to be split between several heavy equipment transporters.[42] Seven trailers would be needed to carry the components: four for the transformers, the smallest of which weighed 25 tonnes; two for the stators; and the last for the upper bracket assembly, which weighed about 15 tonnes. The most critical components were the stators. These had been custom-built, and damage to one of these would probably have resulted in a two-year delay before a replacement could be supplied.[43] To protect the components from the possibility of damage, Royal Electrical and Mechanical Engineers fashioned steel cages from old ISO containers, adding another 28 tonnes of steel to the load.

Despite all the political and military hurdles, a 100-vehicle convoy carrying the turbine parts did eventually leave Kandahar Air Base on 27 August, under command of Lieutenant Colonel Rufus McNeil, the commanding officer of 13 Air Assault Support Regiment. Command of the operation at the Kajaki end was vested in Lieutenant Colonel Huw Williams, the 3 PARA commanding officer. The convoy set off in darkness, pointed itself north, and reached the open plain largely undetected. Within the convoy there was a wide mix of vehicles, reflecting all the different specialists needed to keep the train moving: paratroopers in Jackals protecting the open flanks; Queen's Royal Lancers in Vikings providing close protection with heavy machine guns; and sappers in heavily protected Mastiffs pushing mine rollers. Behind them a line of tractors and dump trucks filled with aggregate stood by to undertake road improvements. The convoy stretched for over 6 miles, creating a dust trail that could be seen for miles. As it snaked past hostile villages it risked attracting volleys of gunfire, but once past areas of habitation the soldiers were driving over a moonscape. The rocky gravel plain north of Kandahar is a barren, deserted area and the only signs of life were the occasional suspected 'dicker' (insurgent spotter). It took four days of hard driving for the convoy to finally reach the mountain pass, placing it just one day's drive away from the dam.

Coincident with the departure of the convoy, clearance operations began at Kajaki itself. The village of Kajai Olya – believed to be harbouring Taliban – was especially targeted. Intelligence had suggested that two compounds were being used as command centres by the insurgents. One of the compounds, codenamed Sentry, was on the eastern bank of the Helmand River. The second compound, Big Top, sat astride Route 611. The ANA *kandak,* under British direction, was tasked to clear both compounds. Once these compounds had been cleared, D Company from 2 PARA would pass through the ANA positions and clear the remainder of the route to FOB Zeebrugge. B Company from 3 PARA would relieve D Company; finally, A Company would secure the coordination point with the convoy on Route Harriet.

Advancing on compound Sentry, the ANA soldiers met little resistance. In an unequal fight, the compound was destroyed by a salvo of GMLRS rockets (over the summer, 16 Air Assault Brigade would launch 197 GMLRS, or over $40 million's worth of rocketry). The biggest challenge for the British mentors proved to be stopping the ANA soldiers from pillaging fruit from a nearby orchard. The ANA companies then reorganized and advanced on the second compound from which they received sporadic fire. This position was also quickly overcome by a massive use of firepower – 150 artillery shells, as well as mortar and aerial bombs, rained down on Big Top. By the time the paratroopers arrived on their start lines to take over from the ANA *kandak* there was nothing left to do. Any insurgents and all locals had fled the area.

For the convoy, this last stretch was the most treacherous. The reconnaissance had not properly assessed the state of the track through Ghowrak Pass and it was discovered that some impromptu road-building was required to allow the passage of the heavy equipment transporters. Having negotiated the mountain pass, the trucks then had to cover a 10-kilometre length of Route 611 that wound past Kajaki Olya before following the bend of the river into FOB Zeebrugge.

The urgency – and the successful delivery of the $200 million project – now fell on the shoulders of a captain in his twenties, Liam Fitzgerald-Finch. Captain Fitzgerald-Finch's unenviable task was to find and defuse the IEDs on Route 611 and to do it quickly. Keeping calm, despite temperatures soaring above 40 degrees, he began the lonely and dangerous task. It was not long before he began to uncover the roadside bombs. Progress slowed, and it appeared the convoy would have to spend another day in the open, vulnerable to attack. Aware of this possibility, Fitzgerald-Finch took the bold decision to continue the fingertip search for IEDs in the dark, a procedure not normally practised because of the self-evident dangers to the bomb disposal officer. In total, 13 IEDs were found and defused. For this action, Fitzgerald-Finch was awarded the Queen's Gallantry Medal.

Five days after the convoy set off, the third turbine was finally delivered to Kajaki Dam at 0230hrs on 2 September. The British had taken no chances. Virtually the entire brigade had been employed in some way to undertake Operation *Oqab Tsuka*, and a massive amount of firepower had been expended to deliver Kajaki Dam's third turbine. A Canadian soldier was killed by a roadside bomb and a British soldier suffered a crushed pelvis in a road accident. One ANA soldier was electrocuted fishing in the river with an illegally commandeered power cable. It was later claimed 250 Taliban were killed, but this was a gross exaggeration. The main experience for the common soldier had been the boredom of spending hours crawling along the desert plateau clad in heavy body armour and helmet in high temperatures: 'Eating sand for hours on end, sweating my proverbials off with barely enough room to swing a cat,' as one sapper remembered.[44] To mark the successful delivery of the turbine, a photograph was taken showing the local governor passing under a ribbon held by Afghan soldiers, but this had been, from start to finish, an ISAF operation.

Operation *Oqab Tsuka* was unarguably a considerable logistic feat and the MOD spin machine was quick to crow about the epic mission. The presentation of a pleasing reality, rather than facing actual reality, had become the British way of warfare. The brigade commander was regrettably quoted in the *Daily Mail* declaring that this operation marked the beginning of the end, inviting the riposte – whose end? Even the prime minister gleaned some reflected glory from the operation by publishing an adulatory article in the popular tabloid the *Sun*. This ghost-written piece omitted to mention that this was an American-financed operation undertaken against opposition from the FCO, and which only came about as a result of pressure from an increasingly exasperated American ambassador in Kabul.

British self-congratulation was both premature and unjustified. Within a few days the de facto front line would reassert itself again and the two-year-old standoff in Kajaki resumed. More pertinently, the delivery of the turbine did not improve the supply of electricity to Helmand or Kandahar provinces. Following the operation, the project remained stalled because of technical difficulties and a lack of security. Not a single volt of electricity would be added to the power grid.*

Operation *Oqab Tsuka* dominated 16 Air Assault Brigade's tour in Helmand, and it was easy to forget that elsewhere the war continued unabated, regardless of the headline-grabbing events at Kajaki.

In Musa Qaleh, The Argylls (5 SCOTS) were fighting a constant game of cat and mouse with the local Alizai insurgents. This unit was led by Lieutenant Colonel Nicholas Borton, who had taken over command of the battalion at short notice after the first commanding officer was wounded in a gun battle. The loss of a commanding officer was itself a noteworthy event – the last time the British Army had suffered such a high-ranking casualty was in the Falklands Conflict, almost quarter of a century earlier. The circumstances of Lieutenant Colonel David Richmond's wounding (he suffered a gunshot wound to the thigh that fractured his femur) were typical of the types of operations which the Jocks† undertook during their six-month tour as Battlegroup North-West.[45]

*The third turbine was finally connected in 2016 after ISAF's departure. A Turkish company completed the project in 2022. At the time of writing, Kajaki Dam has the capacity to generate roughly 150MW of electricity. Seventy years after US firm Morrison–Knudsen initiated the project, it finally came to fruition.

†Since before World War I, 'the Jocks' has been the title of admiration and pride for the non-commissioned fighting men of Scottish regiments. The Jocks proudly refer to themselves by this sobriquet.

Intelligence had been received of a possible Taliban bomb-making factory in a village called Karyeh-ye Kats Sharbat, about 8 kilometres north of Musa Qaleh. The village sat at the confluence of a wadi that debouched into the Musa Qaleh River, immediately west of the prominent mountain known to the troops as 'Mount Doom'. Mount Doom was over 1,600 metres high and completely dominated the surrounding countryside. It rose steeply from the plain north of Musa Qaleh and its slopes were strewn with large boulders. To approach Karyeh-ye Kats Sharbat from the south meant either channelling troops along a narrow corridor west of the mountain, or detouring around the mountain and approaching from the north. The western approach was too obvious and would be 'dicked' by Taliban spotters, so Lieutenant Colonel Richmond decided to strike from the north, taking the longer approach route around Mount Doom.

To distract attention away from this covert approach, a reinforced platoon of Warriors crewed by B Company, Highlanders (4 SCOTS) would be used as bait. The Highlanders were based at FOB Edinburgh, about 6 kilometres to the west of Musa Qaleh. Their task would be to drive north-east across two wadis and to take covering positions on high ground, on the western bank of the Musa Qaleh River. With their thermal sights they would be able to pick out any movement in the village and provide supporting fire with their 30mm cannons if necessary. Concurrently, an ANA company mentored by the Royal Irish would infiltrate north and test the Taliban reaction. Before the deployment of the western force, D Company of The Argylls would sneak around the back of Mount Doom at night, in eight Mastiffs, supported by a contingent from 2/7 Marines who were also based at the Musa Qaleh District Centre. Two sections of ANA would accompany this force to show an 'Afghan face'.

The scheme unfolded according to plan. The combined group of Highlanders and ANA soon became engaged by villagers in Karyeh-ye Kats Sharbat. While this was happening and as dawn broke, D Company approached undetected from the north. As the soldiers neared the outskirts of the village, local 'dickers' spotted the advancing Jocks and a gun battle erupted. This acted as a cue for the Mastiffs to roll forward like tanks and provide fire for the infantry assaulting the village. With their .50-calibre machine guns and 30mm grenade launchers they laid down an impressive weight of fire. D Company advanced quickly into the village and the gunmen fled. As invariably happened in these assaults, the Jocks were then shot at by villagers using the warren of alleys in the village as cover. The reported bomb-making factory proved to be false information – nothing of significance was found. After several hours clearing compounds and becoming engaged in random gun battles, the decision was taken to sweep north through the village and flush out any remaining gunmen.

To communicate his orders, Lieutenant Colonel Richmond had to walk to a cemetery on high ground west of the village, where some US Marines had taken up a fire position. The Bowman radios had failed again, and the only way to guarantee the passage of his orders was to return to World War I-style communications using runners or communicating the orders in person. It was while he was standing on this hillock explaining the next phase of the operation that Lieutenant Colonel Richmond was shot in the leg. The call 'Sunray is down' ('Sunray' was the radio codeword for commander) electrified the British force. In Normandy the life expectancy of an infantry commanding officer was a matter of a few weeks. To post-war generations of soldiers, the loss of a commanding officer was a rarity and novelty. The operation was aborted, and Lieutenant Colonel Richmond was duly evacuated to Camp Bastion field hospital, in pain but alive. The severity of the fracture was such that Richmond would require two years of rehabilitation. Moved by this experience, he subsequently became a champion for wounded soldiers.

On completion of the tour, The Argylls would be scathing of a radio system that almost cost the life of their commander.[46] The weight of the radios was 'very problematic'; the HF radio 'useless'; the VHF range 'generally poor in this terrain'; and the digital applications supposed to modernize army communications (known as BCIP and ComBAT*) 'not used'. Overall, the radio system was judged 'not fit for purpose'. This vituperation had been widespread in unit post-operational reports since the beginning of the mission, After *Herrick 8* – it appears due to a ministry-level injunction – the criticisms abruptly stopped.

The Argylls' commanding officer had been felled by a stray, long-range shot. Many of the gun fights experienced by the Jocks were much more close range and 'personal'. At the age of 24, Lieutenant James Adamson had already earned a Mention in Dispatches for demonstrating coolness

*Bowman Common Information Platform, and Bowman Common Battlefield Application Toolset.

under enemy fire. In early October, as the brigade were preparing to hand over to the marines, his platoon once again found itself involved in heavy fighting. Separated from his sections and with only a mortar fire controller and interpreter as cover, he began to negotiate a shallow stream to rejoin his troops when two gunmen appeared 5 metres in front of the group and opened fire with a machine gun. Miraculously, the insurgents missed the startled British soldiers. Acting on instinct, Lieutenant Adamson bayonet charged the gunmen. For this 'supreme physical courage', Adamson was awarded the Military Cross.

Like the Royal Irish, The Argylls would quit the province having suffered only one fatality, a Lance Corporal James Johnson, killed not at Musa Qaleh but at Lashkar Gah manning a checkpoint. The Jocks proved far cannier than their opponents (the superb performance of this regiment did not save it from defence cuts; The Argyll and Sutherland Highlanders, famous for 'the thin red line',* would be reduced to a ceremonial Balaklava Company).

Over the course of the summer the British would incur over 25 fatalities in Helmand's Green Zone, the majority suffered by 2 PARA patrols operating from FOBs Gibraltar and Inkerman. Among the dead was Lance Corporal Kenneth Rowe, an army dog handler who had volunteered to remain at FOB Inkerman to support a 2 PARA search task. He had been due to leave the besieged base the day before he died. He was killed, alongside the search dog Sasha, when they were caught by an RPG rocket. By curious, dark coincidence the military working dog should not have been there either as it belonged to another handler, but was borrowed by Rowe. Loyalty to the fallen was extended to this canine servant. When it was discovered in the confusion of the casualty evacuation (conducted in darkness) that Sasha had been left behind, a second patrol was mounted to recover the lifeless dog.

These casualty figures – which at the time seemed shocking – contrasted sharply with those of 3 PARA, the sister parachute battalion commanded by Lieutenant Colonel Huw Williams, deployed to Kandahar as the theatre reserve. 3 PARA had been the popular heroes of Operation *Herrick 4*. More books had been written about this battalion than any other unit in the British Army, causing a predictable rush of young men keen to join

*Involving the 93rd Sutherland Highlanders.

3 PARA to collect some of this reflected glory. The new recruits found the action they craved, but what was striking about 3 PARA's tour of southern Afghanistan in the summer of 2008 was that the battalion did not suffer a single fatality, and only suffered four wounded in action.

The reasons for the remarkably low casualty rate were twofold. First, the battalion largely encountered weak and even non-existent opposition. But second, while the sister 2 PARA was dispersed and mired in static, attrition warfare, 3 PARA was concentrated and engaged in mobile warfare. The results spoke for themselves. 3 PARA displayed the highest operational tempo of any unit in 16 Air Assault Brigade and suffered the least number of casualties. The same would be true of every British battalion that took on the role of the theatre reserve until the outgoing Labour government ended this commitment in the autumn of 2009. It was one of the perverse aspects of the war in Helmand that the single approach that was yielding the most success – if success could be measured crudely by the number of operations undertaken against casualties incurred – was the one approach that was not (or could not be) exploited by the British. If the British had stuck to their own doctrine of 'the manoeuvrist approach', or more plainly a philosophy of mobile warfare, the statistics suggest their casualties would have numbered in the tens, not the hundreds.

The principal problem for 3 PARA proved to be not the enemy, but rather like The Argylls, the ongoing saga with the Bowman radios. The radios needed to be 'filled' with the crypto, or code, that allowed secure communications before an operation. In an unforeseen development, heliborne operations involving CH-47s and Black Hawks had a tendency to provoke 'comms fratricide', or cause the radios to drop their fills. This meant an unlucky signaller had to race around the entire company, refilling each radio individually, to restore the net, a task that could take half an hour and result in all loss of surprise.[47] Deep discharging of the batteries was described as 'common' and the range and reliability of the radios inadequate. Across the battlegroup there was 'very low confidence in BOWMAN at all ranks'.

Like the Gurkhas before them, 3 PARA discovered that what really mattered was the quality of the intelligence. The paratroopers were adept at mounting air assault operations and catching the Taliban by surprise. But if the intelligence was weak – as it too often was – it amounted to chasing phantoms in the hills. If Brigadier Carleton-Smith's wish had been realized none of this military action would have been necessary anyway. His brigade had deployed to Helmand to assist in the spread of governance and to allow reconstruction: this was the message he had promoted on his many unit visits. How was this crucial pillar of the British 'comprehensive approach' faring, two years after the first paratroopers arrived in Helmand?

According to DfID, around £23.7 million had now been spent on reconstruction in Helmand since 2006, out of a total commitment of £30 million. This represented less than 5 per cent of pledged British aid to Afghanistan.[48] The money, wherever it was being spent, was not following the bullets. The 'comprehensive approach' – at least in Helmand, where British soldiers were now dying at an alarming rate – was a sham.

By 2008, 98 civilians and 48 military personnel were working in CIMIC at the Lashkar Gah PRT. Over the next 12 months, the renamed Civil Stabilization Unit, commonly recruiting ex-military personnel rather than civil servants, would swell to 140 strong based at Lashkar Gah and five other locations. The military Construction and Supervision Cell (CSC) remained small – just five soldiers – and district centres relied on their own Development and Influence Teams, or DITs. To counter mounting criticism, DfID listed reconstruction successes in Helmand on its website. The long lists of wells dug, schools repainted and mosques repaired drew a sceptical response. An anonymous officer, weary of the parallel reality of aid euphemisms, wrote: 'Need for a comprehensive plan (not just Approach), which is signed up to by all and delivers action not activity.'[49] Embedded journalists were also discovering a quite different reality to that portrayed by DfID.

One such journalist was Anthony Loyd, reporting for *The Times*. He visited Musa Qaleh in the summer of 2008, then being held up as a model of British reconstruction (based on American funds), and wrote a critical report on what he uncovered. It had taken seven months for a civilian stabilization advisor to be posted to Musa Qaleh. Much of the reconstruction money had been squandered on bribes or embezzled. The biggest scam was multiple sub-contracting, invariably between tribal or family members, with each sub-contractor taking a cut but not actually providing a service. About £100,000 was donated towards asphalting the main bazaar road in Musa Qaleh, and within a few months it was filled with cracks and potholes due to the poor workmanship. A further £115,000 was donated towards refurbishing the main clinic in the town, but it remained unused because there was no running water or electricity.

The lack of electricity remained a significant complaint (echoing the problems the British faced in Basra). Under the Taliban electricity had been rationed to alternate days. Now that the British were back, the town was receiving a few hours of reliable supply every four days. The destroyed mosque had still not been rebuilt. The much-vaunted Cash for Works programme (which was actually paying a lower daily rate than the Taliban were offering their fighters) collapsed after the corrupt contractor failed to present satisfactory accounts. How many locals were actually employed on this scheme and where the money went would never be determined with any certainty. Mullah Salaam, Karzai's appointee governor, was actively siphoning off some of the reconstruction money, as were his unpaid policemen.

Christina Lamb was similarly unimpressed by the 'success statistics' culture when she visited Lashkar Gah at the end of the brigade's tour. 'A day spent in this Foreign Office fantasy land was reminiscent of a propaganda tour I was taken on by the Russians in the dying days of their occupation in the late 1980s,' she wrote.[50] The Taliban were just 7 miles away across the river, 'but earnest civil servants boast of British success in winning over the population'. The more than 100 civil servants of the district centre spent their time creating PowerPoints, meeting 'targets' and seldom stepped outside. 'The place has the feel of a cult where the mantra is "Believe",' she concluded, 'and anyone who dares question the enterprise is regarded as a Jeremiah.'

One of the favourite statistics quoted by DfID was the number of re-opened schools (the school at Musa Qaleh closed by the Taliban would be restored to its proper use). But the bald statistics – 59 schools were reportedly functioning in Helmand in the summer of 2008 – barely told the truth.[51] The Helmand provincial council told a visiting group of MPs that there had actually been over 200 schools *before* the British arrived. It had been the fighting that had provoked the closure of schools, not Taliban opposition to education.[52] A veneer of reconstruction based on misleading statistics was constantly being drip fed, creating a false picture of British aid efforts in Helmand Province. The soldiers remained sceptical. One remarked to Loyd: 'They wouldn't know how to pour piss from a boot if the instructions were on the heel. That's the PRT.'

As concerning was the lack of any suggestion that DfID's attitudes to working in Afghanistan had changed. When the House of Commons

International Development Committee delivered its fourth report on reconstruction in Afghanistan, one of the hot topics discussed was the paucity of social life in Kabul, which implied DfID staff needed more leave periods in Britain to recuperate from this unfortunate deprivation.[53] A view was offered:

> Since the attacks on foreign targets near the DFID houses in November 2007 and on the Serena Hotel in January 2008, the opportunities for social life outside the Embassy have been severely curtailed. This has impacted on the opportunities staff have to get 'down time'. In this climate, it is judged that it would not be appropriate to extend the length of the work/breather break cycle beyond six weeks on, two weeks off.

A soldier risking life and limb and earning pennies compared to the generously remunerated DfID staff had no hope of 'social life' in hotels, never mind hiving off back to Britain after only six weeks in-country.

The failure of British reconstruction in Helmand Province was amplified by a self-defeating stinginess on the part of some civil servants entrusted with running important programmes. One such programme was the Helmand PTS (Proceay-e Tahkeem-e Solha, or Peace and Reconciliation Commission). This was studied by the academic and defence advisor Matt Waldeman, who interviewed a number of former Taliban. He discovered that the total budget for the Helmand PTS was $600 *a month*. Fighters who agreed to reconcile were being offered 150 Afghanis, or about three dollars. This derisory amount was much less than the daily wage offered by the insurgency, and as Waldeman observed, this barely covered their travelling costs. Far from providing an inducement to reconciliation, he concluded that the Helmand PTS was perceived as a great insult: 'Given the importance of *eftekhar* or *namus* (honour/dignity) and *sharm* (shame) in Pashtun culture, core insurgents are unlikely to reintegrate unless they can do so with a degree of honour and respectability.'[54]

In answer to a Freedom of Information request by a television broadcaster, it transpired that the British had admitted to causing 104 civilian deaths and that $200,000 had been disbursed in various compensation payments in the last 18 months.[55] These statistics also barely told the story. A British officer working in the Lashkar Gah PRT was appalled to discover that it was taking weeks for compensation claims to be honoured for killed relatives, resulting in the pitiful sight of beggarly widows returning day after day in the vain hope of receiving some compensation. Another commanding officer was horrified that a family that lost eight relatives in an air strike was told to return in 45 days to claim a payment, while at the same time, 'BGs [battlegroups] can waste £69,000 at will firing Javelin missiles at the behest of a JNCO.'[56] The amounts being paid out just added insult to the injury of the bureaucratic foot-dragging. The cost of the life of a woman accidentally killed by British military action was just £127 (it paid to be killed by American forces, literally, as compensation was set at $2,500, far more even than the Taliban were paying the families of suicide bomb volunteers). This stinginess, incidentally, had precedent in Northern Ireland. To give one example, when two young men, Seamus Cusack and Desmond Beattie, were shot and killed by British troops in the course of a riot in Londonderry in July 1971, their relatives received just £415 in compensation, after a four-year wait.[57]

By mid-2009 the British government would admit to paying out around 200 such claims in Afghanistan. Given the small amounts of compensation being disbursed (amounting to much less than the average ammunition expenditure of a platoon in a morning's gun battle), it seemed unfathomable that bureaucracy was not waved aside. By the summer of that year the task force had been resupplied with 198,000 rounds of .50 cal, 2,370,400 rounds of 5.56mm, 2,233,800 rounds of 7.62mm as well as a staggering 38,868 81mm mortar bombs.[58] The cost of this ammunition ran into tens of millions of pounds. A petty concern over paying out false claims seemed to override the immense damage that civil servant parsimony was creating to the perceptions of bereaved Helmandis, leaving aside the physical damage left behind in the wake of military operations.

The experience of two senior NCOs working in Gereshk was typical of the frustrations being experienced all across Helmand in reconstruction efforts. When Staff Sergeant Davidson and Sergeant Needham set up a registration clinic in the town to collect names of potential contractors and tradesmen, they were bemused to find that 'first at the door was the Mayor of Gereshk's son to register as a mechanic; no pressure from dad there then!' Eventually they did register nine bona fide contractors, but the two soldiers honestly conceded that this was a 'pebble thrown in the pond in terms of reconstruction and development progress in Gereshk, Helmand Province'. A week later at the Bost Hotel in Lashkar Gah – the town's only hotel that adjoined the governor's home – an inaugural Helmand contractors conference was held, attended by 61 Afghans representing 55 construction companies. This conference would lead to over 30 local projects supervised by the Royal Engineers, but again the honest soldiers admitted that their projects generated neither popular support nor significant employment. This candour from the soldiers contrasted sharply with the spin offered by DfID.

It was a credit to the spirit of the British Army that such disappointments did not translate into dead cynicism. Soldiers were genuinely moved by the routine poverty in Helmand. The sentiment that the British Army was doing some good was commonly expressed. When Lieutenant Alison Macdonald, working at the Joint District Coordination Cell in Gereshk, visited the town's only school for girls, she was stirred by the reception she received:

> The warmth of the greeting from staff and students was palpable; I was treated like royalty with two bunches of flowers and an offer of a most welcome cold drink. The setup for the visit was an open forum and on arriving in the room I went round and shook the hands of all the female teachers and a selection of the students, and they were all so welcoming and friendly. This was their opportunity to have their say and outline what we might be able to do for them. Their requests were so simple ranging from – fans and fridges, soap and shampoo and milk for the youngest children. All things that we accept as normal but items that can make such a difference to their lives. They were particularly pleased to see a female visiting the school and to have the opportunity to meet and talk to a female officer was a novelty.[59]

It was experiences like this that offered some recompense in the otherwise daily round of frustrations.

For Brigadier Carleton-Smith, these small victories could not hide the larger and much grimmer picture. As the six-month deployment neared its end, his assessment of the situation was sober and realistic. In his post-operational report he warned the mission was heading for 'strategic failure'. The pessimism was echoed in Washington, with National Security Advisor General Jim Jones sentencing, 'Make no mistake, NATO is not winning in Afghanistan.'[60] Carleton-Smith was not a seer and he could not have foreseen the end, as it played out, in the summer of 2021. But it was notable that 17 brigadiers served in Helmand (the last did not deploy due to the short tour) but only one wrote those words.

The reason why: the terrorist attacks of September 11, 2001.
(Spencer Platt/Getty Images)

Prime Minister Tony Blair and President Hamid Karzai in Kabul, 2006 – Blair would leave office in controversy while Karzai would regret the British ever entering Helmand.
(Paula Bronstein/Getty Images)

Defence Secretary John Reid and Brigadier Ed Butler: the two personalities had different perspectives on the Helmand mission. A pensive CGS General Sir Richard Dannatt follows behind. (John D. McHugh/AFP via Getty Images)

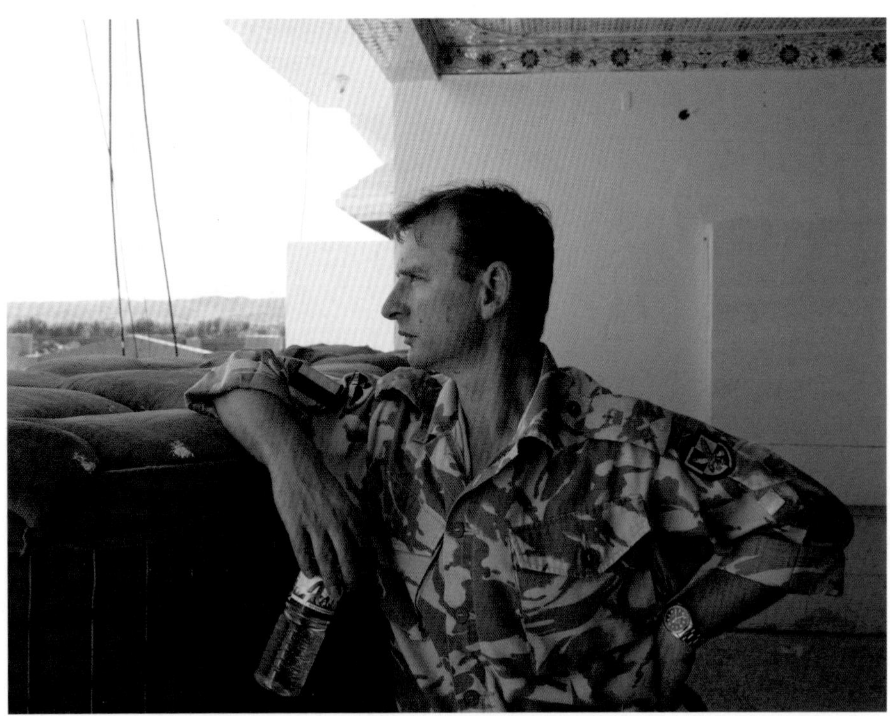

Brigadier Mark Carleton-Smith in Sangin in July 2008 – he was the only task force commander to warn that the mission was heading for 'strategic failure'. (Marco Di Lauro/Getty Images)

Major General Gordon Messenger, Royal Marines, receives a bar to his DSO at Buckingham Palace in December 2009. The absence of leadership in the MOD and PJHQ meant that his plan for Helmand in the winter of 2008–09 effectively became the British campaign plan for the remainder of the war. (Lewis Whyld/WPA Pool/Getty Images)

General Sir Richard Dannatt, Chief of the General Staff from 2006 to 2009. He did more than any other senior officer to raise the profile of the British Army and garner public support for the returning soldiers. (Matt Cardy/Getty Images)

Left 'Kabul Richards': Acting General David Richards. He would put the British Army on a campaign footing, which it badly needed. (SHAH MARAI/AFP via Getty Images)

Below The Helmand River – without it the region would be barren desert. (WAKIL KOHSAR/AFP via Getty Images)

Harvesting the opium poppy sap in Gereshk District. Afghanistan was the world's top opium producer with the epicentre of the trade in Helmand Province. (NOOR MOHAMMAD/AFP via Getty Images)

A gunner corporal gives covering fire to fellow soldiers in the BRF in early 2013. The British Army's standard rifle – the SA80 – gained many enhancements over the course of the war. (Sgt Rupert Frere RLC/Crown Copyright 2019)

2 PARA in the Upper Gereshk Valley in July 2008 – looking warlike was part of the image. (Marco Di Lauro/Getty Images)

Grenadier Guards undertake a joint patrol with the ANA in the Sangin Valley in June 2007. (Marco Di Lauro/Getty Images)

Soldiers from 1 Rifles take cover in a ditch in Nawa-e Barakzai, south of the capital Lashkar Gah, in March 2009. The rifleman in the foreground is carrying a Vallon mine detector. (POA(Phot) Dave Husbands/Crown Copyright)

Welsh Guardsmen return fire from a compound on Operation *Panchai Palang* ('Panther's Claw') in the summer of 2009. (Cpl Dan Bardsley RLC/Crown Copyright)

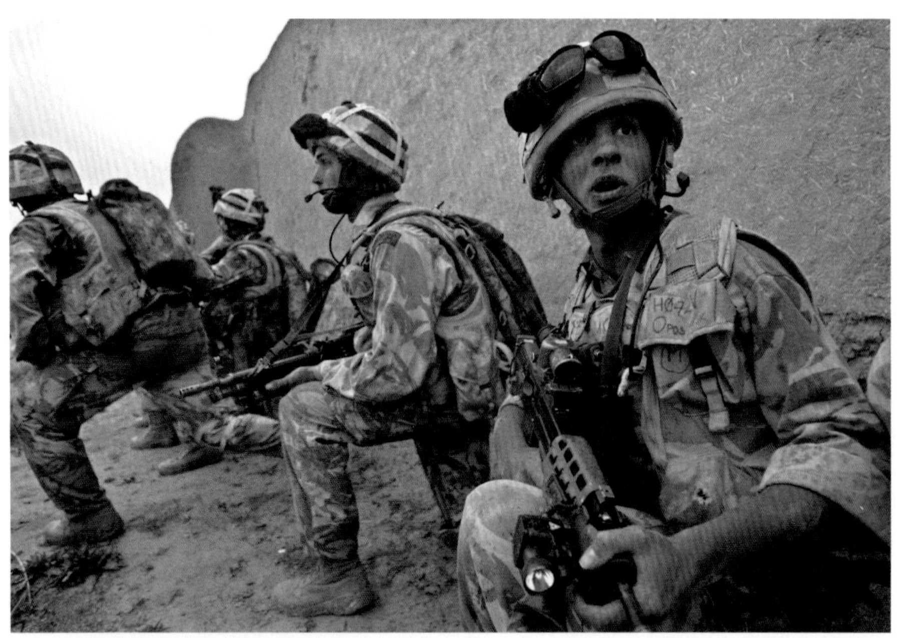

Royal Marines from 42 Commando conduct a village assault near Kajaki in March 2007. (John Moore/Getty Images)

Royal Tank Regiment troopers engage targets from Vikings in June 2009. The Viking was highly manoeuvrable in Helmand's Green Zone but the flat-bottomed design was vulnerable to IEDs. (Cpl Dan Bardsley RLC/Crown Copyright)

The US Cougar was renamed the Mastiff by the British Army. Countless British soldiers owed their lives and limbs to this example of solid American engineering. (Marco Di Lauro/Getty Images)

Royal Marines from 3 Commando Brigade on a Jackal in February 2009. This British-designed vehicle placed the commander and driver directly over the wheel arches, with deleterious consequences if the vehicle struck an IED. More British soldiers and marines were killed or maimed on Jackals than on the Land Rover Snatch that attracted critical media attention. In the background is 'Mount Doom' near Musa Qaleh. (POA(Phot) Dave Husbands/Crown Copyright)

The 'Antiques Roadshow': cavalrymen joked over the Scimitar, a vehicle older than the crews. The inability of the MOD to secure a replacement for this 1970s-era vehicle was one of the worst procurement sagas of the period. The image shows Light Dragoons in southern Helmand in May 2007.
(Marco Di Lauro/Getty Images)

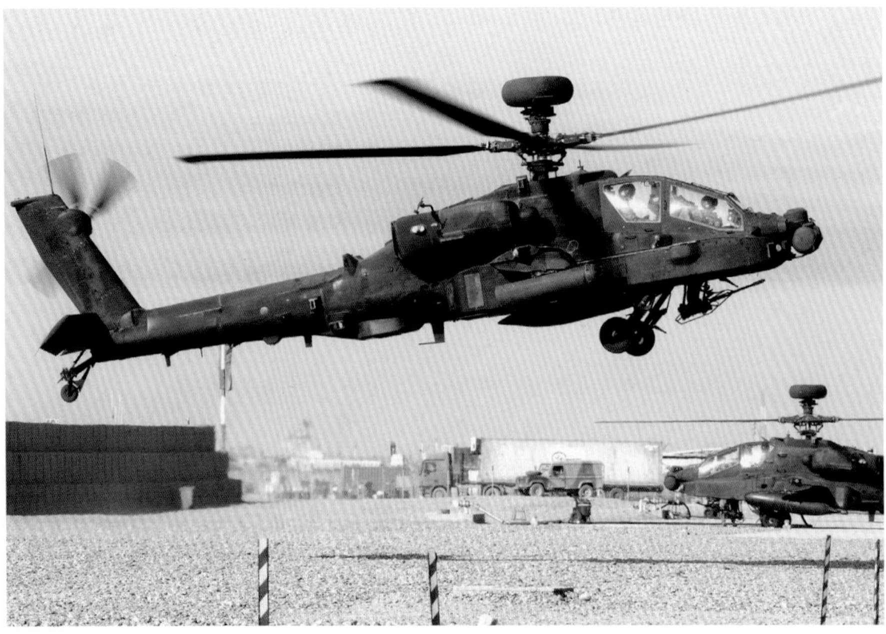

The Apache helicopter was feared by the insurgents. (POA(Phot) Mez Merrill/Crown Copyright)

'Brown out' – a RAF CH-47 Chinook delivers supplies to Royal Marines in Garmsir in February 2007. There were never enough helicopters to support Task Force Helmand. (POA(Phot) Sean Clee/Crown Copyright, 2023)

An RAF Tornado GR4 in August 2009: ISAF was criticised for accidental killings of civilians. In fact, the targeting process was meticulous and pilots elected not to drop ordnance in the overwhelming majority of strike missions. (Flt Lt Joe Marlowe/Crown Copyright)

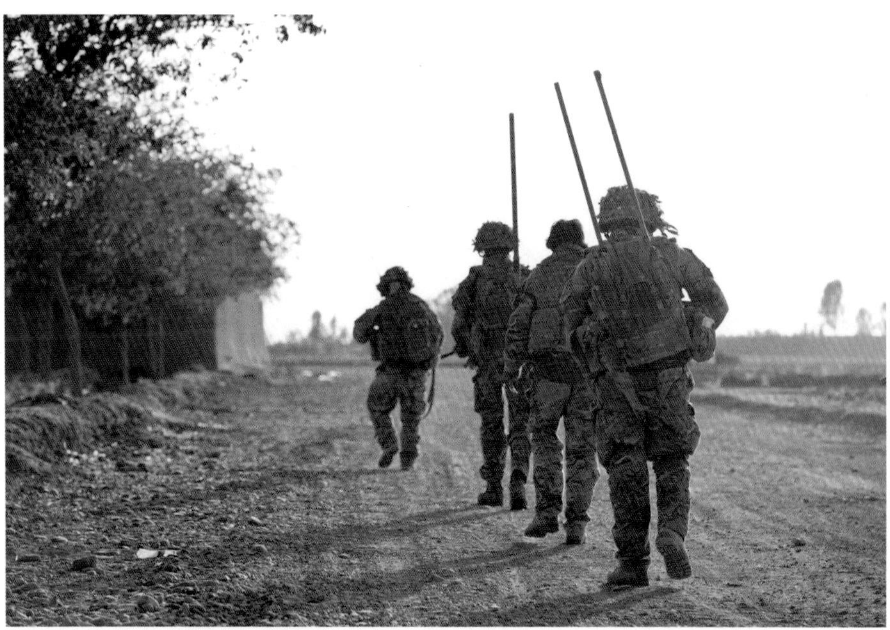

Above A 5 Rifles section at the end of a day's patrol in August 2014. The soldiers are weighed down with electronic countermeasures equipment designed to defeat IEDs. (Cpl Daniel Wiepen/ Crown Copyright)

Left A Royal Anglian soldier checks his map. The British Army turned to gridded satellite imagery for mapping rather than using the digital mapping of the unpopular Bowman radio system. (Cpl Paul Morrison/ Crown Copyright)

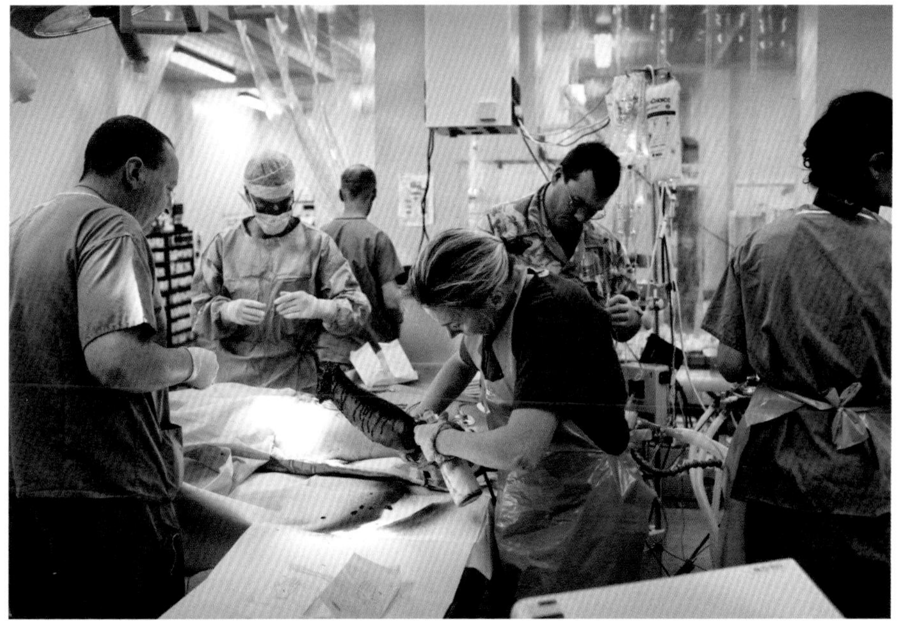

The life-saving Role 1 hospital at Camp Bastion. The soldier on the operating table has lost his left hand. (Marco Di Lauro/Edit by Getty Images)

A Combat Logistic Patrol winds its way through the desert. By the second half of the war, simply resupplying the large, dispersed force had become the principal activity of Task Force Helmand. (THOMAS COEX/AFP via Getty Images)

Winning 'hearts and minds' – or mutual incomprehension? (John Moore/Getty Images)

A Royal Navy Sea King Mk4 flies over Camp Bastion. Over time, Camp Bastion and the adjoining US Marine Corps Camp Leatherneck became the largest settlement in Helmand. The military hubs developed into significant commercial centres, creating local jobs and 'doing good' but perhaps not as aid agencies imagined. (POA(Phot) Mez Merrill/ Crown Copyright)

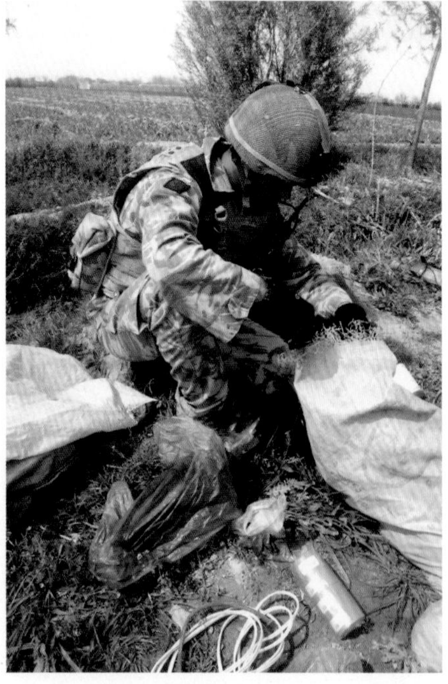

A Royal Welsh soldier examines a cache of bomb-making equipment. IEDs were manufactured on an industrial scale in Helmand's Green Zone. (MoD/Crown Copyright)

The ANA takes over responsibility for the security of Lashkar Gah in July 2011. (POA(Phot) Hamish Burke/Crown Copyright)

Homecoming – Britain rediscovered pride in its soldiers. Here Royal Scots Dragoon Guards march down the Royal Mile in Edinburgh in December 2011. (Jeff J. Mitchell/Getty Images)

Wootton Bassett. It became harder to justify the mounting dead to a sceptical British public. (Matt Cardy/Getty Images)

The fallen. (Cpl Mark Webster/Crown Copyright)

Carleton-Smith's post-operational report was also the last in which a task force commander expressed an opinion. After Operation *Herrick 8* the post-operational reports became bland documents sinning by omission. MOD Orwellian newspeak was the order of the day for the rest of the war. Carleton-Smith's civilian counterpart was the colourful Ambassador Cowper-Coles. He may have played controversial roles but he was the only civilian to admit – after leaving the FCO – it had all amounted to 'a massive act of collective self-deception',[61] from which he did not excuse himself. Over eight years, scores of politicians and senior civil servants played parts in the Helmand imbroglio. For too many, that self-deception had been conscious, not a forgivable error. Only one had the integrity to say it had been a dishonest mission.

The brigade had managed to hold the ring, but to what purpose, as there was no obvious military outcome to the insurgency? Carleton-Smith went further: the Taliban could not be beaten by military force alone and it was unlikely the movement would accept any form of negotiation as long as a single Western soldier was present in Afghanistan. Britain was being faced with the prospect of a long-term military campaign in a harsh and difficult environment which could, conceivably, dribble on for years. Did anyone seriously believe a British electorate would tolerate such a sacrifice for a war the public neither understood nor fully supported? Would a British government stand 'a long war'? According to the brigade, 30 soldiers had been killed and 154 had been wounded in action. This implied that one in 15 soldiers had been wounded and one in 80 had been killed. From this total, 81 per cent of the casualties had been caused by IEDs (an average of four incidents daily).

The list of failures was long. With the exception of Governor Gulab Mangal, there was no credible governance across the province. Reconstruction projects were too small and too slow. As one general candidly stated that summer, 'The problem is that DfID do not see themselves as part of our foreign policy.'[62] A senior DfID official himself confessed that 'we don't do bricks and mortar' but did not elaborate what exactly DfID did do.[63] Counter-narcotics initiatives were failing badly. The Afghan narcotics trade had reaped its biggest harvest to date. Over the 2007–08 season it was estimated the country produced a whopping 8,200 tonnes of raw opium.[64] The enemy had become more adept and more deadly. There was still an inherent tension between the ISAF mission that sought to widen the presence of Western soldiers and the British impulse to remain in situ and 'deepen' the mission. Task Force 42 – the British special forces contingent – had killed half a dozen Taliban commanders, including two key IED facilitators called Bismillah and Sadiqullah, but these targeted killings were making no real impact on the overall war. The latest American special forces group, Task Force 71, was also making its presence felt, but not always in helpful ways. The IED was threatening to become the battle-winning weapon of the war. As the paratroopers returned to their home base in Colchester, they echoed their brigadier's misgivings: if the blokes in a year's time were still fighting over the same hedgerows in the Green Zone, a sergeant major told a television crew, then the whole war was a waste of time. The Taliban, far from being beaten, were getting stronger and better at the game. As one section commander who had taken part in the battles of 2006 observed: 'This tour as a whole has been much riskier than the last time. HERRICK 4 was nothing compared to this. Every contact has been more intense. The Taliban have been far more accurate, professional and determined. I guess the stupid ones are all dead.'[65]

The 2008 campaign had been bloody and it was reflected in the operational honours. There were 23 gallantry awards, including 16 Military Crosses. A total of 59 soldiers were Mentioned in Dispatches.[66] If there was a certain regimental rivalry then the race was between the Parachute Regiment and the Royal Irish Regiment. The paratroopers picked up 20 gallantry awards, overtaking the Ulstermen, who bagged 16 awards including the only three Conspicuous Gallantry Crosses of the tour. A George Medal was awarded to a bomb disposal officer, Staff Sergeant Stuart Dickson, who collected nearly 40 IEDs at mortal risk to himself, rather than undertaking the safer procedure of destroying them remotely, to better understand the construction of these improvised bombs. The intelligence gleaned from this selfless courage proved invaluable.

Some gallantry medals were awarded for a peculiarly British sense of bloody-mindedness that thrived against difficult odds. Typical of this spirit was a Royal Engineer, Captain Russell Archer, who threw away his spade and picked up a rifle to defend a remote outpost in the Nawa-e Barakzai District, just south of Lashkar Gah. Captain Archer was sent with a seven-man section to bolster an ANA platoon in a house which had been taken over as a patrol base. The task was only meant to last two days. Instead, the team found themselves besieged for a month by dozens of gunmen. Like a latter-day Gordon of Khartoum, Captain Archer stayed put even though his food supplies ran out and his Bowman radios packed up. Even after the besieged men began to take casualties, he remained in the pockmarked building, refusing to surrender this little piece of British resistance. In one attack the building was subjected to a sustained three-hour hail of fire with bullets cracking through the rooms. Over a two-week period the insurgents made nine attempts to overrun the building.[67] Captain Archer's steadfastness was not just a measure of his personal courage. It was also a measure of just how beleaguered and stretched the British task force had become. The platoon house sieges, which had marked the initial British deployment, were still being played out two years on.

8

Serving in Hell-Land

Major Paddy Sherrard, a gunner serving with 19 Regiment Royal Artillery, summed up the journey that 140,000 British servicemen and women would take to Helmand over the course of the war: 'A military move is like being on a long conveyor belt: you know when and where you get on it, but don't necessarily know where you will end up, nor how long the journey will take.'[1]

Soldiers are used to being treated like human freight, but even by the normal standards of military transportation, just getting to Afghanistan from scattered home bases in mainland Britain and elsewhere almost always proved a gruelling experience that rudely ushered in the personal transition from garrison life to the gypsy existence of soldiering on operations. Nobody pretended that land-locked Afghanistan was an easy country to reach, but British soldiers at the beginning of the 21st century could still be dismayed by how much more difficult movements and transport staff seemed to make that long journey.

Lance Corporal Preston was a young sapper serving with 23 Engineer Regiment in the spring of 2008. His journey was typical of the two-day ordeal, travelling from barracks in Britain to Camp Bastion:

> We left Rock Barracks late evening on Tuesday 12th March to start our long journey to Afghanistan. We got to South Cerny [sic], near Cirencester and went through the usual safety brief then checked in. We had some scoff then got bussed to RAF Brize Norton for our flight … The flight was long and most people slept all the way, others listen to there [sic] Gucci Ipods or MP3 players. It was late Wednesday night when we arrived in Kandahar. Everyone was tired, but the travelling

> wasn't over, just our transfers to Camp Bastion remained. We were spread across three Hercs and flown to Camp Bastion, with the last arriving at 0330hrs Thursday … then shown to our accommodation for some much needed sleep.[2]

A raft of regulations and interminable briefs only compounded the irritation endured by soldiers going to war.

At the beginning of the campaign, an air bridge was the only viable way of transferring men and materials to Helmand. The problem facing the military planners was: how do you do it with insufficient aircraft and without a graded runway anywhere close to your area of operations? When the British began planning their mission to Helmand in 2005, the closest working airport was the American-built Kandahar Air Base, known as KAF, about 150 kilometres east of where they wanted to be. In military parlance this was the nearest APOD, or Air Point of Disembarkation. Over time KAF became home to 30,000 soldiers, airmen and civilians and gained a reputation as 'slipper city', or congenial posting with home comforts. At the height of operations, KAF handled 5,000 flights per week and was the permanent home to 300 aircraft of various types, making it the busiest single runway in the world. There was still a danger of unexploded ordnance in the environs of the base. Four RAF Regiment Senior Aircraftsmen – Christopher Bridge, Graham Livingstone, Gary Thompson and Luke Southgate – would lose their lives to IEDs from 2007 to 2010. Nevertheless, the insurgent threat always remained relatively low in what was the most comfortable of all the ISAF bases in south-west Afghanistan. Where else could you order cappuccinos and ice creams?

The only existing runway in Helmand was at Bost Airport, located about 1 kilometre south of the town centre in Lashkar Gah. Bost Airport had also been a Russian air base, used mostly by helicopters and transport aircraft. From the ground, Bost Airport was barely distinguishable from the surrounding countryside. Running north to south through the old airport was a single 2,000-metre gravel runway. The 'control tower' was a run-down, one-storey building without reliable electricity or running water. When the RAF attempted to land a C-130 at this airstrip (reportedly carrying special forces soldiers and buckets of cash), the aircraft appeared to detonate an old mine, or possibly a deliberately planted IED, causing the loss of the aircraft and its precious cargo. The experiment was not repeated and Bost Airport would have to wait until 2009 before the runway was finally asphalted, by the Americans. The only other runway in central Helmand was the single runway later constructed by Royal Engineers, at Camp Bastion. This 'expeditionary runway' was suitable for medium transport aircraft like the C-130 but required upgrading to accept larger aircraft.

The lack of a local air base infrastructure was only half of the problem facing the air staffs. The RAF faced serious problems supporting an operation in Helmand due to successive defence cuts that left the service without a credible, strategic transport fleet (the second Wilson government dealt the mortal blow, chopping the fleet by over half to stop the generals from getting ideas in their heads over conducting operations 'east of Suez'). As one disgruntled RAF officer put it: 'While men in suits are arguing over pathetic amounts of money we have to move heaven and earth to patch together vintage aircraft.'[3] In the late 1960s the RAF had managed a fleet of around 200 strategic transport aircraft. At the beginning of the 21st century it operated three ex-Pan Am Tristars.

The crisis became so acute following the invasion of Iraq in 2003 that four C-17A Globemasters were leased from the United States. These were being flown by 99 Squadron and were working flat out supporting the continuing operation in southern Iraq. The rude fact was that the downsized RAF could not support an air bridge to south-west Afghanistan. The only feasible way the British could sustain a military operation in Helmand was through civilian charter flights. This meant long journeys via transit airports in the Middle East, before taking onward flights to Kandahar Air Base. At Kandahar Air Base the troops could then be ferried in RAF C-130s to Camp Bastion.

In 2006 the RAF reorganized into American-style 'Expeditionary Air Wings', to better support Operations *Telic* and *Herrick*. The reorganization could not hide the fact that the vital element of these 'agile, adaptable and scaleable' military organizations, to use the euphemistic jargon, was in fact the civil air industry. The RAF could no longer run an expeditionary war except with the assistance of civilian airlines. To offer one example, between February 2007 and October 2008, Britain's war in Afghanistan was only possible thanks to the contracting of 613 civilian aircraft.[4] Civilian contract did not necessarily imply a more agreeable service. Airport delays and groundings affected these military chartered flights as much as normal civil flights. For the majority this meant 'painful' stays in RAF transit accommodation. On rare occasions the chartered airlines were faced with a contractual obligation to accommodate the soldiers in hotels. When C Company of The Black Watch (3 SCOTS) was delayed at Edinburgh Airport due to adverse weather, they were put up in a four-star hotel. On their last night of freedom the delighted Jocks managed to rack up a £14,000 bill, which included a lobster dinner.

After finally arriving at Camp Bastion, and allowed to catch up on sleep, the soldiers would begin their RSOI, or Reception, Staging and Onward Integration. This leaden abbreviation meant training. At the beginning of the war, RSOI perhaps lasted two days and included some range work and briefs on the tactical situation. By the end of the war, RSOI had swelled into an eight-day 'death by PowerPoint' ordeal. When the time taken to deploy to Helmand was accounted, this implied that some units were taking over a month to arrive in theatre and prepare themselves for operations. Mid-tour R&R could swallow another month (due to the lack of helicopters and the problem of coordinating chartered flights) and the recovery of a unit back to Britain could also take a month. For some soldiers, a six-month tour of duty in Afghanistan actually amounted to about four months. One-third of the time could simply be spent in transit from one place to the next. This was a debilitating waste of manpower the British could ill afford. Despite strong arguments that six-month tours were seriously undermining the British war effort, the system was essentially retained for the duration of the war. The unwillingness to countenance long tours would have surprised old soldiers. Half a century earlier, a battalion of the Suffolk Regiment served a straight three-year tour fighting insurgents in Malaya. This was considered normal. Its modern successor – 1 Royal Anglian – served six months in Helmand.

Camp Bastion on initial impressions was a vast, confusing military camp stuck in the middle of the desert. Over time, it would expand into the biggest settlement by circumference in Helmand, occupying over 35 square kilometres and housing over 20,000 soldiers and civilians. When combined with Kandahar Air Base, this implied some 50,000 servicemen and contractors were deployed in just two bases. In south-west Afghanistan, the imbalance of front-line soldier to base rat was plain to anyone with an abacus.

In addition to the original encampment, more bases would spring up or grow: the ANA Camp Shorabak and the US Marine base, Camp Leatherneck. An Afghan shanty town would grow alongside the vast military complex. To satisfy the water requirements of this military city, four 150-metre boreholes were dug into the coral strata that underlay the desert floor. Daily, these sucked up 100,000 litres of clean water that had made the underground journey from the Hindu Kush. The surplus was bottled in a bottling plant and transported to the patrol bases.[5] A mock Afghan village would be built alongside the base to enhance the realism of the training, peopled by locally employed villagers.

The massive military presence inevitably provoked a mini economic boom in the area, clearly doing 'good' but not as do-gooders imagined – Bastion did more for Helmand than all DfID's programmes combined. Towards the end of the war, over 10,000 civilians and 60,000 vehicles were recorded on the camp's databases – Bastion had become a commercial hub. In fact, by the height of the war some 35 per cent of Task Force Helmand comprised civilians (4,867 employees from 67 companies, not counting the locally employed civilians).[6] Not all business was licit – at least on the Afghan side. Soldiers manning the entrances routinely intercepted around 20 drug parcels every day, which represented a tiny fraction of the drugs smuggled into the complex. The ANA Camp Shorabak was probably one of the bigger drug bazaars in central Helmand.

Perhaps the outstanding feature of Camp Bastion was the air traffic. The base had originally been built by 38 Royal Engineers in April 2006. A two-man RAF Tactical Air Traffic Control Unit was posted to the camp operating from a rudimentary control tower. Just over an hour after this first air traffic control team declared the gravel landing strip open, the first military flight landed. The dirt strip runway was designed to take just three aircraft per week. Within two years the runway at Bastion (later expanded to two runways) would handle hundreds of thousands of flights. In 2007 the runway was hardened, allowing several hundred flights per day. By the following year Camp Bastion was handling 400 daily flights or 12,000 per month. This meant Bastion was handling more traffic than Birmingham, Luton and Edinburgh airports, and only ranked below Stansted Airport in terms of volume of traffic.[7] With the arrival of US Marines in 2009, air traffic spiked. In one week in 2011, over 3,000 flights were handled at Camp Bastion.[8]

For Sapper 'JT' Toher, Afghanistan was 'hot, dusty and generally just uncomfortable'.[9] His immediate priority was to bag a bunk in one of the air-conditioned tents at Camp Bastion, adding with the cynicism of an experienced soldier, 'that's if you can find a tent where the air con is working'. The baking heat impressed the young Briton as did the fine talcum powder sand which got everywhere – 'in your ears, up your nose, in your sleeping bag and anywhere you could imagine'. After settling into one of the large transit tents 'that look like they were used for scouts camping in the 80s', Toher faced the inevitable RSOI training package. The experience seemed to leave him jaded: 'The next morning we were up to start a four day training package for all newly arriving personnel; not being used to the heat, we were all suffering a bit and to top it off we were subjected to 6 hours of PowerPoint presentations updating us in great detail of the current situation. 20 power point in a day.'

The second day of training was spent on the ranges:

> That sounds easy enough, but getting there was a different story. It was a short walk of less than 2km, but with all the heat sand and dust, it felt much longer and the relief was clearly visible on everyone's faces when we arrived. When that was finished, the rest of the day was spent in briefings, mostly on first aid and the communications equipment we would be using in theatre.

It was not all hardship for the young sapper. After a couple of days in this unfamiliar environment, Toher seemed to cheer up:

> We all started to find our feet (and our way round the camp). There are plenty of welfare facilities to keep ourselves entertained in our downtime, the camp even has it's [sic] own little Pizza Hut as well as the internet and telephone suites along with a few local market stall traders selling additional bits and pieces, not bad for a camp in the middle of the desert.

On completion of the RSOI training package, units were broken up and deployed to their respective patrol bases, another long and delayed process because of the shortage of helicopters. For some, the experience of being plucked from the relative comforts of Camp Bastion to an 'austere' patrol base came as a shock – one soldier felt he had been deposited in 'the arse end of nowhere'. The phrase 'polishing my austere' was coined, mixing a masturbatory metaphor with the cleaning chores that accompany the life of a soldier. In the first two years of the war, such hardship was the rule for most soldiers. Over time, an intensive programme of base upgrades undertaken by Royal Engineers gradually improved living conditions.

Some locations, like FOB Inkerman, would always feel like forts marooned in the middle of enemy territory.

Despite the medieval poverty, by the middle of the war, a British soldier in Helmand could reasonably expect to be connected to the modern world and enjoy some distractions for off-duty entertainment. Sapper Hunt, a keen Portsmouth supporter, was genuinely surprised by his new surroundings:

> I was impressed with the amount of activities that were available, when there is down time. There's a TV room, where I can watch Portsmouth FC smash everyone up and down the Premiership. Also a ping-pong table is available when the Gurkhas aren't on it. There is also the world's slowest internet terminal where we believe a hamster is inside controlling the Web. For the more active ones there is a multi-activity gym, with free weights for sculpting the Guns. It is Fijian free as they're to [sic] busy bench-pressing the ISO containers around the corner … On a serious note I didn't expect half the stuff at this FOB, and shows the British Army is prepared and facilitated better than is made out in the press.[10]

For most soldiers the simple provision of an internet connection and the opportunity to telephone home were among the most valued assets at patrol bases.

In the second half of the war, the outside world began visiting the more isolated patrol bases. Entertainment shows had previously been restricted to the large bases. By the summer of 2011 a soldier serving with A Company, 1 Rifles could record the arrival of a dance troupe: 'The show went down a storm, with several Riflemen promptly falling in love with the dancers and trying to abscond with them on the helicopter which came to pick them up later that night.'[11]

Other aspects of patrol base existence, as one Argyll recalled, seemed universal and unchanging:

> Some things, however, never change. Comms are terrible. Cigarettes are consumed apace. Goat bearded scientists in far-off laboratories contrive well-meant and poorly named pieces of equipment in order to further the war effort, all of which share the defining characteristic of being really heavy, and must be carried everywhere. The Corned Beef Hash supply chain remains unbroken, but morale remains high.[12]

Many soldiers were unquestionably moved by the strangeness and mystery of this central Asian country as well as by its abiding beauty. This beauty provided some distraction from the undeniable squalor of daily life. Urinals – known as 'desert roses' – comprised plastic pipes buried in the ground at an angle. Latrines were constructed from old barrels, testing the resolve of even those with insensitive noses and strong stomachs. A consequence of living in such confined environments was the risk of diarrhoea and vomiting (D&V). Few soldiers escaped a bout of D&V during a tour of Helmand, and their condition only served to worsen the state of routinely nauseating latrines. Every day the waste from latrines had to be taken away for incineration. It was the most distasteful job in the bases and nobody got used to stirring and burning the daily slop of human excrement.

The unpopularity of the improvised 'long drop' toilets encouraged technological innovations, some of which required a manual adeptness which, if bungled, could have disastrous consequences for the unfortunate soldier:

> The toilets are wooden cubicles and not the long drops that were used in the past. At this point in the letter it's best not to be eating or about to eat. We now have state of the art zip closed silver bags which come in a white bag which you dispose of in the bin, the silver bag gets burnt once used. When opened there is another bag inside which you open, put over the toilet opening and well you know the rest. However it is always best to know what you are doing the first time you use this apparatus unlike Cpl McEvoy who in the middle of the night had a nature call and having not used this method before picked up a silver bag and not a white one ie a used bag. He then went through the opening procedure and proceeded to put his hand in to open the bottom just that little bit more, well he got a little more than he expected let's put it that way.[13]

Soldiers on patrol, of course, could avoid these difficult rituals and return to nature. Crapping has a special place in soldiers' hearts, for reasons only a Freudian psychologist can probably explain. This description by Sergeant Douglas Craig, a gunner who served in Helmand in 2007, perfectly captured the spirit of the deed, if not the smell:

> I yomp my way up the western concave slope of the horseshoe and notice a slight overhang of rock. I squat and 'lay a cable'. There's a fine

> sense of peace when the wind is blowing through your bollocks as they dangle and you're squeezing a good shit out. These softly paper towels are a fucking godsend. Your finger don't go through them when you're wiping your arse and you get about ten sheets in there ... I stand up like a caveman for all the gun position to see, cock out to the world ...[14]

Ablutions were commonly little more than a hose connected to a cold water tank. Showers were taken using solar bags, an experience that could be 'emotional' in the depth of an Afghan winter when the sun barely warmed the bags. Washing clothes was improvised in canals or using cement mixers as washing machines. One officer was horrified by the smell emanating from his socks after being forced to wear the same pair for a month through a shortage of water at his patrol base. Soldiering in Helmand was not for the faint-hearted.

Given the primitive conditions of life in the patrol bases, many of the normal regulations of military life necessarily were suspended. Hair length – a topic of perpetual fascination in armies and a subject explored in Norman Dixon's classic *On the Psychology of Military Incompetence* – was one such regulation. Soldiers in isolated outposts took the opportunity to grow their hair long, to the despair of visiting regimental sergeant majors, who threatened all manner of sanctions against these 'long-haired lovers from Liverpool' when they returned to one of the main bases. Without the provision of a barber, there was little soldiers could do to keep their hair length trim, unless they were willing to risk the hairdressing skills of an ANA soldier claiming to be a barber in a former life (many did, to make extra income from British soldiers). Moustaches and beards also sprouted in the early years of the war, provoking indignant comments from senior officers about 'scruffy soldiers', as well as jokes from fellow soldiers. For the common soldier this hirsute anarchy represented a sort of liberation and psychological valve from the daily dangers faced on patrols. The early period of anarchy, naturally, was never going to last. By the end of the war, British soldiers conformed to Queen's Regulations in all matters, including the permissible length of head and facial hair.

Keeping up morale in the patrol bases was vital to seeing out a six-month tour in Helmand. One of the most important contributors to morale was undoubtedly mail. Soldiers have always craved news from home, and the servicemen and women deployed to Helmand were no exception to this rule. D Company, 2 PARA were astonished by the amount of mail they received addressed simply to 'A soldier':

> We are receiving plenty of anonymous parcels from charity groups, rotary clubs, veterans and random strangers, all addressed to 'A Soldier'. All contain letters, and I make sure that we reply to all of them. It is astonishingly generous of these people to send us teabags, toothbrushes, soap and little snacks. Most of them are sent by the older generation or from someone who understands what military service means. It is quite humbling to read some of those letters, and yours of course, all of which add a little escapism to our lives here.[15]

By 2009, some quarter of a million parcels were being posted to the task force, with some individual soldiers receiving several hundred unsolicited parcels. The amount of mail soldiers received became so great – especially at Christmas – the ministry was eventually forced to make an appeal not to send unsolicited mail and gifts to Helmand because of the logistic burden this created.

Keeping in touch with home was expressed in other ways. All the major public events of this period – the royal wedding of Prince William and Catherine Middleton, the Queen's Jubilee and the Olympic Games – were celebrated in Helmand. Bunting, party hats and mountains of food made their appearance, to the probable perplexity of Afghans, as British soldiers sought to recreate the mood of the nation in their isolated patrol bases. On the occasion of the Jubilee, every member of 3 Yorks (Duke of Wellington's) received a Fortnum & Mason gift box, echoing the tin gift boxes sent to soldiers in World War I.

Another morale booster was pets. Soldiering on a front line is a life starved of moments of affection. Comradeship bonds soldiers in adversity but does not fill this emotional gap. Pets, and especially dogs, have always provided a source of solace and readily requited companionship. Afghanistan had a large population of ill-treated dogs, some mangy, some bred for fighting, with clipped ears, and some simply abandoned. A dog had starred in the famous British defeat at the Battle of Maiwand. Over time, many bases acquired a resident dog spoiled by British soldiers who imported different cultural attitudes towards animals compared to their Afghan counterparts.

When 3 Troop of 51 Parachute Squadron took over a patrol base in Nad-e Ali, they shared it with 'the other occupants of the compound ... 3 cows,

3 goats and 2 chickens. Not forgetting the infamous Cockerel which would haunt Sappers Chiocci, Sampson & myself through the night.'[16] As was the common experience for soldiers serving in World War I, unwanted animals like mice could be a problem, encouraging mice-hunting competitions:

> Since we arrived at PB1 we have been terrorised by mice chewing through welfare packages and our personal packages so we started laying traps for them. This has taken off as the sport of the PB as we now have a kill board and rather than laying traps in and around our welfare room we now have them hidden around the entire PB in a bid to take the lead. Some have even gone to the lengths of waking up half an hour early to get to the top of the leader board which is currently Sapper Swinfield with 17 kills.[17]

Some soldiers became so attached to their patrol base pets they adopted them. An enterprising Royal Marine NCO serving at Kajaki was taken by two abandoned fighting dogs and successfully brought them back to Britain. The handsome pair lived out the rest of their days in the more peaceful surroundings of southern England. In the summer of 2010 a Gurkha company based in Babaji adopted a local stray and named it Brin. The stumpy-legged mongrel enjoyed going for walks with the patrols. More usefully, the soldiers discovered that its natural inquisitiveness sometimes led Brin to uncover IEDs. By the end of the tour the Gurkhas were so grateful to the animal that the sum of £4,000 was raised to bring Brin home. He was eventually adopted by a teacher in East Sussex. In 2011, the family of a Territorial Army paratrooper killed in Nad-e Ali – Conrad Lewis – moved a mountain of bureaucratic obstruction to bring home a stray dog he had befriended before he died. Pegasus had no idea of her emotional value to the bereaved family, but she almost certainly appreciated the miraculous change from patrol base existence to life in an English suburb.

An unusual pet was a donkey that wandered into a patrol base manned by fusiliers just south of Sangin. Despite protestations from an army vet, the errant animal was swiftly adopted by the soldiers, who gave it a name ('Dave the Donkey') and added a seaside hat to its head. Not everyone judged the opportunistic adoption a good idea when it was discovered the donkey had a habit of braying loudly at dawn. Eventually the animal was reunited with its rightful owner, no worse the wear for its brief service with the British Army. In Babaji, paratroopers serving with B Company, 2 PARA actually bought two mules from villagers – naming them Pegasus and Princess – and used them to ferry supplies in the absence of motorized transport. Pegasus proved docile, but the stubborn Princess seemed less keen to support the British war effort.

Inevitably, serving in a patrol base meant long periods of boredom and monotonous guard duties. Each patrol base was effectively a small fort planted in a hostile landscape. The modern equivalent of the stone-built castle turret was the sandbag sangar, a word imported from colonial India. Sangars came in many shapes and sizes – single sangars, double sangars, 'super sangars' and Cuplock sangars. Competitions were run between Royal Engineer units to see who could build the sangar the fastest (it took less than a day with adequate manpower and resources), and all had to be manned 24 hours a day, which implied hours spent staring out across an unchanging landscape. There were moments of occasional light relief as a Lance Corporal Mark Allen discovered on one shift, but these were rare:

> Taking over the sangar for my second shift I noticed that several kids had gathered in front. This provided some light hearted entertainment at first as they started talking to me (speaking better English than me with my Belfast accent). My first mistake was telling them my name, as then everything was 'Mark, throw me sweets', 'Mark, throw me sun cream' and then they wanted cylume glow sticks as they must have been planning a rave that night. After about 30 minutes of not giving them anything I then learnt that 'I was a bad person' and 'Mark doesn't like Muslims.'[18]

Filling the time at patrol bases, even with the provision of internet connections and televisions, demanded ingenuity and everybody went about it in different ways. Lieutenant Newton, serving with Number 3 Company, Coldstream Guards perfectly sketched the slightly mad relationships that grow between soldiers forced to live cheek by jowl in unpleasant and dangerous circumstances:

> Despite being busy, boredom is still a major issue to contend with. Everyone deals with it in their own way. LSgt Gill and Gdsm Hemans play dominos and talk 'Jamaican' to each other, Dmr 'Ikea' Blakelock builds things (and then watches them fall apart again), Gdsm Dellar likes his sudoku and his dairy milk, whilst Gdsm Oliver is partial to

> listening to criminally bad music on his Ipod and reading footy mags. Gdsm Naylor talks non stop and always seems to have eaten too many skittles, LCpl Jones continually upgrades his sleeping area and tells Naylor to keep the noise down (when not falling down wells – another story), and Gdsm Skelton tells us in an extremely manly fashion how he cant wait to 'get my hair and nails done and go shopping' when he gets back. Gdsm Bourke reminisces about his days as a 'raver' in 'Dony,' while Murphy plays quite remarkable games of chess with LCpl Crombie (both lose all their main pieces within the first dozen moves, and then battle it out for hours with pawns), LCpl Hawksby reads, drinks tea and admires his beard, Dmr Brownlie gets his head down whenever possible (being a Scotsman probably dreaming about how much money he is saving), Gdsm Schofield runs a cafe, Gdsm Etherington is always looking for something he's lost, Gdsm Pontone always seems to be nattering away about something he knows nothing about, and Gdsm Murphy, our resident Essex wide boy entertains himself by pretending to listen. LSgt Staker looks across at the state of my living area and shakes his head, or laments with any Geordie he can find about the state of the Magpies [Newcastle United], whilst LSgt Laws takes matters into his own hands and leads them to Premiership and European Glory on the game 'Championship Manager'. Needless to say Sgt Wilson tends to spend his spare time trying to organise me, and there was me thinking I'd left the days of being told to tidy my room behind.[19]

It would be difficult to find a more representative pen picture of the cross-section of young men Britain sent to war in Helmand Province.

Alcoholic drink, of course, was a taboo. For decades the British Army had taken a relaxed approach to drinking on operations, generally allowing a maximum of two pints daily at the larger bases. In World War I, an alcohol ban would have provoked mutiny – 'No Whiskey – No War' was the cry from the trenches. In World War II, the notion of stopping soldiers (or God forbid, officers) from drinking would have been treated like the suggestion of a madman. These laissez faire attitudes still persisted during the early stages of British Army operations in Iraq in 2003, but under the influence of an American ally that enforced a policy of strict prohibition, British forces duly promulgated a total alcohol ban. Other NATO allies refused to endorse this po-faced Anglo-Saxon ban on drinking. A few years later, a

British soldier serving in Afghanistan had little or no chance of getting his hands on his favourite tipple, although the Kabul contingent did manage a few 'reconnaissance trips' to international hotels. However, there was also sufficient anecdotal evidence to suggest that alcoholic spirits did reach remote patrol bases, concealed in food parcels, and masked as energy or health drinks. For some, the total alcohol ban just seemed to be an example of British pragmatism bowing to American Puritanism.

Denied alcohol, food became an obsession. For some visitors, however, the British provision of rations was a surprise. The American journalist Michael Yon was amazed to witness British soldiers enduring weeks on hard rations: 'The morale of British troops is unmistakeably good, which cannot be attributed to the terrible rations they eat. After more than a month with British combat troops in the Green Zone, I hadn't seen a piece of fresh fruit on a base, despite that we are surrounded by farms.'[20]

Yon's surprise at the stoicism of the British soldier did not fully reflect efforts made by the modern army to improve this staple of field living. For individual soldiers, the 24-hour Operational Ration Pack had been revolutionized beyond the imagination of previous generations. For decades, soldiers had subsisted on the unimaginatively named Menus A, B, C or D. Some of the contents of these uninspiring 'rat packs' had entered army folklore: 'Biscuit Brown', which broke your teeth, and 'Screech Powder', which made your gums screech, to name two. In contrast, by the end of the first decade of the 21st century, a British soldier had a choice of 20 ration packs, including six options for vegetarian, Halal, and Sikh or Hindu palates. Options included: Thai chicken curry, sweet salmon pasta, mixed bean salad, paella, beef and cassava, Oreo cookies, Shrewsbury biscuits and stem ginger biscuits.[21] These were unheard-of delicacies. As one of the catering warrant officers who trialled the new ration packs explained, this was a better-fed, more cosmopolitan and brand-orientated generation of soldiers. The High Street had come to the battlefield.

However, for army chefs, finding imaginative ways to cook monotonous ten-man ration packs remained a thankless task. A Royal Irish Ranger based at Sangin was unsparingly critical of his daily fare:

> The food in Sangin District Centre is actually getting worse and worse. The so called Army Cooks (note I'm still not prepared to call them chefs) seem as interested in cooking as Hitler was in joining the Peaceniks. Corned beef trash has become our staple diet, but we keep

> getting told the cooks are 'trying'. Yes they are trying, 'Trying' to starve us out of Sangin, if you were to ask anybody who has to eat their muck.[22]

This recalled the old army joke that the chef's course was the hardest in the armed forces because nobody passed it, but the criticism was unfair. At the time, Sangin District Centre had just two qualified army chefs who had the nearly impossible task of trying to satisfy the mouths of about 350 hungry soldiers on the slimmest of resources and in field conditions. Along with army engineers and vehicle mechanics, army chefs were probably the hardest working and least thanked soldiers in the task force.

The gruelling work routine facing army chefs in Helmand can be illustrated by the experiences of Corporal Hodgson who served on Operation *Herrick 12*. Hodgson arrived in Camp Bastion in early March 2010, and after completing the mandatory six-day RSOI package, was assigned to the camp 'super kitchen'. His first job was to supervise four chefs working on the advance preparation team. This small team had the daily chore of preparing potatoes and vegetables for between 4,000 and 5,000 personnel daily, as well as preparing up to 1,400 individual meals. It meant getting up well before sunrise and working flat out until the middle shift took over. Shortly afterwards, Corporal Hodgson was moved to this second shift and found himself responsible for feeding up to 7,000 personnel for the evening meal.[23] The scale of the operation made Camp Bastion the largest kitchen run by the British Army in modern times. In any one week diners consumed 8.8 tonnes of potatoes, 7.7 tonnes of chips, 1.4 tonnes of sausages, 2.3 tonnes of bacon, 5.7 tonnes of beef and 12.7 tonnes of chicken. All this stock arrived by sea and then across the overland route from Karachi, with as many as 40 ISO containers arriving every three days at the camp gates.[24] At a patrol base like Shahzad in northern Nad-e Ali, generally reckoned to be relatively austere even in the summer of 2011, marine chefs feeding the 250-strong contingent over a six-month period worked through 12,150 slices of bacon, 3,024 tins of beans, 8,400 baguettes, 5,880 slices of pizza, 1,200 whole chickens, 1,150 sacks of potatoes and no fewer than 3,840 steaks.[25]

At a main base like Camp Bastion there could be no complaints about the quality or quantity of 'scoff'. Breakfast was traditional and included a choice of porridge, bacon and sausage, fried, scrambled or boiled eggs, baked beans, plum tomatoes, mushrooms and black pudding. For those who preferred, there was a continental breakfast of sliced meats, cheese and croissants. At lunch time four hot choices were available, one of which was always a pasta or rice dish. There was also a salad bar, a jacket potato bar with four fillings, a panini bar with four choices and an assorted rolls bar with five choices. For those who missed lunch because they were working or catching up on sleep after a night stag, six choices were offered at the evening meal, including three potato dishes and three vegetable choices. For those with a sweet tooth there were at least two hot deserts and a selection of cold sweets. On Sundays the troops were treated to a traditional Sunday roast, and every two weeks the chefs put on a themed night. With its shops and pizza outlets nobody based at Camp Bastion faced the prospect of shedding weight over the course of a six-month tour. On special occasions – such as Christmas – an effort was made to ensure that even the most remote locations received a traditional festive fare, as these Royal Irish serving with A Company in Nad-e Ali recalled:

> The Christmas Day dinner run was an event that is worthy of a mention in dispatches all of its own. Our chef here in Saidabad had the task of producing over 300 Christmas dinners to be sent out to all the checkpoints and locations within our AO [area of operations]. As well as cooking for A Coy he had to produce meals for D Coy, CO's TAC, the Engr Troop, and our C-IED section. So with seven locations to deliver to the CSM 'Billy Roy' bedecked the quad with antlers and a flashing red nose and we set off to make to make sure all A Coy soldiers received a hot turkey dinner on Christmas day.[26]

Outside Camp Bastion, at locations like the district centre at Sangin, resources and choice were much more circumscribed. At a base like FOB Inkerman the sheer difficulties of resupply encouraged a more tolerant spirit. A 2 Rifles soldier was more than understanding of the challenge facing the army chefs at FOB Inkerman:

> The chefs do an excellent job, when you consider the ingredients they have to work with. Try creating 6 months worth of meals out of corn-beef hash, pineapple slices, a couple of tonnes of rice and half a million jars of peanut butter. Hours are spent opening the 500 tins required to feed the FOB on a daily basis (they have already worn out 5 can openers in 6 weeks).[27]

Overland supply was too dangerous, and helicopter resupply (by contracted civilian helicopters due to the lack of military helicopters) only took place once a month. This meant troops at FOB Inkerman had to be resupplied by air drop.

Corporal McLachlan was a Royal Engineer serving at FOB Inkerman on Operation *Herrick 10*. Whenever an air drop was scheduled he and a three man team had to clear a route to the drop zone. This could take as long as three hours, in darkness. Describing a typical air drop, Corporal McLachlan remembered:

> The plane passed over twice, each time dropping 8 pallets underneath 8 of the biggest parachutes you've ever seen, bearing in mind each parachute was lowering a one tonne weight underneath it. Each pallet had to be closely watched to see where it landed. Once all the pallets had landed the four sappers then had to clear a safe route to pallets which inevitably meant a race against local tribesmen intent on stealing the cargo. On this occasion a Fire Support Group 'fired some warning shots to try and scare them off but it didn't work.'[28]

After a further three hours all the pallets had been secured. To the amusement of the soldiers, the thieves had disdained stealing British Army rations. Corporal McLachlan and his team finally returned safely to FOB Inkerman and got to bed at 0400hrs, a full 12 hours after they had started the task to recover the precious pallets.

Turning the contents of these pallets into three daily meals was the job of the Inkerman chefs. The fare may have been monotonous but it was not unhealthy. Breakfast comprised of fried spam slices, canned chipolata, baked beans and powdered scrambled egg (which one soldier thought shared 'a remarkable similarity to lumpy milk of magnesia'). For those who preferred a continental breakfast, the continent, one wag remarked, was 'waiting to be confirmed'. There was also a choice of muesli or cereal with 'white water' (powdered milk). Copious quantities of sugar were used 'to disguise the taste'. Lunch comprised tinned soup, more spam, more baked beans, noodles or rice and tinned tuna. Boiled sweets and cooking chocolate were served as a dessert. For the evening meal the chefs were at last liberated from the tyranny of spam. This last meal might comprise a beef satay (with extra quantities of peanut butter, again to disguise the taste), a chicken and herb crumble, powdered mustard mash and sweet corn. A typical dessert was pineapple rings in custard. The only drinks on offer throughout the day were 'warmed tropical flavoured chlorinated water or a choice of tea and coffee'. It all smacked of wartime austerity and English boarding schools.

Potable water was a constant problem. Equipped with generator-powered water production units that frequently broke down, most small bases had no choice but to heavily chlorinate the local water, creating an unpalatable drink. Unwilling to drink this chemical brew, soldiers demanded bottled water, which created one of the biggest logistical nightmares facing the British. Soon, the task force was spending around £15 million every year on bottled water, and water pallets became one of the largest (and heaviest) routine loads on resupply runs.

Over time, in areas where the fighting did diminish near British patrol bases, enterprising Afghans set up stalls, knowing that soldiers crave little luxuries like fizzy drinks and, of course, fags. British reports of bazaars reopening following the expulsion of the Taliban sometimes confused genuine economic growth with the simple opportunism of locals trying to make the most of the British military presence.

Commonly, holding *shuras* and doing business became natural bedfellows, as Burma Company recalled:

> 5 Platoon in Check Point (CP) Perkha are doing really well. They have built up a network of friendly locals who are truly grateful for the security they provide. At a recent *shura* (meeting) over thirty locals attended for a cup of *chai* and discussed a wide-range of issues. A budding Afghan entrepreneur has spotted a business opportunity and crates of coca-cola often appear after a touch of bartering! The locals now know most of 5 Platoon by name and as they patrol through the village the locals shout out 'Commander Jamie' or 'Mac' and come over to talk and offer *chai*.[29]

The ANA, by the middle of the war, had become the British Army's main effort. It would only be through the mentoring and training of the Afghan soldier that the British soldier would be able to come home. Much would be written about the vices and virtues of Afghanistan's fledgling army. Perhaps much of this literature ignored the central and not insignificant fact that the British genuinely got on with their Afghan colleagues, without being too rose-tinted and despite all the frustrations. This never happened in Iraq, but it became crucial in Afghanistan. The British love affair with central Asian tribesmen had a long history. Army pamphlets from the wars on the North-West Frontier averred that 'whatever may be the characteristics of the Pathan … it is beyond question that he appeals strongly to and enlists the sympathy of British officers who have had dealings with him politically or when associated with him in the Army'.[30] Perhaps it was Edwardian notions of masculinity that won over the British, who were quick to see in these hardy specimens mirrors of their own fortitude: 'His manliness is at once apparent, and his proverbial hospitality, courtesy, courage, cheerfulness, and loyalty, make him an excellent companion, a valuable soldier, and entitle him to respect and admiration'. The Pathan may not have learned his game on the playing fields of Eton, but he acted as if he had.

A Lance Corporal Waite, who served with a 2 Mercian (Worcesters and Foresters) OMLT in 2009, found the experience of mentoring the ANA enjoyable:

> Working with the ANA has been an experience. We have been on foot patrols with them on a nearly daily basis. They are a very different army to ours with the soldiers seemingly having the choice about whether they wear body armour, helmets or T-shirts and a baseball cap! On patrol they appear to follow orders without question and keep well spaced on the ground. Under contact I noticed that certain soldiers would not take cover until rounds were landing at their feet! … I have found my time working with the ANA enjoyably educational. They are friendly and generous with a good sense of humour.[31]

Sergeant Dave Cooper, serving with 5 Battery, 19 Regiment Royal Artillery was more prosaic in his assessment:

> Afghan soldiers reflect the society from which they are drawn and thus 70% of them are illiterate and they all share an Afghan approach to soldiering that is somewhat different from that which we are used to. This makes for a colourful, if occasionally frustrating, time and we have had to learn how to understand and work with the Afghan way.[32]

For one Royal Irish officer, the whole experience was likened more humorously to 'a shot gun wedding with an Albanian drug lord's hairy stepsister'.

ANA indolence had its amusing moments. Afghan soldiers enjoyed taking on their British counterparts in volleyball or football matches, but were less keen on PT sessions. Among the excuses offered by reluctant soldiers were 'I've got bees in my head' and 'I've run out of blood' – rationales that would surely have found a place in Spike Milligan's war memoirs.

ANA soldiers needed education before bullets, and it was to the great credit of the British Army that valiant attempts were made to fill this terrible gap in the recruits' lives with two-week crash courses in basic literacy. English lessons were also popular, possibly because the teachers were not uncommonly blonde female soldiers, a novelty to the average Afghan recruit. Ubiquitous *Nuts* and *Zoo* magazines were also appreciated, although it was suspected ANA officers were not asking to borrow back copies to improve their English.

A general indiscipline was exacerbated by widespread drug-taking, even on operations. One of many false arguments made by the Taliban was that drug consumption was a Western addiction. In fact, marijuana smoking was rife in Afghanistan, once an obligatory stop on the hippy trail, and heroin addiction was climbing steeply, as it had done in Iran and Pakistan. It is a consistent fallacy of drug-producing countries that addiction is an exported problem that does not threaten the producer countries. Afghanistan was no exception to this rule. Marijuana was abundant in Helmand (by 2010 it began to rival the opium poppy), and ANA soldiers did not hesitate to avail themselves of this ready narcotic. Major Vance Crow, a tough, rugby-playing South African serving with the Royal Irish, was less than impressed by one of his ANA recruits who managed to shoot his own foot in a drug induced state:

> [The] second patient, an Afghan soldier, also far too familiar with marijuana for his own good, recently decide to clip his toe nails using an M16 rifle. In attempting to clip his nails this young man managed to shot his own foot. Fortunately he didn't damage himself too badly and should shortly be returned to his unit ... Don't ever say there was a dull moment in Helmand.[33]

The British could do little to interfere with this national custom, but it certainly made some soldiers wary when shooting broke out.

When the British first deployed to Helmand they were entrusted with training 3/205 'Heroes' Corps, led by Brigadier Mohayadin, a task they inherited from the American PRT at Lashkar Gah. About the only good word that could be said about this formation was that it had a competent overall commander. Mohayadin was an Afghan veteran of many wars with a colourful past. Everything else, unfortunately, was broken. The American-built Camp Shorabak was already showing signs of pillaging. The brigade-sized force could only muster a single *kandak* (battalion). There were no reliable personnel or quartermaster systems in place. The formation was unable to mount independent operations, except under the wing of the British task force. Even after three years of constant mentoring, 3/205 Corps was only used cosmetically (to provide an 'Afghan face') in two major operations: the retaking of Musa Qaleh and the delivery of the third turbine to Kajaki. In the British Army's last two significant operations in Helmand, Operations *Panchai Palang* and *Moshtarak*, the ANA was largely invisible, despite the spin suggesting otherwise. This invisibility, as much as anything, revealed the worrying failure of the mentoring experiment. Living alongside an ANA platoon in a patrol base and undertaking combined patrols was not raising the operational effectiveness of the ANA in meaningful ways. 'Patrolling' was something the Afghan soldier could do without British prodding. Running a modern conventional army in an even modestly competent fashion remained beyond the realistic aspirations of Afghanistan's reconstituted Ministry of Defence, despite the billions of dollars that were being poured into the project.

In the summer of 2010, following a general reorganization of ISAF forces in south-western Afghanistan, Task Force Helmand took over the mentoring of 3/215 Maiwand Corps. This was meant to be a fresh start under McChrystal's policy of 'embedded partnering'. This formation, compared to its predecessor, was at least fully established, comprising four infantry *kandaks*, a highway *kandak*, a combat support *kandak* and combat and service support *kandaks*. But the problems persisted. These included poor leadership, woeful personnel management, terrible living conditions and an unreliable pay system, with its inevitable consequence – a large outflow of demoralized recruits. The British Army's assessment of this brigade was realistic, but a picture of a gradually improving Afghan Army was nonetheless presented in public as the ticket home for British troops.

In any one month only about half of 3/215 Brigade's strength was actually deployed. One quarter were either on leave, AWOL or simply posted as 'absent'. Among the worst offenders were the officers who cited privilege as an excuse to be absent from their units. The remainder camped in Shorabak, where they contributed marginally to the counter-insurgency but at least were being fed properly. The headquarters itself was only a third manned, many of the staff were illiterate and only a few were fully IT literate. Some Afghan officers still wore their Soviet ranks and medals. Many were authoritarian, lazy bullies. Just agreeing on what day of the week it was offered challenges, as the Afghan Army insisted on using the unique Afghan calendar which differed both from the Islamic and Gregorian calendars. It was unsurprising that British guidance on mentoring the ANA philosophically concluded that it was an experience in sharing pain.

For the majority of British soldiers, contact with Afghans meant contact with the ANA or with their poor cousins, the ANP (later AUP, or Afghan Uniformed Police). As the former recruited heavily from non-Pushtun groups, this meant that British soldiers were predominantly dealing with Uzbeks, Tajiks, Turkmen or Hazaras, rather than with the ethnic group whose 'hearts and minds' they were trying to win. Soldiers sent on crash courses in Pashto found that their interlocutors were in fact Dari speakers.

Even with the benefit of some basic language training any conversation beyond commonplace pleasantries almost always required the services of the Terps, or locally employed interpreters (many of whom lost life and limb in service with the British Army). By the middle of the war, the British Army was employing 630 Afghan interpreters.[34] Although not combat trained or armed, Terps braved fire to help wounded soldiers, and at least two received commendations for bravery. The MOD did not release figures for the number of Terp casualties, but it is almost certain that a not small number were killed or seriously injured alongside the British soldiers they were helping. For some, employment with the British Army was a lifeline. For others, it turned into a sour experience, viewed as traitors and in fear of their lives. A handful made the painful choice of seeking political asylum and found life equally tough in council flats in Glasgow and elsewhere. A necessary reliance on interpreters contributed to the illusion that 'hearts and minds' were being won. In *No Worse Enemy*, documentary-maker Ben Anderson recorded how interpreters routinely tried to save face by not translating honestly what the elders were telling Western soldiers.[35] Too often, the villagers simply wanted the soldiers to go away, but this message was not passed on. The experience left Anderson deeply disillusioned and convinced that Afghanistan was heading for another civil war.

The main form of contact, other than random exchanges with farmers, was the *shura* – the traditional form of communal debate used throughout Afghanistan to resolve disputes. The British got good at *shuras* and even wrote a doctrine note on the subject. Even so, the experience still tested the physical and mental resources of some participants:

> All Shura's [sic] then require one to be a contortionist. Having removed your shoes you attempt to sit on the floor of your hosts' accommodation with your legs tucked away. For the first 10 minutes it's tolerable, within 15 minutes it's a mild form of torture and mentally you can only focus on the pain slowly creeping up your legs. Within 20 minutes you're no longer able to physically deal with the pain and you rudely start fidgeting, shitting [sic] your legs in as many different ways possible as to not show the soles of ones feet (an act the Afghans apparently find mildly offensive). Most Westerns [sic] in my opinion end up with the attitude of 'sorry mate but between temporary paralysis and showing the soles of my feet I hope you're not a podiatrist [sic]?'[36]

The trick was not to get down to business too quickly. Afghans loved to talk and found Western urgency irksome. Telling jokes was another way to break the ice. One officer recalled telling a joke that seemed to leave his interlocutors in stitches, even though he struggled to understand the humour:

> Mullah Nasrudin said that he was as strong now as he had been as a youth. When asked for proof, he said, 'When I was a youth, there was a huge boulder that I was not able to lift. I am still not able to lift that same boulder, so you can see that I am as strong now as I was then.'[37]

A strong stomach was another advantage. More than one British soldier found himself heading straight for the latrines following a well-fed *shura*. The key to these meetings, always, was never to promise what could not be delivered.

Whether or not the British were actually winning 'hearts and minds', there was no question the majority of soldiers empathized with the locals, and, over time, this empathy was reciprocated. The violence of the early tours was eventually replaced with a more considered approach, although military operations always have a way of disturbing civilian life, as one officer humorously recalled: 'WO2 Whitehouse is certainly a big hit with the local nationals; they love seeing his wagon steam into view over the horizon leaving a trail of destroyed fields and flattened cooking pots.'[38] As a result of these 'reckless meanderings', the nearby platoon was 'forced to act more like an AXA Insurance than a rifle platoon, shelling out 10,000 Afghanis in compensation in one 24 hour period'.

Death and wounding are facts of war. For British soldiers deploying to Helmand, there was the sober knowledge that some among their number would be returning home on an aero-medical evacuation flight or in a coffin. This was a novelty to an army accustomed to peacetime soldiering, but the soldiers at least had the reassurance that military medical care had improved dramatically since their forefathers had gone to war.

For soldiers in Helmand, however, the majority cause of wounding was not the bullet – it was the roadside bomb or IED. To ensure the best survival prospects for soldiers, a three-part strategy needed to be implemented: better personal protection; better immediate care at the moment of injury; and rapid evacuation to a field hospital. In all three areas, dramatic improvements were made in Helmand.

Soldiers cursed the weight of the Osprey body armour, but it unquestionably saved lives. There were numerous incidents involving soldiers shot in the armour plates and surviving the encounter with no more than severe bruising. The number of fatalities from IED attacks would almost certainly have doubled or tripled if it had not been for the weighty carapace of armour worn by every soldier operating 'outside the wire'. By the end of the war, a three-figure number of soldiers had been struck on the Osprey body armour and owed their lives to the protective plates. The consequences of survival were many more amputees who would have died in previous wars. Just one British triple amputee is believed to have survived World War I. By the mid-point of the war in Helmand, Britain had over 100 single and double amputees and nearly 20 triple amputees in medical care. A year before withdrawal, the total number had climbed to 207. The British Army had also experienced its first-ever surviving quadruple amputee. Jacobean playwright John Webster wrote, 'for a soldier that hazards his limbs in a battle; nothing but a kind of geometry is his last supportation'.[39] This was still true in the 21st century, but the geometry of an amputee was now supported by the best technology, allowing these maimed soldiers to rebuild their lives and pursue activities that would have been unthinkable even a generation past.

The military had always spoken of the 'golden hour', a phrase borrowed from civilian paramedic practice. If a casualty could be rushed from the point of injury to an operating table within an hour, his chances of survival greatly improved. In fact, in Helmand, this 'golden hour' was commonly not achievable: the average casevac time in the first half of the war was over an hour and a half. In the second half, this time did improve. Now the military spoke of the 'platinum 10 minutes'. This was the immediate first aid rendered to a serious trauma casualty by the combat medics on the front line. First aid in the army had previously been taught in an amateurish manner – the lack of real experience in war had diluted the urgency of this vital skill. During the 30-year campaign in Northern Ireland, soldiers carried a single, World War II-era field dressing in their jacket pockets. The war in Helmand, by contrast, transformed British Army first aid practice. Army combat medics now had the tools (American tourniquets, 'quick-clot' bandages and Celox gauzes) as well as the skills to save lives that would otherwise have been lost within minutes of injury. Countless lives were saved by soldiers applying simple techniques and critically staunching blood loss in the first minutes following a traumatic injury.

Britain also went to war with downsized medical defence services and a barely adequate military medical infrastructure. The damage was done by the 1994 *Front Line First: The Defence Costs Study* that witnessed a number of key defence functions, such as the medical services, privatized under the newly fashionable Private Finance Initiatives, or PFIs. The consequent unpreparedness for war provoked a scandal demanding improvements that were quickly implemented as the casualties mounted. So-called 'Role 1' facilities were expanded throughout all the main operating bases, forward operating bases and some of the larger patrol bases. These provided primary health care and pre-hospital emergency treatment. 'Role 2' and 'Role 3' facilities that offered surgical care were established at the main operating bases along with dental, physiotherapy and mental health facilities. These offered intensive care as well as high-dependency treatment, x-ray, CT and laboratory facilities. The main UK hospital was the Anglo-American Role 3 hospital at Camp Bastion, also supported by Danish and Estonian medical personnel. Although the main priority of this hospital was to treat the military wounded, it also handled hundreds of civilian casualties injured in the fighting or in other ways. In any one deployment, over 400 British military medical staff were based in Helmand, the majority located in Camp Bastion.

As a result of successive defence cuts, the medical services of the armed forces (now amalgamated and renamed the Defence Medical Services) were about 6,500 strong. To support the war, the DMS inevitably had to call on the services of reservists as well as the National Health Service. Scores volunteered over the course of the war, providing vital manpower.

The outrage that Lieutenant Colonel Tootal experienced when he witnessed the shabby treatment offered to his injured paratroopers in Britain was addressed by a nervous Labour government, keen to improve its tarnished image with the electorate. At any one time there were between 60 and 75 injured military personnel in NHS hospitals. To cope with the constant influx of patients, five MOD hospital units were established across Britain. The main unit was Selly Oak Hospital, part of the University Hospital Birmingham Foundation Trust. Selly Oak became synonymous with the agony of families making the difficult journey to the bedside of a loved one, now wrecked, missing limbs or in a coma. These destroyed young people would find themselves in the Military Managed Ward, based in the trauma and orthopaedic wards. The Military Managed Ward, as its name suggested, had a military ward manager and military nurses. This single measure – separating military from civilian patients – boosted morale enormously. What injured soldiers needed, as much as the expert medical treatment, was the sense that they were still part of the military family. The psychological value of being able to share experiences with fellow injured soldiers was unquantifiable. Catering was also improved, and to assist the families of injured personnel at Selly Oak, three flats for overnight accommodation were provided by the wartime charity SSAFA. In 2010, the facilities at the University Hospital Birmingham Foundation Trust were expanded with the opening of the £545 million Queen Elizabeth Hospital, the largest acute trauma hospital in Europe. This also included a Military Managed Ward with 30 beds as well as facilities for rehabilitation. A purpose-built accommodation block was added for military families within walking distance of the hospital.

The other medical facility that became synonymous with the war was the Defence Medical Rehabilitation Centre at Headley Court. Over time Headley Court gained the status of places like Craiglockhart in World War I. Around 300 staff worked at Headley Court, teaching the severely injured how to walk again, how to hold a spoon with a prosthetic arm or how to articulate words through a shattered jaw. In typically British fashion, several charities committed to improving the facilities at Headley Court (which was itself owned by a charitable trust). These included the massively successful Help for Heroes as well as older charities like the Royal British Legion, SSAFA and the Army Benevolent Fund. Headley Court grew to become a world-class rehabilitation centre. The credit went entirely to the dedicated staff that nursed, coaxed and encouraged the wounded back into restarting their now terribly changed lives. By 2011 it was clear Headley Court could no longer cope with the growing roll call of the disabled, and a decision was taken to create a Defence and Rehabilitation Centre in the Midlands. For many, Headley Court would always remain the place that restored them to life. A symbolic reversal of the 1994 decision to privatize defence medical services came in May 2014 when the Duchess of Cornwall opened a £138 million facility for defence medical training in Whittington, Staffordshire. This also served as the new headquarters for Defence Medical Services. The funding and management of the facility was, in fact, multifaceted – DMS Whittington was not a 'renationalization'. But it was an important commitment, and it signalled that a British government was once again re-investing in this critical service.

Physical wounds were visible. Mental wounds were not. Unlike the long campaign in Northern Ireland (and the short but intense Falklands Conflict), there was a recognition in the armed forces that shell shock – known by its modern clinical name of Post-Traumatic Stress Disorder – was a real and long-term problem for some soldiers who had experienced traumatic events. Training to identify and to deal with PTSD in Helmand was vastly improved. Mostly this involved relearning old lessons. Courage was like a bank account, and the stress of continuous fighting (and the ever-present threat of IEDs) depleted that account rapidly. Everybody had a threshold. Just offering individual soldiers a short break from front-line duties could make all the difference. For longer term care there were 15 military Departments of Community Mental Health (DCMH). The DCMHs were established in regions where there were large military garrisons. The geographical spread of the DCMH ensured that soldiers could receive mental health care closer to their base stations, which perhaps provided the best, intangible mental health care simply by keeping them within the bosom of their regiment. Specialist and dedicated psychiatric care was provided by the National Health Service as the armed forces had long lost this independent capability.

For many, it was the upset of witnessing civilian deaths, and in particular children, that caused mental turmoil. One example was the experience of Sapper Ryan Pavey, a bomb disposal officer deployed on the notorious Route 611 on Operation *Herrick 15*. The clearance teams had closed off a section of the road, but an Afghan minibus carrying 18 women and children ignored the block and tried to drive around the soldiers, triggering a massive IED. There were only five survivors. Ignoring the threat of secondary IEDs, Pavey rushed to the destroyed van and found a four-year old boy with a severed leg. His prompt actions saved the boy's life. In his words, 'It's harder when the casualties are civilian … when you deploy you have to ready yourself for the possibility of soldiers being injured, but seeing a child hurt is a lot harder than seeing a grown up.' For this selfless act, Pavey was awarded a Queen's Commendation for Bravery.[40]

Incidents like this revealed the great gap in attitudes towards saving life that existed between soldiers and an obsessive safety culture back in Britain. Over this period, first responders to Islamist terrorist attacks in Britain were delayed from attending to victims due to a raft of exaggerated procedures and regulations; injured died who could otherwise have been saved (directly contradicting the unfathomable judgement following the 2005 London Underground bombing that 'they would have died anyway'). Pavey *knew* there was a high likelihood of secondary devices, and still acted. Over the course of the war, hundreds of soldiers acted similarly and saved the lives of fellow soldiers who were only going 'to die anyway' if they were not treated promptly. Fortunately, they were. The British Army's only quadruple amputee survived his injuries.

For others, like Guardsman Jordan Pearson, mental turmoil followed physical injury. Caught in an IED blast, Pearson suffered a range of serious wounds: his rifle muzzle was driven into his chest, narrowly missing his heart; his radio was driven through his arm; and his back was peppered by shrapnel. The explosion killed a colleague, wounded another and left him without trousers, shredded and blown off his body. In his words, dealing with the aftermath of this incident proved a difficult experience:

> Everyone says just man up, and that's what I had been doing for so long, but it came to a point where I couldn't man up any more. I had to go get help to get through it because it was only going to get worse, not better.

> I was short-tempered and angry, drinking too much and arguing, and I was having difficulty sleeping. I was getting paranoid about sleeping in the same room as the other blokes in case they took the mick out of me for screaming in the night from the nightmares.[41]

Thanks to an understanding family, not least his wife Loren, Pearson was encouraged to seek treatment for his diagnosed 'survivor guilt'. While acknowledging that there would be no quick therapy, over time, the guardsman found that he began to experience 'more good days than bad'.

Despite perennial and critical media articles on the subject of PTSD, clinically diagnosed soldiers with mental health problems never rose above one per thousand servicemen. This was not only a testament to enlightened attitudes and better treatment but also perhaps reflected the nature of the war in Helmand. Academic Joanna Bourke's study *An Intimate History of Killing* remains the outstanding work on men engaged in warfare in the modern period.[42] Features of wars that cause subsequent mental health problems, such as massacres described by Bourke in her book, were simply absent in Helmand. In this sense, the war in Helmand was 'a good war' that was always unlikely to result in numerous psychological casualties. This contrasted with the war in Iraq, which did leave a bitter aftertaste in the army.

Despite the uncertain start and lack of infrastructure, the provision of medical care on Operation *Herrick* became one of the unqualified successes of the war. World-class medicine was given to the wounded. Important lessons were learned that increased the sum of knowledge of battlefield medicine. One of the most effective innovations was an aggressive transfusion protocol based on a 1:1 ratio of red cell concentrate (RCC) to fresh frozen plasma (FFP), with platelet component support when needed. This proved highly effective in reducing coagulopathy, one of the lethal triads in massive trauma victim.

No better tribute could be paid to the doctors and nurses of Camp Bastion Field Hospital – British, American, Danish and Estonian – than the statistic that 98 per cent of the casualties that passed through the doors of this hospital lived.[43] Field medicine practised at the Camp Bastion hospital, coupled with better personal protection, reduced the number of wounded who die in war to an historical low.

For the wounded soldier, the reassurance that casevac had finally arrived was signalled by the sound of helicopter rotor blades. Operating miles from the nearest field hospital, the war in Helmand, like the war in Vietnam, relied wholly on helicopter casevac. The risks undertaken by the casevac helicopters were immense. Some 60 per cent of these air ambulances would be engaged by insurgent fire, and the British would take to accompanying the casevac helicopters with a pair of Apaches to offer protection. In 2010 an American escort helicopter protecting the casevac of wounded Royal Marines would be shot down over Sangin. In the same year a British Chinook pilot was shot in the helmet, the round ricocheting off and splitting the helmet shell but fortunately failing to seriously injure the stunned airman. The Taliban should have downed many more helicopters. Luck and pilot skill saved the day.

British casevac was undertaken by MERTs, or Medical Emergency Response Teams, using the wide-bodied Chinook helicopter (in Iraq, the Merlin was used for this purpose). The British were proud of the MERT concept, judging they had got the balance right between getting the casualty as quickly as possible to surgery (the American practice) and providing life-saving capabilities on the aircraft itself. Unlike any other casevac helicopters, the British MERTs offered blood and plasma transfusion, ventilation and hypothermia prevention capabilities. A MERT helicopter, medical team and QRF were on permanent duty 24 hours a day, seven days of the week, at Camp Bastion. On average, MERTs were called out four or five times daily. The medical team included an emergency specialist, an anaesthetist and two medical nurses. It was a relentless job made more difficult in cases involving mass casualties. The target was to achieve 'wheels up' within ten minutes of receiving a '9 Liner', or casualty evacuation request. This was almost always achieved. The real delays in casevac were imposed by the difficulties of securing a safe EHLS or Emergency Helicopter Landing Site. Although there was a certain national bravado over which pilots were the most 'cabby', the fact was that pilots of all nationalities took great risks at some point to recover Category A casualties, ignoring the safety norms and landing under fire to make the vital rescue.

Recovering the casualty was just the start. The back of a Chinook was noisy, dusty and dark. The frame vibrated, and the floor became slippery with blood. Yet these were the vital moments when a wounded soldier had to be stabilized before being admitted to surgery. On landing at Camp Bastion, ambulances would then rush the wounded across a 200-metre strip to the field hospital. Nobody who worked on the MERTs could fail to be moved by the sad cargo of broken bodies recovered on a daily basis from the front lines. Lieutenant Colonel Ian Nesbitt – in civilian life a consultant anaesthetist in Newcastle upon Tyne – soberly observed: 'I have seen more trauma here in a few weeks than I would see in 15 years in the UK.'[44]

With the arrival of American reinforcements, more medical helicopters joined the airborne ferrying service of the wounded and killed in the form of UH-60L Black Hawk 'Dustoffs' and HH-60 Pave Hawk 'Pedros' ('Dustoff' was the call sign of the first medical helicopter shot down in the Vietnam War; the nickname has persisted in its honour). These latter were crewed by highly trained USAF personnel (known as 'PJs'), with a reputation for conducting hazardous rescue missions. PJs held American civilian registration as paramedics, making them probably the best qualified airborne paramedics in the world. The PJs had a nickname for the killed – they called them 'angels'. One PJ who served with 2 Rifles in Sangin summed up their robust attitude to life on the front line: 'I'm not a political guy. While I wish that there were more helicopters to do the job better, I don't give a shit why or how. All I know is that I was glad to be one of the guys that made sure that so many will get to be with one of their families again.'[45]

Medical treatment and evacuation were also offered to Afghan civilians and the Taliban, an experience probably as disorientating as the original injury. As one medical squadron remembered, the range of Afghan patients was very wide:

> Our case mix has been impressive, not least because of the bizarre array of accidents and emergencies that occur among the local population, for which care is often sought here. We have treated – both out on patrol and in the DC compound – injuries including domestic burns in babies and young children; an opium overdose in an infant who drank 'poppy washings'; victims from road traffic accidents, including a child run over by his father's tractor; anaphylaxis from an insect-sting; scorpion bites; electrocutions; 'punishment shooting' gunshot wounds; a stabbing resulting from a family row; and a dramatic suicide attempt involving a large knife and a wheelbarrow.[46]

The saddest case the medical staff had to deal with was a child quadruple amputee.

Over the course of the war, Camp Bastion Role 3 Hospital treated hundreds of Afghans and saved countless of lives. This workload was augmented by a legal requirement to give a medical check-up to any detainees picked up by British forces. This added hundreds more cases in every brigade rotation. In any one week, Bastion's three surgical tables were witnessing on average 120 hours of life-saving surgery.[47] By far the biggest case load was provided by routine medical problems: every six months, the close support medical regiment had to deal with around 30,000 ailments of one type or other. It was like running the busiest of National Health hospitals with the added burden of a daily intake of multiple trauma casualties.

A fascinating change in the British Army serving in Helmand was the growth of religious sentiment. The peacetime army reflected society, and Britain had become an irreligious island with poor church attendance. Perhaps one in ten of the population attended a religious service, but some studies suggested that perhaps it was as few as one in 20. As a result, the role of the padre had shrunk to near irrelevance. During World War II, padres were ubiquitous – the sheer number of battlefield burials meant every unit needed a padre. Padres had won four Victoria Crosses and over 400 Military Crosses, more than would be awarded to the army as a whole for the entire war in Helmand. The last famous padre had been 2 PARA's padre in the Falklands Conflict, David Cooper, a tough character who fitted in with the airborne ethos and who later went on to teach at Eton College. In the modern army they had become nearly invisible. The war in Helmand (and Iraq) once again raised the importance of the padre as an indispensable figure in a fighting unit. Soldiers who would never normally attend a religious service found themselves queuing to pray at makeshift altars in dusty front-line chapels. A Major Richard Streatfield serving with the Rifles put it this way:

> Riflemen are not usually a religious bunch but I can guarantee more prayers have been offered in the last six months than ever before. Early in the tour I heard a section praying before they went out. 'Lo, though I walk through the valley of the shadow of death … ' it was moving and frightening at the same time. One of our soldiers who was killed in action had a prayer found in his helmet. No one carried or wore a crucifix in UK, now they are as common as not. One doesn't find too many atheists on the battlefield.[48]

The influence of one group of soldiers – the Fijians – played its part in redeeming religion among the cynical British soldiery. The Fijians were not only deeply masculine – in an organization that prized a cult of masculinity – they were also deeply religious. They sang moving laments to their fallen comrades and demonstrated to a teenager from Colchester, Liverpool or Leeds that you could be both soldier and religious. The cliché of Fijian 'gentle giants' was not far wrong.

Like other services in the army, the Royal Army Chaplain's Department had suffered cutbacks. Finding sufficient padres to fill the growing need for religious succour proved a problem. Typical of those who stepped forward to fill the vacancies was the Reverend Dr David Latimer, a Presbyterian minister from Londonderry in Northern Ireland.[49] Reverend Latimer was a Territorial Army officer, an indication of the lack of padres within the Regular Army. Within 24 hours of arriving in the province he was dealing with his first casualties, appropriately fellow Ulstermen from the Royal Irish. The padre proved a popular figure riding a quad bike with its own call sign (13) and an identifying placard ('God's 2ic'). When his six-month deployment ended, 400 soldiers attended his farewell service – an unthinkable church attendance only a few years previously. Back in Britain, thanksgiving and memorial services became packed. Cathedrals that had become museums and which reserved side chapels for the dusty colours of disbanded regiments once again witnessed ranks of soldiers passing through their portals.

In its colonial past, the British Army had raised some of the biggest Muslim armies in history, notably in India, but also in Iraq, Egypt, Libya and elsewhere (Gaddafi was trained by the British, who described him as cheerful, amusing and hard-working). In the post-imperial army Muslim numbers dwindled and were eclipsed by two other groups: Gurkhas and Sikhs. Nonetheless, Muslim soldiers could be found in Helmand, and the armed forces head imam Asim Hafiz became an important figure, reconciling potentially divisive issues of Western soldiers in Muslim lands.

The need for religious consolation had a visible symbol. Crosses began to spring up all over the province (incidentally causing no offence to the Muslim soldiers of the ANA). They were typically made from spent shell cases and served as monuments to the fallen, whose names were inscribed at the base of the cross. Over time the crosses became formal places for remembrance and the base plaques filled with names. When the bases closed or were handed over to the Afghan army, the crosses and plaques were retrieved as if they embodied the very spirits of those who had sacrificed their lives and whose names now glinted in brass.

Like soldiers of all eras, British soldiers and marines serving in Helmand brought with them their own tribal language. A good soldier was someone who 'cracked on' or who 'smashed it out'. An idle or useless soldier might be referred to as a 'mong' or 'oxygen-thief'. Every soldier wanted to look 'ally'. An 'ally' soldier was 'warry' – he looked good and 'tooled up' for battle. No soldier wanted to 'stag on', which inevitably implied a boring guard duty in a sangar. Soldiers ate 'scoff' in the 'cookhouse', and marines ate 'scran' in the 'galleys'. Everyone crawled into a 'doss bag' (sleeping bag) at the end of the day.

Despite constant education to the contrary, sexist biases of the average soldier could not be wholly transformed by watching equal opportunities videos (which could barely compete anyway with the industrial levels of pornography watching in the army, as in civilian society). Despite comprising almost 12 per cent of the army's strength, the proportion of deployed servicewomen was actually much lower (less than 1 per cent). This was not due to an unwillingness to serve but rather the insurmountable difficulties of deploying female soldiers outside main bases. The weight problem was another factor. Fit young men were struggling to carry the loads imposed on soldiers. Asking female soldiers to bear the same weights was just not realistic in many cases. The problem of sexism had a darker side in the interactions with Afghan soldiers, for whom a Western female soldier was a sexually exciting novelty. This was not helped by a cultural prejudice (fostered by the widely available pornography) that Westerners were basically decadent. One servicewoman recalled being treated like exotica by the Afghan soldiers:

> Initially we were regarded with extreme curiosity as a unique female partnership. The more junior soldiers would just stare at us, whereas the officers looked at us with puzzled expressions and asked 'why are you in the Army working with men if you are a girl?' Having a mobile phone camera shoved in our faces every five minutes and having a swarm of ANA soldiers following us wherever we went turned into the norm. We were such a novelty to them, and everyone wanted to have their picture taken with us.[50]

Female soldiers were invaluable because they could interact with Afghan women without causing offence. In time, American-style FETs or Female Engagement Teams were established. Able Seaman Class 1 Kate Nesbitt became the second woman to be awarded the Military Cross when she dealt with a casualty under fire. Many more servicewomen would follow in her footsteps and be similarly recognized for gallantry under fire. Courage was not solely a male attribute.

The peculiarities of military language were also evident in the enduring love affair with abbreviations and acronyms. Soldiers themselves found the impenetrability of the jargon amusing, as this engineer recalled:

> The Regiment have just completed the BOO, prior to this the LSI, and before that the ECI ... The BOWO has visited as well as the FOWO to advise us on jobs that must be completed ASAP. The TQ along with the RQ and RQ(T) advised the QM's and SQ's on the way forward. Lots of 6535's, 8088's, ARB's, P1954's, 1033's to be re-signed and checked ... and if anyone can understand the above, please come and translate.[51]

If some aspects of military language were enduring, others had changed. A Falklands generation soldier might have been called Thomas, Jones or McKay. In Helmand you were equally likely to find a Madratabuia, Raiola or Kuku. Nicknames also changed. They ranged from the traditional (Robbo, Scouse and Ginge), to the more exotic (Slumdog, Morgs and Stripper). Under the influence of American forces that owned the electromagnetic spectrum, traditionally dull British military call signs became suggestive of a mythological world peopled with cartoon characters: Maverick, Hades, Greeneyes, Brimstone and Ugly.

The war in Helmand did not produce a Wilfred Owen or Keith Douglas, but more than one amateur poet was moved by the experience of warfare to express himself in verse. The most unlikely such poet was Senior Air Craftsman Craig Blackwell, who served in the humble role of fireman. Blackwell never saw action, but a verse he wrote, 'The Helmand Poem', became a sort of unofficial epitaph for the British sacrifice in Afghanistan.[52]

> In poppy fields you were to fall,
> St Peter was to hear your call,
> And take your soul for God to keep,
> And help embrace that endless sleep.

Your friends will mourn,
Your wife will weep,
Your son will see you in his sleep.
You are another hero lost
Another son this war has cost.
And with your name upon the wall,
With other friends that were to fall,
And died upon their country's call.
In poppy fields they still stand tall.

An anonymous patrol base poet took the most famous poem in the English language on soldiering in Afghanistan (Kipling's 'Square') and cleverly subverted it:

When the gimpy [machine gun] has jammed and you're
Down to one round,
And the faith that you'd lost is suddenly found,
When the Taliban horde is close up to the fort,
And you pray that the arty don't
Drop a round short …

Then, just as the reader thinks he is being led down a familiar path of stiff upper lips and straight backs, there is a rude volte-face. All this, the author muses, for 'three fifty an hour', or less than the minimum wage; for a 'missus at home in a foul married quarter'; for 'damp on the walls and a roof leaking water'; and for children missing their father and 'the childhood that they should have had'. The stern rebuke to Britain's politicians ends:

The Brits will fight on 'till the battle is over,
You may treat him like dirt but nowt will
Unnerve him,
But I wonder sometimes, if the country
Deserves him.[53]

It could have been the words of a soldier fighting in the Crimean War, and many expeditionary campaigns since.

In 2011, the publishing house Ebury would collect 100 war poems in *Heroes*, a book printed to raise awareness and money for service charities.

There were no contenders for a modern version of *Dulce et Decorum*, but the sincerity of the emotions expressed in the poems was undeniable.

The Taliban also wrote verse, drawing on a long oral tradition of poetry in central Asia. In 2011, the publisher Hurst and Co. collected 235 such poems and published them in Britain. This drew harrumphing criticism from a retired senior army officer and regular contributor to *The Times* who argued that publishing enemy poetry was somehow giving wind to 'fascist, murdering thugs'. Setting aside the misuse of 'fascist', which revealed how little this individual seemed to understand of the complexity of the war in Helmand, the charge was silly. Some were love poems rooted in genres dating back to the 17th century. Many war ballads were universal and could have been penned by any soldier in any period. Tellingly, the editor of *Heroes*, a former army captain who had actually served on the front line, unlike the senior officer, had no difficulties with Taliban poetry, observing that the average British soldier had more empathy with his enemy than with the politicians placing him in the firing line – which is another universal feeling shared by soldiery.

Like the largely static World War I, soldiers found time to create front-line newspapers. Several sprang up: the *Musa Qaleh Times*, the *Helmand Highlander* and the *Ripon Sapper*, to name three. The tone was always light-hearted and upbeat. Mostly the soldiers wrote to amuse themselves, their mates and their families.

Surprisingly, the most notable difference between the Helmand front-line newspapers and the earlier genre typified by *The Wipers Times*, was that World War I soldiers were far more subversive and critical than the popular image of a submissive and obedient generation suggests. *The Wipers Times* was peppered with criticism of officers and tactics ('Are you offensive enough?' was a standard joke). No Helmand author dared indulge in such questioning, as it would have contradicted 'the narrative', or the spin of a successful mission. Nor would any modern soldier have dared craft jokes around a fictitious but identifiable General Bertram Rudolph de Rogerum – the inspiration, it may be surmised, for the character General Melchett in the popular comedy series *Blackadder*. In Helmand, lampooning your senior officers was as taboo as questioning the point of the war.

The mismanaged war in Iraq had provoked extreme nervousness in the Labour government. If the government was now keen to restrict the amount of information leaking from Afghanistan, the enterprise was doomed to failure. Soon the British public was being treated to a rash of war memoirs that rolled off the printing press more quickly than the brigades were rotating through Helmand (nearly 30 titles were published by the mid-point in the war). In this respect the war in Afghanistan was different from the ugly and messy confrontation in Basra. Afghanistan had all the appeal of a bygone imperial age, and indeed the ancestors of these war memoirs were the late Victorian and Edwardian tales of derring-do that filled magazines like *Chums*, and newspapers like the *Illustrated London News* and the *Graphic*. The three previous Anglo-Afghan wars had generated a crop of books from protagonists keen to cash in on their experiences, and this latest war was no different. The modern inspiration came from the lurid, sensational bestseller *Bravo Two Zero* (1993), the book which set the house style for modern British war memoirs.

The Helmand war memoirs were packed with a mix of heightened truths and eyewitness accounts of dramatic gun battles. The cinematic titles announced themselves like the tap-tap of a 9mm pistol: *Ground Truth*, *Danger Close* and *Blood Clot* were typical examples. The succeeding pages were filled with the cacophony of whizzing bullets and exploding RPGs. Hardship, heat and dust served as the backdrop to the extraordinary events that were happening on this modern-day North-West Frontier. The general public was let into a whole new range of military terms like novitiates being offered a glimpse into a secret priesthood with its own arcane language. These books secreted testosterone and they sold like hot cakes.

Few authors questioned the merits or the direction of the war, although the now retired Colonel Tootal did use his memoirs to make an impassioned plea for better treatment of serving and retired soldiers. Mostly they glorified the war. The reader was left in no doubt that one was a lesser person for not having served the Queen's Colours, and they no doubt acted as formidable recruiting agents. The Parachute Regiment was particularly successful at exploiting the seductive appeal of war memoirs. No less than four books appeared in very short order describing the exploits of 3 PARA in the torrid summer of 2006. A soldier like Doug Beattie became a one-man advertisement for the heroics of the Royal Irish. Mick Flynn played the same role for the Household Cavalry.

If the war memoirs could be criticized for a certain, self-regarding macho streak, they could not be faulted for their candour. These were mostly the stories of soldiers speaking as soldiers, and stories they had to tell were mostly true, if jazzed-up. They faithfully portrayed the humour, the endurance and the surprising compassion of young men lifted from poor backgrounds, inculcated with military values, and sent to fight a war in a faraway land, like so many of their forebears. They told stories of indisputable heroism in an age when wartime heroics had almost become consigned to grainy, black-and-white, world-war movies. They seemed to redeem a youth that had become characterized as an empty-headed 'Nintendo generation'. For a brief interlude Britain's appalling drugs, drink and teenage pregnancy statistics could be suspended by the thought that somewhere out there a teenager was risking life and limb in the service of his country. The Helmand war memoirs also served a more important purpose. They brought home to the casual reader that this truly was war. The levels of violence may not have been as great as that experienced in the Korean War, as was claimed, but they were certainly severe. Millions of bullets were being expended. Thousands of tonnes of high explosive were being dropped. A virgin army was being 'transformed in contact', as General Dannatt put it.

The war only produced one literary work, *The Junior Officers' Reading Club*, written by Patrick Hennessey, a young Grenadier Guards officer who served in both Iraq and Afghanistan.[54] Much of the work was actually not about war at all. Rather, it examined the psychological paradox of a young man with a profound aversion to the protocols of militarism – bullshit, in common parlance – drawn to serve, for reasons of social prestige it had to be surmised, in a regiment of the Foot Guards where these very traits were most pronounced. In many ways the most vivid and entertaining section of the entire work described Hennessey's passage through basic military training at the Royal Military Academy Sandhurst – the pinnacle of the Guards ethos – an experience he seemed to find at best irksome and at worst traumatic. This was the universal and intelligent civilian protesting at the inanity of polishing boots until, as he put it, your platoon sergeant could see his soul in them. Modestly, the author did not inform the reader that he was actually awarded the Queen's Medal at Sandhurst.

Hennessey was a Balliol graduate (in English Language and Literature). Interestingly, the other three intelligent books on the war – which is not to devalue the popular books or their authors – were also written by young men who went to Oxford or Cambridge. They included Frank Ledwidge's *Losing Small Wars*, Emile Simpson's *War from the Ground Up*, and Mike Martin's *An Intimate War: An Oral History of the Helmand Conflict*. They all left the army, and in the case of Martin, he was shamefully asked to leave on the same day the Foreign Office had organized a book launch to promote *An Intimate War* – raising questions over the army's attitudes to thinking critically. The other relevant question was why no senior officer authored a serious, thoughtful book.

In an age of digital photography, imagery abounded in Helmand. Every soldier could be his own combat cameraman. Helmet cameras became popular, capturing the raw, unedited confusion of a gun battle through jerky shots and the cacophony of automatic weapons. It was such footage – passed to the media – that first alerted the British public in the summer of 2006 that the purported stabilization mission in Afghanistan was going horribly wrong. On rare occasions a helmet camera captured the moment of detonation of an IED, recording the awesome power of high explosives. 'Warry' videos were prized and video swapping became a cottage industry. All such footage legally belonged to the MOD. In an enlightened decision, the ministry allowed the BBC to trawl through hundreds of hours of Helmand combat camera footage. The result was a three-part series called *Our War*, screened in the summer of 2011, that vividly portrayed the realities of front-line soldiering. *Our War* revealed the basic humanity of British soldiers that no amount of words could convey. Supplementing this work were popular series made by presenters like television actor Ross Kemp, who offered flattering but not dishonest documentaries of life on the front line.

Thousands of still photographs were taken by soldiers of their experiences in Helmand. The majority showed mates posing, lounging, cooking, larking about and playing games – all the activities that make up the experience of soldiering. Team photographs were especially poignant, as the fatality and wounding statistics implied that at least one of the faces in the line-up was likely to end up in a hospital or mortuary. This body of photography captured in an unselfconscious way all the universals of warfare – youthful grinning faces, cockiness and war glamour, the squalor of the front line and the contrasting beauty of nature. This was the profound innocence of Philip Larkin's 'MCMXIV' – 'never such innocence/never before or since'. Curiously, despite the obvious photogenic potential of the war in Helmand, no young Don McCullin came forward to make his name as a war photographer. The single Briton who was establishing himself as a classic war photographer, Tim Hetherington, tragically lost his life in Libya in the spring of 2011.

In Helmand, there was one outstanding exception to this rule. In 2007 Brigadier Mackay invited the London-based commercial photographer Robert Wilson to visit 52 Brigade as war artist, not photographer. Wilson visited the brigade over a two-week period armed with a large-format Hasselblad and 35mm Canon camera. Over this period he took over 12,000 images, of which around 300 were selected for an exhibition and book, *Helmand: Faces of Conflict*.[55] In his words:

> My days in Afghanistan were some of the most amazing of my life. It was a rare and fantastic opportunity to capture moments in time which were not only visually stunning but historic. I felt it was important to depict the war through the men who are fighting it, by portraying their world and giving a sense of how they live.

The most intense period was a five-day stint at Musa Qaleh, where Wilson was able to witness and live life on the front line. The majority of the images chosen for *Helmand: Faces of Conflict* were drawn from this period.

Wilson's faces were arresting close-up portraits. They depicted exhausted soldiers, covered in dust, staring directly at the camera. Every one had a dulled, faraway look that spoke of combat fatigue. The use of large-format prints revealed every crease and shadow in the worn faces. Photographed in flat winter sunlight, the resultant bleached look reinforced the sense that the sitters were living in a quite different and alien world. There was an undeniable painterly beauty to the opus that deservedly placed it as classic and not commercial war photography.

The trade of war artist – which emerged in Britain during World War I as a powerful social as well as artistic record of conflict – was also practised in Helmand. Unlike photographers working in Helmand, an artist had to contend with tricky environmental conditions. In the Falklands Conflict, the war artist Linda Kitson had suffered numb fingers, driving sleet and strong winds. In Helmand, the main challenges were the debilitating heat and dust. Two media suited these difficult conditions: acrylic inks and charcoal. Both were easily transportable, they produced quick results and they could readily capture an often-fleeting subject matter.

The artist who best exploited acrylics was the Territorial Army soldier and professional illustrator Matthew Cook. Cook was both a highly experienced soldier and artist. He served with 7 Rifles in the first Gulf

War and subsequently undertook a commission for *The Times* newspaper in the 2003 invasion of Iraq. He returned to Iraq the following year with the London Regiment, as a reservist. In 2006 he deployed to Afghanistan as the official war artist of the Royal Gloucestershire, Berkshire and Wiltshire Regiment and then returned again in the winter of 2009 as the brigade war artist in Helmand. Cook's main inspirations were the war art he had viewed as a young boy in the Imperial War Museum, and the influence of the war artists Feliks Topolski (under whom he served an apprenticeship) and John Piper. His ambition was to be artist as recorder: 'Unlike a lot of traditional war artists that are either anti-war or portraying a very spectacular battle or defeat, I'm not trying to achieve either of those, it is purely a record.'[56]

In this he was uniquely placed, as his eye for accurate military detail was based on personal experience as a serving soldier. As he put it, he had no excuses: 'I do notice in other people's paintings if they get things wrong – if an ammo pouch is the wrong size or things generally don't look right.' His subject matter was the mundane, everyday lives of servicemen in a war zone: a soldier relieving himself along a row of urinals, the domestic details of soldiers having a brew or cooking, the boredom of sentry duty. His tools were just three primary colours, yellow, blue and red – and a set of brushes (that became an exhibition at the National Army Museum). The light in Afghanistan represented a stiff test for any painter, but Cook was able to skilfully record both the spectacular sunsets and the deep shadows thrown by the blinding Afghan sun.

The other artist who left behind a valuable record of life on the front line was Arabella Dorman.[57] This Chelsea-based artist could not have picked a more difficult location or time to practise her trade. In the summer of 2009 she spent a month with 2 Rifles at the Sangin District Centre. By the time this battalion recovered from the town in September, 23 soldiers had been killed and over 100 had been injured. Like photographer Robert Wilson, Dorman had a talent for portraiture, and the medium she chose to capture her subjects with was charcoal and chalk. Dorman had previously spent some weeks with a Rifles battlegroup in Iraq so she was not entirely unfamiliar with soldiery. Nonetheless, the conditions and especially the fatalism of the soldiers deeply moved her. 'The riflemen were so young,' she remembered, 'they were babies.'[58] Before going out on patrol – a moment of nervous tension – riflemen approached her to have their portraits drawn: 'They'd all come to me and say how fast can you do a portrait? And you'd know why they wanted it done. They would talk to me about "if" I get back home, not "when" I get back home.'

On another occasion, when she drew an Afghan gardener working at the British base, he miserably told her: 'You haven't captured the hate in my eyes. I love nothing and I have never known a day of peace.' One of the portraits she drew was of Rifleman Daniel Wilde, one of three teenagers who died together in a single incident when a patrol was struck by multiple IEDs. He had been carrying a wounded colleague when he stepped on a second IED. Dorman's work in Helmand was in the best tradition of classic charcoal and chalk portraiture. Moved by her experience, she returned to Afghanistan the following year, and then revisited the task force for a final trip before withdrawal. She entitled the exhibition of her paintings *New Dawn*. For all its travails, she judged Afghanistan faced 'the hope of a new day but all the uncertainty of what the day will bring'.[59]

Soldiers have always been necessarily fatalistic. There is probably no other way of coping with the knowledge that every day you wake up may be your last, or may end in terrible injury. Corporal Jim White, a Royal Marine on his third tour of Afghanistan, described the surreal dislocation provoked by sudden death on the battlefield: 'To see guys who one minute are in our gym working out doing pull ups and the next you are picking them up off the ground, limbless, it's just a bizarre place, how quickly it changes for the blokes. It can happen in just a second.'[60]

This is what the average British soldier and marine had to face whenever he stepped outside the front gate of his patrol base. At the vast MOD depot at Ashchurch, two aircraft-sized hangars were reserved for casualty vehicles from the war. These were recovered to Britain, like their former occupants, for coroner reports and forensic examination. The row upon row of split and shattered vehicles was a sobering sight. For a soldier contemplating this wreckage of war the question was always: what are my chances?

At the beginning of Operation *Herrick* the intensity of the fighting had been compared to that experienced in the Korean War. This was an exaggerated comparison. As in all wars, risk depended on where you were serving and your role. It was nonetheless the case that the British Army in Helmand experienced a casualty rate that it had become quite unused to, and this was both an institutional and personal shock. Every six-month rotation routinely resulted in the loss of a battalion's worth of soldiers to combat and non-combat injuries (a deficit that was in part compensated by the battalion's worth of Territorial Army soldiers who volunteered for active service). From 2009, battle casualty replacements and reinforcement companies had to be deployed to Helmand to make up the losses. 3 Commando Brigade on Operation *Herrick 9* estimated that only 80 per cent of the deployed force was actually available to the task force commander at any one time because 7 per cent were disease and non-battlefield injury (DNBI), 6 per cent were on leave, 2 per cent were on compassionate leave, 4 per cent were WIA and 1 per cent were KIA. Some estimates suggested that as many as one in six soldiers succumbed to an illness or non-battlefield injury. Over 2007–10, 17 per cent of soldiers flown home early were as a consequence of DNBI. Sixty-five per cent of the Camp Bastion hospital admissions were for the same reason, using up valuable resources.[61]

These overall figures masked significant local variations. The 3 Rifles battlegroup deployed to Sangin over 2009–10 suffered 30 fatalities and over 100 wounded – effectively an entire company had been wiped off the battlegroup's order of battle. The 2 PARA rifle companies that served in the Green Zone in the torrid summer of 2008 reckoned that one in three of their number suffered some form of injury or illness at some point in the tour. 1 Royal Anglian in the previous summer had lost one-fifth of its strength – 165 men. As in previous wars, the infantry bore the brunt of the casualties: three-fifths of all British fatalities were infantrymen. The most dangerous rank to serve in was the lance corporal and corporal rank band. In proportion to their numbers in the army, junior NCOs suffered more fatalities than any other rank. The war was borne by 20-something-year-olds who daily carried the responsibility for the safety of their sections and who frequently paid for this responsibility with their lives. By the mid-point of the war, 27 teenagers had been killed and not a small number were amputees. Kids with barely any other experience of life were repatriated in coffins.

Officers, by contrast, survived the war well. The officer to other ranks fatality ratio was less than 1:10. This did not imply that officers shirked danger. It was just not the type of war where officers had to lead from the front (although many did to give encouragement to wearying soldiers). In World War II, a bolshie conscript army had to be cajoled and even threatened into taking risk by an officer class that paid a high concomitant price. In Korea, the same problem bedevilled the British war effort, based on pressed and reluctant national servicemen. In Helmand, an all-professional and well-motivated volunteer force did not require this kind of leadership. Just one commanding officer was killed in the war – Lieutenant Colonel Rupert Thorneloe of the Welsh Guards – an event that provoked great media commotion.

The mortality and wounding statistics told the story of a war that reached its crescendo in 2009–10 (at least for the British) and then declined. In 2006, 85 soldiers were wounded in action.[62] In the subsequent two years, the numbers jumped to 234 and 235. In 2009, there was a leap – 509 soldiers were wounded in action, an unprecedented number outside the recent experience of the British Army. Disease and non-battlefield injury numbers similarly manifested an upward trajectory. In 2006, 156 soldiers fell ill or were injured. In the succeeding three years, the numbers were 598, 773 and 721. The consequence of this spreadsheet of injury and illness was a daily ferrying of casualties to Britain for medical treatment. There were 262 aero-medical evacuations in 2006. By mid-2010 there had been 3,504. As was frequently pointed out, just five British soldiers died in Afghanistan from 2001 to 2005. For the British the war truly started in Helmand Province. This low early fatality rate was probably one of the contributing factors to the wide-eyed optimism with which the British deployed to southern Afghanistan. The WIA:KIA ratio roughly remained at 4:1, although it did improve towards the end of the war. The VSI/SI (very seriously injured/seriously injured) to lightly wounded ratio was roughly 1:4:5, although there were variations across tours. The lightly wounded were returned to front-line service in theatre, but the constant drain of the lightly wounded was a loss of manpower that commanders could ill afford. For every one soldier lost in combat (killed or wounded), two were being lost through disease and non-battlefield injury. The arithmetic of war has never been reasonable.

The frequency of deployments was inevitably reflected in the regimental fatality league tables. The Rifles 'super regiment' (five amalgamated battalions) that served almost continuously through the height of the war suffered the most fatalities of all the line regiments (55 KIA/252 VSI). The Royal Marines and Parachute Regiment with their multiple deployments also suffered significant losses – 61/170 and 28/151 respectively. The Guards Division lost 36 men and 246 were very seriously wounded. The Mercians also suffered badly, partly because of multiple deployments but also from the bad luck of serving in the worst corner of Babaji (23/155). The five Scots battalions recorded 20 KIA and 111 VSI, a relatively low bill. Mere frequency of deployment, however, was not the determining factor and there were exceptions to the rule. By 2010, the Gurkhas had deployed four times to Afghanistan and had suffered just four combat fatalities, manifesting the lowest fatality rate per deployment of any infantry battalion.[63] This remarkable record could not just be attributed to luck or location – smart soldiering must surely have played a role. The Coldstream Guards in the winter of 2007 uniquely saw out their tour in Helmand without suffering a single fatality, although their good fortune would run out when they returned to Helmand on their second tour. Again this could not just be attributed to chance – the guardsmen managed their war with intelligence and skill. In 2008, as we have seen in a previous chapter, the canny Royal Irish survived six months in Sangin and almost got away without suffering a single fatality – a unique accomplishment. 3 PARA did complete their 2008 tour in Kandahar without suffering a fatality and almost repeated the feat in 2011. Reducing casualty rates was not just about adding more and more layers of armour, and buying more and more expensive equipment – good leadership, clever soldiering and tactics counted for an awful lot.

The infantry were not the only arm to suffer high casualty rates: gunners, engineers, signallers, mechanics, logisticians, policemen and two dog handlers added over 50 names to the roll call of the dead. Twenty bomb disposal officers and search engineers (the RESAs and RESTs*) lost their lives. A staggering 96 were injured, which included 48 T1 casualties (or amputees). Ten Fijians, eight Nepalese, five South Africans, an Australian, a New Zealander and one American all died in the service of the Crown. The Commonwealth still answered the call of the mother country, if in fewer numbers and only as volunteers. Twenty-one Territorial Army soldiers gave their lives. Three servicewomen, Captain Lisa Head, Corporal Sarah Bryant, and Corporal Channing Day, were killed in action. Three military working dogs – Sasha, Treo and Theo – were known to have died, but the true figure was probably higher as special forces used dogs, and even parachuted with them. Nine British soldiers were killed by friendly fire, just under half by American aircraft, although in no incident was the American pilot to blame. The British in turn killed two Danish soldiers and at least four ANA soldiers. Total fratricide deaths from the

*Royal Engineer Search Advisor and Royal Engineer Search Team.

beginning to the end of the mission totalled 18 with 39 soldiers wounded. Despite the obvious psychological and media value of suicide bombing, only 16 British soldiers were killed in suicide attacks. It always remained the rarest form of attack.

Determining your personal probability of death or injury through reading the runes of these statistics was, in the end, a fruitless activity. Everybody knew that Sangin was the most dangerous town in Helmand, but a tour guarding the dam at Kajaki could probably be seen out with little chance of experiencing harm. Fortune in war seemed to escape both quantification and logic. An anti-personnel mine should result in death or traumatic amputation of both limbs, but at least one soldier (a Gurkha) who stepped on a land mine got away with a broken ankle. Another soldier, Corporal Peter Docherty, serving with 27 Transport Regiment, spent a night in the open near FOB Arnhem lying on a camp bed that he unknowingly placed directly over an IED. The following morning he got up, reversed his Land Rover over the spot where he had been sleeping and set the bomb off (but was uninjured).

The Vallon man sweeping ahead of a patrol was always judged to be the most dangerous job, with reason, but your position in a patrol was no guarantee of your safety. On more than one occasion, several members of a patrol stepped on a concealed IED but failed to set it off before a heavier (or weighed down) soldier at the back of the patrol did set it off. On Operation *Herrick 12*, a routine patrol in the vicinity of PB Nahidullah in Lashkar Gah District set off with 25 soldiers. The patrol arrived at an improvised footbridge comprising two logs thrown across the waterway. When the penultimate man in the patrol crossed the footbridge he set off the IED, concealed in the eastern bank. How could this be explained or rationalized? Twenty-three soldiers had cheated fate. The 24th – a young man barely out his teens – became a triple amputee. The same phenomenon was experienced in vehicle convoys. Your position in a vehicle convoy had no bearing on whether you were likely to strike an IED. Vehicles at the front were the most vulnerable, but vehicles in the middle and rear of convoys all struck IEDs at different times. The indiscriminate nature of IEDs spared no one. Once the Taliban began sowing IED-fields there was always the possibility that multiple casualties would be caused as soldiers rushed to help injured comrades. Despite the guidance not to approach an injured soldier without first sweeping the ground, many soldiers, responding instinctively to the distress of a friend, did just that and became casualties themselves. Soldiers who did everything right, through sheer bad luck, got caught out. Soldiers who patrolled casually came home unscathed.

Luck could be capricious but it could also be kind. Hundreds of patrols were conducted over the course of every six-month rotation. On Operation *Herrick 11*, one such routine patrol set off from PB Wahid in Nad-e Ali District. The patrol comprised a rifle platoon and a fire support group. After two hours in the Green Zone the soldiers began to receive fire from concealed insurgent positions. While searching for the enemy firing points, one of the patrol members – Lance Corporal Maynard – felt a sudden blow to his head that propelled him 2 metres in the air and deposited him on his back. To his amazement, he had been hit by a bullet that struck 2 centimetres above his left eye. His helmet stopped the bullet, but only by a matter of millimetres. Lance Corporal Maynard's story was not unique. Several soldiers would survive the same near-death encounter with a high-velocity round.

In the spring of 2010, Lieutenant David Robertson, a Highlander officer mentoring an ANA company in Musa Qaleh, survived an even more remarkable brush with death. He had been leading a combined patrol mounted on Warrior APCs when they came under fire from Taliban in a tree line. The ANA soldiers dismounted and started advancing on the insurgent positions using the Warriors for cover. As the Warriors crested a small hill near a graveyard, they were met by a volley of RPGs. Robertson was commanding his Warrior in the open hatch position – with his head and chest outside the turret. By a considerable fluke, one of the RPG warheads spinning through the air struck him in the chest. Robertson recalled: 'I was knocked backwards. I hit the back of the turret pretty hard.' The impact would have been considerable – the equivalent of being hit by a cricket ball travelling at 300 metres per second. He then described what happened:

> I remember a big bang and a heat wave and then felt burning in my arm and side. I radioed back to report what had happened and then we started to extract some of the ANA casualties who had been injured. One of my lads took a look at my arm which was stinging and felt hot and sore, he whacked a dressing on it and we carried on. We went forward again with the wagon and brought back another ANA casualty and then supported with fire support.[64]

Robertson had been freakishly lucky. The warhead had glanced off his chest armour, breaking into three parts. The piezo-electric fuze on the nose of the warhead detonated when it struck the empty gunner's turret. Had it detonated on initial impact Robertson's upper torso would have been severed. This was the daily experience in Helmand for the front-line soldier – it was a place where the difference between life and death was measured in inches, and courage measured in miles.

9

The Commandos Return

Operation *Herrick 9*, October 2008–April 2009

In the normal course of events, a military commander devises a plan and then executes that plan. In 2005, Colonel Gordon Messenger was serving as chief of staff at PJHQ. Along with a small team of staff officers, Colonel Messenger co-authored the Helmand Plan, or plan for the British deployment to Helmand Province. Messenger, however, never saw the plan through. Instead, he was posted to the National Defence Academy at Shrivenham, where he attended the Higher Command and Staff Course. From there he was appointed aide-de-camp to Elizabeth II, where he may have cut a slightly incongruous figure with his weathered face and appearance of a retired boxer. It was certainly a world away from his roots in the Royal Marines in which he had served for the last 26 years of his life. Like many young men, Messenger had joined up for adventure, but mostly found a life of routine training. This all changed in 2000, when he deployed with the British task force to Kosovo. At the conclusion of this operation he was appointed an OBE. Three years later, he found himself in command of 40 Commando, landing on the Al-Faw peninsula east of Basra, during the 2003 Anglo-American invasion of Iraq. Iraqi resistance was patchy and even pitiful, but at least this was war. A Distinguished Service Order followed. At the conclusion of Operation *Telic 1* Messenger was posted to PJHQ, and it was here that his career first intersected with Helmand Province. Three years later, he was returning to the province as commander of 3 Commando Brigade. The appointment was doubly unexpected as the brigade commander earmarked to take 3 Commando Brigade to Helmand – Brigadier

'Buster' Howes – fractured his pelvis in an accident one month before the deployment, necessitating the sudden change of command. Surveying the wreckage of a plan he had once drafted, what did Messenger make of his appointment and the task ahead of him?

The see-saw of expectations had swung decisively downwards when the marines began to take over from the paratroopers in the autumn of 2008. The symbolic threshold of 100 fatalities had been passed. His predecessor, Brigadier Carleton-Smith, had no doubt communicated his pessimism over the conduct of the war. The media, with Iraq now shifting from the public consciousness, had swung its attentions to Afghanistan. The whiff of a second fiasco was in the air. Faced with another Afghan winter, Messenger was both realistic and cautious. 'I think good enough is what we should look for,' he told an interviewer before deploying to Afghanistan, adding, 'there is a new realism in the air.' This new realism was certainly evident among his political masters. On 3 October, John Hutton took over as the third Secretary of State for Defence in as many years. At the time he was mainly known – at least in the popular press – as the man who confided that the Chancellor Gordon Brown would be 'a fucking disaster' as a prime minister. Unusually for a defence secretary, Hutton had a personal interest in military affairs and had written a well-received regimental history based on the experiences of the King's Own Royal Lancasters during World War I. In the end, he would serve less than a year, resigning in the summer of 2009. Nevertheless, in his short tenure Hutton impressed as a competent minister who was long on honest argument and short on spin.

The circumstances of his appointment were poor. The Brown honeymoon was over, and the government was being wracked by a periodic leadership challenge. Hutton's immediate priority was not Afghanistan but rather closing the final chapter on Iraq. In the week before he assumed his ministerial post, the troublesome Anbar Province had been handed over to the Iraqi authorities. Wasit and Babil provinces exchanged hands over the next month. A more pressing concern – and a cause of great embarrassment to the British government – was the expiry of UN Security Council Resolution 1790 on 31 December. Angered by a perceived British surrender in the south, the Iraqi government, led by Prime Minister Nouri al-Maliki, had foot-dragged over negotiations on the legal status of the remaining British forces camped in the airport outside the city. If the negotiations had failed the British would have found themselves in the humiliating position of having to quit the country, effectively expelled rather than thanked for their efforts. In the end, common sense won the day, and the last fragment of British sovereignty was handed back to the Iraqis on 1 January 2009, in a carefully choreographed ceremony at Basra International Airport. The relief on Foreign Secretary David Miliband's face was undisguised.

The coincidence of the final handover in Iraq with 3 Commando Brigade's second tour of Helmand meant the machinery of the MOD could now be devoted to a single theatre of operations. This was noticeable to the soldiers who deployed with the brigade. A gunner officer, Lieutenant Colonel Neil Wilson, wrote approvingly:

> Much has changed since between [sic] last time we were here on Op HERRICK 5 and this time, Op HERRICK 9 – some for the better and some for the worse. Most noticeable is the campaign footing that the Helmand Task Force is now clearly on – no longer fighting from one day to the next, but taking a far more considered and long-term approach.[1]

He was referring to Operation *Entirety*, an initiative promoted by General Sir David Richards, now C-in-C Land Forces (it would be formally implemented at the beginning of 2009). Operation *Entirety* was not entirely new; many of the initiatives and programmes were already underway. But what Richards did was order, structure and galvanize these various separate efforts *to win*. Up to this point, the notion that the British Army had to succeed was not fully grasped. A staff officer serving under Richards jokingly warned that he was not important enough to declare war on his own, but this is more or less what he did.[2] And it was precisely what the army needed. Two years after British forces first entered Helmand, and despite the obvious unravelling of the campaign, Whitehall and the PJHQ were still in denial that the euphemistic 'operation' was in fact a full-blown war. It was a measure of the lack of accountability of those in senior posts responsible for the prosecution of the war – the operational command chain that stretched from the CDS to the in-theatre brigade commander – that nobody had stepped forward to take charge. What was striking about Operation *Entirety* was that it was championed by someone *outside* the operational command chain, who essentially butted in and took responsibility for the war. As C-in-C Land, Richards had no operational responsibility for Operation *Herrick*. His role was to generate the land forces (regiments, battalions, sub-units and so on), which were then 'handed over' to PJHQ every six months to fulfil the rotations. PJHQ commanded Operation *Herrick* – or should have. As Richards later described in his autobiography *Taking Command*, the problem of a lack of accountability and responsibility in senior posts had become endemic in an army obsessed with processes and committees and somewhat less zealous on straightforward leadership. Retired Royal Engineer Major General Christopher Elliott would later author a book – *High Command* – critical of the dysfunctional British leadership.[3] Over time, Operation *Entirety* introduced a raft of measures and equipment that transformed the British war, helped by Richards's ascendency to the posts of CGS and eventually CDS.

Actually, in the short term, Lieutenant Colonel Wilson could not have been more wrong. 3 Commando Brigade deployed to Helmand with no plan except to consolidate the fragile gains made by their predecessors. Messenger – only one month in the job – anticipated no major operations over the winter, the traditional off-season for fighting in Afghanistan. This, incidentally, puts paid to the allegation that British commanders were deploying to Helmand intent on undertaking 'signature operations' to make their name.

One event changed all this. On the evening of 10 October, two days after the formal handover ceremony between the paratroopers and the marines, as many as four reported Taliban columns began marching on the provincial capital from Nad-e Ali. This was highly unusual and had not been witnessed before. The main group appeared to be driving towards Bolan Bridge from the area of Luy Bagh ('Big Garden') in Nad-e Ali. Two other groups appeared to be marching from the north and south. A last group appeared to be gathering in the east. In the ensuing scramble to intercept the Taliban an ANA *kandak* and an Afghan special forces detachment were despatched to block the advance from Nad-e Ali, and Apache helicopters did the rest. The threat had been exaggerated. Perhaps 150 fighters were involved, and it appeared that at least a third of these were killed or wounded in what amounted to a nocturnal duck shoot for the Apache crews.

There was speculation that the insurgents had tried to exploit the handover; or perhaps that Sher Mohammed Akhundzada had been behind the attack to discredit Governor Mangal; or that inter-tribal rivalry over the government-led eradication programme had caused the flare-up (the Noorzai-dominated police had a habit of pushing eradication teams into lands belonging to tribal enemies). Abdul Rahman Jan, the former sacked police chief with significant poppy cultivations in Nad-e Ali, may have been complicit. Michael Martin argues that it was an Akhundzada–Jan double act, but this allegation came from the Nad-e Ali Governor Habibullah who might be expected to discredit his enemies.[4] Whatever the truth, the event shook both Mangal and the task force, and it completely changed the course of the commandos' tour. There were discussions over moving the PRT to a safe location like Camp Bastion – an indication of just how febrile and exaggerated the atmosphere became in the brigade HQ.[5] This proposal was wisely dismissed. Such a move would have been viewed as a 'defeat' of the British, much like the withdrawal from Basra Palace.

In the end, Messenger resolved that the first priority for 3 Commando Brigade would be to secure Nad-e Ali District – the original Afghan Development Zone. It was an index of the lack of campaign direction offered by PJHQ that, two years into the war, this became the adopted plan. By the time 19 Light Brigade arrived in the spring the plan gained coherence with the decision to secure neighbouring Babaji District, but the coherence was entirely illusory. There had been no long-term plan – it all stemmed from an abortive and over-ambitious Taliban attempt to march on the capital and Messenger's swift response to the potential crisis. In this respect, Gordon Messenger holds a central place in the British involvement in Helmand, albeit thanks to the strange Taliban attack. It was this Royal Marine's plan that effectively became the British campaign scheme for the remainder of the war.

The second important consequence of the 10 October attack was the creation of a new Battlegroup Centre South, commanded by the Deputy Brigade Commander, Colonel Martin Smith (although finding troops for this battlegroup would prove a challenge throughout the tour). At the time, the only British presence in Nad-e Ali was a beleaguered B Company of The Argyll and Sutherland Highlanders (5 SCOTS), due to be replaced by J Company of 42 Commando, with reinforcements from 2 Princess of Wales's Royal Regiment (2 PWRR). These soldiers were holed up in an abandoned school, renamed PB Argyll, in Nad-e Ali bazaar. The Argylls at this base illustrated all the problems besetting undermanned British infantry battalions. This company was in fact made up from a hotch-potch of attachments and had no fire support. Nonetheless, the company commander remained determined to push the insurgents away from the abandoned bazaar, and mounted at least one fighting patrol every day for a period of six weeks. In only two of those patrols did The Argylls not end up in a gun battle.

3 Commando Brigade deployed with two of its commandos – 42 and 45 Commando. The latter mustered five companies but was actually more than 200 men short of the manpower generated by 2 PARA battlegroup, which it replaced, because of the withdrawal of an American unit and other commitments.[6] Whiskey Company initially deployed to FOB Jackson in Sangin; Yankee Company relieved FOB Inkerman; X-Ray Company eventually moved into the newly built FOB Nolay after FOB Robinson was abandoned; Zulu Company deployed north of Gereshk in FOB Gibraltar; and Victor Company guarded Kajaki Dam. In the case of 42 Commando, the unit was just over half strength (436 marines, rather than 800) due to a government financial cap, and it deployed as the theatre reserve in Kandahar.[7]

In addition to the Royal Marine commandos, the brigade was now supported by two army battalions and several sub-units. 1 Rifles under Lieutenant Colonel Joe Cavanagh was deployed to Sangin, the first of a succession of deployments of this regiment to the hostile town that would cost the Rifles so much blood. Of the four companies in this regiment, only E Company, however, was deployed to the district centre. With an expanded geographical presence inherited from 16 Air Assault Brigade, B Company was attached to the 1st The Queen's Dragoon Guards (QDG) battlegroup in Garmsir in the south; and A and Support Companies along with other elements were deployed to Nad-e Ali District, the new area of interest for the British. A Company was subsequently redeployed as an OMLT to Musa Qaleh, working under the 2 Royal Gurkha Rifles (2 RGR) battlegroup, sharing facilities with a US Marine Corps sub-unit that was engaged in mentoring the ANP. At the mid-point in the tour Support Company would swap with A Company, which would redeploy to Camp Shorabak.

2 RGR under Lieutenant Colonel Chris Darby was deployed to the Battlegroup North-West area of operations encompassing principally Musa Qaleh, but also Now Zad. The battlegroup was an eclectic mix of sub-units and nationalities all commanded by the battlegroup HQ based at the Musa Qaleh District Centre. In addition to B Company and the Gurkha reconnaissance group, the battlegroup was reinforced by a Warrior company group from 1 Princess of Wales's Royal Regiment (1 PWRR) and a Mastiff squadron crewed by the QDG. Artillery

support was provided by 29 Commando Regiment Royal Artillery. Engineer tasks, of which there would be several as the Gurkhas expanded the security cordon in Musa Qaleh, fell to 77 Squadron Royal Engineers. Musa Qaleh also hosted an entire ANA *kandak* as well as the company of ANP mentored by US Marines.

The remainder of 2 RGR were dispersed throughout Helmand. One company provided police mentoring in Lashkar Gah; a second supported the 1st QDG Battlegroup South; one platoon provided force protection for the Combat Logistic Patrols (CLPs); and a second platoon reinforced the Danish battlegroup in Nahr-e Saraj. This wide dispersion of soldiers from a single battalion was not unusual – indeed, very few commanding officers in Helmand ever enjoyed the privilege of commanding their battalions as a single unit. Most faced the inevitable break-up of their battalions into penny-packet company and platoon groups. This dispersion of forces inevitably carried a massive logistic bill: just two months into the tour, the brigade logistic regiment was forced to mount 11 CLPs. These were significant undertakings. A typical CLP comprised over 200 trucks and escorts and took 45 minutes to overtake. Each aimed to deliver around 3,000 tonnes of supplies, including 680,000 litres of fuel, to the matrix of FOBs and patrol bases.[8] Every three months 20,000 batteries were being consumed.[9] The bottled water demand was prodigious. On many levels, the biggest single endeavour of the dispersed British task force had simply become administering and feeding itself.

When Lieutenant Colonel Darby surveyed his new domain in Musa Qaleh, he found many reasons for dissatisfaction. The area of operations inherited by Battlegroup North-West was 'not secure'.[10] To the north of the district centre there was 'an obvious gap in the Patrol base ring'. This meant that there was 'an enduring direct fire threat to the DC; significant intimidation of Local Nationals in the Green Zone and Desert Compounds; and a durable and evolving IED threat'. To the south he faced a more 'traditional' front line, with a 'strong defensive belt' that had been established only half an hour's walk away from the centre of the town. This front line included 'bunkers and trench systems supported by IED concentrations and long-range heavy automatic weapon fire'. To consolidate the security bubble around Musa Qaleh, 2 RGR would have to expand that bubble north and south, forcing the Alizai insurgents further away from the town. Lieutenant Colonel Darby had insufficient forces to conduct a simultaneous operation on both sides of the town, so the decision was taken to conduct two separate and sequential operations, known as Operations *Mar Nonu 1* and *2*.

Darby's operational concerns were not the only problems that would beset the 2 RGR company at Musa Qaleh. Just living healthily at the district centre presented a challenge. By the end of the six months, the Gurkhas calculated they had spent 90 per cent of the tour living off rations. The British had still not found a way to get fresh food to one of their major flagship bases.

The aim of the first operation – *Mar Nonu 1* – was to push back the insurgents a further 3 kilometres south of Musa Qaleh, an area from which they were routinely attacking the patrol bases ringing the town. 'Route Pink', the main track leading south out of Musa Qaleh, which was heavily seeded with IEDs, would be cleared, as well as about 50 compounds, some of which were abandoned and known to harbour insurgents.

The operation was undertaken in the first week of November, led by B Company under Major Ross Daines. To achieve surprise, the company undertook a five-hour tactical march in darkness to reach the start lines on the east–west wadi that defines the southern edge of Musa Qaleh. Weighed down like pack mules with ammunition, the Gurkhas arrived at their battle positions damp with sweat despite the night chill. As daylight broke they could see the lines of compounds ahead of them, across perilously open corn fields broken by irrigation ditches. Even these fit mountain men were going to struggle to make good speed across this ground. To provide fire support for the infantrymen, a QDG squadron of Mastiffs had been manoeuvred to the north-west of the B Company start line. Following on behind was an ANA *kandak*, mentored by a 1 Rifles OMLT whose role would be to secure and search the compounds seized by the Gurkhas. The reserve, which would strike at depth positions, was provided by a Warrior company crewed by soldiers from B Company, 1 PWRR. At H-Hour the three platoons in B Company rose from their concealed positions and began the advance. Whether as a result of achieving surprise, or because the Taliban were gauging the British strength, very little resistance was experienced, and B Company reached its first phase line intact.

The lull proved deceptive. Second Lieutenant 'Oli' Cochrane was reorganizing his platoon in preparation for an advance to the second phase line when the soldiers came under accurate fire from a series of compounds to their west. In the confusion Rifleman Yubraj Rai was hit by small arms fire and fell, mortally wounded. To make matters worse, Cochrane had also been hit, but the rounds had been stopped by his radio, rendering it inoperable. The nearest soldier to Rai was Rifleman Dhan Gurung, who immediately went to his aid and frantically started trying to save his life, despite being under fire himself. Seeing that the casualty needed urgent evacuation, Lance Corporal Gajendra, closely followed by Rifleman Manju, sprinted 100 metres across the bullet-swept field to reach the stricken Rai. It was a scenario that would be played out countless times in Helmand as soldiers ignored personal safety in a bid to save the life of a comrade. With Rifleman Gurung providing covering fire, the three men struggled to carry Rai into dead ground – not an easy task, as the weight of a fully laden rifleman could easily exceed 15 stone. Their efforts were in vain. The round had missed the body armour and the wound was not survivable. The fallen Rai had a typical Gurkha background; he had been the main bread winner of the family supporting a mother, sister and three brothers on his rifleman's salary.

For the next six hours B Company found itself locked in fierce gun fights with insurgents fighting from concealed and prepared positions. Each compound had to be cleared individually and each carried the risk of an ambush or IED. With ammunition running low and with the gunmen giving little sign that they were yielding to the pressure, artillery fire was called on the suspected enemy positions, which was provided by 29 Commando Regiment. Apache helicopters were also tasked to snipe at insurgents careless enough to expose themselves to aerial observation.

By the late afternoon it was clear that the reserve had to be committed. Using 'Route Pink' as an axis of advance, the Warrior company joined the fray. The Taliban were normally wary of any armoured personnel carriers which they dubbed 'tanks', but in this case they stood their ground, perhaps confident that the combination of the difficult ground and threat of IEDs would keep the Warriors at bay. The soldiers from B Company, 1 PWRR cleared ten compounds, a task that took all night and was only finally completed at dawn the following day. Weapons, drugs and IEDs were all discovered in the now deserted compounds. Like a wartime scene, the Gurkhas were warmly greeted the following morning by American soldiers who had stuck it out in 'US PB' (a small patrol base used by the Green Berets) despite their isolated position.

In the commanding officer's words:

> The first MAR NONU operation sought to redefine a well established defensive line on our terms. The battle was fought over open farm land interspersed with groups of compounds and the insurgents had established defensive mine fields in support of well prepared defensive positions. These positions were linked to each other and to the rear by communications [sic] trenches, rat runs and kariz lines [underground aquifers], and the primary Command and Control location lay some 2km to the south and west across a wadi and well out of direct fire range. This complex terrain was further complicated by the presence of standing corn that provided cover from view and which we could not easily remove for fear of alienating those farmers that did remain.[11]

By a mixture of careful planning and determined execution, Operation *Mar Nonu 1* succeeded in pushing back the Taliban front line a further 3 kilometres, a significant advance in a war where advances were commonly measured in field lengths.

The plan for Operation *Mar Nonu 2* was significantly different from the first operation. In this case, it was decided that rather than advancing frontally against the Taliban, the key would be to unhinge the insurgent positions by threatening their rear. The Taliban stronghold in the village of Kats Sharbat provided the perfect target for this ruse.

The operation started with the deployment before dusk of the battlegroup tactical headquarters to the Roshan Tower overlooking the Green Zone north of the town. From this eyrie, Lieutenant Colonel Danby would be able to watch the battle unfold as well as coordinate fire support more effectively. Simultaneously, the Gurkha reconnaissance platoon mounted in Jackals married up with a half squadron of Mastiffs crewed by C Squadron, 1st QDG at an observation post called Himal, to the west of the town. This group would act as the deception force. At daybreak the following morning, the deception force advanced north-west along the Farhad Mandah, the major wadi west of the town.

As the deception group struggled up the rocky ridgeline overlooking Kats Sharbat, B Company set off under a waning moon towards the Taliban front line. The progress of B Company was observed by a pair of US Navy F-18s and by a Hermes 450 UAV flying at lower level. There was no Taliban sentry line – a serious mistake on the part of the insurgents – allowing the Gurkhas to make good progress undetected.

Further to the north, the crested vehicles of the deception group had their anticipated effect. Shortly after dawn ICOM intercepts revealed that the Taliban had spotted the British vehicles and that preparations were underway for a fight. This was confirmed by a mass exodus of women and children who headed west into the safety of the Green Zone. The British soldiers were amazed to see what appeared to be hundreds of civilians seemingly appear out of nowhere and then disappear again, all in a matter of 15 minutes. Very probably this was a rehearsed response by a civilian population that had suffered the experience of Russian vehicles overlooking the village from the very same positions the British now occupied. When it was judged that all the civilians had cleared the area, a large smoke and illumination barrage was ordered across the western edge of Kats Sharbat. The exploding shells caused no damage, but the smoke and incandescent flares falling on the ends of parachutes served to increase the confusion in the insurgents' minds. To reinforce the sense that the British were about to assault, several vehicles in the deception group made feinting movements, raising dust and making a lot of noise.

Almost three hours after daybreak, in Lieutenant Colonel Danby's words:

> B Coy 2 RGR had cleared up to its line of departure and without pause rolled through picking up an Afghan National Army company on its eastern flank. Together these sub-units pushed north through the fields, streams and desert compounds of the northern MSQ [Musa Qaleh Wadi] while around them nothing moved. There were no civilians in the fields, no children in the streets and no animals released to pasture. This continued throughout the day; an interesting development for an area that until the day before had either been subject to predictable civilian activity, or a significant number of large-scale small arms attacks.[12]

To the south, by mid-afternoon, B Company had seized the compound that would be used as the new patrol base. Not a single shot had been fired, vindicating the deception plan and infiltration. Indeed, the entire operation had met very little resistance. Over the next day, sappers set to work on building the patrol base, and 24 hours later PB Woqab was ready for occupation – an important consideration, as within 48 hours the new base began to receive incoming fire. For the rest of the month the new base was attacked every day.

For 2 RGR, as the commanding officer recorded in his blog, Operation *Mar Nonu 2* had been 'a complete success'. Crucially, Lieutenant Colonel Danby had made both his land grabs at the beginning of the battlegroup's six-month deployment. This meant that the Gurkhas could now switch their efforts to consolidating their gains, winning the trust of the locals that now fell within the enlarged security bubble, and interdicting insurgents attempting to penetrate the cordon. This cordon was further reinforced at the end of the tour, in March, by 8 (Alma) Commando Battery, which set up a 105mm light gun at the Roshan Tower. Within days of surveying this gun – nicknamed the 'Dragon' – it was in action firing in the direct fire role against insurgent gangs threatening Gurkha patrols. The surprise was considerable.

The commanding officer of 2 RGR judged the consolidation of the security bubble around Musa Qaleh fundamental to calming the situation in the town. The Gurkhas would only suffer one more fatality in their entire tour – a Colour Sergeant Krishnabahadur Dura, killed when the Warrior he was commanding struck an IED. The driver of the vehicle became a double amputee, and a female gunner officer riding in the back of the vehicle also suffered an amputation (the Gurkha – Kushal Limbu – would later make the news as the first double amputee to learn how to ride a specially converted 800cc Suzuki bike, apparently to his wife's displeasure).[13] Over the course of the six-month tour, 2 RGR was attacked 206 times, but crucially all the attacks were against the perimeter of the cordon.[14] There were no attacks at all against the district centre (although there was a successful suicide attack against the deputy police chief, possibly orchestrated by the police chief himself to get rid of the troublesome rival). The goal of creating a secure development zone appeared at last to have been achieved – at least in Musa Qaleh.

Whereas in 2006 the elders had viewed the arrival of the British with some suspicion and then despair, they now saw the foreigners as allies against the far worse threat of freebooting drug barons, assorted criminals and gun-toting Taliban. This switch of allegiance was the very trick the British were trying to pull off everywhere in Helmand. That it happened in Musa Qaleh in the winter of 2008 must be credited to the intelligent leadership displayed by Lieutenant Colonel Danby, and to the patient soldiering of his men. But it was also a success borne from continuity of purpose. The foundations had been laid by Brigadier Mackay in the previous winter. These foundations had been cemented by The Argyll and Sutherland Highlanders (5 SCOTS) during the summer, and the edifice had finally been completed by the Gurkhas.

This was the upbeat picture 2 RGR would present of their tour, but it could not hide some less palatable facts. Local acceptance of the British was fragile and based on an understanding – never stated but always implicit – that the foreigners would not interfere with the poppy crop or raid drug laboratories. The Gurkhas never did. In effect, the British in Musa Qaleh acted as a guarantor of the peace for all the vested interests in the narcotics trade. And just beyond the weapon ranges of the ring of patrol bases was an entrenched enemy. 2 Royal Regiment of Fusiliers would take over from the Gurkhas and suffer seven fatalities, with many more seriously wounded. Musa Qaleh town was secured, but Musa Qaleh District remained at war.

1 Rifles, the second infantry battlegroup in 3 Commando Brigade, experienced a much less focused tour compared to the Gurkhas in the north. Led by Lieutenant Colonel Joe Cavanagh but without the responsibility for a discreet geographical area, the battlegroup was frequently used to make up numbers for other units' operations. Many of these operations were piecemeal and anti-climactic.

The disparate operations, nonetheless, caused attrition in the ranks of 1 Rifles. In the week before Christmas, a 21-year-old Australian named Stuart Nash, who had only served in the British Army for nine months, was shot and killed. The New Year then started badly for the battlegroup with the death of Serjeant* Chris Reed, killed on New Year's Day. Reed was a Territorial Army soldier who worked in a firm building luxury yachts in Plymouth. He had already completed a tour with the regiment in Iraq and this was his second operational tour. On the day he left for Afghanistan, he became engaged to his fiancée, a local girl called Heather. The amount of mail ('blueys', from the colour of the paper) that passed between the couple amazed his fellow riflemen. The last set never reached Garmsir where he was based and would remain unread. Two more NCOs were subsequently killed that month, one in Sangin and a second in Musa Qaleh. Then on 25 February a convoy travelling near Gereshk struck a large IED. Three riflemen died. One of the soldiers, Lance Corporal Paul

*In the Rifles, 'sergeant' is spelt 'serjeant'.

Upton, had left the army several years previously and had only re-enlisted just in time to join the battalion on its tour of Helmand.

3 Commando Brigade, as we have seen, deployed with two of its commandos: 45 Commando led by Lieutenant Colonel Jim Morris, and 42 Commando led by Lieutenant Colonel Charlie Stickland. The two units had quite different tours. The former was committed to the static, defensive holding role in Battlegroup North-West, and the latter was deployed as the mobile reserve for Regional Command South-West. The difference between the two tasks was stark. Charlie Stickland would enthuse about his war in a manner that Jim Morris could not share. Where 42 Commando found itself undertaking classic Royal Marine operations, 45 Commando became mired in the slog of attrition warfare in the Green Zone. Over the course of their difficult tour there was a 94 per cent increase in the number of IED finds in Sangin, and the number of gun fights shot up by a fifth.[15] Some 131 devices were found, and Whiskey Company suffered 36 IED strikes. Sangin's awful reputation was becoming well established.

The marines had started tentatively, and it was not until the second week of November that they experienced their first fatalities when a vehicle from the BRF ran over an IED, killing two experienced crewmen, Marines Neil Dunstan and Robert McKibben. The third marine in the vehicle was severely injured. The Royal Marines commonly liked to think of themselves as 'thinking soldiers'. These two men certainly offered an example of this rule: both were university graduates, which would have been highly unusual in an army unit. McKibben, from County Mayo, had followed in the footsteps of tens of thousands of Irishmen in the service of the British Crown.

The vehicle in which they had been travelling – the Jackal – was originally procured by 22 SAS as a replacement for the long-serving Land Rover. It then migrated to the wider army when the utility of this vehicle for reconnaissance became evident. The open-top Jackal was popular – robust, with good visibility and capable of negotiating difficult terrain. It suffered, however, from an unanticipated fatal design flaw. Both commander and driver sat directly over the front wheel arches, the most vulnerable points if a vehicle ran over an IED. Despite the V-shaped bottom, only so much blast could be deflected. An impressive amount of science was thrown at the problem and improvements were made, in particular to the two front seats, to mitigate the effects of a high-explosive detonation. Lives were saved by these improvements, but the vehicle remained vulnerable. The only design that protected the occupants of a vehicle from the effects of an IED was the standard American design that placed the engine block and wheel arches well forward of the two front crewmen. The number of soldiers and marines killed and injured in this vehicle would exceed the casualty rates suffered in the much-criticized Land Rover Snatch, but somehow the media, fixated by the festering Snatch story, missed the sequel.* The father of one of the victims did not miss this pattern. Under a Freedom of Information Act request, the bereaved father collated data on Jackal fatalities and conclusively demonstrated its vulnerability. This protest fell flat, as much as anything it seemed, because the Jackal was the only British designed and built vehicle in the fleet. Jobs in southern England seemed to carry some weight when determining the worth of vehicles. Indeed, the Jackal would be migrated into the post-Helmand army, despite its vulnerability.

This setback and three more fatalities suffered in November were eclipsed by an event in Sangin which angered the brigade. On 12 November a QRF from X-Ray Company set out from the Sangin District Centre in support of an ongoing operation. As the small force paused on Route 611, south of the district centre, a 13-year-old boy pushing a barrow approached the marines. Seconds later the barrow detonated, killing the boy along with Sergeant John Manuel, Corporal Marc Birch and Marine Damian Davies. Davies left behind a young family and an unborn child. Birch, his friend, had the unusual distinction of being the only marine to have scored a goal against an international football team – in his case, the Sierra Leone national squad. The suicide attack that left three commandos dead caused great shock on a day when the brigade had already suffered a fatality after another Jackal drove over an IED, killing the commander, Lance Corporal Steven Fellows. It seemed particularly low that the Taliban should be using a young boy as the vehicle for a suicide attack. Despite this second setback, the pace of operations continued without interruption. Five more marines and soldiers were killed before the end of the year, including one poignantly killed on Christmas Eve and a second killed on New Year's Eve.

*This author had cause to visit the depot at MOD Ashchurch where casualty vehicles were stored in Britain. From examination of the Jackal commander and driver stations it was plain what was happening when a crew drove over an IED. The state of the flat-bottomed Vikings was also sobering. Both vehicles have been retained post-conflict despite their inherent danger to troops.

Some operations conducted over this period had a certain novelty. It was a remarkable fact that almost three years elapsed between the deployment of a British task force to Helmand Province and the first significant counter-narcotics raid by that force (Operations *Mar Kheshta* and *Ghartse Dagger* had been more modest affairs). The belatedness seemed to mirror the general sluggishness of the British response to a war that had begun to slip out of control. Ironically, it was Brigadier Messenger's marines – the commander who had vowed that British troops would not become involved in counter-narcotics – who launched this first major raid.

Operation *Diesel* took weeks to plan and was mounted in the first and second weeks of February. The mission unfolded in cold but sunny conditions, against a ring of drug laboratories in the Alikozai and Alizai tribal lands of Sapwan Qala, in the Upper Sangin Valley. This was the same area that had been visited just 11 months previously by 40 Commando during Operation *Ghartse Dagger*. A total of 700 men took part, making it one of the largest operations mounted by the commandos during their tour. The entire operation was led by Lieutenant Colonel Jim Morris, the commanding officer of 45 Commando. The strike force comprised companies from 42 and 45 Commandos, supported by an armoured infantry company from 1 PWRR mounted in Warriors. Reconnaissance and cut-off forces were provided by the BRF, the reconnaissance platoon of 1 PWRR. A British special forces element and the American Task Force 31 also took part. The Afghan Army provided an ANA company and Combined Force 333, a counter-narcotics team.[16]

In total, the operation would last two days, during which time there were intermittent gun battles with local villagers, narcotics dealers and insurgents vainly trying to distract and harass the troops. The sheer amount of firepower mustered for Operation *Diesel* ensured that any attempts to disrupt the raid would fail. The marines reckoned that between 20 and 30 insurgents were killed, mainly by circling Apache helicopters that were quick to detect any incursions on the security cordons established by the ground forces.

The haul from the raid was certainly impressive. Destroyed precursor chemicals included 5,000 kilograms of ammonium chloride, 1,025 kilograms of acetic anhydride, 300 kilograms of calcium hydroxide and 1,000 kilograms of salt. Around 1,295 kilograms of wet opium were seized, creating a headline figure for the British media of opium seized worth

£50 million. This exaggerated figure somewhat distracted from the real cost of the haul to the Taliban – a far smaller figure, and the cost that really mattered. The seizure represented less than one six-thousandth of the total opium production in Afghanistan from the previous planting season.

While 45 Commando slugged it out in the Green Zone, Charlie Stickland's commando struck right across the geographical span of Regional Command South. By the end of the six months this battalion conducted almost 20 air assault missions, ten company operations and 30 odd tasks involving road moves, a truly impressive tempo of operations. These operations lasted from 36 hours to one month in duration, and by the end of the tour the commandos reckoned that they had conservatively accounted for about 150 insurgents. The marines uncovered about 2 tonnes of explosives and over 180 IEDs hidden in caches, as good a haul as any unit would manage.

All these operations were a prelude to what would be the main effort for 3 Commando Brigade on Operation *Herrick 9*: wresting Nad-e Ali District back into government hands. The situation in Nad-e Ali in the winter of 2008 was complex, contradictory and, in the long term, intolerable to the provincial government in Lashkar Gah. All that separated Lashkar Gah from Nad-e Ali District was a stretch of the Helmand River and Bolan Bridge. Governor Mangal's writ really only extended as far as the last grubby police post on the western end of the bridge. Beyond that, powerful landowners, narcotics traffickers and freelancing insurgent gangs were the real powerbrokers. As Michael Martin's outstanding study *War on its Head* has argued: 'Apart from the Taliban-era, there were no centrally appointed, non-indigenous, non-mujahidin officials in Nad-e Ali between Habibullah leaving in 1990 as Chief of Police and returning in 2008 with the support of the British as District Governor.'[17] Instead, there were over 20 competing tribal groups compressed in Nad-e Ali and a large annual poppy harvest that meant the district was highly valued by the insurgency as a source of funds. Alongside Marjah and Nawa-e Barakzai districts, Nad-e Ali encompassed some of the richest agricultural lands in Helmand. It had also become a place where former officials with grudges against the new order had retired to their estates, stirring trouble. In the late summer of 2008, as we have seen, this antagonism appeared to erupt in a march on the capital by a large number of insurgents. The march fizzled out, but the governor was alarmed enough to determine that the barbarians on the other side of the river had to be dealt with once and for all.

Nad-e Ali District had a broader significance to the British. This was the original Afghan Development Zone that had been proposed in the 2006 Helmand Plan and which had been completely ignored as the British task force found itself dragged away from the provincial capital to far-flung outposts of the province. The majority of Helmand's population lived in this central area. The British would now attempt to impose order in Nad-e Ali, almost three years later, but the prize, if they succeeded, would be great. The war was never going to be won in towns like Sangin. In Nad-e Ali the British had some hope of demonstrating success and withdrawing, eventually, with dignity.

Operation *Sond Chara* ('Red Dagger', after the commando insignia) was the largest operation of the tour and it coincided with appalling winter weather. Tracks became rutted, ditches burst their banks and fields became flooded. For many of the marines who took part in the operation, the mud and cold became the chief enemy. For their commander, Brigadier Messenger, the principal challenge was numerical. Nad-e Ali District roughly encompassed an area of 200 square kilometres. The three battlegroups under his immediate command – 45 Commando, 2 RGR and 1 Rifles – were all committed to holding a string of FOBs and patrol bases across the province. This meant that Messenger only had the theatre reserve, 42 Commando, at his disposal to support the newly created Battlegroup Centre South, commanded by Colonel Martin Smith. This force would only be able to concentrate in a limited geographical area, and, crucially, would not be able to remain behind to hold any ground cleared of insurgents. If the strategy was clear-hold-build, then the brigade would only be solving the first part of the formula, for a period of two weeks, and in a small number of areas.

This, in effect, is what transpired. Every village the marines tackled had to be revisited again by successor units within months: Khowshal Kalay in April (Operation *Tor Paraang*), which led to the building of CPs Paraang and Haji Alem; Zarghun Kalay in June (Operation *Tor Had Jaar*), which was consolidated with PB Khuday Noor; Gorup-e Shesh Kalay ('Group Six Village') in August, which was secured with PB Shamal Storrai; and Shin Kalay in November (Operation *Tor Sara*), which resulted in the construction of several more checkpoints. In 2010, the Grenadier Guards would find themselves repeating the whole process once again. They would be followed by the kingsmen from the Duke of Lancaster's Regiment, and it was not until the completion of the Royal Irish tour in the spring of 2011 that the areas visited by the marines could finally be judged to be relatively secure. Two years later, a village like Zarghun Kalay, which featured prominently in *Sond Chara*, would still be proving troublesome in an area known as the 'Red Wedge'. Operation *Sond Chara* was only ever going to be the start of a very long game. The subsequent brigade would have to begin exploiting any successes gained by the marines when it arrived in the spring. Without a well-resourced reconstruction plan in place to follow the marines, Operation *Sond Chara* represented the last time the British 'mowed the lawn'.

3 Commando Brigade naturally promoted Operation *Sond Chara*, but in truth it was both an unrealistic and over-ambitious mission. A measure of the unrealism was the fact that the brigade HQ was already planning the second phase – Operation *Sond Chara 2* – which would have seen the marines assaulting villages in neighbouring Babaji District. *Sond Chara 2* eventually became the genesis of Operation *Panchai Palang* ('Panther's Claw') executed by 19 Light Brigade in the summer.[18]

Because Operation *Sond Chara* was intended as the centrepiece of the tour, Messenger was able to scrape soldiers from other parts of the brigade, as well as from allies, eventually mustering a 1,500-strong force. In addition to 42 Commando, British units involved included B Company, 1 Rifles; C Company, 2 PWRR; a reinforced A Squadron QDG; and elements from 29 Commando Royal Artillery and 24 Commando Engineer Regiment. The Danish Jutland Dragoons Regiment provided a mechanized company, additional engineers and a troop of Leopard tanks. An Estonian mechanized company, mortar platoon and ANA *kandak* also joined the operation. Special force elements were provided by the American Task Force 71. The use of main battle tanks on Operation *Sond Chara* meant that the Royal Marines became the first British contingent to use these powerful platforms to support an operation. The Taliban feared tanks, perhaps from mujahidin memories of a Soviet tank regiment that swept through Nad-e Ali in 1983, blasting their positions with impunity. The British never demonstrated the will or desire to overcome the logistic difficulties of deploying a tank troop to Helmand. Cost constraints also played a part in the usual way.

H-Hour for the main phase of Operation *Sond Chara* was set at 1900hrs on the night of 11 December.[19] Kilo Company was lifted by helicopter to a point in the desert immediately west of Khowshal Kalay codenamed Barbarian, which would become the location of PB 1.

The idea seems to have been to create an anchor at this point to secure an 8-kilometre levee track that paralleled the Trik Zabur Canal south-east to a second major crossroads. This was where the BRF that had been hiding in the desert would establish PB 9, also known as Stella. The levee track, nicknamed Route Somerset, would act as the supply route between the two patrol bases. The crossroads, known as Five-Ways Junction, would become a key disputed node in Operation *Moshtarak* 12 months later in the winter of 2010.

Both Kilo Company and the BRF immediately met significant resistance. It was clear villagers at Khowshal Kalay and Five-Ways Junction were extremely hostile to the presence of ISAF. Despite this reception, Lima Company, supported by sappers from 24 Commando Engineer Regiment, and with a gun troop from 29 Commando Regiment in tow, then proceeded down Route Somerset to set up a third patrol base and gun line. With all three sub-units in place, it was judged that phase one had been successfully completed.

This proved wishful thinking. The heavens opened, making resupply difficult. Besieged by increasingly accurate fire, the marines responded with even greater amounts of firepower. The stalemate continued for a matter of days before the marines were pulled out to support subsequent phases of the operation. Route Somerset would become one of the most heavily seeded tracks with IEDs in Nad-e Ali, and PB 1 would be abandoned (later re-established as PB Silab). In the case of PB 9 (Stella), no British unit would ever reach that far south again, a measure of the over-ambition of *Sond Chara*. Eventually, a USMC detachment would establish a security post at this important junction and rename it PB Reilly.

The key objective of Operation *Sond Chara* was Nad-e Ali itself, the settlement that gave its name to the district, and the location where The Argylls and latterly Juliet Company had set up a patrol base. This was the objective for the second phase of the operation.

Nad-e Ali was the site of an old fort which the British had reputedly once invested. The fort itself pre-dated the Anglo-Afghan Wars and was now in a completely derelict state, with only two turrets and its walls standing. The central courtyard, a flat dust bowl, was the size of a large football pitch. This was what the British were after. Nad-e Ali offered the ideal location for a substantial base in the centre of this lawless district. Once established, this base could act as a mother ship for an expanding matrix of patrol bases across the district. American engineers that worked on the canal projects in the 1950s had similarly based themselves here in what was then known as 'Fort Nad-i-ali', before moving to the expanding Lashkar Gah. Aside from the fort, Nad-e Ali was also important because it was a focal point for trading in the local area. Over decades, perhaps originally encouraged by the presence of a garrison, a cruciform of bazaars had grown alongside the fort. These shops sprawled for several hundred metres along the four points of the compass. The only other buildings of note were the disused school (PB Argyll); and a handful of prefabricated buildings on the southern edge of the fort, which the marines would later rename Minerva Lines. The silhouette of two Roshan towers in the centre of the settlement fixed it on the skyline for miles around.

The plan for the investment of Nad-e Ali was described by Lieutenant Colonel Stickland in these words. 'We assaulted at night,' he wrote, 'K Company went to an area of compounds ... then we pushed Lima Company some 6 km to the south east to act as a block to cut off the routes from the South. Simultaneous with that we moved our Commando Recce Force in from the eastern side again to seize another area [on] a main dominating route.'[20]

The nighttime assault came as a complete surprise, and without an insurgent presence in the bazaar area itself Kilo Company was able to quickly establish a patrol base with little interference. As in previous operations of this type, the insertion and initial lodgement were the least difficult tasks. Once the local villagers had sized up the marines in their midst, 'fierce fighting ensued'.[21] These over-excited attempts to dislodge the marines were easily repulsed. Many of the gunmen firing on the marines were very probably just local farmers reacting reflexively to the arrival of Western soldiers in their fields. Over the next 12 months, Nad-e Ali would settle down again, and much like Musa Qaleh, re-establish itself as a narcotics trading hub, but under the protection of the British. For the stall holders, it little mattered who was in charge as long as they were allowed to pursue their lucrative business.

As the immediate environs of Nad-e Ali were being secured, Juliet Company, supported by C Company, 2 PWRR and an Afghan platoon, advanced on the village of Shin Kalay, which lay just 2 kilometres east of Nad-e Ali. The shortest resupply route from Camp Bastion to Nad-e Ali lay through Shin Kalay. This village of around 100 compounds illustrated some of the contradictions the British would be facing in Nad-e Ali District. It was entirely populated by Kharotei who ran their own village militia, not to protect themselves against the Taliban who respected and generally avoided their lands, but to ward off the rapacious Noorzai policemen. To complicate the picture, there were significant local rivalries within the community, and good evidence that the ISI (Pakistani secret services), or proxies, had destroyed the school in the settlement.[22] The approaching marines were predictably met by hails of gunfire, and Juliet Company responded heavy-handedly by calling in support from Apaches, Cobras and F-16s. After about two hours of fruitless exchanges of fire, the fighting suddenly stopped and the marines found themselves being welcomed into the village – as long as they kept the Afghan police out, a promise they could not reasonably keep. 'Green flags of celebration were seen flying over residential compound,' it was reported, and the white flags of the Taliban disappeared.[23]

At this stage of Operation *Sond Chara* the marines basically had a toehold in Nad-e Ali and a second further south. Messenger knew he had to maintain momentum and push on to the next objective. To this end, 42 Commando regrouped and were joined by the Estonian mechanized company for the next phase of the operation – the clearance of Zarghun Kalay ('Green Village'), a village 4 kilometres to the north-west of Nad-e Ali. This operation was again commanded by Colonel Martin Smith, leaving Stickland to consolidate his gains in central Nad-e Ali.

Zarghun Kalay, from the air, was a model American-built village. Perfectly square and laid out within a 1-kilometre grid pattern, the carefully ordered tidiness had since become compromised by Afghan indifference to the right angle, but it still looked quite unlike most other Afghan villages. During the Soviet–Afghan War this settlement had suffered extensive damage. Memories of the fighting were long and foreign soldiers were not welcome. Ironically, because of the resistance put up by the village, the marines were forced to indulge in a little destruction themselves, adding to the prejudice against foreigners.

Zarghun Kalay differed from typical Afghan villages in another important way – the land had been distributed equally among almost 20 different tribes, which left the village without an obvious leader, a vacuum that the Taliban filled. Intelligence suggested that insurgents were now camped in strength at Zarghun Kalay, and they were supported by foreign fighters. According to Michael Martin, a call went out for defenders across Nad-e Ali. This received a good response: as many as 11 known commanders pitched up with their men.[24] The entire operation, therefore, was conducted much like an old-fashioned village assault a wartime veteran might have recognized. The last significant feature of Zarghun Kalay was that it sat in the middle of an expanse of flat, open fields. At the height of winter, the cover offered by the few hedgerows and tree lines that delineated field boundaries was poor. The advancing marines would be very exposed.

The plan for assaulting Zarghun Kalay effectively involved surrounding the village from three sides. The Estonian mechanized company would bypass north to a settlement named Chah-e Anjir Kalay ('Fig Tree Well'). This was a key village astride a wadi at the base of the block of land known as the 'Chah-e Anjir Triangle' or CAT. The PWRR reconnaissance platoon mounted in Scimitars would feint north to Chah-e Mirza ('Mirza's Well') and then swing right to support the assault from the west. Juliet Company would secure a start line about 2 kilometres south of the village in the vicinity of Luy Bagh. Finally, Lima Company, which had marched all the way from Route Somerset in the south, would pass through Juliet Company and attack on an axis south to north.[25]

The assault on Zarghun Kalay began on the morning of 17 December in a tremendous downpour of rain. It did not stop raining for the next three days – the time it took to secure the village and the surrounding area. As one gunner who took part in the operation wrote: 'we were up to our ankles in muddy water … with the rain bouncing off our faces'.[26] This had a deleterious effect on any airborne sensors, whether a UAV or a pilot's targeting pod, but it also had a terrible effect on ground systems, in particular the Bowman radios, which were prone to failure in the heavy rain. Vehicle-mounted radios were especially vulnerable as water entered vital electronic components. In the face of these appalling conditions, the battle to clear the village was described as 'gritty', and it 'saw the fiercest and most sustained fighting of the operation, taking two days to break into the town'.[27]

In the end, aerial pummelling by American Cobras and British Apaches proved decisive. By now Smith had surrounded the village on three flanks, leaving only the northern side open. This was the route the insurgents chose to make good their getaway. It took a further 24 hours for the village to be secured, compound by compound, and no bodies were found. On 19 December, a village *shura* was convened attended by over 200 local men. Governor Habibullah and Colonel Allawullah, the Afghan *kandak* commander, presented the Afghan face at the meeting. Smith attended but remained in the background. The *shura* was almost certainly attended by some of the fighters, curious to see their recent enemy. Like the villagers at Shin Kalay, this was another community that initially appeared to need little persuasion to switch to the government side. A patrol base would be built on a crossroads north of Zarghun Kalay (PB Khuday Noor), but Zarghun Kalay would then lapse back into the hands of the insurgency, especially in the area west of the village.

The next objective lay 3 kilometres further north in the sprawling settlement of Chah-e Anjir. This was really two settlements separated by a ford that crossed an east–west running wadi. The Shamalan Canal ('North Wind Canal'), an important waterway that defined the border between Nad-e Ali and Babaji districts ran just east of Chah-e Anjir, eventually joining the River Helmand further downstream on a prominent bend. The ground here was quite different from central Nad-e Ali, being more broken and with many uncultivated patches. To the west of the town was an area of derelict factories and run-down modern buildings which the British would grab and transform into PB Shahzad ('Prince'). This was where the Helmand Construction Corporation had once based itself, providing local employment to the area. The Russians occupied the very same spot, and just north of the abandoned industrial site was a large graveyard of vehicles, including military vehicles. The 'tank park', as it became known, was a salutary reminder of the fate of the last foreign army that tried its luck in northern Nad-e Ali, a fate the British were keen to avoid. Chah-e Anjir was a fault line of tribal enmities. The dominant Noorzai were hated by the Kharotei, and this encouraged the latter to join the insurgency. The Kharotei in turn were hated by the Popalzai, who bore an ancient grudge against the former, and this encouraged the Popalzai to become insurgents. The British were now about to become yet another party to this feuding.

The assault on Chah-e Anjir began in the early hours of Christmas morning, an awkward emotional moment for the troops who knew that elsewhere in Helmand their fellow marines and soldiers would be suspending operations – albeit briefly – to celebrate the festivities. Accurate intelligence had identified an insurgent compound, and this was quickly occupied. Finds included drugs, bomb-making kits and weapons. After an 'initially fierce break-in battle', the insurgents packed in the fight and dispersed from the area.[28] Unbeknown to the marines, the lack of resistance may have been largely attributable to a complex web of family relations in Chah-e Anjir that kept the 'Taliban' out of the settlement, and as importantly, maintained a monopoly over the drugs bazaar.[29]

Whatever its faults, Operation *Sond Chara* had been a testament to the endurance of the marines and soldiers who took part in the operation. The weather had been appalling. Lima Company reportedly marched 60 kilometres over the course of the two weeks, recalling the more famous yomps of the Falklands Conflict.[30] The meticulous sequencing of the operation across such a large block of Green Zone had resembled a complicated chess game.

Most strikingly – and in contrast to the later Operation *Panchai Palang* conducted by 19 Light Brigade in Babaji District – the marines set about their task with tremendous tempo. No other British brigade would cover so much ground so quickly in the entire war. This was partly attributable to the lack of IEDs. Just 11 were found. It was never clear, however, whether this reflected a lack of insurgent bomb-making skills in Nad-e Ali, or whether the speed of operations and the switches in direction and effort meant that insurgent gangs were never able to successfully target the marines. The latter explanation is not implausible – once the troops became static in the patrol bases in Nad-e Ali, they were quickly surrounded by IED fields. Speed and mobility had been the keys to the tactical success of the operation.

Colonel Martin Smith was being overly optimistic when he commented at the conclusion of the operation that 'peace is returning to the heart of the district'.[31] More realistically, he did concede that permanent security would require more effort, an effort beyond his battlegroup. Satisfactory security would only truly begin to be established 18 months later, when the British area of operations was effectively reduced to Nad-e Ali and the adjoining Babaji District. A Military Stabilization and Support Team (MSST) was despatched to the area, but without a credible reconstruction plan to follow on the military operation, this represented a token gesture. Although Operation *Sond Chara* was only a beginning, the British enjoyed a crucial trump card that would help every succeeding brigade deployed to Nad-e Ali. To date the British had had awful luck with the district governors who as a class had proved to be a gang of corrupt incompetents. Governor Habibullah, an ex-Communist-era police chief, was the exception that proved the rule. Industrious and relatively honest, he was the perfect ally. When a Guards battalion assumed control of the area the following spring, they cultivated him with the customary social charm of the Guards. Habibullah was nobody's fool (and his record as the former police chief of Gereshk was dubious), but a little grace and courtesy certainly helped to oil the relationship. Crucially, Habibullah knew many of the Taliban commanders personally and was able to use his influence on these personalities to maintain a relative peace. In other words, he was at district level what Sher Akhundzada had been at provincial level, if the Foreign Office and SIS had not foolishly conspired to remove him in 2005, thus eliminating the one person who could have helped the British in Helmand.

The successful conclusion of Operation *Sond Chara* came with a cost. Lance Corporal Ben Whatley was killed on Christmas Eve in the battle for Zarghun Kalay. This had been his second tour of Afghanistan. Marines Georgie Evans and Tony Sparks had earlier been killed when they were struck by an RPG on a rooftop. Sparks was a teenager who had only passed out of basic training the previous July. Corporal Robert Deering was killed rushing to save colleagues in a Viking personnel carrier that had struck an IED. He stepped on a second IED, a common occurrence in incidents of this type. Deering had already served in Iraq and Afghanistan on previous tours. Rifleman Nash, a 21-year-old mechanical engineer from Sydney who joined the British Army for adventure, was shot and killed, also at Zarghun Kalay. Enemy losses were uncertain, but the marines estimated that perhaps as many as 30 insurgents were killed.

The close and treacherous nature of the fighting in the Green Zone continued to inspire acts of great bravery. On 9 February, Lance Corporal Matthew Croucher – a reservist – found himself undertaking a compound search with the BRF. As he led the way through a darkened room, he set off a tripwire. Looking down, he caught sight of a live grenade at his feet. In his own words, he 'felt a bit guilty for setting the device off', and took the decision to lie backwards on the grenade to protect his comrades. His backpack and body armour took the force of the blast and he miraculously escaped without serious injury.[32] The ruptured backpack was eventually retired to the Imperial War Museum. Croucher collected a George Cross for this act of selflessness.

For 42 Commando, Operation *Sond Chara* was barely concluded when the unit was called forward again to take part in a combined operation in the Kandahar area. Operation *Shahi Tandar* ('Royal Storm') took place in miserable weather north of Kandahar on 7–9 January. Smaller operations followed, but these were all a prelude to the last big push which 3 Commando Brigade would make before handing over to the successor brigade. For this last phase, the attention of the marines turned southward again.

Southern Helmand seemed to hold a fascination for the commandos. No other units would spend as much time in Reg and Dishu districts, or drive as many miles over this largely uninhabited area. British maps ran out before the Pakistan border (incidentally scotching conspiracy theories that the British were conducting covert cross-border raids). The entire area was a lawless smugglers' paradise and major transit point for the narcotics trade, most notably at Bahram Chah, where opium was traded openly. The end-of-the world feeling of this desolate border area was magnified by the extreme poverty of its inhabitants. There were no schools, clinics or roads anywhere south of the Helmand River. Electricity was non-existent. The mostly Baluchi and Achakzai population lived a marginal existence in every sense of the word, and a majority would have been quite content for the war to pass them by like a sandstorm on the horizon. The Kuchi nomads that criss-crossed the ill-defined border area remained oblivious to the modern world and observed British patrols with the indifference of a people that had witnessed many comings and goings in the past.

ISAF would also have probably preferred to ignore this area altogether except that it represented a major transit route for the insurgency. The Green Zone of Darvishan – the only major town in the south – had been mainly populated by Ishaqzai. South of this tribal group, Alizai settlements had grown on the bend of the Helmand River. A string of Noorzai and more Ishaqzai villages followed the course of the river to its final destination in the Sistani marshlands. All these communities had links with fellow tribesmen in Taliban strongholds like Sangin. The Noorzai were heavily represented in the ANP, driven by poverty to become policemen rather than by notions of serving the community. They brought with them clannish ways and a corrupt accommodation with fellow Noorzai who had opted to join the insurgency instead to make a living. The border police were evenly split between Noorzai and Achakzai. To avoid drug disputes, police operations were run on tribal lines, each leaning favourably towards their own kinsmen. The British did not have the strength to secure southern Helmand, but neither was Messenger prepared simply to ignore this southern flank. Some of the marines' most daring raids had been conducted south of Darvishan in the winter of 2006–07. This would be the last fling before the British abandoned the area and handed it over to US Marines in the summer.

Southern Helmand was the responsibility of the 1st QDG battlegroup, led by Lieutenant Colonel Alan Richmond. The task facing this commanding officer was quite beyond his resources. The battlegroup comprised two infantry companies – both of which were needed to hold Darvishan and the surrounding satellite patrol bases – one formation reconnaissance squadron, and half a dozen Mastiffs. On any given day Richmond had fewer than 20 'runners' or serviceable vehicles to patrol an area of more than 15,000 square kilometres (an area roughly the size of the Scottish Highlands). Because this battlegroup was not considered the main British effort, Richmond had no mortars (a boon for the Taliban, who could mortar at will without fear of retaliation), and the cavalrymen were at the bottom of the pile when bidding for scarce helicopters. The best Richmond could do was to secure Darvishan – which his soldiers managed after a fashion; gun battles declined from one a day to one every three days – and prevent Taliban infiltration up the 'Snakes Head', the meander of the river south of Darvishan. The pity was that a genuine local desire to see off the Taliban, or at least end the fighting, seemed to exist in the area. A *shura* organized at the beginning of the tour attracted 1,200 locals clamouring for security and development. The British could only placate, make promises and wait for the US Marines to arrive. To take the fight to the insurgents would have required the deployment of a second full infantry battalion, which the British did not have.

Nevertheless, the south could not be ignored. On 2 February, 42 Commando began what would be a month-long series of operations codenamed *Aabi Toorah* ('Blue Sword'). These were really a series of sequenced missions. The overall aim of the *Aabi Toorah* operations was information-gathering. At the time, what the British knew about these areas could be summarized in a single thin brief. Staying in the field for a month demanded endurance and severely stretched the resources of the Joint Helicopter Force. By the end of the operation almost 70 tonnes of supplies were either heli-lifted or air-dropped to the marines from RAF C-130s. This was true expeditionary warfare. To alleviate the problem of resupply and to provide additional firepower, 42 Commando split into two groupings: a Manoeuvre Operations Group, or MOG, that included Viking, Jackals and resupply trucks; and a heliborne element that secured areas ahead of the MOG.

The insertion into the Fish Hook proceeded without incident. The MOG drove the 100 kilometres south from Camp Bastion and pre-positioned itself in the desert west of the Green Zone. With this force in place, 300 marines and an ANA company were dropped by Chinook in the vicinity of a village called Divalak, on the banks of the Helmand River. At this point in the course of the river, the Green Zone was barely 1 kilometre wide and much of the land was uncultivated scrub. There were a number of 'significant contacts' with local tribesmen but little sign of Taliban strongholds.[33] Impromptu *shuras* were held, but it is difficult to believe the marines were met with anything less than scepticism, if not outright puzzlement. There was no concentration of Taliban in this area (two years later, following a successful special forces operation against Bahram Chah which left over 50 insurgents dead including foreign fighters, the bazaar at Safar on the Fish Hook would become a major transit point). The main Taliban enclave was 20 kilometres to the west, in a settlement called Khan Neshin.

Khan Neshin had once been a military garrison, established by a forgotten potentate on a strategic fording point on the Helmand River. A village had grown to the north-west of the fort – Zaman Khan Kalay – and a second fort, Kala Shureh, stood 3 kilometres to the west. These medieval forts were now in ruins, and indeed the entire area was littered with abandoned compounds that were slowly being reclaimed by the elements, all of which created a perfect stronghold for narco-traffickers and insurgents alike. Among these were Pakistani foreign fighters. From a distance there was almost a romantic appeal to Khan Neshin, with its once proud ramparts defining the horizon and with the U-bend of the river as a backdrop. Closer inspection revealed dilapidation, decay and scores of ditches, which the marines would have to negotiate on foot to reach their objective.

One week after arriving in the area – on 29 February – the combined force gathered to the north-west of the town in preparation for the assault. Intelligence had suggested Khan Neshin was a 'hotbed of Taliban activity', and so it proved. Lima Company was transported by Vikings in darkness to the start lines and then completed a 6-kilometre approach march across very difficult ground broken by numerous deep ditches. The BRF, mounted on Jackals, covered their approach from a western flank. Kilo Company was inserted by helicopter south-west of their objectives. At dawn, Lima Company advanced cautiously into the settlement, which appeared deserted. This proved to be a lull before the storm. Shortly after 0930hrs gunfire erupted, which would last most of the rest of the morning. The fighting intensified around the bazaar area, where it became desperately close, with both sides trading hand grenades at one stage. A more unpleasant surprise was two suicide bombers who attempted to assail the marines of Kilo Company. Both managed to get close to their targets before detonating their explosive vests. No marine was injured but the spectacle of dismembered body parts turned stomachs. Eventually an Apache put paid to this resistance and scattered the remaining gunmen. Fleeing south and east, they were not seen again. Six dead insurgents were found, along with a large amount of weapons and drugs.[34]

The second phase of Operation *Aabi Toorah* – *Aabi Toorah 2c* – started in the third week of March and lasted three days. As in Operation *Sond Chara*, the marines called on the services of the Danish Leopard tanks. For the Danish tank crews based at FOB Price this was a considerable hike – 40 kilometres as the crow flies – disproving doubters who argued that main battle tanks would be unable to cope with the demands of the unforgiving terrain. The remainder of the 700-strong force comprised 42 Commando and an ANA contingent mentored by 1 Rifles. The American Task Force 31 also took part in the operation. About a third of the battlegroup was lifted into the target area by Chinooks, Royal Navy Sea Kings and USMC Sea Stallions. The remainder made the approach in a convoy protected by Vikings. Fire support was lavish: Apaches, Cobras, an American B1-B bomber, GMLRS and the light guns of 29 Commando Regiment were all made available to Lieutenant Colonel Stickland.

The aim of the operation was to disrupt Taliban groups operating in the Nawa-e Barakzai area. This was 'mowing the lawn' by any other name (or 'Attrit, Disperse, Leave' as Anthony Cordesman wrote with his flair for pithy tags), because the British did not have the numbers to permanently hold this area and there was no follow-up reconstruction plan.[35] Nawa-e Barakzai was a triangle of Green Zone west of Lashkar Gah, on the elbow joint of Nad-e Ali and Marjah districts. The area was broken by a complex pattern of canals and ditches that made access, except on foot, very challenging. The tribal layout was mixed and fractious.

Kilo Company was inserted first at dawn, followed by the BRF, to form an outer cordon. The former landed in what became a running mêlée of anti-aircraft and ground fire from 23 separate firing points.[36] The insurgent armoury included heavy machine guns as well as a rare Chinese truck-mounted SPG-9 recoilless rifle. In the ensuing confusion, three insurgents who accidentally drove their saloon car into the middle of the marines' position were shot dead.[37] More insurgents were subsequently killed in close fighting. As at Khan Neshin, at one stage the marines found themselves trading hand grenades between lines of ditches.

Lima Company then followed, dropped off in the desert west of the first target known as Objective Silver. Each marine was carrying around 100 kilograms in weight, a load greater than the body weight of the average man. Unlike the hot landing experienced by their sister company, Lima Company found a scene of tranquillity. Sapper Jay McIntosh of 25 Field Squadron recalled the sense of dislocation of the heliborne insertion:

> Within a minute of boarding the Chinook we were airborne, the chopping of the blades drowning out the few words that were spoken. I looked out of the window as day broke at the vast landscape and minutes later we touched down in unfamiliar surroundings, dismounted the aircraft in tandem and set up a textbook all-round defence. As the Chinooks disappeared into the distance I took time to look around and saw Danish tanks up on the hill ahead of me looking into the area held by the enemy. As we waited, we stayed focussed, watching our arcs and ready to react in an instant. We were accompanied only by the tweeting of birds, which seemed strange but pleasant given the circumstances.[38]

This sudden serenity was a feature that struck many soldiers tipped into the Green Zone from the noisy bellies of the Chinooks.

Burdened like donkeys – a nickname that the Taliban used for British soldiers – the commandos then yomped across the desert to the edge of the target area. McIntosh and his fellow sappers were needed because Objective Silver was located behind a canal which would have to be crossed by laying an infantry bridge. The sections of this bridge were manhandled by the sappers and the bridge was quickly erected:

> We eventually started patrolling forward, toward an infantry assault bridge which was to be our method of crossing the canal to get to the compounds we were to assault. I admit the speed with which the bridge had been put up surprised me, and I was at the rehearsals! As we approached the bridge, rounds started coming in, landing at my feet and whistling past my head, that's when the section took better cover behind a raised mound, which I'm still thankful for. Despite the Taliban not being the best shots, there were too many rounds to dodge. We crossed

> the everlasting bridge one by one, I could feel it wobbling as I held on to the rails and kept my head down.

Once over the bridge the marines had to force entry into the suspect compound. McIntosh carried the charges: barmines specially adapted to blow holes in the thick compound walls. The sappers relished the work, not just because it gave them an excuse to blow things up, but also because it reduced their load:

> On the other side we found further cover and moved towards a compound before assessing how to enter it. We avoided the door because of the risk of IEDs and placed a half-barmine on the outer wall, blowing an entrance which allowed the Commandos to invade and engage the enemy. Before resting we had to blow some 'murder holes' in the walls with PE4 to allow the Commandos to observe and fire from the compound.

While Lima Company was assaulting Objective Silver, the BRF had been landed directly on Objective Platinum to achieve maximum surprise. A measure of the resistance they met can be gauged from the fact that by the following morning they were still fighting from a compound just 300 metres from where they had been landed.[39] Kilo Company in the meantime had secured a canal crossing point north of the objectives, which would be used to resupply the marines. With Silver cleared, Lima Company then proceeded to a major track junction – Objective Brass – to block the movement of fleeing gunmen, as well as to deter gunmen intent on reinforcing from the west in Marjah District. This carefully orchestrated manoeuvre was covered by the Danish Leopards that laid down accurate fire on dug-in enemy positions. It was a model assault that left the insurgents 'surprised and confused'. A heavy expenditure of Hellfire missiles and several 2,000-pound bombs also helped.

By dusk, Lima Company had moved south to a school that was suspected to be an IED factory. The closing of schools and the conversion of these into insurgent bases, on the assumption that ISAF would not attack school buildings, was a common, cynical and mistaken Taliban tactic. The marines pummelled the building, as McIntosh recalled: 'The most impressive display of firepower I had ever seen as the Taliban were forced out and we moved in.' The intelligence in this case had been accurate. Inside the now damaged building the commandos found pressure plates and other IED components as well as Taliban 'ATM cards' – the inevitable 10-kilogram bags of opium. The following morning, fighters attempted to counter-attack the marines but were met by a volley of mortars, Javelin missiles and machine-gun fire.

Operations like *Aabi Toorah* did not have lasting effects. After three days of almost continuous gun battles the insurgents melted away but they would recover, make good their material and human losses and reassert control of Nawa-e Barakzai. The fault lay not in the idea but in the numbers. Operation *Aabi Toorah* had been based on sound intelligence and the marines had faultlessly executed an imaginative plan. But they could not simultaneously wage this form of mobile warfare and man the dozens of British patrol bases that had sprung up in the last two years. When 3 Commando Brigade arrived in the autumn they inherited 38 bases, the majority manned by no more than a platoon of soldiers. They left only adding another four to the total. Over the course of the war and the three tours undertaken by 3 Commando Brigade, the marines contributed around 26 of the roughly 200 patrol bases and checkpoints built by the British. It was the army that was obsessed with holding ground and which sacrificed mobility for static warfare, not the Royal Marines who appeared instinctively to understand the importance of mobility and agility.

Mobile operations of this type had to be conducted on a weekly basis, relentlessly and without respite – as General Challe had fought the second half of the Algerian War – wearing down the insurgency by never allowing the insurgents to rest or feel safe, anywhere. Eventually, the British did follow this course in the form of 'targeting operations', involving both special forces and the task force. 'Mowing the lawn' had its critics, but in part it was self-defeating not because it was an essentially flawed strategy, but because the British were not doing it enough, or ruthlessly. In Algeria, to invoke the comparison again, the French raised two airmobile *divisions* and built up a force of several hundred helicopters. The British were trying to mount mobile operations with single companies and three or four helicopters. More troops and more helicopters would have been required to pursue a decisive mobile campaign and neither was forthcoming. Static, attrition warfare was always likely to be the order of the day.

The winter had not witnessed the traditional Afghan lull in hostilities. In total, the brigade suffered one more fatality than the paratroopers in the summer – the first tour in which the winter fatality total had exceeded the summer total. Two Conspicuous Gallantry Crosses and 14 Military Crosses would be awarded to the brigade. As in the previous three years, many of these gallantry awards were won by marines and soldiers trying to save stricken comrades under fire. Typical of these was Marine Samuel Alexander, a machine gunner who ran out of ammunition for his GPMG, pulled out a pistol and continued to engage the Taliban at close range, thus allowing the safe extraction of a casualty. One of the more unusual acts of bravery was carried out by Sergeant Noel Connolly, who was alert enough to spot a would-be suicide bomber and courageous enough to rugby tackle the assailant. Able Seaman Class 1 Kate Nesbitt became the first Royal Naval recipient of the Military Cross (and the second ever female recipient) since World War II.

Operation *Herrick 9* marked an important milestone in the war. 3 Commando Brigade's second deployment to Helmand would prove to be the limit of British expansion and ambition. Marines had fought from Kajaki in the far north to the dwindling course of the Helmand River in the far south. Commandos had roamed across Uruzgan, Kandahar and Helmand provinces. In the spring the Americans would be arriving, and the British area of responsibility would naturally contract. At this juncture, it was worth posing the question: what had been achieved?

After three years of fighting, the British desperately wanted and needed to believe that their presence in Helmand was making a difference for the better. Inevitably, there were Panglossian voices that viewed events in the province in the best possible light. An example of this wishful reporting, below, showed just how far some views were from the reality of Helmand:

> With the ANA brigade commander this afternoon I met a gathering of Nad e Ali elders ... There was absolutely no doubt in the minds of these village elders that the actions of the ANA and their OMLT mentors had made a profound difference to the area and their lives. With the greater security provided, normal life has resumed to some extent and these wise, bearded men were obviously deeply grateful for the combined efforts of the Afghan and British soldiers. And similar effects and gratitude have been observed and reported elsewhere, of course.[40]

This was, unfortunately, rose-tinted nonsense. The only certain 'of course' in Nad-e Ali was that the fighting was far from over.

If this officer was seeing peace breaking out, the evidence from nationwide polling was suggesting a quite different picture. At the beginning of 2009 all polls were pointing in the wrong direction. The BBC, in conjunction with two other international broadcasters, had annually surveyed Afghan national opinion on a range of issues. The results of the fourth such poll were dispiriting. Confidence in the security situation and the economy had diminished. The slide towards disillusion and discontent had accelerated. Perhaps the most interesting Afghan perception was one that was never revealed by the extensive polling, conducted not just by the BBC, but by many other organizations. An undercutting irony of the war, adumbrated by Michael Martin, was that despite all the huffing and puffing of the last three years, many Helmandis believed the British were fighting *with* the Taliban, not against them. This myth, however preposterous to a Westerner, was both durable and widely believed. Karzai repeated it and Talibs even believed it.

Many strands contributed to this view: the perfidious *angrez* ('English') were up to their old tricks and were trying to weaken Afghanistan by fomenting conflict; Britain's support for Pakistan was confusingly interpreted as support for the ISI, which everybody knew was supporting the Taliban (how else could DfID's wish to make Pakistan the largest recipient of UK aid money be explained, never mind justifying this perverse policy to the family of a fallen soldier or marine?); British restraint was interpreted as a bargain with the Taliban; and the 'Musa Qaleh deal' was cited as incontrovertible proof that the British were in cahoots with the insurgents. This myth was not just entrenched in Helmand's villages. As Martin points out, educated Afghans also believed it, as did senators in Kabul who were highly critical of the British. When the US Marines deployed to Helmand, the myth gained another chapter. Noting the differences between the two contingents, Helmandis concluded that the British and Americans were in fact conducting some sort of civil war between themselves, with the Taliban fighting on the British side. Laughing off such conspiracy theories was inadequate: they spoke of a profound failure of ISAF to get its message across, as well as a failure to pursue a strategy that made any sense to ordinary Afghans.

Brigadier Messenger, unlike his predecessor, saw some hope in these mixed messages. The strategy of clear-hold-build was working. It just needed more time and probably more troops. As by this stage the British really had no option left but to follow this strategy to which they had committed all their resources, it was perhaps unsurprising that Brigadier Messenger felt obliged to offer an upbeat assessment. Messenger was clear, however, that this strategy should not be an excuse for the British to take ownership of the strings of bases springing up all over the province. The task force could not have done so, even if it had wanted to, because there were insufficient troops. The key was Afghan ownership – the same point made by Ed Butler, the first commander in Helmand, and reiterated by every successive brigade commander. The Afghans had to be prodded, cajoled and coached into taking charge of the war. The problem was that after three years of mentoring, the ANA in Helmand was no nearer to standing on its feet without ISAF assistance. The fault for this lay on both sides: the British had become distracted by the more compelling draw of fighting the Taliban (the mentoring role was seen as a second-class job); and the Afghans had been slow to awaken to the reality that the ISAF milk cow was not going to allow her teats to be suckled for ever. The war would have to wait until the arrival of General McChrystal, who would transform mentoring into more meaningful and durable partnering. Other factors, such as the steep rise in British casualties after the marines departed in the spring of 2009, as well as the fast-approaching British general election, also served to sharpen the British strategy.

Poor intelligence management continued to be a hindrance to coherent operations. The marines found the lack of a central intelligence database 'staggering'. The entire process of collating, fusing and disseminating intelligence was judged 'critically flawed'. Individuals kept information in their heads which was lost when they departed from the province. Archived databases 15 folders deep were found, making it quite impossible for anyone without intimate knowledge of the database to actually find a piece of information in any reasonable time. There were no or few Intelligence Corps soldiers on the front lines (where the majority of useful intelligence was actually being generated by the marines themselves), and there were no electronic means of passing classified intelligence to front-line companies from the brigade headquarters. Understanding of Helmand's political and tribal dynamics remained poor.

Had you joined the army 30 years previously, and attended the intelligence officers' course at the old depot at Ashford, you would have been taught 'there should be a single, centralised and integrated intelligence organisation controlled either by a specially appointed Director of Intelligence or the senior intelligence officer in the area of operations'.[41] Operation *Herrick* never resulted in the appointment of a Director of Intelligence, or indeed a campaign director to take charge and responsibility for the war. There was never a 'single, centralised and integrated intelligence organisation'. The British did know how to do counter-insurgency, or 'revolutionary warfare' as it was then termed – in Malaya, Kenya, Oman and elsewhere. Over the years, the hard-won lessons from Britain's 'small wars' had been forgotten.

Attrition also continued to be a problem. The brigade suffered over 60 per cent of its casualties as a result of IEDs, yet roadside bombs had been comparatively few. What would be the effect if the Taliban began laying these devices in earnest, in belts, or in 'IED fields'? The answer would come later that year. Even without the threat of IEDs, the drain on manpower was debilitating. In total the brigade would lose 379 soldiers to disease and non-battlefield injury, a loss rate it could not make up because there was no battle casualty replacement system. The marines had tried to wrest the initiative from the insurgents, but like the paratroopers before them, they reckoned that nine out of ten gun fights were started by the enemy.

The uneven and in some cases non-existent 'comprehensive approach' appeared to be entrenching itself more meaningfully in the British strategy. But it was slow – far too slow and too modest. 3 Commando Brigade managed to initiate and in part complete around 60 reconstruction projects, committing just under $8 million to these tasks. This was the best record to date of any of the British brigades. Overall, the British task force had committed in the order of $20 million to reconstruction in its three years in Helmand Province.[42]

An example of the work undertaken by soldiers can be drawn from the experiences of Warrant Officer Second Class Ben Fouracre (24 Commando Engineers), who led a Construction and Supervision Team at Garmsir. Fouracre had three big jobs on his books: refurbishing the district centre hospital, a large, rural clinic which on occasions received as many as 200 patients a day; refurbishing the local school; and refurbishing the governor's house and offices. This last task was one which the British routinely undertook in the hope that the flattered and grateful governors would repay the British with loyalty, if not honesty. These hopes were not uncommonly dashed (a common scam was 'losing' generators and requesting replacements from the British). Another seven projects were in the pipeline, including the clean-up of the trashed bazaar, which had already been transformed by the provision of 36 solar street lights. The twin challenges Fouracre faced were securing funds from the system, in the first instance, and preventing the dissipation of these funds through corruption: 'There is a lack of finances to get the tasks started which is frustrating and there is also speculation of corruption which doesn't help things.'[43]

The British were not just committing insufficient funds to reconstruction; they were, as Ben Fouracre complained, releasing these funds with an incomprehensible miserliness. Form-filling (to get approval for a project and therefore the release of funds) could strain credulity. DfID 'box-ticking' included such questions as: how will the project promote understanding across ethnic, religious and social divides? How will women play a part in the implementation of the project? Is the project environmentally friendly? Never mind that Helmand's farmers represented a near-biblical, misogynistic lot as far from DfID's millennium goals as Earth was from Pluto. Did the proposed project agree with the priorities set by the local authorities and lead humanitarian agency? This may have been a relevant question to ask if there had been recognizable, corruption-free, local authorities, and if all the humanitarian agencies, including DfID staff, had not abandoned south-west Afghanistan three years previously.

As 3 Commando Brigade prepared to leave Helmand, dust clouds on the horizon signalled the arrival of American forces. These conventional military forces represented only a proportion of armed Americans and other nationalities in Afghanistan, as a significant slice of reconstruction budgets was simply being swallowed up by security companies. Eight years after the start of Operation *Enduring Freedom*, there were 39 registered private security companies operating in Afghanistan. The number of security contractors employed by the Department of Defense alone amounted to nearly 60 per cent of the entire British military task force. If the total number of legal and illegal security personnel had been calculable, the number would certainly have exceeded the British military contribution to ISAF by some margin. Nobody really knew with precision how many security personnel were being employed in Afghanistan because the country was awash with arms, and anyone with money and a sufficiently vulnerable profile employed armed security guards. One source reckoned that between 10 and 20 per cent of the reconstruction budget was going straight into the pockets of the security firms.[44] One Afghan government official calculated that funding of foreign security firms amounted to three times the salaries of the fledgling Afghan army and police combined.[45] Working in an often-lawless environment, and fuelled by boredom and alcohol, the private security firms soon developed a poor reputation. There were incidents of ill discipline and allegations of illegal 'black ops' and interrogations. These activities – verified or not – created suspicion among Afghan hosts, who increasingly viewed Westerners as lawless and gun-toting (a rich irony, it may be noted).

Westerners working on the fringes of the law were not the only headache. Contracts were granted to ex-warlords and local bullies who effectively became paid mercenaries of ISAF. The Australians in Uruzgan were sustaining a 2,000-strong paramilitary force; the Canadians in Kandahar were employing a local crook to guard camps; and in the German area of responsibility a known opium baron was being funded by ISAF to provide an armed security force.[46] The fickleness of these militias was laid bare when a score of Afghan security contractors rode out of a US special forces base to 'rescue' one of their comrades who had been arrested by the Afghan police. In the ensuing gun battle (inside the police HQ in Kandahar city), they killed the provincial police chief and several policemen.

The employment of private security firms was just the tip of a very large contractor iceberg which was turning Afghanistan into a lucrative market just as operations in Iraq were beginning to wind down. By 2009, and for the first time in the US Army's history, more civilians were being employed in a theatre of war than soldiers (68,197 contractors versus 52,300 soldiers).[47] By the following year, with the 'Obama surge', the disparity would grow. In fact, Department of Defense civilian employees exceeded the entire military contribution of the other 41 nations in ISAF – an indication of how this was an American war and how little the European allies were contributing to the war effort. As the winter of 2009 thawed, giving way to another Afghan spring, the imbalance between America and its allies was about to tell again, but in more positive ways. The Messiah McChrystal was on his way.

10

Crisis Year

Operation *Herrick 10*, April 2009–October 2009

At the beginning of 2009 *The Economist* ran a feature on the state of the British Army. The leader was entitled 'Overstretched, overwhelmed and over there'.[1] The journal warned that Britain's penny-pinching governments had run down the armed forces, while faced with a need to keep pace with the American-led operation in Afghanistan. However, this was not a time to give up: 'Abandoning Afghanistan, leaving a vacuum for the Taliban to fill, would mean a victory for extremism everywhere, a destabilized Pakistan and a less safe world. Losing today's war could make tomorrow's wars more likely.'

Over the years, British governments had systematically underfunded the armed forces, the journal argued. Large, technologically glitzy projects had soaked up funds required for equipment to fight today's wars. British confidence over 'how to do small wars' had turned to hubris. The withdrawal from Basra had been a humiliation, saved by American intervention in the subsequent Iraqi operation to retake the city, Operation *Charge of the Knights*. Worryingly, *The Economist* reported, senior American commanders were voicing a lack of confidence in the British. The following year, embarrassing disclosures on the controversial website Wikileaks would reveal the depth of this American disquiet. The British themselves seemed drained of confidence.

This public pessimism over the conduct of the war was reflected in discourse in military periodicals. An article published in the spring of 2009 in the US Army's house magazine captured the new mood, quite devoid of the triumphalism that marked the early years of the Bush presidency.[2]

Quoting the defense secretary, the article asserted: 'If our goal is to create some sort of Asian Valhalla, we will lose. Nobody has the time, the patience or the money to do that ... We need more concrete goals that can be achieved realistically within three to five years.'

The article itemized the many failures besetting the war. There had been insufficient troops, which had allowed the Taliban to dominate large swathes of the country. Despite the growing consensus that more troops were needed, the defense secretary remained sceptical that reinforcements, beyond the 30,000 soldiers that would be sent after months of lobbying by General McKiernan, would make a great difference. Roadside bombs (3,276 in the previous year) were continuing to cause attrition. Supply lines from Pakistan were being attacked. A plan to create village militias had stalled. President Karzai's power did not extend beyond Kabul, and the licit economy was 'practically nonexistent'. Dennis Steele, the staff writer, concluded gloomily that after eight years of fighting and the expenditure of billions of dollars, Operation *Enduring Freedom* had only brought Afghanistan 'to within sight of a starting point'.

Certainly there was an overwhelming sense that the war had become beleaguered at the beginning of 2009 and that some radical changes needed to be implemented. The inauguration of the new American president – America's first black incumbent of the White House – had been accompanied by a wave of semi-hysterical, global adulation. The new commander-in-chief had promised to make Afghanistan a top priority. His advisors, unaffected by the election hoopla, remained lugubrious and short on inspiration. The redoubtable Richard Holbrooke, no stranger to intractable conflicts, candidly admitted: 'I have never seen anything like the mess we have inherited.' As if to underline the mess, he began using the term 'Afpak War' – not to save syllables, he told a European audience at a security conference in Munich – but because this is what it had become, a much broader cross-border war encompassing two unstable Muslim countries. His counterpart in the Department of Defense, Robert Gates, a dutiful servant of the previous Republican administration who agreed to stay in post under new masters, was equally pessimistic. America should no longer seek to rebuild the derelict that Afghanistan had become after a quarter of a century of fighting. Rather, it should set out to beat its real enemy – al-Qaeda – while maintaining more modest aims in reconstruction and development. European NATO allies plainly had to do more. America could and ultimately would not pull the cart alone.

In Britain, the new realism was captured by Foreign Secretary David Miliband. With refreshing honesty, Miliband conceded the Taliban had fought ISAF to a standstill. A new strategy – and crucially new civilian heads of mission – had to be found to reinvigorate Britain's floundering engagement in Afghanistan. The British ambassador in Kabul, Sherard Cowper-Coles, who himself had been appointed to give the operation more clout, had suffered uneven relations with British military commanders in Helmand, and reportedly lost the confidence of the American ambassador in Kabul (which was easily lost, as Karl Eikenberry cast a long and critical shadow over much of the ISAF operation). Cowper-Coles was appointed special envoy to the region, working alongside the American special envoy Richard Holbrooke. This was a sideways promotion which unfortunately cast the British diplomat in a worse light. Compared to the pugilistic Holbrooke, Cowper-Coles seemed too obviously 'British' – a character suited to clever social intercourse but not hard negotiations with Pakistan's generals. Within a year Cowper-Coles would resign anyway.

A former Islamabad diplomat, Mark Sedwill, replaced him. Mark Sedwill would eventually assume the role of senior ISAF civilian representative in Afghanistan. Sedwill could hardly have been phlegmatic about his new appointment. Support for the British had been steadily declining since the intervention: a stunningly low 6 per cent of Afghans thought that the British were doing a good job in Afghanistan.[3] This was a level of ingratitude not seen since the Korean War, when President Rhee suggested the British contingent should quit the country because it was contributing little.

Another stalemated fighting season had brought the West's strained relations with President Karzai to the fore. This was election year in Afghanistan, and the prospect of another Karzai term in the presidency filled Western politicians with foreboding. The most important of these relations was that between the US State Department and President Karzai, and this was at an all-time low. The new foreign secretary, Hillary Clinton, openly described Afghanistan as a narco-state. Vice President Joe Biden walked out of a state dinner. Richard Holbrooke, predictably, had a blazing row with the Afghan president soon after taking up his appointment. Everywhere there was evidence that the American–Afghan relationship was fraying, perhaps beyond repair.

The use of air power was one of the more controversial aspects of the war and one that inevitably generated fallacies and myths. Mistakes were made and civilians were killed, but the real story was the extreme reticence by ISAF to bomb, and the severe constraints placed on target planners and pilots alike. The professionalism and meticulousness of military targeting boards and pilots were features of the war that were simply never reported. In the year the British task force deployed to Helmand, ISAF air forces mounted 11,528 close air support missions.[4] As the fighting intensified, this number rose to just over 19,000 missions. But even at the peak in 2008, just 1,170 of the 19,000 missions actually dropped ordnance.[5] Over the succeeding years, the numbers were 7.4 per cent of missions (2009); 7.6 per cent (2010); 7.8 per cent (2011); and 6.8 per cent (2012).[6] After 2012, air strikes dropped away steeply. Overall, around 93 per cent of ISAF strike sorties were electing *not* to drop ordnance rather than risk causing civilian casualties. This statistic never entered the canon of articles condemning ISAF's use of air power in Afghanistan.

The long-awaited reinforcement of American forces in Afghanistan brought with it an unexpected change of command. On 11 May the respected General McKiernan found himself in a position not unfamiliar to that of former wartime commanders – he was sacked. The sacking disappointed his staff but reportedly drew little sympathy from his civilian boss, the US defense secretary. To outside observers, the abrupt dismissal seemed unfair. McKiernan had consistently argued that ISAF, and more pointedly the United States, needed to commit more troops to the Afghan campaign. Frustrated by the previous administration, which had been obsessed with a chaotic Iraq, the call for additional troops had finally been acknowledged but McKiernan would not now command these extra troops. Instead, he was going home. A general who had been his subordinate in the invasion of Iraq, General David Petraeus – the hero of America's revived fortunes in Baghdad – would assume command of CENTCOM (Central Command). His representative on the ground would be a special forces general, Stanley McChrystal, and his deputy would be a former commander of the 82nd Airborne Division, General David Rodriguez. To all appearances, a special forces and airborne mafia had taken over the show, sidelining a diligent general who had led the campaign with inadequate forces and weak political support.

It was rumoured Karl Eikenberry, himself a former commander of American forces in Afghanistan, had played a role in the sacking because he had found working with McKiernan difficult. It also appeared that a whispering campaign was mounted against him in Washington. Whatever the truth in the rumors, the appointment of Stanley McChrystal was clearly not going to represent a simple change of command. McChrystal arrived with the full weight of expectation of a new Democrat government intent on undoing the mistakes of the past and resolving the conundrum of Operation *Enduring Freedom*. Whatever confident public pronouncements were being made over the appointment of a new command team, it was almost certainly known in private that the McChrystal promotion represented a risk. The general was not a comfortable figure in the Washington beltway, and he in turn seemed to find politicians discomfited by him. The son of a general (all four siblings served in the armed forces), it was not obvious the younger Stanley was destined for the top. His early career was not spectacular. He took seven years to rise from captain to the next rank band and five years to rise again to lieutenant colonel. Promotion to brigadier took a further 11 years. Then war entered McChrystal's life, something for which he had prepared himself assiduously with service in the 82nd Airborne Division, the Green Berets and 75th Ranger Regiment, a unit which he commanded. With the rocket fuel of battle, his ascent was meteoric. In eight years McChrystal rose from one-star brigadier to four-star general. His five-year tenure with the Joint Special Operations Command (JSOC) was pivotal to this ascent.

The American change of command was matched by a British change of command. At the end of August, Richard Dannatt handed over to David Richards, who had gained the nickname 'Kabul Richards' because of his previous experience as commander of ISAF forces in south-west Afghanistan. Crucially, Richards had been the general commanding ISAF forces when British forces first deployed to Helmand. This gave him a unique perspective on the war. In what had now become a customary speech at Chatham House, General Richards (who had only just returned the previous day from another flying visit to Helmand) reiterated the now orthodox view that the British Army could not be allowed to fail in Afghanistan. 'We must remain absolutely focussed on delivering success in Afghanistan,' he warned his audience, but the message was probably intended for the government.[7]

There was a flat note to this game of military musical chairs. Changing generals did not alter the facts on the ground. The newly appointed McChrystal was as constrained as his predecessor and under even greater pressure to achieve success. The foundations which McKiernan had left could not be changed fundamentally.

The ISAF command inherited by General McChrystal had swelled to over 58,000 troops. There were 42 contributing nations. The smallest, Georgia, supplied just one liaison officer. The largest, the United States, was providing over 26,000 soldiers. In between these two extremes were a host of minnows undertaking tasks of varied usefulness: 170 Macedonians, 120 Albanians and 70 Slovenians laboured somewhere within the ISAF ark. Larger contributors such as Italy (2,350 soldiers), Spain (780 soldiers) and most notably Germany (3,465 soldiers) deliberately avoided being drawn into fighting. When the numbers were summed, too many nations were 'peripherals' and too many were offering 'stand aside' forces, using Anthony Cordesman's terms. Only about 15 per cent of ISAF was actually committed to the fight, the majority of which were American forces.

McChrystal did not have time on his hands. He arrived in theatre just as the fighting season was getting underway and with McKiernan's reinforcement plan already too advanced to be substantially changed. What he did have was the opportunity to take a blank sheet of paper and rethink the entire strategy in Afghanistan. Supported by a small team of hand-picked military officers and outsider civilian experts like the academic Anthony Cordesman, McChrystal keenly seized this opportunity. These civilians worked *pro bono* and even paid for their own air flights, a reflection of the sense of duty in American public service. This attitude was unfortunately absent in a Britain where an ex-defence secretary would describe himself as a 'taxi for hire', and quote preposterous £5,000 daily consultancy fees, once out of office.

The product of the intensive, three-month-long brainstorming session – succinctly subtitled 'Commander's Initial Assessment' – was presented to Defense Secretary Gates on 30 August.[8] The anticipation that attended the publication of this study was high and its readers were not disappointed. McChrystal displayed clarity both in thought and prose.

The problem was simply expressed: could ISAF achieve its mission? And if so, how and with what resources? Acknowledging that ISAF faced a deteriorating situation and a growing insurgency, McChrystal offered three key ideas. First, ISAF had to redefine the fight. 'Our objective,' he wrote, 'must be the population.' This was not a new mantra, either to the Americans or to the British who had argued this view most forcibly under Brigadier Mackay two years previously. 'Population-centric COIN', to use the jargon, had been, at least in theory, one of the foundations of the American strategy in Vietnam. 'The Vietnamese people are and must remain,' Chief of Staff General Harold Johnson wrote in 1966, 'the true and paramount objective of all U.S. Government efforts in Vietnam.' McChrystal was repeating this very old refrain.

Second, ISAF had to win short – in the next 12 months – in order to gain long term. As one of McChrystal's staff put it, the war could well last another ten years, but it would be decided in the next 12 months. Making a decisive difference could no longer be postponed. Third, ISAF had to change its culture in two principal ways: the Western alliance had to better connect with Afghans and better connect with itself, operating in a more unified manner. Drawing from these fundamental concepts, McChrystal proposed four pillars to the new strategy: closer mentoring of the Afghan forces (a policy that would become known as 'embedded partnering' to distinguish it from previous training assistance programmes); better governance, a key plank over which ISAF in practice had little control; a regaining of the initiative, for which McChrystal planned to ramp up special forces operations (Joint Detention Operation 435); and the geographic refocusing of resources where they were most needed. In the short term, this would be south-west Afghanistan. On an organizational level, McChrystal made two significant changes: he established the NATO Training Mission in Afghanistan (NTM-A) on a firm footing, and he rationalized the ISAF Joint Command.

This, in essence, was the 'McChrystal Plan', and very little of it was new, a point McChrystal generously conceded. All of McChrystal's predecessors, from McNeill onwards (2002–03), had broadly followed these policies and programmes. A line could be drawn even further back, to various Vietnam-era programmes. McChrystal was a diligent student of the Vietnam War and in fact over the summer had reread Stanley Karnow's seminal history of the conflict.

It followed with an unfortunate logic that McChrystal could correspondingly not avoid the same problems that beset the Vietnam War, or the 'avoided issues', to borrow a phrase coined by one of the anonymous authors of the leaked Pentagon Papers.[9] In the earlier war, there was the flawed assumption that more American advisors ('mentoring', in the modern term) would result in greater effectiveness in the ARVN (Army of the Republic of Vietnam). But as the Pentagon Papers argued, this assumption was exceedingly hard to prove and, with hindsight, easy to disprove. More in the end did not increase quality – it simply turned out more bad soldiers. Then there was the 'chicken-and-egg argument' over security which bedeviled the Vietnam War. Was pacification (securing the population) the precondition for winning the loyalty of Vietnamese farmers (hearts and minds), or did that loyalty have to won first by good governance, in order for pacification to stand any chance of success? Was it realistic to expect Western soldiers to pacify and win hearts and minds – to protect the population, in McChrystal's strategy – if that population did not support the government? There was no certain answer to this question, and few alternative ideas.

What imbued the 'McChrystal Plan' with special purpose was the man himself. McChrystal succeeded where his predecessors had failed in stamping his considerable reputation and personality on the plan – perhaps the vital ingredient a general brings to a battlefield. McChrystal had an electric effect all the way down the rank structure, so that even the lowest private sensed there was a new commander in charge, and importantly that the new brass hat was playing to win. The feeling that you are on the winning side is a battle fought in men's minds, and it was McChrystal's genius to win this battle within the first few months of his command.

The second battle, with the perceptions of the Afghan people, was naturally going to prove a much tougher fight. McChrystal liked to use the analogy of Afghanistan as a room full of argumentative and violent people. ISAF, acting as a moderator, could not settle the argument. The people of Afghanistan would decide which speaker offered the most compelling and attractive argument. ISAF's role was to ensure that the people were given a fair chance to make this choice in a stable and lawful country. This was why McChrystal emphasized in his directive, 'Focus 95% of your time building relationships with them [the Afghans], and together with the Afghan government, meeting their needs', adding sentiments that a Vietnam-era general would never have uttered: 'We will not win by simply killing insurgents.' This was the most important difference between the two wars – Westmoreland's 'body count' had so scarred the American military establishment that no American general would ever countenance revisiting those painful days and arguments. As a result, McChrystal would be associated with the opposite strategy, or the draconian policy of 'courageous restraint', a point that was not actually made with any force in his original assessment, but which fell out as the natural corollary from a need to protect the population.

The hidden contradiction in the 'McChrystal Plan' was one which President Obama himself created and which lay at the heart of America's confusion over its war in Afghanistan. Under the new Democrat administration, America's mission was now firmly to 'disrupt, dismantle and eventually defeat al-Qaeda and prevent their return to Afghanistan'. This was a Biden-championed mission, promulgated as presidential policy on 27 March, that relegated the more nobly unmanageable task of reinventing Afghanistan as a prosperous, benign democratic state. This was also the mission clearly supported by Defense Secretary Robert Gates.

If this was the new mission, then was McChrystal even fighting the right war? Defeating al-Qaeda by waging a narco-nationalist war against Afghan Pashtuns – for this was the war McChrystal was really fighting – seemed a costly and odd way of going about this probably impossible task. When McChrystal stated that his mission was to defeat the Taliban (to be fair, this mission was given to him by the Joint Chiefs), the proposition was straight away challenged by the civilians in the National Security Council. What was the point of defeating the Taliban? How did this serve America's national security interest? In this respect McChrystal had been asked, like General Creighton Abrams in Vietnam, to preside over the funeral rites of an unpopular war by his political masters. Even as McChrystal threw all his intellectual rigour at the problem of winning a counter-insurgency war, influential voices in Washington were already beginning to view the entire American commitment in central Asia in a very different light. Exit and not victory strategies were being sketched.

Perhaps the real flaw lay in none of these divergent views but in McChrystal's conviction that this was a war that *could* be won. Clearly, general rank is achieved by individuals who believe the victory laurel can be grasped. So much is unremarkable. But in holding this belief McChrystal unfortunately joined the band of Vietnam generals who placed hope above realism. It was a measure of his self-scrutiny and honesty that he was not so blind to this jeopardy. The war could be won, *if* Washington willed it (the same advice chairman of the Joint Chiefs Wheeler gave to Lyndon Johnson; he didn't, any more than Obama). Over the three months of the assessment period, it became increasingly apparent to him that this was not the case.

In the *White House Years*, Kissinger wrote with characteristic wisdom:

> ... the most difficult lesson for a national leader to learn is that with respect to the use of military force, his basic choice is to act or to refrain from acting. He will not be able to take away the moral curse of using

> force by employing it halfheartedly or incompetently. There are no rewards for exhibiting one's doubts in vacillation; statesmen get no prizes for failing with restraint. Once committed they must prevail.[10]

McChrystal understood this viscerally, as a military commander does. But President Obama also probably understood this. However, he had not committed America's armed forces in the first place – he had inherited the clumsy decisions of the previous administration and did not feel beholden to prevail in dubious ventures he did not start. As he would later demonstrate when turmoil swept across the Middle East during his second presidential term, Obama was almost dogmatically inclined to refrain from acting, rather than involve America in intractable foreign squabbles. In the end, there was little likelihood the president and his appointed superstar commander would have ever agreed on this point – the couple were ill matched and heading for a bust-up, long before that bust-up eventually happened the following year.

In his second ISAF directive McChrystal subsequently ordered that in future all operations be undertaken jointly with the Afghan National Army. 'We will live, train, plan, control and execute operations together at all command echelons,' he wrote, adding, 'from the Government Ministries down to platoon level.'[11] This was a clear signal that ISAF's exit strategy was being pinned on building up the Afghan security forces to the point where Western forces could start withdrawing. It was the only viable exit strategy left to ISAF, but the fact remained the British task force had been operating jointly with ANA since the beginning and the latter's capacity to operate independently was limited at best.

However, self-deluding reporting about the capabilities of the ANA had become an unfortunate feature of the war. The reality was somewhat grimmer. The ANA and ANP were wholly dependent on Western (almost exclusively American) funding. Just to sustain the present Afghan security forces would probably cost the US taxpayer $10–20 billion over the next two presidential terms.[12] As worryingly, ISAF claims of the ANA's preparedness to assume responsibility for the security of Afghanistan simply did not match the reality on the ground. Later in the year, when the commander of the US Marines in Helmand was asked what his number one problem was, he replied baldly: 'the ANA'. In the spring of 2011, a more honest assessment of the ANA would conclude that in fact just one battalion was capable of independent operations.

If the build-up of the ANA was failing, there was one aspect of the war that seemed to be going well, and which strengthened the argument in Washington that America was fighting the wrong kind of war – a costly counter-insurgency war rather than smart counter-terrorist war. The American reinforcement in Helmand had coincided with a ratcheting up of America's covert strikes against the Taliban and al-Qaeda leadership (known as HVTs or High Value Targets), using armed drones to attack their Pakistani sanctuaries. The controversial strikes, run under a CIA-led programme and conducted by the aptly named Predator UAV, were proving highly successful – at least in terms of killing insurgent and terrorist leadership figures. In the 1990s the Clinton administration had agonized over using armed drones to kill Osama bin Laden. The sticking point had always been a fear that innocent civilians would be killed in a missile strike. Ten years later, such ethical and legal debates had lost their weight. America was at war and it had the means to strike (with Pakistani compliance) its enemies. There had only been one Predator strike in 2004, and one in the following year. By 2008 a cross-border attack was being conducted every ten days, and by 2009 every few days.[13] By the time the British launched Operation *Panther's Claw* in the summer of 2009, there had been 31 Predator strikes against Taliban and al-Qaeda leadership targets in Pakistan.

This then was the backdrop the British faced when, on 10 April, 3 Commando Brigade officially handed over to 19 Light Brigade, commanded by Brigadier Tim Radford. This brigade had only recently left Catterick in Yorkshire and had been relocated to Northern Ireland. Two of the infantry battalions were drawn from bases in Northern Ireland (2 Rifles and 2 Mercians), but the other infantry battalions were collected from across the mainland. These included the Welsh Guards, 2 Royal Regiment of Fusiliers and The Black Watch, based at Inverness. The brigade's cavalry regiment of Light Dragoons, a Geordie outfit, was ironically based in Swanton Morley, in deepest, rural Norfolk. Almost all the combat support units, including the brigade's gunners and sappers, were drawn from Northern Ireland.

The brigade was known as the 'Black Panthers' and it sported a panther's head on a green triangle as its logo. 19 Light Brigade had already been deployed at the beginning of the Iraq campaign as well as on the violent Operation *Telic 9* in the summer of 2007. In total, the brigade numbered about 8,100 all ranks.

For any unit deploying to Afghanistan, the luck of location had become all-important. Since the beginning of 2008, 79 per cent of all British fatalities had been as a consequence of IEDs.[14] 2 Rifles drew the short straw and was deployed to the most dangerous location of all – Sangin. The commanding officer, Lieutenant Colonel Rob Thomson, described what he found: 'Our area of operations, the patch, was about the same size as Dorset, approximately 2,225 km^2, a massive area for a Battle Group numbering 1,100 soldiers; there were over 25 different cap badges represented in our ranks including the RAF and one sailor!'[15]

To make up the numbers the battlegroup was reinforced by A Company from 2 Royal Regiment of Fusiliers, thus creating five line companies. A Company was deployed to FOB Jackson in Sangin; B Company was dispersed between FOB Inkerman, FOB Wishtan and FOB Gibraltar, the most dangerous locations; C Company took over FOB Nolay and a number of southern bases; and I Company was given the relatively benign task of securing Kajaki Dam. As well as a virulent and confident insurgency, 2 Rifles faced the additional challenge that the official governor of Sangin, an Alikozai named Haji Faisal, was proving as useless as his counterpart in Musa Qaleh, Mullah Salaam. By contrast, the unofficial Taliban governor, Mullah Abdul Khaliq, was demonstrating all the qualities that the British were seeking in a governor: decisive leadership and respect from the tribes.

The Black Watch, 3rd Battalion, The Royal Regiment of Scotland (3 SCOTS) commanded by Lieutenant Colonel Stephen Cartwright, assumed the role of the theatre reserve battalion based at Kandahar. This battlegroup would be reinforced by 46 Territorial Army soldiers, an impressive commitment from Britain's citizen soldiers. The battalion would be busy: The Black Watch undertook 13 battlegroup and seven company operations (including 14 air assaults) during its tour, but everyone knew from the casualty statistics that the Kandahar-based battalion undertaking mobile operations suffered the least fatalities of all the British infantry units deployed in Afghanistan.[16] What nobody could have guessed in the spring was that The Black Watch would be the last British battalion to undertake this role. In October, a panicked government would announce that Britain would no longer deploy an infantry battalion to Kandahar, in order to concentrate its forces in Helmand. The most effective British battalion in south-west Afghanistan would be withdrawn to meet the political imperative of demonstrating to a critical electorate that more troops were being sent to Helmand.

The Welsh Guards, commanded by Lieutenant Colonel Rupert Thorneloe, took over in central Helmand, now viewed as the district of greatest importance to the British campaign. Number IX Company, a composite sub-unit led by Major Sean Burchill, was initially deployed to Lashkar Gah as the protection company for the brigade HQ and PRT. Prince of Wales's Company took over PBs Argyll, Pimon and the checkpoint (CP) at Blue 29; Number 2 Company took over PBs Silab and Tanda, along with CPs Paraang and Haji Alem; Number 3 Company, divided into four OMLTs, was detached to 2 Mercians in the Sangin area; and a 'Task Force Nawa' was deployed to PB Jaker, which would eventually be handed over to US Marines. Prince of Wales's Company was then subsequently deployed to Chah-e-Anjir ('Fig Tree Well') and named their patrol bases 'Shahzad' or 'Prince'.[17] The oddly titled IX Company was, in fact, a romantic resurrection of 1 Company, 2 Welsh Guards, a battalion placed in suspended animation in 1947. A second and much smaller X Company was also established to train the ANA. These ad hoc reorganizations pointed to the deeper malaise within even the well-recruited Guards Division: the British Army simply did not have enough infantrymen.

The Worcestershire and Sherwood Foresters, now renamed 2 Mercians, were on their third tour of Afghanistan. Lieutenant Colonel Simon Banton found himself in the familiar position of previous infantry commanding officers in Helmand without a coherent command. A Company was deployed to Darvishan, in the south, under command of a Light Dragoons battlegroup. This was where the company had been deployed just 18 months previously, before the surge by 24th MEU that finally expelled the Taliban from the environs of the town. The contrast was plain to Captain Simon Cupples, who had served in the previous tour:

> What was once a deserted town with only enemy in the area is now a hustling [sic] bazaar with many shops offering a wide selection of goods. There has been a project to tarmac the road that runs through the District Centre, and to install solar powered street lights. This is an amazing achievement; bearing in mind some of the locals will have never driven on or even seen a tarmac road before![18]

Other elements of the battalion were deployed as OMLTs in central Helmand, taking over from 1 Rifles.

The fourth infantry battalion in the brigade was 2 Royal Regiment of Fusiliers. This was deployed to Battlegroup North-West, centered on Musa Qaleh. C Company held the district centre in the town itself, and B Company deployed to PB Woqab. A Company was detached to FOB Nolay in support of the 2 Rifles battlegroup in Sangin. Unbeknown to the soldiers the battalion would be chopped in imminent defence cuts – this would be the unit's last sacrifice.

19 Light Brigade deployed to Helmand knowing that it would embark on one of the biggest operations of the war to date. On 5 June, on the eve of this operation, John Hutton, the Secretary of State for Defence, resigned, simultaneously announcing that he would not stand as an MP at the next general election. Once again, there would be a change of personality at ministerial level in the British war in Helmand at exactly the wrong juncture – a poor contrast to the American practice of five-year terms of service across different administrations. From the perspective of a personality like Defense Secretary Gates, it may have seemed that Britain's political classes were simply not taking the war seriously enough.

Hutton was succeeded by Bob Ainsworth, the Minister of State for the Armed Forces, a former trade unionist at Jaguar Cars before joining the Labour Party. The new incumbent arrived with spoonfuls of self-abasement. In an interview with the *Daily Telegraph* he confessed:

> I have strengths and I have weaknesses. I don't pretend to be able to write a great thesis or doctorate … I don't try to second guess decisions that are quite properly taken in the military chain of command. I don't try to pretend I am cleverer than a general or the Chief of the Defence Staff … I speak with a Midlands accent. I drop my aitches. I suffer with an asthmatic-related condition that means I speak with a gravelly voice. I have a moustache that some people appear to take offence to.[19]

But behind this faux humility was a determined personality (even, it appeared, in matters of self-interest – when the scandal over MP expenses broke out in 2009 it emerged he was the joint highest claimant for a second home allowance among his fellow MPs, although there were no suggestions of impropriety). He would need this determination in the closing battles fought between the Treasury and the MOD in the last months of the Brown government. Bob Ainsworth was also one of the most attentive defence secretaries across Operation *Herrick*. He seemed to genuinely empathize with the ordinary men and women who were risking their lives in Helmand, seeing perhaps in their commonness a mirror of his own humble background. His tenure in the end was short, but honest.

19 Light Brigade began its tour by launching Operation *Zafar*.[20] This took place in an area 7 kilometres north of Lashkar Gah, in the south-east corner of Nad-e Ali and Babaji districts. *Zafar* illustrated all the problems besetting British operations in Helmand, as well as the idealism of the soldiers tasked to undertake these operations. The aim of the operation was to clear a Taliban gang from a small village called Basharan astride the Shamalan Canal. But the problem in Basharan was not the lawlessness provoked by insurgents, but rather by poor local governance. Basharan was a failed village. Dominated by Barakazi (there were nine sub-clans compressed in this area), Basharan had witnessed an influx of Saids, Noorzais, Baluchis, Zakzais and Tarikzais. Poor water management following the extension of the Shamalan Canal had resulted in salination, loss of productive lands and reduced acreage. The land west of the village had reverted to semi-desert. During the Soviet period the village had become a front line. Old Russian positions were still visible north of the settlement. An even older ruined fort, known to the locals as the 'British Fort', testified to the Anglo-Afghan wars. For the villagers with long memories, foreign soldiers meant fighting. What Basharan badly needed was modest investment, but all the British were about to offer was more bullets and bombs. The village also desperately needed corruption-free police, but as IX Company of the Welsh Guards discovered, the local ANP were a bunch of virtually useless drug addicts. In these circumstances, it was entirely unsurprising the villagers wanted nothing to do with the local government, and were even less impressed with the notion of British soldiers 'liberating' them from the Taliban. Basharan in this respect encapsulated a paradox that the British were well aware of: that by supporting a corrupt government they were necessarily casting themselves as enemies of the very people whose 'hearts and minds' they were trying to win.

Zafar was billed as an operation led by the Afghan National Security Forces, but from start to finish it was British-led and largely fell on the shoulders of Major Sean Burchill, the officer commanding IX Company. The police were so poor, Burchill gave up on them. The ANA, mentored by British troops, proved equally useless and disinterested. As a consequence, IX Company was forced to assume responsibility for the operation but had too few soldiers. Eventually, Basharan did 'fall' after significant damage had been wrought and the civilian population displaced. Burchill was so moved by the ruined state of the school in the village (which had reportedly been closed by the Taliban after executing the head teacher), he resolved to make the restoration of the building his personal mission. This idealistic, South African-born officer moved bureaucratic mountains to revive a rudimentary education system in Basharan, but he would not see the fruits of his efforts. In June he was killed by an IED, travelling in a Jackal, near the village he had adopted as his own.

In the second half of June – and coinciding with Operation *Khanjar* ('Strike of the Sword'), an offensive in southern Helmand conducted by US Marines – the British launched Operation *Panchai Palang* ('Panther's Claw'). This was to have been the second half of Operation *Sond Chara*, mounted by 3 Commando Brigade in the previous tour, but the marines ran out of time and resources. The aim of Operation *Panchai Palang* was to clear an area north of the provincial capital that had become a safe haven for the Taliban. As Brigadier Radford put it, the operation would 'liberate' 80,000 Helmandis who were living under the oppressive rule of the Taliban and who would now be able to vote in the forthcoming elections. In this hope at least, the British would be sorely disappointed.

The ground over which the operation was conducted was classic Helmand Green Zone: a patchwork of fields, irrigation ditches, tree lines and compound farm buildings. This was bocage country in stifling heat and with an elusive enemy. Babaji and Malgir districts were sandwiched between Helmand's two principal towns: Gereshk and Lashkar Gah. The British were surprised to discover that some of the tribesmen in this area had no clue that they were actually residents of any particular district – there was no government at all. Instead there were over 20 villages, each headed by an elder, and no overall district leader. The overwhelming majority of the inhabitants of these districts – perhaps 95 per cent – were Barakzai. This tribe was heavily involved in the opium trade and had little incentive to support the British. There was not one hospital or recognized school in the entire area. The poverty was stunning.

Panchai Palang had four 'objectives' in the classic military sense. From east to west, these were the Barakzai villages of Char Coucha, Paind Kalay, Rahim Kalay and Walizai. From top to bottom, the valley resembled a triangle tipped on its right side. At the apex of the triangle, in Malgir District, the Green Zone was no more than 2 kilometres wide. At the base of the triangle, on the boundary of Babaji and Nad-e Ali districts, the Green Zone stretched for almost 15 kilometres. In total, the British would have to cover about 20 kilometres of difficult ground contested by tribesmen who were likely to put up a fight. As the entire operation lasted about five weeks, this meant that 19 Light Brigade achieved a rate of advance of around 500 metres per day, or slower than a formation in Normandy. In fact, the brigade never reached its final objective, the south-west corner of Babaji known as Loy Adera (later nicknamed the 'Babaji Pear' by the soldiers because of its shape). This contrasted with the far swifter US Marine Operation *Khanjar*, which concluded within one week, and which greatly resembled a Vietnam-era air mobility operation. Why were the British so much slower?

The plan for Operation *Panchai Palang* was undermined by several factors. The first flaw was purely conceptual: Malgir and Babaji could not be 'liberated' as if they were a piece of land 'occupied' by an enemy. In this respect, *Panchai Palang* repeated the fallacy of Operation *Sond Chara*, conducted by 3 Commando Brigade the previous winter, from which it was derived. The likelihood was that a grand sweep through the area would provoke a strong tribal response, with or without the incitement of insurgent gangs. This is exactly what happened. Indeed, it would take three more years to 'liberate' Babaji, by which time the British were handing over to local forces and withdrawing. Ironically (or perhaps predictably), the Afghan security forces would only remain in situ for about a year before abandoning every British-built patrol base and checkpoint, and calling into question what had been the point of 'liberating' Babaji in the first place.

The second and critical weakness in the plan was the axis of advance. The brigade proposed to squeeze its entire force down a single, gravel track known as the Old Babaji Road, which ran down the spine of the valley. This was a huge risk. The track followed a wavy line, joining clusters of *kalays* or villages, and was believed to be the only trafficable route in the entire area. In the event, the heavy military traffic collapsed every single culvert on the Old Babaji Road. As the British lacked the necessary engineer resources to keep their battlegroups moving (fascines and trackway), this meant every culvert became a major obstacle which ground the advance to a standstill. For the local villagers, the British brigade became a slow-moving caravan of vehicles which could be blocked at the front and readily picked off from the sides. In the west, the Welsh Guards would also advance on a single track, again with deleterious consequences. Other elements then compounded these difficulties: an extreme risk aversion to the threat of IEDs; logistic difficulties resupplying and sustaining the advancing battlegroup; and the debilitating effects of the heat.

A critical third factor was simply a lack of troops, especially infantrymen. In World War II, an objective like Malgir and Babaji districts would have been a divisional task. Radford was being asked to complete the task with one Light Dragoons battlegroup. In fact, he was attempting the job with an understrength and ad hoc unit. The Light Dragoons was actually made up from one formation reconnaissance squadron; a depleted A (Grenadier) Company, 2 Mercians; and B Company, 2 Mercians. Egypt Squadron, 2nd Royal Tank Regiment mounted in Vikings was being used in a resupply role, and the few Mastiffs available to the battlegroup were used both as a brigade HQ and as a ferrying service. This was a completely inadequate force.

Lastly, *Panchai Palang* appeared to illustrate an unfortunate inverse correlation between the distance and speed covered by a British Army brigade, and the amount of paperwork it generated. The embarrassing fact was that the modern British Army, obsessed with a plethora of 'processes' – all dipped in acid baths of euphemisms and buzz-phrases – could no longer devise plans without cranking through sand-clogged gears of byzantine, unnecessary staff work, still less execute those plans quickly. Ironically, the mountain of staff effort was largely redundant anyway, because the British actually knew very little about the area they were about to invest. The failure of the Intelligence Corps to collate intelligence in a half-competent manner meant Brigadier Radford would have to start from an almost blank piece of paper, three years after the British had deployed to the province. As the brigade chief of staff later recalled, the first good intelligence came when a colonel took it upon himself to walk into a refugee camp and ask the simple question: 'Who comes from Babaji?'[21] Good intelligence also began to flow when the Light Dragoons clashed with armed gangs, old-fashioned 'reconnaissance by fire' making up for the intelligence deficit.

About 3,000 troops were committed to Operation *Panchai Palang*, including two mechanized companies from the Danish battlegroup and companies from the ANA 3/205 Brigade. The hard fighting, however, was undertaken by the British. The estimated number of enemy fighters in Babaji and Malgir districts was 500, although this was just a wild guess. The large number of troops involved on the fringes of the operation only added to 19 Light Brigade's logistic problems.

The prelude to Operation *Panchai Palang* began on 19 June, under the cover of darkness. About 350 men from 3 SCOTS were lifted by helicopter to the southern crossing point in Babaji, on a bend in the Nahr-e Bughra Canal. On the eve of the operation, the troops observed a moving tribute to one of their recently fallen comrades, Sergeant Sean Binnie, who had been killed in Musa Qaleh, before gorging on hamburgers and chips and mounting the awaiting helicopters.[22] The unlucky Binnie had posted a grenade through a door only for the gunman to jump out and shoot him at point-blank range.

Panchai Palang was the largest British Army air assault operation in many years, and it required the entire lift of available Chinook helicopters (12 aircraft) to transport the Jocks. Due to a lack of British Chinooks, six of these helicopters were provided by the USMC, an embarrassing reflection of the ongoing problem the British were experiencing in providing sufficient helicopters for the British task force three years after entering Helmand Province. The total package included: 12 Chinooks, two Sea Kings (used as sniper platforms), three UH-60 Black Hawks, two AH-64 Apaches, one AC-130 Spectre gunship, a pair of Harriers and two Predator armed UAVs. Four of the helicopters took off from Bastion with the commanding officer's tactical party and B Company under Major Al Steele. The other six flew the longer distance from Kandahar carrying A (Grenadier) Company, led by Major Matt Munro.

3 SCOTS's target was a well-known narcotics bazaar and a collection of compounds near the village of Lakhshak Kalay. This was divided into two objectives: Zermatt, the bazaar itself that would be secured by A Company; and Whistler, the western end of the wadi that fell to B Company.[23] As dawn broke it became evident the entire area was deserted. The opium bazaar that had been described as a major narcotics hub was also empty, although there was enough detritus to suggest the market stalls had been used to trade in opium. In anticipation of the arrival of the British the Taliban had laid eight IEDs in the bazaar, each one of which had to be laboriously cleared.[24] In total, A Company would clear 22 IEDs, with a further 13 IEDs discovered by B Company. All the surrounding farmhouses were empty, and the 'goodies' which the soldiers had brought with them (gifts for children) proved useless – there were no children anywhere. B Company would not find a single civilian until the fourth day of the operation, when a teenage boy was found scavenging for bread, and an old man with bad legs was discovered sitting outside a shack.[25]

The lodgement the Jocks established over the next few days was not entirely peaceful. There were some sporadic gun battles, but these were desultory affairs. Serious resistance to the British presence only lasted about two days. At one point a group of gunmen crawled to within 100 metres of 1 (Minden) Platoon's position, but they were seen off with a withering amount of machine-gun fire, mortars and artillery.[26] On another occasion, three gunmen were spotted by a circling Reaper UAV. The UAV pilot launched a Hellfire missile and killed one of the men (at $100,000 per shot, this was an expensive way to kill a villager with a rifle). With no civilians to worry about, the defenders could afford to lavish large amounts of ordnance on anyone suspicious approaching the compounds the Jocks had taken over as patrol bases. On another occasion, a 500-pound bomb was dropped on a compound from an American B1-B bomber, one of only ten bombs dropped in the entire operation.[27] At FOB Wahid, the name given to the newly established company base, two snipers took pot shots at the Jocks for almost the entire duration of their two-week stay. Eventually, '5 Pl was tasked to mount an ambush patrol to try to catch the perpetrators who were becoming increasingly brazen. In position by 4am, the ambush was triggered at 8am as one of the sections saw two insurgents moving into position at close quarters. In the ensuing fight they killed one and an UAV was able to track and stop the other.'[28] The lack of enemy activity did not mean rest for the soldiers. Building a FOB (and second patrol base at a point called Crossing Point 1) required heavy manual labour. Although there were Royal Engineers on hand to provide some of the heavy lift, the infantrymen still had to fill over 3,000 sandbags to bolster their defences.[29]

These gun battles remained intermittent, and over time the appetite for challenging the British presence waned. The 3 SCOTS Reconnaissance Platoon conducted mounted patrols in Jackals to reassure any returning locals they could find, but these were few and far between. The Mortar Platoon, fulfilling the reputation of mortar platoons in infantry battalions, settled into its own luxurious compound decorated with Afghan tapestries and containing a prized bed. The most serious injuries experienced by 3 SCOTS were a twisted ankle and a swollen eye from an insect bite.[30] By the time the Jocks were relieved by Number 2 Company of the Welsh Guards on 4 July – 11 days after they had seized the lodgement – they were entertaining themselves swimming in the Shamalan Canal. The enterprising soldiers had even built themselves a diving board. Others fished, adding carp and crab to the menu of rations. According to the battlegroup, as many as 48 insurgents were killed, but no bodies were recovered, and this was probably an overestimation.[31]

For the Welsh Guards who relieved the 3 SCOTS, operations began on 25 June in the bottom corner of Babaji with the investment of Chah-e Anjir by the Prince of Wales's Company. The battlegroup axis of advance then took it east of the town of Chah-e Anjir, where the marines had raided a Taliban cache the previous winter, veering north and running a further 6 kilometres to the junction of the Shamalan and Nahr-e Bughra canals. The guardsmen's mission was to advance along a levee track (Route Cornwall) that ran parallel to the canal and to block or destroy 14 crossing points, ranging from footbridges to road bridges. Running almost parallel to this canal track was Route 603 to the west (Route Dorset), a straight gravel track which American contractors had built in the 1950s. In effect, the Welsh Guards would be slamming shut the door before a sweep was conducted from east to west by the Light Dragoons and 2 Mercians (Worcesters and Foresters) battlegroup, preparing to deploy from the area of Gereshk.

This was the plan, but it contained serious flaws. The original area of operations ascribed to Lieutenant Colonel Thorneloe was so unfeasibly large he felt obliged to protest to the brigade HQ, forcing a readjustment of boundaries. The proposition that the guardsmen could somehow seal off the Shamalan Canal was also fanciful. The lack of helicopters was worrisome. Most acutely, the battlegroup was being asked to advance along a single narrow axis – the levee track – which could easily be interdicted by seeding IEDs. Inevitably, this is what happened.

Progress was slow for the heavily laden infantrymen. Conscious of the danger of roadside bombs, the Welsh Guards advanced cautiously, clearing and marking safe lanes for follow-on vehicles carrying resupplies and stores. There was intermittent resistance, and it was obvious that the Welsh Guards' progress north was being watched by the locals. A favoured tactic was to allow a convoy of vehicles to pass and then activate a roadside bomb (by connecting a battery to the circuit) to catch the convoy on its return journey. It was on returning from such a journey in a Viking that Lieutenant Colonel Thorneloe was killed, alongside his teenage driver, Trooper Joshua Hammond, serving with 2nd Royal Tank Regiment. Thorneloe's death – he was the most senior British officer killed in Helmand – caused great commotion in Britain. Pictures of his widow, fists clenched on the steps of the Guards Memorial Chapel, were splashed on the front pages of all the newspapers. Prince Charles, who had known Thorneloe personally, attended the funeral service, as did former Secretary of State for Defence, Des Browne, whom he had served as a military assistant. The well-attended funeral service did not quite bury the commanding officer, whose death would have one more twist. In October, a Conservative MP and former guardsman received an unsolicited email from a friend which included secret extracts from an email sent by the officer just before his death. Thorneloe had already begun to gain a reputation within the brigade for his outspoken manner, which caused tensions with the brigade headquarters. In the extracts, he almost presaged his own demise, lamenting that he had 'virtually no' helicopters to transport his soldiers and this was forcing him to undertake risky road moves. Damningly, he asserted that ISAF helicopter management was 'not fit for purpose'. Three weeks after sending this email he was dead, and his words ended up in the *Daily Mail* newspaper.

The death of these two soldiers marked the beginning of what would prove to be the bloodiest month for the British task force in Helmand. The Welsh Guardsmen reached the Black Watch lodgement 11 days after they left their start lines, but the cost had been high. At the beginning of July – at the height of Operation *Panchai Palang* – a grim milestone was reached. After a bloody week of fighting British fatalities suffered in Afghanistan exceeded the number suffered in the unpopular war in Iraq. Fifteen soldiers were killed in just over a week and eight were killed in just one 24-hour period (an event that would provoke the mothers of the fallen soldiers to start a bereavement support group). At the field hospital in Camp Bastion medical staff worked overtime to save lives. A total of 656 patients would be received over the course of the operation, and at one point half of Britain's blood supplies were being diverted to Afghanistan.[32] For Commander Surgeon Sarah Stapley, who served for nine weeks at the hospital, Operation *Panchai Palang* was a conveyer belt of amputations. By the end of her tour she had amputated 62 limbs, including eight limbs in one frenetic day.[33] The total number of British soldiers killed in Helmand now stood at 184. In the smoke and mirrors of Whitehall it was rumoured the Labour government was planning to cut and run – a charge quickly countered by the nervous prime minister in a letter to MPs.

It was clear by the summer that opinion on the war had become angrily divided. The camp that argued for an immediate withdrawal (which included the distinguished British military historian Correlli Barnett) was challenged by a bullish camp that pressed for more troops and an

American-style surge – the sacrifice would have to continue until success had been achieved. This was a classic sunk-cost fallacy. Nobody wanted to be the first person to write off the moral debt to the dead. It was a former Russian general, quoted in a British newspaper, who summed up what some feared but dare not express in public: 'I believed as sincerely as US officers do now that we were fighting there to help make our country safer. After the war … I could see this war had been pointless.'[34]

The problem the government faced was that there was little to show for three years of sacrifice. What exactly was the war being fought for? ISAF (or more properly the American-led Operation *Enduring Freedom*) was no closer to finding Osama bin Laden (or eradicating al-Qaeda and its allies in Afghanistan). The jihadist domino theory argument that waging war in Afghanistan meant that terrorism was being kept at bay from Britain's shores was not credible. The war was provoking the possibility of terrorism, and Britain's home-grown terrorists had no links with Afghanistan anyway – they were mainly, but not exclusively, drawn from disaffected ranks of young Pakistanis. The conflict had spread instability across the entire region, honest governance had not been brought to Afghanistan and the Taliban seemed to be getting stronger. By all measures, the war seemed to be going backwards.

For the soldiers, isolated from this mounting concern at home, the operation continued to unfold despite the setbacks. The day after Lieutenant Colonel Thorneloe was killed, two Danish mechanized companies supported by a troop of tanks seized crossing points south of Gereshk. The third phase of Operation *Panchai Palang* was about to be executed. With the crossing points secured, the Light Dragoons battlegroup passed through the Danish positions and began to advance south-west. For a combination of reasons, Lieutenant Colonel Gus Fair's men arrived on their start lines in some disorder. The exhausted cavalrymen were then surprised by the mirage-like vision of some Danish female APC crews wandering across the battlefield dressed in shorts and vest tops.

This area of Malgir District was fiendishly difficult ground. The battlegroup would have to negotiate a ring of villages separated by intensively cultivated farmland. The most common annotation on the maps carried by the soldiers was the phrase 'numerous ditches'. Every hundred metres the soldiers faced an obstacle that could conceal a firing point, or bog down their vehicles. Acting Corporal Pattenden, serving with 25 Field Squadron Royal Engineers, described some of these difficulties when his section was tasked to open a route over a stream, a task that was expected to take a few hours and in the end took four days:

> Our effort was to get routes open, enabling convoys of mastiffs to get forward to the troops in forward locations. One of the first tasks required was a route upgrade about a kilometre from A1 echelon. SSgt Pascoe had recced it and we were briefed that it required about 2 hours work to put in a fascine across a pretty small stream about a meter wide. In reality this was a lot more complicated! Work lasted all day, then the following day work carried on with just about every vehicle coming through getting bogged in and the plant operated by Spr Cormack had to recover them. After 4 days the job was finally complete.[35]

One of the problems facing these young sappers was that the Royal Engineers no longer held route-opening equipment developed from the experience of World War II. The kit that did exist, such as trackway and fascine-layers, had not been deployed to Helmand at all or in sufficient numbers, despite previous commanders noting that obstacle-crossing equipment was imperative to negotiate Helmand's Green Zone.

It took the Light Dragoons 36 hours to clear through the first village. A Scimitar was destroyed, but the crew miraculously crawled away from the vehicle unscathed. By the morning of 5 June the advance was resumed, with A Company on the right and B Company on the left clearing the area of Abpashak Wadi. Straight away, the battlegroup was engaged by fleeting gunmen. To add to the friction, the point sections began finding IEDs, some double-stacked and containing large charges. In one incident the uncovered IED was so large it completely cratered the route and blocked any further movement. An American Paladin counter-IED team was forced to blow down a wall and dozer the earth into the crater to allow the advance to continue. In the meantime, B Company had stumbled into an ambush and suffered multiple casualties. By the end of the day, the Light Dragoons had advanced a mere 400 metres.

The following morning it was A Company's turn. Within half an hour of advancing from nighttime harbours the forward left platoon was caught in an ambush and suffered seven casualties. Unfortunately, the stricken platoon was on the wrong side of an unfordable ditch, which significantly complicated the casualty evacuation. The inconclusive fighting then continued for the rest of the day, with neither side making great headway. By the second night, the battlegroup had only managed to push the insurgents back a few fields, despite support from Apaches, artillery and mortars.

On the third morning, a decision was taken to use air strikes to end the stalemate. This proved decisive. Four bombs were dropped on a compound 200 metres forward of A Company, and this seemed to unlock the gate. The subsequent advance was not, however, without resistance. More casualties were sustained, and Trooper Christopher Whiteside, a 21-year-old from Blackpool who had overcome a serious knee injury to serve with the Light Dragoons, was killed by an IED. By the fourth night, Emsdorf Troop, which had lent ten men to A Company, was down to two survivors. Overall, a troop that started with with just over 30 soldiers would be left with eight survivors – three were killed and 20 injured. This troop was led by a Lieutenant Tresham Gregg, who would subsequently be awarded the Military Cross. Gregg was another example of the family sacrifice in the British Army: he was the grandson of the wartime Royal Tank Regiment officer, Colonel Tresham Gregg, a distinguished officer who served in several theatres and who fought as a partisan in Italy. The subaltern's father, another Tresham Gregg, was also a serving officer in the Light Dragoons.[36]

Every track had to be checked for roadside bombs, so the battlegroup continued to advance at the pace of the slowest mine-sweeping solder. As the insurgents were laying IEDs 'like minefields', that pace was slow. It took a further five days for the battlegroup to cover just 4 kilometres. Commonly, IED belts were covered by ambush parties. Four days into the operation, Lance Corporal Kyle Smith, serving with the Mercians, was leading his section across an open field when the soldiers were ambushed. Four soldiers fell in a hail of automatic fire. Smith attended to the nearest casualty, exposing himself to the Taliban fire over 100 metres as he pulled the wounded soldier into cover. Having rescued one comrade, Smith again risked his life dragging a second casualty into cover. For these acts of bravery, Lance Corporal Smith was awarded the Conspicuous Gallantry Cross.[37] In a similar incident, Corporal Craig Adkin, a company medic also serving with the Mercians, found himself criss-crossing bullet-swept fields to tend to casualties from an RPG strike. He would be awarded a Military Cross for this courage under fire.[38]

IEDs had undoubtedly become the biggest single menace facing British soldiers in Helmand, and the summer of 2009 was the period when this menace spiked dramatically on every graph. By the mid-point of the tour, 19 Light Brigade had found over 900 of these roadside bombs. Across Helmand, every sixteenth patrol was experiencing an IED strike. In areas like Sangin, every sixth patrol was now encountering an IED. The psychological impact of these odds – particularly for the Rifles deployed in Sangin – could not be overstated. Morale became volatile. For the first time in the war, units had to deal with soldiers who struggled to step beyond the front gate of the patrol base and go 'outside the wire'. For the first time in a generation there were incidents of soldiers shooting themselves in the foot to escape the front line, as well as 'refusals' (soldiers refusing to patrol).[39] The number of non-battle injuries and illnesses at Bastion Hospital rose steeply, raising suspicions that many soldiers were resorting to malingering. Was it coincidence that the location with the most soldiers reporting non-battle injuries and illnesses, by a significant margin, was Sangin? Over the course of *Herrick 10*, there were more than 3,000 cases of soldiers reporting gastro-intestinal sickness in Sangin.[40] Close to 2,000 cases of skin problems were recorded. As 'runny tummy' or rashes gave you a ticket to light duties, or even a day off, the conclusion one could draw was obvious. Lieutenant Colonel Rob Thomson put on a brave face in Sangin – what else could he do? – but the numbers suggested that he was commanding a battalion on the edge. In a previous generation such soldiers might have faced court martial. A modern generation treated the issue more sensitively, and nobody was in a mood to start prosecuting soldiers whose nerves were frayed beyond any reasonable level.

A total of 176 of these devices would be discovered on Operation *Panchai Palang*, accounting for nine out of the ten fatalities experienced on the operation, but the true number laid by the insurgents to stall the British advance was many times higher. Not every bomb could be found, and the Taliban recovered devices that had been inadvertently bypassed by the British. The fatalities provoked by IEDs across the past two years of the war told their own story. In 2007 just 11 British soldiers had been killed by IEDs and 16 had been wounded. By the following year the figures had risen to 38 and 113 respectively. In 2009 – the year in which the Taliban began mass-laying of IEDs – casualty figures almost became unsustainable. Seventy-eight British soldiers were killed, and a staggering 328 were injured – an entire battalion was written off from this hidden menace. Over 70 per cent of British fatalities were being caused by IEDs, and the soldiers facing this daily threat were well aware of the statistic.

The majority of the roadside bombs encountered by the soldiers on Operation *Panchai Palang* continued to be the simple pressure-plate variety, commonly using saw blades freely given to farmers in aid programmes. This exploitation of cheap materials was also evident in the growing use of fertilizers to make homemade explosives – a phenomenon which had echoes of IRA homemade bombs (Afghan tribesmen actually proved to be more resourceful bomb-makers than Irish nationalists). As the British improved the protection levels of their vehicles, so the local bomb-makers increased the size of their IEDs. It was a deadly arms race played out on the tracks and trails that criss-crossed the Green Zone. Ammonium nitrate mixed with a tell-tale grey aluminium powder were the favoured ingredients used to fill 10-litre plastic containers, pressure cookers or small drums. A frustration for bomb disposal officers was that agencies promoting reconstruction in Helmand were deliberately supplying high nitrogen content fertilizers to the farmers – the very type that made the best bombs.[41] Eventually the British would attempt to ban the import of this fertilizer to Helmand with mixed success.

The size of IEDs was not the only concern. Over the 2008–09 fighting seasons, it became increasingly obvious that the Taliban were no longer planting single roadside bombs. They were planting 'IED fields', a sort of nuisance minefield designed to trap British forces in a maze of bombs. In the summer of 2008, the discovery of six roadside bombs in one day by the Royal Irish in Sangin was considered newsworthy. By the following summer, 2 Rifles located at the same base would find five times this number of bombs in one day. These IED fields presented a terrible hazard to soldiers responding instinctively to save a comrade injured by an IED, who then became injured or killed themselves. Bomb disposal officers found that they were being especially targeted either by the design of the IED, or the cunning manner in which they were emplaced.

The devices the soldiers were finding were also becoming increasingly sophisticated. The command wire IED was perhaps the simplest form of remote device, but examples were now being found where several hundred metres of wire were being pre-buried in anticipation of the opportune moment to connect a bomb to the end of the wire. The bombers were also beginning to experiment with the radio-controlled bomb, using different types of Dual Tone Modulated Frequency (DTMF) receivers in an attempt to defeat British ECM. Directional mines, essentially tins filled with nails or ball bearings, set at waist or head height, were beginning to appear in

Helmand. One bomb disposal operator found the parts of half a motorcycle embedded in a bomb to create shrapnel.[42]

The Taliban were not just laying cleverer devices; they also pressed children and animals into the game. 'Donkey IEDs' were perhaps the strangest permutation in the armoury. The British experienced at least three of these: one in Sangin, another in Garmsir and a third described thus by an officer who witnessed the demise of the animal:

> Then in the afternoon the gate guard realised there was something suspicious going on. A group had just let go of a donkey a short way from camp and hurried off. He tried to divert the animal with flares and other warnings. Obstinacy not being the best quality in that situation, the beast of burden eventually had to be stopped by a rifle shot. The team went out and established there was something very suspicious under the bundle of hay carried by the donkey. Eventually one brave ANA warrior set fire to the hay with a flare from a distance, and 30 seconds later there was a considerable explosion. No one was hurt.[43]

By the summer of 2009, when Operation *Panchai Palang* was mounted, there was irrefutable evidence of Iranian and Pakistani complicity in the bomb-making. The ISI had a long history of transferring bomb-making skills to the mujahidin. The Iranian al Quds force had been a source of IED and other war materials in Iraq. Now it appeared they were assisting the Taliban against the common Western enemy. In the spring of 2009 an American-led special forces operation against a bazaar in Marjah District led to the biggest ever drug bust in Afghanistan's history. But what was noteworthy about this raid was what else was found: 44 blocks of Iranian plastic explosives, hundreds of blasting caps, hundreds of kilos of opium base, 27,000kg of ammonium nitrate (a sufficient quantity to make literally hundreds of powerful roadside bombs) and three police cars. There could be no clearer example of the nexus between Iranian arms traffickers, Afghan drug traffickers and the corrupt Afghan police. At the conclusion of the raid American fighter-bombers flattened the bazaar.

These developments were concerning, but the single evolution in IED design that radically changed the nature of the war in Helmand was the introduction of low metal content IEDs (LMCIEDs). If one weapon might be described as the Taliban's Stinger (the American anti-aircraft missile that changed the dynamics of the Soviet–Afghan War), this was it.

LMCIEDs used carbon rods instead of metal parts, such as the ubiquitous saw blades, to make the electrical connections to detonate the bomb. LMCIEDs could not be readily detected, if at all, by the Vallon mine detectors issued to the soldiers, and even some of the more sophisticated detectors later introduced into service struggled to detect such devices. A lessons document worryingly recorded, 'Due to the nature of these devices it is difficult for VALLON to detect them. It is made all the more difficult when operating within confined spaces or areas with no ground sign or markers … As yet there is no technical solution to this issue.'[44]

The devices did not come from Afghanistan. Pakistanis taught the Taliban how to make these difficult-to-detect roadside bombs (the directional mines or EFPs, Explosively Formed Projectiles, came from Iran). For soldiers sweeping for IEDs, the only sure ways to find the devices were detecting the battery pack (before stepping on the pressure plate) or ground sign (evidence of digging). One soldier sardonically noted that during his training he had been told to look for disturbed earth, but nobody told him that everywhere was disturbed earth.

Over time, LMCIEDs proliferated, soon becoming the most common type of IED in Helmand. This created a terrible moral dilemma for commanders. Before the introduction of these devices, soldiers were leaving the safety of their bases with the knowledge they had a fighting chance of beating the bombers, if they undertook their drills correctly. Now this was no longer the case. A patrol could carry out all the correct drills and still fall victim to an IED that was very difficult to detect. This, with a sickening inevitability, is what began to happen over the months that followed. LMCIEDs were a far graver problem than the lack of protection on the Land Rover Snatch or the lack of helicopters – two issues highlighted by the media during the war – because there was no 'silver bullet' technological solution to the problem. Either the British had to concede the ground to the Taliban, or the patrolling had to continue with the certain knowledge that soldiers would be killed and maimed. Conceding ground was not an option, so the patrolling continued and the casualties mounted.

Despite the increasing number and sophistication of the roadside bombs, it was a reflection of the success of the *range* of British counter-measures that a minority of these devices successfully detonated and claimed casualties. This was the key. There was no single technological solution, and no counter-IED drills could cope with every situation. The combination of aerial surveillance and ground surveillance technologies provided one important layer of protection. The second vital layer was provided by the Afghan security forces and locals who pointed out the location of IEDs to British patrols. They were far more attuned to the environment than the average British soldier and could more readily spot something that was out of place. 'Turn-ins', as they were known, were often done at risk to the farmer who faced the wrath of the insurgents after the British bomb disposal team had left the area. On many occasions, the farmers dug up the IEDs themselves and deposited them at the nearest British base, to the consternation of the sangar sentries. The last important element was simply leadership. LMCIEDs had a profound psychological effect on soldiers sweeping with the Vallon detectors – especially in the summer of 2009 when they first began to proliferate. It was clear to everyone the risks had multiplied enormously. On more than one occasion, platoon commanders, sergeants and even company commanders took over from their privates and led patrols to restore confidence in shaken troops. Lieutenant Colonel Thorneloe himself had taken the place of a private soldier and swept for IEDs before he was killed. This was leadership of the highest order.

ISAF, ultimately, was very fortunate the Taliban evolution of IEDs effectively ended with the LMCIED. Over time, mine-sweeping soldiers became extremely skilled in detecting the tell-tale signs of a buried bomb, partly from enhanced training, partly from the accumulated experiences of successive brigades and lastly because of the introduction of specialized detectors. Military working dogs (codenamed 'BEEKs') also proved invaluable. Towards the end of the war the majority of patrols were supported by a sniffer dog.

By 9 July another phase of Operation *Panchai Palang* was drawing to a conclusion. After five days pushing south-west, the Light Dragoons battlegroup had reached a line astride the largest cluster of settlements in the northern half of Malgir District. The battlegroup had been operating in a bottleneck barely 3 kilometres wide where it had faced determined resistance. Once past these villages the Green Zone widened, allowing the spear point to probe around insurgent positions. The wider frontage also meant that insurgents could more easily escape the advancing force, constrained to the central axis, because of the lack of trafficable routes on the flanks. The arrival of two reinforcing companies also added to the momentum of the battlegroup. In the first week, an advance of a few hundred metres was considered good. By the second week, the Light Dragoons were achieving 1-kilometre bounds.

Optimism over a possible collapse of resistance, however, proved premature. Several insurgent gangs had either been bypassed, or deliberately allowed the British convoy of vehicles to pass. These now began to harass the extended military cavalcade. To prevent more enemy reinforcements entering the area, a decision was taken to mount a second heliborne operation. This would act as a block ahead of the Light Dragoons. The task fell to B Company, 3 SCOTS, which had only just been extracted from Babaji. Overcoming its tiredness, the company duly launched again on 10 July, seizing two objectives named Mull and Eigg. The block remained in place for five days, but in fact encountered no enemy.

This cued the second push by the Light Dragoons. Paind Kalay, the brigade's second objective, was secured on 13 July without a fight. Two days later, the third objective, Rahim Kalay, was also grabbed bloodlessly. The battlegroup had now reached the center of Babaji District. By now, it was evident that resistance against the British was evaporating. Many of the insurgent foot soldiers who had decided to contest the ground had been killed and commanders were losing heart. Faced with the possibility of being overrun, insurgent gangs were now fleeing the area, creating lucrative targets for the Apache.

The final phase of the operation was initiated on 20 July with a third heliborne assault on Loy Aderah, this time mounted by A Company, 3 SCOTS, who linked up with C Company, 2 Royal Welsh, a sub-unit that boasted 22 Warriors. The Royal Welsh had driven their vehicles across 8 kilometres of Green Zone in an armoured sweep towards the east bank of the Luy Mandah Wadi. This was the first time the heavy armoured vehicles had been risked in this way, and they were helped on their way by the hard, dry ground.

The deployment of the Royal Welsh had been a necessary but unplanned last roll of the dice. By this stage, the Light Dragoons battlegroup was exhausted and the brigade was still short of its final objective. Brigadier Radford needed to find fresh troops, but from where? At short notice, C Company was ordered to make the 100-kilometre drive south from Musa Qaleh and was given just four days to prepare for battle. As it chanced, the area they entered had largely been deserted by insurgents and the 35-tonne vehicles were able to use existing tracks rather than destroy crops by traversing farmers' fields (platoons were handing out bags of cash to immediately compensate farmers anyway). Unfortunately, this decision, taken from good intentions, led to collapsed culverts and a headache for sappers tasked to repair the damage behind the advancing company group. For most locals, and especially the children, there seems to have been a certain excitement over the appearance of the Warriors. On one occasion, villagers actually joined in to assist a crew which had thrown a track. Over the next few days the company cleared 198 compounds and held three village *shuras*. There was virtually no fighting.[45]

On 25 July Operation *Panchai Palang* was officially declared over. In total, 23 British soldiers were killed, although only ten died on the operation itself. The remainder were killed in fighting that flared up elsewhere in Helmand, especially in the Sangin area. Three times this number of soldiers were seriously injured, and many more were lightly injured. With Operation *Panchai Palang*, 19 Light Brigade shot its bolt. Although the brigade was still two months short of the end of its tour, no further brigade-level operations would be attempted. The limits of British combat power had been reached.

Regardless of the military success of the operation, everyone was aware that *Panchai Palang*'s true success could only be measured in the future by the security and development delivered to the districts. As a British military spokesman put it:

> Our intention with this operation was, in the short term, to clear the area in advance of the presidential and provincial elections so that we could ensure that the Afghan people were free to exercise their democratic rights. In the longer term, it was to remove the insurgents and hold the region, alongside Afghan forces, to allow reconstruction and development to take place.[46]

Achieving these longer-term aims, of course, would always be much harder. Within days it was evident that the Taliban had re-infiltrated the area and were already threatening any locals who cooperated with the British. Newly constructed checkpoints manned by Afghan police proved useless. It was too easy to bribe an Afghan policeman. Some had relatives among the gunmen. Within a month of the conclusion of Operation *Panchai Palang*, five more British soldiers were killed in Babaji. The hard truth was that the area had largely reverted back to less conspicuous but no less threatening Taliban control.

British commanders like Lieutenant Colonel Gus Fair who commanded the Light Dragoons battlegroup, and whose dusty, tanned face appeared on several BBC news bulletins, would have disputed this pessimistic view. Fair believed at the conclusion of the operation that 'more than ever this is a winnable campaign'. In the long term, Fair would be proved right (in most areas of Babaji), in the sense that local, tribal governance would reassert itself, and the Taliban would be forced out. But it would take another two years of hard fighting, and a further year consolidating the gains.

Following the conclusion of *Panchai Palang*, Task Force Helmand would mount eight major operations and countless company-level operations to subdue the insurgency in Babaji. They included *Kapcha Azadi* on Route Trident (winter 2009); *Kapcha Sarek* in Rahim Kalay (July 2010); *Kapcha Luma* in Char Coucha (October 2010); *Kapcha Bambarak* in Tor Ghai (December 2010); *Kapcha Kwandi*, which revisited Char Coucha (January–February 2011); *Omid Shash* in Kopak (February 2011); *Kapcha Lewe* in Kopak and Malgir (March–April 2011); and *Omid Haft* in Kopak and Padaka (May–June 2011). This relentless effort finally yielded the prize, but first the British would suffer another reverse.

From the beginning, the forthcoming presidential election had been set up as a measure of the success of Operation *Panchai Palang*. This proved an unfortunate misjudgement. As the election drew nearer, the omens looked increasingly poor. To cope with the largely illiterate Afghan population, voting would be cast by fingerprint. The Taliban threatened to cut off the fingers of anyone who voted by checking for the tell-tale signs of indelible ink. The campaign of intimidation appeared to be succeeding, and all the indicators were suggesting that the rural population of Helmand would not vote. At one point the new British ambassador, Mark Sedwill, visited Nad-e Ali District, pointedly refusing to wear a ballistic vest to show that it was safe to walk the streets, but the gesture meant little to ordinary Helmandis. With a population of just over 800,000, it had originally been planned to open as many as 222 polling stations across the province to cater for about 600,000 potential voters. It soon became apparent that this plan was wholly unrealistic. In the end only 107 polling stations would be opened, but the British hoped that at least this reduced number would still capture the majority of the voting population.[47]

The detailed picture, however, remained disappointing. The ambassador's upbeat claim that 'we are confident that the majority of eligible voters in Helmand who want to will be able to vote' was for the cameras, but the claim was wildly off the mark.[48] Perhaps the most disappointing numbers emerged from Nad-e Ali District itself, which the ambassador visited. This was Helmand's most populous rural district, with a population of over 100,000. British operations in this district, since the autumn of 2008, had been promoted as a move to liberate the villages from the stranglehold of the insurgency, and 13 polling stations were opened. On the eve of polling just 625 people had bothered to register in Nad-e Ali, and nobody was expecting more. It was rapidly becoming apparent, even to the most determined optimist, that the voting in Helmand would be a fiasco.

When voting day arrived on 20 August it turned into the disaster doomsayers had predicted. There were 139 gunfights across the British-held areas, the most violent day of the entire tour. Nobody voted in Garmsir, newly 'secured' by US Marines. Perhaps 150 people voted in Babaji.[49] The claim that 80,000 more Helmandis would now be able to vote, following the end of Operation *Panchai Palang*, rebounded spectacularly. In Nad-e Ali, possibly 800 fraudulent votes were cast. The numbers elsewhere were similarly disappointing; Chah-e Anjir (2,297); Luy Bagh (321); Zarghun Kalay (231); and Shin Kalay, just one (presumably the self-appointed village elder).[50] In Sangin, within minutes of opening the polling stations, gun battles erupted around the district centre. The local Taliban kept up this barrage of fire for the rest of the day. The riflemen defending the district centre enjoyed the punch-up, but for the 16,000-odd registered voters in the town, voting day was a surreal experience punctuated by Apache helicopters, bombing runs from coalition aircraft and artillery fire. A pall of smoke drifted across the town by the end of the day. The questionable report that 500 people had still managed to vote was hardly the victory for democracy the British had lauded. In nearby FOB Inkerman the fighting was no less intense. By the end of the day, the riflemen had lobbed 133 mortars and 172 artillery shells at insurgent positions. Supporting Apaches fired about 500 30mm cannon rounds and loosed off 28 flechette rockets and a Hellfire. British Tornados, American A-10s and Belgian F-16s joined the fight. Two 500-pound bombs were also dropped to fend off the attacks.[51]

In some locations, such as Chah-e Anjir, where Prince of Wales's Company, Welsh Guards was based, the fighting became the entertainment:

> The finest example of how simple communication turns a crowd was on Election Day when the town's perimeter was attacked around thirty times resulting in AH fire missions, GMLRS and many small arms

> engagements. By using a sound commander on the polling centre roof to give voters prior warning of our fire missions, at times whilst the indirect rounds were actually in the air, voters knew the reason for the bangs. Indeed, after the first few rounds the crowds began to cheer every subsequent explosion knowing the enemy were being hit. We had generated a carnival atmosphere.[52]

In Musa Qaleh, a deal with the Taliban to allow voters to cast their vote for Karzai appeared to fizzle out, if it was ever really agreed. Hardly anyone bothered to vote, but somehow about 9,000 votes had been cast for Karzai. The wily Akhundzada appears to have been behind the vote-rigging. These were his tribal heartlands, and he would decide the outcome of the Musa Qaleh vote. Across the province, perhaps 8 per cent of the electorate had managed to vote, principally in the safe towns of Lashkar Gah and Gereshk. Nationwide, perhaps 30 per cent of the electorate had voted, and there had been numerous attacks, with about two dozen people killed.

The initial electoral report from Helmand indicated that about 50,000 people had voted. Within a week that number had climbed to 300,000. Bitterly, the British had to concede (in private) that they had presided over a massive exercise in ballot stuffing. Nobody could pretend the vote in Helmand had been fair or open. The Taliban had won an unlikely victory and could truthfully claim they had thwarted the elections.

Nationwide, the election results were no less disastrous. It rapidly became apparent that there had been widespread electoral fraud. As President Karzai inched towards the required 50 per cent threshold needed to avoid a second-round run-off, the scale of the fraud became clearer. Perhaps a third of the votes were tainted, mostly in favour of the Pashtun president. Richard Galbraith, serving as deputy to the UN mission in Afghanistan, resigned following allegations that his Norwegian boss tried to suppress his strong criticism of the election process. Five other members of staff also submitted their resignations. In the end ISAF was left with two irreducible and irreconcilable facts: the election results were illegitimate, and Karzai had won the necessary majority of that illegitimate vote. None of the options open to address this fraudulent outcome was palatable. A re-run appeared logistically impossible, and it was doubtful that Afghans would wish to vote again. Forcing a second-round vote would be unlikely to reverse the outcome anyway and could make matters worse. Forming a national coalition government seemed impossible, as Dr Abdullah Abdullah – his rival – had vowed that he would not serve in a Karzai government.

The flawed Afghan presidential elections were a serious blow to the West and a significant coup for the Taliban. The capstone of ISAF's strategy was that it was supporting legitimate political governance. It was now unarguable that Western soldiers were propping up a corrupt and crooked government without a legitimate mandate. Echoes of Vietnam once again sounded in Washington. In a sense, however, nothing had changed. Karzai had always been expected to win. But the manner in which he won seemed to strike a near mortal blow to an increased American commitment to Afghanistan. President Obama would be awarded the Nobel Peace Prize less than two months later – the first time this award had been granted to a serving US president since 1919 – but this was poor consolation now that 'Obama's war' in Afghanistan had turned sour.

For British infantrymen on the front line, Afghanistan's political shenanigans were a remote concern. Nowhere was this truer than in Sangin, where 2 Rifles was slugging it out with an implacable enemy. Over the course of their tour the riflemen had to deal with over 200 roadside bombs.[53] A single rifleman was responsible for finding 19 of these devices. Twenty-four soldiers in the 2 Rifles battlegroup were killed and a further 80 were seriously wounded. As many as one in five of the battlegroup sustained some sort of injury. These were World War II casualty rates, and they were just not sustainable. For the first time, the British were forced to send battle casualty replacements (BCRs) to make up for the combat losses. In this case, a company from 3 Yorks (Duke of Wellington's) was despatched at short notice from its base in Warminster. The Taliban did not have it all their way. Four bomb-making teams were killed, but this had no impact on the threat of IEDs as bomb-making skills had proliferated.

The American journalist and ex-special forces soldier Michael Yon, who spent a month with 2 Rifles over the course of that torrid summer, vividly described the experiences of the soldiers caught, as he put it, in a 'daily struggle for tiny pieces of real estate'.[54] The picture he painted was bleak and honest. Despite the best efforts to apply a 'hearts and minds' approach, Yon concluded that 'cooperation from locals is almost non-existent in many places', and interaction between the two sides 'nearly zero'.[55]

His view of defence departments was also pessimistic: 'The Pentagon and British MoD spin lies (though I have found Secretary Gates talks straight), but veins of pure truth can be found right here with these soldiers … nothing coming from Kabul, London, or Washington should be trusted.'[56] Yon provided some of the most vivid and honest reporting of the British in Helmand until his embed with 2 Rifles was terminated by the MOD, it was suspected because he was too honest.

The madness that Sangin had become was illustrated by the experiences of Corporal Henry Sanday, one of several Fijians serving in 2 Rifles.[57] In the early hours of the morning on 11 August, 2 Rifles began Operation *Flint*, a mission whose aim was to open an 800-metre road between FOB Jackson and PB Wishtan, to allow a resupply of the patrol base. Wishtan summed up everything that had gone wrong with the British presence in Sangin. Nobody actually wanted this area of largely deserted compounds, the size of about half a dozen football pitches, and it had become a lethal no man's land. The high compound walls and numerous alleyways created a perfect environment for the insurgents to lay numerous traps with IEDs, without being observed. For the British it was imperative a resupply route be kept open to the isolated patrol base, and that route was the notorious Pharmacy Road, in fact no more than a wide dirt track. Scores of IEDs would be laid in the vicinity of Pharmacy Road, and 2 Rifles would eventually suffer 20 casualties in Wishtan just trying to keep the lifeline open. It was probably not an exaggeration to state that Pharmacy Road became the most dangerous road in the world in the summer of 2009.

A low point was experienced on 10 July in an incident that effectively wiped out a platoon. Three sections had set off down the Wishtan bazaar road to rendezvous with an ANA platoon. The lead Vallon men continually received double-tone warnings indicating the presence of IEDs, so it was decided to take an alternative route through a compound. This compound had also been laced with IEDs. A rifleman inadvertently set off an IED that killed him and severely wounded six other soldiers. Among the casualties were the company commander and platoon commander. The first proposed emergency helicopter landing site proved unfeasible because of the large number of IEDs. Eventually it was decided everyone should make their way back to PB Wishtan, divided into three groups, and each carrying casualties. One of these groups set off another IED, killing four riflemen and wounding several more. Three teenagers were among the dead: Riflemen William Aldridge, James Backhouse and Joseph Murphy.

The commanding officer remained defiant in the face of these losses: 'It has been a grim day here in Sangin … the Bugle Major sounded the advance and it would have been heard right across the valley as the sun slipped behind the ridge. We turned to our right, saluted the fallen and the wounded, picked up our rifles and returned to the ramparts.'[58]

But what the British were achieving by basing themselves in the middle of this death trap was an open question. The majority of locals had long fled the area. To avoid the IEDs the soldiers took to 'grand nationaling' (after the steeplechase race) – using ladders to cross-grain the area by climbing over the compound walls and thus avoiding the tracks. It was insane: the soldiers were being forced to keep their feet off the very earth they were supposed to be claiming. On occasions 'grand-nationaling' was not possible, either because the compound walls were too high, or because the loads the soldiers carrying were too heavy, or because vehicles had to be used to carry stocks. Then the riflemen predictably struck IEDs.

Operation *Flint* took two days to complete. Almost 200 men were needed to secure the short stretch of road. It was conducted in 50-degree heat, and the soldiers were carrying in excess of 60 pounds of equipment. The counter-IED teams led by Staff Sergeant Olaf Schmid, who would later be killed by an IED, spent 22 hours clearing IEDs from the Pharmacy Road. By the end of the operation they had uncovered 31 – a record for one day. One of the British armoured tractors ran over an IED and had to be abandoned. The following day a curious local went to investigate and was killed by a Taliban booby trap. The next day a second local was killed when he used a parallel route which he believed had been cleared by the British. This highlighted the danger that only a proportion of the roadside bombs had been found. Many more were still buried somewhere in the warren of alleys, waiting for victims.

Sanday and his men left their patrol base early on the morning of 13 August, the day after Operation *Flint* had been officially closed. At just before 0530hrs they struck an IED that wounded Lance Bombardier Matthew Hatton and two others. Captain Mark Hale and Rifleman Daniel Wild went forward to help the injured Hatton, and they inadvertently set off another IED, killing all three men. Sanday now had five casualties on his hands. The 43-year-old Hale had served in the army since the age of 16 when he joined up as boy soldier. The youngest fatality, Daniel Wild, was just 19. In the previous year he had ironically been prevented from deploying to Kosovo on the grounds of his age. Faced with the probability that the entire area was seeded with IEDs, Sanday tried to get the medevac helicopter (in this case an American Pedro) to land on a roof, but this proved impossible. Eventually, a landing site was found and the three dead and two wounded soldiers were extracted.

Sanday, who was the acting platoon sergeant, then had to pick up the pieces of his shaken patrol and continue with the task. What followed is best described in Yon's words:

> Later that evening, when the mission had been completed and the soldiers were moving back to FOB Jackson, they were hit by a third bomb leaving two casualties. Sanday was setting up another helicopter extraction when a fourth bomb detonated and an interpreter turned into a 'white mist' leaving only a leg … Sanday was down to four unwounded soldiers in his section and in Sangin the IEDs often seem come in big clusters. No matter which way you go, there is a high probability of more. Two interpreters were killed in the strike and three [soldiers] were wounded. Some of the men were in shock and did not react to Sanday's commands. They were seriously battle-affected and refusing orders …[59]

The body of the interpreter who disappeared was eventually found 20 miles away, floating in the Helmand River.

Sanday's trial was not yet over. The following morning he set off again to support a second operation to clear Route Sparta – a 700-metre stretch of track that connected FOB Jackson with PB Nolay, held by the Royal Regiment of Fusiliers. Eventually 21 IEDs would be discovered on this track. He had not patrolled long when an IED detonated 100 metres in front of him, killing three fusiliers. While setting up the helicopter extraction, another soldier stepped on an IED, causing further casualties. Over the course of 24 hours, Sanday witnessed the deaths of six soldiers and two interpreters. He also witnessed multiple traumatic amputations and had to deal with soldiers on the edge of nervous breakdowns. This was not an extraordinary sequence of events. This was what Sangin had become every other week.

Immediately north and south of Sangin, little had changed since 2 PARA fought their bitter battles in the previous summer. The officer commanding B Company of 2 Rifles, based at FOB Inkerman, likened his company to 'a big block of cheese'. Every day his men set out and patrolled the Green Zone, and every day the Taliban watched and waited.

> Once they are confident that they are in a safe position, especially with adequate safe routes to extract, they open up on us with everything they have got. It is very difficult to see the insurgents before the contact because of the thickness of the vegetation, the numerous compounds and rat runs all provide ample cover from view. At this stage, the mouse has the upper hand but not for long.

The British response was always overwhelming firepower and more destruction: 'Once the firing points have been located, the company puts down a staggering amount of small arms fire which results in the suppression of their firing points. We then set about trapping the mouse with artillery and mortars, using aircraft and attack.'[60]

These daily skirmishes achieved nothing. Once the dust settled and the front line had coagulated again, both sides resupplied their ammunition stocks and prepared for another round of confrontation. The officer commanding FOB Inkerman was putting a brave face on a dire situation. Remarkably, *every* Rifles patrol that stepped out of FOB Inkerman that summer was attacked by gunmen, without exception. The local villagers could not have sent the British a more explicit message – clear off. The density of IEDs meant that patrols could no longer fire and manoeuvre, which was why the riflemen resorted to calling in artillery fire or aircraft support.

Every patrol had to follow the 'Afghan Snake', or march in single file behind the Vallon men. The fear of IEDs was so great that even when under fire individual soldiers elected to remain where they were and take their chances, rather than risk diving for cover and setting off an IED. The loads carried by some soldiers were so great that if they got down, they struggled to get up again. Despite the array of surveillance technologies ranged against the insurgents, the riflemen discovered it was very hard to spot the gunmen at the height of the summer, hidden in dense vegetation or behind head-height crops. In the previous year the paratroopers had been able to reach the banks of the Helmand River from FOB Inkerman. The Rifles could not extend their presence further than the weapon range of the sangar sentries. The front line was retracting, not expanding. By the time B Company quit the base, IEDs were being laid within 200 metres of the front gate (which resulted in multiple amputations to two soldiers in separate incidents). The isolated soldiers at FOB Inkerman, three years into the war, were also still fighting battles on other fronts as well. On one occasion, due to poor logistic planning, the company ate nothing but ration pack Menu B for an entire month. By the end of the tour, the average rifleman had shed about an eighth of his body weight.

This same pattern was repeated even in areas considered a 'success story', such as PB Shahzad, held by Prince of Wales's Company of the Welsh Guards. The guardsmen did win 'hearts and minds' at their base at Chah-e-Anjir, but it counted for little. Over a three-month period they were attacked 140 times. Every attack took place within half a kilometre of the town centre, and the majority within 200 metres.[61] It was a siege situation, however hard a propaganda machine tried to suggest that progress was being made.

Fighting in the Green Zone remained as treacherous as ever. In early June, a 2 Rifles patrol stepped out of FOB Gibraltar, led by Lieutenant Paul Mervis. Mervis was typical of the changing demography in the British Army. He was an academically gifted child from a middle-class background who read philosophy at university. Before joining the army he had travelled widely and worked for *The Spectator*. He may have not been the most military of officers but he was loved by his soldiers. That morning, as soon as the riflemen began to patrol, the platoon sensed there would be trouble. In the words of the post-incident report: 'It soon became apparent to both multiples [patrols] that the atmospherics in the area were deteriorating fast. At 0610D* H31B and the sangar sentries in FOB GIB both reported that local farmers and their families were rapidly leaving the fields and moving west out of the area through which H31 were moving.'[62]

To pre-empt the insurgents, Mervis ordered his section to occupy a compound from which the soldiers would be able to enjoy a dominating position over the fields. The compound was entered through a side gate after carefully sweeping for IEDs. Two Vallon men then began to sweep the roof, where the section intended to take up fire positions. They completed their sweep, found nothing, and the rest of the section was called to the roof. The section commander then made one last check before Mervis and the GPMG gunner moved to occupy a corner of the roof. As the GPMG gunner laid his gun down, there was an explosion that collapsed the roof. Mervis, who was closest to the IED, was mortally wounded by the bomb and a second soldier was injured. The section had done everything right and had still been caught out. The C Company sergeant major later wrote of the young officer: 'I have never met, nor am I likely to meet, a man who cared so much about his men.'

Far to the north in Musa Qaleh, where the remainder of the Fusiliers battlegroup was based, with C Company in the district centre and B Company in PB Woqab, the soldiers found the same levels of indifference, fear and hostility. The Gurkhas who preceded the Fusiliers had expanded the security bubble around the town with the *Mar Nonu* sequence of operations. The Fusiliers would continue this tactic of incremental land grabs over the course of their six-month tour. Like the Gurkhas before them, the Fusiliers would look back on their tour of Musa Qaleh with the satisfaction that the security bubble had been expanded and consolidated. It was true that the front line had expanded outwards, but it remained a permeable skin.

The experiences of 7 Platoon at PB Woqab were typical of the daily routine of fruitless skirmishes across no man's land. From June to August the platoon was under daily attacks from concealed insurgent firing positions. There was no follow-up to these attacks because the platoon was undermanned and dared not risk being ambushed.

This rule was broken in late July when a sangar sentry reported that an enemy machine gunner had been hit in a hedge line about 500 metres north of the base. As in almost all such cases, this was a speculative and optimistic call. The fact was that the British were firing tens of thousands of rounds from patrol bases and hitting nothing. The base platoon commander nonetheless took a decision to search the hedge line with two sections. Due to the continuing manpower shortages, this was the largest-sized force the patrol base could afford to release. What followed was a predictable sequence of events which had been replayed countless times in the Green Zone over the last three years. There was no dead Taliban machine-gunner, but there were gunmen out there who quickly set up an ambush and caught one of the sections in the open. Overwhelmed by the weight of small-arms fire and unable to manoeuvre because of the weights they were carrying, the soldiers fell back on the staple British response – even heavier retaliatory firepower. The light gun perched on Roshan Tower joined in the scrap. Mortar missions were called. Eventually, an aircraft was tasked to drop a bomb on the suspected enemy firing points. To the young lieutenant's amazement, none of this stopped the enemy fire, which only died off once the soldiers had retreated back to PB Woqab and closed the door behind them. Probably every patrol base commander in Helmand that summer, without exception, could have related such a story.

Holding this front line did not come cheaply in lives or bullets. Seven fusiliers lost their lives, including three on a single day. Many more were terribly injured, a toll which included numerous amputees. The three fusiliers killed in the single incident were Lance Corporal James Fullarton, Fusilier Simon Annis and Fusilier Louis Carter. The mother of Fusilier Annis – Ann Annis – would later write a poignant tribute to her son, *Butterflies and Feathers*, a counterpoint to the industrial output of *Bravo Two Zero*-style books that the war was beginning to generate. Her book opened a door to the very real and lifelong emotional war the relatives of the bereaved faced. Typically, the three fusiliers were killed by an IED in Sangin. Two of the soldiers were teenagers. Carter had only passed out of the army's Infantry Training Centre at Catterick that summer. He joined his regiment and then immediately lost his life stepping on a second IED while trying to save his section commander who had been mortally wounded by an initial explosion. Ann Annis's book would be followed by Dr Margaret Evison's *Death of a Soldier*. Her son, the handsome and charismatic Lieutenant Mark Evison, was shot and killed by Kharotei tribesmen near a village called Noor Mohammed Kalay in Nad-e Ali (subsequent investigation suggested that he may have been killed by friendly fire from one of the GPMGs firing from the patrol base).[63] Thanks to the proliferation of GoPro cameras, the last hour of his life was captured, and with it the controversy over his death and delayed evacuation. Why did it take the mother of a fallen soldier to make the obvious and honest observation? 'It was a war very slow in its winning,' Margaret Evison wrote, 'if it was being won at all.'[64]

The bullets, unlike the lives, were expendable, and as far as the soldiers were concerned the more they fired off, the better. The fire support group based at the Roshan Tower reckoned that by the time they packed their bags and handed over to the incoming brigade they had launched £1.75 million's worth of Javelin missiles, or about 10 per cent of the British reconstruction budget in Helmand since operations began in 2006 (by December 2009, the MOD was obliged to order an additional 1,300 Javelin missiles to replace expended stocks).[65]

If the Rifles and the Fusiliers could reflect on a bitter and bloody summer, 3 SCOTS experienced a very different tour. Other than D Company, which was deployed in support of the 2 Royal Regiment of Fusiliers battlegroup in Musa Qaleh, the remainder of the battalion was based at Kandahar as the Regional Battlegroup South, supporting operations in both Kandahar and Helmand provinces.

On 11 April, the day after formally taking over from 42 Commando, A Company, commanded by Major Matt Munro, was collected by helicopters and dropped off near a suspected Taliban-dominated village called Nasser, in Kandahar Province (Operation *Tyruna 1A*). In the resultant 36-hour operation, the Jocks uncovered small caches of anti-personnel mines, mortars and rocket-propelled grenades. The operation was mostly remembered for 'two incredible storms' that tested the endurance of soldiers who had left behind warm clothing and sleeping bags to reduce the weight of their packs.[66] This was followed by Operation *Sarak 1*, a six-day surge in the area of Band-e Timor, which yielded nothing of significance. The biggest challenges were the extreme weights carried by the soldiers and the weather: four soldiers were evacuated with back injuries, two from heat exhaustion and one with torn ligaments.[67] This was followed by *Sarak 3*, a Soviet-style operation to clear insurgents away from Highway 1 and Route 601. It proved as forlorn. Ambushing road travellers was national sport across central Asia, and Highway 1 would continue to suffer attacks for the remainder of the war. Most of the fighting centred on an area called Yakchal, which the British would still be contesting three years later. Over the course of the operation, the Jocks confiscated a hoard of over 7 million Afghanis (£140,000). For the British this was drug money. For villagers it was not unlikely this stash was part of a nexus of credits and debits on which their livelihoods rested.

The first major operation undertaken by 3 SCOTS in Helmand was Operation *Ouba 3*, a drug-busting raid conducted in the Upper Sangin Valley in the first week of June. A total of 450 soldiers were involved in this two-phase operation, as well as over 100 ANA. B Company led the operation, supported by the ANA contingent. The first phase targeted predominantly Alizai villages 10 kilometres south of Kajaki: Sar Puzay, Nangazi and Barakzai (an area of operations known as 'Black Rock'). The second targeted 'Brown Rock', another 7 kilometres further south, which included the villages of Chahardah and Bustanzay.

Operation *Ouba 3* was the largest British-led counter-narcotics raid to date. Ten laboratories were uncovered and destroyed, which the battlegroup reckoned amounted to 15 per cent of the narcotic-processing capability in the Upper Sangin Valley.[68] More than 5,000 kilograms of opium paste was also destroyed. Other items discovered included 220 kilograms of morphine, 60 kilograms of heroin, 148 kilograms of cannabis, 5,800 kilograms of ammonium chloride and 2,500 kilograms of sulphur. Eight AK-47 machine guns and three pistols were also recovered.[69] The air support for this operation had come from American F-18s operating from the USS *Eisenhower* in the Indian Ocean, demonstrating the impressive reach of the US Navy's air wing.

In mid-June, it was once again the turn of the battlegroup to undertake a raid against a suspected Taliban weapon and drugs cache as part of a wider disruption effort prior to the Afghan national elections.[70] Operation *Tora Arwa* was mounted on 10 June and eventually lasted six days. The Jocks were airlifted to the target area in Zhari District in six Canadian Chinooks, supported by American fighters. This was an area known as the 'heart of darkness', and indeed ISAF would never succeed in pacifying the tribes in Zhari. The intense gun battle that followed lasted for several hours before the superior firepower of the Jocks forced the insurgents to retreat from their positions. At one point, the insurgents lobbed Chinese rockets at the Jocks. One platoon commander described it as 'the most terrifying firework display I've ever been [to]'.[71] Numerous weapons were found as well as 118 kilograms of wet opium, 190 kilograms of marijuana and over 100 kilograms of marijuana seeds. The marijuana finds in this and previous raids pointed to a new trend. By the subsequent year, marijuana would be competing with the opium poppy as farmers in south-west Afghanistan sought to diversify their income streams. The fighting was mostly concluded when Private Robert McLaren, from Kintra on the Isle of Mull, was killed after stepping on an IED. McLaren, who had passed out of basic training in April, was the first fatality experienced by the 3 SCOTS battlegroup since the start of operations two months earlier. A mobile rather than static approach to counter-insurgency was demonstrably costing fewer lives.

More operations followed through a broiling August: *Tyruna 2C* in Panjwai District (14–15 August); *Aabi Toorha*, providing security for the elections (16–23 August); *Tor Shakatcha*, which cost the lives of Sergeant Gus Millar and Private Kevin Elliott (29 August–2 September); and *Burs Simi* in the Upper Gereshk Valley (5–7 September).

It was not all operations for the soldiers based at Kandahar. The air base not only boasted restaurants and coffee houses but also hosted shows, recalling the entertainment that was laid on for soldiers during World War II. One soldier serving with A Company remembered with particular fondness the arrival of an obscure popular band called Electric Mayhem, but not for the music:

> There is no doubt that for many the highlight of the week was the arrival of the Combined Services Entertainment (CSE) show … A stone cold sober and male dominated audience cannot be every rockers [sic] dream, but to their credit they worked the crowd to as much of a frenzy as you can, particularly when the show was halted midway through by a rocket attack. There was, however, one particular aspect that may have been mostly responsible for the charged atmosphere and that was the CSE dancers. With three very tantalising young girls wearing the absolute minimum and flaunting themselves on stage, it is not wholly surprising the show was a success with the jocks.[72]

If 19 Light Brigade could claim that the fighting campaign, though bloody, had achieved its aims by the beginning of the autumn, how was the wider British campaign faring? The human cost over the summer had been high. Seventy-six soldiers were killed (54 from IEDs), and 340 wounded in action. Thirty more amputees were added to the roll call of Britain's war disabled. FOB Gibraltar was abandoned, a base which had cost 11 British lives. Several hundred insurgents were claimed to have been killed or wounded and the brigade admitted the accidental deaths of as many as 20 civilians, overwhelmingly by air strikes (the Taliban well understood the significance of civilian deaths; on occasions they would deliberately provoke a fight from a compound in which they would padlock women and children in the expectation the British would retaliate and kill the civilians).[73]

A measure of the mismatch between the local fighters and the task force can be gauged from the number of gun battles. There were 1,990, but these only resulted in the deaths of four British soldiers. The villagers were firing off thousands of rounds and completely failing to hit anyone. Reportedly, Task Force 42, the British special forces contingent, had accounted for 65 of 240 insurgent leaders on the 'kill or capture' list.[74] A snapshot of one battlegroup, the Welsh Guards, revealed the scale of the fighting. Over the course of their tour, they were involved in 1,463 gun fights, they encountered 303 IEDs (of which 96 detonated) and they suffered 16 fatalities. The battlegroup claimed to have killed 438 fighters (from a highly exaggerated brigade total claim of 3,100).[75] The brigade as a whole faced 1,780 IEDs, of which 571 detonated. This was a 300 per cent increase on the previous summer.[76]

The brigade had undertaken one major operation in an area it knew very little about, and then, having fulfilled its part of the bargain, could only watch as the political side of the bargain unravelled in corrupt elections. This was a grave setback, but the British could at least claim they had now established a credible military hold on central Helmand. The arrival of a US Marine task force was about to turn the British into junior partners but this suited all parties. Despite undeniable improvements in all areas of the British task force, old complaints continued to resurface. There were insufficient helicopters. The supply chain was slow and clogged. More funds were required for reconstruction and the release of these funds had to be quickened. The management of intelligence remained poor and its dissemination a constant challenge. The brigade was effectively fixed and it lacked the capability to conduct mobile operations in the Green Zone. The Bowman radio system remained unpopular and the ability to send secure data across networks remained limited. Soldiers were still being forced to carry loads that would break mules.

This larger and widely dispersed British task force implied a larger logistics bill. The brigade logistics infrastructure now encompassed over 3,000 military personnel, civilian contractors and locally employed contractors, or LECs (Camp Bastion would eventually host as many as 10,000 civilian contractors). The camp had swelled to accommodate this increase in manpower, and an Afghan shanty town had encrusted itself to the perimeter of the camp. The economic stimulus generated by this vast military hub almost certainly exceeded the plethora of reconstruction projects designed to create employment in Helmand. The logistics headquarters staffs, for example, were responsible for the 1,100-kilometre resupply route from Karachi. This was a road paved with gold for all the trucking companies that won contracts with the British Army, as well as for all the checkpoints, legal and illegal, that collected bribes to allow the trucks to pass. No British study was ever undertaken to determine how much money passed hands in bribes from the port of disembarkation in Karachi to Camp Bastion, but the figure would have been in the thousands of dollars per truck. Whatever else Operation *Herrick* was achieving, it was, without argument, a bonanza for Pakistani trucking mafias and parasitic militias and police forces that 'secured' the supply routes.

Within the theatre of operations, the logistics staffs were responsible for about 10,300 military and civilian personnel, 1,550 vehicles and over 16,000 different weapon systems.[77] This implied holding front-line stocks of 700,000 rations, 3 million litres of water, 4 million litres of fuel and 3,000 tonnes of ammunition. Roughly every ten days, a Combat Logistic Patrol (CLP) left the safety of Camp Bastion and snaked its way around the dispersed FOBs and patrol bases, distributing 350 tonnes of these supplies. It was a punishing schedule for men and machines, even without the threat of insurgent attacks.

The difficulties of moving anywhere freely in Helmand continued to hamper military operations. By 2009, the army had procured nearly 500 new protected vehicles for operations in Afghanistan. Only a proportion of these were actually deployed on the front line. The capacity of the army to receive, train on and deploy new vehicles was being far outstripped by the rate at which the American manufacturers were supplying the units. There was no point transporting an upgraded Mastiff 2 to Helmand if the vehicle had not been fitted out with the correct equipment, if it lacked a trained driver, if there was no crew at the other end or if the repair chain lacked the necessary spares. All these factors took time to resolve in an army that was 'running hot'. The lack of military helicopters, exacerbated by restrictions on the use of civilian helicopters, only made matters worse.

Over the summer, as we have seen, American journalist and former special forces soldier Michael Yon spent several weeks embedded with 2 Rifles. The manner in which British forces had become effectively fixed by the threat of roadside bombs amazed him. In his words:

> Enemy control of the terrain is so complete in the area between Sangin and Kajaki that when my embed was to switch from FOB Jackson to FOB Inkerman – only seven kilometers (about four miles) away – we could not walk or drive from Jackson to Inkerman. Routes are deemed too dangerous. Helicopter lift was required. The helicopter shortage is causing crippling delays in troop movements. It's common to see a soldier waiting ten days for a simple flight. When my embed was to move the four miles from Jackson to Inkerman, a scheduled helicopter picked me up at Jackson and flew probably eighty miles to places like Lashkar Gah, and finally set down at Camp Bastion. The helicopter journey from Jackson began on 12 August and ended at Inkerman on the 17th. About

five days was spent – along with many thousands of dollars in helicopter time – to travel four miles.[78]

Yon's experience was not exceptional but rather the weekly reality for British soldiers serving in Helmand.

Protecting this enlarged force demanded mammoth efforts from 38 Engineer Regiment, the unit that supported 19 Light Brigade over its six-month tour. By October, it was estimated that the brigade's sappers had erected 67.2 kilometres of Hesco bastion, or as one officer put it, 'enough to surround Wembley football pitch 192 times'. This could have been viewed as a significant engineering achievement, or as a metaphor for the separation between British soldiers and villagers whose 'hearts and minds' they were trying to win.

The constraints on movements inevitably affected reconstruction efforts. According to DfID, over 2009, £190 million had been invested in Helmand through the PRT (£50 million from the UK and £70 million from the US, the two majority donors). This grossly misrepresented the sum of funds actually disbursed, or wisely spent. A sample of projects undertaken suggested a far more modest outlay: $257,000 was disbursed in 443 micro loans – commonly the most effective disbursement of aid. Maintenance work on the Shamalan Canal attracted $1.3 million in funds. Four schools were built, and eight refurbished by the British, in three years. It was claimed there were now 81 schools open in Helmand, attended by 45,037 boys and 14,214 girls. In Sangin, new government offices, a school and a clinic were opened (although the latter would remain unused and without equipment when the brigade returned to the UK).

The most significant projects were undertaken in the relatively benign provincial capital. Around $10 million was disbursed in 80 projects. A headquarters for the counter-narcotics police was added to a police compound built earlier in the year. A new prison capable of holding 700 inmates was built – this proved to be a good long-term investment as ISAF ramped up detention operations in the last years of the war. The hospital received two ambulances (which was a start, given that Lashkar Gah had precisely no ambulances). Four vital signs monitors, two portable ventilators, an operating table and ten computers were also donated to the Italian-run hospital. RTA (Radio Television Afghanistan) gained a fancy new television and radio station, although very few Helmandis actually owned televisions.

Whatever DfID's dogmatic misgivings about military involvement in reconstruction and development, it was thanks to a small eight-man team of Royal Engineers (522 Specialist Team Royal Engineers) that projects like these were driven forward with some success, despite huge frustrations, and in some cases at all. As Christina Lamb critically reported, in the previous year DfID and FCO personnel at the PRT rarely ventured outside the compound walls.[79] 'Those who occasionally brave the five-minute drive to the governor's office,' she observed, 'do so in armed convoys, surrounded by bodyguards and travelling at high speed. The cracks on the vehicles' windows from rocks thrown almost every time they go out are a measure of the locals' appreciation.' Perhaps an indication that life was becoming normal, if not enjoyable, for the citizens of Lashkar Gah was the restoration of Tortank Stadium. Fallen into disuse, it had become no more than a dustbowl surrounded by graffiti-defaced high walls. By 2009, almost 30 clubs had established themselves in the refurbished facilities, offering sports as diverse as basketball, tennis and cycling. Bodybuilding and martial arts – two traditional Afghan sports – unsurprisingly proved to be the most popular activities. The Taliban had banned organized football. Now Lashkar Gah boasted two football leagues. By the following year, an Afghan pop star would be crooning to an excited crowd at this stadium.

The biggest spender in Helmand, since 2006, was in fact USAID. The gravel airstrip at Bost Airport was asphalted, and the new airport was opened by the American ambassador, Karl Eikenberry (at a cost of $45 million, or as much as DfID's entire budget for Helmand for three years).[80] In a second phase of development, an agricultural business park was built alongside the airport. This proved a white elephant. Four years later, the agricultural business park, like the Kajaki Dam project, remained a mirage of dashed hopes. A $3 million cold storage facility in Gereshk went the same way – unused and abandoned.

These reconstruction projects demonstrated greater British engagement in the so-called 'comprehensive approach', however flawed, but the British contribution remained small, and the reality at the sharp end, outside the city limits of Lashkar Gah, could not be disguised. On election day in Sangin more money was expended on ammunition than was spent in the entire year's reconstruction budget for that district.[81] The dollars were still following the bullets. A company commander put it this way, 'We are effectively engaged in an armed debate with the insurgents as to who can best meet the needs and hopes of the people … In this we both risk failure because what we are offering is unwanted, transient, unconvincing, poorly delivered or insubstantial compared to the commitment, risk or inconvenience it entails.'[82]

The operational gallantry awards, as in previous tours, told their own story. Six Conspicuous Gallantry Crosses, 17 Military Crosses and four Queen's Gallantry Medals were awarded. Major Jo Butterfill, a fusilier, won his Military Cross leading his company south of Sangin, where his men found 63 IEDs and suffered 12 IED strikes. Lieutenant William Hignett, a Rifles platoon commander, led his men in the most evil place in Helmand, Wishtan, finding 44 IEDs and barely suffering any casualties. Corporal Christopher Reynolds, a sniper, demonstrated a special brand of Celtic bellicosity. Locked in a gunfight, he ran out of ammunition for his sniper rifle, picked up an assault rifle and continued engaging the enemy with this weapon, fully exposed to the return fire. When this weapon ran out of ammunition, he continued the fight by commandeering a machine gun. Gunner Steven Gadsby was awarded the Conspicuous Gallantry Medal for carrying two casualties over an exposed bridge, under enemy fire, rather than using a longer covered route, in an effort to get the casualties evacuated as quickly as possible. Sergeant Matthew Turrall, an Irish Guardsman, risked his own life to save three Afghan children caught in a crossfire. He was awarded the Military Cross for this action and later said that he had been led by a 'fatherly urge' to protect the children. Two guardsmen who refused to follow him in this mad dash received a good bollocking. In every rank band and in every regiment, acts of bravery were being recorded.

Four George Medals would be awarded. The first went to Rifleman Paul Jacobs, a Vallon operator who was caught in multiple IED blasts, seriously wounded and rendered almost blind. Despite these injuries, he retained sufficient composure to drag himself to safety through an area strewn with these deadly devices. The second went to Staff Sergeant Kim Hughes, a bomb disposal operator. Hughes was called to deal with one of the most appalling incidents endured by 2 Rifles during their difficult tour. A section caught in an IED field set off a device, killing one of the riflemen. Two stretcher bearers then set off a second device. Both men were killed instantly and four were seriously wounded, one of whom would subsequently die of his wounds. Hughes manually cleared the area at enormous risk to himself to allow the safe extraction of the casualties. His citation read: 'Dealing with any form of IED is dangerous; to deal with seven VOIEDs [Victim Operated IEDs] linked in a single circuit, in a mass casualty scenario, using manual neutralisation techniques once, never mind three times, is the single most outstanding act of explosive ordnance disposal ever recorded in Afghanistan.'

Two posthumous medals were awarded. A George Medal was awarded to Captain Daniel Shepherd, another bomb disposal operator who in one gruelling 36-hour period disposed of 13 IEDs, using only manual means and fingertip searching. In a number of these clearances, he found himself under enemy fire. A George Cross went to Staff Sergeant Olaf Schmid. Before he was killed, Schmid personally dealt with 64 confirmed IEDs. Schmid led the clearance of Pharmacy Road in Wishtan on the day when 31 bombs were discovered. Later he manually defused a radio-controlled device attached to an artillery shell that might have killed and injured a large number of civilians in the bazaar in Sangin. He lost his life in an alleyway attempting to defuse a daisy chain of three IEDs on the day before he was due to return home.

11

All Change

Operations *Herrick 11* and *12*, October 2009–October 2010

19 Light Brigade handed over to its successor brigade, 11 Light Brigade, on 10 October 2009. The new brigade commander, Brigadier James Cowan, had been the last operational commanding officer of The Black Watch before it was amalgamated into The Royal Regiment of Scotland. He led the battalion in the 2004 US-led operation to retake Fallujah, Operation *Phantom Fury*, which proved a bitter experience for this proud regiment. As if to underline the difficulties 11 Light Brigade would face, three of his soldiers were killed in separate incidents before Cowan had even formally assumed command. One month after the brigade handover in Helmand, there was also a change at the top of the British command structure, with Major General Nick Carter taking command of Regional Command South from the outgoing Dutch Major General Mart de Kruif. Like several senior British officers, this was Carter's second tour of Afghanistan. He would be joined by a fellow Green Jacket officer, Lieutenant General Nick Parker, who served as Deputy Commander ISAF. Parker's son – an officer in the Rifles – would become a double amputee from the war. This was family sacrifice common to a wartime generation but unheard of in modern Britain.

Cowan announced his arrival with the necessary soapy statement:

> Only the people of Afghanistan can provide the lasting solution … we will do everything we can to help achieve this goal. To this end, we will consolidate our close relationship with our friends in the US Marine Corps and our civilian counterparts in the Provincial Reconstruction Team in order to bring prosperity to the people of Helmand.[1]

Behind this rhetoric, however, was a thoughtful mind with a good understanding of Afghanistan's history and the recent tensions that were fuelling the insurgency in Helmand. Every tribal community, Cowan appreciated, was subtly different. There was no single monolithic insurgency but rather several overlapping local insurgencies fuelled by different grievances. In Nad-e Ali, land disputes and tribal squabbles predominated. In Sangin, the Ishaqzai felt downtrodden and marginalized by President Karzai. The British had to make sense of these differences to make progress in the war. Cowan still lacked sufficient troops to decisively turn the British-held areas of Helmand, but he enjoyed other advantages. For the first time since the beginning of the war, Task Force Helmand was firmly placed within an efficient and purposeful chain of command: from McChrystal, through his deputy General Rodriguez, down to the British general, Nick Carter. The special forces campaign, for so long independent if not counter-productive to the overall war, was being ramped up. Cowan was also aware that a British Army that espoused a 'manoeuvrist approach' had become fixed. He would urge the brigade to think in a manoeuvrist fashion, but the reality for the average soldier marooned in a patrol base would continue to be attrition warfare.

The deployment of the fresh brigade was accompanied by the announcement of a new course from the prime minister, when Parliament returned from its summer recess. This was perhaps Gordon Brown's worst statement on the war and certainly the least credible. After a sombre reading of the names of the 37 servicemen who had died over the summer, Brown described how the task force would embark on an ambitious training programme of the Afghan National Security Forces (ANSF). This accorded with General McChrystal's overall policy of 'Afghanization', and in effect it signalled the initiation of a British exit strategy. The announced plan was both ambitious and disingenuous. The British would establish a police academy at Lashkar Gah and train up to 1,000 policemen a month for three years. This announcement was not untypical of a government that had got into the habit portraying past events as future initiatives, despite being caught out by the media when it played this game. The police training facility already existed. Known as the IHPTC (Interim Helmand Police Training Centre), it had been opened in the spring and it had been built with American dollars. And nobody seriously believed that the academy could churn out 12,000 trained and competent police officers every calendar year for the next three years. This was a fantastic number, and it suggested the prime minister had been fed exaggerated targets by an aide.

The real figures, once the training regime became established, were more modest. The first 138 police recruits were trained in January 2010 (the intention had been to train 150 recruits in each cycle).[2] By March it was hoped that three cycles might run simultaneously, totalling 450 recruits and as many as 2,550 trainees per year. In fact, the British and contract trainers more or less kept to this goal, and the 1,000th police recruit passed out in July 2010. The 2,000th recruit received his pass certificate in January 2011. These numbers were not bad but they were far from the unrealistic figures presented to Parliament by the beleaguered prime minister.

The proposed numbers for the ANA were even more fantastic: British forces would train 40,000 ANA in 2010 (the task force was currently mentoring fewer than 2,000 reliable ANA, and even this small commitment stretched British resources). A further 900 Afghan officers would be trained every month in Helmand. By the end of 2010, it was claimed, the British task force would be partnering a 10,000-strong ANA division. Again, this was so exaggerated a proposal that the lack of challenge it received from the suntanned MPs was surprising, the tans possibly offering a clue as to where their minds were still basking. Gordon Brown's integrity was not in question: it appears pleasing noughts were added to the numbers, which the prime minister duly and without intention to mislead announced.

In a sleight of hand that again no MP challenged, Brown also announced the British regional battlegroup would redeploy to central Helmand. This referred to the unit based at Kandahar. This battlegroup, as we have seen, had conducted an independent and successful campaign for the last two years with a mobile approach to counter-insurgency, unlike the other British battlegroups that were fixed in the Green Zone. It was the battlegroup that suffered the least casualties and manifested the highest tempo of operations. Four units had served in this role (1 Royal Gurkha Rifles, supported by a Royal Welsh company; 3 PARA; 42 Commando; and 3 SCOTS). Between them they had suffered just eight fatalities.[3] The remainder of the task force had passed the 200th fatality mark. Now the regional reserve would adopt a static role and suffer attrition like the other infantry battlegroups. The ISAF regional commander would lose his best asset, but British troop numbers in Helmand would be bumped up, a useful political consideration for the next occasion when the prime minister had to answer questions on troop levels in Helmand Province.

It was clear from these announcements that the casualty rates over the summer had panicked a government staring at electoral meltdown in the spring. Faced with a fight for its survival, the Labour government would force the hand of the armed forces. Ironically, even as the army was promulgating a new counter-insurgency doctrine, it was effectively being told to curtail fighting and start training Afghan soldiers and policemen as quickly as possible. The single most important priority was to avoid British casualties and limit the electoral liability of the Afghan war before the general election. An offer to send an additional 500 soldiers (from 2 Royal Welsh) came across as a pre-election bribe: they would only be sent if the Afghans contributed more forces, if ISAF European partners increased their troop contributions and if they were 'properly equipped'. This announcement was also disingenuous. 2 Royal Welsh was held back from deploying with 11 Light Brigade not to meet any of the conditions outlined to Parliament but to coincide with the anticipated American announcement of further troop reinforcements. Only too late, it appears, the government appreciated that the forthcoming Obama surge would leave Britain in the embarrassing position of not being able to reciprocate with its own 'mini-surge'. This was especially embarrassing because Britain had vociferously criticized European allies for a lack of commitment. The only solution was to hold back the Royal Welsh (the commanding officer was only informed as he was about to deploy with his battalion to Helmand), and subsequently to release the battalion following the American announcement, which was only finally made in early December. The appearance was thus given that London was 'doing its bit' in synchronicity with Washington. The Royal Welsh paid for this politicking, spending the next two months kicking its heels and with families living with the uncertainty of not knowing when loved ones would be deployed, or for how long.

The problem, put simply, was that Britain had run out of infantry. Throughout the 1990s, infantry 'overstretch' had been a festering sore in parliamentary debates. The voices that warned of serious consequences if the number of county battalions was cut were not heeded. A Conservative government made deep cuts in Options for Change 1991, and the Labour government downsized the infantry further under the controversial Future Army Structures 2003–06 programme. By late 2009, the crisis in infantry manpower had become so acute (even with the end of operations in Iraq), the army was forced to re-role the surviving, merged infantry battalions. Four battalions (The Highlanders, 1 Duke of Lancaster's Regiment,

1 Royal Anglian and 4 Rifles) were plucked out of their existing armoured and mechanized roles and converted into light infantry battalions. The arithmetic of war could no longer be pushed aside. To sustain the campaign in Helmand into 2011 the army needed a minimum of 30 light infantry battalions. It only had 22. The addition of four battalions would provide additional manpower, by which time, hopefully, a British withdrawal would solve the problem.

For Britain, as well as all the other ISAF partners, America's next step in the war in Afghanistan remained the key, and the man holding that key – President Obama – was giving nothing away. From September to the beginning of November, numerous meetings were held in camera with the Joint Chiefs of Staff and civilian agencies at the White House. In a mirror image of the Vietnam War, the various actors played their familiar roles: the Joint Chiefs arguing for escalation and State arguing for a political solution. However, journalists trying to read the runes were disappointed. Following an earlier leaking of General McChrystal's draft report, tight security was imposed on the meetings. Critics accused the president of dithering and European allies fretted in the wings.

The main obstacle holding back an announcement of the president's new strategy for Afghanistan was the still-awaited outcome of the Afghan presidential elections. This messy election was finally resolved in the beginning of November when Dr Abdullah Abdullah, financially broke and without reasonable hope of beating Hamid Karzai, withdrew from the second-round run-off. The Afghan electoral commission promptly awarded the election to Karzai, confirming him in office for the next five years. The deep disappointment in the West over the flawed elections could hardly be disguised. Karzai was always likely to have been the winner – the polls had consistently placed him as a clear favourite – but the manner in which he won, with over a million fraudulent votes, tarnished the result and made his government appear illegitimate, not only in Western eyes but also among many Afghans. For the soldiers in Helmand, the cancellation of the second-round run-off, just one week before the due date, was an immense relief. Nobody had been looking forward to a re-run of the fiasco of the first-round elections.

This relief was quickly shattered by an incident that rocked public opinion in Britain. Shortly after midday on 3 November, a combined British–Afghan patrol operating near the Kharotei village of Shin Kalay, in Nad-e Ali District, returned to CP Blue 25 to rest and debrief. As was customary, the soldiers stripped off their body armour and sat in a circle with their ANP counterparts to discuss the patrol. Above them in a sangar, a policeman manned the checkpoint machine gun that normally faced outwards towards the insurgent threat. The policeman was a man named Gulbuddin, a resident of Musa Qaleh who had served in the ANP for about two years. Later it would be alleged that he had an argument with a superior, or that he may have been high on opiates. In a moment of madness, Gulbuddin picked up the machine gun, pointed it at the British soldiers below him and opened fire. Three Grenadier Guardsmen and two Royal Military Policemen were killed instantly. Among the dead were the Regimental Sergeant Major of the Grenadier Guards, a teenager and a Territorial Army volunteer. Six other soldiers were grievously injured. He also managed to wound his ANP commander and another policeman. He made his escape on foot, reportedly wounded in the leg by glancing shot.

The last victim of this attack may have been a seven-week-old baby named Khloe Abrams in Northampton. Among the wounded had been a Lance Corporal Liam Culverhouse. He lost an eye and was subsequently discharged from the army. The civilian Culverhouse failed to settle down and led a somewhat chaotic and on occasions violent life. Three years after he was attacked, he attacked his daughter Khloe, smashing her skull and many other bones. She died 18 months later in a hospice.[4]

As 11 Light Brigade units began to fan out across the British-held areas of Helmand, the soldiers knew that this tour would represent the beginning of the British contraction. Southern Helmand, where a British contingent had only truly held the town of Darvishan and its environs, had been handed over to the US Marine Corps. Now Zad, where the British misadventure had begun, was also being handed over to American forces. With the arrival of a further US Marine brigade, the remainder of northern Helmand would follow, reducing the British area of responsibility to central Helmand. The brigade also knew that it would embark on one last major British operation – Operation *Moshtarak* ('Together' in Dari) – to clear the Chah-e Anjir Triangle (CAT) between Nad-e Ali and Babaji districts. This would coincide with an American operation to clear Marjah District to the south. These operations were a prelude for the wider Operation *Hamkari* that would take place the following year across south-west Afghanistan, effectively ISAF's last roll of the dice against the Pashtun insurgency.[5] Operation *Moshtarak* had been discussed since the summer. It was an open secret in Helmand that the Americans and British were about to clear the last two ungoverned areas of central Helmand. The combination of the flawed Afghan elections and President Obama's long consultation over the conduct of the war would effectively delay the start of the operation until the beginning of 2010. Finally clearing central Helmand, creating protected communities and opening the roads would be the themes dominating the brigade's deployment.

The Household Cavalry Regiment (HCR), a unit with almost uninterrupted service in Iraq and Afghanistan since 2001, was deployed to the northern battlegroup based at Musa Qaleh. Lieutenant Colonel Fullerton, who took a measured approach to this last British deployment in the town, described the disposition of his battlegroup thus:

> We find ourselves spread out across the Task Force Helmand area, with the Battle Group Headquarters, a troop from A Squadron and C Squadron in Musa Qaleh, A and B Squadron in Babaji, although this does change according to Brigade Reconnaissance Force taskings, and HQ Squadron split between Camp Bastion, FOB [Forward Operating Base] Edinburgh, just west of Musa Qaleh, and Musa Qaleh district centre. I have also formed E Squadron, consisting of both Household Cavalrymen and attached arms, who work as the Influence Group in Musa Qaleh; a most vital role in winning the support and consent of the local population.[6]

This last British contingent in Musa Qaleh was ironically the most generously manned. The Fusiliers and Gurkhas before them had struggled to expand the security bubble around the town for want of sufficient troops. The HCR battlegroup was supported by A Company, 2 Royal Welsh (mounted in Warriors); A Company, 1 Royal Anglian (who shamefully received just five weeks' notice of their deployment); B Company, 2 Yorks (Green Howards); L (Néry) Battery from 1 Royal Horse Artillery, and supporting engineers, mechanics and signallers. The battlegroup would consolidate rather than expand the security bubble, drawing public criticism from the incoming US Marine commander who would interpret this as an indication of a British lack of fight. For Fullerton this was a misreading of the situation in Musa Qaleh. The British had effectively secured the town and its immediate perimeter. Taking the fight to the Alizai tribesmen in petty gun battles in the Green Zone was benefiting nobody, least of all the civilian population the cavalrymen were supposed to be protecting (the battlegroup was proud to report that no civilians were killed during its six-month tenure of Musa Qaleh). It was also unfair criticism in other respects: the battlegroup suffered a total of 96 casualties, over 200 IEDs were encountered and Fullerton's men were engaged in over 200 gun fights. Fifteen Mastiffs suffered IED strikes but the crews survived (including an IED that detonated under the commanding officer's vehicle). The Warrior crews were less fortunate, and two drivers were killed. The statistics speak for themselves: the HCR did not sidle out of Musa Qaleh.

In central Helmand, the Grenadier Guards, commanded by Lieutenant Colonel Roly Walker, took over from the Welsh Guards. Walker, like Fullerton, would also survive an IED strike, travelling in a Ridgeback, which implies that at least two British commanding officers owed their legs if not their lives to sound American engineering (unlike Lieutenant Colonel Thorneloe, who was killed in the inadequate Viking, a vehicle that was retained post-Helmand, like the Jackal, regardless that it was vulnerable). The outgoing Lieutenant Colonel Antelme who had assumed command following Thorneloe's death ensured a smooth handover by organizing a dinner with Habibullah, the district governor. The Afghan was no doubt impressed by the suaveness of his hosts. The geographical centre of the Grenadier Guards' area of responsibility – FOB Shawqat – was held by Nijmegen Company. The old PB Argyll, a school adjoining FOB Shawqat, reverted to its former use, and Governor Mangal was invited to cut the ribbon in a school reopening ceremony. Queen's Company was deployed to Lashkar Gah, and Number 2 Company was despatched to PB Wahid on the edge of the Green Zone. The Estonian armoured infantry company supporting the Grenadier Guards was deployed to PB Pimon, another base established on the edge of the Green Zone, overlooking the Nahr-e Bughra Canal. Support Company from 2 Yorks (Green Howards) provided the OMLTs training ANA and ANP personnel. E Battery, 1 Royal Horse Artillery was also based at PB Pimon, along with elements from the Combat Service and Support Company.

The last company in the battlegroup – Inkerman Company – was deployed to the Chah-e Anjir Triangle, taking over PB Shahzad. This was the large patrol base located within the buildings of the former Helmand Construction Company, immediately west of Chah-e Anjir. Inkerman Company was dispersed between Shahzad and several satellite bases: Five Tanks (named after prominent water tanks in the vicinity of the base), School House CP, Compound 23, Crossing Point 11 and Yellow 12.

The Grenadier Guards' tour had begun with the setback of the death of RSM Darren Chant. This would prove to be the only major setback of the tour. For the remainder of their deployment, the Grenadier Guards would pursue a patient and cunning campaign, luring the insurgents into traps and commonly outwitting them. In this respect, the battalion demonstrated how a counter-insurgency campaign might be 'won' – at least tactically – from a matrix of fixed bases, by using these as secure locations from which to deploy and ambush insurgent gangs. Tribal dynamics and the presence of an effective and pro-British governor greatly aided the guardsmen, but the manner in which Lieutenant Colonel Roly Walker went about the business of securing Nad-e Ali nonetheless deserved recognition. At the heart of the scheme was a policy 'to develop a series of check points and patrol bases away from the populated areas to allow the locals to live in a normal enviroment [sic]. It also means that if fighting does take place, then at least it will be directed at the ISAF bases, therefore not endangering the lives of the locals.'[7] This was pursued in an incremental manner, gradually rather than forcefully squeezing the troublemakers away from the villages. In his words, 'The most important [task] was protecting the people and improving their freedom to move, as much to contrast how the situation used to be, with what it was now, and what it could be in the future; as it was to restore governance, stimulate trade and commerce, and resurrect the social fabric of damaged communities.'[8] Although Walker could not have known this at the time, his battalion laid the foundation for the pacification of Nad-e Ali. The British would win this war of attrition and grind out a sort of victory, but it would take a further two years of sacrifice.

In keeping with this new philosophy, the British began to deploy a wide array of psychological techniques to win over the villagers to the government side. Much of this work was undertaken by 15 Psychological Operations Group, a small band of dedicated servicemen and women, many reservists, who became skilled at their trade and scored some genuine successes. Initiatives included Sound Commander (essentially a loudspeaker mounted in patrol bases), Radio-in-a-Box or RIAB, billboards, notice boards and vehicle banners. The simple trick of flying Afghan flags and bunting had an effect. The launch of Radio Nad-e Ali in early January 2010 proved a big success, particularly with women who previously had no voice. In a sure sign that the British were beginning to understand who mattered in Helmandi society, mullahs were invited to speak on radio shows. Another initiative was the '110 Tip Line', which offered villagers a chance to tip off the security forces anonymously. Very soon it was receiving some 600 calls every week, a measure of just how frustrated ordinary farmers were with the continuing insurgency. The British also promoted community reward schemes, youth activities and village projects. There were frustrations and a good deal of corruption, but through this patient incremental approach a suspicious population gradually warmed to the 'Angrez' and their ways. The key to all this work, as the Grenadier Guards realized, was honesty. 'We had to take care to acknowledge publicly our weaknesses and our cock-ups,' as one Grenadier officer put it, adding mischievously, 'perhaps in a way our politicians can avoid.'[9]

Although Operation *Moshtarak* would not start until the New Year, subsidiary operations were undertaken to nibble away at the insurgent safe havens in northern Nad-e Ali. The dangers were ever-present notwithstanding the beginnings of success enjoyed by the British.

Private Robert Hayes was a 19-year-old serving with Essex Company, 1 Royal Anglian. He had only served in the army 11 months when he was attached to the Grenadier Guards in Nad-e Ali. Posted to PB Paraang, a small base located south of the village of Khowshal Kalay, he and his comrades found that virtually every patrol was being ambushed by locals hiding behind compound walls and using virtually undetectable 'murder holes' to fire on the soldiers. The Welsh Guards before them had lived with the same predicament. Employing ICOM scanners to monitor insurgent radio chat, it was also apparent that the village of Khowshal Kalay was supplying a dicking screen that monitored the movements of the soldiers whenever they left their patrol base.

On 3 January a patrol set out as usual across the open fields surrounding the base. At just after 1000hrs the soldiers were ambushed and one was wounded. Certain that they had been caught inside an IED field (the insurgents typically initiated their ambushes when patrols were in an area sown with IEDs), the patrol requested fire support. A volley of Javelin and Hellfire missiles was loosed at the suspected firing points, allowing the patrol to extract and evacuate the casualty. One particular compound was judged to have been the principal enemy firing point. This unoccupied compound had been searched before by the platoon, so no chances were taken and a hole was blown in a side door, rather than using the obvious entrance that was probably mined. The suspected insurgent firing point was in a small tower in a corner of the compound. Private Hayes led the way, sweeping the ground with his Vallon for possible IEDs. When he reached the base of the tower, he paused at a wooden stairway leading to the roof. Hayes then made the fateful decision to climb the stairway. As he reached the top, he set off an IED that killed him and buried his section commander in rubble. The shaken soldiers later recalled the Taliban crowing at their success over the ICOM chatter.

Throughout Nad-e Ali the guardsmen tried to implement the new McChrystal policy of 'courageous restraint' while not allowing the insurgents to feel the pressure against them was being relaxed. It was 'a phrase easier to say than actually execute', as the battalion reported, but the statistics showed the British were indeed scaling back their level of firepower within the district. It was with some pride, for example, that Inkerman Company at Chah-e Anjir, like the cavalrymen in Musa Qaleh, completed its six-month tour without killing a single civilian. The argument whether courageous restraint was in fact causing more ISAF casualties proved difficult to settle. By the mid-way point of the tour, the battlegroup had suffered eight fatalities. Three times this number of soldiers had been wounded, a toll that included amputees. By the end of the tour, the battlegroup had suffered 15 fatalities and 69 wounded. Just under 100 soldiers were sent back to Britain as a result of non-battle injuries, illustrating how manpower was drained in the infantry battlegroups, even without enemy action.

The Grenadier Guards did succeed in creating 'protected communities', but equally, insurgent gangs in Nad-e Ali proved tenacious. The guardsmen and attached infantry companies were involved in over 1,300 gun fights and found more than 500 IEDs (62 of which detonated, mostly harmlessly against the better-protected American vehicles). The Royal Engineers attached to the battlegroup built 20 new police checkpoints in Nad-e Ali District, a punishing work schedule over six months. Insurgent casualty figures remained controversial. The guardsmen estimated the number of insurgents killed was 'north of 600'. With some honesty, the guardsmen conceded that 36 civilians were killed, but only eight were directly attributable to British fire. Regardless of the true figure of enemy dead, when 2 Duke of Lancaster's Regiment took over Nad-e Ali in the autumn it was undeniable the district was no longer an insurgent safe haven, a not insignificant achievement on the part of the Grenadiers.

To the north-east of Nad-e Ali, a sister regiment, the Coldstream Guards, took over from the Light Dragoons battlegroup that had fought to clear Babaji District during Operation *Panchai Palang*. Led by Lieutenant Colonel Toby Gray, the battlegroup was dispersed between four main patrol bases (unimaginatively named PBs 1, 2, 3 and 4), as well as a number of satellite bases that appeared to have been named by someone with a surfeit of imagination (PBs Hansel and Gretel, for example). Number 2 Company assumed a police mentoring role, but the battlegroup gained a Mastiff group crewed by cavalrymen from the King's Royal Hussars, as well as a company from 3 Yorks (Duke of Wellington's). It would prove too difficult to use the Mastiff group effectively in Babaji because of the lack of trafficable routes. The majority of the battlegroup was concentrated at PB 4, which inevitably became the focus of insurgent mortar and RPG attacks. Frustratingly for the British, PB 4 happened to be the compound of a notable whose nephew was a well-known Taliban commander, Sur Gul. 19 Light Brigade had been ignorant of this fact when the compound was first occupied. As was customary, the uncle was paid not ungenerous rent, a proportion of which he passed to his insurgent nephew. This went on for three years. As Michael Martin points out, this unusual arrangement caused some confusion among locals who believed the British were in some cunning way conspiring with the Taliban (the same was true, of course, in locations like Sangin and Musa Qaleh, where the British were tenants in the properties of known villains, creating the impression they were secretly in cahoots with these individuals).[10]

Lieutenant Colonel Toby Gray saw similarities between Babaji and the experience of counter-terrorism in Ulster:

> Operations are constant and, in much the way that we did in Northern Ireland, the Battle Group has set out to dominate our 'patch' with constant and aggressive patrolling. Whilst it's demanding, it ensures that the enemy is given little space to operate and, ultimately, makes life a lot safer for our troops and the people amongst whom we operate. The areas in which the companies work vary – some, especially in the north east of the AO [area of operations] are much more developed and are being targeted for work such as setting up schools and clinics, developing agriculture and improving employment opportunities. Other areas, such as in the west where Numbers One and Three Company are operating,

> are very much less so and the task there is to win the trust of the people and put the insurgent onto the back foot – needless to say, they are up to the job and are making great strides in an area that, until last June, had never seen ISAF troops and was firmly in Taliban control.[11]

The Coldstream Guards were able to start a number of reconstruction efforts, including mosque rebuilds and various agricultural projects. The largest such endeavour was the construction of Route Trident, the first road-building project undertaken by the British Army, so it was claimed, since the Dhofar War (1963–76). When 19 Light Brigade fought its way down the central spine of Babaji, it became apparent that this neglected district did not have the route-carrying capacity for heavy military traffic. This also affected the locals, who were unable to carry their produce to markets in Gereshk or Lashkar Gah. The single available route had also become dangerous for British soldiers – 19 casualties had been suffered since the end of Operation *Panther's Claw* by convoys transiting between the bases, forcing air resupply, which in some cases had to be fought over with the insurgents (and which contributed to the myth that the British were in fact supplying the Taliban).

The proposed solution was to build a military road joining PB 1 in the east to PB 4 in the west, along the line of an existing track. The distance was a mere 8 kilometres, but in Helmand even a short stretch of track presented significant obstacles. Culverts would have to be strengthened and in some cases replaced (a total of 17 eventually). Landowners would have to be compensated where the road diverted from the original track. The Taliban were hardly likely to allow this work to proceed uninterrupted, which meant that the work gangs would have to be protected every step of the way. At first, road-building under fire seemed an amusing novelty to the soldiers but the joke soon wore thin.

The work was entrusted to Support Troop, 23 Amphibious Engineer Squadron, commanded by a Lieutenant Helen Ladd. After a reconnaissance and trials, the sappers began building the road in mid-December, starting in the village of Gholam Dastagir Kalay near PB 1. The road itself was constructed from a material called Neoweb, a honeycomb geotextile concertina, overlaid by soil and aggregate supplied by unreliable local contractors. Despite the difficulties, the building of Route Trident was completed by the end of the tour (at a painful pace of about 100 metres per day), and the work stimulated employment for 70 locals prepared to brave Taliban intimidation. A journey which before was reckoned to take about 36 hours was reduced to four hours. As importantly for the British, Neoweb could not be readily dug up, and this greatly reduced the threat of roadside bombs. Eventually, Route Trident would be extended to join up with a Route Morpheus to improve road links between Lashkar Gah and Gereshk. By 2012–13, black-topped roads had begun to be laid to replace these rudimentary routes.

For the average guardsman, life in Babaji was a mix of boredom, frustration with the ANP and occasional danger. Sharp contrasts in fate seemed to colour their experience. Lieutenant Douglas Dalzell joined the Coldstream Guards in 2008, having just missed the last deployment of the battalion to Helmand, and was posted to Number 3 Company. When the battalion returned to the province, only 18 months later, he was transferred to Number 1 Company and assumed command of 2 Platoon. Dalzell was both a popular and conscientious officer 'devoted to his platoon'. When the guardsmen deployed to Babaji, they were confident that everything had been done to prepare them for their tour. However well prepared, 2 Platoon seemed fated to experience bad luck. On 30 November the platoon sergeant John Amer was killed in an IED strike. This was a severe blow. More battle and non-battlefield casualties followed, depleting the platoon. This run of bad luck was briefly put aside on Christmas day when the surprised platoon found themselves hosting General McChrystal for lunch. This was typical of McChrystal, who sought to spend as much time with allies, listening and learning from their experiences, as with American soldiers. For Dalzell and his guardsmen, hosting a celebrity commander like McChrystal was a dazzling experience. In the New Year, 2 Platoon were once again embroiled in operations, leading to the biggest offensive of the tour, Operation *Moshtarak*. On 18 February, a bright, cold day, Dalzell celebrated his birthday – and like every other day, the young officer set off with his platoon on another patrol. The task on this day was to search a compound which was a suspected Taliban firing point. The platoon approached the compound, taking care to sweep the track leading to the main entrance. When they reached the doorway the lead Vallon man carefully checked for IEDs. Receiving no warning tones on his metal detector, he stepped inside. The next man to follow was Dalzell. He stepped on the pressure plate of an IED which the Vallon had missed and suffered a traumatic amputation. In the ensuing scramble to call a medevac helicopter, a signaller moved to the corner of an adjoining compound to get a better signal. He set off a second IED and suffered a double amputation. The stricken signaller lived. Dalzell died of his wounds.

To the north, Sangin remained by far the worst place in Helmand, a town bleeding the task force with a thousand cuts. 3 Rifles assumed command of Sangin on 19 October, taking over from the sister regiment 2 Rifles. As if to underline the level of fighting in the area, Witchcraft 22, a Fire Support Team based at FOB Armadillo, recorded that the day before the handover it had fired off 64 artillery shells, two Hellfire missiles, two 500-pound bombs and two GMLRS rockets.

The 3 Rifles commanding officer, Lieutenant Colonel Nick Kitson, was a relative of General Sir Frank Kitson, the hard-nosed British commander who snuffed out the Mau Mau rebellion in Kenya in the 1950s. The two Kitsons could not have been further apart. Mass hangings, a policy which no doubt would have had a strong effect in Sangin, were no longer a weapon in the armoury of British commanders. Nor could the modern Kitson employ the sanction ordered by Lord Roberts in 1880 – that any Afghan found bearing arms within a 5-mile radius of his base should be promptly shot, a measure, incidentally, which had the effect of reducing attacks against the British and Indian soldiers to zero. He would have to fight within modern rules of engagement, and what a tough fight this would prove.

A Company was deployed to FOB Nolay; B Company drew the short straw and was posted to the district centre and satellite bases; and C Company found itself in the relatively peaceful FOB Zeebrugge at Kajaki. As with every other infantry battalion struggling to make up numbers, 3 Rifles was reinforced by A Company, 4 Rifles, deployed to FOB Inkerman, and B Company, The Royal Scots Borderers (1 SCOTS), deployed to FOB Wishtan. Fire support was provided by Chestnut Troop, 1 Royal Horse Artillery, and engineer support by 42 Squadron, 28 Engineer Regiment. Various other attachments completed the organization that like its predecessor was over 1,400 strong.

Kitson believed in the strategy of clear-hold-build. This Petraean doctrine was energetically promoted by what would be the last British Army unit to serve in Sangin. Towards the end of the tour Kitson wrote:

> Now that we are genuinely their neighbours in a large number of places (there are 29 security force locations of various shapes and sizes in the BG area, of which we are present in 23), we can communicate with the

> locals on a continuous basis, understand their hopes and fears and tell them the truth about what we are trying to do.[12]

This policy rested on the blind hope that the predominantly Ishaqzai and Alikozai tribesmen of Sangin wanted to communicate with the British. The experience since 2006 had been that the only communication the locals wished to exchange with foreign soldiers was gunfire. 2 Rifles had suffered grievously in Sangin. 3 Rifles would experience an even bloodier tour as Kitson attempted to spread British influence by dispersing his battlegroup among the hostile population.

3 Rifles' last foray at solving the problem of Sangin proved controversial and costly in lives. The desperate conditions of ordinary riflemen can be illustrated by the sombre and terse record left by the company sergeant major of A Company at Nolay. With the officer commanding the company on his mid-tour leave, it fell to the warrant officer to maintain the company blog:

> The company was deeply saddened to lose five members of its team. Lance Corporal Christopher Roney (2 Platoon) was killed in an Incident at PB ALMAS on 21st December 2009, Corporal Lee Brownson and Rifleman Luke Farmer (2 Platoon) in a contact IED on 15th Jan 2010 during a night patrol and LCpl Daniel Cooper (2 Platoon) in a contact IED on 24th Jan 2010 whilst leading a resupply patrol. We have also suffered a number of other casualties, Rifleman Deare in a contact IED strike at PB HANJAR on 15th December, Rifleman Parkes and Neville in a contact IED strike at PB JAMIL on 16th December 2009, LCpl Williams, Rifleman Swinhoe, Wildman, Cowd, and Woodford were injured in an incident at PB ALMAS on 21st December 2009, and Lance Bombardier Philips who received a gunshot wound to the thigh only last week.

This was a rate of attrition no battlegroup could sustain for more than a few months. Experienced and over-tasked soldiers were being lost. In his short career, Brownson, mentioned in the sergeant major's despatch, had served in Kosovo, Iraq and Afghanistan. The home towns of the fallen servicemen revealed how many communities were being touched by the war: Bishop Auckland, Sunderland, Pontefract and Hereford. And the cost at home was mounting in other ways – two more widows and four more children had been added to the roll call of the bereaved from A Company's recent losses.

Despite such setbacks, Kitson put a brave face on the situation. More patrol bases were built and more casualties incurred. 3 Rifles would man the most bases in Sangin of any British unit, and suffer the highest number of casualties. A possible correlation between being fixed and dispersed and high casualty counts was not drawn. Instead, an aggressive narrative was offered. 'The insurgents cannot keep it up for long,' Kitson reported, 'we hit them hard when they show themselves and most of the population in the new areas welcome us.'[13]

This latter point was more wishful thinking than fact. Kitson was right that Sangin was war weary, but locals associated the war not with the Taliban, their kinsmen and relatives, but with the presence of the British, who had provoked the fighting in the summer of 2006. Eighty per cent of the population of Sangin District, according to a British estimate, was directly or indirectly involved in the illicit opium trade. The British and Americans after them would always hold on to the hope that somehow Sangin – a town at the centre of Afghanistan's narcotics trade – could be turned to the government side. This consistently proved a forlorn hope. And nor were the insurgents tiring. In the weeks following the clearance of Route 611 from Sangin to FOB Inkerman – a distance of no more than 5 kilometres – Sergeant Major Patrick Hyde, the A Company warrant officer responsible for ensuring the resupply of the new bases, would personally experience 14 IED strikes (and survive them all, again, thanks to the American vehicles).[14] This unstoppable warrant officer would eventually experience 17 IED strikes over the course of multiple tours, and be awarded a fully deserved Military Cross. His laconic comment at setting some sort of record was, 'I don't like driving a desk. I want to be a soldier.'[15] On Christmas day alone, 13 IEDs were cleared in the vicinity of the notorious FOB Wishtan.[16]

Kitson drove his men in what amounted to a last British gamble in Sangin. 2 Rifles had averaged around ten patrols a day. Kitson pushed this up to 50. The sister battalion had mounted around 800 patrols in its six-month tour. Kitson raised this number to 1,000 *per month*. Inevitably, the casualty clock started ticking and rang alarm tones by the time 3 Rifles handed over to 40 Commando. A total of 27 soldiers lost their lives in Sangin, including soldiers from other regiments attached to the 3 Rifles battlegroup. Well over 100 were injured, a total that included several single and double amputees. Not everyone would have agreed that this human cost was being reflected by 'progress' in Sangin.

On 2 December President Obama made the long-awaited announcement on the future of America's commitment to the war in Afghanistan. It sounded like 'the latest treatment for a dying patient', in journalist Michael Yon's words.[17] Symbolically, the announcement was made in a speech to army cadets at West Point Military Academy. After 93 days of deliberation – dithering in the view of critics – and ten gruelling meetings with an inner council of advisors, expectations were high. If the audience expected a dramatic announcement, they left disappointed. As anticipated, a surge of 30,000 troops would be authorized, with the bulk of the troops arriving in Afghanistan by the middle of the following year. General McChrystal would be 10,000 troops short of the reinforcement he requested at the beginning of the year, but at least he could be satisfied that his overall strategy had been approved. The British also had reason to be satisfied: a further US Marine brigade would be deployed to Helmand. In an unfortunate parallel, the American surge, together with the smaller increases promised by other NATO countries, meant that total ISAF troop numbers deployed in Afghanistan would now match Soviet troop levels at the height of the Soviet–Afghan War – a point not missed by critics of the war.

Questions over whether the American strategy would work were not foremost in all minds. What made the champagne corks pop in London (and in other European capitals) was not the announcement of an American surge, but the announcement of an American withdrawal. In a break from the Bush administration that studiously avoided committing America to withdrawal timetables, President Obama made the bold announcement that American troops would start withdrawing from Afghanistan in the summer of 2011 – or in time for the next American presidential race. The war, now routinely dubbed 'Obama's War' by the media, had a finite timetable. Afghanistan would not sink his chances of re-election. One American president had drawn European allies into an unpopular war, and now a second American president was abandoning the ship, or at least returning the ship to harbour. For most European leaders, the question was no longer could the war be 'won' – a possibility that few countenanced – but would the war still sink their own electoral chances?

No European leader was more pressed by this question than the British prime minister, Gordon Brown. Facing an election in five months, and trailing badly in the polls, the Labour government needed to exploit President Obama's announcement of a withdrawal by laying out the road map of a British withdrawal before the next general election. He also needed success on the battlefield.

Operation *Moshtarak* was a hugely important operation in the story of Britain's war in Helmand. It was not only the last major operation undertaken by Task Force Helmand, at the height of its strength, but it also represented the culmination of almost four years of painfully won lessons. If *Moshtarak* were bungled, the British might as well pack up and go home. It also illustrated the limits of British military power. In *Moshtarak* the entire resources of a British Army brigade were concentrated on a piece of land shaped like an upside-down triangle whose sides measured no more than 5 kilometres. The main objectives of the operation were just two small villages – Showal and Naqelabad Kalay – and the enemy was a small number of insurgents armed with light weapons. There were believed to be perhaps 100–150 insurgents in the area, and possibly the same number in adjoining Babaji. In this respect, Operation *Moshtarak* was a hubristic finale to the self-delusion that had permeated the Ministry of Defence for the last two decades.

The Chah-e Anjir Triangle, or CAT for short, was the elbow joint that joined Nad-e Ali and Babaji districts (it was also confusingly known as 'Area 31', which gave birth to Combined Force 31 for the operation). A British presence had been established at the bottom apex of the triangle, at Chah-e Anjir itself, and a second British base had been established at the entrance of the main wadi in the north, but the rest of the ground remained 'Taliban country'. Just north of Chah-e Anjir was the small village of Abdul Wahid Kalay, dominated by Noorzai and hostile to the British. This village would have to be secured to ensure further progress into the centre of the triangle. At the top of the triangle were the two villages that were the main objectives of the operation. Adjoining the Nahr-e Bughra Canal was Showal (literally 'crane', named after an abandoned crane which the Taliban used to fly their flag). This was a predominantly Kharotei village of fewer than 1,000 inhabitants. Further south was Naqelabad Kalay, another mainly Kharotei settlement. Further to the east was a collection of compounds on the southern bank of the canal near a wadi called Naray Mandeh. This had a mixed population. In fact, there were over 12 tribal groups living in the area, including Tajiks and Hazaras. CAT had few vehicle-capable tracks, and the few that existed were extensively seeded with IEDs. Clearing the area would be a foot slog. Perhaps 14,000 tribesmen lived within this small triangle of land.

Operation *Moshtarak* was part of a wider three-phase strategy. The first phase involved the reorganization of forces around Kandahar city, a measure made necessary by the imminent withdrawal of Canadian forces from Afghanistan (the Dutch in Uruzgan had already left in the summer, the first ISAF contingent to quit the war). This reorganization had already largely been completed. The second phase was the clearance of central Helmand, which included Operation *Moshtarak*. The last phase (Operation *Hamkari*), anticipated to take place in the spring, would involve a major effort to restore governance in Kandahar.

The main phase of Operation *Moshtarak* began on Saturday 13 February. Over 15,000 troops took part in the operation, although this figure was highly misleading, as the proportion of front-line troops was actually much smaller. The watchword of the operation was articulated by Major General Messenger as lead spokesman on British operations in Afghanistan: 'Where we go, we will stay. Where we stay, we will build.' On the British side, the major units involved included the Grenadier Guards, the Coldstream Guards, 1 Royal Welsh and the Household Cavalry. On the American side, the assault forces included 1/3 Marines, 1/6 Marines, 3/6 Marines, 4/23 Marines (a Stryker battalion) and a LARR (Light Armoured Reconnaissance Regiment). Extensive combat engineer resources were made available as well as lavish ground-attack and helicopter support.

The operation began with a massive heliborne insertion of around 1,200 soldiers. This was the most complex and demanding air control operation mounted by the RAF in Helmand, and it required every available transport helicopter in south-west Afghanistan. At any one stage over 60 aircraft were operating in relatively confined airspace, at night and against a demanding schedule. The fact that this part of the operation was completed on time and without incident was a great testament to the planning staffs, pilots and ground crew of the Joint Helicopter Force. Flight Lieutenant 'Haz' Hasley, one of the Chinook pilots, described the excitement of that night:

> We struck out at low level under the moonless night towards our objective which was the insurgent held town of Showal. En route to target the ambient light levels were so poor that even our NVGs

> [Night Vision Goggles] struggled to provide much more than a dark green nothingness. However, with only a few short miles to go the goggles erupted in a bright and clear picture provided by infrared flares invisible to the naked eye, dropped from a circling C-130 Hercules from overhead. On short finals to the target, the formation of Chinooks tightened spacing and pitched noses up hard to decelerate quickly. The back wheels dug into the soft ground of the muddy field and we disgorged our complement of Royal Welsh and ANA troops. Seconds later we were wheels up and racing back to Bastion airfield to pick up our next chalk of soldiers.[18]

Over the course of the night, Hasley and the other three British Chinooks in his flight ferried 650 British and Afghan soldiers to their start lines in a relay that lasted two hours.

The airborne assault, spearheaded by A Company, 1 Royal Welsh and 1/3/201 Kandak of the ANA, met no opposition. The 240-strong B Company landed in Shaheed, two hours before first light, securing three objectives with the assistance of an Afghan 'Tiger Team'. Unusually, the ANA *kandak* was drawn from Kabul and included an 86-strong French contingent, the only occasion in the war when Gallic soldiers fought alongside British soldiers. Eventually, the Royal Welsh secured eight small settlements at the northern end of CAT, all but one without a fight. There were no casualties, as far as anyone could tell on either side, and no civilians were injured.

To the south-west, the Grenadier Guards, with an Estonian mechanized company and 1/3/215 Kandak, began to advance north from Chah-e Anjir. Progress for the Grenadiers was slow and deliberate. On 5 February the guardsmen had already cleared a vital node known as Shirin Jan junction near Chah-e Anjir. This operation had not been without its difficulties, as one guardsman recalled with a Milliganesque touch:

> We set off in the pitch blackness across some of the worse terrain we'd experienced in Afghanistan with Gdsm Heaton checking for IED's [sic] the whole way. It will be remembered by all as the insertion from hell. Gdsm Challinor summed it up when he was heard saying 'I can't go on anymore, just leave me here I'll be alright!' LSgt Mann decided that he needed a wash and fell in a river where he had to be rescued by WO1 Stevens.[19]

The object of these night infiltrations, which the guardsmen used to great effect, was to get behind the Taliban screen. The far harder task was clearing the kilometre stretch of a track known as Washir Road to a point called Yellow 11. An American engineer team, Task Force Thor, struck an IED and had to retire. A second team found eight IEDs, and a further four were turned in by local villagers. The insurgents naturally tried to impede this route clearance, and eventually it took three days of repeated clearances before the Washir Road could be declared safe.

The British had hoped that the fighting phase of Operation *Moshtarak* would be concluded swiftly and bloodlessly, and this wish came to pass. Just one hellfire missile was launched in the entire operation. No bombs were dropped and the guns stayed silent. Not a single civilian was killed. This was a vindication of an approach that prized subtlety over brute force and words over bullets. Within 24 hours the British were convening *shuras* to explain to the locals the purpose of their presence and their intentions for the future. The *shura* at Showal was attended by about 150 Kharotei, an indication that this former Taliban enclave was at least prepared to listen to the foreigners. In the bazaar in Showal alone, bomb disposal teams had to clear 29 IEDs. Further route clearance operations were undertaken and more caches were uncovered (the Royal Welsh found 13 IEDs in one compound alone). Patrol bases were built alongside the newly invested villages and on major track junctions. In total, 24 new checkpoints and PBs would be built. Patrols were sent out to map the 'human terrain', the laborious process of trying to find out who exactly lived in which compounds and where their loyalties lay. This was what the British called 'hot stabilization' and was crucial to reinforcing a perception in the local tribes that this time government forces had come to stay. It was unsurprising that when Brigadier Cowan returned from his first *shura* he was reported to be 'very pleased'.

What did *Moshtarak* achieve and what was learnt? Several months of careful preparation had been rewarded. The military outcome had always been subordinated to the main effort, which was to protect the people and not to kill insurgents. The two governors, Mangal and Habibullah, had been intimately engaged throughout the planning process. Local advice had been assiduously sought. As one officer explained: 'We asked the district governor to identify the most important villages, the most important routes, and what would define normalcy [in our area of operations], and these three things became our objectives.'[20]

The brigade drew up a list of 18 indicators of success, and the first six all related to governance.[21] The British had successfully followed up the military operation with 'government in a box' (a phrase reportedly coined by General McChrystal, although some questioned whether it mutated too easily into 'government in a coffin'). This was a dramatic change of attitude from that of just two years previously, when a British brigade might have judged the success of an operation by the body count.

When Brigadier Cowan handed over command of Task Force Helmand on 10 April, his verdict was honest and measured:

> In a population-centred counter-insurgency, empowering the people is essential. The local leaders are the people who should lead on achieving security and through the district governors we have been creating a comprehensive network of village security shuras so every community is responsible for its own destiny. This is a hard fight and it will continue to remain so. This is not a campaign that anyone expects to win anytime soon.[22]

To support this strategy of 'protected communities', the Royal Engineers had built 22 new patrol bases, 88 checkpoints and 61 sangars, a phenomenal achievement of military engineering.[23] A further 16 bridges were constructed, opening routes for the locals and soldiers alike.

The winter fighting season had not proved to be a respite. The task force suffered 61 fatalities and around 1,000 wounded. This tally included 12 medics wounded while attempting to save the lives of stricken soldiers.[24] In a district like Babaji, where the task force was now expanding its presence, fatalities doubled and the number of wounded tripled. A measure of the busyness of the medical teams can be gauged by the humble but vital role played by the ambulance crews at Bastion helipad that ferried the casualties from incoming helicopters across the short strip to the hospital. Over the course of six months they made this urgent journey 2,614 times.[25]

On average, the brigade had mounted around 400 patrols a week, and one in four of these had resulted in a TiC (Troops in Contact), a euphemism for a gunfight. One in eight patrols had encountered IEDs. Despite the policy of 'courageous restraint', ammunition expenditure had been colossal. There had been 258 breach operations alone (using explosive entry to search a compound).[26] The average village in Nad-e

Ali or Babaji comprised fewer than 100 compounds. The British had effectively damaged two villages' worth of compounds in the course of their operations just through this technique alone. By Christmas 2009, the US Army and Marines had deployed six GMLRS (Guided Multiple Launch Rocket System) and 19 HIMARS (High Mobility Artillery Rocket System) to Helmand. The British had just four GMLRS launchers.[27] But the ammunition expenditure told a very different story. By the autumn of that year, a total of 1,433 rockets had been launched in Helmand. The US Army had launched 707 rockets (49 per cent of the total), and the US Marines had launched just 70 (5 per cent). The Royal Artillery, with its mere four launchers, accounted for 656 rockets, or 45 per cent of the total.

Cowan was awarded the Distinguished Service Order for his leadership of 11 Light Brigade. That such awards were routinely handed out to senior British officers did not lessen the merit that was attached to this particular award. There was an irony that after four years of trying the British had finally got it right, even as they were preparing to relinquish responsibility for all but three districts in Helmand to the US Marine Corps. 11 Light Brigade could not redeem the previous wasted years, but the brigade could and did set the foundations for a dignified withdrawal. Over the course of their six-month tour, Cowan's men racked up the gallantry awards. 'Courageous restraint' did not imply lack of courage. Five Conspicuous Gallantry Crosses, 18 Military Crosses, three Distinguished Flying Crosses and seven Queen's Gallantry Medals were awarded to the brigade. Thirty-eight soldiers were Mentioned in Dispatches, and 12 received Queen's Commendations for Bravery. Acting Corporal Sarah Louise Bushbye of the Royal Army Medical Corps was one of the Military Cross recipients, the third servicewoman to receive this award. Sixty-three of the awards went to the infantry, five of which were posthumous, demonstrating that in other respects nothing had changed. The war was being carried, as in the past, by the poor bloody infantry.

Cowan's replacement was Brigadier Richard Felton, an officer whose career bridged the recent history of the British Army. Felton had been originally commissioned into the Gloucestershire Regiment. The 'Glorious Glosters' had made their famous last stand against the Chinese at the Imjin River but were unable to make a similar heroic stand against Treasury cuts. Like so many county regiments on which Britain's fortunes had rested in past wars, the Gloucestershire Regiment disappeared within a larger merged regiment that barely lasted another decade before it too was culled.* By this time Felton had served in Northern Ireland, and in Bosnia as chief of staff to 7th Armoured Brigade. In 1998 he took the decision to transfer to the most modern part of the army, the Army Air Corps. By the following year he had assumed command of 669 Squadron. Staff appointments followed, and in 2003 he volunteered to undertake the arduous Apache conversion course, the first of its type. He passed out in April 2004 and assumed command of 9 Regiment. The timing could not have been more fortuitous. Two years later, he was commanding the Joint Helicopter Force on Operation *Herrick 4*. Two promotions followed and now Felton found himself in the unusual position of being Britain's first Army Air Corps brigadier in command of a mechanized brigade in a war.

4th Mechanized Brigade, or 'The Black Rats', owed its lineage to the original Desert Rats. This famous division had originally comprised a light armoured cars brigade that eventually became 7th Armoured Brigade, and a heavy brigade, 4th Armoured Brigade. This heavier brigade was equipped with cruiser tanks and consisted of 1st and 6th Royal Tank Regiments. Decimation in battle and other reorganizations would jumble up the units, but the original brigade designations stuck. The rat was in fact a desert jerboa, a symbol adopted at the beginning of 1940.

The brigade deployed on the eve of the most hotly contested and surreal British general election fought in a generation. Two weeks before the polling stations opened, a volcanic eruption in Iceland encouraged a handful of British officials to cause more damage to the economies of the European Union than the September 11 attacks, the very event that had led to Britain becoming embroiled in a war in Afghanistan. As a result of a particle dispersion model used by the London-based Volcanic Ash Advisory Centre, all flights were grounded across Europe for six days. Around 7 million passengers found themselves inconvenienced and in many cases out of pocket. The total cost of this fiasco was estimated at over £2 billion. Since the 1950s, there had been just 126 reported incidents involving civil airliners flying into volcanic ash, of which just ten had resulted in partial or complete engine failure. None had resulted in a crash.[28] Disproportionate British exaggeration was never going to stand with European authorities. First France and

*The Gloucestershire, Berkshire and Wiltshire Regiment, formerly Duke of Edinburgh's Royal Regiment.

then Germany rebelled against the British judgement, and these were soon followed by other European countries. All of Europe opened up, but British officialdom continued to insist it was too dangerous to fly (ironically, Europe enjoyed high pressure and clear blue skies that week, making the British alarm-ringing even stranger). Finally, the British Airways chairman, exasperated with the damage caused to the airline industry, seized the initiative and ordered his stranded aircraft to fly back to Britain. At the eleventh hour, even as the aircraft were approaching British airspace, the ban was lifted.

This bizarre distraction provided only temporary respite for a Labour government which was nearing the end of its 13-year hold on power. The 2010 general election witnessed the first television debates in British history. The surprising star of these shows was the Liberal Democrat leader Nick Clegg. The Labour camp muttered about the importance of 'substance over style', but the British seemed to prefer style over substance. In the event, the Labour Party was not wiped out, and the Liberal Democrats lost seats, but the Conservative Party, led by David Cameron, failed to gain a parliamentary majority, securing just 306 seats. As the three main parties scrambled to woo each other to form a coalition government, the country was again distracted by the nail-biting culmination of the football Premier League (won by Chelsea, with an 8-0 thumping of Wigan, breaking several records along the way). Late in the evening on Tuesday 10 May, the incumbent Gordon Brown finally bowed to the inevitable and resigned his premiership with great dignity. Released from the necessity to spin a war he did not start, the rock-faced Scotsman paid a moving tribute to the armed forces in his valedictory speech. Ironically, it was in these last few minutes of his premiership that the private individual came to the fore, expressing the depth of his feelings over soldiers whose lives had been lost, 'in honour', as he put it. Perhaps Gordon Brown never did 'get the war', but he most certainly got its human sacrifice.

With a change of government came a new defence secretary, and the man entrusted with this difficult post was another Scotsman, Dr Liam Fox. Conservative policy towards the war in Afghanistan in the run-up the general election had been contradictory. In television interviews Fox had emphasized withdrawing as quickly as possible and handing over security responsibilities to the Afghans. His master, David Cameron, had preferred to offer the more statesman-like pledge that a British withdrawal would not be dictated by an artificial timetable but by results on the ground, unwisely holding himself hostage to an uncertain future. Now the Conservative defence secretary was in coalition with the Liberal Democrats whose views on defence were radically different to his own party's policies.

The coalition government wasted no time in addressing the Afghan war. Within a week of assuming power, the new foreign secretary, William Hague, paid a visit to his American counterpart, Hillary Clinton. Clinton had been charmed by the previous foreign secretary, David Miliband (so youthful, she sighed). William Hague clearly deployed all his reserves of charm, because the body language at the joint press conference was good. The 'special relationship' was safe under the novel arrangements for sharing power being concocted in Westminster. By the end of the month, a high-level delegation travelled to Helmand, which was upstaged by the surprise visit of England's iconic footballer David Beckham. Defying the cliché that footballers are born with blessed feet but inarticulate tongues, Beckham spoke as movingly as anyone at the memorial plinth at Camp Bastion. A patriot to his metatarsals, the former England captain boosted the morale of the troops in a way that politicians could only envy.

The reason for all this urgency was an imminent and significant change to the command arrangements in south-west Afghanistan. Just as in Normandy British commanders had bowed to the inevitable numerical ascendancy of American troops and leadership as the bridgehead expanded, so in Helmand the exclusively British war was about to become an American war, commanded by an American general.

The new command arrangements were announced on 21 May. The old Regional Command South would be split into two headquarters. A new Regional Command South-West would assume responsibility for Helmand and Nimroz provinces (the latter a desert area with no ISAF presence). The new Regional Command South would now control the smaller but no less volatile Kandahar, Uruzgan, Daykundi and Zabul provinces. The Dutch had already quit and the Canadians were about to follow, so this would become an almost exclusively American command. On the ANA side, 215 Corps would be partnered by Regional Command South-West, and 205 Corps would revert to Kandahar. Overall troop levels matched the split in command, rising from 35,000 in October 2009 to over 50,000 by the summer of 2010. Major General Richard Mills (USMC) duly assumed command of Regional Command South-West, but in an important concession to the British it was agreed this command would rotate between an American and a British general. Effectively, all of south-west Afghanistan would now be back under American leadership, and this gave the campaign a coherence (and resources) that it had lacked in the last four years.

The key announcement, however, related to the allocation of district responsibilities in Helmand. In a widely anticipated move it was announced British troops would hand over Battlegroup North-West to US Marines. This area encompassed Kajaki and Sangin. First there would be an interim arrangement, in which the British battlegroup (made up from 40 Commando) would fall under the command of an American Regimental Combat Team (North), but now everyone knew that the end was in sight. Astonishingly, delay in handing over Sangin to the US Marines had come from the Brown government, which feared a loss of reputation. Jack Fairweather has expressed this decision in polite terms: 'These political risks [being perceived to be cutting and running], they apparently calculated, were greater than those resulting from a few more British deaths in Sangin.'[29] The 'few more deaths' were the lives of 14 marines. Their comrades would probably not have shared in this political equation of death.

The transfer in command took place on 1 June, and the first steps of the British withdrawal took place at the end of the month. Royal Marines who had wrested the mountain overlooking Kajaki Dam in 2007 handed over their perch to American counterparts. FOB Zeebrugge would now be a US Marine Corps outpost. Behind these new arrangements, NATO was manoeuvring itself for an ultimate and final withdrawal. On 22–23 April a conference had been held in Tallinn, Estonia. The theme of the conference was the handover of security to the Afghan Army and police. The idealistic agendas of previous conferences had been knocked sideways by the more pragmatic and pressing question of ending an inconclusive and unpopular war. The conference closed with a resolution to meet in Lisbon, in November, to present defined and concrete conditions for ISAF's withdrawal from Afghanistan.

The withdrawal of the marines from Kajaki allowed Lieutenant Colonel Paul James, the commanding officer of 40 Commando, to concentrate his marines in Sangin. James would be the last British officer to command troops in Sangin. He was ably helped in this difficult task by RSM Pelling, who in 2007 had taken part in the abortive assault at Jugroom Fort. Pelling had been one of the bulwarks of that tour and his inner strength would be needed on this last tour. The fact that James was the last British commander in Sangin in a way liberated this officer from making the usual hollow statements over progress in the town. 'The greatest reason why there is instability in Sangin,' he said, 'is … the narcotics trade … We can just keep killing people every day but actually the only real way to overcome this is by sheer economics, by offering the youth better incentives, a better job, better education.'[30]

The marines' last tour of Sangin would be grim. As well as suffering 14 fatalities, over 50 would be seriously injured, including another marine triple amputee, joining Mark Ormrod from the first 3 Commando Brigade tour of Helmand. A 300-metre patrol was considered a good day.[31] Despite using even more sophisticated equipment, the marines found their metal detectors missed eight out of ten IEDs.[32] In the worst-hit troop in 40 Commando, two out of three casualties was a Vallon man.[33] Whatever postures commanders adopted, they faced terrible dilemmas. In the end, there were no easy tactical answers in Sangin.

On 20 June another grim milestone was passed when the 300th British fatality from the war in Afghanistan died in Queen Elizabeth Hospital in Birmingham from wounds sustained in an IED strike. He was Marine Richard Hollington of B Company, 40 Commando. His death was announced just two days before the Conservative chancellor, George Osborne, presented a budget to Parliament that included the most swingeing cuts in public expenditure in a generation. The media were quick to note that in the newly dubbed 'age of austerity', Britain's two wars in Iraq and Afghanistan had cost the nation over £20 billion. The Blairite readiness to intervene in Muslim countries had proved, and was still proving, expensive to the nation's coffers. Did making Britain 'safe from terrorism' – a home-grown terrorism that the previous Labour government had incited through participation in the Anglo-American invasion of Iraq – truly justify such a high cost in lives and treasure? Few in the summer of 2010 continued to believe so.

The bad news then worsened, from an entirely unexpected quarter. The front cover of that summer's double issue of *Rolling Stone* magazine displayed a flamboyant popular singer named Lady Gaga sporting two automatic rifles for breasts, and little else. The contents of the magazine were no less eye-catching. Over a series of unguarded moments with freelance journalist Michael Hastings, General McChrystal and his staff had given a highly damaging insight into the poisonous web of relationships at the top of the American national security apparatus. McChrystal had already tested President Obama's patience twice in the previous year. During the period of consultation over a new strategy in Afghanistan, details of McChrystal's preferred strategy had been leaked to the media (but not by the general or his staffs). The leaks had been exacerbated by a speech delivered in London in which McChrystal seemed to throw a gauntlet down to his political masters to back him or sack him. The October speech drew a panicked response from the White House and a staged meeting between the president and his general. If the president's staff hoped the wayward McChrystal would now conform, they were hoping against human nature.

McChrystal had to go. He had violated the fundamental relationship between civilian and military leaders in a democratic society. The sadness was that the obsessed and driven McChrystal, who had spent the last nine years of his life almost continuously at war, did represent ISAF's best hope of success. McChrystal was the great *entr'acte* of the war. MacArthur had been an indifferent general but a tireless self-promoter. McChrystal could point to genuine accomplishment in Iraq. His military record in two intractably difficult wars was unimpeachable. There *was* no better American general than Stanley McChrystal, a point made starkly evident as the White House scrambled to find a replacement. Summoned back to Washington, he handed in his resignation after a half-hour private meeting with President Obama. The resignation letter was brusque, offered no apology to the insulted and spoke instead of the importance of the mission. To the last McChrystal remained the committed soldier. With no obvious replacement, the White House fell on submitting the candidacy of General David Petraeus to Congress (which implied a step down for the 62-year-old, who was holding the post of CENTCOM commander). In the interim, Lieutenant General Nick Parker found himself in charge of the biggest land force commanded by a British general since World War II. The Taliban, predictably, celebrated the scandal.

For the British, the worsening situation was emphasized by the sudden spike in casualties. In one week in June, 11 soldiers and marines were killed. Four soldiers serving with 1 Mercians (Cheshires) drowned at night in a ghastly road accident: Colour Sergeant Martyn Horton, Lance Corporal David Ramsden, Private Douglas Halliday and Private Alex Isaac. Horton left behind a nine-year-old son and infant step-daughter. Ramsden had left the army but decided to re-enlist as a reservist and serve a tour in Afghanistan. In Sangin, marines continued to fall to sniper fire and IEDs. In early July, Sergeant Talib Hussein, an ANA soldier based at PB 3 in Babaji District, murdered the British company commander, Major Joshua Bowman, in his sleep. He then entered the operations room and killed the two soldiers manning the radios, Lieutenant Neal Turkington, an Ulsterman, and Corporal Arjun Purja Pun, a Gurkha. The assailant fled into the night and got away.

In the winter of 2007 Rory Stewart had presciently observed that policymakers, 'worried about lack of progress, are in danger of flipping from troop increase to flight'.[34] This prophecy appeared to be unfolding. McChrystal's resignation coincided with the long-term transition from a counter-insurgency campaign to a counter-terrorist campaign favoured by Vice President Biden. Prime Minister Cameron reiterated that British troops would quit Afghanistan by 2015, while General Richards hinted that peace talks should start at once. The Pentagon continued to promote the fallacy that although the war was not winnable in a conventional sense, the Taliban were beatable, and beating the Taliban was an essential precursor to successful negotiations and withdrawal. This was the same fallacy promoted in the long and painful withdrawal from Vietnam. Both President Obama and Biden favoured a limited counter-terrorist war but simultaneously wanted the counter-insurgency war to succeed. The former implied chasing a target that had long dispersed and mutated into a wider regional and global phenomenon, and the latter was never going to succeed, as much as anything, because a political will to win had evaporated. As if to confirm the weakening political will, Japanese, American and European donor countries all suspended or withheld over $8 billion of aid money within the space of six weeks.

At least – it seemed – special forces operations were reaping success. On assuming command General Petraeus informed his congressional interrogators that special operations – the controversial 'night raids' – had killed or captured 130 Taliban commanders in the previous four months. This had all the hallmarks of a McChrystal-inspired strategy of industrial-level special operations. Hitting at least one target every night had been a McChrystal mantra, and the figures suggested that this target was being over-achieved. From February 2009 and December 2010, there was a five-fold increase in night raids. Over one three-month period, an average of around 20 raids was being conducted *every night*. In April, over a 24-hour period, as many as 40 raids had been undertaken.[35] ISAF claimed that eight out of ten raids succeeded in capturing or killing an insurgent commander, but critics were less sure. Chest-thumping in the media over these numbers disguised that the majority of the 'downed' commanders were mid- or low-level figures. The success rate against 'Tier 1 Taliban' was less impressive. Lost commanders were replaced within one or two weeks, and the disruption to insurgent networks was always transient and 'reversible' – a phrase frequently repeated as ISAF began to withdraw.

On 7 July, the Defence Secretary Liam Fox rose to the despatch box and informed the House of Commons that British troops would be handing over Sangin to US Marines. The significance of the announcement escaped no one. This was the great symbolic step in the British withdrawal from Helmand Province. Sangin – the very name had become etched in British Army folklore – was being surrendered. This was the town that British troops had entered thoughtlessly and precipitously in the summer of 2006. A two-day mission turned into a costly platoon house siege. A staff officer serving with the brigade had resigned over the stupidity of the act. The town elders had begged the British to leave because their presence would only inflame an already simmering inter-tribal conflict. Four years later the British reaped the reward the elders had predicted. Despite Fox's claim that the British were leaving Sangin 'a better place', by every measure, Sangin was a much worse place.

One-third of all British casualties were suffered in Sangin at the time of withdrawal, but this figure was misleading. Less than 10 per cent of the task force was based in Sangin. By proportion to deployed numbers and in absolute terms Sangin was, by some distance, the most dangerous place to serve in Helmand Province. Over 100 British soldiers and marines died in Sangin. Withdrawal from Sangin offered the tempting political prize of an automatic halving of British casualties, which is what happened.

The handover finally took place at 0630hrs on 20 September with 3/7 Marines. The last British gun in Sangin was manned by 3/29 (Corunna Battery). The American marines brought heavier 155mm artillery pieces, which they were quick to use. There was no great fanfare. The defence secretary and several senior officers spoke of the British sacrifice in the town, but a departing marine simply said that he felt 'hollow'. Another laconically remarked that 'they're welcome to it'. The US Marines immediately began closing down a number of the small bases which the British (principally 3 Rifles) had erected, arguing that this policy had effectively fixed the British. Restoring mobility to the battlefield, the very argument that had raged in the summer of 2006, had still not been settled.

Ironically, the British ended up exactly where they started – stuck in a building leased from one of Sangin's prominent narcotics barons. They left as they arrived, by helicopter, not daring to test the veracity of the renamed Avenue of Hope by attempting a road move through the town. The last British serviceman to die in Sangin was Marine Adam Brown, killed on 1 August. Like so many others, he died in the immediate vicinity of his patrol base after stepping on an IED. He left behind a widow, his childhood sweetheart.

The sequel to this departure revealed the depth of infantile debate over the conduct of the war, at least among armchair generals. Suddenly, Sangin became the place where US Marines were going to show 'the Brits' how it should be done. To be fair, this bravado was not coming from the unfortunate unit posted to Sangin – 3/7 Marines – whose motto was 'Get Some'. The young American marines soon did get some. Fortunately short-toured, this unit then handed over to 3/5 Marines 'Darkhorse'. By January, the replacement unit had suffered as many fatalities as the Rifles in their entire tour. Over a hundred had been wounded, a tally that included triple amputees. More than a thousand IEDs were encountered. This was both a predictable and avoidable misfortune. 3/5 Marines was new to Afghanistan and had been pitched in the worst place. The precipitate withdrawal from the old British bases had fired up the insurgents, who were now lapping against the breakwaters of FOB Jackson. The tactic of closing bases was duly reversed with levels of violence the British would have never dared employ. To re-invest the abandoned FOB Wishtan, every compound 100 metres either side of Pharmacy Road was flattened. Sangin was being destroyed in order to save it. Counter-claims of how many Taliban were being killed were meaningless. When most of the Upper Sangin Valley was in open insurrection against you, proffering exaggerated body counts was as futile as the body counts of the Vietnam War.

Quitting Sangin meant that Brigadier Felton could concentrate on what had become the main British effort: Nad-e Ali and Babaji districts. Deployed in this area were three infantry battalions and two cavalry regiments, as well as additional sub-units drawn from the Scots Guards and Royal Scots Borderers (1 SCOTS) mainly tasked with mentoring the ANA and ANP.

The 1st Royal Dragoon Guards, commanded by Lieutenant Colonel Carr-Smith, split into three squadron groups: B Squadron mounted in Mastiffs acted in support of the Gurkhas in Babaji and the Lancasters in Nad-e Ali; C Squadron re-roled as infantry; and D Squadron took over the role of the armoured support group mounted in Vikings.

The Queen's Royal Lancers assumed the role of the BRF, which deployed as far away as Kandahar. The centre of the reduced British area of responsibility was entrusted to 1 Duke of Lancaster's Regiment, a unit recently formed from the amalgamation of the King's Regiment and the Queen's Lancashire Regiment. Later in the tour, Arnhem and Blenheim Companies from 2 Lancs would be deployed to Helmand, marking the first occasion when both the new battalions were committed to operations. Lieutenant Colonel Frazer Lawrence, based at FOB Shawqat, inherited a more pacified Nad-e Ali from the Grenadier Guards. His main task now was to consolidate the gains and to keep pushing the Taliban into outlying areas and away from the villages. By the time the Lancasters quit Nad-e Ali, the commanding officer would dare venture into the bazaar in a beret rather than helmet.

The precision of combat operations contrasted sharply with the weekly administration of moving sub-units between locations and ensuring their resupply. This was actually the main business of any battlegroup tasked with holding a matrix of patrol bases, and it amounted to a sort of organized chaos which the soldiers bore with stoicism and humour. When 1 Platoon, A Company was told that it was being sent to CP Folad near Shaheed to relieve the Royal Welsh, it responded to the news enthusiastically. Shaheed had a reputation for regular gun fights with the Taliban (the platoon commander was caught in four such encounters soon after arriving ahead of his platoon). On completion of the reconnaissance of the new base, a transport helicopter managed to disembark a further six soldiers, but then the handover plan began to unravel. The events that followed were probably embellished by the kingsman blogger, but perhaps not that much:

> Days passed, smoke was thrown on the HLS at passing helicopters, but still no 1 Pl. Just when we thought all hope was lost another six men arrived and the entire Royal Welsh Pl disappeared. Where were the rest of the Pl? Harvey and Baines quickly found themselves in contact on

> the Sanger within two hours of their arrival. Eventually the rest of the Pl arrived cursing Shawqat, the Navy, the RAF and anyone else who caused the delay on there [sic] arrival to the PB. The RAF set about trying to destroy all our communications with Coy HQ. The plan was to refill the radios by helicopter then filling them [sic]. A helicopter arrived, and the man on the back purged our radios then flew away. Another helicopter arrived and an Engineer got off, much to our surprise. The man on the back of the helicopter then took the radios again and took them to Bastion leaving us with no comms. The next day he returned with the radios but they still were not filled. Kgn Cooper then got excited when he saw an Apache flying overhead and popped smoke anticipating that it would land and sort all our problems. Eventually the radios were fixed, however this was not to be the end of our dramas with the RAF. The very next day saw the R&R [Rest and Recuperation] plot kicking in and Cpl Walsh and Bdr Todd were to be extracted by helicopter. The helicopter arrived, the Engineer jumped off again much to our surprise, then took off leaving a stunned Cpl Walsh ready to cry in the middle of the HLS … thereby missing his cousins [sic] wedding.[36]

The consolation for the kingsmen was that they did find the action they craved – apart from 3 Section, which somehow kept missing the insurgents, resulting in teasing from the other two sections.

In neighbouring Babaji there were equally contrasting fortunes. This district had been split between the Gurkhas and 1 Mercians (Cheshires), commanded by Lieutenant Colonel Andrew Hadfield. For B (Malta) Company of the Mercians, the deployment to CP Kings Hill proved hellish (the base hung a sign over the entrance that read 'Welcome to Hell'). Kings Hill was built within the territory of probably the most resourceful insurgent gang in Babaji, and one almost certainly abetted by foreign fighters. The ground favoured the insurgents with numerous hedges and orchards that allowed a covert approach to the base. Kings Hill was soon ringed by IEDs, as one soldier warned a visiting reporter from the *Sun*: 'Walk out there on your own and you would be dead in seconds. That field is full of IEDs and the ditches around it are even worse.'[37]

The front line extended to a radius of just a few hundred metres, and the soldiers were completely hemmed in by constant sniping. Malta Company, led by Major Richard Grover, seemed destined to experience bad luck. The simple task of chopping down a tree in front of a sangar left one soldier dead and four others injured as the Taliban had succeeded in planting IEDs right under the shadow of the patrol base walls. A patrol venturing outside unknowingly passed over an IED and almost escaped unharmed, but the ninth man finally applied the necessary pressure to detonate the device and lost a leg. Another IED strike resulted in a triple amputation. Patrols got shot at with accurate fire. On one patrol, two soldiers, Corporal Terry Webster and Lance Corporal Alan Cochran, were both shot dead. Other fatalities included Lieutenant John Sanderson, a 'big man with a heart of gold', who was killed in an IED strike, and Lance Corporal Andrew Breeze, also killed by an IED. Remarkably, Breeze, a 31-year-old from Manchester, was on his *sixth* operational tour. Grover was contemptuous of this 'coward's way to fight a war', but it was also an effective way to fight.[38] Over five weeks the company suffered nine fatalities and 12 soldiers were seriously injured. An entire platoon had been effectively wiped out by these invisible killers.

Another particularly bad area was the 'Babaji Pear', in the south-west corner of the district, which had mostly been avoided by ISAF. This fell to Left Flank Company Scots Guards, and their tour proved hectic. Between 22 April and 1 October, not one day passed when the guardsmen were not involved in a gun fight. Eventually there were a total of 650 such spats, and the soldiers fired off more than 350,000 rounds. Over the course of the summer there were 78 incidents involving IEDs, and three IED factories were discovered. Some 150 insurgents were reckoned to have been killed. It was a tribute to the soldiers that despite the heavy levels of fighting, just three guardsmen were killed and 20 injured. IED detection skills also improved: for every one that detonated, nine were being found.[39]

The Gurkhas, who concentrated their campaign on securing the Barakzai villages of Rahim Kalay and Paind Kalay, got off much more lightly.[40] Aside from the incident on 13 July in which the rogue ANA soldier killed three soldiers before fleeing PB 3, the battalion suffered no fatalities over several weeks. This was not due to a lack of insurgent activity, especially at PBs 1 and 4. Over the summer months, the Gurkhas found that every third patrol was engaged in gun battles, and immediately following the poppy harvest virtually every patrol entering a new area came under fire from the local Barakzai. Luck may have played a part, but the Gurkhas also made their own luck. As one rifleman recalled, the company knew that it had won over the trust of the locals when they started selling chickens to the soldiers at local prices. Another surprising measure of the build-up of trust was the arrival of two unaccompanied women at PBs 2 and 4 to attend compensation clinics. This was unheard of in Helmand. One of the women had been widowed in the previous summer during Operation *Panchai Palang*. It had taken her a year to find the courage and confidence to approach the British in person, without a male escort, to seek compensation. Later in the war, the British would be approached by Afghan women seeking protection from violent relatives. These remarkable if rare episodes revealed that Afghan women, far from being ignorant and illiterate, had a very shrewd idea of where they might find justice. It was not in the medieval sharia law foisted on them by village mullahs but in the fairness displayed by Western soldiers whose language they did not even speak. These incidents spoke eloquently of the tragedy suffered by Afghanistan's perennial victims of war – its womenfolk.

Raw courage also played a part in the Gurkhas' war, as it had done in past tours. Acting Sergeant Dipprasad Pun was acting as night sentry at a patrol base near Rahim Kalay when he became aware of a digging noise outside the front gate.[41] On investigating, to his amazement, he found a group of insurgents digging in an IED under the very noses of the British. In the ensuing gun battle, Pun single-handedly fought off the insurgent gang, killing three, and at one stage hurling a machine-gun tripod at an assailant who had climbed the base perimeter wall, when he ran out of ammunition. Over the course of this desperate action Pun fired off all his magazines, a belt of machine-gun ammunition and threw 17 grenades to keep the attackers at bay. The assault was only finally broken off when Pun detonated a Claymore mine. For this action, Dipprasad Pun, whose grandfather and father both held gallantry awards, was awarded the Conspicuous Gallantry Cross.

The luck would run out right at the end of the tour, when a suicide bomber killed Rifleman Suraj Gurung, a recently married soldier from Gorkha in the foothills of the Himalayas. Reflecting the frustrating unpredictability of insurgent tactics, the suicide bomber had been squatting beside a stream washing his feet. As the patrol approached, he stood up to hail the approaching Gurkhas before detonating his bomb. No training could prepare the soldiers for this kind of behaviour. Body parts of the bomber were later found 100 metres from the detonation point.

The diminishing area of British responsibility in Helmand was reflected in the realities of life on the front line. In 2008 a British patrol may have spent a day outside a patrol base roaming over several kilometres. By the summer of 2010 the average patrol length had been reduced to just 90 minutes, and patrols were only straying a few hundred metres from their patrol bases, taking care to remain within the weapon ranges of the sangars. The British were literally holding fortified Alamos, to use Michael Yon's phrase (over 90 now across Task Force Helmand), and nothing else. The clear-hold-build strategy was remorselessly being reduced to a costly strategy of mostly holding existing bases. Twenty-four of the brigade's 26 available companies were in the 'ground-holding role' – that is, fixed in a patrol base or FOB. The number of bases manned by British soldiers (in partnership with the ANA or ANP) jumped from 53 to 119 – the biggest single expansion of any British brigade. These bases continued to attract violence. In 2009 there had been an average of around 300 TiCs per month. In the summer of 2010, this number had risen to 400, and there had been a 200 per cent increase in the number of IEDs. 'Fighting the FOB' – as it became known – was the logical and inevitable consequence of a process that had been started by 12th Mechanized Brigade in the summer of 2007, when it steamed over the Green Zone, leaving behind patrol bases in its wash. Every succeeding brigade had added to the matrix of patrol bases. And every single new base – without exception – became another platoon house under siege.

The answer to this dilemma for the British was to procure American technology, rather than a revision of tactics. Britain's downsized army was mirrored by an eviscerated British land defence industry that could no longer respond quickly or at all to the operational requirements of the army. When Britain went to war over the Falkland Islands in 1982, virtually all the equipment fielded by the army was British manufactured (although its beef steaks came from Argentina, a situation that was quickly rectified by finding an alternative supplier). One generation later, virtually all new equipment was foreign made. This was a dramatic historic reversal of the British experience of warfare and it was not inevitable. Political ideology – 'Thatcherism' in a broad sense – paradoxically disarmed Britain. The state was not so much rolled back as left completely naked.

An inventory of new equipment the Labour government was forced to procure to support the armed forces as Urgent Operational Requirements (UORs), and other programmes that made it possible for Britain to fight its wars at all, illustrates how America, overwhelmingly, became Britain's armourer. By March 2009, the Ministry of Defence had spent £4.2 billion on these emergency procurements.[42] The list below is not exhaustive, but the absence of the word 'British' is obvious. It is included in this book so the reader may properly appreciate the sheer scale of British dependence on the American defence industry.

Aircraft included the C-17 heavy transport aircraft, Shadow R1 surveillance aircraft, Sentinel R1 surveillance aircraft (Canadian-American) and WAH-64D Apache helicopter. UAVs were the Desert Hawk, Predator B, Scan Eagle and Tarantula. Patrol and other vehicles included Mastiff (Cougar), Ridgeback, Wolfhound and Husky. Weapon systems bought included the Guided Multiple Launch Rocket System (GMLRS), Javelin anti-tank missile, the M203 underslung grenade launcher, the 66mm LASM rocket, Sharpshooter rifle, Barrett .5-calibre sniper rifle, and .5-calibre Browning (American-Belgian). Vital surveillance and detection systems included the Lightweight Counter-Mortar Radar (LCRM), Counter Rocket-Artillery-Mortar (C-RAM) system, Boomerang shot detection system, Persistent Theatre Detection System (PTDS), Persistent Ground Surveillance System (PGSS), Persistent Ground Surveillance Tower (PGST), Revivor balloons, Cortez surveillance system, and a suite of masts and cameras. Sensors and sights included the Sniper pods for the Harrier GR7, the widely used ACOG rifle sight, the VIPR 2 thermal imaging sight, and the Head-Mounted Night Vision Device. Other systems included the vital Firestorm Target Acquisition System, HEATs and GRATs situational awareness systems, Rover III terminals to receive UAV footage, JADOCs command system, PSS-SOF mensuration system for precision attack (pronounced 'piss-off'), TIGR patrol data logging system, and HIIDEs biometric collection system.

America was not the only foreign supplier. Israel provided Litening II/III pods for the Tornado GR4, the Hermes 450 UAV, vehicle up-armour packs and the Spike-NLOS missile, also known as Exactor. German kit included an automatic grenade launcher, the Vallon mine detector, the Laser Light Module Mk3, and a new range of MAN trucks. The army bought the Belgian 5.56mm Minimi machine gun, the Norwegian Black Hornet UAV, and an Italian combat shotgun. Sweden was an especially important supplier, providing NLAW (Next Generation Light Anti-Tank Weapon), the Mamba and Giraffe radars, BvS10 Viking troop carriers, and an Anti-Structure Munition (Swedish-German). Italian Panther and Trakker trucks were procured, along with the Austrian Vector PPV light vehicle and 60mm mortar. The widely used Commanders' Target Location System (PLRF 10/15) was Swiss. The Singaporean Warthog replaced the dangerous Viking. France supplied a range of sensors: Battlegroup Thermal Imaging, the Joint Target Acquisition System, the Surveillance System and Range Finder (SSARF), Sophie smart binoculars, and the SLD-500 sniper detection system. The Seer electronic warfare system was a mix of predominantly French and Italian technology. The popular quad bikes were Japanese.

British defence industry could no longer design or manufacture the most basic tool of a soldier – his rifle. The standard service rifle (SA80) was rescued from its many problems by a German company (Heckler & Koch). This was unsurprising, as both the historic Royal Small Arms Factory at Enfield Lock and Royal Ordnance no longer existed. The latter had been part of the history of the British Isles since the Tudor period. The many modifications added to the weapon in Afghanistan were all foreign: the Lightweight Day Sight (American), ACOG sight (American), Picatinny Rail (American), Laser Light Module (German), Underslung Grenade Launcher (American), and new magazines (American). Even the thousands of foot-slogging kilometres trodden by British infantrymen were creating wealth abroad. The first of the new issue army desert boot was manufactured in Spain. The Meindl boot, widely worn in Helmand, was creating jobs in a small village named Kirchanschöring in Bavaria. The British dead and wounded who could not walk were carried off the battlefield on an American stretcher – the Tallon II. Whether admitted or not, British dead and maimed represented a cash cow for foreign firms.

The point about 'fighting the FOB' was that it was not taking the fight to the enemy – it was mostly just making it much harder for locals to attack the British. This did not imply a tactical victory for the insurgency. From the Taliban perspective, this defensive strategy created significant and even insurmountable problems. Each patrol base line was pushing them further and further away from the population centres. Brendan Hughes, a former Belfast Brigade IRA commander, once confessed that the British Army's surveillance apparatus in Ulster effectively ground his operations to a halt. The same phenomenon was beginning to be witnessed in Helmand. Paradoxically, the British were now winning the match by batting defensively.

These developments emerged against the background of the ninth major international conference held on Afghanistan since the beginning of the war. The 20 July Kabul Conference was significant for several reasons. It was the first such conference held in Afghanistan, despite the security headache incurred by the arrival of over 60 foreign delegations. Media leaks had already revealed that a timetable for ISAF's withdrawal by 2014–15 was the implicit agenda of the conference. To improve the chances of a successful withdrawal, the government made the tactical announcement that British aid to Afghanistan would be increased by 40 per cent, an echo of the Soviet Politburo's last fling of the dice before withdrawing from Afghanistan in the 1980s. The conference passed off peacefully, and all the delegations, save the Iranian representative who jarringly criticized the presence of Western soldiers in Afghanistan, repeated the same tired messages: an end to corruption, the 'Afghanization' of the war and reconstruction. The conference pointedly had little to say about reconciliation or a political solution to the conflict. Hillary Clinton soberly left the conference remarking that success was far from guaranteed.

This show of unity was barely a week old before a massive leak of military secrets detonated in Washington, provoking anger and embarrassment. The source of the leaks appeared to be a baby-faced American soldier working in an intelligence post in Baghdad. Private Bradley Manning – writing under the pseudonym 'Bradass87' – astonishingly appeared to have passed around 90,000 CENTCOM SIGACTs (Significant Actions) and other reports dating from 2004 to 2009 to the popular website Wikileaks, run by the Australian Julian Assange. Manning's motivation seemed unclear. It was apparent that he was a troubled young man whose suitability for intelligence work was open to question. He was an only child from a broken home. He had been rejected by his father (for his homosexuality) and neglected by his Welsh mother who returned to her native Wales. Manning drifted for a while before finally finding a home in the US Army. He struggled to make friendships and remained the slighted and slightly clever loner. Manning felt the need to show off the span of his knowledge to a stranger (in this case a hacker who immediately informed the authorities). If he thought he was going to get away with such a gross act of disclosure, he was naïve. It took just two days to track him down. SIGACTs were ultimately routine secret-level synopses of incidents as well as reports on other matters of general intelligence interest. But the complete ISAF IED database and a database of over 2,000 potential targets for special forces operations were also passed on.

However, the Wikileaks story was soon pushed off the front pages by the continuing problem of corruption at the heart of Afghanistan's government. In early September it emerged that Kabul Bank was close to insolvency. This bank had been established in 2004. Perhaps $1.2 billion had been deposited in the bank since its formation.[43] A proportion of these funds were derived from the narcotics trade, and some accounts were almost certainly stuffed with embezzled aid money. The bank mattered because it accounted for about half of the banking sector in Afghanistan and it was responsible for the payroll of Afghanistan's civil servants and security forces (a contract which it won, according to opponents, because it had funded President Karzai's election campaign). Karzai's brother, Mahmood, was a shareholder and he had been using the bank to fund personal business interests. The vice president's brother, Haseem Fahim, had been repeating the trick. In fact, it transpired that a small clique in Kabul had effectively been using the bank as a personal bank account, awarding themselves loans to fund luxury lifestyles, some with no intention of repaying the loans.

The scale of the fraud cast Western donors in a scandalous and irresponsible light. As a subsequent study noted, 'the bank's structure was created with the prime purpose of committing fraud on a massive scale'.[44] Around 114 fictitious companies and 2,000 false loan accounts were created, which no Western donor or auditing firm appeared to notice, siphoning off an estimated $861 million, or 92 per cent of the bank's loan book, into the pockets of just 12 individuals – the blessed Apostles of Western naïveté.[45] This represented between 6 and 10 per cent of Afghanistan's GDP.[46] There had probably never been such an outright theft of national wealth by so few individuals in modern history. The chairman of the bank, Sherkhan Farnood, bought 16 properties in Abu Dhabi's Palm Jumeirah complex. In total, perhaps some £93 million was invested in properties by the bank's executives in this luxury resort, and in Kabul. Another £37 million vanished in first-class flights and five-star hotels – hardly the purpose of British aid. On one occasion, an Afghan minister arrived in Abu Dhabi with $52 million stuffed in suitcases. Afghan affluence was so brazen locals jokingly nicknamed the cluster of new properties Kabul Bank Street. Another standing joke was Afghan officials turning up at Bagram Airport, under ISAF protection, with suitcases filled with dollars.

DfID suspended aid payments of £80 million, but this was shutting the stable door after the horse had bolted. The organization's arrogance and turning of a blind eye to corruption had been breathtaking. In evidence to the House of Commons International Development Committee it had boasted, 'DFID is a strong advocate of aid effectiveness, and is leading by example.'[47] The reality was that for several years, tens of millions of pounds of British taxpayers' money had been embezzled to fund the luxury lifestyles of corrupt Afghan officials. The embezzled funds would only partially be recovered, and sacked officials would simply move on to graze in some other financial pasture.[48] By 2012, just five individuals had been taken into custody, but for a variety of technical and bureaucratic reasons, none had been taken to court.[49] The ex-governor simply fled to the United States, where he enjoyed legal residency and could not be pursued or prosecuted.

When the Public Accounts Committee sat to deliberate on DfID's financial management in 2011, its findings were predictably severe.[50] The department had stopped monitoring its own finance plan in 2010. It had no credible mechanism to estimate leakage through fraud and embezzlement. It was increasing its aid through multilaterals over which it had little or no visibility. Aid was being channelled through complex and costly delivery chains. Each hand through which the money passed naturally took a cut. In the committee's view, DfID could neither demonstrate that it was achieving value for value, nor indeed whether it had a convincing way of measuring value for money. DfID responded to this inquiry with barely credible assertions, prompting the committee to conclude: 'We were unconvinced that figures of around 0.01% were an accurate reflection of the scale of fraud, and were concerned that no instances of fraud were identified in half of the countries to which the Department gave aid in 2010–11. In our view, current levels of reported fraud are unbelievably low.'

These findings were shocking, as DfID was the single government department whose budget was being increased in order to meet an ideological target of 0.7 per cent of gross national income committed to aid by 2013. A department with a staff of just over 2,000 would be controlling a budget in the order of £11 billion. This was the biggest concentration of taxpayers' money in the hands of the smallest number of individuals, of any government department, the Treasury aside. The lack of transparency and honest reporting was hardly reassuring. The real damage from DfID's denial was on the perceptions of ordinary Helmandis. As Michael Martin astutely pointed out, Helmandis were well aware of the scale of embezzlement and fraud of British aid funds – they were doing it.[51] That the PRT seemed to be turning a blind eye to this truth fostered a conspiracy theory that the

British were effectively laundering their own money and supporting the crooks at the top.

The opium poppy harvest in 2010 provided little solace for ISAF. Forest fires in Russia and devastating floods in Pakistan had not affected the price of wheat, which remained low by historic levels. The incentive for Afghan farmers to grow the illicit opium poppy remained as strong as in previous years. The total hectares devoted to this crop were unchanged, although disease had resulted in a 48 per cent drop in opium production to 3,600 tonnes.[52] This benefited the farmers, as the average farm gate price of dry opium leapt from $64 per kilogram to $169 per kilogram. The gross income per hectare of opium was calculated at $4,900, which amounted to a 39 per cent payrise for Helmand's farmers, or substantially more than the payrise a British soldier protecting the farmers could hope to receive. The total farm gate value of the crop for 2010 was estimated at $604 million (by contrast, British counter-narcotics spend in Helmand for that year was £6.2 million).[53] It was a bonanza for the narcotics traffickers. Helmand, as in previous years, was the champion opium province, accounting for 53 per cent of the total crop. CENTCOM figures for drug busts revealed that the counter-narcotics campaign remained woefully inadequate. There had been 24 such operations over the summer in Helmand.[54] The average find was a couple of 10-kilogram bags of wet opium. The largest was an operation that netted 2 tonnes of raw opium.

The first Operation *Herrick* tour under the new Conservative–Liberal Democrat government concluded in mid-October. The brigade had endured 30 gunfights per day and over 5,000 over the course of the six-month tour.[55] Including six Danes and one Estonian, Brigadier Felton had lost a total of 62 men. Over 400 had been wounded in action, or a battalion's worth of soldiers.[56] The last to die was a kingsman serving with Arnhem Company, 2 Lancs, who stepped on an IED in Babaji District on the eve of the handover to 16 Air Assault Brigade. The brigade claimed to have killed or wounded around 500 insurgents but fewer than ten civilians.[57] This last figure seemed suspect, as there was evidence that a relaxation of 'courageous restraint' had caused civilian casualty figures to rise again.[58] Over 1,500 fire missions had been called, suggesting that the recourse to firepower was creeping back into British tactics. The brigade was awarded three Conspicuous Gallantry Crosses and 15 Military Crosses. The recipients were drawn from all ranks and age groups: the eldest was Lieutenant Colonel James Martin (The Princess of Wales's

Royal Regiment), and one of the youngest was Acting Lance Corporal Kylie Watson, serving with the Royal Army Medical Corps. Posthumous awards were won, as in the past, by soldiers trying to save the lives of wounded comrades. Lance Corporal Stephen Monkhouse (Scots Guards) and Acting Corporal Matthew Stenton (1st Royal Dragoon Guards) were both honoured in this way. The two men died together saving the life of a fellow soldier who had been wounded in the Basharan area, north of Lashkar Gah, where the popular Major Sean Burchill had been killed the previous summer. For the paratroopers now flooding into Helmand Province this was their fourth tour in Afghanistan since 2002. Would they find 'a better place', as the spin claimed?

12

Doing the Hard Yards (Successfully)

Operations *Herrick 13* and *14*, October 2010–October 2011

When the 45-year-old Brigadier James Chiswell assumed command of the British task force in October 2010, at the head of 16 Air Assault Brigade, he bullishly told the media: 'We do difficult and that's why we are here.' The son of a former Parachute Regiment commanding officer, Chiswell had taken part in the rescue mission in Sierra Leone in 2000 (Operation *Barras*) for which he had been awarded a Military Cross. He was now leading the paratroopers for their third tour in four years in Helmand. They would face difficulties, but of a very different order from those faced by their predecessors.

The war in Helmand, at least for the British, had changed dramatically by the end of 2010. Chiswell knew, as did all his successors, that there would now only be retrenchment, not expansion. The British manning high point had been reached. Taking in Lashkar Gah, Nad-e Ali, Nahr-e Saraj (North and South) and Babaji districts, the British were now responsible for about 250,000 Helmandis, yielding a ratio of one soldier per 25 inhabitants.[1] Applying the Quinlivan formula* – a debated ratio – this offered sufficient manpower. Even so, Task Force Helmand was only responsible for about 1 per cent of the total population of Afghanistan, a measure of the scale of the overall task facing ISAF. With the growth of the Afghan security forces, every future brigade would be scaled back and smaller. There would be no more brigade-level British operations. Funding

*The Quinlivan formula – coined by RAND analyst James Quinlivan – posits the bare minimum ratio of security forces required to provide security for the inhabitants of an occupied territory.

for the Military Stabilization and Support Teams (MSSTs) would be cut by 90 per cent, depriving commanders of dollars for 'consent winning activities', such as the Cash for Works programmes. Over the course of the year, stepping stones towards an eventual withdrawal had been laid. These included the US–Afghanistan Strategic Dialogue in May, the National Consultative Peace Jirga in June and the carefully orchestrated Kabul Conference in July.

The height of the American expansion had also been reached. The Obama surge checked the Taliban: in the south-west there had been tangible gains, but eastern Afghanistan seemed to be sliding backwards. As much as anything, the surge had revealed NATO's continuing dependency on American leadership, manpower and firepower. If the Stars and Stripes had been removed from ISAF's command and control structure, there would have been no ISAF.

The military advantage enjoyed by the British task force had increased significantly. It was one of the unfortunate ironies of the war that Task Force Helmand finally managed to swing the war decisively in its favour, but was only really able to exercise this advantage for a period of one and half years before turning to the task of transition and withdrawal. This was not just a matter of being responsible for a smaller geographical area. Intelligence was immeasurably improved, in large part thanks to the Royal Signals, who constructed a modern, if byzantine, communications infrastructure in the middle of the desert. By the winter of 2010 there were over 500 signallers labouring in more than 50 locations.[2] Over 50 ground satellite terminals were established. Thirteen microwave towers linked up the task force. This force was now benefitting from over 700 American TACSAT 117 radios, the principal radio for the command, strike and ISTAR* nets. Importantly, a 62-node digital infrastructure – termed 'Promina' and replicating an existing system in Britain – allowed the transmission of Mission Secret and Top Secret data over 1,500 'Red' and 'Black' telephones. Nearly 60 server stacks were needed to keep this network running, with the concomitant air conditioning bill. It was this

*Intelligence, Surveillance, Target Acquisition and Reconnaissance.

capability – augmented by a staggering 83 applications* – that finally turned around the British intelligence effort.

The fundamental rule of getting intelligence operators to the front line – a bottom-up rather than top-down approach – was implemented through American-style COISTs, or Company Intelligence Support Teams. Where in the past soldiers could not even name the predominant tribe in their area, they now knew the names of the owners of compounds surrounding their bases. The British never attempted a census of Helmand – the task would have overwhelmed their resources – but accumulated local knowledge gradually improved the focus and granularity of their intelligence. Biometric data collection refined this knowledge. Using American technology, British soldiers began imaging, swabbing and finger-printing villagers. Soon, the databases swelled with tens of thousands of profiles. Through patient detective work, profiles were matched to IED finds, and this allowed intelligence officers to generate a much clearer picture of just how many IED teams existed in the British areas. The numbers were not small and they remained intractably difficult to close down decisively.[3]

Voluminous American intelligence at the Joint Special Operations Command (JSOC) was now feeding special forces raids and detention operations. These were being undertaken on an 'industrial' scale. A study by the Afghanistan Analyst Network concluded that between 1 December 2009 and 30 September 2011, there were in the order of 2,365 capture-or-kill raids. These resulted in 3,875 deaths and 7,147 detentions. From these gross numbers, perhaps 174 'leaders' were killed and 501 were detained.[4] This suggested that actually less than 5 per cent of the total deaths were leadership targets. The high point seemed to be reached in June 2011. With the departure of General Petraeus, who had championed the strategy, the numbers began to decline.

The British contribution to this tally was modest (ISAF statistics suggested a figure of less than 5 per cent). Before the arrival of Task Force Leatherneck, British special forces raids had been few, perhaps two or three per month. On the few occasions when British brigade commanders quoted special forces capture-or-kill statistics, the number was somewhere

*The Afghanistan Mission Network (AMN) experienced an 'application explosion', with 83 'necessary' applications and 239 'required' applications.

around one or two dozen over the course of six months. Later, they did ramp up. Following the arrival of the US Marines – over a 21-month period – there were 377 capture-or-kill raids in Helmand.[5] These resulted in 821 deaths and 1,263 captured insurgents. The arrival of the Americans had significantly raised the tempo.

The question of Afghan resentment over night raids was not straightforward. Politically, night raids were a gift to President Karzai, who brazenly exploited them to demonstrate his nationalist credentials. Eventually, his persistence on this issue would result in an almost total cessation of the raids, except in special circumstances and always with an Afghan presence (which contingents like the British were already practising anyway). At local level, the picture was less clear. More than one Afghan confided with the British that these targeting operations were the best thing they were doing. In the summer of 2013 when a prominent and violent insurgent commander in Sangin was finally killed by a Predator, one local worthy congratulated the British and averred this had been the best day in Sangin in the last ten years.

In response to the criticism over the special forces raids, Commander ISAF, General John Allen, was moved to defend his soldiers at the Senate Armed Services Committee. The statistics he offered were insightful, and they contrasted with the Afghanistan Analyst Network findings, albeit they pertained to a later period.[6] Over 2011–12, ISAF conducted 2,200 night raids. In half of these raids the targeted individual was captured or killed. In another third, an associate was found. In one-fifth, the raid was conducted on an apparently innocent party – which was not a small error ratio. But the important point was that in nine out of ten raids, no shots were fired. And the percentage of civilian casualties was just 1.5 per cent. According to Allen, from a total of 9,200 night raids, just 27 innocent civilians had been killed or wounded. This last number seemed low; even so, it appeared equally likely that civilian deaths in night raids were being exaggerated by critics. The overwhelming majority of these raids were essentially nighttime arrest operations in which no shots were fired, as Allen honestly asserted.

There was another more subtle point about special forces operations, cleverly identified by Michael Martin. This related to the other side of special forces missions: the operations deliberately set up to kill an individual, or 'kinetic strikes' in the awful euphemism. Intelligence – virtually all the product of American resources – became excellent by the end of the war. But although ISAF knew who was causing trouble, it did not necessarily know *why* they were causing trouble. Part of the problem was ISAF's mechanistic portrayal of the enemy as a 'network diagram' and applying 'effects' to the network, a methodology championed in an influential article authored by the director of the Iraq JSOC from 2004 to 2007, Colonel Michael Flynn. Flynn's piece attained almost religious status. It resonated with the McChrystal dictum 'attack the network'. Seeking to understand the networks – answering the question but why are these individuals fighting at all? – was not so assiduously followed. The root problem with the dictum 'attack the network' was that Afghan society *was* a network: of family, villages, clans and tribes. A surveillance technology that tracked and linked mobile communications – essentially how the 'networks' were being plotted – was ultimately clumsy. The industrial-level special forces campaign was 'taking down' individuals who in the eyes of many locals were not villains at all, but rather respected personalities. Some raids were actually killing individuals who wanted to reconcile with ISAF. Martin cited the example of a commander killed in Shin Kalay – presumably by the British – whose car became a memorial shrine. At least in this case, striking one more individual off the target list had probably added another ten to the list, an 'effect' totally contrary to what the campaign was hoping to achieve.

The evidence of ISAF's own experience was that no matter how many individuals were eliminated from a network, another simply replaced the captured or killed insurgent. The British recorded this, but whether they reflected on the evidence is another question. By the second half of the war, British intelligence maintained a lengthy PowerPoint presentation – updated on a monthly basis – displaying the networks of insurgent commanders, termed 'Bravos',* across south-west Afghanistan (in British fashion, the areas for special forces operations were named after Greek mythological characters). By this stage there were three special forces task forces operating in Helmand: TF-32, 42 and 318, the latter US Navy SEALs. TF-196 based at Kandahar provided helicopter support. If an insurgent leader was 'taken down', a red 'X' was drawn over the mugshot. Insurgents also transited to and from Pakistan so were not always active.

*'Alphas' were individuals providing support to the insurgency predominantly through the servicing of IED and weapons caches, as well as buildings. 'Charlies' were vehicles.

The pace of operations was certainly unrelenting. From Operation *Herrick 15* through to *Herrick 17* there were over 100 per tour, or roughly one every one or two days (*Herrick 15* – 108, *Herrick 16* – 119 and *Herrick 17* – 111).[7] These resulted in 71, 64 and 65 'kinetic strikes' respectively, or in English, killings. The operations that involved strikes resulted in multiple deaths (115, 105 and 91) from which a proportion of the killed were subsequently confirmed as 'Jackpots', or leaders on the priority targeting list (25, 9 and 26). In military fashion, this list went by the euphemistic abbreviation JPEL, or Joint Prioritized Effects List. Not all operations, however, involved killing. A proportion were High Risk Arrests (HRAs). On Operations *Herrick 15* and *Herrick 17*, less than half were HRAs (37 and 28). *Herrick 16* was the exception, it may be supposed due to the policy adopted by the special forces squadron. On this tour, the 'kinetic strikes' and HRAs roughly matched (64 and 57 respectively). This squadron in fact arrested the largest number of alleged insurgents by some margin (130) of which 18 turned out to be 'Jackpots'. It also killed a large number on the strike operations (105) but only nine were 'Jackpots'.

Regardless of the numbers, the salient feature about the PowerPoint was that it never grew smaller; the opposite happened – it just continued to expand until the British departed. It was also notable that a minority of individuals who found themselves displayed on the PowerPoint, from month to month, were actually 'taken down' or detained. In this respect, the PowerPoint network diagrams seemed to offer portraits of the strategic futility of what ISAF was doing, although not tactical ineffectiveness. For the front-line soldier, any insurgent killed or arrested was one less trying to kill him.

This raised an unavoidable question over the special forces campaign: how was it contributing to the overall war? There was a sense, at least in the American camp, that the industrial-level tempo of operations was a sort of silver bullet, perhaps the silver bullet that would bring the insurgency to its knees. Petraeus was certainly vocal in his defence of the special forces campaign, and who could not be dazzled by the numbers cited by the JSOC? The problem with this view is that it simply does not match the wider statistics published by ISAF. The dramatic ramping up of special forces operations took place roughly between the spring of 2009 and the summer of 2010 (the tenures of McChrystal and Petraeus). It would have been reasonable to expect some positive reflection of this attrition on the battlefield. The opposite was true. From 2009 to 2011, Enemy Initiated

Attacks (EIAs) *increased*, rather than decreased. No matter how many Taliban commanders were reportedly 'taken down', the insurgency got stronger. In fact, it is very difficult to find in any ISAF-published metric evidence of the impact of the special forces campaign. A decline in EIAs became evident, from the spring of 2011, following the large *conventional* operations, particularly in south-west Afghanistan (although it should be noted this was relative). If there was a silver bullet, it seems it was being fired by a humble private in a line regiment, not by a special forces soldier.

One factor that was having a profound impact on the battlefield was the impact of American surveillance assets. By the end of 2010, according to CENTCOM, there were over 60 persistent surveillance systems (aerostats) arrayed over Helmand and Kandahar provinces. These were supplemented by nearly 20 medium and high-altitude UAVs and over 30 fixed wing, multi-intelligence platforms collecting both imagery and signals intelligence. By the end of the war, in a stunning manifestation of the alacrity and depth of America's defence industry, around 25 variants of these 'funnies', or special mission aircraft based on the Beechcraft King Air, had been developed. In comparison, a debilitated British defence industry proved incapable of making a single contribution to this important field.

On a monthly basis, this effort was reinforced by a variety of aircraft flying on average 130 signals intelligence missions, nearly 80 imagery intelligence missions, over 70 measurement and signals intelligence missions and as many as 150 Ground-Moving Target Indicator (GMTI) missions.[8] This implied that on any one day there were somewhere between 15 and 20 American aircraft sucking up the electro-magnetic spectrum and imaging hundreds of square kilometres of south-west Afghanistan to a resolution of less than 1 metre. All these assets were commanded at regional level. At task force and battlegroup level, there were now hundreds of ground and mast-mounted cameras, arrays of Unmanned Ground Sensors (UGS), flocks of smaller tactical and hand-thrown UAVs and scores of Electronic Warfare (EW) Teams, ranging from individuals monitoring ICOM receivers to more sophisticated direction-finding platforms. The average Pashtun farmer may have been forgiven for wondering whether it was now possible to defecate in a field without someone imaging, recording and measuring the act.

At theatre level, in the rarefied world of highly sensitive intelligence, the National Security Agency (NSA) and GCHQ were adding reams of communications intelligence. Post-war, it would be revealed GCHQ staff received 156 campaign medals, an indication of the contribution this organization made to the war effort. Over half of all targeted operations were reportedly cued by the intelligence gleaned by these government mathematicians, scientists and information technology experts, recalling the close relationship that existed between soldiers and scientists in World War II.[9] Where once there had been a paucity of information, there was now a deluge (creating the same problem that beset the Saigon Combined Intelligence Centre in the Vietnam War, which had to process over a tonne of paper every day). This Western effort, of course, could not have succeeded without Afghan intelligence. There was plenty of anecdotal evidence to suggest that much useful intelligence in fact came from Afghan agencies, in particular the National Directorate of Security (NDS). Where interrogation failed, torture was used – an unfortunate practice that forced the British to hold Taliban detainees beyond the regulatory 96-hour detention period, rather than risk handing them over to Afghan colleagues.

Nad-e Ali and Babaji districts were now criss-crossed by a matrix of patrol bases and checkpoints, as many as 200 including police outposts. In some areas there was a security force location every few hundred metres. By the time 16 Air Assault Brigade completed its tour, there were British soldiers based in 120 of these security posts. A map view of central Helmand suggested that the strategy of clear-hold-build had finally been vindicated. In truth, it amounted to old-fashioned population control: were 'hearts and minds' actually won, or were villagers forced to behave cooperatively? In the Second Boer War (1899–1902), the checkpoints would have been called block houses, but were the Boers won over or simply forced to concede to the matrix of British bases? The same question hung over Helmand.

In Nad-e Ali and Babaji, this suffocating presence certainly succeeded in making it very hard for insurgents to move around openly. Over time, Taliban gangs, which historically were not actually that strong in these two districts, found themselves squeezed out to the margins. This was all deeply unfair if you were an insurgent.

3 PARA under Lieutenant Colonel James Coates was based in the Chah-e Anjir Triangle (CAT). This area had been ostensibly cleared during Operation *Moshtarak*, but the lack of numbers meant the British, as usual, only really controlled the immediate orbits of their patrol bases. Indeed, the paratroopers were surprised to discover that the main base, FOB Shahzad, was living under constant attacks from the north. The entire area would need to be cleared again, a task that Coates embraced with aggression and cunning. Four major operations would be mounted over the course of the

tour, which resulted in six communities decisively locked out to the local troublemakers.

It was 3 PARA under Coates that made the important tactical breakthrough in the British war. In this respect, credit must be afforded to this veteran battalion, first pitched into Helmand in the torrid summer of 2006. The tactic was called 'intelligent targeting',[10] and it mostly relied on two American pieces of kit: the sophisticated Apache* and the remarkably simple aerostats. The LEWTs commonly provided the first cue. As one officer later remarked, it was amazing no one had thought of it earlier. At the heart of 'intelligent targeting' was precisely intelligence: understanding the local players and dynamics, distinguishing hardcore insurgents from wavering sympathizers and striking precisely and at a time of your own choosing. The officer commanding ISTAR Company described the tactic thus: '3 PARA deployed on Op HERRICK 13 with a well-rehearsed targeting strategy and approach which, along with the provision of highly effective ISTAR assets, enabled them to dismantle the insurgent networks and establish protected communities across the AO [area of operation] within a very short space of time.'[11] Coates believed the key was answering three questions: who were the British fighting? Why were they fighting? And who should be targeted? Targeting did not necessarily mean killing – it could equally mean talking and persuading. Importantly, 3 PARA insisted that the first principle of 'intelligent targeting' was 'Zero collateral damage i.e. no civcas [civilian casualties] and no significant damage to local property'.[12]

The insurgents in the Chah-e Anjir Triangle seemed unaware of the reach of the aerostats, or believed they could not be seen. In fact, on a clear winter's day, the cameras could confidently identify a human at a considerable range with sufficient granularity to determine whether that person was undertaking some nefarious activity. The paratroopers set about exploiting this system by calling an Apache strike when they were confident the target was valid (necessarily so, as the insurgents were commonly too far away for a foot patrol to reach them). Over the course of their tour, 3 PARA reckoned they caught close to 130 insurgents in

*The American supplied GMLRS rocket and the Israeli Exactor (Spike-NLOS) missile were also used to strike. Base mast-mounted cameras – systems termed Remover, Airliner and Livingstone – also provided visual surveillance. The aerostats were termed Revivor.

this way, three-quarters of which were chased down by Apaches. Only a handful were believed to have got away. They also managed to arrest over 150 suspected insurgents. In total, the American aerostats probably accounted for around 250 local troublemakers.

Some engagements were lightning quick. In one incident, a LEWT detected and fixed the locations of two insurgents known by their call signs 'Zubia' and 'Maboob'. The detection was recorded at 1639hrs. From their transmissions it was evident the pair – loitering by the entrance of a compound – were preparing to attack a patrol. Three minutes later, a base aerostat confirmed the detection (a process known as PID, or Positive Identification, without which no strike was allowed under the rules of engagement). Simultaneously, a drone also got 'eyes on'. Authority to strike was confirmed by the local commander. One minute later, 'Zubia' and 'Maboob' were dead. The entire sequence had lasted four minutes.[13]

Despite this success, the Chah-e Anjir Triangle remained a dangerous area. The paratroopers encountered over 130 IEDs and suffered five serious casualties from these devices. Appreciating that the trick was to get at the insurgents and not wait for them to get at you, the paratroopers also used helicopters extensively – every other day – to mount small raids into areas where insurgents imagined they were safe. By the end, 3 PARA was mounting heliborne raids at a relentless pace, which suffocated gangs in their area. Even allowing for the self-serving reporting of units, it is undeniable that 3 PARA's war over the winter of 2010–11 witnessed the most interesting and effective evolution of tactics, on the British side, since the war became stalemated. Very soon, every other battlegroup was copying 3 PARA, with similar results. Aerostats and 'shooters', in American parlance, had proved the winning tactical combination.

The British were also talking as well as fighting, building as well as destroying. This was what the Royal Irish commanding officer described as 'doing the COIN hard yards'. It was not glamorous work. It required infinite patience and a resignation to 'the Afghan way of doing things'. This was the way the British would be leaving Helmand, tip-toeing out of the room they had carelessly gate-crashed. An RAF sergeant working in an MSST with 2 PARA captured this reality with amused resignation: 'The realities … are long hours; endless Shuras dealing with crowds of LN's [local nationals] all wanting your attention at once, constant demands for money, being worn down and frustrated by daily dealings with the locals.'[14] The worn-down sergeant – known as the 'Bank of Babaji' by local farmers – concluded that 'nothing gets done quickly here', and 'everybody wants something for nothing'.

In Helmand the handover of units proceeded like a well-worn routine. The Irish Guards under Lieutenant Colonel Christopher Ghika took over the mentoring role of 3/215 Corps from The Royal Scots Borderers (1 SCOTS). At Lashkar Gah, The Argyll and Sutherland Highlanders (5 SCOTS) took over the police training role from 1 Mercians (Cheshires). 2 PARA, commanded by Lieutenant Colonel Andy Harrison, did a straight swap with the Gurkhas in Babaji District. This battalion was reinforced by B Company, 3 PARA, and a company from 5 SCOTS. 3 PARA, as we have seen, went to the Chah-e Anjir Triangle. In the centre of the British area, the Royal Irish under Lieutenant Colonel Colin Weir picked up the reins from the Lancasters. Armoured support was provided by 2nd Royal Tank Regiment, which replaced 1st Royal Dragoon Guards.

In southern Nad-e Ali, A Company, 1 Royal Irish, found itself split between six new bases and 'in conflict with the enemy most days, every day in fact'.[15] Eventually a battalion-level operation would be mounted in late October (Operation *Tor Kanjak IV*, or 'Black Thorn') to clear the area. In the north, where a gang of foreign fighters had camped, B Company was experiencing similar high levels of fighting and would lose three rangers, wounded early in the tour by an IED. This prompted the visiting RSM to comment: 'You get a sense of what it must have been like in the Great War, living below parapets where a raised head could attract deadly fire, soldiers huddled together in small groups enjoying a common interest like a card game or amusing story.'[16] When Brigadier Chiswell visited the rangers of B Company, he also found himself under attack.

In October, the new Conservative–Liberal Democrat government was due to publish its first Strategic Defence and Security Review. This publication was preceded by weeks of sniping as retired admirals, generals and air chief marshals drew the battle lines for their respective services. So much hot air and despair had not been witnessed for many years, with some justification. Despite Liam Fox's assurance that Britain's global role was a necessity and not a luxury, it was obvious there would be cuts, probably savage.[17] All the rumours were exaggerated and the strategic arguments and counter-arguments largely pointless. The fact was that the shape and size of Britain's armed forces were largely being determined by constrained budgets and defence contracts to protect 'British jobs'. Future threats and the role of the armed forces were secondary considerations. The Defence

Select Committee was quite right when it later observed that it could 'divine no strategic vision' in the document. The Public Administration Select Committee was similarly scathing. It concluded the answer to the question 'Who does UK national security policy?' was 'no one'.

The army was expected to survive the cuts better than the other two services, but only marginally. A second British government took the historically unprecedented decision to reduce the size of the army (by 7,000 personnel) in the middle of a war. The overall size of the force had now collapsed below the symbolic 100,000 threshold. Six brigades would be reduced to five brigades. Only two infantry battalions were allowed to retain their Warrior APCs. The other 34 infantry battalions were re-roled as light battalions to feed the Afghan war. In effect, the British Army had been propelled back to the 1920s and was now a small motorized force. This was hardly the vision proponents of the 'Revolution in Military Affairs' had imagined just ten years previously.

In early November, the governor of Helmand, Gulab Mangal, visited London. The purpose of this visit was to set the scene for the forthcoming NATO conference in Lisbon. The British government needed the governor to portray a province ripe for handover with a little more work, and Mangal played his part. Statistics demonstrating progress were trotted out to the nodding approval of his hosts. The conclusion that this purported progress offered was that British forces might safely withdraw by 2014, the same message the prime minister was about to deliver at Lisbon.

The 28 members of NATO met at Lisbon on the weekend of 20 November. In Helmand, the British task force had just suffered its 100th fatality that year, Guardsman Christopher Davis, a 22-year-old from St Helens. The Russian president joined the conference to discuss Russian–NATO cooperation, a sign of the long if hesitant thaw in East–West relations (which would be reversed by the Russian annexation of Crimea in 2014). Unfortunately, the conference met against the backdrop of the worst crisis between ISAF and Karzai. In a move that dismayed Petraeus, Karzai threatened to close down all private security companies (PSCs) in Afghanistan. Such a measure would have caused an overnight collapse of the entire development mission – it was only because of the extensive private security provision that aid was being furnished to Afghanistan at all. Following much haggling, it was agreed an Afghan Public Protection Force (APPF) would assume the role of providing convoy and fixed-site protection. The saga that followed would fill a small chapter. Suffice to say that three years later, the APPF, which might better have been titled the 'Afghan Public Extortion Force', had still not been stood up properly and was close to financial meltdown, after it transpired that a small number of individuals had simply siphoned off the funds committed to the force into private bank accounts. The PSCs in the meantime continued to operate, re-branded as 'risk management companies'. The story of the APPF was more complicated than this summary suggests, but what was not problematical was the prediction that this was how the APPF story would end.

The public aim of the Lisbon Conference was to discuss 'transition' – NATO's exit strategy – but the truth was that all the backroom dealing had already been concluded prior to the conference. There would be no haggling or late-night discussions, only a carefully stage-managed statement presented by the triumvirate of President Karzai, Anders Fogh Rasmussen, the NATO Secretary General, and Ban Ki-Moon, the UN Secretary General. The latter stated that 2015 would be the date by which Afghans would be masters of their own house, without elaborating on the state of that house. This was both a timetable for withdrawal and a conditions-based withdrawal, but nobody could convincingly explain this contradiction. The prime minister did not even try. 'I couldn't be more clear about what 2015 is,' Cameron tersely told reporters, 'and what it means.'[18]

In a foretaste of the likely pattern of events once the British started withdrawing, 16 Air Assault Brigade found itself having to recapture ground encroached by emboldened insurgent gangs. In December 2009, the Royal Marines had cleared the village of Zarghun Kalay, in north Nad-e Ali, after a 48-hour battle in miserable weather. Now it was back in Taliban hands. At the end of November, the Royal Irish duly mounted an air assault operation to recapture the village, in an area known as the 'Red Wedge' to the troops, killing 11 insurgents. In fact, in the first two and a half months of their tour, B Company was involved in 546 engagements with insurgents in this area, the majority of which were futile shootouts between the two sides.[19] In Operation *Moshtarak*, the Kharotei village of Naqelabad Kalay had been a main objective, along with the village of Showal. Barely ten months after the Royal Welsh had 'taken' Naqelabad Kalay, 3 PARA had to do it all over again. In the event, A Company was able to walk into the village without firing a shot, thanks to careful preparatory operations in the preceding weeks, including a smart night raid that resulted in seven captured insurgents. The battlegroup followed this up with a night infiltration of Naqelabad Kalay on 10 November. When a group of around 20 insurgents attempted to challenge the paratroopers, an air strike was called that decisively ended the fight. It later transpired that a foreign fighter commander had been killed in the strike.

In the village of Char Coucha ('Four Alleys'), the sister battalion 2 PARA found itself clearing the settlement yet again in Operation *Kapcha Kwandikalay* ('Cobra Safe'). This followed a year of inconclusive fighting which had cost the British eight fatalities and 49 wounded. The epicentre of the trouble was CP Kings Hill, where the Mercians had suffered grievously the previous summer. There was perhaps a personal edge to this operation, as it was here that Private Daniel Prior was killed by an IED in mid-March, helping a fellow paratrooper climbing down a ladder. It took eight days just to clear 50-odd compounds, but only nine IEDs were discovered. This risk aversion was not without justification: five bomb disposal officers had previously been killed or badly injured in this village. The rude fact was it was taking a large number of resources to sterilize single villages, and even after such expenditure there could be no guarantee the insurgents would not return. In the case of Char Coucha, the sacrifice was ultimately rewarded. A Company, 2 RGR took over from the paratroopers and set about consolidating security. Three additional checkpoints were constructed. Over 75 families gradually returned and resumed their lives. A road, mosque and temporary school were built or refurbished. Over the course of six months, not a single IED was laid in the vicinity of the village. As impressively, CP Kings Hill, the worst single patrol base in Babaji, suffered no attacks.

Further south in Shin Kalay, Kharotei tribesmen had once again clashed with their neighbours and blamed the 'Taliban'. The real reason for these clashes probably lay in land disputes exacerbated by the fact that November was the planting season for the opium poppy, but it suited the Kharotei to co-opt British troops into their feuds. In early December, the Royal Irish supported by 5 SCOTS mounted Operation *Tor Kanjak 5* ('Black Thorn'), which led to several arrests and separated the warring parties. The villagers enthusiastically identified 'Taliban' to the Afghan police and expressed solidarity with the government when Governor Habibullah held an impromptu *shura* in the main mosque, as they had done two years previously when Royal Marines first arrived in the settlement. That summer, a Captain John Bethell, serving as the Welsh Guards intelligence officer, wrote a highly perceptive article in *British Army Review*, describing the complex web of relationships in Shin Kalay.[20] These were not remote villages. These were 'cleared' communities within shooting range of British patrol bases. In some areas the insurgents were walking straight back in as soon as they had the measure of the British platoon houses in their midst.

In Sayedabad, which the Lancasters had invested the previous summer during Operation *Tor Shezada* ('Black Prince'), the fighting had never stopped. For A Company, 1 Royal Irish, this was used as an opportunity to finally 'close the Nad-e Ali door and lock it'. When the company first deployed to this corner of the district, it had taken responsibility for five patrol bases, with PB Kalang acting as the company HQ location. On the very day of the handover, the Ulstermen discovered they were unable to patrol 50 metres from the patrol base without coming under sustained fire from the locals. This was an area dominated by Baluchis who were determined to resist encroachment by Western soldiers. They appeared to be backed up by Achakzai and Noorzai, the latter heavily implicated in the narcotics trade. Indeed, it subsequently transpired that one of the principal causes of conflict was local fears over the Government Led Eradication (GLE) programme. Unlike other parts of Nad-e Ali, these communities had not been included in the wheat seed distribution and had consequently grown the opium poppy. If, as Taliban propaganda suggested, the British intended to destroy the poppy crop, it would have spelled the ruin of farmers who had already committed to the planting cycle. Over the next three months, A Company set about leaning against the door, as well as reassuring villagers in countless *shuras*. This determined effort eventually succeeded in advancing the front line a further kilometre south, adding to the matrix of deterrent patrol bases.

Despite these clearances, the southern flank of the Royal Irish would remain persistently troublesome to the end of the tour. In a final operation (*Tora Zhemay VI*, 'Courageous Winter', conducted over 26–28 February), the battlegroup mounted the biggest airborne operation undertaken by an Irish regiment since World War II, in the area of Zaborabad. Eleven helicopters, including four US Marine Sea Stallions, landed A and C Companies, a contingent from 2/8 Marines and an ANA company in an area known as the 'red desert', from the colour of the soil. On the ground, blocking positions were established by Cyclops Squadron, 2 RTR, as well as by soldiers from A and C Companies. The heliborne group was dropped on three landing sites appropriately named Carrick, Derry and Belfast, shortly after daybreak. The overwhelming presence of ISAF soldiers scared away the insurgents and there was no fighting. The two-day operation was marked by torrential rain and 'cloying mud'. Several arrests were made and 14 weapon caches were uncovered. As much as anything *Tora Zhemay VI* demonstrated just how accurate British intelligence had become. A year previously a battalion would have counted uncovering one weapon cache a successful operation.

In Babaji, 2 PARA had taken over from the Gurkhas. Five companies were deployed across the district: D Company to PB 1, C Company to PB 2, E Company to PB 3, B Company to PB 4 and C Company relieving The Argylls at PB 5. Over the course of the winter these companies gradually expanded the security bubbles around their villages, building more checkpoints and pushing the insurgents south across the river.

For the commanding officer, the paratroopers were more involved in a 'gendarmerie role' than in open confrontation with insurgents. Much of the time the paratroopers found themselves engaged in the humdrum business of promoting local governance and reconstruction in villages. At Tor Ghai, the Taliban attempted to reverse the opening of a temporary school by sending the teacher threatening night letters. Major French, commanding E Company, took the unusual measure of writing a threatening letter back to the Taliban. It did the trick. The lower levels of violence were reflected in the casualty statistics, although the poignancy of losing soldiers over the Christmas season never lessened. Civilian casualties from IEDs remained high, tipping the locals towards the paratroopers. It came as a surprise to discover that insurgents were fining villagers $1,000 if a child or animal accidentally set of an IED. In these circumstances, many farmers had had enough and backed the Western soldiers.

Shortly after the tenth anniversary of the war, as Christmas approached, ISAF suffered an unexpected blow with the premature death of Richard Holbrooke from a heart complication (his place was taken in the interim by Frank Ruggiero, later replaced by the veteran diplomat Marc Grossman). Before passing away in a hospital in Washington DC, Holbrooke was visited by grandees of an American establishment bidding farewell not just to their most effective special representative to Afghanistan and Pakistan, but to a man who had been part of American foreign policy for half a century. Reportedly, his last words as he was wheeled into the operating theatre were, 'You've got to fix Afghanistan.' Holbrooke's untimely loss was followed by that of Mark Sedwill, NATO's senior civilian representative in Afghanistan, who left his post in March after serving a year in Kabul. Sedwill had succeeded as much as anyone in restoring British credibility in the capital, and was an effective interlocutor with his American counterpart. His immediate replacement was Sir Simon Gass, no stranger to difficult regimes as he was hopping from the hot post of British ambassador to Iran. This was also an interim posting, and he in turn was replaced by Sir William Patey.

In the week following Holbrooke's premature death, President Obama delivered a promised annual review of the war. After paying tribute to the deceased special representative, the president spelled out America's mission in Afghanistan, a mission of greatly reduced expectations and limited time frame. 'It is important to remember why we remain in Afghanistan,' he said. He continued:

> It's not to defeat every last threat to the security of Afghanistan, because, ultimately, it is Afghans who must secure their country. And it's not nation-building, because it is Afghans who must build their nation. Rather, we are focused on disrupting, dismantling and defeating al-Qaeda in Afghanistan and Pakistan, and preventing its capacity to threaten America and our allies in the future.[21]

This was Biden's counter-terrorism war trumping the prospect of an interminable counter-insurgency war. The British prime minister, coincidentally on a Christmas front-line visit in Helmand, concurred with the Obama strategy.

As 16 Air Assault Brigade prepared to hand over to the commandos, it was clear the winter of 2011 pointed to some sort of turning point in the war. In this sense, Operation *Herrick 13* represented redemption for the paratroopers after the fiasco of *Herrick 4* and the frustrations of *Herrick 8*. The most visible sign of this change was in the casualty statistics – they collapsed significantly, at least in the British-held districts. The brigade suffered the least number of combat deaths from enemy action (18) since 52 Infantry Brigade in the winter of 2007. This was noteworthy, as the preceding brigades had been routinely suffering over 50 fatalities. Taliban activity had not abated – in some areas it had increased – but these insurgent foot soldiers amounted to 'spoilers', in the words of the commanding officer of The Royal Highland Fusiliers, who were finding it increasingly difficult to derail the ISAF train. The JFEOD had dealt with over 1,000 IED callouts, of which around one-fifth had detonated.[22] One IED had successfully detonated for every two and a half that had been defused, damaging or destroying 36 vehicles and killing 12 soldiers (all riding British Jackals; none died in the American-supplied vehicles). Bomb disposal officers and searchers were continuing to pay a high price: three were killed and seven lost limbs, a tally which included triple amputees. These depressing statistics concealed an undoubted success: as many as four out of ten IEDs were now being pointed out to British troops by supportive locals. In fact, twice as many IEDs were being identified as were detonating. It could not be denied the British were at last winning the trust of frustrated villagers.

Elsewhere in Helmand, and especially in Sangin, the same miserable story was being played out, but this was now a narrative being reported in *USA Today* and not *The Times*. British politicians could breathe a sigh of relief and be privately grateful that at last the British war appeared to be heading in the right direction.

The fall in casualties was real, but deceptive in some respects. A large number of soldiers and civilians were still being injured. The commanding officer of 207 Field Hospital – a Territorial Army unit – recalled that in the first three weeks of the tour, his doctors and nurses had to deal with nine double amputations, two triple amputations, two quadruple amputations, multiple gunshot wounds and one unfortunate case involving nine seriously wounded children, one of whom died.[23] In the same period, the Bastion mortuary processed 19 ISAF soldiers killed in action. Over the course of the tour, 3,800 patients passed though Bastion Hospital, including over 1,000 Afghans. A majority were non-battlefield casualties, but this did not diminish the fact that for the medical staffs, the war had not relaxed. Bastion's reputation as the busiest and best trauma hospital in the world was still deserved.

Gold did finally pour into Helmand. Over 2010–11 around $500 million was committed to reconstruction in the province.[24] About half of this was drawn from American CERP funds – effectively, US Marines were leading the rebuilding of Helmand, not civilian government organizations or NGOs. This perhaps provided the counter-proof to the British doctrinal position that soldiers were incapable of understanding development issues, and could not be trusted with aid money except under tight controls. Another fifth of the funds was provided by USAID, and Britain had set up a central 'conflict pool' that contributed around $90 million. Debate over

DfID's commitment to Helmand Province had become, to a certain degree, a stale debate. There were over 100 civilians working in the Lashkar Gah PRT, but only seven were DfID staff. The PRT had become a multi-agency organization, recruiting talent from a variety of organizations including ex-servicemen who were not fussed with living in field conditions. DfID was now the third smallest contributor of aid money to Helmand, after Estonia and Denmark.[25]

Whether this progress could be translated into overall, strategic success remained doubtful. It was revealing that former Defence Secretary Des Browne, questioned by the Defence Select Committee in March, gave this pessimistic answer to the prospects of ultimate British success: 'We don't have the resources or the ability to build a settled, governed community in an environment to which we are culturally not sensitive, and where the people of that country have not known governance for 40 years or more and have a life expectancy of about 46.'[26] Notwithstanding, on 21 March, on the back of this purported progress, President Karzai made the announcement that seven towns and districts would be handed over to Afghan control by the summer, including the British-controlled Lashkar Gah. 'Transition' was coming to Afghanistan, and soon.

The Taliban reacted to this announcement with defiance. In Helmand the entire mobile telephone network was shut down following threats of violence against staff. But this was now a province with a capital that boasted ten internet cafes, over 200 shops selling (immoral) DVDs, a dozen periodicals and radio stations and satellite TV for those with independent electricity supply. You could pass your time away in a coffee shop or ice cream parlour in 'Lash Vegas', as the British soldiers dubbed the town. Modernity had arrived, and there was little that the Taliban or anybody else could do to halt the tide of electronic consumerism.

3 Commando Brigade formally assumed command of the task force on 9 April 2011. The brigade was commanded by Ed Davis who, like his predecessor Brigadier Gordon Messenger, was now on his second tour of Afghanistan. The Royal Marines had been the first British troops to set foot in Afghanistan in the winter of 2001 (aside from the special forces contingent that joined the American Operation *Enduring Freedom*). Since 2006, due to the shortage of infantry battalions, there had been a near continuous presence of commandos in the province. This was the brigade's third full tour, as a brigade, in four years. For Davis, the war in Afghanistan had changed. The phrase 'Afghan good enough' began to creep into literature.

It meant that ISAF's time was now finite and it signalled resignation that a return to 'Afghan ways' was inevitable. This was not cause for a wake:

> Embracing this reality will require both military and civilian colleagues to accept … that for all our human terrain analysis, the influence we can bring to bear is limited … they will find their own way to delivering for themselves and their people … If we fail to grasp this and fail to work with the grain of Afghan society in Central Helmand, we risk not only becoming irrelevant, but also having the Afghans 'pull the wool over our eyes'.[27]

Working with the grain of Afghan society had been the very message General Sir David Richards had proselytized in the summer of 2006. Brigadier Jerry Thomas had argued the same point in the winter of that year. Somehow, in the intervening years, the message had got lost. Davis also clearly saw, perhaps with the benefit of past mistakes, 'how naïve we were being applying western, idealistic notions to our model of society'.

45 Commando, led by Lieutenant Colonel Oliver Lee (also on his second tour) assumed control of Nad-e Ali from the Royal Irish. 3 PARA in the Chah-e Anjir Triangle was replaced by 42 Commando, led by Lieutenant Colonel Ewen Murchison. Further east, 1 Rifles assumed responsibility of Babaji from 2 PARA. This battalion was commanded by Lieutenant Colonel James de Labillière (unrelated to the famous General de la Billière). This battlegroup was augmented by 43 Territorial Army volunteers from 6 Rifles, Kilo Company from 42 Commando and A (Amboor) Company from 2 Royal Gurkha Rifles (2 RGR).

In Lashkar Gah there was a straight handover between two Scottish battalions, with The Royal Highland Fusiliers (2 SCOTS) passing the baton to The Highlanders (4 SCOTS) commanded by Lieutenant Colonel Alastair Aitken. 9/12 Lancers provided the cavalry regiment, taking over from 2 RTR. In a sign of the changing role of the task force, perhaps the most important tasks now fell to Lieutenant Colonel Fraser Rea (2 RGR), who was responsible for the Police Mentoring and Advisory Group at the renamed Regional Training Centre South-West, and Lieutenant Colonel Giles Woodhouse, commanding 3 Mercians (Staffords), who was charged with training the ANA in the Brigade Advisory Group, supported by the Royal Scots Dragoon Guards. The former regiment deployed A and C Companies in the light role under Danish command, in Rahim and Khar Nikah Kalays respectively. B Company assumed the role of the Warrior company. The Gurkhas were also required to detach a B Company to man six checkpoints on the Nahr-e Bughra Canal facing the troublesome *dashte* (desert) to the west.

The newly established 30 Commando also deployed with the brigade. This had roots in the Information Exploitation (IX) Group – a successful idea which had been developed in previous deployments. 30 Commando and its predecessor organizations was one of the successes of the war. By the end of the tour, this unit, working intimately with the BRF, accounted for over half of all detained insurgents and four-fifths of all seizures of homemade explosives (over 6 tonnes, or enough to make 900 IEDs, a measure of the industrial output of these devices across Helmand). Some 4 million Pakistani rupees were seized and £2 million's worth of opium impounded. The number of caches uncovered leapt by 140 per cent compared to the previous brigade, and four out of five operations led either to a find or an arrest.[28] This was a stunning return rate and it signalled that 3 Commando Brigade had truly mastered fusing and acting on intelligence with alacrity. The intelligence was also precise: half of all detainees arrested by the BRF were transferred to the Afghan judicial system, a success rate that exceeded that of all other units in Task Force Helmand.[29]

A third possible training task was also now beginning to emerge with the development of the Afghan Local Police (ALP), essentially village militias that, it was hoped, were untarnished by the brush of corruption of the AUP. The ALP programme was established by presidential decree in August 2010. An officer who witnessed the birth of the fledgling ALP in south Nad-e Ali described them thus:

> Potential recruits are nominated by village elders before being security vetted, biometrically enrolled, drugs tested and registered by the Ministry of Interior (MOI) in exactly the same way as the ANP. Once registered they swear an oath of allegiance to GIRoA [Government of the Republic of Afghanistan] and are paid and equipped by the MOI, receiving 60% of the ANP wage.[30]

In fact, in the usual way, the ALP was the latest in a series of similar initiatives, no sooner conceived than changed by the next Westerner arriving in Afghanistan on a short tour, carrying a knapsack of good ideas. These included the Community-Based Security Solutions (CBSS) programme; the Critical Infrastructure Protection (CIP) programme; the Intermediate Security for Critical Infrastructure (ISCI) scheme; the Afghan Public Protection Programme (AP3) and Local Security Forces (LSF) scheme. All had collapsed – why would the ALP fare any better?

Perhaps the real story behind the ALP was the manner in which ISAF was prepared to clutch at straws, disregarding a history of disappointments and failures with previous attempts to raise local police forces. The fact that an American general was prepared to describe the ALP as a 'potential game changer' in testimony to the House Armed Services Committee suggested a unique desperation.[31] This was the spokesman of a country that had spent over $550 billion dollars in a high-tech war now suggesting that an illiterate villager armed with a rifle might provide the answer. A British officer tasked with training ALP perhaps expressed the problem with the greater honesty: 'Imagine taking a group of young, ill-educated, unemployed young men in the UK, giving them three weeks training, a gun, and posting them into a CP, what do you think would happen?'

The laydown of forces inherited by the marines would contract by the summer (with the handover of Lashkar Gah), which was welcomed as British troops were still scattered across 120 separate FOBs, patrol bases and checkpoints, some only held by sections with ANA support. The outgoing brigadier had emphasized four themes: the continuing erosion of the insurgency, better governance, improved Afghan security forces and reconstruction. 3 Commando Brigade would reinforce these themes and seek to push Taliban gangs still further away from central Helmand.

The question of good governance remained vexed. Power was becoming centralized in a handful of Afghans the British could trust – Governor Mangal and his inner circle of personal appointees. This power was growing at the expense of the formal provincial line ministries and other administrative bodies the British were attempting to establish. Mangal was an effective governor who was instrumental to saving the British cause, but he was not immune to Afghan practices.[32] Ultimately, Mangal knew the British and Americans were acutely dependent on his survival: this card proved an ace.

The challenge of the narco-economy also remained unanswered. According to UNODC, almost 140,000 Helmandi households had cultivated the illicit crop in the previous year – or put another way, roughly half of all of Helmand's farmers were in cahoots with the Taliban. For around a sixth, the opium poppy remained the main crop. Around 8 tonnes of opium had been seized that year, a token amount as the estimated total production was close to 2,000 tonnes. Around 70,000 hectares in Helmand were set aside for the cultivation of the opium poppy, a marginal decrease on the previous year, but this was largely irrelevant as the farm gate price of dry opium had leapt 217 per cent to $254 per kilogram. In fact, the price of opium was now back at the levels it enjoyed when the British first arrived in the province in 2006. If peace was descending in some parts of the British-held province, it was a 'criminalised peace' and at the heart of this criminality was the opium poppy.[33] Even at the spectacular height of the cocaine trade in Colombia, this drug only accounted for around 2 per cent of the South American country's GDP. In Afghanistan, opium still accounted for about a quarter of the country's GDP despite the growth in the licit economy. In Helmand, the dependence was even higher.

3 Commando Brigade's tour started with a tragic setback. Just ten days after the handover, Captain Lisa Head, a bomb disposal officer serving with 11 Explosive Ordnance Regiment, was killed attempting to defuse an IED in an alleyway. Captain Head had been unlucky. One IED had been found and a second had detonated without causing injuries. A third undetected bomb killed her. She was the second servicewoman killed in action in Helmand. Lisa Head was only 29 when she died, but this was already her third operational tour. The rate of operational tours was proving unrelenting for Britain's downsized army.

In Britain, the country was recovering from a double bank holiday and the revelries that followed the marriage of Prince William to his long-term girlfriend Catherine Middleton, when the most unexpected news began to stream from breakfast television channels. Osama bin Laden was dead, killed by American special forces in a raid north of Islamabad. It had taken 3,159 days to track down the fugitive, but America had got its man. It seemed strangely fitting that the news broke on a day of swept blue skies not unlike that terrible morning on September 11. In America, and especially in New York, scenes of euphoria were witnessed as crowds poured onto the streets to celebrate the death of the bogeyman.

Bin Laden had been found living at Number 254, 16 Street, Bilad Town, a quiet suburb in the small garrison town of Abbottabad.[34] The original camp had been founded by a British Army officer, James Abbot, who clearly had an eye for picturesque landscapes. As befitted his style, bin Laden occupied a three-storey but plain villa surrounded by high walls and tranquil views. He seems to have spent the last five years of his life in this secluded house, in a sort of Islamic Garden of Eden surrounded by as many as four women, 13 children and a menagerie of animals. The Pakistan Army officer training academy was less than a mile away, and the suburb was the home of serving and retired army officers. Bin Laden's villa was the largest in the area, immediately raising the question why nobody had apparently sought to establish who occupied the prominent building.

Operation *Neptune Spear* was conducted by the US Navy SEAL Team 6, a well-practised detachment that mounted similar missions in Afghanistan. In an echo of the Desert One fiasco, it almost all went horribly wrong when one of the Black Hawk stealth helicopters carrying the assault groups stalled and crashed against a wall.[35] The luck that deserted one Democrat president smiled on Obama. The loud explosions woke up the neighbourhood (one local Tweeter giving real-time accounts of the activities of the mysterious 'helicopter/UFO' to an unsuspecting audience). The United States had not informed the Pakistani government of the raid, fearing compromise, and the Pakistani reaction on the ground was slow. The assault team from Razor 1 abseiled down and quickly cornered bin Laden in his bedroom with his wife.[36] Ninety seconds after the sailors landed and shortly after midnight on 2 May, Osama bin Laden was reportedly killed by a bullet that passed above his left eye. He was also shot in the chest. Later, a dispute would grow between two of the SEALs involved in the raid – Robert O'Neill and Mark Bissonnette – over who had actually killed bin Laden. This somewhat distracted from the question why it had been necessary to kill the evidently confused 54-year-old. It appears the fatally wounded bin Laden was lying on the floor convulsing when he was finished off.[37] Five minutes appeared to elapse between the first confirmed sighting of bin Laden and his death, reported with the words: 'For God and Country, Geronimo, Geronimo, Geronimo'. Bin Laden had died unarmed, although there was an AK-47 and a pistol in the bedroom. Just 12 shots were fired in the entire raid. Within 24 hours, bin Laden's body was transferred to USS *Carl Vinson* and given an Islamic burial at sea. Thus did the world's most wanted terrorist vanish forever in the turquoise waters of the Arabian Sea.

The death of bin Laden had huge symbolic significance. Al-Qaeda had lost its figurehead and inspiration. For Americans, justice had been done. In other respects, the significance of this event was less important. By the time he was finally killed, the march of history had begun to leave behind the white bearded man living in Abbottabad. The turmoil in the

Arab world and calls for democracy marginalized al-Qaeda, although these developments greatly excited bin Laden as a transformational *hadath ha'il* ('formidable event'). Seventeen declassified letters later released by the Department of Defense revealed an isolated figure with no real control over any of the so-called Al-Qaeda affiliates. One his deepest concerns, which appeared to consume his thoughts, was the manner in which Muslims were slaughtering Muslims. A bin Laden niece had posed half-naked in a Western glamour magazine – the true measure of how far Osama had drifted from a changed world.

His death, rather than capture, left a huge hole in the historical record. The chief witness of the events of September 11 was now mute. With the Egyptian Ayman al-Zawahiri still at large, the world was left with the incarcerated and unreliable Khaled Sheikh Mohammed as keeper of the only substantial version of the September 11 plot. Bin Laden's death had no immediate impact on the war in Afghanistan, which had long mutated into a Pashtun narco-nationalist war. Across the Arab world, from Yemen to North Africa, al-Qaeda-inspired groups had incubated, and in some of these countries, they were flourishing. The spiritual head might have been decapitated but acolytes were still filled with jihadist ardour. Threats of vengeance were now in the air. An American talk show host joked that everyone in al-Qaeda had just got a promotion, but there was an unintended grim flipside to the joke.

In one important respect, the death of bin Laden did have profound consequences on the war in Afghanistan. The passing of this bogeyman marked a psychological watershed that no American legislator could ignore. By coincidence, the US Congress had scheduled an intensive session of testimonies from Afghanistan experts to answer the question: what is the end state in Afghanistan, and how do we get there? Virtually every interlocutor delivered the same message – it is time to unwind the massive commitment and get out. Or in American terms, to liquidate the war.

For 3 Commando Brigade the principal task was clearing the remaining 'ungoverned spaces' in Babaji. Much of the trouble in the district stemmed from the fact that the British had unwittingly backed the Barakzai over the minority tribes on the fringes of Babaji.[38] In one of 2 PARA's last operations (Operation *Omid Shash*, 'Hope Six' – the previous five had not seen 'hope' fulfilled), a 1,000-strong battlegroup including 750 ANA commanded by General Sherin Shah had swept into the villages of Malgir and Kopak, in the north-east corner of the district, meeting little resistance. The operation had lasted two days, and the forces had subsequently withdrawn. The marines would repeat the process but now establish a permanent presence in the villages. Simultaneously, the abandoned village of Loy Mandeh would be tackled, a settlement that had already cost the life of Marine Nigel Mead and which was known to be heavily seeded with IEDs. The three objectives were given the codenames Gold, Silver and Bronze.

Omid Haft ('Hope Seven') involved most of 42 Commando and a contingent from 1 Rifles. These were supported by A and B Companies from The Highlanders (4 SCOTS); D Squadron from the Royal Scots Dragoon Guards (Scots DG) mounted on Warthogs; 9/12 Lancers from the BRF operating on Jackals; and Yankee Company from the 30 Commando Information Exploitation Group.[39] The ANA element was provided by the 6th Kandak from 3/215 Brigade. A total of 22 aircraft were involved ferrying troops or providing air cover and surveillance, an airborne operation that coincided with poor weather.

While the marines fought to clear Loy Mandeh, in the early hours of 26 May and still beset by poor weather, a 300-strong force of 1 Rifles and 6/3/215 ANA mounted a heliborne assault in the areas of Malgir and Kopak villages. Yankee Company acted as a screen. Twelve helicopters were involved, dropping the soldiers at five separate locations near Objective Gold. The assault was supported by 29 Commando Regiment, who fired illumination rounds to assist the helicopter crews struggling with the low light conditions. In coordination with the heliborne deployment, a second 200-strong force secured crossing points over the Nahr-e Bughra Canal at Objectives Silver and Bronze. This action was undertaken by two ANA *tolays* drawn from 3/215 Brigade supported by mentors. Fifty tonnes of stores were subsequently dropped by USMC helicopters on the five helicopter landing sites in the vicinity of Gold. Unlike the marines further south, 1 Rifles at first met virtually no resistance, and by the end of the first day the foundations of five checkpoints had been established. On the second day, A Company was locked in 'a running battle between the company and the insurgents lasting from early morning until after dark'.[40] To break the deadlock, mortars, Apaches and strike aircraft were called against the insurgents, who proved very difficult to spot in the lush vegetation. That night the insurgents got their revenge by opening sluice gates and flooding the field in which the soldiers had leaguered.

When the Chinooks arrived to extract the riflemen, one of shortest men in the company, an unfortunate Lance Corporal Ingram, was up to his chin in water.

To ensure the sustainability of the new checkpoints, a massive engineer effort was undertaken. Sappers from 31 Armoured Engineer Regiment cleared the main route connecting the checkpoints to the spine of Babaji (Route Neptune); other sappers from 39 Armoured Engineer Regiment followed behind, upgrading the route; and a third engineer detachment built a 44-metre temporary General Support Bridge over the Nahr-e Bughra Canal. This allowed the resupply of 60 tonnes of supplies carried by the Close Support Regiment (CSLR). Eventually, the General Support Bridge was replaced by a second permanent bridge, the longest built by the British Army in Helmand. This construction took ten days to complete in temperatures reportedly soaring over 50 degrees. With the closure of *Omid Haft* by the end of May, the task force had effectively cleared the last two substantial areas within the British area of responsibility (only temporarily; as usual, Kopak would flare up again, and Malgir remained hostile). The only disappointment in *Omid Haft* had been the performance of the ANA, who flagged and refused to enter the most dangerous area inhabited by Alikozai. A further three British soldiers were killed in the course of the operation, two shot by Taliban sharpshooters.

The dominance enjoyed by the British task force meant that companies were now effectively engaging in a modern version of imperial policing – perhaps the field where the British Army has always excelled. In the last week of April, D Company, 3 Mercians (Staffords), the Warthog group and the Danish B Mechanized Company, supported by a troop of Leopard tanks, mounted a series of three raids in the Gereshk area that uncovered a large number of IED components, including 70 detonators. Successes such as these could not mask the fact that the Upper Gereshk Valley remained a place of 'angry bushes', as one subaltern wisecracked, violently resistant to any British attempts at pacification. In some villages, like Adinzai and Kwoja Morad, the Taliban openly broadcast messages over mosque loudspeakers, such was their confidence. This was not to argue the insurgents were popular. As Lieutenant Fitzpatrick serving at PB Rahim with A Company, 3 Mercians (Staffords) discovered, farmers would discreetly tell patrols they wanted the British to kill the insurgents. Indeed, it was a constant source of puzzlement and frustration to many farmers why the British did not just see off the insurgency with blunt force. Over time, this led to the improbable conspiracy theory, voiced by Lashkar Gah's burgeoning, chattering class of local journalists, that the British were secretly colluding with the Taliban, to avenge the reverse of the Battle of Maiwand. An important and rare advantage enjoyed by Lieutenant Fitzpatrick was the presence of the ALP unit. These part-time policemen had grown up with the insurgents and knew them by sight. They also knew where all the IEDs were being buried. One policeman achieved a record by personally digging up 28 such devices.

Better intelligence was resulting in the uncovering of large IED factories. Near the village of Aga Khel Kalay, previously cleared in *Omid Haft*, a tip-off led to the discovery of 44 pressure plates, 45 kilograms of high explosives and 81 detonators. A subsequent operation by the BRF netted 75 pressure plates.[41] In late July, Captain Nick Welby-Everard Torbet and Corporal Ed Williams (both serving with 101 Engineer Regiment) endured a marathon in blistering temperatures clearing a compound of IEDs. Eventually they disposed of 87 fully or partially constructed detonators, 56 detonators and sacks of explosives.[42] These successes had to be set against the relentless pace of the insurgent IED campaign, fed by a seemingly inexhaustible supply of these cheap devices.

For most infantrymen a tour in one of the front-line patrol bases was beginning to resemble the experience of patrolling in Northern Ireland, albeit in a very different environment. Private Matt Mortimer, serving with 1 Platoon, A Company, 1 Rifles, captured the typical routine in the company blog:

> For the last 5 days, our Multiple has been on patrols. Each patrol varies in duration, route and purpose. On an average day we would get up at 0700 to wash and shave before breakfast – we get a good choice, sausages, bacon (or Spam!), black pudding, beans, fried bread, pancakes and porridge. The patrol will then set off at a previously specified time, which some days could be as early as 0500. One of our patrols lasted for 4 hours, and the aim was to investigate a well and meet the people who live nearby. When we got back to the PB we had lunch and spent the afternoon playing volleyball, going to the gym and reading after our kit had been checked and cleaned. On the second patrol we went on we set off at 1000. The purpose of this patrol was to investigate a compound which insurgents had used in the past. The Afghan National Army went in to the compound first and detained the owner for being

> an insurgent sympathiser. On the way back we stopped at one of the checkpoints for a debrief with the other multiple which was involved in the patrol, and then headed back to the PB in the late afternoon. The cookhouse put on some sandwiches for us and the rest of the day was ours to relax.
>
> The next day we went on a ground dominating patrol to show the locals [sic] community that we are providing them with security. We got back to the PB at lunchtime, but we had orders for a patrol the following day, which we got up at 0230 for and set off at 0400, patrolling to one of the checkpoints and then to occupy a compound as part of a cordon while the Counter-IED team cleared the area around where a school is being built for local children. The clearance took a long time, so we were out for 15 hours.
>
> Thankfully the next day of patrols was easier, setting off at about midday – which was really hot. We headed out to speak to a local elder regarding some IEDs which may have been planted by the insurgents and went to have a look but we couldn't find it so we came back in. Another early start the next day, as we got up at 0200 (although we did get bacon sandwiches and Weetabix for breakfast)! We left the PB a 0400 and went south to clear some compounds and provide defence for a meeting between the OC and the local community. This went well and were [sic] returned at about 1100, our last patrol before we went on guard to protect the patrol base.[43]

Although soldiers like Private Mortimer could now feel some confidence that the insurgents were on the back foot, the levels of violence remained high. Over the course of the summer there were on average over ten daily attacks, the majority ineffectual, but it meant nobody could relax.

Overall, however, it had to be recognized the British had at last pulled off the trick of pacifying central Helmand. The real measure of this was the unlucky A (Grenadiers) Company, 2 Mercians (Worcesters and Foresters), who assumed responsibility for Kopak, in the south-west corner of Babaji, on the next rotation. Over the winter, this small area accounted for *over half* of all incidents in Task Force Helmand. Miserable weather added to the difficulties experienced by the soldiers. In typical Helmand fashion, and for no apparent reason A Company could fathom, the fighting then suddenly died away the following year. Some NCOs in this company had served on Operations *Herrick 1, 6* and *10* – effectively, the last decade of their lives had been spent either fighting, or training and preparing to redeploy to Afghanistan. Elsewhere in Babaji and Nad-e Ali, soldiers could find themselves manning checkpoints and not firing a single shot from week to week.

The diminishing levels of fighting were now balanced by better organized 'hearts and minds' efforts. Veterinary clinics were mounted, which were hugely popular affairs with Helmand's farmers. The British also learned the value of deploying American-style Female Engagement Teams (FETs). Over six months the brigade would hold 650 *shuras* with villagers, a quite outstanding effort to connect with the local population which would have been impossible even a year previously because of Taliban intimidation. As Brigadier Davis later remarked, he now had tens of thousands of counter-insurgents on his side.

Some aspects of life in the patrol bases remained unchanged: boring guard duties and rude children, as remembered by Lance Corporal Kelly Wolstencroft, a dog handler:

> Earlier today when I was looking out into the green zone at all the poppies I heard kids shouting up to the sangar asking for 'chocolate, chocolate' and 'water, water'. Unfortunately I had nothing with me to give to them and was unable to leave my post, eventually they became annoyed and started throwing rocks and stones at me then left, but not before giving me the middle finger![44]

In a sign of changing social attitudes, Kelly Wolstencroft was lesbian and wrote openly about her girlfriend on the British Army's official website. This was the young woman's second tour of Helmand. A more salient example was the case of Warrant Officer Deborah Penny. Deborah had previously been David. The warrant officer deployed on the last *Herrick* rotation and was the first transgender soldier to serve on an operational tour in the history of the British Army.[45]

This improving picture could not mask the broader strategic and domestic problems facing the defence secretary, Liam Fox, all of which were coming to a head in the month of July. The script should have run something like this: British forces hand over the province of Lashkar Gah to Afghan security forces in a largely peaceful ceremony; a long-awaited report on the role of Britain's reserve forces is released, mixed artfully with the news that a further 18,000 soldiers will be cut from the Regular

Army by 2020; Parliament goes into its summer recess, followed by the Westminster media pack.[46] This was the narrative Liam Fox would have wished but, as always, events intervened again.

In late June, Kabul's long-suffering Intercontinental Hotel was attacked by seven suicide bombers who appeared to have been abetted by hotel security guards. In the end it took the intervention of a detachment of New Zealand SAS to see off the attackers, but not before pictures of the iconic hotel in flames had been transmitted around the world. Then, on 12 July, a former security chief of Ahmed Wali Karzai assassinated his former master in his private residence. The Taliban celebrated the assassination as their most successful operation in ten years, a revealing admission that the heartbeat of the insurgency rested in that most enduring Afghan cultural trait – taking revenge on your enemies. Just hours after the assassination, America's new commander in Afghanistan, General John Allen, formally assumed command from the departing Petraeus. 'There will be tough days ahead,' he said, in an understatement.

In Lashkar Gah, on 20 July, a colourful row of flags fluttered over the heads of dignitaries and senior officers as Britain formally handed over control of the district to the Afghan security forces. In response to Liam Fox's assertion that 'normal life' was returning to large parts of the provincial capital, the Taliban duly overran an ANA patrol base and murdered all its occupants. In the previous fortnight, a combined British–Afghan force had conducted Operation *Pot Khanjer 20*, in yet another attempt to disperse insurgents east of the city (an operation in which a Bombardier James Hallam, now on his third operational tour in Afghanistan, had a lucky brush with death when a bullet severed his helmet strap). The other 19 *Pot Khanjers* had failed to suppress the threat of persistent attacks on Route 601. Two days before the handover, Lance Corporal Paul Watkins, serving with 9/12 Lancers, and Corporal Mark Palin, serving with 1 Rifles, were killed in separate attacks. Watkins was one of a small legion of South Africans now serving in the British Army. Palin left behind a widow and young son. The risks in the handover could hardly have been made more evident.

But as big a gamble for Britain lay in the long term, and in the role being sketched for the future reserve forces. The hand of now-retired Lieutenant General Graeme Lamb was behind Reserve Forces 2020, the document describing the proposed future composition and roles of the Territorial Army, and its much smaller sister organizations in the Royal Navy and RAF.[47] The reality was the modern Territorial Army was incapable of deploying a single battalion. Leaving aside the not-inconsiderable cultural and legal hurdles that would have to be overcome to truly create a British 'National Guard', the numbers simply did not stack up. Reservists were not the answer to the manpower crisis in the army and, crucially, reservist soldiers could not *substitute* for regular soldiers – and this was the argument the government was making. The proposal that Britain could still count on around 100,000 soldiers, because 20,000 lost regular soldiers would be substituted by reservist soldiers, was false. Britain could now count on around 80,000 soldiers and some reinforcements, but nobody could say how many. The government had no real hope of reaching its target of 30,000 trained reservists anyway; within a matter of two years, it became obvious from recruiting numbers the existing Territorial Army was not only not growing, but it was shrinking. The rumour doing the rounds was that more Britons were heading off to Syria to join the insurgent group ISIS than joining the Territorial Army. A botched IT program on which the recruitment drive rested further undermined the policy, forcing the government to move the target date to 2018. The appeal of the Territorial Army to politicians was purely financial, not strategic; the part-time soldiers were costing around 1.5 per cent of the total defence budget. For the relatively cheap price of some transient poor headlines lamenting the further downsizing of the British Army, and some dubious promises to make the reserve forces more effective, Fox had got his cuts. It was a short-term political win, but a headache for all his successors.

3 Commando Brigade handed over to their successors, 20th Mechanized Brigade, commanded by Brigadier Patrick Sanders, on 9 October 2011. Brigadier Ed Davis had every right to feel some satisfaction. Local support for the presence of British troops had grown. The best indicator of this change in the attitude of ordinary Helmandis was the fact that four out of ten IEDs were being reported by locals (although this desire to be helpful could sometimes literally backfire, when local farmers assured patrols that a track was clear of IEDs, only for the patrol to trigger a bomb). Over the course of 3 Commando Brigade's tour, 7,200 kilograms of explosives were seized and over 400 IEDs neutralized. Eleven schools and three bazaars were refurbished, and 47 kilometres of hard-top road were laid. Overall, there was a 45 per cent reduction in attacks across the

British area and an 86 per cent reduction in southern Nad-e Ali (where the ALPs were proving a success).

Pressure had been maintained on insurgent gangs. The Royal Scots Dragoon Guards, crewing the Warthogs, conducted over 20 deliberate operations, the longest of which lasted seven weeks. The squadron reckoned they racked up 85,000 miles on this Singaporean-built vehicle (or drove twice around the world). B Company, 2 RGR, based in Nad-e Ali, conducted over 1,000 patrols by the mid-way point of their tour. By the end of the deployment, this sub-unit alone would conduct 28 deliberate, company-level operations. 9/12 Lancers, mounted in Scimitars, proved indispensable, in one incident crashing through thick undergrowth to reach a soldier who had triggered an IED and lost limbs. Within seven minutes, the soldier had been retrieved and was receiving medical attention. The brigade's Close Support Logistic Regiment (CSLR) delivered over 3,000 vehicle loads of stores and supplies to the scattered patrol bases, perhaps the best measure of the tempo of British operations.

Taliban commanders continued to be targeted, Davis revealing that in the first four months, 16 low-level commanders had been killed or captured. This number was down on the previous brigade, which may have accounted for twice this number, but this suggested that Taliban commanders were electing to remain in Pakistan, which suited the British. This undoubted success had to be tempered by the fact that IED statistics still manifested an upward trend. Putting down what had become a booming cottage industry was proving very hard. At the mid-tour point Davis offered, 'attacks are about 43 per cent down on last summer'. It was undeniably the case that in some localized areas boredom was becoming a factor.

Probably the most significant factor favouring the British was the American biometrics technology.* By the time the marines left, over 100,000 Helmandis had been photographed, finger-printed or swabbed (by October 2011, 68 per cent of military-aged men in Helmand had been swabbed).[48] This patient collection of data proved disastrous for unwary insurgents. Every week, a significant number of local young men were being arrested because they manifested positive matches – over 600 by the end of the tour. Could they have even begun to understand that servers in

* The two systems were HIIDE (Handheld Interagency Identification Detection Equipment) and BAT (Biometric Automated Toolset).

Texas had been their undoing? In fact, more insurgents were now being arrested than killed in gun fights. This was policing rather than soldiering, which also suited the British. British-built checkpoints jumped from 25 to 47, suffocating the insurgency with a denser matrix of bases. A staggering 6,000 patrols had been mounted.

The handover to 20th Mechanized Brigade coincided with the tenth anniversary of the war, which prompted a period of reflection on both sides of the Atlantic. *TIME* magazine ran a feature on the war.[49] The cover photograph showed a mountain road in Afghanistan leading nowhere, with the caption: 'Why the U.S. will never save Afghanistan'. Inside, the staff writer, the Afghan-American Aryn Baker, enumerated the blood and treasure spent over the last decade. Her conclusion was bleak: 'And it simply isn't working.' If *TIME* was the voice of middle America, then that voice was saying, let's cut our losses and leave.

Ironically, even as the British were beginning to reap success in Helmand, controversy engulfed Defence Secretary Liam Fox. The story, involving his best man Adam Werritty posing as an official advisor and handing out business cards with the House of Commons logo, had all the ingredients for a perfect Westminster scandal. Five days after the brigade handover in Helmand, Liam Fox resigned. Britain was now about to get its seventh Secretary of State for Defence in ten years – Philip Hammond, moving from the Department for Transport. At no point in its history had this post been swapped so many times in such a short space of time and against a background of two wars. The turbulence the ministry suffered with the constant changes of government, leadership, policies and budgets had been huge.

The key question hanging over a successful transition was the reliability of the Afghan security forces. At the beginning of May, Corporal Ben Newton-Jones, serving with 3 Platoon, A Company, 1 Rifles took over PB Jaba in the so-called 'Padaka horseshoe'.[50] The name came from the fact that the soldiers were surrounded by IEDs seeded around the village, which was built in a horseshoe shape. This small base was only 600 metres from a major British patrol base (PB 4), but the soldiers found the front line was a matter of a few hundred metres from their sangars. On the eighth day at the base:

> … the enemy attacked. We all moved to our stand-to positions and started to return fire. We had come under fire from multiple firing points from

> the south-west through to the north, with the closest only 60 metres away. The sangar (sentry tower), under the command of LCpl Ashworth, was engaging enemy fighters to the south-west and west, in firing points about 100 to 150 metres away, with the .50 calibre heavy machine gun and the smaller yet equally devastating General Purpose Machine Gun (or GPMG for short).

This was one of many scrapes, and over the course of the summer the riflemen gained in confidence and wiliness to avoid the Taliban traps. When the riflemen quit the base, they felt the area was more secure but conceded that the front line could still be measured in a radius of 'a few hundred metres'. This is what the British had bought with all their blood and treasure. Would the 'few hundred metres' hold after Corporal Newton-Jones handed over to Afghan soldiers?

As many soldiers were killed on Operation *Herrick 14* as on the first Operation *Herrick 4*. It had taken the British ten, six-month rotations – ten brigades over five years – to restore the status quo ante bellum. This had been achieved by a combination of factors: the drastic contraction of the British area of responsibility coupled with the American reinforcement; the exploitation of key American technologies, notably surveillance systems and biometrics; the rush procurement of over £4 billion's worth of new, mostly American vehicles and weapon systems; better continuity and intelligence between the brigades; more astute tactics, particularly against the ever-present threat of IEDs; and finally, a meaningful attempt at reconstruction in Helmand. None of these factors would have counted but for the courage and determination of the soldiers and marines sent to the province. When Whiskey Company, 42 Commando deployed to the north-east corner of Nad-e Ali, assuming control of Zarghun Kalay and Luy Bagh villages, it expected a typical Helmand tour. Some of their number would be killed, many more injured, and there would be gun fights every week. Six months later, to everybody's considerable surprise, the company left without firing a shot. John Reid's wish had come true. In at least one corner of Helmand, peace had been restored. This was the sound of success for the British. Silence.

13

The Rush for the Exit Door

October 2011–December 2014

> Ur out of mind. U and ur people … Tajiks are evrywhere Tajiks and they r a pure nation, moron … U have nothing to do with our culture, history, language, identity, food, roots … etc … today, in Afghanistan we spit in your faces and treat ur worser than u treated Hazaras.[1]

Thus did an anonymous Tajik address a Pashtun blogger in 2011, the year that ISAF finalized the timetable for *Inteqal*, or Transition. This vitriol was not uncommon. Ironically, it was made possible by Western aid money that shifted insults traded with bullets to electronic bulletin boards. The vituperative Tajik was blogging on the most popular forum on *Afghanistanonline* with over 41,000 visitors from a choice of 35 forums.[2] The web master had been compelled to create a separate 'ethnic issues' page because every single forum on the site (covering a range of subjects from sports to books) was being hijacked by ethnic slanging matches. Against such a background, what were the chances of a successful conclusion to ISAF's decade-long war in Afghanistan?

General Petraeus underlined the stakes when he addressed a congressional committee in the spring of that year: ISAF only had one chance, and there would be no more opportunities to redress mistakes: 'As we embark on the process of transition, we should keep in mind the imperative of ensuring that the transition actions we take will be irreversible. As the ambassadors of several ISAF countries emphasized at one recent NATO meeting, we'll get one shot at transition, and we need to get it right.'[3]

He was right, but his testimony raised more questions than answers, not least: did the members of Congress care anymore? Did the member nations in the ISAF ark care, or were the animals that went in two by two about to leap overboard at the soonest opportunity? Transition was a euphemism for withdrawal. In many eyes the sooner the better.

If a date had to be set for the beginning of withdrawal it would be 22 June 2011. On this day, at 7pm Eastern Time, President Obama made a pronouncement, at the same lectern from which he had announced the death of Osama bin Laden one month earlier, that America would withdraw over 30,000 troops from Afghanistan by the following summer – or in time to collect an electoral dividend in the forthcoming presidential elections. Domestic politics had shoved its way to the front of the queue.

Washington was not the only capital now keeping a weather eye on the approaching storm clouds of elections and trimming its Afghan commitments accordingly. In November 2010, President Bronislaw Komorowski of Poland announced Polish troops would be out of Afghanistan by 2012. Prime Minister Julia Gillard followed with an announcement in the spring that Australian troops would quit Uruzgan by 2013, or in time for the August federal elections, as the Australian media was quick to point out. Britain had already signalled that as many as 450 servicemen would be withdrawn by the end of the year, and President Sarkozy hinted that around 10 per cent of the French contingent would withdraw by September, with the remaining forces concentrating in Kapisa Province. President Zapatero of Spain joined in, announcing the contingent in Camp Stoner would pack up, leaving a reduced force in Badghis Province. It little helped, as his party was heading for an historic drubbing in the elections anyway. Sarkozy would also fall, but by a narrow margin. Angela Merkel simultaneously announced Germany would begin withdrawing forces in the autumn. The Dutch and Canadian contingents had already withdrawn or were in the process of withdrawing over 2010–11, the latter having suffered 158 fatalities.

Within a year, this tip-toeing towards the exit had turned into an out-of-breath jog for the last bus by Europe's somewhat overweight, middle-aged heads of state. Following his success in the French elections, President Hollande kept his electoral pledge and announced the total withdrawal of French combat forces by 2013. By this stage, a number of shocking Green-on-Blue incidents had already swung French popular opinion sharply against the war. Merkel followed, pulling all German troops out of Kunduz by October 2013, in time for the general elections which she handsomely won. Other nations on the fringes soon followed with similar announcements: Turkey, Belgium and the Czech Republic. Norway released a statement that it would close its PRT at Maimanah by the end of 2012, an announcement echoed by the Hungarians at Pul-e-Khomri in Baghlan Province.[4] Bulgaria announced the withdrawal of its force protection company from the Kabul Airport by January 2013; the Slovakians announced the withdrawal of their engineers from Kandahar and infantry from Tarin Kowt by December 2012; New Zealand pulled its special forces unit; and Albania halved its commitment in Herat. Bankrupt nations like Greece were already unplugging computers and packing crates with Afghan souvenirs. Ten of the 48 contributing nations in the summer of 2011 had deployed fewer than 50 servicemen anyway: whether they stayed or went would make little difference. Most had avoided fighting and engaged in military 'tokenism'.

The official timetable for withdrawal was actually set at the Lisbon Conference in October 2011, but by then all the major contributing nations had stated their positions. NATO's rubber-stamp was hardly necessary. The NATO Secretary General cautioned: 'We need to be clear about what transition means and doesn't mean. Transition means that Afghan authorities take the lead and we move into a supportive role. But it doesn't mean a rush for the exit.' His words fell on cloth ears; a rush is what it had become.

Other milestones were agreed and later confirmed at the Chicago Conference (20–21 May 2012). The ANSF would assume the lead for security nationwide by 2013. ISAF forces would shift from fighting to training and advising. The mission would officially end on 31 December 2014 (it actually ended on 28 December). NATO would not abandon its 'Afghan friends' at this cliff-hanger date. There would be an 'enduring commitment', but even Washington was avoiding getting drawn into the specifics of what this commitment might entail. Behind all this manoeuvring was the unanswerable and intractable question of long-term funding. The ANSF was an entirely artificial construct propped by Western aid money. In reality, America was supporting the patient with minimal support from partner nations. At Chicago, an American programme to agree a more equitable arrangement for the long-term financial support of the ANSF was rebuffed by nervous and bankrupt Europeans. When Washington's most loyal ally, Britain, was offering less than 1 per cent of the required funds, what hope? Henry Kissinger, no stranger to difficult withdrawals from lost wars, was moved to quip that the exit strategy had become all exit and no strategy.

For the redoubtable Anthony Cordesman, withdrawal was 'a race against time, resources and the enemy'.[5] The pessimists who saw a collapsing edifice were not giving credit to the undeniable reversal of fortunes on the battlefield. The real war was only two years old: the first eight years had been largely wasted. But could this advantage be handed over to Afghans to ensure long-term strategic success? Cordesman was not so sure. Transition was an easily invoked word, but a transition to what? Would the uncertain strategy of clear-hold-build just mutate into withdraw, cease funding and provoke an economic depression?[6] With the clock ticking, it was time to end the 'politically correct, totally dishonest, and vacuous conceptual plans'.[7] Transition was in danger of turning into a liar's contest, if that is not what it had already become. Barbara Stapleton, who so perceptively observed and described the first five years of the ISAF mission, cast her sharp eye over the withdrawal and came to the equally depressing conclusion that it amounted to no strategy at all.[8] Such was the expert opinion, and little was positive.

Over 2004–06, ISAF had unrolled itself like a carpet in an anticlockwise direction across Afghanistan. The carpet had since become frayed and had many holes. In other areas, the thread held. The plan was to hand over security responsibility to the ANSF, in four phases over a period of two years, starting with the most secure areas and ending with the most contested. ISAF programmes invariably begat organizations, and transition was no exception. In this case, it was called the Joint Afghan–NATO Inteqal (Transition) Board, or JANIB. Its main function was to rubber stamp decisions taken elsewhere, and to claim useful salaries.

On 22 March 2011, Karzai duly announced the first phase of transition. This involved the handover of seven districts and provinces, including Lashkar Gah. All but two were in the north and centre of the country, and the latter was, of course, in the British area of responsibility, a public relations boon for the Conservative–Liberal Democrat government that would be able to point to 'progress'. Phase two of transition was announced six months later, on 27 November 2011. This was somewhat more complicated. Six provinces were handed over and a number of districts, including Nad-e Ali in Helmand Province.[9]

The third stage of transition was announced on 13 May 2012. Ashraf Ghani, head of the transition commission, stated: 'the third transition will be difficult, we don't want to lie to the Afghan people'. His nervousness was understandable. In a surprise move, all provincial capitals not already under Afghan control would be transitioned (20 out of 34). In effect, phase three was a truly nationwide transfer of security responsibilities, but in taking this course, Kabul was assuming control of provinces where security was tenuous. The number of provinces where security responsibilities had been completely handed over to Afghans now rose to 11. This implied that three-quarters of the population was now living in areas with no, or minimal, ISAF presence. For the British, the significance of phase three was that it included Nahr-e Saraj District. This was the last area still under British control (Lashkar Gah and Nad-e Ali had been transitioned in the previous year). The last stage – phase four – was declared in the summer of 2013, somewhat ahead of schedule. There was little fanfare, as by now the ANSF were suffering in the order of 300 fatalities a month.

What of the withdrawal from Helmand? For all the mistakes that were made at the beginning of the war, it would be highly ungenerous not to recognize that Task Force Helmand quit the province in good order and with reasons to feel pride. The measure of just how effective the British had become as a counter-insurgent force can be taken from the success ratio of the last actions. Without exception, every deliberate operation from about the summer of 2012 yielded results: a cache, a weapon find or a stash of explosives. Targeting of insurgent commanders became a precise skill and the British got terribly good at it.

Poor intelligence had been transformed into excellent intelligence. Two key meetings were held fortnightly on alternate Sunday mornings, known as the Joint Effects Meeting (JEM) and 'Secrets'.[10] Targeting priorities (which insurgents should be pursued and how) were decided at these meetings. The conventional troops lacked the resources of the special forces but compensated through creating the necessary relationships across the various task force agencies. A lack of access to Top Secret intelligence was one constraint. This was remedied by posting a subaltern to the Operational Intelligence Support Group (OISG) in the task force HQ. Another key was cross-cueing surveillance assets. EW was 'the key capability', also described as 'the only game in town'.[11] This generated Lines of Bearing (LoBs) on insurgent communications, which could then be exploited by tasking imaging assets such as drones or base surveillance cameras. Two-man targeting teams were allocated for each insurgent commander (if only they had known). The job of these teams was to build up knowledge on the individuals. Patience was all-important. Because the Intelligence Corps lacked the manpower, any sensible senior soldier or officer could be allocated to these teams, including spare medical officers. Although 'not sufficiently well resourced in any respect to have a decisive impact on either transition or the insurgency', commented one of the last battery commanders, 'what the combination of JEM and target [Secrets] achieved, however, was to maximise the chances that elements of the TSU would be looking at the right time and in the right place, giving us the best opportunity to make campaign progress through cumulative tactical actions'.[12]

The foundations for the withdrawal were actually laid in the summer of 2011, well in advance of the actual troop withdrawals. The signs that this was a war being wound down not ramped up were everywhere. Half of all infrastructure programmes at Camp Bastion were cancelled; £50 million's worth of ammunition was destroyed or returned to Britain. Eventually as many as 500 tonnes of unusable ammunition had to be destroyed, the British deploying a novel small arms incinerator to complete the task quickly. Over 5,000 tonnes of military equipment made the journey home by sea or air. Another 268 ISO containers were filled with other stores. Aircraft spare parts were reduced by between 25 and 38 per cent. This essential housekeeping was just the beginning of a mammoth exercise for the Royal Mechanical and Electrical Engineers, who would attempt to salvage as much serviceable equipment as possible from Helmand. The fact was that this conflict – like all wars – would result in writing off millions of pounds of equipment and infrastructure investment.

By the summer of 2012, logisticians calculated that around 3,000 vehicles and 11,000 ISO containers would have to be returned to Britain, with an estimated value of £4 billion.[13] Later the numbers were refined to 3,345 vehicles and around 5,500 containers. By the end of 2013, some 1,467 vehicles and 2,000 containers had been flown or shipped back to the UK, but 1,479 containers had been scrapped or sold off.[14] Attempting this task would have been impossible without the battalions of Western civilian contractors and locally employed staff (LES) based at Camp Bastion and elsewhere (as many as 1,000 LECs, or locally employed contractors; 1,600 other contractors; and 2,100 CONDOs, or contractors deployed on operations, were on the books).[15] For the locals, the departure of the British (and Americans at Camp Leatherneck) signalled the end of a good run. The more skilled workers could earn as much as $500 a month, or more than the going rate paid by the insurgency. By the end of the war, the British were providing steady employment for as many as 800 Afghans at Camp Bastion. In a few cases, local staff threatened by the Taliban were generously paid off and relocated by the British. Happily, these cases were relatively few, as more often than not the Taliban themselves were profiting hugely from the ISAF contracts.

By the beginning of 2013, it seemed the arithmetic might not add up and the task force presence would have to be extended to the spring of 2015, with the total closure of all British assets extended to 2016. This estimation proved pessimistic, and the last commander of Joint Force Support (Afghanistan) – Brigadier Darrell Amison – completed the epic task on time. The British effort paled in comparison with the headache presented to American logisticians, faced with recovering around 50,000 vehicles and $50 billion's worth of equipment. About one-tenth of this equipment was scheduled to be left behind, gifted to the ANA or written off.

The saga of communications and IT systems gradually unwound but not without headaches. After all the frictions and cost behind the Bowman radio, it remained a system with limitations. The HF radio was 'used sparingly throughout TFH [Task Force Helmand]' as a secondary or tertiary link, except in the case of the Combat Logistic Patrols (resupply convoys) where it was the primary radio due to convoy length and the absence of ECM fratricide issues.[16] Bowman VHF radios remained the 'mainstay' of company operations and by the end were described as 'performing well in all aspects', but this may have been internal propaganda. The fact was that WGS (World Geo-Reference System) 84 mapping underlying Bowman was not compatible with the gridded, satellite-imagery-based maps actually used by troops: this factor meant it was not possible to call a fire mission using the Bowman digital mapping, or trust the Blue Force tracking due to latency issues (delays in the updating of a friendly force position on the digital map). Consequently, it wasn't used.

By 2013, a radio system that had not even been in service ten years and which had cost an estimated £2.6 billion was already being quietly sidelined and a successor software-defined radio system was being sought (which turned into another procurement horror and is still not resolved at the time of writing of this book). If the phrase 'never again' is applied to the war in Helmand, it will surely apply to the British Army's first attempt at fielding digital communications. To be fair, Task Force Helmand's woes were nothing compared to the wider ISAF communications networks, not least due to crypto compromises (on one occasion a Norwegian patrol lost a PRC117F loaded with seven weeks' worth of keymat (crypto key material), provoking 'coalition wide' consternation until the consequences of the compromise were sanitized). The fact was that every army was struggling to master digital communications and data networks, including the US Army, which wasted billions on inadequate systems. But for the heroic efforts of the Royal Signals, it would have been a lot worse.

The thorny question of Camp Bastion Hospital was one of the more difficult to resolve. In the last two years of the war there were 335 doctors and nurses serving in this facility (240 UK, 85 US and ten Danish). The hope that the ANA would establish its own medical service had been over-optimistic, with the result that everyone depended on this single hospital: ISAF, the ANSF, insurgents and ordinary Helmandis. It had always been the intention to avoid creating a dependency culture, but where else could you find emergency resuscitation, operating tables and intensive care units? Even with the decline in casualties, the casevac helicopters remained busy. As late as the autumn of 2011, around 400 casualty evacuations were being undertaken *every month*.[17] The majority of admissions were British and coalition soldiers, but the majority of surgery hours were actually accounted for by local nationals (as many as 300 hours per month at a peak). Bastion Hospital became what it never intended to be: the default life-saving hospital for everyone in Helmand. Scores of insurgents owed their lives to the operating tables at Bastion (60-odd hours of surgery per month at a peak). This generosity to an enemy some felt utterly undeserving was never reported. One-fifth of patients were Afghan children, whose only hope of survival was Western medicine. The hospital even had to deal with a surprise premature birth within the task force (the mother was Lance Bombardier Lynette Pearce, a Fijian). In the end, Camp Bastion Hospital was a noble if short-lived gift to Helmand. The closure of the hospital was not quite the end of the story. In an equally noble gesture, the US Marines left behind a $10 million, 30-bed hospital for the Afghan security forces.

The last sequence of British brigades, from Operation *Herrick 15* to *20* (October 2011 to October 2014) ran: 20th Armoured Brigade (Brigadier Patrick Sanders); 12th Mechanized Brigade (Brigadier David Chalmers); 4th Mechanized Brigade (Brigadier Bob Bruce); 1st Mechanized Brigade (Brigadier Rupert Jones, son of 'H' Jones killed in the Battle of Goose Green in the 1982 Falklands Conflict); 7th Armoured Brigade (Brigadier James Woodham); and 20th Armoured Brigade (Brigadier James Swift, who did not deploy with his brigade).

Over the first half of 2012, Task Force Helmand collapsed 52 of its bases, leaving British soldiers holding just 34.[18] By the end of Operation *Herrick 17*, British, Danish and Estonian troops were deployed in just 19 patrol bases: the former American FOB Ouelette in 'Ops Box Burma', six patrol bases in Nahr-e Saraj, eight in Nad-e Ali and four in Lashkar Gah.

The final British dispositions were based around five battlegroups: CF (Combined Force) Burma; CF Nahr-e Saraj North; CF Nahr-e Saraj South, Training Support Unit (TSU) Nad-e Ali; and TSU Lashkar Gah. With the completion of Tranche 3 Transition, these gradually collapsed to single TSUs for each district, and then to none by the summer of 2013.

By far the toughest assignment – and the last major bastion of resistance the British faced in Helmand – was Ops Box Burma. This was an area of roughly 500 square kilometres in the Upper Gereshk Valley. Home to possibly 8,000 villagers and located halfway between Gereshk and Sangin, this had been a lawless and untamed swathe of the Green Zone from the beginning. When Task Force Leatherneck inherited Sangin it also inherited the Upper Gereshk Valley. The US Marines built a substantial base on the edge of the Green Zone (FOB Ouelette) but decided they lacked the numbers to invest the valley. Instead, the task became guarding Route 611, the newly hard-topped road joining Gereshk and Sangin. Route 611 thus became a de facto front line. As the majority of compounds straddling the route were abandoned, it became a particularly bloody front line. When the 1,000-odd US Marines withdrew, they handed over to a much smaller 300-strong British force. This was CF Burma and it had no chance of confronting the troublesome tribesmen – indeed, it did not even try.

Like the US Marines before them, the British settled for keeping Route 611 open. Ops Box Burma was finally handed over by the Scots Guards to the ANSF (in fact, to a more trustworthy ANCOP contingent) in December 2012. At the time, this single valley was accounting for a stunning 11 per cent of all violent incidents in Afghanistan. The last British base in the area – FOB Ouelette – was finally handed over in September 2013. Brigadier Jones felt it politic to state that 'the handover of Patrol Base Ouellette is another indicator of the progress of the Afghan security forces', but this was far from the truth. The British only finally managed to extricate themselves after two attempts because the Afghan police refused to take over the dangerous base. The notion that withdrawal was 'conditions-based' was bunkum.

By the summer of 2013, the number of patrol bases was down to 13, and the British had almost entirely withdrawn from Lashkar Gah. By Christmas, it was down to five. By February 2014, the British had concentrated their remaining forces in just three bases, and by the summer all troops were based where the story had begun, in Camp Bastion. The last British outpost to close down was Sterga 2, located on a hilltop east of Bastion, in mid-May. At the time it was manned by around 80 soldiers: Highlanders supported by gunners from 3 Royal Horse Artillery and 32 Regiment Royal Artillery, as well as a small contingent of signallers from 14 Signal Regiment. Their commander was the 26-year-old Captain Edward Challis, who took some pride in being the last of the last. US Marines quit Sangin over the same period. In a modest ceremony, Task Force Helmand officially ceased to exist on 1 April 2014, and the last downsized brigade was subordinated to the American-led Regional Command South.

Concurrently with this drawdown, more than 180 checkpoints and patrol bases were bequeathed or constructed for the ANSF. Within a year, roughly half of these would be abandoned, particularly in remote or indefensible areas. By October 2013, one year before withdrawal, *Pajhwok* news was reporting that many of these old bases that cost so much blood and treasure were now being dismantled.[19] The matrix of British-built forts had barely lasted two years. For the locals, the collapse of British patrol bases provided a bonanza of raw materials: wood, corrugated tin, discarded pallets and the ubiquitous Hesco barriers. Sympathetic British commanders invited friendly villagers to join in the dismantling of the bases, an invitation that was never refused, and an activity which resembled a sort of organized looting.

The British withdrawal did not imply a winding down of patrols or fighting. Over the course of 2012, the last year in which Task Force Helmand maintained a presence across the Green Zone, around 600 patrols were being mounted every week. 12th Mechanized Brigade recorded 75 IED strikes against vehicles, one-fifth resulting in the vehicle being written off. The same formation found over 800 IEDs. A weekly average of 40 attacks was being recorded, the overwhelming majority initiated by insurgents.[20] The argument that ISAF had seized the initiative from the insurgency was always a little over-cooked. These numbers implied a roughly 1 in 15 chance that a British patrol would end up in a gun fight. This broad statistic, however, masked great differences. In some areas of Nad-e Ali, nobody fired a shot for months. In the Upper Gereshk Valley, every patrol was being fired at, as if nothing had changed since the first British troops entered this area in 2006. The British actually suffered more fatalities in 2012 – the year when the withdrawal ramped up – than in the previous year. 12th Mechanized Brigade suffered 22 fatalities and 199 wounded (including 18 amputees). The formation reckoned they accounted for around 450 insurgents, killed or wounded. Over 50 'Jackpots' were recorded – that is, the detention or killing of more high-value insurgents, rather than simple foot soldiers.

The intensity of the fighting was evident in the ammunition expenditure figures. In the last two years of the war – when Task Force Helmand was essentially withdrawing – British soldiers still managed to fire off 7,481,687 rounds of 5.56mm and 1,579,348 rounds of 7.62mm ammunition.[21] As many rounds were fired off in the last six months as in the first Operation *Herrick 4* that witnessed the platoon house sieges. Nor did the use of heavier weaponry entirely subside. On Operation *Herrick 17* (October 2012–March 2013), the task force lobbed 4,119 artillery shells. It quit Helmand to the sound of 1,261 exploding shells (from a total 8,197 from October 2012 to September 2014). The Apaches were also busy. They flew home having rattled off 190,753 30mm cannon rounds. There were no Linebacker II raids* against the Taliban, but air support only truly declined at the very end. Close support sorties with weapons released were 2,517 from 32,928 sorties (2010); 2,678 from 34,282 sorties (2011); 1,974 from 28,640 sorties (2012); and 209 from 3,308 sorties (2013).[22] In one respect, however, the war in Vietnam did repeat itself: it was only when the threat of American air power was finally lifted seven years later that an emboldened Taliban marched on Kabul.

Overall ammunition expenditure told an extraordinary if predictable story. In total, Task Force Helmand expended 47 million bullets in its eight-year war.[23] This illustrated one of the great paradoxes of modern wars, namely that despite being armed with the most advanced rifles in the history of warfare, soldiers fire off thousands of bullets and fail to hit anything. Even making a generous assumption that ten insurgents were killed for every British fatality, this still implied the average front-line soldier was expending many thousands of bullets for every enemy killed. Of course, the musketry of the enemy was equally dire. As the overwhelming

*The 1972 so-called 'Christmas bombings' ordered by Nixon at the end of the Vietnam War.

majority of gun fights took place at long ranges, against an enemy neither side could actually see, it perhaps should not surprise it had amounted to eight years of cacophonous but mostly harmless shooting matches.

A milestone was reached on 15 September 2014, when the British Forces Broadcasting Service (BFBS) closed down its radio and television transmitters for the final time after broadcasting continuously for almost 3,000 days. At its peak the service had maintained nearly 100 transmitters across Helmand and Kabul and broadcast more than 15,000 hours of television programmes (*Downton Abbey* proving a surprise hit with American marines).[24] Operation *Herrick* ended on 31 October, replaced by Operation *Toral*, the successor support operation. On the previous Sunday, 26 October, the Union flag was lowered for the last time in Camp Bastion. It was in a sense an anti-climactic moment. After 13 years, the world had moved on. The last British soldiers to die on Operation *Herrick* were killed in an air accident involving a Lynx that summer. They were Captain Thomas Clarke, Flight Lieutenant Rakesh Chauhan, Warrant Officer Second Class Spencer Faulkner, Corporal James Walters and Lance Corporal Oliver Thomas. The latter was a reservist serving with the Intelligence Corps. Britain's volunteer soldiers had given to the end.

The last Union flag was carried from Camp Bastion by Wing Commander Matt Radnall.[25] This symbolic moment was painted with an exaggerated sense of threat. Both the Americans and British had been keen to avoid a 'Saigon moment'. There was no chance of that, yet Radnall was clad in protective gloves, ballistic goggles, a helmet and Osprey body armour. Above him were circling British Apaches, USMC Super Cobras, RAF Tornado GR4s, USAF B-1 Lancer bombers and Reaper UAVs. Had so much firepower ever been deployed to accompany a flag home? After eight years of fighting, no district in Helmand had passed the Abrams Test.* The province was now less secure than when Task Force Helmand first turned up. The British and Americans left behind 298 concrete buildings, including 14 fully equipped gyms and a 64,000-square-foot $18 million command and control centre that was never used.[26] The two runways and air control facilities were destined to run down due to a lack of maintenance skills and spare parts. The Afghans left behind in the

*The Abrams Test was coined from General Creighton Abrams' observation that if he could not walk somewhere in daylight, or drive by night, without protection, then a district was not secure.

now-empty Camp Bastion began racing around in abandoned American golf carts, to the amusement of the departing British. It seemed a fitting last image. Within a month the Taliban had attacked and entered Camp Bastion. This also seemed fitting.

Task Force Helmand's withdrawal was significantly driven by the withdrawal of Task Force Leatherneck. No British government could afford to be left holding the line in Helmand, and the blame for failure. Promises of a measured and conditions-based withdrawal were abandoned by the Obama administration in the run-up to the 2012 presidential election. In Helmand, this meant a 'steep' and 'painful' rush for the exit by Task Force Leatherneck (against the wishes of the US Marines who perceived premature departure as an insult to their fighting prowess). At one stage, a marine had been located in 250 bases across southern and northern Helmand. By April 2012, this number had fallen to around 100. Just in time for the election, it was reduced again to just 26 bases. In six months, a 19,000-strong force had been reduced to 7,000, including just two infantry battalions. This number was matched by almost exactly the same number of civilians at Camp Leatherneck, tasked with winding down the operation.

Sangin had been the British Army's Passchendaele in Helmand, and so it turned out for the US Marines. In honour of the sacrifice, a marching trail at Quantico boot camp would be named 'Sangin', because it exemplified 'everything that is good about the Marine Corps'. 3/7 Marines had taken over from British counterparts in the summer of 2010. Like all new boys, the unit had ignored the advice of its predecessors and quickly suffered a large number of casualties. This unit handed over to 3/5 Marines 'Darkhorse', which became infamous for suffering the most number of casualties of any marine unit in Afghanistan. By the time the unit handed over to 1/5 Marines in March 2011, it had suffered 25 fatalities and 184 wounded, including 34 amputees. Ironically, Defense Secretary Gates became so concerned with the plight of the marines in Sangin he volunteered to withdraw them, the very strategy the British had proposed at the beginning of the war, and for which they were criticized by a Washington fretting over British 'lack of fight'. The marines refused the offer, predictably.

The last full battalion to serve in Sangin was 1/7 Marines. It left in October 2012, having suffered just six fatalities, but this was attributable to the fact that by then the marines had handed over the problem to the Afghans, with unhappy results. The American marines, much like the British before them, were unwilling to accept the sacrifice had been in vain. It was argued that attacks had fallen to just 25–30 *per day*, and that in the final fighting season in 2012 *only* 570 IEDs had been encountered. Memories were unbelievably short. In 2006, four attacks per day was considered bad, and tens not hundreds of IEDs were being encountered. Sangin was being left in a far worse state.

The truth is nobody succeeded in taming northern Helmand. In December 2010, Task Force Leatherneck took a swing with Operation *Outlaw Wrath*. It enjoyed as little success as British attempts to quell the insurgency. This was followed by Operation *Eastern Storm* in November 2011, and Operation *Branding Iron* in August 2012, the last major USMC operation in Helmand. Ironically, this operation, which involved a drive from Sangin to Kajaki, almost exactly mirrored the last major Soviet operation in Helmand. History had repeated itself, at least on Route 611.

In each case, the results were transient and the insurgents regained lost ground. In the winter of 2012, northern Helmand was taken over by 2/7 Marines. This battalion posted platoon-sized units in Now Zad, Musa Qaleh, Kajaki and the Sangin Valley. Smelling victory, the Alizai and allied tribes moved swiftly. In a matter of two weeks, all the ground from Kajaki to halfway down the Sangin Valley was recaptured. ANA checkpoints were either abandoned, or the occupants were evicted, or deals were struck between the insurgents and the Afghan soldiers. This left a marooned marine platoon at the dam, exactly where the British had started in the spring of 2006. By the summer of 2014, the Taliban, almost certainly abetted by covert Pakistani support, mounted a concerted assault involving hundreds of insurgents. This surge succeeded in recapturing all of northern Helmand, except the main towns.

Unnoticed by commentators, the FCO quietly dropped tackling the opium poppy from the menu of British objectives. The ostensible reason why a British task force had been sent to Helmand proved a grand failure. The reasons were, as ever, complex. Academics like David Mansfield, with extensive field experience, detailed the problems: government corruption, a lack of viable alternatives, token and misconceived Western aid programmes, the persistence of the insurgency and basic survival.[27] His interviews with Helmand farmers offered a window into local attitudes. 'Fuck the government. They destroyed my crop,' one farmer told him in Lashkar Gah District. It could have been an epitaph for the entire project.[28]

From 2006 to 2014 Helmand's farmers produced 26,154 tonnes of opium valued at $3.184 billion at farm gate prices.[29] Interdiction never netted more than about 0.05 per cent of the annual opium production, and eradication never exceeded more than about 3 per cent of the acreage under cultivation. In the last year of ISAF's presence, the now independent Afghan counter-narcotics agencies confiscated around 18 tonnes of opium.[30] Helmand alone had produced almost 3,000 tonnes. By withdrawal, eradication programmes, which had always been token efforts anyway, were virtually abandoned.

But apart from personalities like David Mansfield, no one involved in this gross and predictable waste of British taxpayers' money, in the FCO or elsewhere, honestly and transparently reported the truth. No other possible judgement can be made on the Blair government's decision to lead in counter-narcotics in Afghanistan – it was in the end a dismal failure. Individuals associated with this foolish decision, and its many fruitless programmes, were never summoned to account for the waste. Failure had many orphans.

The fact was that Western countries, led by a misguided Washington, had ultimately spent 14 years fighting 'non-wars' against 'non-terrorists', as Cordesman put it, slipping from chasing down al-Qaeda in the wake of the September 11 attacks, to engaging in two ruinously misconceived exercises in armed nation-building in Iraq and Afghanistan. 'I've never believed,' argued former ambassador Sir Rodric Braithwaite, in evidence to the Defence Select Committee as Operation *Herrick* wound down, 'the argument that by fighting in Helmand you will prevent people plotting in the mountains of Pakistan to blow us up on the streets of London. It seems to me that that is a series of non-sequiturs.'[31] He was right. Successive British governments had justified the war to the electorate on the grounds that it was critical to British domestic security. This argument could be challenged but not disproved as long as British soldiers remained in Afghanistan. With the withdrawal of the British task force, the question could now be posed again with new rigour. If the government argument was right, was Britain now a more dangerous country because British soldiers were no longer fighting Pashtun tribesmen in a corner of south-west Afghanistan? Neither the Taliban nor al-Qaeda had been defeated. They were stronger. The absurdity of the proposition was self-evident to all except those determined to defend the notion that Helmand represented some sort of jihadist domino in the Global War on Terror – a British soldier or marine dying in a street in Sangin was somehow keeping another Briton in a street in Surbiton 'safe'.

The last two years of the war also witnessed successes, too easily forgotten in the broader story of disappointment and withdrawal. Perhaps the most exciting organizational development of the war for the British was the evolution of the BRF as a modern-day successor to the wartime Long Range Desert Group (LRDG). This had been Brigadier Jerry Thomas's original vision and it came to fruition.[32] Much like the wartime LRDG, the BRF rivalled the special forces contingent in the tempo and effectiveness of its operations. The key to the BRF was that it was practising mobile warfare, not static, attritional warfare. On Operation *Herrick 12*, the BRF had mounted 16 operations. Over the next two rotations, the number jumped from 20 to 49 deliberate operations. Working with better intelligence, the BRF accounted for over half of all cached IEDs found by the task force, and four-fifths of all homemade explosive finds (an accumulated total of 6 tonnes, or enough to make a staggering 900 IEDs). The BRF also accounted for the largest number of detentions. By the winter of 2012, the momentum of this impressive unit had become unstoppable. Led by QDG Major Justin Stenhouse, the BRF mounted 70 operations, killed or captured 29 insurgents and facilitators and seized 1.6 tonnes of homemade explosives.[33] In one hectic period, the unit mounted four aviation assaults on the trot. Stenhouse was awarded the Distinguished Service Order but with modesty commented, 'I just did my job', preferring to give all the credit to his soldiers. As the British withdrawal gathered pace, brigade commanders came to increasingly rely on the BRF to mount mobile operations and keep emboldened insurgents on the back foot.

There were also belated attempts to win 'hearts and minds' – belated because the British were off and it did not really matter anymore whether or not Afghan farmers warmed to their Western military neighbours. This did not undermine the sincerity and goodwill demonstrated by individuals like Flight Lieutenant Sttevei Atalla. Blessed with a winning smile, Atalla worked as a stabilization officer in an MSST attached to Delhi Company, 1 Yorks (Prince of Wales's Own).[34] At first she found it difficult to overcome the suspicions of local farmers. Then, as she described it: 'Slowly people started to come to us, first the children then the adults; they would have tea with us.' Over five months, 'the local people became fond of me; they called me "Guwette" which means "desert flower". They started handing in IEDs because they were concerned for my safety.' A small victory had been won in a corner of Helmand. Flight Lieutenant Atalla was awarded the Queen's Commendation for Valuable Service for this work.

Task Force Helmand was withdrawing, but the British Army was conducting a more dramatic withdrawal at home, and the man leading this retreat was the defence secretary. Philip Hammond came with a reputation for chilly precision: 'Forensic Phil'. This did not do justice to a personality with a wry sense of humour. Personality aside, Hammond was the only defence secretary in the first two decades of the 21st century with the intellect and ability to address the persistent, gross financial mismanagement in the MOD.* Unfortunately, the financial discipline would only last as long as he remained in office.

The media had widely reported a £36 billion black hole in the ministry's finances, inherited from the previous government. In fact, as Hammond revealed, the true figure was closer to £74 billion when taking into account manpower costs, the need to cut the defence budget following the 2008 financial crisis and his own government's equipment and support liabilities. The inherited black hole, while deeply unwelcome, amounted to less than half of the problem. In other words, even if the Labour government had passed on a balanced budget, there would still have been cuts, though not as severe. In this respect, the Labour government's financial mismanagement of the defence budget was a political gift behind which the Conservative–Liberal Democrat government was able to carry out its cuts, while blaming the last mob. They were, in any case, necessarily deep.

With one year to go before the official end of the ISAF mission, around 80 per cent of over 800 bases in Afghanistan had been handed over to Afghans. Shutting down the Lashkar Gah PRT involved packing 1,400 computers and 10 miles of cables. At the height of the British 'boots on the ground', there had been around 200 patrol bases and checkpoints. The majority had already been either abandoned, or deliberately destroyed. By the beginning of 2014, in Nad-e Ali and Nahr-e Saraj, Afghan security forces now maintained a presence in just 30-odd patrol bases. This raised an important question. What had been the point of the Petraean strategy of clear-hold-build which the British task force had dutifully followed? British sappers had expended hundreds of thousands of man-hours erecting

*To be fair to the long-serving Ben Wallace, initiatives to address the MOD's chronic financial mismanagement were also started over the period 2022–23.

a matrix of posts which the Afghans had already abandoned, a full 12 months before the British were due to leave. What had been cleared? What had been held? What purpose had all this effort served? Too many of these had represented transient posts, quickly circumvallated by IEDs, where a British soldier eventually left behind a leg, or his life. Had it been worth it? If the British had followed a mobile, intelligence-led, targeted approach to counter-insurgency, rather than allowing themselves to be dispersed and mired in static, attrition warfare, would they have paid such a high price?

Withdrawal also brought with it the only war crime case recorded in Task Force Helmand. This involved a marine Sergeant Alexander Blackman, who shot a badly wounded insurgent rather than offering medical assistance. The self-rationalization Blackman invoked – that this was exactly how a wounded marine would have been treated by the Taliban – was the same defence deployed 131 years previously in a similar case in Kabul. In this earlier incident, soldiers of the Seaforth Highlanders (then 72nd Highlanders) were accused of setting light to two wounded Afghan fighters, a story scandalously reported in *The Civil and Military Gazette*.[35] A Dr Bourke then intervened and ordered the two men to be shot, judging that 'life was extinct or practically so'. After some investigation it transpired that soldiers from 5 Goorkhas* had in fact been implicated. In their defence, the commanding officer explained, 'his men must have thought the Afghans were dead; he denies that his men would torture the living but admits the possibility of the dead body of a Mohamedan being set on fire by his men as an act of retribution for the mutilations and indignities which their wounded and killed suffer when they fall into the hands of the Mohamedans'. Lord Roberts had high regard if not affection for his Gurkhas, rating them the best of the 'native' troops, but he nonetheless set up a Court of Enquiry and subsequently raised the allegations to the Army Headquarters in India. Sergeant Blackman received a life term for murder,† but it appears the case against 5 Goorkhas was eventually discontinued. In a footnote, an apocryphal tale circulated in Helmand in 2011 that a Gurkha patrol returned to base with the head of an insurgent, offering the explanation that carrying the body back for identification purposes had proved too difficult. This remained a gruesome but unproven story.

*As spelt in the 19th-century Indian Army

†In 2017 the sentence was reduced to manslaughter and Blackman was subsequently released.

On the civilian side, the merry-go-round of civil servant appointments continued to match the rapid rotations of generals. In the spring of 2012, Sir William Patey handed over to Simon Gass, Britain's fifth ambassador in Kabul since 2006. He in turn handed over to Sir Richard Stagg the following year. Trying to keep count of the number of DfID officials that transited through Afghanistan over the same period became a losing game. This latter organization ended the war as it started – poorly. In 2011, it published its Afghanistan 'Operational Plan 2011–2015', a document of wishful thinking, misleading statistics, and meaningless targets, the latter a great obsession of British government departments over this period.

Under 'Peace, Security and Political Stability', it stated that 78 per cent of Afghans believed their provincial government was doing a good or very good job. DfID's target would be to 'contribute to an increase' in this percentage by 2015. Setting aside how anyone could possibly measure whether or not DfID contributed to such an increase, if it happened, this was a gross simplification of the complexities facing local governance in Afghanistan's provinces. The number '78' actually came from the 2010 annual *Asia Foundation Survey*, a 150-page document with thousands of data. DfID was creating a 'target' based on a single datum point, extracted from a thick report with hundreds of graphs.

In another section, DfID set itself the target of creating 200,000 jobs by 2015. Again, how could anyone possibly measure or prove this? Nobody could. Around 400,000 young men were entering the labour market *every year*. The unemployment rate was in the order of 40 per cent and GDP per capita was one of the lowest in the world (215th). Few Afghans outside the large towns had 'jobs'. They had multiple and contingent income streams, as numerous studies showed. Some were licit and some were not. For most Afghans, it was just about daily survival. Setting such a target was asinine.

Perhaps the most gross and misleading statistic of all was the precise figure of 211,900 children enrolled in primary schools by 2015. Astonishingly, this number was derived by dividing the number of children the Kabul government aimed to enrol in schools by DfID's contribution to the proportion of total ARTF funds (the Afghanistan Reconstruction Trust Fund), and other non-ARTF funding allocated to education. The ARTF was an embezzled and wasteful fund. Taking an Afghan government stated goal as a starting point for anything was like consulting a mafia boss on orphan care. DfID had no clue how many children were actually enrolled in primary schools because no DfID officials actually visited schools. These were numbers plucked from the air and crunched through a meaningless formula. Roughly half of Afghanistan's claimed schools did not actually exist. Four-fifths of girls were chucked out at sixth grade without anything that might be described as an education. A third of Afghanistan's districts had no female teachers such was conservative Pashtun resistance to the notion of educated women. The majority of Afghan children left primary school functionally illiterate. How did that stack up against DfID's list of 'positive indicators'? And so it went on, with the usual management platitudes: 'delivery', 'partnership agreements', 'value for money', 'portfolios' and 'action points'. It was a sorry end to a bleak chapter.

Just as Pacification in the Vietnam War generated a raft of false claims, so the many programmes visited on Helmand produced dishonest 'success statistics'. In 2014, wary of a media that was preparing to question the point of the war, the British government published online 'The Story of the UK's work in Afghanistan'.[36] This document was riddled with misleading and untruthful assertions – indeed the casual mendacity was breathtaking. It was claimed, for example, that 260 kilometres of hard-topped roads had been built in Helmand in the previous year. The truth was less than 100 kilometres of roads were hard-topped over eight years, with American dollars. It was also claimed that 89 schools had been built. This was simply untrue. The British refurbished one school in Musa Qaleh, and one in Sangin near the district centre. No attempts were made to build schools in the Sangin or Upper Gereshk Valleys or in Now Zad and Kajaki – it would have been a quite impossible task. In Nad-e Ali, in 2013, just six permanent structure schools had been built, but the British were hoping to add another five before leaving. There were no secondary schools for girls at all in Nad-e Ali, despite the many claims that education for girls had improved. The only meaningful schools for girls in Helmand were in Lashkar Gah and Gereshk. They pre-dated the arrival of the British (built by the Americans during Helmand's golden period), and contrary to myth, they were not closed down by the Taliban. 'The Story of the UK's work in Afghanistan' compounded these false claims by simultaneously asserting that 30,000 girls were now attending school in Helmand. Just one month after the publication of this document, the Nad-e Ali governor was informing *Pajhwok* news that in fact there were 3,500 schoolgirls in the district.

What these assertions and statistics revealed was a government culture of endemic, casual falsehoods, not tangible achievement. An organization like DfID could spout pleasing numbers, safe in the knowledge that no parliamentary select committee, or other inquiry, would ever find the resources to uncover the truth. To invoke Cordesman's phrase, Helmand had indeed become a liar's contest.

Britain, to be just, was not sailing alone on this ship of lying fools. The failures of reconstruction were comprehensively described by the Afghanistan Analysts Network in a series of essays, *Snapshots of an Intervention*, published on the eve of the 2012 Tokyo Conference. The detail in this book was fascinating, but perhaps the foreword said it all:

> Years of following the international efforts had left us with an increasingly strong sense of déjà vu: another conference to demonstrate momentum, another strategy to surpass the ones before, another project that would come and go and be forgotten the moment its progress was no longer being reported on, only to resurface in a new guise a little later ... the short rotations and limited mobility of embassy and donor agency staff, the pressures to spend and deliver and to come up with project-sized solutions for complex problems, the tendency to design programmes by brainstorm, the lack of institutional memory ... money and opportunity were being wasted in an overwhelming manner ...[37]

The consequence of this massive Western failure and mendacity over the true state of Afghanistan was paid for by the Afghan people, who 'were left empty-handed, with promises of security, stability and reconstruction unmet'. In this respect, Tokyo did not disappoint. This conference achieved a sort of baroque of meaningless slogans, false promises couched in technical jargon, pledges that were never going to be fulfilled and unrealistic targets. For Kabul, the vital outcome was continued international (American) funding for the security forces, for a further three years, following ISAF's withdrawal – or as long as Russian funding lasted.

In a final, spasmodic fit of national masochism, the independent and bipartisan US Commission on Wartime Contracting in Iraq and Afghanistan finally concluded a three-year investigation into where all the dollars had gone (no such effort was undertaken in Britain and never would be). Who knows what made the jaw of the average senator drop, but surely these sentences had an effect:

> At least $31 billion, and possibly as much as $60 billion, has been lost to contract waste and fraud in America's contingency operations in Iraq and

> Afghanistan. Much more will turn into waste as attention to continuing operations wanes, and U.S. support for projects and programs in Iraq and Afghanistan declines, and as those efforts are revealed as unsustainable.[38]

British MPs were only saved reading a similar paragraph on British aid because, for political reasons, no inquiry was launched to investigate the gross scale of waste by DfID in Afghanistan.

It was Secretary of State Clinton who had argued the United States was unwilling to disengage from Afghanistan, despite all the difficulties, because 'we have seen this movie before'.[39] Hence the ten-year Enduring Strategic Partnership Agreement (SPA) signed on 1 May 2012. However, this agreement was more rhetoric than concrete steps. The agreement did not have the legal force of a treaty and both sides could withdraw giving a year's notice. With negotiations over the post-2014 status of forces stalled, there was a chance the SPA would fall off the diplomatic cliff. The SPA eventually transmuted into a Bilateral Security Agreement (BSA), which proved an even more unsatisfactory arrangement.

In a fit of pique, justified by disagreements over peace talks and continuing ISAF raids on Afghan homes, Karzai refused to sign the Bilateral Security Agreement. It was the only way he could thumb his nose at Washington, and he did so with grating impudence. Yet, what was America getting for this very generous offer? Very little – Afghanistan promised to fight al-Qaeda, a frankly empty pledge which it could not fulfil, but American troops remaining in Afghanistan would not be allowed to undertake operations against the insurgency, and nor would an American government be allowed to use its bases for other operations in the region. It was not worth the paper it was written on, and too many hard-nosed American negotiators knew it. By this stage, Obama and Karzai were no longer on speaking terms, Secretary of State Kerry was distracted by the Syria crisis and the US Embassy in Kabul, much like the in-country team at the end of the Vietnam War, had the unenviable task of unwinding America's commitment to Afghanistan. Defense Secretary Chuck Hagel, a Vietnam veteran, found himself playing the role of Mel Laird, rebalancing America's armed forces for a post-Afghan future. Regardless of Karzai's refusal to sign the BSA, it made little long-term difference anyway. There was no surprise when President Obama announced that troop levels would be reduced to 9,000 at the end of 2014, and that the Afghan commitment would end completely by 2016 (a decision that would be reversed).

If America was liquidating its Afghanistan war, where did this leave NATO? Asking whether the alliance had won or lost the war became irrelevant. Certainly, nobody in European capitals, or even Washington, was bothering to pose the question. Nonetheless, entirely ducking this thorny question hardly did justice to NATO's first real war, America's longest war and, of course, an unresolved and continuing war for Afghans. ISAF officially stood up on 1 January 2002, and ended the mission on 28 December 2014. Thirteen years of fighting could not be lightly dismissed.

It was a fact that ISAF quit leaving the enemy undefeated. The three principal insurgent leaders – Mullah Omar, Jalaluddin Haqqani and Gulbuddin Hekmatyar – all survived as did their armies (Mullah Omar, of course, died in 2013, but his passing away was kept secret). This was not all down to Pakistan providing sanctuary and support, although this was an important factor in the war. It was more because, in an echo of George Herring's judgement on the Vietnam War, ISAF became embroiled in an unwinnable war, which it did not even try to win except for one brief period. On Tuesday 18 June 2013, the last Afghan district passed to ANSF control. As if to mark the occasion, four US soldiers were killed in Bagram.

The cost to Afghan civilians remained high, although it should be noted that more Iraqis were being killed in now 'liberated' and 'democratic' Iraq than in Afghanistan. And of course, many, many more Muslims were being killed by fellow Muslims as a consequence of the misnamed Arab Spring. The average farmer in the Upper Gereshk Valley had plenty to grumble about over the war, but it could have been a lot worse.

ISAF entered 2014 with all the gloom of a wake. The Consolidated Appropriations Act pushed American support for Afghan reconstruction past the symbolic $100 billion mark. It would eventually surpass all the aid given to 16 European countries under the Marshall Aid programme – a thought that should sober the average American taxpayer. Some $10 billion had now been spent on counter-narcotics programmes. In a classic understatement, the Special Inspector General for Afghanistan Reconstruction (SIGAR) observed, 'The results of all this spending and activity leave something to be desired.'

All roads pointed to the 2014 presidential election and many were predicting disaster. Around 7,200 polling booths were established throughout the country, but some 750 never opened due to security concerns. In Helmand, there were 147 polling booths; however, the voting was largely confined to Lashkar Gah and Gereshk. Nearly 7 million

Afghans voted, of which 34 per cent were women. The Taliban campaign to thwart the election proved a flop: there were more than 900 attacks during election week, roughly the same number as in 2009, but these were ineffectual. The Independent Election Complaints Commission recorded over 2,000 voting irregularities, but it was accepted that the election would be decided by bartering and deals, not the popular vote. The surprise winner in the first round was Abdullah Abdullah, beating Ashraf Ghani into second place. Helmand's favoured candidate – Zalmai Rassoul – only managed to gain 10 per cent of the vote.

The second round of voting proved much less satisfactory. In Helmand, some 60,000 votes were apparently cast (less than 10 per cent of the electorate). Nationwide, massive electoral fraud lifted the Pashtun Ashraf Ghani above Abdullah Abdullah. Having suffered the loss of the last election due to fraud, Abdullah was in no mood to accept the result. After six months of haggling, a John Kerry-brokered deal saw Ghani installed as president and Abdullah assuming the odd post of chief executive officer. Within a week, the crucial BSA and a status of armed forces agreement were signed. There was a collective sigh of relief but, unfortunately, few of Afghanistan's long-term problems were being addressed by these arrangements. A British prime minister was the first international leader to visit the newly installed President Ghani. But it was telling that the first foreign trip made by Afghanistan's new president was to China.

Despite this unseemly scramble for the top post, the office of the president ended much as it began in 2001, as mayor of Kabul. Karzai ended his 13-year marathon as president of the Afghan Interim Authority, and then as full president of the Islamic Republic of Afghanistan, with a characteristically abrupt comment: 'I can't wait to leave.' This was somewhat disingenuous, as before quitting he had ordered the construction of a personal residence within the presidential compound, ensuring he would remain within earshot of the next appointee. Karzai had been the American candidate shoe-horned into the presidency. He left office bickering and criticizing the benefactors who had placed him there. In a typical snub he quit office thanking China, Germany, India, Iran, Japan, Saudi Arabia, South Korea and Turkey, but pointedly not thanking the country that had propped up Afghanistan for the last decade, the United States. Nor did he mention Britain, with whom relations had deteriorated beyond repair. On Helmand, Karzai was also characteristically blunt, and not without justification. The sacking of

Governor Sher Akhundzada, the origin of all the British ills in Helmand, had been a terrible mistake. Why sacking the one man who could control Helmand's tribes was judged a good idea could only be answered by the FCO and SIS officials responsible for the foolish decision. Their names will never be revealed. It would have been better, Karzai offered, if the British had never entered Helmand.

For all his flaws, Karzai proved the great survivor. He was also not without his insights. An idealistic Western intervention did degenerate into a wasteful, corrupting, national chest-thumping competition in which domestic political concerns always trumped the needs of Afghans. American policy was driven from the barrel of a gun, consistently making matters worse. Too many Western experts had descended on Afghanistan, lining their pockets, adding useful bullet points to their CVs and then vanishing as programmes collapsed. His government had been bypassed and his position undermined. Afghanistan had been transformed into a laboratory for 'Coinistas', making their name touting all manner of theories on how to defeat insurgencies. So much promise had turned to dust.

This was the conclusion to ISAF's 'conditions-based' withdrawal – an Afghanistan that looked not dissimilar to the country the Soviet Army quit. And much like the final withdrawal of US combat troops from Vietnam in March 1973, Afghanistan was left with a 'leopard spot' map. In some areas government troops held sway; in others the Taliban now ruled. In Helmand, the game was restarted, as if the British had been nothing more than a passing thunderstorm. Sher Akhundzada and his brother Amir, now governor of Uruzgan, gathered their old allies. These included Abdul Rahman Jan, who had managed to consolidate his power bases in Nad-e Ali and Marjah. Opposing them were the old familiar faces: Rais Baghrani, now a senator; Mohammed Wali, ensconced in the Parliament; the tribal leader Abdul Rahman Khan; and Malim Mir Wali Khan, also squatting in the Kabul legislature. A fragile Afghan army withdrew to the sanctuaries of district centres, and a crooked police force fell back on its old predatory ways.

This pattern was repeated across Afghanistan. All the old warlords resurfaced, in many ways stronger: Ismail Khan in Herat; the indefatigable Abdul Rashid Dostum in Mazar-e-Sharif; Fahim Khan in the deep north; and Haji Muhammad Mohaqiq in central Afghanistan (Khan would die prematurely, provoking a bout of national mourning). The grand exercise in nation-building, the euphemistic 'capacity building', succeeded in producing an astonishing capacity for rampant, institutional corruption, but little more. Democracy was a sham, and the artificially created state was entirely dependent on foreign aid for its survival.

Aid millionaires were created, many now living in the Gulf States (or in comfortable addresses in capitals like London), and modernity did arrive in Kabul and larger provincial cities, but for the majority of rural or displaced Afghans, which is to say the majority of Afghans, life did not greatly change. Much like Saigon, Kabul became a magnet for these peoples. In 2001, the Taliban capital had a population of roughly 1.5 million. By the time ISAF departed, this had swelled to 6 million, the majority living in shanty towns without water, electricity or heat. The best indicator of ISAF's withdrawal proved to be plummeting property prices as wealthy Afghans fled the country. As much as $4.6 billion *in cash* was being expatriated by these nouveaux riches every year – or more than Afghanistan's entire GDP.[40] This was just the licit declared amounts. The true figure of embezzled aid funds was much higher. The majority of Afghans were still living on about three dollars a day. Ethnic divides were as sharp as before; Pashtun pride and resentment were as prickly. Pakistani meddling was unchecked. This was a country experiencing many thousands of insurgent attacks every year (accurate data collection unfortunately collapsed with ISAF's withdrawal, so even vaguely reliable numbers were unavailable).[41] Over 3,500 civilians were being killed annually, but in one sense this number was trivial. This was also a country where roughly half of all children were not reaching the age of five. The lot of an Afghan woman remained irredeemably constricted by custom and religion.

Nobody won the war because the war which began with the Soviet invasion in the 1980s, which descended into civil war in the 1990s, and which became a Western war in the 2000s, remained unfinished business. One cycle of violence had ended, which only implied another would begin. This was Afghanistan at the end of 2014 – a country ripe for a fall.

An argument may be made that the war in Helmand marked a swansong for the historic British Army, if not a requiem for Britain's armed forces. Two successive governments, representing the three main political parties, decisively cut the size of the armed forces in the middle of two wars. This historically unprecedented slicing of Britain's defences meant the British Army was at its smallest size since the 18th century, the moment when the history of the modern British Army began. A 300-year cycle appeared to reach its closing chapter – literally so, as every surviving regiment was lost over a roughly ten-year period, first by Labour and then Conservative cuts. The only non-amalgamated regiments left in the British Army were the five, untouchable Foot Guard regiments, the Royal Tank Regiment, the Parachute Regiment and 22 Special Air Service Regiment. Everybody else had vanished at the strokes of Treasury pens.

The arithmetic was now inescapable. In the first Gulf War, the RAF fielded 33 fighter squadrons. It now had six. The navy halved. With the defence cuts enacted by the 2010 defence review and subsequently, the British Army was effectively emasculated; it was also now half the size of the 1990 army, and hollow. It was ironic that one of the central lessons of the Iraq and Afghanistan wars was that Britain, in the end, paid a higher cost for under-funding and under-resourcing its armed forces. Yet, once again, a British government was in this familiarly uncomfortable position. The country could now deploy a brigade of soldiers, about ten warships and a squadron of strike aircraft. These were trivial forces. When the BBC broadcast its two-part documentary on the British campaign in Helmand, it entitled the series *The Lion's Last Roar?* A telling moment in popular culture came in an edition of the humorous television show *Have I Got News for You*, hosted by Jeremy Clarkson. In response to a brewing crisis in Ukraine in the spring of 2014, four Typhoon jets were deployed to Eastern Europe. 'Four!' Clarkson exclaimed. 'That's the entire air force. Are they crazy?' At least the British could see the funny side of their decline.

If this pessimistic outlook has some redeeming hope, it is courage. Armies are enfeebled by constant cuts, but they cannot survive without courage. Perhaps the outstanding feature of the war in Helmand was the courage displayed by the soldiers, marines, airmen and sailors who fought in that province. The roll call of gallantry medal winners represented public recognition. Behind this public recognition were hundreds of unrecorded acts and moments of private fears overcome by ordinary young men and women. Every patrol that stepped out of its base had to steel itself for the possibility of death or terrible injury. Over the course of the war, tens of thousands of such patrols were mounted. If the war was a swansong for this British Army, then the band played lustily. Tommy Atkins marched away with a flourish of courage.

Roll of Honour – Afghanistan 2002–14

Note: The Ministry of Defence did not routinely release details of fatalities suffered by 22 SAS, the SBS and 1 SRR. If any members of these regiments are missing from the roll of honour, it is for this reason.

2002

Private Darren John George – 1 Royal Anglian
Sergeant Robert Busuttil – Royal Logistic Corps
Corporal John Gregory – Royal Logistic Corps

2004

Lance Corporal Steven Sherwood – 1 Royal Gloucestershire, Berkshire and Wiltshire Light Infantry
Private Jonathan Kitulagoda – Rifle Volunteers (Territorial Army)

2006

Corporal Mark Cridge – 7 Signal Regiment
Lance Corporal Peter Edward Craddock – 1 Royal Gloucestershire, Berkshire and Wiltshire Regiment
Captain Jim Philippson – 7 Parachute Regiment Royal Horse Artillery
Sergeant Paul Bartlett – Royal Marines (SBS)
Captain David Patton – Parachute Regiment (SRR)
Lance Corporal Jabron Hashmi – Intelligence Corps
Corporal Peter Thorpe – Royal Signals
Private Damien Jackson – 3 PARA
Lance Corporal Ross Nicholls – The Blues and Royals
Second Lieutenant Ralph Johnson – Household Cavalry Regiment
Captain Alex Eida – 7 Parachute Regiment Royal Horse Artillery
Private Andrew Cutts – 13 Air Assault Support Regiment (Royal Logistic Corps)
Private Leigh Reeves – Royal Logistic Corps
Lance Corporal Sean Tansey – The Life Guards
Corporal Bryan James Budd VC – 3 PARA
Lance Corporal Jonathan Peter Hetherington – 14 Signal Regiment

Ranger Anare Draiva – 1 Royal Irish
Flight Lieutenant Steven Johnson – 120 Squadron Royal Air Force
Flight Lieutenant Leigh Anthony Mitchelmore – 120 Squadron Royal Air Force
Flight Lieutenant Gareth Rodney Nicholas – 120 Squadron Royal Air Force
Flight Lieutenant Allan James Squires – 120 Squadron Royal Air Force
Flight Lieutenant Steven Swarbrick – 120 Squadron Royal Air Force
Flight Sergeant Gary Wayne Andrews – 120 Squadron Royal Air Force
Flight Sergeant Stephen Beattie – 120 Squadron Royal Air Force
Flight Sergeant Gerard Martin Bell – 120 Squadron Royal Air Force
Flight Sergeant Adrian Davies – 120 Squadron Royal Air Force
Sergeant Benjamin James Knight – 120 Squadron Royal Air Force
Sergeant John Joseph Langton – 120 Squadron Royal Air Force
Sergeant Gary Paul Quilliam – 120 Squadron Royal Air Force
Corporal Oliver Simon Dicketts – Parachute Regiment
Marine Joseph David Windall – Royal Marines
Private Craig O'Donnell – The Argyll and Sutherland Highlanders (5 SCOTS)
Corporal Mark William Wright GC – 3 PARA
Lance Corporal Luke McCulloch – 1 Royal Irish
Lance Corporal Paul Muirhead – 1 Royal Irish
Marine Gary Wright – 45 Commando
Marine Jonathan Wigley – 45 Commando
Marine Richard J. Watson – 42 Commando
Lance Bombardier James Dwyer – 29 Commando Regiment Royal Artillery

2007

Marine Thomas Curry – 42 Commando
Lance Corporal Mathew Ford – 45 Commando
Marine Jonathan Holland – 45 Commando
Marine Scott Summers – 42 Commando
Lance Bombardier Liam McLaughlin – 29 Commando Regiment Royal Artillery
Lance Bombardier Ross Clark – 29 Commando Regiment Royal Artillery
Marine Benjamin Reddy – 42 Commando
Warrant Officer Class 2 Michael Smith – 29 Commando Regiment Royal Artillery
Private Chris Gray – 1 Royal Anglian
Lance Corporal George Russell Davey – 1 Royal Anglian
Guardsman Daniel Probyn – 1 Grenadier Guards
Corporal Darren Bonner – 1 Royal Anglian
Corporal Mike Gilyeat – Royal Military Police
Lance Corporal Paul Sandford – 2 Mercians (Worcesters and Foresters)
Guardsman Simon Davison – 1 Grenadier Guards
Guardsman Neil 'Tony' Downes – 1 Grenadier Guards
Captain Sean Dolan – 2 Mercians (Worcesters and Foresters)
Sergeant Dave Wilkinson – 19 Regiment Royal Artillery
Guardsman Daryl Hickey – 1 Grenadier Guards
Drummer Thomas Wright – 2 Mercians (Worcesters and Foresters)
Lance Corporal Alex Hawkins – 1 Royal Anglian
Guardsman David Atherton – 1 Grenadier Guards

Sergeant Barry Keen – 14 Signal Regiment
Private Tony Rawson – 1 Royal Anglian
Captain David Hicks MC – 1 Royal Anglian
Private John Thrumble – 1 Royal Anglian
Private Robert Foster – 1 Royal Anglian
Private Aaron McClure – 1 Royal Anglian
Senior Aircraftman Christopher Bridge – 51 Squadron Royal Air Force Regiment
Private Ben Ford – 2 Mercians (Worcesters and Foresters)
Captain David Hicks – 1 Royal Anglian
Private Damian Wright – 2 Mercians (Worcesters and Foresters)
Private Johan Botha – 2 Mercians (Worcesters and Foresters)
Sergeant Craig Brelsford MC – 2 Mercians (Worcesters and Foresters)
Corporal Ivano Violino – 36 Engineer Regiment
Private Brian Tunnicliffe – 2 Mercians (Worcesters and Foresters)
Colour Sergeant Phillip Newman – 4 Mercians (Territorial Army)
Major Alexis Roberts – 1 Royal Gurkha Rifles
Lance Corporal Jake Alderton – 36 Engineer Regiment
Captain John McDermid – The Royal Highland Fusiliers (2 SCOTS)
Trooper Jack Sadler – Honourable Artillery Company (Territorial Army)
Lance Corporal Michael Jones – Royal Marines
Sergeant Lee Johnson – 2 Yorks (Green Howards)

2008

Corporal Darryl Gardiner – Royal Electrical and Mechanical Engineers
Corporal Damian Stephen Lawrence – 2 Yorks (Green Howards)
Corporal Damian Mulvihill – 40 Commando
Marine David Marsh – 40 Commando
Lieutenant John Thornton – 40 Commando
Senior Aircraftman Gary Thompson – Royal Auxiliary Air Force Regiment
Senior Aircraftman Graham Livingstone – Royal Air Force Regiment
Trooper Robert Pearson – Queen's Royal Lancers
Trooper Ratu Sakeasi Babakobau – Household Cavalry Regiment
Captain James Christopher Thompson – 23 SAS (R)
Marine Dale Gostick – Armoured Support Company, Royal Marines
Private Charles Murray – 2 PARA
Private Daniel Gamble – 2 PARA
Private Nathan Cuthbertson – 2 PARA
Private Jeff Doherty – 2 PARA
Lance Corporal James Bateman – 2 PARA
Corporal Paul Stout – 23 SAS (R)
Lance Corporal Richard Larkin – 23 SAS (R)
Corporal Sean Robert Reeve – Royal Signals (attached to 23 SAS (R))
Corporal Sarah Bryant – Intelligence Corps
Private Joe John Whittaker – 4 PARA (Territorial Army)
Warrant Officer Class 2 Michael Norman Williams – 2 PARA
Warrant Officer Class 2 Dan Shirley – 13 Air Assault Support Regiment (Royal Logistic Corps)
Lance Corporal James Johnson – The Argyll and Sutherland Highlanders (5 SCOTS)

Corporal Jason Stuart Barnes – Royal Electrical and Mechanical Engineers
Lance Corporal Kenneth Rowe – Royal Army Veterinary Corps
Sergeant Jonathan William Mathews – The Highlanders (4 SCOTS)
Private Peter Joe Cowton – 2 PARA
Signaller Wayne Bland – 16 Signal Regiment
Corporal Barry Dempsey – The Royal Highland Fusiliers (2 SCOTS)
Ranger Justin James Cupples – 1 Royal Irish
Warrant Officer Class 2 Gary O'Donnell GM & Bar – 11 Explosive Ordnance Disposal Regiment (Royal Logistic Corps)
Private Jason Lee Rawstron – 2 PARA
Lance Corporal Nicky Mason – 2 PARA
Trooper James Munday – Household Cavalry Regiment
Rifleman Yubraj Rai – 2 Royal Gurkha Rifles
Marine Robert Joseph McKibben – Brigade Reconnaissance Force
Marine Neil David Dunstan – Brigade Reconnaissance Force
Colour Sergeant Krishnabahadur Dura – 2 Royal Gurkha Rifles
Marine Alexander Lucas – 45 Commando
Marine Georgie Sparks – 42 Commando
Marine Tony Evans – 42 Commando
Corporal Marc Birch – 45 Commando
Sergeant John Manuel – 45 Commando
Marine Damian Davies – Commando Logistic Regiment
Lance Corporal Steven 'Jamie' Fellows – 45 Commando
Lieutenant Aaron Lewis – 29 Commando Regiment Royal Artillery
Rifleman Stuart Nash – 1 Rifles
Corporal Robert Deering – Commando Logistic Regiment
Lance Corporal Benjamin Whatley – 42 Commando
Corporal Liam Elms – 45 Commando

2009

Serjeant Chris Reed – 6 Rifles (Territorial Army)
Marine Travis Mackin – 45 Commando
Corporal Danny Winter – 45 Commando
Captain Tom Herbert John Sawyer – 29 Commando Regiment Royal Artillery
Acting Corporal Richard Robinson – 1 Rifles
Corporal Daniel Nield – 1 Rifles
Marine Darren Smith – 45 Commando
Lance Corporal Stephen Kingscott – 1 Rifles
Rifleman Jamie Gunn – 1 Rifles
Lance Corporal Paul Upton – 1 Rifles
Corporal Tom Gaden – 1 Rifles
Marine Michael Laski – 45 Commando
Lance Corporal Christopher Harkett – 2 Royal Welsh
Corporal Graeme Stiff – Royal Electrical and Mechanical Engineers
Corporal Dean Thomas John – Royal Electrical and Mechanical Engineers
Lance Sergeant Tobie Fasfous – 1 Welsh Guards
Sergeant Sean Binnie – The Black Watch (3 SCOTS)

Rifleman Adrian Sheldon – 2 Rifles
Corporal Kumar Pun – 1 Royal Gurkha Rifles
Lieutenant Mark Evison – 1 Welsh Guards
Marine Jason Mackie – Armoured Support Group Royal Marines
Fusilier Petero Suesue – 2 Royal Regiment of Fusiliers
Sapper Jordan Rossi – 38 Engineer Regiment
Lance Corporal Robert Martin Richards – Armoured Support Group Royal Marines
Lance Corporal Kieron Hill – 2 Mercians (Worcesters and Foresters)
Corporal Stephen Bolger – Parachute Regiment
Lance Corporal Nigel Moffett – Light Dragoons
Rifleman Cyrus Thatcher – 2 Rifles
Private Robert McLaren – The Black Watch (3 SCOTS)
Lieutenant Paul Mervis – 2 Rifles
Major Sean Birchall – 1 Welsh Guards
Trooper Joshua Hammond – 2nd Royal Tank Regiment
Lieutenant Colonel Rupert Thorneloe MBE – 1 Welsh Guards
Private Robert Laws – 2 Mercians (Worcesters and Foresters)
Lance Corporal David Dennis – Light Dragoons
Lance Corporal Dane Elson – 1 Welsh Guards
Captain Ben Babington-Browne – 22 Engineer Regiment
Trooper Christopher Whiteside – Light Dragoons
Rifleman Daniel Hume – 4 Rifles
Private John Brackpool – 1 Welsh Guards
Corporal Lee Scott – 2nd Royal Tank Regiment
Rifleman Daniel Simpson – 2 Rifles
Rifleman Joseph Murphy – 2 Rifles
Rifleman James Backhouse – 2 Rifles
Rifleman William Aldridge – 2 Rifles
Corporal Jonathan Horne – 2 Rifles
Rifleman Aminiasi Toge – 2 Rifles
Corporal Joseph Etchells – 2 Royal Regiment of Fusiliers
Captain Daniel Shepherd GM – 11 Explosive Ordnance Disposal Regiment (Royal Logistic Corps)
Guardsman Christopher King – 1 Coldstream Guards
Bombardier Craig Hopson – 40 Regiment Royal Artillery
Warrant Officer Class 2 Sean Upton – 5 Regiment Royal Artillery
Trooper Phillip Lawrence – Light Dragoons
Craftsman Anthony Lombardi – Royal Electrical and Mechanical Engineers
Private Kyle Adams – Parachute Regiment
Lance Corporal Dale Hopkins – Parachute Regiment
Corporal Kevin Mulligan – Parachute Regiment
Private Jason George Williams – 2 Mercians (Worcesters and Foresters)
Lance Bombardier Matthew Hatton – 40 Regiment Royal Artillery
Rifleman Daniel Wild – 2 Rifles
Captain Mark Hale – 2 Rifles
Private Richard Hunt – 2 Royal Welsh
Sergeant Simon Valentine – 2 Royal Regiment of Fusiliers
Fusilier Louis Carter – 2 Royal Regiment of Fusiliers

Fusilier Simon Annis – 2 Royal Regiment of Fusiliers
Lance Corporal James Fullarton – 2 Royal Regiment of Fusiliers
Private Johnathon Young – 3 Yorks (Duke of Wellington's)
Serjeant Paul McAleese – 2 Rifles
Fusilier Shaun Bush – 2 Royal Regiment of Fusiliers
Sergeant Lee Andrew Houltram – Royal Marines (SBS)
Private Kevin Elliott – The Black Watch (3 SCOTS)
Sergeant Stuart Millar – The Black Watch (3 SCOTS)
Lance Corporal Richard James Brandon – Royal Electrical and Mechanical Engineers
Private Gavin Elliott – 2 Mercians (Worcesters and Foresters)
Corporal John Harrison – Parachute Regiment
Kingsman Jason Dunn-Bridgeman – 2 Duke of Lancaster's Regiment
Trooper Brett Hall – 2nd Royal Tank Regiment
Acting Serjeant Stuart McGrath – 2 Rifles
Acting Sergeant Michael Lockett MC – 2 Mercians (Worcesters and Foresters)
Private James Prosser – 2 Royal Welsh
Acting Corporal Marcin Wojtak – 34 Squadron Royal Air Force Regiment
Guardsman Jamie Janes – 1 Grenadier Guards
Lance Corporal James Hill – 1 Coldstream Guards
Corporal James Oakland – Royal Military Police
Corporal Thomas Mason – The Black Watch (3 SCOTS)
Staff Sergeant Olaf Schmid GC – Royal Logistic Corps
Corporal Nicholas Webster-Smith – Royal Military Police
Corporal Steven Boote – Royal Military Police
Guardsman James Major – 1 Grenadier Guards
Sergeant Matthew Telford – 1 Grenadier Guards
Warrant Officer Class 1 Darren Chant – 1 Grenadier Guards
Serjeant Phillip Scott – 3 Rifles
Rifleman Philip Allen – 2 Rifles
Rifleman Samuel John Bassett – 4 Rifles
Rifleman Andrew Ian Fentiman – 7 Rifles (Territorial Army)
Corporal Loren Marlton-Thomas – 33 Engineer Regiment (EOD)
Sergeant Robert Loughran-Dickson – Royal Military Police
Acting Sergeant John Amer – 1 Coldstream Guards
Lance Corporal Adam Drane – 1 Royal Anglian
Rifleman James Stephen Brown – 3 Rifles
Lance Corporal David Leslie Kirkness – 3 Rifles
Corporal Simon Hornby – 2 Duke of Lancaster's Regiment
Lance Corporal Michael Pritchard – Royal Military Police
Lance Corporal Christopher Roney – 3 Rifles
Lance Corporal Tommy Brown – Parachute Regiment
Rifleman Aidan Howell – 3 Rifles
Sapper David Watson – 33 Engineer Regiment (EOD)

2010
Private Robert Hayes – 1 Royal Anglian
Captain Daniel Read – 11 Explosive Ordnance Disposal Regiment (Royal Logistic Corps)

Rifleman Luke Farmer – 3 Rifles
Corporal Lee Brownson CGC – 3 Rifles
Rifleman Peter Aldridge – 4 Rifles
Lance Corporal Daniel Cooper – 3 Rifles
Lance Corporal Graham Shaw – 3 Yorks (Duke of Wellington's)
Corporal Liam Riley – 3 Yorks (Duke of Wellington's)
Private Sean McDonald – The Royal Scots Borderers (1 SCOTS)
Corporal Johnathan Moore – The Royal Scots Borderers (1 SCOTS)
Warrant Officer Class 2 David Markland – 36 Engineer Regiment
Lance Corporal Darren Hicks – 1 Coldstream Guards
Lance Sergeant Dave Greenhalgh – 1 Grenadier Guards
Rifleman Mark Marshall – 6 Rifles
Kingsman Sean Dawson – 2 Duke of Lancaster's Regiment
Sapper Guy Mellors – 36 Engineer Regiment
Lieutenant Douglas Dalzell MC – 1 Coldstream Guards
Lance Sergeant David Walker – 1 Scots Guards
Senior Aircraftman Luke Southgate – II Squadron Royal Air Force Regiment
Rifleman Martin Kinggett – 4 Rifles
Sergeant Paul Fox – 28 Engineer Regiment
Rifleman Carlo Apolis – 4 Rifles
Corporal Richard Green – 3 Rifles
Rifleman Jonathon Allott – 3 Rifles
Rifleman Liam Maughan – 3 Rifles
Lance Corporal Tom Keogh – 4 Rifles
Corporal Stephen Thompson – 1 Rifles
Captain Martin Driver – 1 Royal Anglian
Private James Grigg – 1 Royal Anglian
Lance Corporal Scott Hardy – 1 Royal Anglian
Serjeant Steven Campbell – 3 Rifles
Lance Corporal of Horse Jonathan Woodgate – Household Cavalry Regiment
Rifleman Daniel Holkham – 3 Rifles
Guardsman Michael Sweeney – 1 Coldstream Guards
Rifleman Mark Turner – 3 Rifles
Fusilier Jonathan Burgess – 1 Royal Welsh
Corporal Harvey Holmes – 1 Mercians (Cheshires)
Lance Corporal Barry Buxton – 21 Engineer Regiment
Sapper Daryn Roy – 21 Engineer Regiment
Corporal Christopher Lewis Harrison – 40 Commando
Corporal Stephen Walker – 40 Commando
Gunner Zak Cusack – 4 Regiment Royal Artillery
Corporal Stephen Curley – 40 Commando
Marine Scott Taylor – 40 Commando
Marine Anthony Hotine – 40 Commando
Lance Corporal Alan Cochran – 1 Mercians (Cheshires)
Corporal Terry Webster – 1 Mercians (Cheshires)
Lance Bombardier Mark Chandler – 3 Regiment Royal Horse Artillery
Private Jonathan Monk – 2 Princess of Wales's Royal Regiment
Lance Corporal Andrew Breeze – 1 Mercians (Cheshires)

Marine Steven James Birdsall – 40 Commando
Kingsman Ponipate Tagitaginimoce – 1 Duke of Lancaster's Regiment
Corporal Taniela Tolevu Rogoiruwai – 1 Duke of Lancaster's Regiment
Trooper Ashley David Smith – Royal Dragoon Guards
Marine Richard Hollington – 40 Commando
Marine Paul Warren – 40 Commando
Lance Corporal Michael Taylor – 40 Commando
Sergeant Steven Darbyshire – 40 Commando
Private Alex Isaac – 1 Mercians (Cheshires)
Private Douglas Halliday – 1 Mercians (Cheshires)
Lance Corporal David Ramsden – 1 Mercians (Cheshires)
Colour Sergeant Martyn Horton – 1 Mercians (Cheshires)
Bombardier Stephen Gilbert – 4 Regiment Royal Artillery
Corporal Jamie Kirkpatrick – 101 Engineer Regiment (EOD)
Corporal Seth Stephens CGC – Royal Marines (SBS)
Trooper James Leverett – Royal Dragoon Guards
Private Thomas Sephton – 1 Mercians (Cheshires)
Bombardier Samuel Robinson – 5 Regiment Royal Artillery
Marine David Hart – 40 Commando
Corporal Arjun Purja Pun – 1 Royal Gurkha Rifles
Lieutenant Neal Turkington – 1 Royal Gurkha Rifles
Major James Joshua Bowman – 1 Royal Gurkha Rifles
Marine Matthew Harrison – 40 Commando
Marine Jonathan David Thomas Crookes – 40 Commando
Senior Aircraftman Gunner Kinikki Griffiths – Royal Air Force Regiment
Sergeant David Thomas Monkhouse – Royal Dragoon Guards
Staff Sergeant Brett Linley GM – 11 Explosive Ordnance Disposal Regiment (Royal Logistic Corps)
Lance Corporal Stephen Daniel Monkhouse MC – 1 Scots Guards
Corporal Matthew James Stenton MC – Royal Dragoon Guards
Sapper Mark Antony Smith – 36 Engineer Regiment
Lance Sergeant Dale Alanzo McCallum – 1 Scots Guards
Marine Adam Brown – 40 Commando
Lieutenant John Charles Sanderson – 1 Mercians (Cheshires)
Rifleman Remand Kulung – 1 Mercians (Cheshires)
Sapper Darren Foster – 21 Engineer Regiment
Sapper Ishwor Gurung – 69 Gurkha Field Squadron, 21 Engineer Regiment
Lance Corporal Jordan Dean Bancroft – 1 Duke of Lancaster's Regiment
Lance Corporal Joseph McFarlane Pool – The Royal Scots Borderers (1 SCOTS)
Captain Andrew Griffiths – 2 Duke of Lancaster's Regiment
Kingsman Darren Deady – 2 Duke of Lancaster's Regiment
Trooper Andrew Martin Howarth – Queen's Royal Lancers
Sergeant Andrew James Jones – Royal Engineers
Corporal Matthew Thomas – Royal Electrical and Mechanical Engineers
Rifleman Suraj Gurung – 1 Royal Gurkha Rifles
Sergeant Peter Anthony Rayner – 2 Duke of Lancaster's Regiment
Corporal David Barnsdale – 33 Engineer Regiment (EOD)
Sapper William Blanchard – 101 (City of London) Engineer Regiment (EOD)

Senior Aircraftman Scott Hughes – Number 1 Squadron Royal Air Force Regiment
Ranger Aaron McCormick – 1 Royal Irish
Guardsman Christopher Davies – 1 Irish Guards
Private John Howard – 3 PARA
Corporal Steven Thomas Dunn – 216 (Parachute) Signal Squadron
Warrant Officer Class 2 Charles Henry Wood – 23 Pioneer Regiment (Royal Logistic Corps)

2011

Private Joseva Saqanagonedau Vatubua – The Argyll and Sutherland Highlanders (5 SCOTS)
Private Martin Bell GM – 2 PARA
Ranger David Dalzell – 1 Royal Irish
Warrant Officer Class 2 Colin Beckett – 3 PARA
Private Lewis Hendry – 3 PARA
Private Conrad Lewis – 4 PARA (Territorial Army)
Lance Corporal Kyle Marshall – 2 PARA
Private Robert Wood – Royal Logistic Corps
Private Dean Hutchinson – Royal Logistic Corps
Lance Corporal Liam Richard Tasker – Royal Army Veterinary Corps
Lance Corporal Stephen McKee – 1 Royal Irish
Private Daniel Steven Prior – 2 PARA
Major Matthew James Collins – 1 Irish Guards
Lance Sergeant Mark Terence Burgan – 1 Irish Guards
Colour Sergeant Alan Cameron – 1 Scots Guards
Captain Lisa Jade Head – 11 Explosive Ordnance Disposal Regiment (Royal Logistic Corps)
Marine Nigel Dean Mead – 42 Commando
Colour Serjeant Kevin Charles Fortuna – 1 Rifles
Marine Samuel Giles William Alexander MC – 42 Commando
Lieutenant Oliver Richard Augustin – 42 Commando
Corporal Michael John Pike – The Highlanders (4 SCOTS)
Lance Corporal Martin Joseph Gill – 42 Commando
Rifleman Martin Jon Lamb – 1 Rifles
Corporal Lloyd Newell – Parachute Regiment (22 SAS)
Craftsman Andrew Found – Royal Electrical and Mechanical Engineers
Private Gareth Leslie William Bellingham – 3 Mercians (Staffords)
Lance Corporal Paul Watkins – 9/12 Lancers
Corporal Mark Anthony Palin – 1 Rifles
Marine James Robert Wright – 42 Commando
Lieutenant Daniel John Clack – 1 Rifles
Sergeant Barry Weston – 42 Commando
Lance Corporal Jonathan James McKinlay – 1 Rifles
Marine David Fairbrother – 42 Commando
Rifleman Vijay Rai – 2 Royal Gurkha Rifles
Private Matthew James Sean Haseldin – 2 Mercians (Worcesters and Foresters)
Private Matthew Thornton – 4 Yorks (Territorial Army)
Lance Corporal Peter Eustace – 2 Rifles
Lieutenant David Boyce – 1 Queen's Dragoon Guards
Lance Corporal Richard Scanlon – 1 Queen's Dragoon Guards

Private Thomas Christopher Lake – 1 Princess of Wales's Royal Regiment
Rifleman Sheldon Lee Jordan Steel – 5 Rifles
Sapper Elijah Bond – 35 Engineer Regiment
Captain Tom Jennings – Royal Marines
Squadron Leader Anthony Downing – Royal Air Force
Private John King – 1 Yorks (Prince of Wales's Own)

2012
Rifleman Sachin Limbu – 1 Royal Gurkha Rifles
Signaller Ian Sartorius-Jones – 20th Armoured Brigade Headquarters and Signal Squadron
Lance Corporal Gajbahadur Gurung – 1 Yorks (2 Royal Gurkha Rifles)
Senior Aircraftman Ryan Tomlin – 2 Squadron Royal Air Force Regiment
Sergeant Nigel Coupe – 1 Duke of Lancaster's Regiment
Corporal Jake Hartley – 3 Yorks (Duke of Wellington's)
Private Anthony Frampton – 3 Yorks (Duke of Wellington's)
Private Christopher Kershaw – 3 Yorks (Duke of Wellington's)
Private Daniel Wade – 3 Yorks (Duke of Wellington's)
Private Daniel Wilford – 3 Yorks (Duke of Wellington's)
Captain Rupert Bowers – 2 Mercians (Worcesters and Foresters)
Sergeant Luke Taylor – Royal Marines
Lance Corporal Michael Foley – Adjutant General's Corps
Corporal Jack Leslie Stanley – Queen's Royal Hussars
Sapper Connor Ray – 33 Engineer Regiment (EOD)
Guardsman Michael Roland – 1 Grenadier Guards
Corporal Andrew Steven Roberts – 23 Pioneer Regiment
Private Ratu Silibaravi – 23 Pioneer Regiment
Corporal Brent John McCarthy – Royal Air Force Police
Lance Corporal Lee Thomas Davies – 1 Welsh Guards
Captain Stephen James Healey – 1 Royal Welsh
Corporal Michael John Thacker – 1 Royal Welsh
Private Gregg Thomas Stone – 3 Yorks (Duke of Wellington's)
Lance Corporal James Ashworth VC – 1 Grenadier Guards
Corporal Alex Guy MC – 1 Royal Anglian
Warrant Officer Class 2 Leonard Thomas – Royal Signals
Guardsman Craig Andrew Roderick – 1 Welsh Guards
Guardsman Apete Tuisovurua – 1 Welsh Guards
Lieutenant Andrew Robert Chesterman – 3 Rifles
Lance Corporal Matthew David Smith – Royal Engineers
Guardsman Jamie Shadrake – 1 Grenadier Guards
Guardsman Karl Whittle – 1 Grenadier Guards
Sergeant Lee Paul Davidson – Light Dragoons
Lance Corporal Duane Groom – 1 Grenadier Guards
Sergeant Gareth Thursby – 3 Yorks (Duke of Wellington's)
Private Thomas Wroe – 3 Yorks (Duke of Wellington's)
Sergeant Jonathan Eric Kups – Royal Electrical and Mechanical Engineers
Captain James Anthony Townley – Royal Engineers
Captain Carl Manley – Royal Marines

Corporal David O'Connor – 40 Commando
Corporal Channing Day – 3 Medical Regiment
Lieutenant Edward Drummond-Baxter – 1 Royal Gurkha Rifles
Lance Corporal Siddhanta Kunwar – 1 Royal Gurkha Rifles
Captain Walter Barrie – Royal Regiment of Scotland (1 SCOTS)

2013
Sapper Richard Reginald Walker – 28 Engineer Regiment
Kingsman David Robert Shaw – 1 Duke of Lancaster's Regiment
Lance Corporal Jamie Webb – 1 Mercians (Cheshires)
Corporal William Savage – The Royal Highland Fusiliers (2 SCOTS)
Fusilier Samuel Flint – The Royal Highland Fusiliers (2 SCOTS)
Private Robert Hetherington – 51st Highland Volunteers (7 SCOTS, Territorial Army)
Lance Corporal James Brynin – Intelligence Corps
Warrant Officer Class 2 Ian Fisher – 3 Mercians (Staffords)
Captain Richard Holloway – Royal Engineers (SBS)

2014
Sapper Adam Moralee – 32 Engineer Regiment
Captain Thomas Clarke – 657 Squadron Army Air Corps
Warrant Officer Class 2 Spencer Faulkner – 657 Squadron Army Air Corps
Flight Lieutenant Rakesh Chauhan – Royal Air Force
Corporal James Walters – 657 Squadron Army Air Corps
Lance Corporal Oliver Thomas – 3 Military Intelligence Battalion (Reserves)

Glossary

ADZ	Afghan Development Zone
AIA	Afghan Interim Authority
ALP	Afghan Local Police
ANA	Afghan National Army
ANP	Afghan National Police
ANSF	Afghan National Security Forces
APPF	Afghan Public Protection Force
ARIB	Afghanistan Roulement Infantry Battalion
ARRC	Allied Rapid Reaction Corps
AUP	Afghan Uniformed Police
BRF	Brigade Reconnaissance Force
BSA	Bilateral Security Agreement
CAT	Chah-e Anjir Triangle
CDS	Chief of the Defence Staff
CERP	Commander's Emergency Response Program
CGS	Chief of the General Staff
CIMIC	Civil Military Cooperation
CJTF	Combined Joint Task Force
COIN	Counter-insurgency
CP	checkpoint
CSIS	Center for Strategic and International Studies
DfID	Department for International Development
DNBI	disease and non-battlefield injury
DOD	US Department of Defense
FCO	Foreign and Commonwealth Office
FOB	forward operating base
GCHQ	British Government Communications Headquarters
GMLRS	Guided Multiple Launch Rocket System
HCR	Household Cavalry Regiment
HEG	Helmand Executive Group
IED	improvised explosive device
ISAF	International Security Assistance Force
ISI	Pakistani Inter-Services Intelligence Directorate
ISTAR	Intelligence, Surveillance, Target Acquisition and Reconnaissance

JFEOD	Joint Force Explosive Ordnance Team
JSOC	Joint Special Operations Command
KRH	King's Royal Hussars
kandak	Afghan battalion
LAV	light armoured vehicle
LEWT	Light Electronic Warfare Team
LMCIED	low metal content IED
MERT	Medical Emergency Response Team
MEU	Marine Expeditionary Unit
MI5	British Security Service
MOD	Ministry of Defence
MOG	Mobile Operations Group
MSST	Military Stabilization and Support Team
MTA	Military Technical Agreement
NGO	Non-Governmental Organization
OMLT	Operational Mentoring and Liaison Team
PB	patrol base
PJHQ	Permanent Joint Headquarters
PRT	Provincial Reconstruction Team
PSC	private security company
PWRR	Princess of Wales's Royal Regiment
QDG	The Queen's Dragoon Guards
QIP	Quick Impact Projects
QRF	Quick Reaction Force
RGR	Royal Gurkha Rifles
RPG	rocket-propelled grenade
RSOI	Reception, Staging and Onward Integration
shura	consultative meeting
SIS	Secret Intelligence Service
TiC	Troops in Contact
tolay	Afghan company
UAV	unmanned aerial vehicle
UNODC	United Nations Office on Drugs and Crime

Bibliography

Allen, Craig, *With the Paras in Helmand, A Photographic Diary*, Pen and Sword Books, 2009.

Anderson, Ben, *No Worse Enemy: The inside story of the chaotic struggle for Afghanistan*, Oneworld, 2011.

Anderson, E. and N. H. Dupree, eds, *The Cultural Basis of Afghan Nationalism*, Pinter Publishers, 1990.

Annett, Roger, *Lifeline in Helmand, RAF Frontline Air Supply in Afghanistan, 1310 Flight in Action*, Pen and Sword Books, 2014.

Annis, Ann, *Butterflies and Feathers*, AuthorHouse UK, 2011.

Bailey, Jonathan, Richard Iron and Hew Strachan, *British Generals in Blair's Wars*, Ashgate, 2013.

Beattie, Doug, *An Ordinary Soldier: Afghanistan: A Ferocious Enemy, A Bloody Conflict, One Man's Impossible Mission*, Simon and Schuster UK Ltd, 2008.

—— *Task Force Helmand*, Simon and Schuster UK Ltd, 2009.

Benitz, Max, *Six Months Without Sundays, The Scots Guards in Afghanistan*, Birlinn Limited, 2011.

Bergen, Peter L., *The Osama bin Laden I Knew, An Oral History of Al-Qaeda's Leader*, Free Press, 2006.

Bird, Tim and Alex Marshall, *Afghanistan: How the West Lost its Way*, Yale University Press, 2011.

Bishop, Patrick, *3 PARA*, Harper Press, 2007.

—— *Ground Truth, 3 PARA: Return to Afghanistan*, Harper Press, 2010.

Black Watch, *Aviation Assault Battlegroup: The 2009 Afghanistan tour of the Black Watch 3rd Battalion the Royal Regiment of Scotland*, Pen and Sword Books, 2011.

Braithwaite, Rodric, *Afgantsy: The Russians in Afghanistan 1979–1989*, Profile, 2011.

Burke, Jason, *The 9/11 Wars*, Allen Lane, 2011.

Bury, Patrick, *Callsign Hades*, Simon & Schuster, 2010.

Caroe, Sir Olaf, *The Pathans*, Macmillan, 1958.

Chalmers, Malcolm, *Paying for Defence: Military Spending and British Decline*, Pluto Press, 1985.

Chandrasekaran, Rajiv, *Little America: The War Within the War for Afghanistan*, Bloomsbury, 2011.

Chayes, Sarah, *The Punishment of Virtue: Inside Afghanistan After the Taliban*, Penguin, 2006.

Chouvy, Pierre Arnuad, *Opium, Uncovering the Politics of the Poppy*, I. B. Taurus, 2009.

Churchill, Winston S., *Malakand Field Force 1897*, Longman's Colonial Library, Project Gutenberg e-Book, 2005.

Coll, Steve, *Ghost Wars: The Secret History of the CIA, Afghanistan and Bin Laden, from the Soviet Invasion to September 10th 2001*, Penguin, 2005.

Cordovez, D. and S. Harrison, *Out of Afghanistan: The Inside Story of the Soviet Withdrawal*, Oxford University Press, 1995.

Cowper-Coles, Sherard, *Kabul: The Inside Story of the West's Afghanistan Campaign*, Harper Press, 2011.

Dalrymple, William, *The Return of the King: The Battle for Afghanistan*, Bloomsbury, 2012.

Docherty, Leo, *Desert of Death: A Soldier's Journey from Iraq to Afghanistan*, Faber and Faber, 2008.

Doherty, Richard, *Helmand Mission: With 1st Royal Ranger Battlegroup in Afghanistan 2008*, Pen and Sword Books, 2009.

Dorman, Andrew, *Crises and reviews in British Defence Policy, Britain and Defence 1945–2000*, Pearson Education, 2001.

Dorronsoro, Gilles, *Revolution Unending: Afghanistan, 1979 to Present*, Columbia University Press, 2005.

Douglas, Craig, *Fire Mission, The Uncensored Truth, The Diary of a Firing Sergeant in Afghanistan*, independently published, 2013.

Dupree, Louis, *Afghanistan*, Princeton University Press, 1980.

Ewans, M., *Afghanistan: A Short History of its People and Politics*, Harper Collins, 2001.

Evison, Margaret, *Death of a Soldier: A Mother's Story*, Biteback, 2012.

Fairweather, Jack, *A War of Choice, The British in Iraq 2003–2009*, Jonathan Cape, 2011.

—— *The Good War: The Battle for Afghanistan 2006–14*, Jonathan Cape, 2014.

Fergusson, James, *A Million Bullets: The real story of the British Army in Afghanistan*, Corgi Books, 2009.

—— *Taliban: The history of the world's most feared fighting force*, Corgi Books, 2010.

Ferguson, Niall, *The Cash Nexus: Money and Power in the Modern World 1700–2000*, Penguin Books, 2001.

Flynn, Mick, *Bullet Magnet*, Wiedenfeld & Nicolson, 2010.

Flynn, Mick, with Will Pearson, *Trigger Time*, Orion Publishing Group, 2011.

Forbes, A., *Britain in Afghanistan: The First Afghan War 1839–42*, Leonaur Ltd, 2007.

—— *Britain in Afghanistan: The Second Afghan War 1878–80*, Leonaur Ltd, 2007.

Freedman, Lawrence, *The Politics of British Defence 1979–1998*, Macmillan Press, 1999.

Fremont-Barnes, G., *The Anglo-Afghan Wars 1839–1919*, Osprey Publishing, 2009.

Gall, Carlotta, *The Wrong Enemy: America in Afghanistan 2001–2014*, Houghton Mifflin Harcourt, 2014.

Gall, Sandy, *War Against the Taliban: Why it All Went Wrong in Afghanistan*, Bloomsbury, 2012.

Giustozzi, Antonio, *War, Politics and Society in Afghanistan, 1978–1992*, C. Hurst and Georgetown University Press, 2000.

—— *Koran, Kalashnikov, and Laptop: The Neo-Taliban Insurgency in Afghanistan*, Columbia University Press, 2006.

—— *Empires of Mud: Wars and Warlords in Afghanistan*, C. Hurst & Co. Ltd, 2009.

Goodson, Larry P., *Afghanistan's Endless War: State Failure, Regional Politics, and the Rise of the Taliban*, University of Washington Press, 2007.

Grahame, Sergeant Paul and Lewis Damien, *Fire Strike 4/7*, Ebury, 2010.

Grau, Lester and Jalali Ali Ahmad, *The Other Side of the Mountain: Mujahideen Tactics in the Soviet-Afghan War*, Foreign Military Studies Office, Fort Leavenworth, 1997.

Grau, Lester, *The Bear Went Over The Mountain: Soviet Combat Tactics in Afghanistan*, National Defense University Press, 1996.

Grau, Lester and Michael A. Gress (trans and eds), The Russian General Staff, *The Soviet Afghan War: How a Superpower Fought and Lost*, University of Kansas Press, 2002.

Grey, Stephen, *Operation Snakebite*, Penguin Books UK, 2009 (reprinted as *Into the Viper's Nest, Task Force 1 Fury and the Battle for Musa Qaleh*, MBI Publishing Company LLB and Zenith Press, 2010.

Gul, Imtiaz, *Pakistan: Before and After Osama*, Roli Books, 2012.

Gunaratna, Rohan, *Inside Al Qaeda, Global Terror Network*, Berkley Books, 2002.
Harnden, Toby, *Dead Men Rise: The Welsh Guards at War*, Quercus, 2011.
Heathcote, T. A., *The Afghan Wars 1839–1919*, Spellmount Ltd, 2007.
Hennessey, Patrick, *The Junior Officers' Reading Club*, Allen Lane, 2010.
—— *Kandak: Fighting with Afghans*, Allen Lane, 2012.
Hill, Christian, *Combat Camera, From Auntie Beeb to the Afghan Frontline*, Alma Books, 2014.
Hunter, Major Chris, *Eight Lives Down*, Corgi Books, 2009.
—— *Extreme Risk*, Corgi Books, 2009.
—— *Tripwire*, Corgi Books, 2009.
Kelley, Kevin J., *The Longest War, Northern Ireland and the I.R.A.*, Zed Books Ltd, 1990.
Kitson, Frank, *Low Intensity Operations: Subversion, Insurgency, Peace-keeping*, Faber and Faber, 1971.
Jones, Seth, *In the Graveyard of Empires: America's War in Afghanistan*, Norton, 2009.
Kemp, Colonel Richard and Christopher Hughes, *Attack State Red*, Penguin Books, 2009.
Kilcullen, David, *The Accidental Guerrilla: Fighting Small Wars in the Midst of a Big One*, Oxford University Press, 2009.
Kiley, Sam, *Desperate Glory: At War in Helmand with Britain's 16 Air Assault Brigade*, Bloomsbury Publishing, 2009.
Ledwidge, Frank, *Losing Small Wars: British Military Failures in Iraq and Afghanistan*, Yale, 2011.
Lee, Graham, *Fighting Season: Tales of a British Officer in Afghanistan*, Duckworth Overlook, 2012.
Lewis, Major Russell, *Company Commander*, Virgin Books, 2012.
Lieven, Anatol, *Pakistan, A Difficult Country*, Penguin Books, 2011.
Loyn, David, *Butcher and Bolt: Two Hundred Years of Foreign Engagement in Afghanistan*, Windmill Books, 2008.
McDonald, David, *Drugs in Afghanistan: Opium, Outlaws and Scorpion Tales*, Pluot Press, 2007.
Macy, Ed, *Apache Down*, Harper Press, 2008.
Martin, Mike, *An Intimate War: An Oral History of the Helmand Conflict*, C. Hurst & Co. Ltd, 2014.
Marsden, P., *Afghanistan: Aid, Armies and Empires*, I. B. Taurus, 2009.
Nojumi, Niamatullah, *The Rise of the Taliban in Afghanistan*, Palgrave, 2002.
Peters, Gretchen, *Seeds of Terror*, Thomas Dunne Books, 2009.
Polman, Linda, *War Games: The Study of Aid and War in Modern Times*, Viking, 2010.
Rashid, Ahmed, *Taliban: Militant Islam, Oil and Fundamentalism in Central Asia*, Yale University Press, 2001.
—— *Descent into Chaos: The U.S. and the Disaster in Pakistan, Afghanistan, and Central Asia*, Penguin, 2008.
Rayment, Sean, *Into the Killing Zone: Dispatches from the Frontline in Afghanistan*, Constable & Robinson Ltd, 2008.
—— *Bomb Hunters: In Afghanistan with Britain's Elite Bomb Disposal Unit*, Collins, 2011.
Robson, Brian, *Crisis on the Frontier: The Third Afghan War and the Campaign in Waziristan 1919–1920*, Spellmount Ltd, 2004.
Ryan, Mike, *Frontline Afghanistan: The Devil's Playground*, Spellmount Ltd, 2010.
Schofield, Victoria, *Afghan Frontier, At the Crossroads of Conflict*, Tauris Parke Paperbacks, 2011.
Semple, Michael, *Reconciliation in Afghanistan*, USIP Press, 2009.
Simpson, Emile, *War from the Ground Up: Twenty-First Century Combat as Politics*, C. Hurst & Co. Ltd, 2012.
Singer, Peter W., *Corporate Warriors*, Cornell University Press, 2003.
Southby-Tailyour, Ewen, *3 Commando Brigade*, Random House Group, 2009.
—— *Helmand Assault*, Random House Group, 2010.
Steele, Jonathan, *Ghosts of Afghanistan: The Haunted Battleground*, Portobello Books Ltd, 2011.

Stewart, J., *Crimson Snow, Britain's First Disaster in Afghanistan*, Sutton Publishing, 2008.
Stewart, Rory and Gerald Knaus, *Can Interventions Work*, Norton, 2011.
Streatfeild, Richard, *Honourable Warriors, Fighting the Taliban in Afghanistan*, Pen and Sword Books, 2014.
Summers, Anthony and Robbyn Swan, *The Eleventh Day: The Full Story of 9/11 and Osama Bin Laden*, Doubleday, 2011.
Sykes, Percy, *A History of Afghanistan*, Vol. 2, Macmillan, 1940.
Taylor, Chantelle, *Battleworn, The Memoir of a Combat Medic in Afghanistan*, iUniverse LLC, 2014.
Tankel, Stephen, *Storming the World Stage: The Story of Lashkar-e-Taiba*, C. Hurst & Co. Ltd, 2011.
Tomsen, Peter, *The Wars of Afghanistan*, Public Affairs, 2011.
Uesseler, Rolf, *Servants of War, Private Military Corporations and the Profits of War*, Soft Skull Press, 2008.
Urban, Mark, *War in Afghanistan*, Macmillan Press, 1988.
US Army Office of the Surgeon General/Borden Institute, *War Surgery in Iraq and Afghanistan: A Series of Cases, 2003–2007*, edited by Shawn Christain Nessen, Dave Edmond Lounsbury and Stephen P. Hetz, 2008.
Weston, Simon, *Helmand: Diaries of Frontline Soldiers*, Osprey Publishing, 2013.
Wilson, Robert, *Helmand: Faces of Conflict*, Jonathan Cape, 2008.
Winn, Matthew, *One Of Many*, Kindle edition, 2014.
Wiseman, David, with Nick Harding, *Helmand to the Himalayas*, Osprey Publishing, 2014.
Wood, Jake, *Among You: The Extraordinary True Story of a Soldier Broken by War*, Mainstream Publishing, 2013.
Yousaf, Mohammad and Mark Adkin, *Afghanistan – The Bear: The Defeat of a Superpower*, Leo Cooper, 1992.
—— *Afghanistan: The Bear Trap*, Leo Cooper, 2001.
Zaeef, Abdul Salam, *My Life With The Taliban*, translated by Alex Strick van Linschoten and Felix Kuehn, C. Hurst & Co Ltd, 2010.

Notes

PREFACE

1 See Niall Ferguson, *The Cash Nexus*, Penguin Books, 2001, Chapter 1.

2 Ibid, p. 46.

3 *British Army Review* (BAR), Spring 2011, Anthony King, 'Military Command in the Last Decade', reprint of an article in *International Affairs*, Volume 87, Issue 21, March 2011.

CHAPTER 1: THE PLANES OPERATION

1 Hansard, International Terrorism and Attacks in the USA HC Deb 14 September 2001, Volume 372, cc. 604–616.

2 The sting was carried out by *Dispatches*, Channel 4.

3 Cordesman's voluminous output on Afghanistan, from 2001 to 2014, was the single most impressive, wise and passionately argued commentary of the war. Nobody did more to warn against and then dissect the folly of the war as it unfolded.

4 Anthony Cordesman, 'Defending America: Redefining the Conceptual Borders of Homeland Defense', 19 September 2001.

5 *The 9/11 Commission Report*, p. 45.

6 Ibid, p. 39.

7 Ibid, p. 58.

8 Peter L. Bergen, *The Osama bin Laden I Knew: An Oral History of Al-Qaeda's Leader*, Free Press, 2006, p. 36.

9 *The 9/11 Commission Report*, p. 59.

10 The full name was Jam'at Qaedat Ansar Allah or 'The Base Group of Allah Supporters'.

11 Bergen, *The Osama bin Laden I Knew*, p. 83.

12 Steve Coll, *The Bin Ladens: The Story of a Family and its Fortune*, Penguin Group, 2008, p. 413.

13 *The 9/11 Commission Report*, p. 109.

14 Ibid, p. 109.

15 Ibid, p. 129.

16 Ibid, p. 140.

17 Ibid, p. 183.

18 Ibid, p. 170.

19 Ibid, p. 146.

20 Bill Roggio, 'AQIS announces death of 2 senior leaders in US operation', *The Long War Journal*, 21 November 2014, www.longwarjournal.org/archives/2014/11/aqis_announces_death.php.

21 Gordon Corera and Steve Swann, 'Khalid Sheikh Mohammed: How "9/11 mastermind" slipped through FBI's fingers', BBC News, 6 September 2021.
22 Broadcast on Al Jazeera television, 1 November 2004.
23 Full text of PM Tony Blair's speech at the Lord Mayor's banquet: www.theguardian.com/world/2001/nov/13/september11.usa1.
24 *The 9/11 Commission Report*, p. 124.
25 Ibid, p. 134.
26 Hansard, Coalition against International Terrorism HC Deb 04 October 2001, Volume 372, cc. 671–688.
27 Ibid.
28 Ibid.
29 Brian Glyn Williams, 'Dostum and the Mazar i Sharif Campaign: new light on the role of the Northern Alliance warlords in Operation Enduring Freedom', *Small Wars & Insurgencies*, 4, 2010, pp. 610–632.
30 US Presidential address to the nation, 7 October 2001.

CHAPTER 2: INTERNATIONAL RESCUE

1 Rohan Gunaratna, *Inside Al Qaeda, Global Network of Terror*, Berkley Books, 2002, p. 303.
2 Williams, 'Dostum and the Mazar i Sharif Campaign', p. 617.
3 Anthony Davis, 'How the Afghan War was won', *Janes Intelligence Review*, 23 January, 2002.
4 Williams, 'Dostum and the Mazar i Sharif Campaign', p. 616.
5 Anthony Cordesman, *The emerging strike patterns in the air war in Afghanistan*, 20 October 2001.
6 Ibid.
7 Davis, 'How the Afghan War was won'.
8 Ibid.
9 CENTCOM commander Tommy Franks would insist that the aim of the operation was to dismantle al-Qaeda, but it is difficult not to view the decapitation of its leader as central to this mission.
10 Williams, 'Dostum and the Mazar i Sharif Campaign', p. 626.
11 Davis, 'How the Afghan War was won'.
12 Ahmed Rashid, *Taliban*, I. B. Taurus and Co. Ltd, 2010, p. 221.
13 Davis, 'How the Afghan War was won'.
14 Rashid, *Taliban*, p. 223.
15 Michael Martin, *War on its Head: An Oral History of the Helmandi conflict 1978–2012*, King's College London Doctoral Thesis, January 2013, p. 149.
16 Martin, *War on its Head*, pp. 148–150.
17 Ibid.
18 Anthony Cordesman, *The Air War Lessons of Afghanistan: Change and Continuity*, December 2001, p. 62. 'Nothing that US and allied forces did … has shown that the US and its Western allies have a solution to the problems associated with combating an enemy whose forces are dispersed, fluid, and not seeking a conventional fight.'
19 Lord Roberts of Kandahar, *41 Years in India*, Richard Bentley and Son, 1897.
20 Footage showed as many as six British special forces soldiers and marines (22 SAS/SBS).
21 This 'incident' in fact lasted four days, and there are numerous conflicting accounts of the sequence of events. The chief charge against the Northern Alliance and Western forces is that they took part in an unjustified massacre of prisoners. This is rebutted by the argument that there was fanatical resistance and prisoners armed themselves from the fort armoury.

22 The data is from www.landmines.org that monitored the problem of unexploded ordnance in Afghanistan.
23 Cordesman, *The Air War Lessons of Afghanistan*, p. 142.
24 The statement was made in January 2002 after the establishment of the rudimentary HQ in Kabul.
25 See Jack Fairweather, *The Good War: The Battle for Afghanistan 2006–2014*, Jonathan Cape, 2014, p. 39.
26 United Nations Peacemaker, Agreement on Provisional Arrangements in Afghanistan Pending the Re-establishment of Permanent Government Institutions (Bonn Agreement), https://peacemaker.un.org/afghanistan-bonnagreement2001.
27 The Brookings Institution, 'Are we winning the war on terrorism? A report from Afghanistan', 19 January 2006.
28 Hansard, International Assistance Force (Kabul), Volume 377: debated on Thursday 10 January 2002.
29 Hansard, International Assistance Force (Kabul), HC Deb 10 January 2002, Volume 377, cc 688–701.
30 'MILITARY TECHNICAL AGREEMENT Between the International Security Assistance Force (ISAF) and the Interim Administration of Afghanistan ("Interim Administration")', http://bits.de/public/documents/US_Terrorist_Attacks/MTA-AFGHFinal.pdf.
31 Alistair Horne, *A Savage War of Peace: Algeria 1954–1962*, Pan Books, 1997, p. 49.
32 UK MOD, INTERNATIONAL SECURITY ASSISTANCE FORCE (OPERATION FINGAL), March 2002, 'disposed of nearly 3 million munitions, 80% of which were anti-personnel landmines'.
33 Ibid.
34 Hansard, Afghanistan HC Deb 18 March 2002, Volume 382, cc. 7–8.
35 Ibid.
36 Hansard, Afghanistan, HC Deb 20 March 2002, Volume 382, cc. 328–373.
37 Ibid.
38 Ibid.
39 Hansard, Afghanistan HC Deb 18 March 2002, Volume 382, cc. 7–8.
40 Ibid.
41 Ibid.
42 HQ 3 Cdo Bdw RM Intelligence Estimate for Potential Offensive Operations in Afghanistan: as at 12 March 2002.
43 Barbara J. Stapleton, 'A Means to What End? Why PRTs are peripheral to the bigger political challenges in Afghanistan', *Journal of Military and Strategic Studies*, Fall 2007, Volume 10, Issue 1.
44 Anthony Cordesman, *The Lessons of Afghanistan: A First Analysis*, February 2002.
45 DOD figures, June 2002.
46 Fry evidence to Defence Committee, 8 February 2011.
47 Byrd, 3 October 2002, Congressional Record, S9873.
48 NATO press release 127, 21 November 2002.
49 Rashid, *Taliban*, p. 225.
50 Ibid.
51 Fairweather, *The Good War*, pp. 126–127.
52 Stapleton, 'A Means to What End?'.
53 Martine van Biljert and Sari Kouvo, *Snapshots of an Intervention: The Unlearned Lessons of Afghanistan's Decade of Assistance (2001–11)*, Afghanistan Analysts Network, 2012, Ch. 4, p. 29.
54 Gerald F. Hyman, *Afghanistan after the Drawdown, U.S. Civilian Engagement in Afghanistan Post-2014*, CSIS, April 2014.

55 Fairweather, *The Good War*, p. 144.
56 van Biljert and Sari, *Snapshots of an Intervention*, p. 30.
57 *ISAF Mirror*, January 2005.
58 *ISAF Mirror*, September 2005.
59 51.5 per cent – MOD figures.
60 van Biljert and Sari, *Snapshots of an Intervention*, p. 55.
61 Hyman, *Afghanistan after the Drawdown*.
62 This unit confusingly appeared to start its deployment as Operation *Herrick 3*, but became merged into Operation *Herrick 4*.
63 David Richards, *Taking Command*, Headline Publishing Group, 2014, p. 182.
64 Reid evidence to Defence Select Committee, 8 February 2011.
65 Ibid.
66 General Richards evidence to Defence Select Committee, 11 May 2011.
67 Richards, *Taking Command*, p. 186.
68 Tom Coghlan, 'Afghan expect record opium poppy crop and the Taliban will reap the rewards', *The Independent*, 11 May 2006.
69 Brigadier Mark Carleton-Smith, 16 Air Assault Brigade.
70 Mike Jackson evidence to Defence Select Committee, 5 May 2011.
71 Ed Butler evidence to Defence Select Committee, 16 December 2014.
72 Reid evidence to Defence Select Committee, 8 February 2011.
73 Defence Committee, Decision making in Defence Policy, HC 682, Dec 14–Jan 15.
74 Houghton evidence to Defence Committee, 11 May 2011.
75 Fairweather, *The Good War*, p. 145.
76 *The Times*, 14 January 2011.
77 *The Times*, 9 June 2010.
78 *The Times*, 5 April 2014.
79 Stapleton, 'A Means to What End?'.
80 Ibid, p. 23.
81 Linda Polman, *War Games: The Study of Aid and War in Modern Times*, Viking, 2010.
82 Jonathan Foreman, *Aiding and Abetting: Foreign Aid Failures and the 0.7% Deception*, Civitas, 2013.
83 Stapleton, 'A Means to What End?'.
84 Ibid.

CHAPTER 3: A PARTICULARLY DIFFICULT OPERATION

1 Reportedly, originally spoken to a *Daily Telegraph* journalist. The quote is also recorded as 'miles and miles of fuck all with a river running through it', www.thedailybeast.com/no-more-friendly-fire.
2 *The Independent*, quoting Major Will Pike in 'The Interview', 9 November 2008.
3 44th Regiment memorial plaque, Essex Regimental Chapel, Warley, Essex.
4 1,150km long from its source in the Hindu Kush mountains, 80 kilometres west of Kabul.
5 Major S. Hill and members of B Company, 2 Mercian, 'Dismounted Close Combat Operations in the Green Zone', *The Infantryman* journal, UK MOD, 2007, p. 117.
6 Jean Mackenzie, 'New America Foundation, Counterterrorism Strategy Initiative Policy Paper', *The Battle for Afghanistan, Militancy and Conflict in Helmand*, September 2010.
7 Report of the Site Selection of the Permanent Administrative Centre of the Helmand Valley Authority, 1953.
8 *Pathans: Handbook of the Indian Army*, The Recruiting Office Peshawar, 1936.
9 Ibid p. 16.
10 Series GSGS 5971, Sheet Tribal Areas in Helmand Province, Edition 1.

11 Michael Yon, *The Afterwar*, 8 December 2011, https://michaelyon.com/dispatches/the-afterwar/.
12 'Platoon Leading in Frontier Warfare', Military Training pamphlet 16 (India), 1945.
13 'British Forces enter "Opiumland"', *Janes Terrorism and Security Monitor*, 6 March 2006.
14 Richards, *Taking Command*, p. 241.
15 Matt Cavanagh, 'Ministerial Decision Making in the Run-up to the Helmand Deployment', *RUSI Journal*, Vol. 157, No. 2, April/May 2012.
16 Royal United Services Institute (RUSI), 'The Afghan Papers: Committing Britain to War in Helmand 2005–2006', 'Cross-Government Planning and the Helmand Decision 2005–2006'.
17 To be fair to the 'Reid Group', many of these questions could only have been answered by a 'Hoon Group', if such an entity existed, but everyone connected with this period has been reticent to speak.
18 John Reid statement to Parliament, 26 January 2006.
19 Ed Butler, 'Setting Ourselves up for a Fall in Afghanistan', *RUSI Journal*, 13 March 2015.
20 Ibid.
21 Wall evidence to Defence Select Committee, 11 May 2011.
22 Butler evidence to Defence Select Committee, 16 December 2014.
23 Ibid.
24 Ibid.
25 Ibid.
26 Martin, *War on its Head*, p. 187.
27 Butler's writings are in his *RUSI* article, 'Setting Ourselves up for a Fall in Afghanistan'; Jack Fairweather, 'The squabbling generals who sent 3 Para into a minefield', *The Times*, 20 November 2014, www.thetimes.com/article/the-squabbling-generals-who-sent-3-para-into-a-minefield-gzlkolzmq36.
28 Defence Secretary Reid statement to the Commons, 26 January 2006.
29 General Wall evidence to Defence Select Committee, 11 May 2011.
30 General Richards evidence to Defence Select Committee, 11 May 2011.
31 Fairweather, *The Good War*, Chapter 8.
32 Colonel Stuart Tootal, *Danger Close*, John Murray, 2009, p. 47.
33 Westminster Hall Debates, 17 June 2008, www.parliament.uk.
34 'A Changing Nation, DfID support for Afghanistan', DFID pamphlet, 2005.
35 Kim Howells evidence to Defence Select Committee, 6 January 2015.
36 Westminster Hall debates, 17 June 2008, www.parliament.uk.
37 *Conduct of Anti-Terrorist Operations in Malaya*, 1958 (First Edition 1952).
38 Butler evidence to Select Defence Committee, 5 May 2011.
39 James Fergusson, *A Million Bullets*, Transworld Publishers, 2008, p. 241.
40 Poll undertaken by Altai Consulting, 10 December 2005.
41 Butler evidence to Select Defence Committee, 5 May 2011.
42 Major General Richards's Directive to ISAF on assuming command of RC (SW).
43 Ibid.
44 UK MOD, *Future Conflict – Insights from interviews with senior commanders*, 30 January 2006.
45 UK MOD, *Military Operations* news article, 'Para soldiers on their way to Afghanistan,' 3 May 2006.
46 Patrick Bishop, *3 PARA*, Harper Press, 2007, p. 19.
47 Combat support and combat service support units included: 13 Air Assault Support Regiment; 16 Close Support Medical Regiment; 156 Provost Company, Royal Military Police; 8 Close Support Squadron, 7 Air Assault Battalion, Royal Electrical and Mechanical Engineers; 216 Signal Squadron and 16 Air Assault Brigade's Headquarters staff.

48 Butler evidence to Select Defence Committee, 5 May 2011.
49 Ibid.
50 National Audit Office (NAO), Support to High Intensity Operations, REPORT BY THE COMPTROLLER AND AUDITOR GENERAL, HC 508 Session 2008–2009, 14 May 2009.
51 Bishop, *3 PARA*, p. 40.
52 Fergusson, *A Million Bullets*, p. 115.
53 Ibid.
54 'Lieutenant general has commanded units in the last three major conflicts', nvdaily.com, 11 October 2008.
55 US Department of Defense, Office of the Assistant Secretary of Defense (Public Affairs) News Transcript, Presenter: Army Maj. Gen. Benjamin Freakley, commander, Combined Task Force 76 and commanding general, 10th Mountain Division.
56 Ibid.
57 Martin, *War on its Head*, p. 171.
58 Fairweather, *The Good War*, p. 162.
59 Ibid, see Chapter 13.
60 Butler, 'Setting Ourselves up for a Fall in Afghanistan'.
61 General Richards evidence to Defence Select Committee, 11 May 2011.
62 *The Daily Telegraph*, 20 November 2010.
63 Martin, *War on its Head*, p. 193.
64 Dr Chris Tripodi published an insightful article on the 'politicals' in the Spring 2008 edition of *British Army Review* (BAR): 'Understanding: Its Utility and Influence: The British Experience on the North-West Frontier 1918–1939'.
65 *The Sunday Times*, Culture section, 6 November 2011.
66 Dr Kim Howells, House of Commons Hansard Debates, 20 February 2007.
67 Butler evidence to Defence Select Committee, 5 May 2010.
68 General Wall evidence to Defence Select Committee, 11 May 2011.
69 According to Michael Martin, the police chief was a Noorzai named Sarwar Jan, *War on its Head*, p. 200.
70 See Section 4.8 of Martin, *War on its Head*.
71 Ibid.
72 Ibid, p. 167.
73 Leo Docherty, *Desert of Death: A Soldier's Journey from Iraq to Afghanistan*, Faber & Faber, 2008.
74 Martin, *War on its Head*, p. 139.
75 Fergusson, *A Million Bullets*, pp. 223–224.
76 Jean Mackenzie, 'New America Foundation, Counterterrorism Strategy Initiative Policy Paper', *The Battle for Afghanistan, Militancy and Conflict in Helmand*, September 2010, p. 9.
77 Bishop, *3 PARA*, p. 83.
78 To be strictly accurate, Pathfinders had exchanged fire with police, who engaged them on 6 April near Now Zad.
79 Anthony King, 'Understanding the Helmand Campaign: British Military Operations in Afghanistan', *International Affairs*, Vol. 86, No. 2, March 2010.
80 Browne evidence to Defence Select Committee, 29 March 2011.
81 Butler, 'Setting Ourselves up for a Fall in Afghanistan'.
82 Browne evidence to Defence Select Committee, 29 March 2011.
83 Browne statement to the Commons, July 2008.
84 Browne evidence to Defence Select Committee, 29 March 2011.
85 Mike Jackson testimony to Defence Select Committee, 5 May 2011.

86 'John Hutton reiterates the case for the Afghanistan operation', *Defence Policy and News*, 11 November 2008.
87 10 Platoon was relieved.
88 Fergusson, *A Million Bullets*, p. 117.
89 UK MOD, *Military Operations* news article, title lost, 2 August 2006.
90 Fergusson, *A Million Bullets*, p. 148.
91 Ibid, p. 157.
92 Ibid, p. 174.
93 Ibid, p. 126.
94 W. L. Spencer Churchill, *Malakand Field Force 1897*, Longmans Colonial Library, p. 84.
95 Fergusson, *A Million Bullets*, p. 179.
96 Martin, *War on its Head*, p. 165.
97 Ibid, p. 200.
98 UKMOD, *The Infantryman* journal, 'Sangin: A Platoon Commander's Recollections', Lt H. Framer, OC 1 Pl 3 PARA, 2006.
99 Bishop, *3 PARA*, p. 115.
100 Ibid, p. 179.
101 Ibid, p. 211.
102 There was a second incident in 2010 involving two soldiers who became trapped in an alleyway blocked by presumed IEDs. In fact, the two IEDs that had already detonated and severely wounded their colleagues were the only IEDs in the alleyway. Rather than take any further chances, an American helicopter with a winch lifted them to safety.
103 James Matthews, 'Afghanistan veteran looks back on Kajaki Dam tragedy', Sky News, 5 July 2021, https://news.sky.com/story/afghanistan-veteran-looks-back-on-kajaki-dam-tragedy-decisions-are-made-by-people-in-suits-who-have-never-fought-a-battle-12348992.
104 'Troops blown up by Afghan mines sue MOD', *The Daily Telegraph*, 28 February 2007.
105 Fergusson, *A Million Bullets*, p. 353.
106 Bishop, *3 PARA*, p. 155.
107 Tootal, *Danger Close*, p. 197.
108 Bishop, *3 PARA*, p. 229.
109 Fergusson, *A Million Bullets*, p. 322.
110 UK MOD, *Military Operations* news article, title lost, 8 August 2006.
111 Bishop, *3 PARA*, p. 227.
112 UK MOD, *Military Operations* news article, title lost, 12 October 2006.
113 Fergusson, *A Million Bullets*, p. 373.
114 UK MOD, *Military Operations* news article, 'Coming home, 3 Para battlegroup talk about their battle with the Taliban', 12 October 2006.
115 Hansard, HC Deb 26 March 2007, c.1232W.
116 Butler, 'Setting Ourselves up for a Fall in Afghanistan'.
117 MOD UK, *Military Operations* news article, title lost, 12 October 2006.

CHAPTER 4: UNFIX THE FORCE

1 UK MOD, Op BANNER, An Analysis of Military Operations in Northern Ireland, AC 71842, July 2006.
2 See *British Army Review* (BAR), Spring 2011, Anthony King, 'Military Command in the Last Decade', reprint of an article in *International Affairs*, Volume 87, Issue 21, March 2011, for discussion on failings of British command.

3 Mungo Melvin made the remark during a presentation at the Royal United Services Institute (RUSI) in the spring of 2014, which this author attended. The event included a number of presenters speaking on a range of subjects. The backdrop was the Russian operation in Crimea.
4 UK MOD, Operation *Desert Sabre*, The Planning Process and Tactics Employed by 1st Armoured Division, 1993.
5 Alex Danchev, *Alchemist of War: The Life of Basil Liddell Hart*, Weidenfeld & Nicholson, 1996.
6 Ibid, p. 149.
7 UK MOD, *The Infantryman* journal, 2007, 42 COMMANDO ROYAL MARINES: UK BATTLE GROUP OBSERVATIONS ON OP HERRICK 5, Lt Col M J Holmes DSO RM – CO 42 Cdo RM, p. 77.
8 Ibid.
9 Ibid.
10 HERRICK 5 SOPs (Standard Operating Procedures), Chapter 4 Comms, undated and no author attribution.
11 UK MOD, 100604, OP TELIC Lessons Learned, Ch. 2 Inform (ISTAR).
12 Anthony Cordesman, *Afghan National Security Forces: What It Will Take to Implement the ISAF Strategy*, CSIS, September 2010, p. iii.
13 All the deployment details in this paragraph come from Ewen Southby-Tailyour, *3 Commando Brigade*, Random House Group, 2009.
14 Southby-Tailyour, *3 Commando Brigade*, p. 83.
15 Fairweather, *The Good War*, pp. 234–235.
16 See Chapter 3 of Southby-Tailyour, *3 Commando Brigade*, for a full description of the operation.
17 Ibid.
18 Ibid.
19 Ibid, p. 233.
20 UK MOD, *The Infantryman*, 2007, MOBILE OPERATIONS GROUP (MOG) ACTIVITIES, Maj (now Lt Col) E Murchison MBE RM – OC J Coy 42 Cdo RM, p. 90.
21 Southby-Tailyour, *3 Commando Brigade*, p. 104.
22 Martin, *War on its Head*, p. 201.
23 Southby-Tailyour, *3 Commando Brigade*, p. 130.
24 Ibid, pp. 133–141 for a detailed description of this operation.
25 Ibid, pp. 166–172 for a detailed description of this operation.
26 UK MOD, *Military Operations* news article, 'Marine attempt daring Apache rescue during Afghanistan operation', 17 January 2007.
27 Gary E. Langar and ABC Polling Unit, ABC News/BBC/ARD poll 'Where things stand in Afghanistan', 3 December 2007.
28 Environics, '2007 Survey of Afghans', 19 October 2007.
29 Gary E. Langar and ABC Polling Unit, ABC News/BBC/ARD poll 'Where things stand in Afghanistan', 3 December 2007.
30 Ibid.

CHAPTER 5: TAKE THE FIGHT TO THE ENEMY

1 'The Taliban's Spring Offensive', *Janes Terrorism and Security Monitor*, 30 March 2007.
2 According to Grenadier officer Patrick Hennessey, author of *The Junior Officers' Reading Club*, this was not the case. A Ugandan prince apparently once served in the Grenadier Guards

as an officer, although it is not clear whether he held honorary rank or actually fulfilled a meaningful role.

3 1 GG Queen's Company blog, 23 March 2007.

4 *Herrick 6* – 19 Regiment RA CO's blog, 23 July 2007.

5 *Helmand Highlander*, Edition 1, undated.

6 Colonel Richard Kemp and Chris Hughes, *Attack State Red*, Penguin Books Ltd, 2010, p. 206.

7 Ibid, p. 43.

8 Ibid, p. 89.

9 Ibid, p. 97.

10 UK MOD, *Military Operations* news article, 'Baptism of fire for Grenadier Guards officer in Afghanistan', 21 May 2007.

11 *Helmand Highlander*, Edition 3, June 2007.

12 Report of the Secretary General of the UN to the General Assembly on the situation in Afghanistan, A/62/345-S/2007/555, 21 September 2007.

13 UK MOD, *Military Operations* news article, 'UK Brigadier discusses way ahead with Afghan tribal elders', 14 May 2007.

14 DfID factsheet, 'Leading the British Government's fight against world poverty', Afghanistan, April 2007.

15 UK MOD, *The Infantryman* journal, 'A Day in the Life of … Pte E Garner – 1 R Anglian', 2007, p. 103.

16 *Helmand Highlander*, Edition 3, June 2007.

17 UK MOD, *Military Operations* news article, 'Success of Sangin operation allows troops to engage with Afghan locals', 4 June 2007.

18 Peter Dahl Thruelsen, *Implementing the Comprehensive Approach in Helmand – Within the Context of Counterinsurgency, Faculty of Strategy and Military Operations*, Royal Danish Defence College, October 2008, p. 32.

19 Pajhwok Afghan News, 3 October 2012.

20 UK MOD, *Military Operations* news article, 'Royal Engineers take on the difficult task of reconstruction in Helmand', 13 August 2007.

21 'Opium and the Afghan Insurgency', *Janes Terrorism and Security Monitor*, 7 September 2007.

22 UK MOD, *Military Operations* news article, Lorraine McBride, 'Vikings recall being under fire', 4 July 2007.

23 Kemp and Hughes, *Attack State Red*, p. 243.

24 The standard army helmet would be redesigned several times, eventually culminating in the Mk7A that did provide better protection against small-calibre fire.

25 UK MOD, *Military Operations* news article, 'Taliban forced back as UK troops build bridges in Helmand', 22 June 2007.

26 UK MOD, *Military Operations* news article, 'Kajaki "Vikings" are kings of the hill', 16 August 2007.

27 Ibid.

28 A single rocket appears to have fallen short in the course of the war.

29 Op *Herrick* 7, 39 Regt RA blog, undated.

30 UK MOD, *Military Operations* news article, 'Equipment and logistics vital to Afghan mission', 15 June 2007.

31 General Sir Andrew Skeen, *Passing it on – Short talks on tribal fighting on the North-West Frontier of India*, Gale and Polden Ltd, 1932, p. 3.

32 UK MOD, *History and Honour* news article, '184 honoured for courage and professionalism on Operations', 7 March 2008.

33 MOD figures sourced from Op *Herrick 7* post-operational reports. The brigade authored an over-arching report. Subordinate battlegroups as well as combat support arms such as Royal Artillery units also published post-operational reports.
34 Ibid, and all other data in this paragraph.
35 US Central Command Air Forces (CENTAF) Combined Air Operations Centre (CAOC) data, 5 December 2007.
36 CIA, Office of Near Eastern and Asian Analysis and Office of Soviet Analysis, *The Soviet Invasion of Afghanistan: 5 Years Later*, May 1985.
37 Post-operational report data can be conflicting. Some data suggests: Op *Herrick 6*, 1,096 and avg. 40; Op *Herrick 5*, 821 and avg. 30; and Op *Herrick 4*, 537 and avg. 20.
38 British ROE were based on the five principles of the Laws of Armed Conflict (military necessity, distinction, discrimination, proportionality and humanity), as well as the requirement to achieve Positive Identification (PID) of the target. The majority of engagements were conducted as self-defence under JSP 398 Card 'Alpha' rules. Attacks were conducted under ROE 421, 422 and 429A, which effectively authorized a British serviceman to conduct offensive engagements against persons judged to be manifesting intent to commit or actually committing hostile acts. Over the course of the war, Task Force Helmand was involved in tens of thousands of engagements with the enemy. Instances where the ROE may have been bypassed or loosely interpreted remained extremely rare. They almost invariably arose from 'fog of war' situations, rather than wilful bending of the rules. The biggest single challenge – despite the deployment of an array of technologies – was achieving PID.
39 UK MOD, *History and Honour* news article, '184 honoured for courage and professionalism on Operations', 7 March 2008.
40 UK MOD, *History and Honour* news article, 'Afghanistan honours "reflect the actions of all"', 7 March 2008.
41 UK MOD, *History and Honour* news article, 'Royal Anglian officer "humbled" by award', 9 March 2008.
42 UK MOD, *The Infantryman* journal 2007, 'The Infantry on Op Herrick 6', Brig J. G. Lorimer MBE – Comd 12 (Mech) Bde, p. 104.
43 Mark Townsend interview with Brigadier Lorimer, *The Guardian*, 5 August 2007.
44 UK MOD, *Defence Policy and Business* news article, 'Defeating the Taliban tactically at every turn: US and UK Defence Secretaries talk common goals', 11 October 2007.
45 WO2 M. J. Pelling RM, 'A Company Sergeant Major's Notes on Op Herrick 5', BAR 144.
46 Global Dashboard, 'Our Man in Kabul', by Alex Evans, 3 October 2007, https://www.globaldashboard.org/2007/10/03/our-man-in-kabul/.

CHAPTER 6: THE PRIZE IS THE POPULATION

1 Stirrup evidence to Defence Select Committee, 11 May 2011.
2 *As You Like It*, Act 2, Scene 7.
3 Donald J. Mrozek, *Air Power & the Ground War in Vietnam*, an AFA Book, Pergammon-Brassey's, 1989, p. 52.
4 Anthony Cordesman, CSIS, 'Assessing the Afghan-Pakistani Conflict', 3 December 2009, p. 5.
5 Ibid, p. 21.
6 'Opium and the Afghan Insurgency', *Janes Terrorism and Security Monitor*, 12 September 2007.
7 Cordesman, 'Assessing the Afghan-Pakistani Conflict', p. 10.
8 Government Accountability Office (GAO), 'Securing, stabilizing, and reconstructing Afghanistan', Report to Congressional Committees, GAO-07-801SP, May 2007.

9 USCENTCOM Brief and UNA/62/722-2/2008/159, 6 March 2008.
10 Anthony Cordesman, CSIS, 'Assessing the Afghan-Pakistani Conflict', 4th Working Draft, December 3, 2007.
11 Anthony Cordesman, adapted from UNAMA, *Suicide Attacks in Afghanistan, 2001–2007*, 1 September 2007 and Martin Linnet, *Afghanistan Index*, October 2007, & UNA/62/722-S/2008/159, 6 March 2008.
12 UN JCMB (the Joint Coordinating and Monitoring Board) Secretariat Report, 3 October 2007.
13 Quoted by Mark Waldeman, *Golden Surrender?*, Afghanistan Analysts Network, p. 4.
14 1 Coldstream Guards Op *Herrick* 7 blog.
15 Ibid.
16 Ibid.
17 'Scorpion Reconnaissance Vehicle', *Janes Armour and Artillery*,.
18 Peter Viggo Jakobsen and Peter Dahl Thruelsen, *Clear, Hold, Train: Denmark's Military Operations in Helmand 2006–2010*, Danish Foreign Policy Yearbook 2011.
19 UK MOD, *Equipment and Logistics* news article, 'RAF Reaper fires weapons for first time', 6 June 2008.
20 UK MOD, COIN in Helmand, Task Force Operational Design, 30 October 2007.
21 Ibid.
22 UK MOD, Commander British Forces Op HERRICK 7, COUNTERINSURGENCY IN HELMAND TASK FORCE OPERATIONAL DESIGN, TFH/ COMD/DO 7, 1 January 2008, p. 5.
23 UK MOD, COIN in Helmand, Task Force Operational Design, 30 October 2007.
24 Andrew Mackay and Steve Tatham, *Behavioural Conflict, From General to Strategic Corporal: Complexity, Adaptation and Influence*, The Shrivenham Papers, No. 9, December 2009.
25 UK MOD, Commander British Forces Op HERRICK 7, COUNTERINSURGENCY IN HELMAND TASK FORCE OPERATIONAL DESIGN, TFH/ COMD/DO 7, 1 January 2008, p. 6.
26 Mackay and Tatham, *Behavioural Conflict*.
27 Ibid.
28 Ibid.
29 Number 3 Company blog, 1 Coldstream Guards, Op *Herrick* 7.
30 1 Coldstream Guards, Op *Herrick* 7 blog.
31 Number 3 Company blog, 1 Coldstream Guards, Op *Herrick* 7.
32 Ibid.
33 UK MOD figures from Joint Doctrine Note (JDN) 2/08.
34 UK MOD figures from operational reporting and all other data in this paragraph .
35 Martin, *War on its Head*, p. 209.
36 Retired Major General Andrew Mackay, 'The Art of Influence: How the Taliban were driven from a strategic Afghan town', BBC News, 17 Sep 2015, www.bbc.co.uk/news/resources/idt-ff9a9c01-faa4-4038-b4e9-83e619460e1f.
37 Stephen Grey, *Operation Snakebite*, Penguin Books UK, 2009 (reprinted as *Into the Viper's Nest, Task Force 1 Fury and the Battle for Musa Qaleh*, MBI Publishing Company LLB and Zenith Press, 2010), p. 102.
38 Ibid, p. 122.
39 Ibid, p. 124.
40 See Chapter 18 of Grey, *Operation Snakebite*.
41 Ibid, pp.147–148.

42 See Chapter 19 of Grey, *Operation Snakebite.*
43 Ibid, p. 152.
44 Ibid, pp. 174–177.
45 Ibid, p. 193.
46 Ibid, pp. 194–201.
47 See Chapter 24 of Grey, *Operation Snakebite.*
48 Ibid, p. 273.
49 UK MOD, Commander British Forces Op HERRICK 7, COUNTERINSURGENCY IN HELMAND TASK FORCE OPERATIONAL DESIGN, TFH/ COMD/DO 7, 1 January 2008, p. 2.
50 UK MOD, *Equipment and Logistics* news article, 'Final Posting Dates to Theatre', 1 December 2008.
51 1 Coldstream Guards, Op *Herrick* 7 blog.
52 Grey, *Operation Snakebite*, p. 82.
53 Ibid.
54 B Company, 1 RGR blog, Op *Herrick* 7.
55 Ibid.
56 QM blog, 1 RGR, Op *Herrick* 7.
57 Carl Forsberg, Institute for the Study of War, *The Taliban's Campaign for Kandahar*, 2009, p. 23.
58 A Company blog, 1 RGR, Op *Herrick* 7.
59 UK MOD, *History and Honour* news article, 'Gurkhas honoured by Queen for bravery in Afghanistan', 5 November 2008.
60 See Mackay and Tatham, *Behavioural Conflict.*
61 The detailed and highly useful 125-page *Operation HERRICK 7: October 2007 – April 2008 'Counterinsurgency in Helmand – Company Level Tactics – March 2008'*. This would be the first of a stream of publications as successive task forces built on the knowledge and experiences of predecessor brigades.

CHAPTER 7: FIXED AGAIN

1 23 Engineer Regiment (Air Assault) Newsletter, 17 March 2008.
2 BAR 144, originally from an article in *Prospect* in which Rory Stewart and Sherard-Cowper Coles exchanged views on Afghanistan in the form of letters.
3 *Afghanistan Study Group Report*, 'Revitalizing our efforts, Rethinking our strategy', Gen James L. Jones USMC (Retd) and Ambassador Thomas R. Pickering, 30 January 2008.
4 Anthony Cordesman, CSIS, *The Ongoing Lessons of the Afghan and Iraq Wars*, April 11, 2008, pp. 3–5.
5 On the record discussions with General McNeill and farewell briefing at the Pentagon, 13 June 2008.
6 Sam Kiley, *Desperate Glory At War in Helmand with Britain's 16 Air Assault Brigade*, Bloomsbury Publishing, 2009, p. 7.
7 Anthony Cordesman, *Ongoing Lessons of the Afghan Conflict*, 6 May 2004, p. 8.
8 Patrick Bishop, *Ground Truth*, Harper Press 2009, pp. 18–19.
9 Ibid.
10 UK MOD, AC 71876, Army Doctrine Publication, *Countering Insurgency – A Guide for Commanders*, March 2008.
11 *ISAF Mirror*, July 2008.
12 Ibid.

13 1 R Irish blog, Op *Herrick 8.*
14 Lt Peter Gavin blog, 1 R Irish, Op *Herrick 8.*
15 Cpl Walden, 4 Platoon, B Company, 2 PARA blog, Op *Herrick 8.*
16 Pte Adams, 5 Platoon, B Company, 2 PARA blog, Op *Herrick 8.*
17 D Company, 2 PARA blog, updated 27 June 2008.
18 5 SCOTS blog, Operation *Herrick 8.*
19 Rupert Pengelly, 'Infantry look to C4I aids for tempo without torment', *Janes Intelligence Defence Review* (JIDR), 9 July 2009.
20 UK MOD, *Equipment and Logistics* article, 'Bullet magnet praises body armour for twice saving life', 6 January 2011.
21 'Donkeys led by Lions', BAR 150, Summer 2008.
22 16 Air Assault Brigade Briefing Day, 3 December 2008.
23 2 PARA blog, Private Smith 23 from Nottingham, B Company, 4 Platoon, undated.
24 2 PARA blog, Private Goodall 24 from Northampton, B Company, 4 Platoon, undated.
25 D Company, 2 PARA blog, Op *Herrick 8.*
26 Pte Smith, 4 Platoon, B Company, 2 PARA blog, Op *Herrick 8.*
27 Kiley, *Desperate Glory*, p. 179.
28 General Sir Andrew Skeen, *Passing it on – Short talks on tribal fighting on the North-West Frontier of India*, Gale and Polden Ltd, 1932, p. 11.
29 He was killed on 27 June 2010 near CP Kings Hill in Nahr-e Saraj.
30 Helmand Province, Westminster Hall debates, 17 June 2008.
31 Mrozek, *Air Power & the Ground War in Vietnam*, p. 123.
32 See Chapter 1 of Kiley, *Desperate Glory*.
33 See CRS Report for Congress, *NATO in Afghanistan: A Test of the Transatlantic Alliance*, 23 October 2008.
34 *The Times*, 26 November 2008.
35 UK MOD, *Defence Policy and Business* news article, 12 March 2008.
36 This was the reported NACMO cost (Net Additional Costs of Military Operations) by the UK MOD.
37 'BAE Systems ramps up ammo production', *Janes Defence Weekly* (JDW), 25 September 2009.
38 See Chapter 7 of Kiley, *Desperate Glory*.
39 Ibid.
40 Kiley, *Desperate Glory*, p. 182.
41 Guenter Lewy, *America in Vietnam*, Oxford University Press, 1980, p. 118.
42 See Michael Yon's account of Operation *Oqab Tsuka*: Where Eagles Dare, 6 September 2008, https://michaelyon.com/dispatches/where-eagles-dare/ and Correction and update: Where Eagles Dare, 9 Sep 2008, https://michaelyon.com/dispatches/correction-and-update-where-eagles-dare/. Yon published some of the most forthright and valuable front-line reporting of the war.
43 Ibid.
44 23 Engineer Regiment (Air Assault) Newsletter, Op *Herrick 8*, undated.
45 See Chapter 4 of Kiley, *Desperate Glory*.
46 16 AA Bde HERRICK 8 Post Operational Overview, December 2008.
47 Loose Minute: OpIss4R Summary – 16 AA Bde – HERRICK 8 Briefing day, 3 December 2008.
48 Aid to Helmand as a proportion of spent funds may have been higher (10–15 per cent) as there was a difference between pledged money and spent money. Over FY 2006–07, for example, DfID spend in Helmand was 16 per cent of total UK spend in Afghanistan.

49 UK MOD, 16 AIR ASSLT BDE 03 DEC 08 COLLECTIVE DEBRIEF- INTERVIEW KEY POINT SUMMARY (as at 29 Jan 09), ANNEX A TO 3073/L2/WARDEV/LWC DATED 03 MAR 09.
50 Christina Lamb, 'Grim reality of life beyond Helmand, British officials are pleased with their reconstruction. Our correspondent finds little for them to crow about', *The Times*, 5 October 2008.
51 Bishop, *Ground Truth*, p. 221.
52 Westminster Hall debates, 17 June 2008, quoted by Mark Lancaster, Shadow Minister for International Development.
53 House of Commons International Development Committee, *Reconstructing Afghanistan: Government Response to the Committee's Fourth Report of Session 2007–08*, 24 April 2008.
54 Mark Waldeman, *Golden Surrenders?*, Afghan Analysis Network, p. 6.
55 Channel 4 News, 'Afghan casualties: number of UK payouts "treble"', updated on 24 June 2010.
56 The remark was made by the commanding officer of 4 Rifles.
57 Kevin J. Kelley, *The Longest War, Northern Ireland and the I.R.A.*, Zed Books Ltd, 1990, p. 153.
58 UK MOD, *Equipment and Logistics* news article, 'Getting the right kit to the right place and on time', 12 August 2008.
59 Lt Alison Macdonald, JDCC blog, Op *Herrick 8*.
60 Anthony Cordesman, Adam Mausner and David Kasten, CSIS, *Winning in Afghanistan, Creating Effective Afghan Security Forces*, May 2009, p. 7.
61 Defence Select Committee, Oral evidence: 'Decision-making in Defence Policy', HC 682, 16 December 2014, p. 11.
62 Quoted by Adam Holloway MP in the Westminster Hall debates, 17 June 2008.
63 Ibid.
64 UNODC data.
65 16 Air Assault Brigade Briefing Day, 3 December 2008.
66 UK MOD, *History and Honour* news article, 'Operational Honours and Awards List', 6 March 2009.
67 Ibid.

CHAPTER 8: SERVING IN HELL-LAND

1 19 Regt RA blog, Op *Herrick 7*.
2 23 Engineer Regiment (Air Assault) Newsletter, 25 March 2008.
3 'RAF Tristar stands idle as contract wrangle continues', *Janes Defence Weekly*, 7 June 2011.
4 National Audit Office (NAO), Support to High Intensity Operations, REPORT BY THE COMPTROLLER AND AUDITOR GENERAL | HC 508 Session 2008-2009 | 14 May 2009, p. 28.
5 UK MOD, *Equipment and Logistics* news article, 'Supplying troops in Helmand with water', 27 January 2011.
6 Malcolm Chalmers, Joel Rogers de Waal, Professor Michael Clarke and Trevor Taylor, 'Wars in Peace, British Military Operations since 1991', RUSI, 26 March 2014, p. 312.
7 UK MOD, *Estate and Environment* news article, 'Camp Bastion – the fifth busiest UK airport', 24 August 2009.
8 UK MOD, *Estate and Environment* news article, 'New control tower for Bastion', 8 June 2011.
9 28 Engineer Regiment Newsletter, 22 September 2009.
10 23 Engineer Regiment (Air Assault) Newsletter, 25 March 2008.
11 A Company, 1 Rifles blog, Op *Herrick 14*.

12 2 Platoon, 5 SCOTS blog, Op *Herrick 13*.
13 B Company, 2 PARA blog, Op *Herrick 13*.
14 Craig Douglas, *Fire Mission, The Uncensored Truth*, e-book, 2013, diary entry 15 October 2007.
15 D Company, 2 PARA blog, Op *Herrick 8*.
16 23 Engineer Regiment (Air Assault) Newsletter, Edition 7, Op *Herrick 13*.
17 Ibid, Edition 6.
18 38 Engineer Regiment Newsletter, Edition 3, Op *Herrick 10*.
19 Number 3 Company, 1 Coldstream Guards blog, Op *Herrick 7*.
20 Michael Yon, 'British Operations in Afghanistan', 13 September 2008, www.michaelyon-online.com.
21 UK MOD, *Equipment and Logistics* news article, 'New ration packs provide variety for troops', 10 February 2010.
22 1 Royal Irish blog, Op *Herrick 8*.
23 *The Ripon Sapper*, Edition 5, Operation *Herrick 12*.
24 UK MOD, *Equipment and Logistics* article, 'Bastion forces keep forces fed in Helmand', 20 April 2011.
25 UK MOD, *Military Operations* news article, 'Royal Marines chefs feed the front line', 20 June 2011.
26 A Company, 1 R Irish blog, Op *Herrick 13*.
27 2 Rifles blog, OC B Company, May 2009.
28 38 Engineer Regiment Newsletter, Edition 5, Op *Herrick 10*.
29 *Akhbar*, 3rd Battalion of the Yorkshire Regiment Newsletter 4, June 2012.
30 *Pathans: Handbook of the Indian Army*, The Recruiting Office Peshawar, 1936.
31 UK MOD, *The Infantryman*, 2008–09.
32 5 Bty update, Sergeant Dave Cooper, 19 RA Regiment blog, 5 June 2007.
33 1 R Irish Blog, Maj Vance Crow, Op *Herrick 8*.
34 UK MOD, *Military Operations* news article, 'The vital role of interpreters in Helmand', 3 June 2011.
35 Ben Andersen, *No Worse Enemy: The inside story of the chaotic struggle for Afghanistan*, Oneworld Publications, 2012.
36 1 R Irish Blog, Maj Vance Crow, Op *Herrick 8*.
37 UK MOD, Op *Herrick 10*, Tactical COIN vignettes – Key Leader Engagement, 10 November 2009.
38 *Akhbar*, 3rd Battalion of the Yorkshire Regiment Newsletter 3, June 2012.
39 *The Duchess of Malfi*, Act 1, Scene 1, Bosola.
40 UK MOD, *History and Honour* news article, 'Soldier who saved Afghan child's life and receives bravery award', 9 October 2012.
41 UK MOD, *People in Defence* article, 'Living through survivor guilt', 10 October 2012.
42 Joanna Bourke, *An Intimate History of Killing*, Granta Books, 1999.
43 Terri Judd, *The Independent Magazine*, feature on Camp Bastion field hospital, 3 October 2009.
44 MOD *Military Operations* news article, reference lost.
45 Michael Yon, 'Dispatches, Pedros', 13 September 2009, https://michaelyon.com/dispatches/pedros/.
46 23 Air Assault Medical Squadron blog, Op *Herrick 8*.
47 3 Medical Regiment, Op *Herrick 12*.
48 From the BBC Radio 4 *Today* series of 21 battlefield vignettes.
49 'God's Squad', *Soldier, October* 2008.
50 UK MOD, *The Infantryman*, 2008–09.

51 23 Engineer Regiment (Air Assault) Newsletter, 10 August 2008.
52 First published in a MOD *Defence News* article, reference lost.
53 The anonymous poem 'Afghanistan (with apologies to Kipling)' was posted on: http://laurenofarabia.blogspot.com/2010_05_01_archive.html.
54 Patrick Hennessey, *The Junior Officers' Reading Club: Killing Time and Fighting Wars*, Penguin Books, 2009.
55 Robert Wilson, *Helmand: Faces of Conflict*, Jonathan Cape, 2008.
56 UK MOD, *Defence News* article, reference lost.
57 See *The Times*, 1 December 2009 for a review.
58 Ibid, and all other quotes in this paragraph.
59 *The Times*, 18 October 2014.
60 40 Commando blog, Op *Herrick 12*.
61 LWX Newsletter, Directorate of Land Warfare, Land Warfare Centre, April 2012.
62 All data in this paragraph from UK MOD figures.
63 Including one British officer.
64 UK MOD news article, title and date lost, Operation *Herrick 10*.

CHAPTER 9: THE COMMANDOS RETURN

1 Lt Col Neil Wilson, 29 Commando Royal Artillery, 25 November 2008.
2 Richards, *Taking Command*, p. 287.
3 Christopher L. Elliott, *High Command, British Military Leadership in the Iraq and Afghanistan Wars*, C. Hurst & Co. Ltd, 2015.
4 Martin, *War on its Head*, p. 219.
5 See Southby-Tailyour, *Helmand Assault*, p. 67.
6 Ibid, for a fuller account of the orbats and numbers.
7 Ibid p. 199.
8 UK MOD, *Military Operations* news article, 'Supplying Helmand's Front Line', 8 November 2009.
9 National Audit Office, Support to High Intensity Operations. REPORT BY THE COMPTROLLER AND AUDITOR GENERAL | HC 508 Session 2008-2009 | 14 May 2009, p. 20.
10 2 RGR Newsletter, Op *Herrick 9*.
11 Ibid.
12 Ibid.
13 *The Times*, 3 April 2011.
14 2 RGR Newsletter, Op *Herrick 9*.
15 Southby-Tailyour, *Helmand Assault*, p. 158.
16 Kim Sengupta, 'Troops seize £50m of Afghan Opium', *The Independent*, 18 February 2009, and UK MOD *Military Operations* news article, 'Helicopter-borne troops strike at Taliban's drug industry', 18 February 2009.
17 Martin, *War on its Head*, p. 114.
18 Southby-Tailyour, *Helmand Assault*, p. 37.
19 Ibid, p. 105 and remainder of chapter.
20 UK MOD, *Military Operations* news article on Op *Sond Chara*.
21 Ibid.
22 Martin, *War on its Head*, pp. 221–223.
23 Ibid.

24 Ibid, p. 224.
25 See Southby-Tailyour, *Helmand Assault*, Chapter 4, for a detailed description of the battle.
26 UK MOD, *Military Operations* news article, 'IN PICTURES: Op *Red Dagger* strikes in Helmand', 5 January 2009.
27 Ibid.
28 Ibid.
29 Martin, *War on its Head*, p. 225.
30 Southby-Tailyour, *Helmand Assault*, p. 145.
31 Ibid.
32 UK MOD, *History and Honour* news article, 'George Cross presented to Royal marine Reservist', 30 October 2008.
33 UK MOD, *Military Operations* news article, 'IN PICTURES: Marines take on Taliban in the Fish Hook', 20 March 2009.
34 See Southby-Tailyour, *Helmand Assault*, Chapter 6, for a detailed description of this action.
35 Anthony Cordesman, CSIS, *Armed Nation Building: The Real Challenge in Afghanistan*, November 2007, p. 13.
36 Southby-Tailyour, *Helmand Assault*, p. 249.
37 Ibid, p. 247.
38 38 Engineer Regiment Joint Force Engineer Group, Newsletter, Edition 3, 20 April 2009, *Herrick 10*, Op ABBI TORA 2C – Spr Jay McIntosh.
39 Southby-Tailyour, *Helmand Assault*, p. 254.
40 1 Rifles BG, Op *Herrick 9*.
41 Defence Intelligence and Security School Ashford, Intelligence in Revolutionary Warfare, author's 'Student Notes', 1981.
42 The rough expenditures were: Op *H4* $500,000, Op *H5* $1.8 million, Op *H6* $2 million, Op *H7* $3 million, Op *H8* $4.5 million, Op *H9* $8 million (UK MOD).
43 24 Commando Engineer blog, Op *Herrick 9*.
44 Jake Sherman and Victoria Di Domenico, Centre on International Cooperation, *The Public Cost of Private Security in Afghanistan*, September 2009.
45 Ibid.
46 Ibid.
47 Ibid.

CHAPTER 10: CRISIS YEAR

1 *The Economist*, 29 January 2009.
2 US DOD, *Army* magazine, 'Afghanistan: America's Main Effort Redux', March 2009.
3 ABC/BBC/ARD Poll 5 February 2009.
4 United States Air Forces Central Command (AFCENT), Combined Air Operations Command, (CAOC) Airpower Summary, Combined Forces Air Component Commander statistics; NEWS RELEASE U.S. Air Forces Central Command Public Affairs, February 5, 2012 Release Number 01-02-12, https://www.afcent.af.mil/Portals/82/Documents/Airpower%20summary/AFD-120208-021.pdf.
5 Anthony Cordesman, *The Afghan-Pakistan War: The Air War*, 12 August 2009.
6 AFCENT data, op cit.
7 Chatham House, 17 September 2009.
8 Initial United States Forces – Afghanistan (USFOR-A) Assessment, 30 August 2009.
9 Pentagon Papers, Part IV-B-3, p. 12.

10 Henry Kissinger, *White House Years*, Volume I, Weidenfeld and Nicolson, 1979, p. 498.

11 ISAF Partnering Directive 29 August 2009.

12 Center on International Cooperation, Jake Sherman and Victoria Di Domenico, *The Private Cost of Public Security in Afghanistan*, September 2009.

13 See *The Long War Journal*: www.longwarjournal.org/archives/2009/07/us_predator_strikes.3php.

14 UK MOD, 19 Bde C-IED Study Day PowerPoint, Land Warfare Centre, undated and no author attribution.

15 2 Rifles blog, Op *Herrick 10*.

16 Black Watch, *Aviation Assault Battlegroup: The 2009 Afghanistan tour of the Black Watch 3rd Battalion the Royal Regiment of Scotland*, Pen and Sword Military, 2011, p. 16.

17 Toby Harnden, *Dead Men Risen*, Quercus, 2011, p. 30.

18 A Company blog, 2 Mercians, Op *Herrick 10*.

19 Defence Secretary Ainsworth interview with the *Daily Telegraph* newspaper, July 2009.

20 See Harnden, *Dead Men Risen* for a detailed description of this operation.

21 Army Field Manual (AFM) Intelligence, Surveillance, Target Acquisition and Reconnaissance (ISTAR) V6, Annex A to Chapter 1.

22 Jon Boone, 'Battle of Babaji – a battle for hearts and minds, but none to be found', *The Guardian*, 25 July 2009.

23 Black Watch, *Aviation Assault Battlegroup*, p. 139.

24 Ibid.

25 Ibid.

26 Black Watch blog, Op *Herrick 10*, 6 July 2009.

27 Boone, 'Battle of Babaji – a battle for hearts and minds, but none to be found'.

28 UK MOD, *The Infantryman*, 2010.

29 Black Watch blog, Op *Herrick 10*, 6 July 2009.

30 Ibid.

31 Black Watch, *Aviation Assault Battlegroup*, p. 145.

32 Terri Judd, *The Independent Magazine*, feature on Camp Bastion hospital, 3 October 2009.

33 Ibid.

34 Pavel Grachev, quoted in *The Independent*, 12 July 2009.

35 38 Engineer Regiment Newsletter, Edition 11, Op *Herrick 10*.

36 *The Times* obituaries, 17 April 2014.

37 UK MOD, *History and Honour* news article, 'Mercian soldiers receive gallantry awards', 12 July 2010.

38 Ibid.

39 Harnden, *Dead Men Risen*, 2011, p. 524.

40 MOD figures via Defence Analytical Services Agency (DASA).

41 'Home-made Horror', *Janes Terrorism and Security Monitor*, 7 September 2009.

42 Ibid.

43 UK MOD, *The Infantryman*, 'Behind the Headlines: What is it like to fight in Afghanistan?' A series of vignettes on the BBC Radio 4 *Today* programme, Winter 2009/10, Maj R. G. Streatfield MBE – OC A Coy, 4 Rifles, at 3 Rifles BG, 2011.

44 UK MOD, RAPID OLAAAR1 DEDUCTIONS/LESSONS OP HERRICK 13 – April 2011, LXC 4_3_14_1, 19 April 2011.

45 Ibid.

46 UK MOD, *Military Operations* news article, 'Armoured thrust clears final Taliban from "Panther"'s Claw', 27 July 2009.

47 *The Times*, 19 August 2009.
48 Ibid.
49 *The Times*, 21 August 2009.
50 Harnden, *Dead Men Risen*, p. 490.
51 Michael Yon, *New York Daily News*, 6 September 2009.
52 UK MOD, *The Infantryman*, 2010.
53 CO 2 Rifles blog, Op *Herrick 10*.
54 Michael Yon, *New York Daily News*, 6 September 2009.
55 Ibid.
56 Michael Yon, 'Precision Voting', 31 August 2009, https://michaelyon.com/dispatches/precision-voting/.
57 'On the frontline with 2 Rifles', 25 August 2009, www.defenceviewpoints.co.uk/military-operations/on-the-front-line-with-2-rifles.
58 2 Rifles blog, Op *Herrick 10*.
59 Michael Yon, 'On the frontline with 2 Rifles', 25 August 2009, www.defenceviewpoints.co.uk/military-operations/on-the-front-line-with-2-rifles.
60 2 Rifles blog, OC B Company, Op *Herrick 10*, June 2009.
61 Harnden, *Dead Men Risen*, 2011, p. 501.
62 C Coy, Op *Herrick 10*, CONTACT IED IVO FOB GIB ON 12/06/09 WHICH RESULTED IN 1x UK KIA.
63 *The Sunday Times*, 16 November 2014.
64 Margaret Evison, *Death of a Soldier*, Biteback Publishing, 2012, p. 231.
65 *Land Warfare International*, January 2011.
66 Black Watch, *Aviation Assault Battlegroup*, p. 30.
67 Ibid, p. 43.
68 Ibid, p. 89.
69 UK MOD, *Military Operations* news article, 'Black Watch smash Taliban drugs factory', 8 June 2009.
70 Black Watch, *Aviation Assault Battlegroup*, p. 110.
71 Ibid, p. 125.
72 A (Grenadier) Company blog, 1 Black Watch, Op *Herrick 10*.
73 UK MOD, Lessons Update AFG – July 2008.
74 Harnden, *Dead Men Risen*, p. 538.
75 Ibid, p. 542.
76 UK MOD, *The Infantryman*, 2010.
77 UK MOD, *Military Operations* news article, 'Logistics Ops fuel the fight against the Taliban', 31 December 2009.
78 Michael Yon, *New York Daily News*, 6 September 2009.
79 Christina Lamb, 'Grim Reality of life beyond Helmand', *The Sunday Times*, 5 October 2008.
80 DfID's Helmand Agriculture and Rural Development Programme (HARDP) for 2006–09 broke down as: $12.5 million for the National Rural Access Programme, $3.1 million for the Rural Water Supply and Sanitation Programme, $3.1 million for the Microfinance Support Facility and $15.6 million for the National Solidarity Programme.
81 Anthony Loyd, 'Weary troops are fighting a losing battle, not a lost cause', *The Times*, 23 September 2009.
82 UK MOD, TACTICAL COIN VIGNETTES – OP HERRICK 11, LXC/Vignettes/ Apr 10 20 May 10, Op Vignette 8: THE CHALLENGES OF Company COMMAND IN A COIN ENVIRONMENT.

CHAPTER 11: ALL CHANGE

1 UK MOD, *Soldier* Magazine, October 2009.
2 UK MOD, *Defence Policy and Business* news article, 'First Afghan Police Graduate from Helmand Training Centre', 29 January 2010.
3 1 RGR (1), 3 Para (Nil), 42 Commando (3), the 3 SCOTS (4).
4 *The Times*, 18 January 2014.
5 See Brett Van Ess, 'The Fight for Marjah: Recent Counterinsurgency Operations in Southern Afghanistan', *The Small Wars Journal* and Institute of War, 30 September 2010, for a detailed description of the USMC operation in Marjah and its aftermath.
6 HCR blog, Op *Herrick 11*.
7 1 Grenadier Guards blog, Op *Herrick 10*.
8 UK MOD, *The Infantryman*, 2011.
9 Ibid.
10 Martin, *War on its Head*, p. 232.
11 1 Coldstream Guards blog, Op *Herrick 11*.
12 3 Rifles blog, Op *Herrick 11*.
13 UK MOD, *Military Operations* news article, '3 RIFLES CO "People Power is Coming to Sangin"', 1 April 2010 and 3 Rifles blog, Op *Herrick 11*.
14 UK MOD, 'The Story of 3 Rifles Battlegroup, Operation *Herrick 11*, Oct 09 – Apr 10'.
15 *The Sunday Times*, 23 March 2014.
16 UK MOD, 'The Story of 3 Rifles Battlegroup, Operation *Herrick 11*, Oct 09 – Apr 10'.
17 Michael Yon, *New York Daily News*, 6 September 2009.
18 UK MOD, *Military Operations* news article, reference lost.
19 The Inkerman Company blog, Grenadier Guards, Op *Herrick 11*.
20 Theo Farrell, *Appraising Moshtarak: The Campaign in Nad-e Ali District, Helmand*, Royal United Services Institute (RUSI).
21 Ibid, p. 4.
22 UK MOD, *Military Operations* news article, 'Commander of Task Force Helmand – 'We're winning but it's not over yet', 25 March 2010.
23 28 Regiment Royal Engineers Newsletter, Op *Herrick 12*.
24 3 Medical Regiment (Close Support Medical Regiment), Op *Herrick 12*.
25 Ibid.
26 28 Regiment Royal Engineers Newsletter, Op *Herrick 12*.
27 'UK makes the most of GMLRS in Afghanistan', *Janes International Defence Review*, 10 November 2009.
28 USGS, 'Encounters of Aircraft with Volcanic Ash Clouds: A Compilation of Known Incidents, 1953–2009', 2010.
29 Fairweather, *The Good War*, p. 355.
30 Thomas Harding, 'In Sangin, most dangerous Afghan district, British troops fear war will last 10 years', *Daily Telegraph*, 3 July 2010, www.telegraph.co.uk/news/worldnews/asia/afghanistan/7870537/In-Sangin-most-dangerous-Afghan-district-British-troops-fear-war-will-last-10-years.html.
31 *The Guardian*, 17 November 2010.
32 Ibid.
33 Ibid.
34 BAR 144, originally from *Prospect*.
35 The Open Society Foundations Regional Policy Initiative on Afghanistan and Pakistan, *The Cost of Kill/Capture: Impact of the Night Raid Surge on Afghan Civilians*, 19 September 2011, p. 2.

36 1 Lancs blog, Op *Herrick 12*.

37 Spoken to Duncan Larcombe, the *Sun*, the reference and date are lost.

38 Duncan Larcombe, 'Heroes in the heat of battle', 3 July 2010, http://helmandblog.blogspot.com/2010/07/heroes-in-heat-of-battle.html.

39 UK MOD, *The Infantryman*, 2011.

40 This is a relative judgement, as the battlegroup suffered over 150 casualties from battle and non-battle causes. Fatalities, however, remained very low.

41 *The Times*, 25 March 2011.

42 National Audit Office (NAO), Support to High Intensity Operations, REPORT BY THE COMPTROLLER AND AUDITOR GENERAL | HC 508 Session 2008-2009 | 14 May 2009, p. 7.

43 Jerome Starkey, 'Bank woes worsen as owners are accused of lending to themselves', *The Times*, 6 September 2010.

44 Miles Amoore, 'Executives took £600m from Kabul bank set up for fraud', *The Times*, 13 November 2011.

45 Independent Joint Anti-Corruption Monitoring and Evaluation Committee, *Report of the Public Inquiry into the Kabul Bank Crisis*, 15 November 2012.

46 *The Times*, 25 May 2011.

47 House of Commons International Development Committee, 'Reconstructing Afghanistan: Government Response to the Committee's Fourth Report of Session 2007–08', Third Special Report of Session 2007–08.

48 Around 8 per cent or £46 million had been recovered by late November 2011. By 2012, a reported $128.3 million in cash had been recovered, as well as assets worth around $100 million. At the time of withdrawal at the end of 2014, it was reported that $150 million in cash assets had been recovered.

49 Eventually, 21 convictions were reportedly secured, *The Times*, 1 October 2014.

50 Public Accounts Committee 52nd Report, 19 October 2011.

51 Martin, *War on its Head*, p. 254.

52 UNODC, *Afghanistan Opium Survey*, September 2010.

53 Figures from FCO website – UK Afghan Drugs Interdepartmental Unit.

54 Special Inspector General for Afghanistan Reconstruction (SIGAR), Quarterly Report, July 2010, p. 109.

55 MOD figures: 32 contacts per day and 5,372 SIGACTs.

56 MOD figures: 421 WIA.

57 MOD figures: 478 EKIA, 233 EWIA, 8 CIVCAS.

58 A high figure of 285 CIVCAS was reported but it is unclear whether this encompassed all CIVCAS incidents across south-west Afghanistan. Such a figure would more closely tally with CIVCAS statistics offered by organisations like the UN.

CHAPTER 12: DOING THE HARD YARDS (SUCCESSFULLY)

1 Lashkar Gah 140,000, Babaji 36,000, Chah-e Anjir 14,000, Nad-e Ali 60,000.

2 UK MOD, 'Operation HERRICK Capability Overview', PowerPoint presentation, October 2010.

3 To give a sense of numbers, by Operation *Herrick 12*, over 17,000 profiles had been collected, creating around 100 matches to IEDs, and suggesting between 20 and 40 teams.

4 Alex Strick van Linschoten and Felix Kuehn, *A Knock on the Door: 22 Months of ISAF Press Releases*, Afghanistan Analysis Network, 2011.

5 Ibid.

6 Allen Testimony, Senate Armed Services Committee, 22 March 2012.
7 UK MOD, 20130618-4X-MXS-_TFH_Presentation-v3-RO3_G35.
8 Unclassified presentation: 'A Regional Commander's Perspective on the Campaign in Afghanistan', Major General Nick Carter, recently COM RC (South).
9 *The Times*, 31 December 2014.
10 The approach would be summarized in a PowerPoint 'CF [Combined Force] Targeting' dated January 2012 authored by the SO1 Jt Fires CSTTG. The 'best practice' was taken from 3 PARA in *H13* and 1 Rifles in *H14*.
11 UK MOD, *Combat* 2012 journal, E-Supplement, 'Tactical Lessons in Battlegroup Targeting', Maj C. Hitchins-OC ISTAR Coy, 3 PARA, p. 18.
12 Ibid.
13 UK MOD, PowerPoint, 'COIN Targeting', no date and no author attribution but known to be from the period *H13–H14*.
14 Sergeant Andrew Coull RAF, 2 PARA, Op *Herrick 13*.
15 1 R Irish blog, Op *Herrick 13*.
16 Ibid.
17 Speech to Chatham House, 13 July 2010.
18 *The Independent*, 20 November 2010.
19 UK MOD, *Military Operations* news article, 'Helping Afghans build their future', 25 January 2011.
20 Captain John Bethell, 'Accidental Counterinsurgents: Nad-e Ali, Hybrid War and the Future of the British Army', *British Army Review* (BAR) 149, Summer 2010.
21 President Obama, Afghanistan–Pakistan annual review: www.whitehouse.gov/the-press-office/2010/12/16/statement-president-afghanistan-pakistan-annual-review.
22 UK MOD figures.
23 Colonel Robin Jackson, PowerPoint presentation: 'Medical lessons learned from H13'.
24 UK MOD figures and all other data in this paragraph.
25 DfID: $38 million, Denmark: $15 million; Estonia: $0.5 million.
26 Browne evidence to Defence Select Committee, 29 March 2011.
27 UK MOD, *Combat* journal, 'People First, Insurgent Second', Brig E. G. M. Davis OBE – Comd 3 Cdo Bde and Comd TFH, 2012, p. 74.
28 UK MOD, *Combat* journal, 'Task Force Helmand Information Exploitation Group', Lt Col M. Stovin-Bradford RM – CO 30 Cdo IX Gp, 2012, p. 78.
29 Ibid.
30 UK MOD, *Combat* journal 'Taking a Stand, Forming the Afghan Local Police in Nad-e Ali', SO3 Afghan Local Police Combined Force Nad-e Ali (South), 2013, p. 26.
31 Seth A. Shreckengast, *The Only Game in Town: Assessing the Effectiveness of Village Stability Operations and the Afghan Local Police*, 27 March 2012.
32 Martin, *War on its Head*, pp. 256–257.
33 See Citha D. Maass, *Afghanistan's Drug Career*, Afghan Analysts Network, March 2011.
34 *The Sunday Times*, 8 May 2011, gave bin Laden's address as House No. 3, Streret No. 8-A, Garga Road, Thanda Chowa, Hashmi Colony, Abbottabad.
35 The aborted raid to rescue the Iranian Embassy hostages on 24–25 April 1980.
36 Four helicopters were involved, Razor 1 and 2 carrying the assault teams in Black Hawk stealth helicopters, and two Chinooks.
37 According to Matt Bissonnette, a member of SEAL Team 6 and author of *No Easy Day*, Dutton Penguin, 2012.
38 Martin, *War on its Head*, p. 236.

39 UK MOD, *Military Operations* news article, 'Op OMID HAFT clears insurgents from Loy Mandeh area of Afghanistan', 31 May 2011.
40 A Company, 1 Rifles blog, Op *Herrick 14*.
41 UK MOD, *Military Operations* news article, title lost, 22 June 2011.
42 UK MOD, *Military Operations* news article, 'Bomb disposal pair clears Taliban IED factory', 25 July 2011.
43 1 Rifles, A Company blog, date lost.
44 UK MOD, British Army Helmand blog, *Herrick 14*.
45 *The Evening Standard*, 20 April 2014.
46 Future Reserves 2020, The Independent Commission to Review the United Kingdom's Reserve Forces, July 2011.
47 The other two co-authors were the later CDS Nick Houghton, and the later Minister for Reserves Julian Brazier.
48 UK MOD, PowerPoint, 'COIN Targeting', undated and with no author attribution but known to be from the period of *H13–H14*.
49 *TIME*, 24 October 2011.
50 A Company, 1 Rifles blog, Op *Herrick 14*.

CHAPTER 13: THE RUSH FOR THE EXIT DOOR

1 Afghanistanonlineforums.com.
2 The extract is from a blog in the spring of 2011.
3 General Petraeus testimony to US Congress 16 March 2011.
4 Hungary announced it would reduce its commitment at the Pul-e-Khomri PRT from 255 to 190 in March 2012.
5 Adam Mausner with Anthony Cordesman, *The War in Afghanistan: A Trip Report*, 20 June 2011.
6 Anthony Cordesman, *Afghanistan Win or Lose: Transition and Coming Resource Crisis*, 22 September 2011.
7 Ibid.
8 Barbara J. Stapleton, *Beating a Retreat, Prospects for the Transition Process in Afghanistan*, Afghanistan Analysts Network, 2012.
9 Anthony Cordesman, *Afghanistan: The Timetable for Security Transition*, 1 December 2011.
10 UK MOD, BATTLEGROUP DELIBERATE TARGETING ON OP HERRICK 17, TSUNDA/G2/Targeting, 26 March 2013.
11 UK MOD, BC NDA, Company DELIBERATE TARGETING ON OP HERRICK 17, TSUNDA/H17/J2/Targeting, 26 March 2013.
12 UK MOD, BATTLEGROUP DELIBERATE TARGETING ON OP HERRICK 17, TSUNDA/G2/Targeting, 26 March 2013.
13 MOD figures.
14 *The Times*, 6 January 2014.
15 UK MOD, PowerPoint, Op HERRICK 17 / JFSp(A)15 MXS Syndicate Discussion 3: Redeployment, COS JFSp(A)15, undated.
16 UK MOD, OP HERRICK 12-2 TACCIS UPDATE, Ref: J6/3100/12-2, 13 September 2010.
17 ISAF figures.
18 *The Times*, 14 September 2012.
19 *Pajhwok Afghan News*: www.pajhwok.com/en/2013/10/03/british-bases-helmand-being-destroyed.

20 Op *Herrick 16*, Comd TFH Post-Op Presentation, Version 10, undated but known to be from the period October 2012.
21 This total included training ammunition. The source is the UK website ThinkDefence.com. The reference is lost and a search on the ThinkDefence website no longer retrieves the original article.
22 AFCENT data, Combined Forces Air Component Commander 2008–2013 Airpower statistics: Number of weapons released.
23 Darren Boyle, 'British forces fired 10,000 rounds every day during eight year conflict with the Taliban', MailOnline, 8 April 2015.
24 UK MOD, *Defence Focus* news article, title lost, 22 September 2014.
25 *The Times*, 2 November 2014.
26 US DOD, *Stars and Stripes* newspaper: www.stripes.com/news/middle-east/marine-pullout-offers-preview-of-what-us-leaves-behind-for-afghan-troops-1.313791.
27 David Mansfield, *Between a Rock and a Hard Place*, 10 October 2011.
28 Ibid, p. 33.
29 UNODC data – the cumulative totals taken from annual reports.
30 US DOD, 'Report towards Security and Stability in Afghanistan', October 2014.
31 Sir Rodric Braithwaite evidence to Defence Select Committee, 4 September 2012.
32 Inherited from 3 PARA, who lacked the numbers and opportunities to expand the concept.
33 UK MOD, *History and Honour* news article, 'DSO for Army Major who charged enemy lines', 5 October 2012.
34 UK MOD, *History and Honour* news article, 'Royal Air Force officer honoured for work with local Afghans', 19 October 2012.
35 *Roberts in India, The military papers of Lord Roberts, 1876–1893*, Military Records Society, p. 136.
36 Gov.UK, 'The UK's work in Afghanistan', 14 January 2014, https://www.gov.uk/government/publications/uks-work-in-afghanistan/the-uks-work-in-afghanistan.
37 Martine van Bijlert and Sari Kouvo (editors), *Snapshots of an Intervention: The Unlearned Lessons of Afghanistan's Decade of Assistance (2001–11)*, Afghanistan Analysts Network, 2012.
38 US Congress, Commission on Wartime Contracting in Iraq and Afghanistan, Transforming Wartime Contracting: Controlling Costs, Reducing Risks, 31 August 2011.
39 Testimony to the Senate Foreign Affairs Committee, 23 June 2011.
40 *The New York Times*, 30 March, 2012.
41 A maximum of more than 35,000 annual insurgent attacks, and over 10,000 IED incidents was suggested. By contrast the US State Department, quoting the START database, suggested just over 1,000 'terrorist' incidents per year. When ISAF stopped collecting in the winter of 2013, there were around 2,000 incidents every month.

Index